ASSESSMENT
IN SPECIAL AND INCLUSIVE EDUCATION

THIRTEENTH EDITION

JOHN SALVIA
The Pennsylvania
State University

JAMES E. YSSELDYKE
University of
Minnesota

SARA WITMER
Michigan State
University

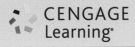
CENGAGE
Learning·

Australia • Brazil • Mexico • Singapore • United Kingdom • United States

ASSESSMENT
IN SPECIAL AND
INCLUSIVE EDUCATION

Assessment in Special and Inclusive Education, **Thirteenth Edition**
John Salvia, James E. Ysseldyke, and Sara Witmer

Product Director: Marta Lee-Perriard

Product Manager: Cheri-Ann Nakamaru

Content Developer: Kassi Radomski

Product Assistant: Stephen Lagos

Content Project Manager: Samen Iqbal

Art Director: Andrei Pasternak

Manufacturing Planner: Doug Bertke

Production Service: Lori Hazzard, MPS Limited

Intellectual Property Analyst: Jennifer Nonenmacher

Photo Researcher: Sathya Pandi

Text Researcher: Kanchana Vijayarangan

Copy Editor: Bill Clark

Cover and Text Designer: Jennifer Wahi

Cover Image Credit: iStockphoto.com /malerapaso

Compositor: MPS Limited

For product information and technology assistance, contact us at **Cengage Learning Customer & Sales Support, 1-800-354-9706.**

For permission to use material from this text or product, submit all requests online at **www.cengage.com/permissions**. Further permissions questions can be e-mailed to **permissionrequest@cengage.com**.

Library of Congress Control Number: 2015949536

Student Edition:
ISBN: 978-1-305-64235-5

Loose-leaf Edition:
ISBN: 978-1-305-64264-5

Cengage Learning
20 Channel Center Street
Boston, MA 02210
USA

Cengage Learning is a leading provider of customized learning solutions with employees residing in nearly 40 different countries and sales in more than 125 countries around the world. Find your local representative at **www.cengage.com**.

Cengage Learning products are represented in Canada by Nelson Education, Ltd.

To learn more about Cengage Learning Solutions, visit **www.cengage.com**. Purchase any of our products at your local college store or at our preferred online store **www.cengagebrain.com**.

Printed in the United States of America
Print Number: 01   Print Year: 2016

CONTENTS

Part 4: Using Assessment Results to Make Educational Decisions 280

20 MAKING INSTRUCTIONAL DECISIONS 280

21 MAKING SPECIAL EDUCATION ELIGIBILITY DECISIONS 302

PREFACE

As indicated by the title of the thirteenth edition, *Assessment in Special and Inclusive Education*, we continue to be concerned about assessing the performance and progress of students with disabilities, regardless of whether their education occurs in general or special education settings. We are also concerned with assessment that occurs in classrooms to identify and address the needs of students requiring additional academic and social–emotional support. Educational assessment has undergone substantial change since the first publication of *Assessment in Special and Inclusive Education* in 1978. Improvement and expansion in assessment tools and strategies are certainly evident. New models and technologies for assessment in school settings have emerged in an attempt to more efficiently address the increasingly diverse needs of students today. Federal laws and regulations related to school assessment practices have been revised in attempts to promote improvements in student outcomes, and they are in the midst of revision as we complete this most recent edition.

Throughout these changes, we have remained committed to assessment approaches that promote data-based decision making, and we believe many concepts and ideas that were presented in the original edition are still essential for our readers to understand and know how to apply. Philosophical differences continue to divide the assessment community. Disputes continue over the value of standardized and nonstandardized test administration, objective and subjective scoring, generalizable and nongeneralizable measurement, interpersonal and intrapersonal comparisons, and so forth. In the midst of these differences, we believe students and society are best served by the objective, reliable, and valid assessment of student abilities and skills and by meaningful links between assessment results and intervention.

Our position is based on several conclusions. First, the IDEA requires objective assessment, largely because it usually leads to better decision making. Second, we are encouraged by the substantial improvement in assessment devices and practices over the past 30-plus years. Third, although some alternatives are merely unproven, other innovative approaches to assessment—especially those that celebrate subjectivity—have severe shortcomings that have been understood since the early 1900s. Fortunately, much of the initial enthusiasm for those approaches has waned. Fourth, we believe it is unwise to abandon effective procedures without substantial evidence that the proposed alternatives really are better. Too often, we learned that an educational innovation was ineffective after it had already failed far too many students.

Our focus is on assessment that matters; assessment that will bring important changes that enhance the lives of the students served. By equipping our readers with knowledge and understanding of key assessment concepts and principles that can be readily applied in school settings, we believe they will be prepared to engage in work that will indeed improve the academic and social–emotional outcomes of the students they serve.

AUDIENCE FOR THIS BOOK

Assessment in Special and Inclusive Education, Thirteenth Edition, is intended for a first course in assessment taken by those whose careers require understanding and informed use of assessment data. The primary audience is made up of those who are or will be teachers in special education at the elementary or secondary level. The secondary audience is the large support system for special educators: school psychologists, child development specialists, counselors, educational administrators, nurses, reading specialists, social workers, speech and language specialists, and specialists in therapeutic recreation. Additionally, in today's reform climate, many classroom teachers enroll in the assessment course as part of their own professional development. In writing for those who are taking their first course in assessment, we have assumed no prior knowledge of measurement and statistical concepts.

PURPOSE

Students with disabilities have the right to an appropriate evaluation and to an appropriate education in the least restrictive educational environment. Those who assess have a tremendous responsibility; assessment results are used to make decisions that directly and significantly affect students' lives. Those who assess are responsible for knowing the devices and procedures they use and for understanding the limitations of those devices and procedures. Decisions about a student's eligibility for special education and related services must be based on accurate and reliable information; decisions about how and where to educate students with disabilities must be based on accurate and reliable data. Best practices in assessment can help support the learning and development of not just those with disabilities, but all students needing a variety of different levels of support, and so we intend for many of the concepts presented to facilitate best practices for all students, and not just those with disabilities.

NEW TO THIS EDITION

The thirteenth edition continues to offer straightforward and clear coverage of basic assessment concepts, evenhanded evaluations of standardized tests in each domain, and illustrations of applications to the decision-making process. All chapters have been updated, several have been revised substantially, and a few have been eliminated to allow for a clear focus on assessment that matters for promoting academic and social–emotional outcomes.

OVERALL CHANGES

Throughout the revision process, our primary goal was to focus on essential assessment concepts, principles, and practices necessary for serving students in school settings. The development and availability of assessment tools, particularly for the purpose of systematic monitoring of student progress, have increased dramatically in recent years, and websites now provide information to facilitate our readers' own reviews of these tools. Therefore, instead of providing numerous detailed reviews of available instruments, we decided to focus our efforts on effectively communicating the key characteristics readers should look for when evaluating the multitude of options available. We have further focused this edition on basic information necessary for generalists (as opposed to specialists) who are seeking to use assessment to improve academic and social–emotional functioning of school-age students. As such, we have reduced coverage of topics that are not closely aligned with this purpose. In order to better facilitate our readers' ability to access the content offered, all available content is present directly in the book rather than in both the book and a separate website. Furthermore, instead of including a separate chapter on technology, we have incorporated discussion of new technologies within the chapters with which they most closely align. Finally, we know that many school systems are moving toward use of models involving a multi-tiered system of supports (MTSS), and we therefore considered it necessary to provide more background for readers on these models for assessment and intervention. In doing so, we revised the associated chapters to focus on basic assessment concepts and principles that are important to understand when applying these models, define important keywords that are increasingly being used in the application of these models, and provide examples of how these models are applied in schools. Overall, our goal is to provide readers with a comprehensive textbook that provides easy access to the assessment concepts and ideas necessary to facilitate the academic and social–emotional competence of all students in schools today.

NEW FEATURES

In addition to important content revisions, we have incorporated several new pedagogical features across chapters.

- At the beginning of each chapter, we now display professional standards and specific learning objectives. Each learning objective is linked directly to a major chapter heading, and to associated comprehension questions at the end of the chapter.

- Keywords are bolded, with definitions included in the narrative.

- Each scenario is explicitly referenced to basic concepts and ideas presented in the chapter.

- Advanced content, previously located on the book's CourseMate website, which is for students in upper-level or graduate courses, is uniquely formatted to convey that it is advanced material.

MAJOR CHAPTER REVISIONS

Although all chapters that were maintained for the thirteenth edition have been updated, major updates were made in the following chapters:

- Chapter 1: Assessment in Social and Educational Contexts

  Revised to provide a brief introduction to basic assessment concepts and themes that are elaborated on in later chapters.

- Chapter 5: Technical Requirements

  Advanced content that was previously displayed only on the CourseMate website is now incorporated within this chapter, and it is formatted to indicate that it represents advanced information.

- Chapter 10: Monitoring Student Progress Toward Instructional Goals

  Instead of providing reviews of specific progress monitoring tools, we highlight key features that are important to look for when evaluating the associated tools.

- Chapter 12: Response to Intervention (RTI) and a Multi-Tiered System of Supports

  New keywords that correspond to the evolving application of these models in schools are defined, and an additional scenario is provided to describe how these models are applied within school settings.

- Chapter 19: Using Measures of Social and Emotional Behavior

  To ensure readers have information on assessing adaptive behavior, content on this topic has been incorporated into the chapter.

- Chapter 22: Making Decisions About Participation in Accountability Programs

  This chapter has been revised to focus on information essential for those making decisions about how individual students should participate in large-scale assessment used for accountability purposes, rather than focusing on information that is important primarily for policymaking at the state level.

- Technological advancements in assessment, previously located in one chapter (23), are now embedded within existing chapters with related content.

- In addition, we deleted chapters that were deemed either particularly specialized, focused on nonobjective assessment practices, or not well aligned with our focus on promoting academic and social–emotional outcomes. More specifically, we have deleted content on the assessment of sensory acuity and oral language (Chapters 14 and 20), portfolio assessment (Chapter 25), perceptual-motor assessment (Chapter 16), and assessment of infants, toddlers, and preschoolers (Chapter 19).

REVISED TESTS

Several tests that are very commonly used to assess students with disabilities have been released with new editions. Reviews of the following recently updated tests are included in corresponding chapters of the book:

- Woodcock–Johnson Tests of Achievement and Cognitive Abilities–Fourth Edition (WJ-COG-4; WJ-ACH-4)

- Wechsler Intelligence Scales for Children–Fifth Edition (WISC-V)

- Oral and Written Language Scales–Second Edition (OWLS-2)

- Behavior Assessment System for Children–Third Edition (BASC-3)

- Gray Oral Reading Test–Fifth Edition (GORT-5)

- Diagnostic Achievement Battery–Fourth Edition (DAB-4)

ORGANIZATION

Part 1, "Overview and Basic Considerations," places testing in the broader context of assessment.

- In Chapter 1, "Assessment in Social and Educational Contexts," we describe the challenge of addressing the needs of diverse students in schools today, and introduce basic concepts and principles that will be covered in greater depth later in the book.

- In Chapter 2, "Assessment and Decision Making in Schools," we describe the four main methods for collecting assessment information, and the main types of decisions made in school settings for which assessment is necessary.

- In Chapter 3, "Laws, Ethical Codes, and Professional Standards That Impact Assessment," we discuss the ways assessment practices are regulated and mandated by legislation and litigation, and various ethical principles that may be used to guide assessment practices.

- In Chapter 4, "What Test Scores Mean," we describe the commonly used ways to quantify test performance and provide interpretative data.

- In Chapter 5, "Technical Requirements," we explain the basic measurement concepts of reliability and validity, and incorporate advanced content related to these concepts for those who want to know more.

- In Chapter 6, "Cultural and Linguistic Considerations," we discuss various cultural and linguistic factors that need to be considered when collecting and interpreting assessment information, related legal requirements, and suggested guidelines for assessment practices.

- In Chapter 7, "Using Test Adaptations and Accommodations," we explain the need for some students to have changes made in how various tests are administered, and provide associated guidance for making accommodation decisions during eligibility and accountability testing.

Part 2, "Assessment in Classrooms," provides readers with fundamental knowledge necessary to conduct assessments in the classroom, and information about new technologies that can facilitate efficient collection and summarization of data for use in making decisions in the classroom.

- Chapter 8, "Teacher-Made Tests of Achievement," provides a systematic overview of tests that teachers can create to measure students' learning and progress in the curriculum.

- Chapter 9, "Assessing Behavior Through Observation," explains the major concepts in conducting systematic observations of student behavior.

- Chapter 10, "Monitoring Student Progress Toward Instructional Goals," describes concepts, ideas, and strategies that can be used to measure student academic progress.

- Chapter 11, "Managing Classroom Assessment," is devoted to helping educators plan assessment programs that are efficient and effective in the use of both teacher and student time.

- Chapter 12, "Response to Intervention (RTI) and a Multi-Tiered System of Supports," provides information on how assessment information can inform decisions made within these innovative models, and guidance for ensuring that appropriate practices are put into place when applying these models,

In Part 3, "Assessment Using Formal Measures," we provide information about the abilities and skills most commonly tested in the schools.

- Part 3 begins with Chapter 13, "How to Evaluate a Test." This chapter is a primer on what to look for when considering the use of a commercially produced test.

- The next six chapters in Part 3 provide an overview of various domains that are assessed in schools using formal measures, and reviews of the most frequently used measures: Chapter 14, "Assessment of Academic Achievement with Multiple-Skill Devices"; Chapter 15, "Using Diagnostic Reading Measures"; Chapter 16, "Using Diagnostic Mathematics Measures"; Chapter 17, "Using Measures of Written Language"; Chapter 18, "Using Measures of Intelligence"; Chapter 19, "Using Measures of Social and Emotional Behavior."

In Part 4, "Using Assessment Results to Make Educational Decisions," we discuss the most important decisions educators make on behalf of students with disabilities.

- In Chapter 20, "Making Instructional Decisions," we discuss the decisions that are made prior to a student's referral for special education and those that are made in special education settings.

- In Chapter 21, "Making Special Education Eligibility Decisions," we discuss the role of multidisciplinary teams and the process for determining a student's eligibility for special education and related services. In a new section we describe approaches using information on a student's Response to Intervention in making eligibility decisions.

- In Chapter 22, "Making Decisions About Participation in Accountability Programs," we explain the legal requirements for states and districts to meet the standards of No Child Left Behind and IDEA, and important considerations in making decisions about how a student participates in the accountability program.

- In Chapter 23, "Collaborative Team Decision Making," we provide an overview of communicating with school teams about assessment and decision making, and include information about the characteristics of effective school teams, strategies for effectively communicating assessment information to parents and students, and the rules concerning data collection and record keeping.

ONLINE RESOURCES FOR INSTRUCTORS

ONLINE INSTRUCTOR'S MANUAL WITH TEST BANK

An online instructor's manual accompanies this book. It contains information to assist the instructor in designing the course, including sample syllabi, discussion questions, teaching and learning activities, field experiences, learning objectives, and additional online resources. For assessment support, the updated test bank includes true–false, multiple-choice, matching, short-answer, and essay questions for each chapter.

POWERPOINT LECTURE SLIDES

These vibrant Microsoft PowerPoint lecture slides for each chapter assist you with your lecture by providing concept coverage using images, figures, and tables directly from the textbook.

COGNERO

Cengage Learning testing, powered by Cognero, is a flexible online system that allows you to author, edit, and manage test bank content from multiple Cengage Learning solutions; create multiple test versions in an instant; and deliver tests from your learning management system, your classroom, or wherever you want.

ACKNOWLEDGMENTS

Over the years, many people have assisted in our efforts. In the preparation of this edition, we express our sincere appreciation to Kassi Radomski for her assistance throughout its development, Mark Kerr, product manager, for his dedication to this edition; and Samen Iqbal and Lori Hazzard for their help. We also appreciate the assistance of Kristen Schrauben for her work on the Instructor's Resource Manual with Test Items, which accompanies this text.

Finally, a specific thanks to the reviewers of the twelfth edition who helped us shape this new edition: Mishaleen Allen, Texas A&M University-San Antonio; Deborah Anne Banker, Angelo State University; Andy Beigel, Keuka College; Donna Bergman, Spring Arbor University; Kerry Burd, Rockford University; Nancy Burton, Concord University; Laura Carpenter, Auburn University at Montgomery; Steve Chamberlain, University of Texas at Brownsville; Jennifer Desiderio, Eastern Michigan University; Caroline DiPipi-Hoy Femstrom, East Stroudsburg University; Pam Chaney, University of North Alabama; Daniel Grace, Morehead State University; Alice Graham, Salve Regina University; David Griffin, Nova Southeastern University; Diane Harr, Concordia University, St. Paul; Juliet Hart Barnett, Arizona State University; Caryn Huss, Manhattanville College; Jason Kight, California University of Pennsylvania; Susan Lamprecht, The College of William and Mary; Debra Leach, Winthrop University; Linda Lind, Iowa State University; Jessica Lisa, St. Joseph's College; Sandy Long, Carson-Newman University; Patricia

Luebke, Alverno College; Corissa Mazurkiewicz, Concordia University; Ted Miller, University of Tennessee at Chattanooga; Anjali Misra, State University of New York Potsdam; Denise O'Connell, Bay Path University; Pamela Peak, University of North Texas; Kathy Ryan, Carthage College; Michael Shaughnessy, Eastern New Mexico University; James Shriner, University of Illinois at Urbana-Champaign; Maria Stetter, Roosevelt University; Douglas Sturgeon, Shawnee State University; Justyn Thoren, Rivier University; Lisa Turner, Clarion University; and Jie Zhang, The College at Brockport, State University of New York.

John Salvia • Jim Ysseldyke • Sara Witmer

CHAPTER

1

ASSESSMENT IN SOCIAL AND EDUCATIONAL CONTEXTS

LEARNING OBJECTIVES

1-1 Determine individual differences in skills, abilities, and behaviors and how these differences can require different levels of support to succeed in school.

1-2 Ascertain why assessment is important in school and society.

1-3 Explain why assessment is important in special and inclusive education.

1-4 Articulate key themes that are important to understand for engaging in best practices in assessment.

1-5 Discuss that significant improvements in assessment have happened and continue to happen.

STANDARDS ADDRESSED IN THIS CHAPTER

 CEC Initial Preparation Standards

Standard 1: Learner Development and Individual Learning Differences

1.0 Beginning special education professionals understand how exceptionalities may interact with development and learning and use this knowledge to provide meaningful and challenging learning experiences for individuals with exceptionalities.

Standard 4: Assessment

4.0 Beginning special education professionals use multiple methods of assessment and data-sources in making educational decisions.

 CEC Advanced Preparation Standards

Standard 1: Assessment

1.0 Special education specialists use valid and reliable assessment practices to minimize bias.

Ψ **National Association of School Psychologists Domains**

1 Data-Based Decision Making and Accountability

8 Diversity in Development and Learning

Education is intended to provide *all* students with the skills and competencies they need to enhance their lives and the lives of their fellow citizens. School personnel are expected to provide all students with a predetermined set of competencies, usually those specified in national common core content standards or in specific state education standards. This function would be extremely difficult even if all students entered school with the same abilities and competencies and even if all students learned in the same way and at the same rate. However, they do not. For example, it is the first day of school at Stevenson Elementary, and several students show up for kindergarten:

- Kim is dropped off at the front door. He speaks no English and the school staff had no idea he was coming.
- Marshall comes knowing how to read, print, add, and subtract.
- Joyce is afraid to come to school and cries incessantly when her mother tries to leave.
- Kamryn and her mother arrive with a folder that includes all of her preschool records, her immunization and medical records, and reports from the two psychologists she has been seeing since age 2.
- Mike doesn't show up. The school has his name on a list, his completed registration records, and notes from a social worker indicating that he is eligible for free and reduced-price lunch.

Not only do students not begin school with the same skills and abilities, they make progress through the curriculum at different rates and have different instructional needs. For example, midway through the first grade, Sally has picked up all she has been taught with no additional help. She just "gets it." Bill needs instruction specifically targeted to help him overcome his deficiencies in letter–sound correspondence; he sees a tutor twice a week. Joe needs so much help that he receives intensive special education services.

Students attending schools today are a much more diverse group than in the past. Today's classrooms are multicultural and multilingual. Students demonstrate a significant range of academic skills; for example, in some large urban environments 75 percent of sixth graders are reading more than two years below grade level, and there is as much as a 10-year range in skill level in math in a sixth-grade classroom. More than 6.5 million children and youth with disabilities (approximately 13 percent of the school-age population) receive special education and related services. Most of these children and youth are attending schools in their own neighborhoods in classes with their peers—this was not always the case in the past—and fewer students with disabilities receive special education services in separate buildings or separate classes.

The focus of this book is on students in both special and inclusive education. **Special education** is a set of unique educational services and supports provided to students with disabilities who meet particular disability criteria; these may include services provided in separate settings or services provided in settings comprising both students with and without disabilities. **Inclusive education** refers to educational approaches that facilitate learning of all students, including those with and without disabilities, within the same environment.

1-1 Individual Students Need Different Levels of Support to Succeed

We as teachers and related services personnel are faced with providing education matched to the needs of students with few skills and those with highly developed skills in the same class. No matter what level of skills they bring with them and no matter how motivated students are to learn, it is our job to enhance their competence and to build the capacity of schools together with families, community agencies, churches, and other factors that influence students' development to meet their needs. In a larger social context, the assessor or a case coordinator must take into account these multiple influences as he or she assesses students and develops supports to meet individual student needs. For example, the tutoring Rosa is receiving at the local Hispanic community center could actually be interfering rather than helping. Or we may find that a really effective way to help Mohammed is to work with the local Somali neighborhood organization that provides students with homework help. As citizens and members of a variety of communities, we are also interested in the capacity of systems to support students in these ways, and we can enhance our effectiveness by taking into account these multiple perspectives and systems. To discuss all these influences is beyond the scope of this text, yet we will be taking many such factors into consideration as we talk about appropriate assessment and decision making in school and community settings.

Schools must provide multiple levels of support to enable each student to be successful in attaining the common core standards as required by state and federal regulations. School personnel must decide who gets what kinds of support and the level of instructional intensity needed by a student, how instruction will be delivered, and the extent to which instruction is working. **Differentiated instruction** is a process that involves matching the content and instructional approach to individual students' learning needs in order to accelerate the learning of all students. Within one first-grade class, some students may not have mastered single-digit addition and subtraction, whereas other students may have mastered this skill and may be ready to learn the strategies of carrying and borrowing associated with double-digit addition and subtraction. Some students may need the teacher to provide 10 examples of carrying within a double-digit additional problem and other students may need just two examples. Only with appropriate and ongoing assessment can one ensure that the content and instructional approaches selected truly match students' needs, and that they are effective. **Assessment** is the process of collecting information (data) for the purpose of making decisions for or about individuals. Knowledge and application of best practices in assessment can help a teacher provide differentiated instruction that optimizes student learning. Read the chapter scenario and associated questions to think more carefully about how a teacher may need to use information to guide the instruction that she will provide to a variety of students in her classroom.

Differentiated instruction is something that all teachers, including both general and special education teachers, strive to incorporate for all of their students, regardless of whether or not the students have disabilities and require special education services. When teaching students who have disabilities that require special education services, general educators and special educators work together to determine how to best match academic instruction to any given student's needs. Students eligible for special education services may receive some or all of their instruction in a separate setting. However, regardless of where a student with a disability is taught, it is important for general and special education teachers to work together to develop, implement, monitor, and evaluate plans for differentiating instruction to ensure the student has adequate access to the general curriculum. General educators tend to be most familiar with the general curriculum, and therefore are able to articulate what the content of instruction should be. Special educators tend to be most familiar with the unique needs of students with disabilities, and can therefore help identify potential barriers to accessing the general curriculum and propose ways to reduce those barriers. Beyond the school setting, there are often additional sources of support, including community centers, faith-based organizations, and mental health providers that school teams may communicate with to help address the unique needs of students, both those with and without disabilities. The use of assessment tools and strategies can go a long way in helping teachers decide what supports are necessary.

Although differentiated instruction is often applied at the classroom level, there are often procedures used at the school level to facilitate differentiated instruction. In the past decade, many districts and schools have begun using Multi-Tiered System of

SCENARIO IN ASSESSMENT

MRS. JOHNSON | Mrs. Johnson's fourth-grade class is a heterogeneous group, and includes the following: four students who are receiving enrichment for one hour per week, two students who receive speech therapy for 30 minutes twice a week, two students with learning disabilities who receive itinerant (special education) services daily, 12 students who are functioning at grade level in all academic areas, and six students who are functioning below average in one or more academic areas. She also has two students whose educational records have yet to arrive from out-of-state.

Mrs. Johnson intends to spend the first week of school in a review of academic content and assessment of each student's prior knowledge so that she can differentiate her instruction. She will meet with the following specialists who will be providing pull-out services to her students: the itinerant special education teacher,

to begin coordinating the instructional support that her two students with learning disabilities receive; the speech therapist, to schedule times when the two students needing therapy will be removed from her class; and the enrichment teacher, to schedule times when the four gifted students will be seen for enrichment activities that will also be part of her curriculum. It looks like another busy year in her fourth-grade class.

This scenario highlights the wide range of students that a teacher may have in class. These students are likely to have very different instructional needs. Additional information about these students' skills and prior learning experiences may help inform this teacher's instructional decision making so that student learning is optimized. What additional information do you think might be helpful to collect, in order to inform instructional decision making?

Supports (MTSS) models to more effectively match the content, method, and intensity of instruction to individual students' needs. Those students who are particularly low in certain skills and not progressing at an expected rate are identified for more intensive instruction and intervention. The goal of using these models is to ensure that resources are allocated in such a way that all students receive the support they need to be successful. Students' instructional needs are identified and their progress is monitored so that instruction can be adapted when necessary. As with differentiated instruction at the classroom level, assessment can play a very important role within MTSS models. MTSS and the role of assessment within MTSS models are further explained in Chapter 12.

1-2 The Importance of Assessment in Schools and Society

The end goal of assessment is improved educational outcomes for students. This is where teachers, school psychologists, speech and language pathologists, administrators, and other school personnel get their rewards: seeing students become more competent over time. School personnel tell us this is exciting work.

Assessment touches everyone's life. It especially affects the lives of people who work with children and youth, and who work in schools. Test scores, in particular, are now used to make a variety of important decisions. Here are just a few examples of the ways in which test scores affect people's lives:

- You learn that, as part of the state certification process, you must take tests that assess your knowledge of teaching practices, learning, and child development.

- Mr. and Mrs. Johnson receive a call from their daughter Morgan's third-grade teacher, who says he is concerned about her performance on a reading test. He would like to refer Morgan for further testing to determine whether she has a learning disability.

- Mr. and Mrs. Erffmeyer tell you that their son is not eligible for special education services because he scored "too high" on an intelligence test.

- In response to publication of test results showing that U.S. students rank low in comparison to students in other industrialized nations, the U.S. Secretary of Education issues a call for more rigorous educational standards for all students and for increased federal aid.

- The superintendent of schools in a large urban district learns that only 40 percent of the students in her school district passed the state graduation test.

- Your local school district asks for volunteers to serve on a task force to design a measure of technological literacy to use as a test with students.

In the United States, almost everyone goes to school. And it seems like everyone has an opinion about testing. **Testing** is administering a predetermined set of questions or tasks, for which predetermined types of behavioral responses are sought, to an individual or group of individuals in order to obtain a score. It is important to realize that there are many assessment methods apart from testing. Furthermore, best practices in assessment, as opposed to testing, involve more than just administration of a test to obtain a score. Considerations such as the types of decisions for which a particular test score is truly helpful, and the conditions under which the test score can be deemed valid must be taken into account when using tests. However, it remains the case that testing is often the "go to" method for making important decisions that affect people's lives.

The procedures for gathering data and conducting assessments are matters that are rightfully of great concern to the general public—both individuals who are directly affected by the assessments (such as parents, students, and classroom teachers) and individuals who are indirectly affected (for example, taxpayers and elected officials). These matters are also of great concern to individuals and agencies that license or certify assessors to work in the schools. Finally, these matters are of great concern to the assessment community. For convenience, the concerns of these groups are discussed separately; however, the reader should recognize that many of the concerns overlap and are not the exclusive domain of one group or another.

1-2a CONCERNS OF STUDENTS, THEIR FAMILIES, AND TEACHERS

People react strongly when test scores are used to make interpersonal comparisons in which they or those they love look inferior. We expect parents to react strongly when test scores are used to make decisions about their children's life opportunities—for example, whether their child could enter college, pass a class, be promoted to the next grade, receive special education, or be placed in a program for gifted and talented students. Parents never want to hear that their children are not succeeding or that their children's prospects for adult life are limited. Students do not want to hear that they are different or not doing as well as their peers; they certainly do not want to be called handicapped or disabled. Poor student performance also affects teachers. Some teachers deny that student achievement really is inadequate; they opine that tests measure trivial knowledge (not the important things they teach), decontextualize knowledge, make it fragmented and artificial, and so on. Other teachers accept their students' failures as a fact of life (these teachers burn out). The good teachers work harder (for example, by learning instructional techniques that actually work and individualize instruction).

Unwanted outcomes of assessment often lead to questions about the kinds of tests used, the skills or behaviors they measure, and their technical adequacy. Decisions about special and remedial education have consequences. Some consequences are desired, such as extra services for students who are entitled to special education. Other consequences are unwanted, such as denial of special education services or diminished self-esteem resulting from a disability label.

1-2b CONCERNS OF THE GENERAL PUBLIC

Entire communities are keenly interested when test scores from their schools are reported and compared with scores from schools in other communities. Districts with "good" test scores are desirable, and real estate prices reflect the fact that parents want to live in those districts. This is especially true for parents of students who have disabilities. Good special education programs are a magnet for many such parents. Read the upcoming Scenario in Assessment and associated questions to think about how school district test scores may influence communities.

Often, test results are used to make high-stakes decisions that may have a direct and significant effect on the continued funding or even closing of schools and school systems, modifying state curricula, and salary negotiations. Finally, individuals who take tests outside of the schools are also affected. We take a test to earn the privilege of a driver's license. We usually have to take tests to gain admission to college. When test results restrict access to privileges, those denied access often view the tests as undemocratic, elitist, or simply unfair.

1-2c CONCERNS OF CERTIFICATION BOARDS

Certification and licensure boards establish standards to ensure that assessors are appropriately qualified to conduct assessments. Test administration, scoring, and interpretation require different degrees of training and expertise, depending on the kind of test being administered. All states certify teachers and psychologists who work in the schools; all states require formal training, and some require competency testing. Although most teachers can readily administer or learn to administer group intelligence and achievement tests as well as classroom assessments of achievement, a person must have considerable training to score and interpret most individual intelligence and personality tests. **Competency-based assessment** refers to assessment of very specific knowledge and skills using authentic or simulated situations in which the knowledge and skill can be demonstrated. This assessment approach is being used more frequently to ensure that those administering and using tests to make important decisions truly have the necessary testing skills and knowledge. When pupils are tested, we should be able to assume that the person doing the testing has adequate training to conduct the testing correctly (that is, establish rapport, administer the test correctly, score the test, and accurately interpret the test).

The joint committee of three professional associations that developed a set of standards for test construction and use has addressed the importance of testing:

> *Educational and psychological testing are among the most important contributions of cognitive and behavioral sciences to our society, providing fundamental and significant sources of information about individuals and groups. Not all tests are well developed, nor are all testing practices wise or beneficial, but there is extensive evidence documenting the usefulness of well-constructed, well-interpreted tests. Well-constructed tests that are valid for their intended purposes have the potential to provide substantial benefits for test takers and test users. Their proper use can result in better decisions about individuals and programs than would result without their use and can also provide a route to broader and more equitable access to education and employment.*

SCENARIO IN ASSESSMENT

MICHAEL | Businessman Sam has just been promoted and transferred to a different state. He and his wife, Virginia, and their three children are house hunting. Their son Michael is a student with autism; one of the family's primary considerations in selecting a new home is the school district's programs for students with autism.

The area where the family is moving is served by three school districts, one religious school, and one charter school. School district one has three students with autism (one who is about the same age as Michael), and those students are placed in classrooms for students with intellectual disabilities. School district two is more rural and buses all of its elementary students with autism to one classroom, where they are educated and included in activities with nondisabled peers. School district three is the largest and maintains classes for students with varying degrees of autism (i.e., both higher- and lower-functioning students) in several school buildings. The charter school has no students with disabilities. Students

with disabilities in the religious school are fully included and may receive speech, occupational, and physical therapies through school district three. Sam and Virginia contact the local autism support group to see if it has a recommendation about the school systems. The group strongly recommends school district three. Besides having an excellent special education program, it is known to provide strong education for students without disabilities. Annual state testing results show that most students in school district three, including many students with disabilities, meet grade-level expectations. Even though houses cost several thousand dollars more in school district three, Sam and Virginia purchase their new home there.

This scenario provides an example of how important test scores can be to decision making. In this case, school test scores influenced a family's decision about where to live. How have test scores been used to make important decisions that have affected your life?

The improper use of tests, on the other hand, can cause considerable harm to test takers and other parties affected by test-based decisions.(American Educational Research Association, American Psychological Association, and National Council on Measurement in Education, 2014, p. 1).

1-3 Why Learn About Assessment in Special and Inclusive Education?

Educational professionals must assess and understand the results of assessments that they and others administer. Assessment is a critical practice that serves the purpose of matching instruction to the level of students' skills, monitoring student progress, modifying instruction, and working hard to enhance student competence. It is a critical component of teaching, and so it is necessary for teachers to have good skills in assessment and a good understanding of assessment information.

Although assessment can be a scary topic for practicing professionals as well as individuals training to become professionals, learning its different important facets helps people become less apprehensive. Educational assessments always have consequences that are important for students and their families. We can expect that good assessments lead to good decisions—decisions that facilitate a student's progress toward the desired goal (especially long term) of becoming a happy, well-adjusted, independent, productive member of society. Poor assessments can slow, stop, and sometimes reverse progress. The assessment process can also be intimidating because there is so much to know; a student of assessment can easily get lost in the details of measurement theory, legal requirements, teaching implications, and national politics.

Things were much simpler when the first edition of this book was published in 1978. The federal legislation and court cases that governed assessment were minimal. Some states had various legal protections for the assessment of students; others did not. There were fewer tests used with students in special education, and many of them were technically inadequate (that is, they lacked validity for various reasons). Psychologists decided if a student was entitled to special education, and students did not have individualized educational programs (IEPs). Back then, the major problems we addressed were how to choose a technically adequate test, how to use it appropriately, and how to interpret test scores correctly. Although the quality of published tests has increased dramatically throughout the years, there are still poor tests being used.

Things are more complex today. Federal law regulates the assessment of children for and in special education. Educators and psychologists have many more tools at their disposal—some excellent, some not so good. Educators and psychologists must make more difficult decisions than ever before. For example, the law recognizes a greater number of disabilities, and educators need to be able to distinguish important differences among them.

Measurement theory and scoring remain difficult but integral parts of assessment. Failure to understand the basic requirements for valid measurement or the precise meaning of test scores inescapably leads to faulty decision making. Through reading and contemplating the information presented in the chapters that follow, we believe you will gain valuable knowledge and skills for selecting and using assessment methods that can improve decision making in schools, particularly those that relate to meeting the needs of a diverse student population.

1-4 Important Assessment Concepts to Understand

Models, methods, and materials used for assessment are constantly evolving. In the past four decades that we have been writing and updating this book, we have seen schools engage in many different assessment practices, both good and bad. We highlight here some foundational concepts that we believe are important to understand as you learn more about assessment, with additional information on the chapters in which these concepts are covered in greater depth. A comprehensive understanding of these concepts will help you as you seek to apply assessment knowledge in your school-based practices.

1-4a LEVEL VS. RATE OF PROGRESS

Instructional decision making can be best informed by knowing both (a) a student's *current level* of performance and (b) his or her *rate* of progress, and it is important to understand the difference between the two. Other words that are sometimes used to refer to the same concepts are status and rate of improvement. Suppose that at the end of a week of instruction, Cara correctly spelled 12 out of 20 targeted spelling words, and Callie correctly spelled 20 out of the same 20 targeted spelling words. Although Callie appears to have greater current skill in spelling the targeted set of words, the extent to which she benefited from the instruction that was provided remains unclear. Suppose that at the beginning of the week the teacher collected information to know that Cara spelled only one out of the 20 targeted words correctly and Callie spelled 18 out of the 20 targeted words correctly. Cara therefore learned how to spell at a rate of 11 words per week (i.e., 12 − 1); Callie learned how to spell at a rate of just two words per week (i.e., 20 − 18). Cara appears to have a much higher rate of progress, suggesting that the instruction was particularly effective for her; however, she has not yet mastered the set of words. Although Callie has mastered the targeted words, it is questionable whether the instruction was particularly effective for her—she might have learned more had she been given the opportunity. Determination of performance level can be important for making decisions about what to teach, as well as deciding whether a student has mastered a skill. But information on rate of progress is needed to know whether instruction is particularly effective. In this book, you will learn about different instruments and methods for measuring both level and rate of progress. Some tools are primarily developed and used for measuring level, others are developed to allow for measurement of both level and rate of progress. Chapters 8–11 provide more information on how performance level and rate of progress can be measured in classroom settings, and Chapter 12 explains how these are often used as a part of MTSS.

1-4b DIFFERENT DECISIONS OFTEN REQUIRE DIFFERENT DATA

Decisions made within school settings vary considerably in terms of the consequences or stakes attached. In some cases, decisions may have relatively minor implications for student learning. For instance, a high school teacher may want information to decide whether to focus more instructional time during a particular class period on the causes of the Civil War, or whether it would be better to move on to teaching about the various battles in the war. In this case, the teacher might quickly develop a very brief measure to find out whether the majority of the class knows several identified causes of the war. In other cases, a decision may have major implications for students. For example, determining whether a student has a disability and qualifies for special education services can have very important implications for the student's future. Such a decision should be informed by data that are collected carefully over time and that have strong evidence of reliability (i.e., they measure consistently) and validity (i.e., they measure what they propose to measure). Although data with strong technical characteristics (i.e., reliability and validity) are desirable, they are not always necessary. In some cases reliance on a high standard for reliability and validity may prolong decision making that needs to be made more quickly to be effective. It is therefore important to consider the stakes of the decision being made to know how technically adequate the assessment tools should be. Chapters 4, 5, and 13 provide information on technical characteristics that should be considered when deciding which assessment tools to use. The chapters within Part 2 of the book

(Chapters 8, 9, 10, 11, and 12) discuss assessment methods and tools that are typically used to make decisions about teaching and learning within the classroom for a variety of students. The chapters within Part 3 of the book (Chapters 14, 15, 16, 17, 18, and 19) describe assessment tools that are typically used in decision making for students who may ultimately need more substantial resources than what are available in many classrooms, including those students needing special education services. Chapters 20, 21, 22, and 23 describe assessment processes that are used when making different types of decisions.

1-4c DIFFERENT METHODS MAY BE NEEDED FOR DIFFERENT STUDENTS

Test developers typically try to make their tests accessible to a wide range of individuals. However, characteristics of how the test is administered, how those being tested are expected to provide their responses, and characteristics of the norm group to whom students are compared may influence the extent to which a given test is appropriate for a particular student. For example, some tests that are intended to measure math skills are written in a way that students ultimately need to have vision and competent reading skills to understand the test items. Such a test may not accurately measure the math skills of a student who is blind or has a reading disability. Students who do not have proficiency with the English language or who are from particularly unique cultures may not have the prerequisite language and cultural knowledge to demonstrate their cognitive abilities on tests that have been developed and normed in the mainstream culture. In such cases, one must be careful to either identify and use tests that are more appropriate for students with the given characteristics, consider accommodations that might be made to allow the test to be more appropriate for the given student, or use alternative methods of assessment. Chapters 6 and 7 discuss important considerations for the assessment of two unique groups of students: those who are English language learners and those who have disabilities. Chapter 22 highlights important considerations for effectively including student with disabilities in accountability assessment programs.

1-4d DIFFERENT SKILLS OFTEN REQUIRE DIFFERENT METHODS

In Chapter 2, you will learn about the four primary methods used for collecting data on students' academic and social emotional skills: record review, interview, observation, and testing. Because testing can be done in a particularly objective manner, it is often a preferred method for collecting data on students. However, some skills that we want to measure are highly context-dependent, meaning that students may only show them under particular conditions or in particular settings. Attempts to create "tests" for these skills may therefore be difficult, so it can be helpful to rely more heavily on interviews with individuals who observe the student's use of skills in different settings, as well as on observations conducted in different settings. For example, it would be hard to develop a test of anger management skills. Authentic opportunities to collect data on such skills happen in the moment; administering a predetermined set of tasks or questions at a particular time to find out about a student's anger management skills will not likely provide useful information. Instead, one might rely more heavily on a teacher's or parent's report of the student's skills in this area, which represents their use of the skills in authentic situations. Chapters 14–19 discuss various methods and measures that are used for specific academic and social–emotional skills.

1-4e ONLY PRESENT BEHAVIOR IS OBSERVED

When students take tests we only observe what they do. We never observe what they can do. If a student spells half of the words correctly on a spelling test, we know that she spelled half of the words correctly. We do not know that she *can* only spell half of the words correctly or that she will do so in the future. Any statement about future performance is an inference. Many factors determine a student's performance on a given day on a given test, and it is important to remember that we only observe what the student *does*, not what he or she *can do*.

1-4f HIGH- AND LOW-INFERENCE DECISION MAKING

In assessment we typically make inferences about a student's level and rate of progress using a sample of information. However, a high level of inference making can be problematic. Inference making is particularly evident and potentially problematic when (a) there are only a few items or tasks that sample a particular behavior or skill of interest, and (b) the skills needed to complete the items or tasks do not adequately reflect the skills targeted for measurement. For example, use of a brief, three-item multiple-choice test to measure a student's math problem-solving skills involves a high level of inference because (a) it includes just a few items and (b) the task ultimately requires mere selection from the listed responses for each item rather than actual completion of a math problem. A student could earn (merely by chance!) a high score on such a test and not ultimately have strong math problem-solving skills. In such a situation, the inference that the resulting test score offers an accurate indication of the student's math problem-solving skills would be incorrect. A test requiring less inference would be one that requires the student to actually solve the problem on his or her own, without providing a list of potentially correct responses.

Furthermore, some constructs currently being measured in school settings are only tangentially related to academic and social–emotional skills. When tests of these constructs are used, high-level inferences are needed to connect the information in a way that can meaningfully inform instruction. For example, although there is information to suggest that short-term memory (a construct commonly measured on tests of intelligence) is related to academic performance, knowing that a student performed low on a test of short-term memory does not provide targeted guidance on what or how to teach. Although it may suggest a student needs more repetitions to master a particular skill, one could arrive at that conclusion with greater confidence if tests more directly measured the number of repetitions the student required to learn something.

It is our belief that one should avoid use of assessment tools that require a high level of inference making. This is because results obtained through use of such tools may (a) misrepresent the students' actual skills, and (b) lead to conclusions that are not helpful for informing instruction. Instead, we prefer direct measurement of actual academic and behavioral skills that can be altered through instruction. Characteristics and examples of direct assessment are described in Chapter 10. Chapters 8–19 include information on assessment tools that vary considerably in the level of inference required for instructional decision making.

1-4g ACCURACY IN COLLECTING, SCORING, INTERPRETING, AND COMMUNICATING ASSESSMENT INFORMATION

Assessment tools often have very specific rules about how they are to be administered and scored. These rules are developed to ensure that the tool allows for accurate and meaningful measurement of the target skill. Deviation from these rules can result in scores that do not accurately reflect a student's level of competence in the targeted area, and ultimately can lead to poor decision making. Therefore, great care must be taken to ensure that the data are collected carefully and with due attention to any administration and scoring rules.

However, merely attending to accuracy in the collection of data is not enough. The data are only helpful if they are used in an appropriate manner for decision making. All too often we hear of situations in which schools have collected a large amount of data, but the data never go on to facilitate improvements in instruction because no one either has or takes the time to use them, or they use them in ways that they were not intended to be used. Even before data are collected, it is important to clarify how they will be used and ensure that the use of the given data for the given purpose is justified. In many cases, data are used to inform the decision making of teams of individuals. In these cases, it is important to ensure that the assessment information is communicated well to all team members. Chapter 3 discusses rules and ethics surrounding the collection and use of data in school settings, and Chapter 23 offers ideas for ensuring that data are communicated well to team members.

1-4h FAIRNESS IS PARAMOUNT

Fairness is a guiding principle in assessment and throughout this textbook. School personnel should always work to maximize fairness in assessment. This means choosing tests that are technically adequate and that are relevant to improved instructional outcomes, always taking into account the nature of students' social and cultural backgrounds, learning histories, and opportunities to learn, and always being sensitive to individual differences and disabilities. Fairness and absence of bias are guiding principles as we discuss basic concepts of assessment and technical adequacy in Part 1, classroom assessment practices in Part 2, evaluate formal assessments in Part 3, and apply assessment to decision making in Part 4.

1-4i ASSESSMENT THAT MATTERS

There are four kinds of assessment practices that take place in today's schools: assessment that matters but is technically inadequate, assessment that is technically adequate but does not matter, assessment that is neither technically adequate nor matters, and assessment that is both technically adequate and matters. The fundamental purpose of assessment is gathering information that leads to improvement in students' competencies in relevant domains of behavior and achievement. If assessment practices do not do so, they do not matter. Assessment that is related to and supports the development of effective interventions is worthwhile and clearly in the best interests of individuals, families, schools, communities, and society.

1-4j ASSESSMENT PRACTICES ARE DYNAMIC

Educational personnel regularly change their assessment practices. New federal or state laws, regulations, or guidelines specify—and, in some cases, mandate—new assessment practices. New tests become available, and old ones go away. States change their special education eligibility criteria, and technological advances enable us to gather data in new and more efficient ways. The population of students attending schools also changes, bringing new challenges to the educational personnel who are working to enhance the academic and behavioral competence of all students. Therefore, although this section of the chapter is focused on highlighting key concepts that are universal, it is important to note that one of those concepts is that assessment practices change. By becoming familiar with the fundamental concepts presented here and throughout this book, we anticipate that you will have some beginning skills to evaluate future assessment practices and adopt those practices that not only meet legal and ethical guidelines but also help to promote student learning.

1-5 Good News: Significant Improvements in Assessment Have Happened and Continue to Happen

The good news is that there have been significant improvements in assessment since the first edition of *Assessment* in 1978. Assessment is evolving in a number of important ways.

- Methods of test construction have changed.
- Better statistical analyses have enabled test authors to do a better job of building their assessments.

- Skills and abilities that we assess have changed as theory and knowledge have evolved. We recognize attention deficit hyperactivity disorder and autism as separate disabilities; intelligence tests reflect theories of intelligence; measures of achievement are more closely aligned with the way in which students learn.

- Each state once had separate standards, which resulted in confusing comparisons among states. In the past few years, a large number of states have worked together to create a common core set of standards in reading and math that are considered important for all students to achieve.

- Better assessment methods have worked their way into practice, including systematic observation, functional assessment, curriculum-based measurement, curriculum-based assessment, and technology-enhanced assessment and instructional management.

- The adoption by states and school districts of the concept of multi-tiered system of support (MTSS) has led to assessment practices that are focused on instruction and instructional interventions designed to enhance student competence and build the capacity of systems to meet students' needs.

- Advancements in technology are making the collection, storage, and analysis of assessment data much more manageable and user-friendly.

- Federal laws prescribe the procedures that schools must follow in conducting assessments and hold schools more accountable for the assessments they conduct.

We have every reason to expect that assessment practices will continue to change for the better.

Chapter Comprehension Questions

Write your answers to each of the following questions and then compare your responses to the text.

1. What is meant by "individual differences"? Give two examples and indicate why it is important to take individual differences into account as we endeavor to help students succeed in school.

2. State reasons why assessment is important in school and society.

3. How do educational personnel decide what supports students need to succeed in school?

4. Describe at least five key concepts that are important to understand that will be the focus of later chapters in this book.

5. Provide two examples of how assessment practices have improved in recent years.

CHAPTER

2

ASSESSMENT AND DECISION MAKING IN SCHOOLS

LEARNING OBJECTIVES

2-1 Describe four ways in which assessment information is collected.

2-2 Explain seven kinds of educational decisions made using assessment information.

2-3 Discuss the sequence of activities and decisions that are made at each tier (universal, targeted, intensive) in the assessment process.

STANDARDS ADDRESSED IN THIS CHAPTER

CEC **CEC Initial Preparation Standards**

Standard 4: Assessment
4.0 Beginning special education professionals use multiple methods of assessment and data-sources in making educational decisions.

Standard 5: Instructional Planning Strategies
5.0 Beginning special education professionals select, adapt, and use a repertoire of evidence-based instructional strategies to advance learning of individuals with exceptionalities.

CEC **CEC Advanced Preparation Standards**
ADVANCED

Standard 1: Assessment
1.0 Special education specialists use valid and reliable assessment practices to minimize bias.

 National Association of School Psychologists Domains
1 Data-Based Decision Making and Accountability
5 School-Wide Practices to Promote Learning

Assessment is a process of collecting information for the purpose of making decisions for or about students. In this chapter we describe four major ways in which assessment information is collected, and we describe seven major kinds of decisions made using assessment information. We conclude the chapter by describing the assessment process in schools.

2-1 How Are Assessment Data Collected?

When most people hear the term "assessment," they think of testing. Assessment is broader than testing. **Testing** consists of administering a particular set of questions to an individual or group of individuals to obtain a score. That score is the end product of testing. A test is only one of several assessment techniques or procedures for gathering information. During the process of assessment, data from record reviews, interviews, observations, and tests all come into play. To be most efficient, it can be helpful to first seek relevant information through a review of records, followed by interviews with those with special expertise and those who know the individuals(s) well, and then through observations. The use of testing can be reserved for the collection of more targeted information that can inform instructional changes, and for those decisions that require the use of very current and highly precise information about student skills and behavior. You may find it helpful to think of the mnemonic R.I.O.T. first used by Kenneth Howell (Hosp, Hosp, Howell & Allison, 2014; Howell & Morehead, 1987) as a handy way to remember the four ways of collecting assessment information.

2-1a RECORD REVIEW

Record review is an assessment method involving review of student cumulative records or medical records. In student records, school personnel retain demographic information, previous test scores, attendance data, and teacher-verified comments about student behavior and performance. Assessors nearly always examine the prior records of the individual students with whom they work. Record reviews are useful in documenting when problems first appeared, their severity, and the interventions attempted. Similarly, record reviews are helpful when a student has not previously demonstrated difficulties. Assessors may also review the nature of instructional demands in classrooms and compare these to products of individual students' work, in order to get at any discrepancies between the skills students have and the nature of the tasks they are being asked to complete.

2-1b INTERVIEWS

Recollections, or recalled observations and interpretations of behavior and events, are frequently used as an additional source of information. People who are familiar with the student can be very useful in providing information through interviews and rating scales. An **interview** is an assessment method involving a conversation between two or more people where questions are asked by the interviewer to elicit facts or statements from the interviewee. Interviews can range in structure from casual conversations to highly structured processes in which the interviewer has a predetermined set of questions that are asked in a specified sequence. Unstructured interviews are discussions with loosely defined questions and open-ended responses. Semi-structured interviews include a standardized set of questions and open-ended responses. Structured interviews standardize both the questions and possible responses. Examples of structured interviews are the Behavioral Assessment Scale for Children-3 (Reynolds and Kamphaus, 2015) and the Gilliam Autism Rating Scale 3 (2014). Generally, the more structured the interview, the more accurate are the comparisons of the results of several different interviews. Rating scales can be considered the most formal type of interview. Rating scales allow questions to be asked in a standardized way and to be accompanied by the same stimulus materials, and they provide a standardized and limited set of response options.

2-1c OBSERVATIONS

Observations can provide highly accurate, detailed, and verifiable information not only about the person being assessed but also about the surrounding contexts. Observations can be categorized as either nonsystematic or systematic. In **nonsystematic**, or **informal**, **observation**, the observer simply watches an individual in his or her environment and notes the behaviors, characteristics, and personal interactions that seem significant. In **systematic observation**, the observer sets out to observe one or more precisely defined behaviors. The observer specifies observable events that define the behavior and then counts the frequency or measures the frequency, duration, amplitude, or latency of the behaviors.

2-1d TESTS

A **test** is a predetermined set of questions or tasks for which predetermined types of behavioral responses are sought. Tests are particularly useful because they permit tasks and questions to be presented in exactly the same way to each person tested. Because a tester elicits and scores behavior in a predetermined and consistent manner, the performances of several different test takers can be compared, no matter who does the testing. Hence, tests tend to make many contextual factors in assessment consistent for all those tested. The price of this consistency is that the predetermined questions, tasks, and responses may not be equally relevant to all students. Tests yield two types of information—quantitative and qualitative. **Quantitative data** are observations that have been tabulated or otherwise given numerical values. They are the actual scores achieved on the test. An example of quantitative data is Lee's score of 80 on her math test. **Qualitative data** are pieces of information collected based on nonsystematic and unquantified observations. These may consist of other observations made while a student is tested; they tell us how Lee achieved her score. For example, Lee may have solved all of the addition and subtraction problems with the exception of those that required regrouping. When tests are used, we usually want to know both the scores and how the student earned those scores.

2-2 Types of Assessment Decisions Made by Educators

When you work in schools you will gather and use assessment information to make decisions for or about students. Educational assessment decisions address problems. Some of these assessment decisions involve problem identification (deciding whether there is a problem), whereas others address problem analysis and problem solving. Most educational problems begin as discrepancies between our expectations for students and their actual performance. Students may be discrepant academically (they are not learning as fast as they are expected), behaviorally (they are not acting as they are expected), or physically (they are not able to sense or respond as expected). At some point, a discrepancy is sufficiently large that it is seen as a problem rather than as a benign human variation. The crossover point between a discrepancy and a problem is a function of many factors: the importance of the discrepancy (for example, the inability to print a letter versus forgetting to dot the "i"), the intensiveness of the discrepancy (for example, a throat-clearing tic versus shouting obscenities in class), and so forth. Other assessment decisions address problem solving (how to solve problems and thereby improve students' education). Table 2.1 lists the kinds of decisions school personnel make using assessment information. Read the upcoming Scenario in Assessment and associated question for an example of a situation in which a team will need to use assessment data to inform decisions about a student with a disability.

TABLE 2.1	Decisions Made Using Assessment Information
Screening	Are there unrecognized problems?
Progress monitoring	Is the student making adequate progress? Toward individual goals Toward state or common core standards
Instructional planning and modification	What can we do to enhance competence and build capacity, and how can we do it?
Resource allocation	Are additional resources needed?
Eligibility for special education services	Is the student eligible for special education and related services?
Program evaluation	Are the instructional programs that are being used effective?
Accountability	Are we achieving desired outcomes?

© Cengage Learning

2-2a SCREENING DECISIONS: ARE THERE UNRECOGNIZED PROBLEMS?

Screening decisions involve the collection of assessment information for the purpose of deciding whether students have unrecognized problems. Educators now know that it is very important to identify physical, academic, and behavior problems early in students' school careers. Early identification enables us to develop treatments or interventions that may alleviate or eliminate difficulties. Educators also understand that it is important to screen for specific conditions, such as visual difficulties, because prescription of corrective lenses enables students to be more successful in school. School personnel engage in universal screening (they test everyone) for some kinds of potential problems. All young children are screened for vision or hearing problems with the understanding that identification of sensory problems allows us to prescribe corrective measures (glasses, contacts, hearing aids, or amplification equipment) that will alleviate the problems. All students are required to have a physical examination, and most students are assessed for "school readiness" prior to entrance into school. Screening tests typically are given to all students in regular classes to identify students who are discrepant from an expected level of performance. Such screening is called universal screening.

2-2b PROGRESS MONITORING DECISIONS: IS THE STUDENT MAKING ADEQUATE PROGRESS?

School personnel assess students for the purpose of making two kinds of **progress monitoring decisions**: (1) Is the student making adequate progress toward individual goals? and (2) Is the student making adequate progress toward common core standards or specified state standards?

Monitoring Progress Toward Individual Goals

School personnel regularly assess the specific skills that students do or do not have in specific academic content areas such as decoding words, comprehending what they read, performing math calculations, solving math problems, and writing. We want to know whether the student's rate of acquisition will allow the completion of all instructional goals within the time allotted (for example, by the end of the school year or by the completion of secondary education). The data are collected for the purpose of making decisions about what to teach and the level at which to teach. For example, students who have mastered single-digit addition need no further instruction (although they may still need practice) in single-digit addition. Students who do not demonstrate those skills need further instruction. The specific goals and objectives for students who receive special education services are listed in their individualized educational programs (IEPs).

We monitor progress toward the competencies we want individuals to attain so that we can modify instruction or interventions that are not having desired outcomes. Progress may be monitored continuously or periodically to ensure students have acquired the information and skills being taught, can maintain the newly acquired skills and information over time, and can appropriately generalize the newly acquired skills and information. The IEPs of students who receive special education services must contain statements about the methods that will be used to assess their progress toward attaining individualized goals. In any case, the information is used to make decisions about whether the instruction or intervention is working and whether there is a need to alter instruction.

Monitoring Progress toward Common Core State Standards or Specific State Standards

School personnel set goals/standards/expectations for performance of schools, classes, and individual students. The U.S. Department of Education has developed a list of what are called Common Core State Standards, which all students are expected to meet. Some states use these standards as the basis for their state assessment and accountability systems. A website devoted entirely to the Common Core State Standards Initiative contains the latest information on that federal effort. All states have identified academic content and performance standards that specify what students are expected to learn in reading, mathematics, social studies, science, and so forth. Students with significant disabilities may be required to work toward a set of alternative achievement standards (this is discussed in detail in Chapter 22). Moreover, states are required by law to have in place a system of assessments aligned with their goals/standards/expectations. The assessments that are used to identify the standing of groups are also used to ascertain if individuals have met or exceeded state standards/goals. The Common Core State Standards Initiative likely will change significantly over time. Be sure to search the Internet for "Common Core State Standards changes" and "NCLB changes" for the most recent information.

2-2c INSTRUCTIONAL PLANNING AND MODIFICATION DECISIONS: WHAT CAN WE DO TO ENHANCE COMPETENCE AND BUILD CAPACITY, AND HOW CAN WE DO IT?

Instructional planning and modification decisions involve the collection of assessment information for the purpose of planning individualized instruction or making changes in the instruction students are receiving. Inclusive education teachers are able to take a standard curriculum and plan instruction based on it. Although curricula vary from district to district—largely as a function of the values of the community and school—they are appropriate for most students at a given age or grade level. However, what should teachers do for those students who differ significantly from their peers or from district standards in their academic and behavioral competencies? These students need special help to benefit from the classroom curriculum and instruction, and school personnel must gather data to plan special programs for these students.

Three kinds of decisions are made in instructional planning: (1) what to teach, (2) how to teach it, and (3) what expectations are realistic. Deciding what to teach is a content decision usually made on the basis of a systematic analysis of the skills that students do and do not have. Scores on tests and other information help teachers decide whether students have specific competencies. Test information may be used to determine placement in reading groups or assignment to specific compensatory or remedial programs. Teachers also use information gathered from observations and interviews in deciding what to teach. They obtain information about how to teach by trying different methods of teaching and monitoring students' progress toward instructional goals. Finally, decisions about realistic expectations are always inferences, based largely on observations of performance in school settings and performance on tests.

One of the provisions of the No Child Left Behind Act, the major federal law governing delivery of elementary and secondary education, states that schools are to use "evidence-based" instructional practices. There are a number of interventions with empirical evidence to support their use with students with special needs. A number of websites are devoted to evidence-based teaching, including the National Center on Intensive Intervention, the National Center on Response to Intervention, Intervention Central, and the What Works Clearinghouse from the U.S. Department of Education.

2-2d RESOURCE ALLOCATION DECISIONS: ARE ADDITIONAL RESOURCES NECESSARY?

Resource allocation decisions involve the collection and use of assessment information for the purpose of deciding what kinds of resources and supports individual students need in order to be successful in school. Assessment results may indicate that individual students need special help or enrichment. These students may be referred to a teacher assistance team,[1] or they may be referred for evaluation to a multidisciplinary team that will decide whether these students are entitled to special education services.[2] School personnel gather data on student social-emotional difficulties or on academic skills for the purpose of deciding whether additional resources are necessary. They also use assessment information to make decisions about how to enlist parents, schools, teachers, and community agencies in enhancing student competence.

When it is clear that many or all students require additional programs or support, system change and increased capacity may be indicated. Clear examples of building the capacity of schools to meet student needs include preschool education for all, federal funding to increase student competence in math and science, implementation of positive behavior support programs, and federal requirements for school personnel to develop individualized plans to guide the transition from high school to post-school employment.

2-2e ELIGIBILITY FOR SPECIAL EDUCATION SERVICES DECISIONS: IS THE STUDENT ELIGIBLE FOR SPECIAL EDUCATION AND RELATED SERVICES?

Eligibility decisions involve the collection and use of assessment information to decide whether a student meets the state criteria for a disability condition and needs special education services to be successful in school. Before a student may be declared eligible for special education services, he or she must be shown to be exceptional (have a disability) *and* to have special learning needs. This is an important point

[1] Two kinds of teams typically operate in schools. The first, usually composed of teachers only, is designed as a first line of assistance to help classroom teachers solve problems with individual students in their class. These teams, often called teacher assistance teams, mainstream assistance teams, or schoolwide assistance teams, meet regularly to brainstorm possible solutions to problems that teachers confront. The second kind of team is the multidisciplinary team that is required by law for purposes of making special education eligibility decisions. These teams are usually made up of a principal; regular and special education teachers; and related services personnel, such as school psychologists, speech and language pathologists, occupational therapists, and nurses. These teams have different names in different places. Most often they are called child study teams, but in Minneapolis, for example, they are called special education referral committees or IEP teams.

[2] Students who are gifted and talented are considered exceptional. Yet, they are not entitled to special education services under IDEA. Some states have special provisions that entitle gifted and talented students to receive special services. Be sure to check your state department of education website to see whether and how gifted and talented students are entitled to special services.

especially relevant to assessment in schools. It is not enough to be disabled *or* to have special learning needs. Students can be disabled and not require special education services. For example, they can be blind, and the blindness may not be interfering with their academic performance. Similarly, students can have special learning needs but not meet the state criteria for being declared disabled. For example, there is no federal mandate for provision of special education services to students with behavior disorders, and in many states students with behavior disorders are not eligible for special education services (students need to be identified as emotionally disturbed to receive special education services). Students who receive special education (1) have diagnosed disabilities and (2) need special education services to achieve educational outcomes.

In addition to the classification system employed by the federal government, every state has an education code that specifies the kinds of students who are considered disabled. States may have different names for the same disability. For example, in California, some students are called "deaf" or "hard of hearing"; in other states, such as Colorado, the same kinds of students are called "hearing impaired." States may expand special education services to provide for students with disabilities that are not listed in the Individuals with Disabilities Education Improvement Act (IDEA), but states may not exclude from services the disabilities listed in the IDEA. Finally, while a state may provide gifted students with special programs and protections, gifted students are not included in the IDEA and are not entitled to federal funding for special education. We expand on these concepts in the chapter on Making Eligibility Decisions.

2-2f PROGRAM EVALUATION: ARE INSTRUCTIONAL PROGRAMS EFFECTIVE?

Assessment data are collected to evaluate specific programs. **Program evaluation decisions** are those in which the emphasis is on gauging the effectiveness of the curriculum in meeting the goals and objectives of the school. School personnel typically use this information for schoolwide curriculum planning. For example, schools can compare two approaches to teaching in a content area by (1) giving tests at the beginning of the year, (2) teaching comparable groups two different ways, and (3) giving tests at the end of the year. By comparing students' performances before and after, the schools are able to evaluate the effectiveness of the two competing approaches.

The process of assessing educational programs can be complex if numerous students are involved and if the criteria for making decisions are written in statistical terms. For example, an evaluation of two instructional programs might involve gathering data from hundreds of students and comparing their performances and applying many statistical tests. Program costs, teacher and student opinions, and the nature of each program's goals and objectives might be compared to determine which program is more effective. This kind of large-scale evaluation probably would be undertaken by a group of administrators working for a school district. Of course, program evaluations can be much less formal. For example, Mackenzie is a third-grade teacher. When Mackenzie wants to know the effectiveness of an instructional method she is using, she does her own evaluation. Recently, she wanted to know whether phonics instruction in reading is better than using flashcards to teach word recognition. She used both approaches for three weeks and found that students learned to recognize words much more rapidly when she used a phonics approach.

2-2g ACCOUNTABILITY DECISIONS: DOES WHAT WE DO LEAD TO DESIRED OUTCOMES?

Accountability decisions are those in which assessment information is used to decide the extent to which school districts, schools, and individual teachers are making adequate progress with the students they teach. Under the provisions of the No Child Left Behind Act, schools, school districts, and state education agencies are now held

JOAN | Joan is an eighth-grader who was retained in first grade and identified as a student with a learning disability at the end of the third grade. She has progressed from grade to grade and remained in special education since that time. Currently, Joan receives resource services and in-class support for English, mathematics, science, and social studies taken in the general education classroom. In her resource room she receives instruction in writing (especially spelling) and in reading, where her lack of fluency hampers her comprehension.

Joan does have a number of strengths. She attends school regularly and, until recently, enthusiastically. She demonstrates excellent auditory comprehension and her attention to task is above average. She actively participates in class activities and discussions. She has good ideas and communicates them well orally. She asks for and accepts help from her teachers and is well accepted by her peers.

Recently, however, she has begun to exhibit signs of low self-esteem. Joan's parents are becoming concerned. Because Joan will be entering high school next year, her parents are concerned that time is running out and that Joan really needs to feel better about herself and how far she has come. So her parents ask for an IEP team meeting to address their concerns about Joan's reading, writing, and self-esteem. They wonder if Joan needs a more intensive special education program.

This scenario highlights a situation in which information is needed to inform decision-making about a student receiving special education services. Using Table 2.1 and the associated descriptions of decision types, how would you categorize the specific decisions for which information is needed to address the concerns noted by Joan's parents?

accountable for individual student performance and progress.[3] School districts must report annually, to their state's department of education, the performance of all students, including students with disabilities, on tests the state requires students to take. By law, states, districts, and individual schools must demonstrate that the students they teach are making adequate yearly progress (AYP). When it is judged by the state that a school is not making AYP, or when specified subgroups of students (disadvantaged students, students with disabilities, or specific racial/ethnic groups) are not making AYP, sanctions are applied. The school is said to be a school in need of improvement. When schools fail to make AYP for two years, parents of the children who attend those schools are permitted to transfer their children to other schools that are not considered in need of improvement. When the school fails to make AYP for three years, students are entitled to supplemental educational services (usually after-school tutoring). Failure to make AYP for longer periods of time results in increasing sanctions until finally the state can take over the school or district and reconstitute it.

2-3 The Assessment Process

The assessment and decision-making process differs for individual students, but there are commonalities in the sequence of activities that take place. Figure 2.1 shows the flow of activities from initial concern by a classroom teacher to the implementation of prereferral interventions in the general education classroom. Student progress is monitored and, depending on how students perform, they receive either more or less intensive services. Also illustrated is the fact that assessment information is collected for the purpose of deciding whether students are eligible for special education services and for the purpose of making accountability decisions. This simple chart is intended to illustrate the process in general. Recognize that for individual students, the process may include some extra steps, and that certainly it takes varying amounts of time for different individuals to proceed through the steps. Recognize also that many students with disabilities receive special education services before they enter school. This is especially true for students who are blind, deaf, have medical conditions that interfere with learning, or have multiple disabilities.

Let's walk through the steps in the assessment and decision-making process. A student, let's call her Sara, is enrolled in the general education classroom. Universal screening (screening tests given to all students in her grade) reveal a difference between her reading level (the observed level on the screening test) and the level of

---

[3] It is important to note that many states have applied for and received waivers of these requirements. What is mentioned is what is the case based on the No Child Left Behind Act of 2001.

FIGURE 2.1
The Assessment Process

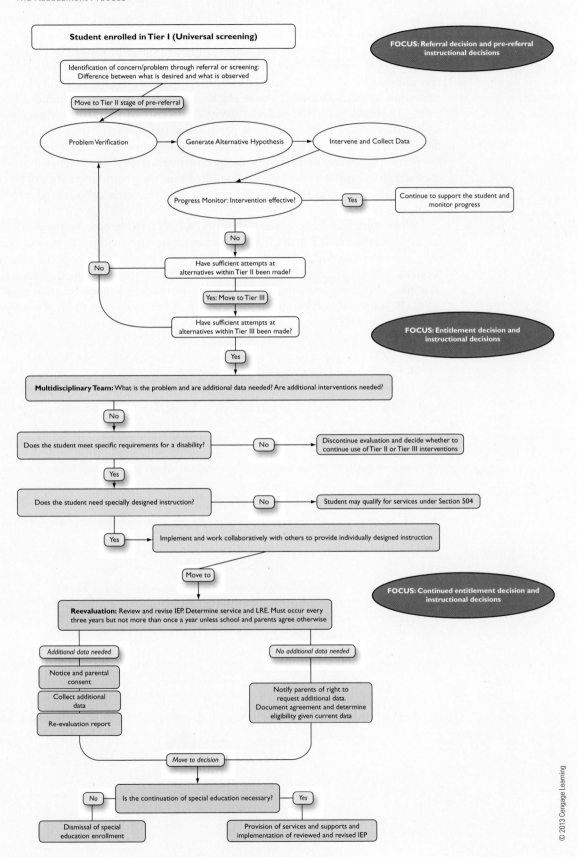

Student enrolled in Tier I (Universal screening)

FOCUS: Referral decision and pre-referral instructional decisions

Identification of concern/problem through referral or screening: Difference between what is desired and what is observed

Move to Tier II stage of pre-referral

Problem Verification → Generate Alternative Hypothesis → Intervene and Collect Data

Progress Monitor: Intervention effective? — Yes → Continue to support the student and monitor progress

No

Have sufficient attempts at alternatives within Tier II been made? — No

Yes: Move to Tier III

Have sufficient attempts at alternatives within Tier III been made?

Yes

FOCUS: Entitlement decision and instructional decisions

Multidisciplinary Team: What is the problem and are additional data needed? Are additional interventions needed?

No

Does the student meet specific requirements for a disability? — No → Discontinue evaluation and decide whether to continue use of Tier II or Tier III interventions

Yes

Does the student need specially designed instruction? — No → Student may qualify for services under Section 504

Yes

Implement and work collaboratively with others to provide individually designed instruction

Move to

FOCUS: Continued entitlement decision and instructional decisions

Reevaluation: Review and revise IEP. Determine service and LRE. Must occur every three years but not more than once a year unless school and parents agree otherwise

Additional data needed

Notice and parental consent

Collect additional data

Re-evaluation report

No additional data needed

Notify parents of right to request additional data. Document agreement and determine eligibility given current data

Move to decision

No — Is the continuation of special education necessary? — Yes

Dismissal of special education enrollment

Provision of services and supports and implementation of reviewed and revised IEP

the materials in which she is placed. A decision is made to move to targeted interventions (tier 2) in an effort to attempt to overcome Sara's deficit in reading skills. The problem is verified, alternative hypotheses are generated about how best to address the problem, interventions are tried, and assessment data are collected. If sufficient progress is not evidenced after application of multiple interventions, a decision is made to move to more intensive (tier 3) interventions. Once sufficient attempts at intervening in a variety of ways are made, and if Sara fails to make sufficient progress, she may be referred for further assessment to determine her eligibility for special education services. Decisions about eligibility must be made by a multidisciplinary team of professionals that includes general and special educators, administrators, school psychologists, and others, depending on the nature of the case. The multidisiciplinary team develops an individualized educational plan, specifying short- and long-term objectives for Sara and the specific instructional approaches that will be used to achieve those objectives. It is expected that the long-term goals will be based on the state education standards. The goals are thus often called standards-based goals.

When students receive special education services, teachers are expected to monitor progress toward IEP goals. School personnel are also required to review periodically the extent to which the student continues to be eligible for special education services, and if not, they must discontinue such services. Screening, instructional planning, eligibility, and progress evaluation decisions are made for individual students. Resource allocation decisions are system decisions that apply to individual students. Program evaluation and accountability decisions typically are made for groups rather than individuals.

Chapter Comprehension Questions

Write your answers to each of the following questions and then compare your responses to the text.

1. List and briefly describe the four major ways in which assessment information is collected.

2. List and describe the seven kinds of decisions made using assessment information.

3. Describe the sequence of activities that take place at the prereferral, eligibility, and reevaluation stages of the assessment process.

CHAPTER

3

LAWS, ETHICAL CODES, AND PROFESSIONAL STANDARDS THAT IMPACT ASSESSMENT

LEARNING OBJECTIVES

3-1 Articulate the major laws that affect assessment, and the specific provisions (for example, individualized education program, least restrictive environment, and due process) of the laws.

3-2 Describe broad ethical principles and standards for assessment that have been developed by professional associations, and a process for addressing situations in which the most ethical approach is ambiguous.

3-3 Explain how test standards promote the development of tests with greater technical adequacy.

STANDARDS ADDRESSED IN THIS CHAPTER

CEC CEC Initial Preparation Standards

Standard 4: Assessment

4.0 Beginning special education professionals use multiple methods of assessment and data-sources in making educational decisions.

Standard 6: Professional Learning and Ethical Practice

6.0 Beginning special education professionals use foundational knowledge of the field and their professional Ethical Principles and Practice Standards to inform special education practice, to engage in lifelong learning, and to advance the profession.

CEC CEC Advanced Preparation Standards
ADVANCED

Standard 1: Assessment

1.0 Special education specialists use valid and reliable assessment practices to minimize bias.

Bill Aron/PhotoEdit

23

Standard 6: Professional and Ethical Practice
6.0 Special education specialists use foundational knowledge of the field and professional Ethical Principles and Practice Standards to inform special education practice, engage in lifelong learning, advance the profession, and perform leadership responsibilities to promote the success of professional colleagues and individuals with exceptionalities.

 National Association of School Psychologists Domains
1 Data-Based Decision Making and Accountability
10 Legal, Ethical, and Professional Practice

Much of the practice of assessing students is the direct result of federal laws, court rulings, and professional standards and ethics. Federal laws mandate that students be assessed before they are entitled to special education services. Federal laws also mandate that there be an individualized education program for every student with a disability; that instructional objectives for each of these students be derived from a comprehensive individualized assessment; and that states provide an annual report to the U.S. Department of Education on the academic performance of all students, including students with disabilities. Professional associations (for example, the Council for Exceptional Children, the National Association of School Psychologists, and the American Psychological Association) specify standards for good professional practice and ethical principles to guide the behavior of those who assess students.

3-1 Laws

Laws, rules, and regulations change frequently. They are fueled by information provided to policymakers, which convinces them that the respective changes will be helpful. Changes often come about when there is a lack of clarity in the associated laws, rules, and regulations, as evidenced by court cases that are needed to clarify how the law should be interpreted in various ambiguous situations. As you read this chapter, we suggest that you enter "IDEA changes," "ESEA changes," or "NCLB changes" into a search engine and read the latest changes to the law.

It is very important that you understand the history of federal legislation on the education and assessment of individuals with disabilities. Prior to 1975, there was no federal requirement that students with disabilities attend school, or that schools should make an effort to teach students with disabilities. Requirements were on a state-by-state basis, and they differed and were applied differently in the states. Since the mid-1970s, the delivery of services to students in special and inclusive education has been governed by federal laws. An important federal law, called **Section 504 of the Rehabilitation Act of 1973**, gave individuals with disabilities equal access to programs and services funded by federal monies. In 1975, Congress passed the **Education for All Handicapped Children Act (Public Law 94-142)**, which was a law that included many instructional and assessment requirements for serving and identifying students with disabilities in need of specially designed instruction. The law was reauthorized, amended, and updated in 1986, 1990, 1997, and 2004. In 1990, the law was given a new name: the **Individuals with Disabilities Education Act (IDEA)**, and as with other reauthorizations, it included updated provisions for identifying and serving students with disabilities. To reflect contemporary practices, Congress replaced references to "handicapped children" with "children with disabilities." In the 2004 reauthorization, the law was again retitled, as the Individuals with Disabilities Education Improvement Act, to highlight the fact that the major intent of the law is to improve educational services for students with disabilities.

The 2001 Elementary and Secondary Education Act (commonly referred to as the No Child Left Behind Act (NCLB)), is another federal law that is especially important to contemporary assessment practices, because it requires that states report to the U.S. Department of Education every year data on the performance and progress of all students. States get the information from districts, so this law requires that school districts report to state departments of education on the performance and progress of all students, including students with disabilities and English learners. Table 3.1 lists the federal laws that are especially important to assessment practices, and the major new provisions of each of the laws are highlighted.

3-1a SECTION 504 OF THE REHABILITATION ACT OF 1973

Section 504 of the Rehabilitation Act of 1973 is civil rights legislation that prohibits discrimination against persons with disabilities. The act states:

No otherwise qualified handicapped individual shall, solely by reason of his handicap, be excluded from the participation in, be denied the benefits of, or be subjected to discrimination in any program or activity receiving federal financial assistance.

Section 504 (1) prohibits schools from excluding students with disabilities from any activities solely because of their disability, (2) requires schools to take reasonable steps to prevent harassment based on disability, and (3) requires schools to make those accommodations necessary to enable students with disabilities to participate in all its activities and services (Jacob, Decker, & Hartshorne, 2011). If the Office of Civil Rights (OCR) of the U.S. Department of Education finds that a state education agency (SEA) or local education agency (LEA) is not in compliance with Section 504, and that a state or district chooses not to act to correct the noncompliance, the OCR may withhold federal funds from that SEA or LEA.

Most of the provisions of Section 504 were incorporated into and expanded in the Education for All Handicapped Children Act of 1975 (Public Law 94-142) and are a part of the Individuals with Disabilities Education Improvement Act of 2004. Section 504 is broader than those other acts because its provisions are not restricted to a specific age group or to education.

Section 504 has been used to secure services for students with conditions not formally listed in the disabilities education legislation. The most frequent of these conditions is attention deficit hyperactivity disorder (ADHD). Unlike IDEA, Section 504 does not provide any funds to schools. Yet, any school that receives federal funds for any purpose at all must comply with the provisions of Section 504 or they lose their funds. And, to make matters more complex, Section 504 and the Americans with Disabilities Act Amendments of 2008 require that schools must provide students with the necessary accommodations to participate in individual and standards-based assessments. It is illegal to refuse to let students use accommodations (like extra time, testing sessions broken into short intervals, or sign language) necessary to be successful in school and/or to participate in individual or standards-based assessment. Those who assess students are required to evaluate the extent to which they are eligible for accommodations in classrooms and/or those necessary to take tests. The accommodations must always be determined by a group of people (usually the child study or IEP team) and they must be based on individual student need rather than on disability type or category.

3-1b MAJOR ASSESSMENT PROVISIONS OF THE INDIVIDUALS WITH DISABILITIES EDUCATION IMPROVEMENT ACT

When Congress passed the Education for All Handicapped Children Act in 1975, it included four major requirements relative to assessment: (1) an individualized education program (IEP) for each student with a disability, (2) protection in evaluation

TABLE 3.1	Major Federal Laws and Their Key Provisions Relevant to Assessment

Act	Provisions
Section 504 of the Rehabilitation Act of 1973 (Public Law 93-112)	It is illegal to deny participation in activities or benefits of programs, or to in any way discriminate against a person with a disability solely because of the disability. Individuals with disabilities must have equal access to programs and services. Auxiliary aids must be provided to individuals with impaired speaking, manual, or sensory skills.
Family Educational Rights and Privacy Act (Public Law 93-380)	Educational agencies that accept federal funding must grant parents the opportunity to inspect and challenge student records, as well as require parent consent for release of identifiable data. Once the child turns 18, these rights are transferred to the child.
Education for All Handicapped Children Act of 1975 (Public Law 94-142)	Students with disabilities have the right to a free, appropriate public education. Schools must have on file an individualized education program for each student determined to be eligible for services under the act. Parents have the right to inspect school records on their children. When changes are made in a student's educational placement or program, parents must be informed. Parents have the right to challenge what is in records or to challenge changes in placement. Students with disabilities have the right to be educated in the least restrictive educational environment. Students with disabilities must be assessed in ways that are considered fair and nondiscriminatory. They have specific protections.
1986 Amendments to the Education for All Handicapped Children Act (Public Law 99-457)	All rights of the Education for All Handicapped Children Act are extended to preschoolers with disabilities. Each school district must conduct a multidisciplinary assessment and develop an individualized family service plan for each preschool child with a disability.
Individuals with Disabilities Education Act of 1990 (Public Law 101-476)	This act reauthorizes the Education for All Handicapped Children Act. Two new disability categories (traumatic brain injury and autism) are added to the definition of students with disabilities. A comprehensive definition of transition services is added.
1990 Americans with Disabilities Act	Guarantees equal opportunity to individuals with disabilities in employment, public services, transportation, state and local government services, and telecommunications.
1997 Amendments to the Individuals with Disabilities Education Act (IDEA; Public Law 105-17)	These amendments add a number of significant provisions to IDEA and restructure the law. A number of changes in the individualized education program and participation of students with disabilities in state and district assessments are mandated. Significant provisions on mediation of disputes and discipline of students with disabilities are added.
2001 Elementary and Secondary Education Act (No Child Left Behind Act; Public Law 107-110)	Targeted resources are provided to help ensure that disadvantaged students have access to a quality public education (Title I funds). The act aims to maximize student learning, provide for teacher development, and enhance school system capacity. The act requires states and districts to report on annual yearly progress for all students, including students with disabilities. The act provides increased flexibility to districts in exchange for increased accountability. The act gives parents whose children attend schools on state "failing schools list" for two years the right to transfer their children to another school. Students in "failing schools" for three years are eligible for supplemental education services.
2004 Reauthorization of IDEA	New approaches are introduced to prevent overidentification by race or ethnicity. States must have measurable annual objectives for students with disabilities. Districts are not required to use severe discrepancy between ability and achievement in identifying students with learning disabilities.
2008 Americans with Disabilities Act Amendments	This act further defines and clarifies criteria necessary for determining whether a student has a disability under ADA and Section 504.

procedures, (3) education in the least restrictive appropriate environment (LRE), and (4) due process rights. The provisions of federal law continued with the 2004 reauthorized Individuals with Disabilities Education Improvement Act.

The Individualized Education Program (IEP) Provisions

Public Law 94-142 (the Education for All Handicapped Children Act of 1975) specified that all students with disabilities have the right to a free, appropriate public education and that schools must have an IEP for each student with a disability who is determined to need specially designed instruction. An **Individualized Education Program (IEP)** is a legal document that describes the services that are to be provided to a student with a disability who qualifies for special education services. In the IEP, school personnel must specify the long- and short-term goals of the instructional program. IEPs must be based on a comprehensive assessment by a multidisciplinary team. We stress that assessment data are collected for the purpose of helping team members specify the components of the IEP. The team must specify not only goals and objectives but also plans for implementing the instructional program. They must specify how and when progress toward accomplishment of objectives will be evaluated. Note that specific assessment activities that form the basis of the program are listed, as are specific instructional goals or objectives. IEPs are to be formulated by a multidisciplinary child study team that meets with the parents. Parents have the right to agree or disagree with the contents of the program. Read the upcoming Scenario in Assessment and associated question to consider how legal requirements surrounding IEPs influence the experiences of students with disabilities.

In the 1997 amendments, Congress mandated a number of changes to the IEP. The core IEP team was expanded to include both a special education teacher and a general education teacher. The 1997 law also specified that students with disabilities are to be included in state- and districtwide assessments and that states must report annually on the performance and progress of all students, including students with disabilities. The IEP team must decide whether the student will take the assessments with or without accommodations or take an alternate assessment.

Protection in Evaluation Procedures Provisions

Congress included a number of specific requirements in Public Law 94-142. These requirements were designed to protect students and help ensure that assessment procedures and activities would be fair, equitable, and nondiscriminatory. Specifically, Congress mandated eight provisions:

1. Tests are to be selected and administered so as to be racially and culturally nondiscriminatory.
2. To the extent feasible, students are to be assessed in their native language or primary mode of communication (such as American Sign Language or communication board).
3. Tests must have been validated for the specific purpose for which they are used.
4. Tests must be administered by trained personnel in conformance with the instructions provided by the test producer.
5. Tests used with students must include those designed to provide information about specific educational needs, not just a general intelligence quotient.
6. Decisions about students are to be based on more than their performance on a single test.
7. Evaluations are to be made by a multidisciplinary team that includes at least one teacher or other specialist with knowledge in the area of suspected disability.
8. Children must be assessed in all areas related to a specific disability, including—where appropriate—health, vision, hearing, social and emotional status, general intelligence, academic performance, communicative skills, and motor skills.

SCENARIO IN ASSESSMENT

LEE | Lee is a young man with a moderate intellectual disability. He was diagnosed at birth with a genetic syndrome that is closely associated with intellectual disability. Consequently, Lee's parents were concerned with his development and monitored it closely. Unfortunately, it soon became clear that he was lagging in passing developmental milestones such as recognizing faces, sitting up, making prespeech sounds, and so forth. At age 2, he was identified as eligible for early intervention services because of his delayed development. An Individual Family Service Plan (see Part C of IDEA) was developed. Not only did Lee receive special services, but also his family received various support services. Lee and his family continued to receive special education services when he enrolled in his neighborhood school, where he received a free, appropriate public education as described in an individualized educational plan (IEP) that his parents helped develop. In the primary grades, Lee also received speech therapy for articulation problems and occupational therapy for pencil and scissor use. Lee's parents received parent counseling to learn how to manage bedtime and toileting behavior. Lee made good progress throughout his elementary school program. He mastered self-help skills, some sight vocabulary, coin recognition, etc. In short, he met the annual goals in his IEP, seemed to enjoy school, and made friends, mostly in his special education classroom.

The year Lee entered high school he turned 14, and his education emphasized preparing Lee for postsecondary training, employment, and community living. It stressed helping Lee become more independent in life after high school. Therefore, his progress was measured in the areas of employment options and preferences, recreation and leisure activities, personal management (e.g., using public transportation, doing laundry, money management, etc.), family and social relationships, and advocacy. Lee participated in a work-study program and had a job coach for his job at a local supermarket. Lee continued his public education until the year he turned 21.

Today, Lee lives in a subsidized apartment, works full-time at the same supermarket, and has several friends. He plans on marrying his long-time girlfriend in the near future. He has an advocate who advises him on a number of topics.

Fifty years ago—before PL 94-142, IDEA, and PL 99-457, and before states and the federal government began guaranteeing educational rights for students with moderate or severe disabilities—Lee would have faced a much different life. There would not have been an early education or a public education. Lee would not have been prepared to live so independently—to work, to have his own home, etc.

This scenario highlights how federal law guarantees students with disabilities a free and appropriate public education. IEPs are developed to address individual student needs, and involve monitoring of progress in areas targeted for measurement for the individual student. How might have Lee's education looked different if there were not rules requiring that an IEP be developed and informed by an assessment process?

© Cengage Learning

In passing the 1997 amendments and the 2004 amendments, Congress reauthorized these provisions.

Least Restrictive Environment Provisions

In writing the 1975 Education for All Handicapped Children Act, Congress wanted to ensure that, to the greatest extent appropriate, students with disabilities would be placed in settings that would maximize their opportunities to interact with students without disabilities. **Least Restrictive Environment (LRE)** is now defined in Section 612(a)(5) (A) of IDEA 2004, which states:

> *To the maximum extent appropriate, children with disabilities . . . are educated with children who are not disabled, and special classes, separate schooling, or other removal of children with disabilities from the regular educational environment occurs only when the nature or severity of the disability of a child is such that education in regular classes with the use of supplementary aids and services cannot be achieved satisfactorily.*

The LRE provisions arose out of court cases in which state and federal courts had ruled that when two equally appropriate placements were available for a student with a disability, the most normal (that is, least restrictive) placement was preferred. The LRE provisions were reauthorized in all revisions of the law.

Due Process Provisions

In Public Law 94-142, Congress specified the procedures that schools and school personnel would have to follow to ensure due process in decision making, which is commonly referred to as "**due process**." Specifically, when a decision affecting identification, evaluation, or placement of a student with disabilities is to be made, the student's parents or guardians must be given both the opportunity to be heard and the right to have an impartial due process hearing to resolve conflicting opinions.

Schools must provide opportunities for parents to inspect the records that are kept on their children and to challenge material that they believe should not be included in those records. Parents have the right to have their child evaluated by an independent party and to have the results of that evaluation considered when psychoeducational decisions are made. In addition, parents must receive written notification before any education agency can begin an evaluation that might result in changes in the placement of a student.

In the 1997 amendments to IDEA, Congress specified that states must offer mediation as a voluntary option to parents and educators as an initial part of dispute resolution. If mediation is not successful, either party may request a due process hearing. The due process provisions were reauthorized in the 2004 IDEA.

3-1c THE NO CHILD LEFT BEHIND ACT OF 2001

The **No Child Left Behind Act of 2001** is the reform of the federal Elementary and Secondary Education Act, which was signed into law on January 8, 2002, and has several major provisions that affect assessment and instruction of students with disabilities and disadvantaged students. The law requires stronger accountability for results by specifying that states must have challenging state educational standards, test children in grades 3–8 every year, and specify statewide progress objectives that ensure proficiency of every child by grade 12. The law also provides increased flexibility and local control, specifying that states can decide their standards and procedures but at the same time must be held accountable for results. Parents are given expanded educational options under this law, and students who are attending schools judged to be "failing schools" have the right to enroll in other public schools, including public charter schools. A major provision of this law is called "putting reading first," a set of provisions ensuring an all-out effort to have every child reading by the end of third grade. These provisions provide funding to schools for intensive reading interventions for children in grades K–3. Finally, the law specifies that all students have the right to be taught using "**evidence-based instructional methods**"—that is, teaching methods proven to work. The provisions of this law require that states include all students, among them students with disabilities and English-language learners, in their statewide accountability systems.

The Elementary and Special Education Act (i.e., No Child Left Behind Act of 2001) was due for reauthorization in 2007; however, as of the writing of this text, Congress had not yet taken the associated actions. In response to the lack of reauthorization, President Obama offered flexibility to states with regard to the specific requirements of the law if they submitted accountability plans demonstrating a strong commitment to improving the outcomes of all students. In addition, **Race to the Top** was initiated, which is a federal program that has granted funds to two consortia of states for the development of common assessments that measure student achievement against standards that represent what is needed to be successful in the workplace and college. At the same time, **Common Core State Standards** have been developed by state leaders to allow for greater consistency in what is taught and measured across states. More information about these developments is available in Chapter 22. Although not federally mandated, many states have decided to participate in these initiatives and thereby receive the associated funding.

3-1d 2004 REAUTHORIZATION OF IDEA

The Individuals with Disabilities Education Act was reauthorized in 2004. Several of the new requirements of the law have special implications for assessment of students with disabilities.[1] After much debate, Congress removed the requirement

---

[1] The law was retitled the Individuals with Disabilities Education Improvement Act, but the acronym IDEA is still used to refer to the new law.

that students must have a severe discrepancy between ability and achievement in order to be considered as having a learning disability. It replaced this provision with permission to states and districts to use data on student responsiveness to intervention in making service eligibility decisions. We provide an extensive discussion of assessing response to intervention in Chapter 12. Congress also specified that states must have measurable goals, standards, or objectives for all students with disabilities.

3-1e AMERICANS WITH DISABILITIES ACT OF 1990 (ADA)

The Americans with Disabilities Act (ADA) is the law that requires agencies receiving federal funding to provide appropriate access to their activities for individuals with disabilities. It is the most often cited law in court cases involving either employment of people with disabilities or appropriate education in colleges and universities for students with disabilities. Simply put, any agency or organization that receives federal funds must provide access (like building ramps), transportation (like special buses or wheelchair lifts), or accommodations (like sign language interpreters at plays and musical events) necessary to enable students with disabilities to participate in its services and events.

3-1f AMERICANS WITH DISABILITIES ACT AMENDMENTS OF 2008 (ADAA)

In 2008, Congress reauthorized and revised the Americans with Disabilities Act. The **Americans with Disabilities Act Amendments of 2008 (ADAA)** is the name of the new law, and includes changes primarily for the purpose of clarifying the criteria for making decisions about eligibility for entitlements like special education services. The term "504/ADAA impairment" is used to refer to those students who qualify as having a disability under Section 504/ADAA, but who are not eligible for special education and related services under IDEA. As long as they also meet the "need" criterion, they are entitled to special education services as a protection under Section 504/ADAA.

3-1g FAMILY EDUCATIONAL RIGHTS AND PRIVACY ACT OF 1974 (FERPA)

Through this act, educational agencies that receive federal funds must allow all parents access to, and the ability to amend, their child's educational records until the child turns 18, at which time the associated rights are conferred to the student. In order to share identifiable information outside of the school setting, consent from the respective individuals is needed. The associated rules are further explained in Chapter 23 on Collaborative Team Decision Making, and they are also incorporated within IDEA.

3-2 Ethical Considerations

Professionals who assess students have the responsibility to engage in ethical behavior. Most professional associations have put together sets of standards to guide the ethical practice of their members; many of these standards relate directly to assessment practices. Those most relevant to the concerns of education professionals are the ethical principles of the Council for Exceptional Children, National Education Association, American Federation of Teachers, National Association of School Psychologists, and American Psychological Association. (All of these can be found on the respective organization's website.) In our work with teachers and related services personnel, we consistently have found that the most helpful set of ethical principles and guidelines are those of the National Association of School Psychologists (these are based heavily on the ethical principles of the Canadian Psychological Association).

In publishing ethical and professional standards, the associations express serious commitment to promoting high technical standards for assessment instruments and high ethical standards for the behavior of individuals who work with assessments. Here, we cite a number of important ethical considerations, borrowing heavily from the **National Association of School Psychologists' (2010)** *Principles for Professional Ethics*, the **American Psychological Association's (2010)** *Ethical Principles of Psychologists and Code of Conduct for Psychologists*, and the **National Education Association's** *Code of Ethics of the Education Profession*, which each represent the ethical codes for the respective professional organizations. We have not cited the standards explicitly, but we have distilled from them a number of broad ethical principles that guide assessment practice and behavior.

The term *ethics* generally refers to a system of principles of conduct that guide the behavior of an individual. Codes of ethics serve to protect the public. However, ethical conduct is not synonymous with simple conformity to a set of rules outlined as principles and professional standards. Instead, it often requires careful thought and use of a decision-making process. Given that every situation is different, it is impossible to provide an ethical approach for each situation one might encounter. A professional must have good knowledge of the given situation to know how best to apply the relevant principles and standards in a given context. NASP's Code of Ethics of 2010 is organized around four broad ethical themes: Respecting the Dignity and Rights of All Persons; Professional Competence and Responsibility; Honesty and Integrity in Professional Relationships; and Responsibility to Schools, Families, Communities, the Profession, and Society" (Jacob, Decker, & Hartshorne, 2011, p. 9). We briefly describe these four broad ethical themes in the sections that follow, and describe a process to guide ethical decision making for situations where you are uncertain how to proceed.

3-2a FOUR BROAD ETHICAL PRINCIPLES

Respect for the Dignity of Persons

School personnel are committed to "promoting improvement in the quality of life for all students, their families and school communities" (Jacob et al., 2011). (For a fuller discussion of these principles see Jacob et al., 2011). The discussion applies equally to all school personnel. In brief, this broad principle means that we always recognize that students and their families have the right to participate in decisions that affect student welfare, and that students have the right to decide for themselves whether they want to share their thoughts, feelings, and behaviors.

Those who assess students regularly obtain a considerable amount of very personal information about those students. Such information must be held in strict confidence. A general ethical principle held by most professional organizations is that confidentiality may be broken only when there is clear and imminent danger to an individual or to society. Results of pupil performance on tests must not be discussed informally with school staff members. Formal reports of pupil performance on tests must be released only with the permission of the persons tested or their parents or guardians.

Those who assess students are to make provisions for maintaining confidentiality in the storage and disposal of records. When working with minors or other persons who are unable to give voluntary informed consent, assessors are to take special care to protect these persons' best interests. Those who assess students are expected to maintain test security. It is expected that assessors will not reveal to others the content of specific tests or test items. At the same time, assessors must be willing and able to back up with test data decisions that may adversely affect individuals.

Professional Competence and Responsibility (Responsible Caring and Beneficence)

The ethical codes of all helping professions share a common theme referred to generally as the *beneficence* principle. **Beneficence**, or responsible caring, means educational professionals do things that are likely to maximize benefits to students, or at least do no harm. This means that educational professionals always act in the best interests of the students they serve. The assessment of students is a social act that has specific social and educational consequences. Those who assess students use assessment data to make decisions about the students, and these decisions can significantly affect an individual's life opportunities. Those who assess students must accept responsibility for the consequences of their work, and they must make every effort to be certain that their services are used appropriately. In short, they are committed to the application of professional expertise to promote improvement in the quality of life available to the student, family, school, and community. For the individual who assesses students, this ethical standard may mean refusing to engage in assessment activities that are desired by a school system but that are clearly inappropriate.

Honesty and Integrity in Professional Relationships

We must all recognize the boundaries of our professional competence. Those who are entrusted with the responsibility for assessing and making decisions about students have differing degrees of competence. Not only must professionals regularly engage in self-assessment to be aware of their own limitations, but also they should recognize the limitations of the techniques they use. For individuals, this sometimes means refusing to engage in activities in areas in which they lack competence. It also means using techniques that meet recognized standards and engaging in the continuing education necessary to maintain high standards of competence. As a professional who will assess students, it is imperative that you accept responsibility for the consequences of your work and that you endeavor to offset any negative consequences of your work.

As schools become increasingly diverse, professionals must demonstrate sensitivity in working with people from different cultural and linguistic backgrounds and with children who have different types of disabling conditions. Assessors should have experience working with students of diverse backgrounds and should demonstrate competence in doing so, or they should refrain from assessing and making decisions about such students.

Responsibility to Schools, Families, Communities, One's Profession, and Society

Those who are entrusted to educate students have responsibilities to the societies and communities in which they work. This means behaving professionally and not doing things that reflect badly on one's employer or profession. As professionals, we are responsible for promoting healthy school, family, and community environments, respecting and obeying laws, contributing to our profession by supervising, mentoring, and educating professional colleagues, and ensuring that *all* students can attend school, learn, and develop their personal identities in environments free from discrimination, harassment, violence, and abuse (Jacob et al., 2011). Often the students with whom we work (especially students with disabilities) are among the most vulnerable members of society. We have a responsibility to protect their rights.

Those who assess students are responsible for selecting and administering tests in a fair and nonbiased manner. Assessment approaches must be selected that are valid, provide an accurate representation of students' skills and abilities, and also avoid being influenced by their disabilities. Tests are to be selected and administered so as to be racially and culturally nondiscriminatory, and students should be assessed in their native language or primary mode of communication (for example, Braille or communication boards).

HOW DO YOU RESOLVE AN ETHICAL DILEMMA?

How do you decide what kinds of actions are ethical?

Jacob et al. (2011) provide an eight-step problem-solving model that walks us through the following steps:

1. Describe the parameters of the situation.
2. Define the potential ethical–legal issues involved.
3. Consult ethical and legal guidelines and district policies that might apply to resolution of each issue.
4. Evaluate the rights, responsibilities, and welfare of all affected persons (students, peers, teachers, other school staff, parents, siblings).
5. Generate a list of alternative things you could do in response to the situation.
6. List the consequences of taking each action.
7. Consider any evidence that the various consequences or benefits resulting from each decision will actually happen (conduct a risk–benefit analysis).
8. Make the decision.

If you encounter another professional who you believe is behaving unethically, the following steps are to be used:

1. Speak personally about what you have observed with the person who has committed the behavior. Let him or her know that the behavior might be considered illegal or unethical. Often, people do not know or recognize that what they are doing is illegal, wrong, or harmful. (Of course, they often do).
2. If the behavior persists (e.g., repeated use of technically inadequate tests), take another professional with you and talk to the person about what the two of you have observed.
3. If the behavior persists, report the behavior to the person's supervisor and ask the supervisor to take action. If your school district has an attorney, include the attorney in this discussion.
4. If the behavior persists, either report the behavior to the relevant ethics board or committee or let the school attorney take action deemed necessary.

Adapted from Jacob, S., Decker, D., and Hartshorne, T. *Ethics and Law for School Psychologists*, 6th ed.

3-3 Test Standards

Those who assess students adhere to professional standards on assessment.

The ***Standards for Educational and Psychological Testing*** were developed by a joint committee of the American Educational Research Association, the American Psychological Association, and the National Council on Measurement in Education (2014), and they specify a set of requirements for test development and use. It is imperative that those who develop tests behave in accordance with the standards, and that those who assess students use instruments and techniques that meet the standards.

In Part 3 of this text, we review commonly used tests and discuss the extent to which those tests meet the standards specified in *Standards for Educational and Psychological Testing*. We provide information to help test users make informed judgments about the technical adequacy of specific tests. There is no federal or state agency that acts to limit the publication or use of technically inadequate tests. Only by refusing to use technically inadequate tests will users force developers to improve them. After all, if you were a test developer, would you continue to publish a test that few people purchased and used? Would you invest your company's resources to make changes in a technically inadequate test that yielded a large annual profit to your firm if people continued to buy and use it the way it was without any changes?

Chapter Comprehension Questions

Write your answers to each of the following questions and then compare your responses to the text.

1. What are three major laws that affect assessment practices?
2. How do the major components of IDEA (individualized educational plan, least restrictive environment, protection in evaluation procedures, and due process) affect assessment practices?

3. Special education is a field of acronyms. SWD are entitled to services under IDEA; others, who are labeled ADHD, are not eligible for services under IDEA but once received services under ADA and are now eligible under ADAA/504. Because of NCLB, Title I students are eligible for services. Students with disabilities are put on an IEP, but school personnel do not have to write one for SW/OD. Students with disabilities are entitled to a FAPE, PEP, and education in the LRE. Translate these sentences in a way that your mother or grandmother could understand.

4. Identify the ethical principles that you believe should guide the behavior of individuals in two of the following professions: plumber, stockbroker, grocery store manager, used car salesman, physician, bartender, and professor. Then write a brief paragraph on why you selected the principles and how they differ for different professions. Are there commonalities?

5. How do the broad ethical principles of beneficence, competence boundaries, respect for the dignity of persons, confidentiality, and fairness affect assessment practices?

6. What are two practices in which you can engage to support the development of technically adequate tests?

CHAPTER

4

WHAT TEST SCORES MEAN

LEARNING OBJECTIVES

4-1 Describe the basic quantitative concepts that deal with scales of measurement, characteristics of distributions, average scores, measures of dispersion, and correlation.

4-2 Explain how test performances are made meaningful through criterion-referenced, achievement standards-referenced, and norm-referenced interpretations.

4-3 Describe how norms are constructed to be proportionally representative of the population in terms of important personal characteristics (for example, gender and age), must contain a large number of people, must be representative of today's population, and must be relevant for the purposes of assessment.

STANDARDS ADDRESSED IN THIS CHAPTER

 CEC Initial Preparation Standards

Standard 4: Assessment

4.0 Beginning special education professionals use multiple methods of assessment and data-sources in making educational decisions.

 CEC Advanced Preparation Standards

Standard 1: Assessment

1.0 Special education specialists use valid and reliable assessment practices to minimize bias.

 National Association of School Psychologists Domains

1 Data-Based Decision Making and Accountability

9 Research and Program Evaluation

School personnel are expected to use the results of tests that they receive throughout their professional careers. Correct usage requires educators to understand the meaning of the scores reported for those tests. Suppose you decide to review the school folders of students who will be in your class in the fall. You learn that Willis has an IQ of 87 and scored at the 22nd percentile on a measure of reading vocabulary. Elaine earned a grade equivalent of 4.2 on a math test. Overall, 65 percent of your students earned scores of "proficient" in reading on the state test last spring; 22 percent of your students earned scores of "basic." Most of your class also scored at the state median on the measure of writing. Obviously, this information is supposed to mean something to you and could affect how you will teach. What do these scores mean? Should they affect the instructional decisions you will make?

Understanding the meaning of many test scores requires knowledge of basic statistical concepts. The first part of this chapter reviews basic quantitative concepts that will be needed by those who want to understand assessment and the use of assessment information to make decisions about students in special and inclusive education.

4-1 Descriptive Statistics

We use descriptive statistics to describe or summarize data. In testing, the data are scores: several scores on one individual, one score on several individuals, or several scores on several individuals. Descriptive statistics are calculated using the basic mathematical operations of addition, subtraction, multiplication, and division, as well as simple exponential operations (squares and square roots); advanced knowledge of mathematics is not required. Although many calculations are repetitive and tedious, calculators and computers facilitate these calculations, and test authors usually provide tables of all the pertinent descriptive statistics. This chapter deals with the basic concepts needed for an understanding of descriptive statistics: scales of measurement, distributions, measures of central tendency, measures of dispersion, and measures of relationship (correlation).

4-1a BASIC STATISTICAL NOTATION

A number of symbols are used in statistics, and different authors use different symbols. Table 4.1 lists the symbols that we use in this book. The summation sign (Σ) means "add the following"; X denotes any score. The number of scores in a distribution is symbolized by N; n denotes the number of scores in a subset of a distribution. The arithmetic average (mean) of a distribution is denoted by $\overline{X}$. The variance of a distribution is symbolized by S^2, and the standard deviation by S.

TABLE 4.1	Commonly Used Statistical Symbols
Symbol	**Meaning**
Σ	Summation sign
X	Any score
N	Number of cases
n	Number in subset
$\overline{X}$	Mean
S^2	Variance
S	Standard deviation

4-1b SCALES OF MEASUREMENT

The ways in which data can be summarized depend on the kind of scale in which the scores are expressed. There are four types of measurement scales: nominal, ordinal, ratio, and equal interval (Stevens, 1951).

The four scales are distinguished on the basis of the relationship between adjacent, or consecutive, values on the measurement scale. An adjacent value in this case means a potential or possible scale value, rather than an obtained or measured value. In Figure 4.1, the possible values between 2 inches and 6 inches, measured in intervals of eighths of an inch, are depicted. Any two consecutive points on the scale (for instance 3 1/8 and 3 1/4 inches) are adjacent values. Any two points on the scale that have values between them (for instance 3 1/8 inches and 4 1/8 inches) are not adjacent points. Of course different scales have different adjacent values—adjacent intervals larger or smaller than 1/8 of an inch.

Nominal scales name the values of the scale, but adjacent values have no inherent relationship. These values can describe attributes (for example, gender, eye color, race), geographic region where a person resides (for example, the Pacific Northwest), educational classification (for example, learning disabled or emotionally disturbed), and so forth.

Because adjacent values on nominal scales have no inherent relationship, the various mathematical operations cannot be performed on them. For example, numbers on athletic shirts have no mathematical relationship to each other. The player who wears number 80 is not necessarily a better or larger or older player than the player who wears number 79 or number 70; they are just different players. There is no implied rank ordering in the numbers worn on the shirts. It would not make any sense to add up shirt numbers to determine which athletic team is the best. Mathematically, all we can do with nominal scales is determine the frequency of each value (for example, the number of boys and girls).

Ordinal scales order values from worse to better (for example, pass-fail, or poor-OK-good-better-best), and there is a relationship among adjacent scores. Higher scores are better than lower scores, but the magnitude of the difference between adjacent values is unknown and unlikely to be equal. Thus, we cannot determine how much better a *better* performance is than a *good* performance or if the difference between *good* and *better* is the same as the difference between *better* and *best*. Because the differences between adjacent values are unknown and presumed unequal, ordinal scores cannot be added, multiplied, divided, or averaged.

Ratio scales not only order values but also have two very important characteristics: (1) the magnitude of the difference between adjacent values is known and is equal, and (2) each scale has an absolute and logical zero. Equal differences between adjacent values means that the difference between 4 and 5 pounds, for example, is the same as the difference between 40 and 41 pounds and is the same

FIGURE 4.1
Adjacent and
Nonadjacent Values

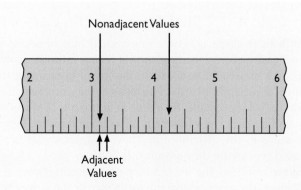

FIGURE 4.2
The Measurement of
Lines as a Function
of the Starting Point

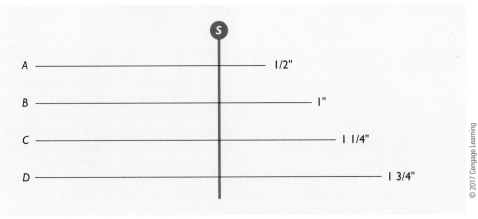

as the difference between 555 and 556 pounds. Because the differences between adjacent values on equal interval scales are equal, scores can be manipulated mathematically (e.g., added, multiplied, squared, and so forth). Having an absolute and logical difference means that we can create ratios with any two variables. For example, if John weighs 300 pounds and Bob weighs 150 pounds, John weighs twice as much as Bob.

Equal-Interval scales are ratio scales that do not have an absolute and logical zero. Consider the information in Figure 4.2. The differences among lines A, B, C, and D are readily measured. We can start measuring from any point, such as from the point where Line S intersects Lines A, B, C, and D. The portion of Line A to the right of S is 1/2 inch long; that of Line B to the right of S is 1 inch long; that of Line C to the right of S is 1 1/4 inches long; and that of Line D to the right of S is 1 3/4 inches long. The lines are measured on an equal-interval scale, and the differences among the lines would be the same no matter where the starting point S was located. However, because S is not a logical and absolute zero, we cannot make ratio comparisons among the lines. Although, when we began measuring from S, we found Line A to measure 1/2 inch from S and Line B to measure 1 inch from S, the whole of Line B is obviously not twice as long as the whole of Line A.

Most tests do not have a logical or absolute zero. Classroom tests, such as Ms. Smith's arithmetic test (Table 4.2), also lack an absolute zero. Because a student gets no problem correct does not mean that the student knows absolutely nothing about arithmetic. Because equal-interval scales lack an absolute zero, we cannot construct ratios with data measured on these scales. For example, Sam does not know twice as much about arithmetic as Carole. Later in this chapter you will learn that all standard scores are equal-interval scales. That we can add, subtract, multiply, and divide data measured on these scales makes them very useful in making complex interpretations of test scores.

4-1c CHARACTERISTICS OF DISTRIBUTIONS

A **distribution's shape** is a two-dimensional plot of scores by the number of people earning each score. Distributions of equal-interval scores (for example, student scores on a classroom test) can be described in terms of four characteristics: mean, variance, skew, and kurtosis. The **mean** is the arithmetic average of the scores in the distribution (for example, the mean height for U.S. women is the average of all U.S. women's heights). The **variance** is an average distance between each score and every other score in the distribution. These characteristics are very important and are discussed repeatedly throughout this book.

Skew refers to the asymmetry of a distribution of scores. In a **symmetrical distribution,** the scores above the mean mirror the scores below the mean. Easy ques-

TABLE 4.2	Ranking of Students in Ms. Smith's Arithmetic Class		

Student	Raw-Score Total	Rank	Difference Between Score and Next Higher Score
Bob	27	1	0
Lucy	26	2	1
Sam	22	3	4
Mary	20	4	2
Luis	18	5	2
Barbara	17	6	1
Carmen	16		
Jane	16	8	1
Charles J.	16		
Hector	14		
Virginia	14		
Frankie	14		
Sean	14	13	2
Joanne	14		
Jim	14		
John	14		
Charles B.	12		
Jing-Jen	12	18	2
Ron	12		
Carole	11	20	1
Bernice	10	21	1
Hugh	8	22	2
Lance	6	23	2
Ludwig	2	24	4
Harpo	1	25	1

tions are balanced by difficult questions. However, a distribution will be **negatively skewed** when it is easy and many students earn high scores and fewer students earn low scores. That distribution of scores will not be symmetrical. There will be more scores above the mean that are balanced by fewer but more extreme scores below the mean, as shown in Figure 4.3. **Positively skewed distributions** occur when a test is difficult, and many students earn low scores while a few students earn high scores.

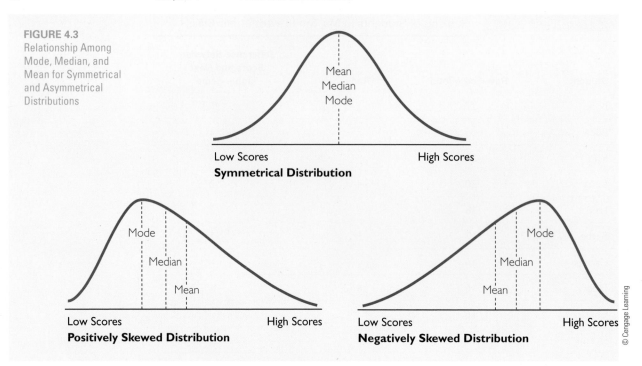

© Cengage Learning

FIGURE 4.3
Relationship Among
Mode, Median, and
Mean for Symmetrical
and Asymmetrical
Distributions

There are more scores below the mean that are balanced by fewer but more extreme scores above the mean, as shown in Figure 4.3.

Kurtosis describes the peakedness of a curve—that is, the rate at which a curve rises and falls. Relatively flat distributions spread out test takers and are called **platykurtic**. (The prefix *plat-* means flat, as in platypus or plateau.) **Leptokurtic** are fast-rising distributions with strong peaks. Figure 4.4 illustrates a platykurtic and a leptokurtic curve.

The normal curve is a particular symmetrical curve. Many variables are distributed normally in nature; many are not. The only value of the normal curve lies in the fact that, for this curve, the proportion of cases that fall between any two points on the horizontal axis of the curve is known exactly.

4-1d AVERAGE SCORES

An average gives us a general description of how a group as a whole performed. There are three different averages: mode, median, and mean. The **mode** is defined as the score most frequently obtained. A mode (if there is one) can be found for data on nominal, ordinal, ratio, or equal-interval scales. Distributions may have two modes (if they do, they are called "bimodal distributions"), or they may have more than two.

FIGURE 4.4
Platykurtic and
Leptokurtic Curves

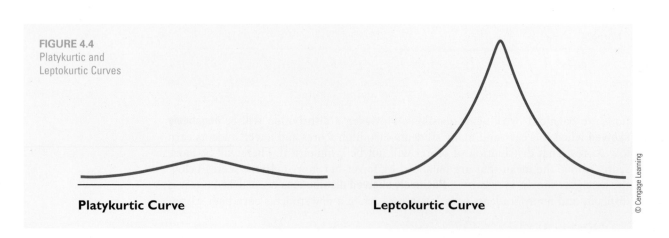

© Cengage Learning

The **median** is the point in a distribution above which are 50 percent of test takers (not test scores) and below which are 50 percent of test takers (not test scores). Medians can be found for data on ordinal, equal-interval, and ratio scales; they must not be used with nominal scales. The median score may or may not actually be earned by a student. For the set of scores 4, 5, 7, and 8, the median is 6, although no one earned a score of 6. For the set of scores 14, 15, 16, 17, and 18, the median is 16, and someone earned that score.

The **mean** is the arithmetic average of the scores in a distribution and is the most important average for use in assessment. It is the sum of the scores (ΣX) divided by the number of scores (N); its symbol *is* $\overline{X}$. The mean, like the median, may or may not be earned by any child in the distribution. Means should be computed only for data on equal-interval and ratio scales.

Mean $= \overline{X} = \Sigma X/N$ **Equation 4.1**

4-1e MEASURES OF DISPERSION

Dispersion tells us how scores are spread out above and below the average score. Three measures of dispersion are range, variance, and standard deviation. The **range** is the distance between the extremes of a distribution; it is usually defined as the highest score less the lowest score. It is a relatively crude measure of dispersion because it is based on only two pieces of information. Range cannot be calculated with nominal data.

The variance and the standard deviation are the most important indexes of dispersion. The **variance** is a numerical index describing the dispersion of a set of scores around the mean of the distribution, and is calculated using equation 4.2. The symbol S^2 is used when describing the variance of a sample; the symbol σ^2 is used when describing the variance of a population. Because the variance is an average, the number of cases in the set or the distribution does not affect it. Large sets of scores may have large or small variances; small sets of scores may have large or small variances. In addition, because the variance is measured in terms of distance from the mean, it is not related to the actual value of the mean. Distributions with large means may have large or small variances; distributions with small means may have large or small variances. The variance of a distribution may be computed with Equation 4.2. The variance (S^2) equals the sum (Σ) of the square of each score less the mean $(X - \overline{X})^2$ divided by the number of scores (N).

$S^2 = \Sigma(X - \overline{X})^2/N$ **Equation 4.2**

Computational Example

As an example, we use the scores from Ms. Smith's arithmetic test to compute variance (see Table 4.2). Column B in Table 4.2 contains the score earned by each student. The first step in computing the variance is to find the mean. Therefore, the scores are added, and the sum (350) is divided by the number of scores (25). The mean in this example is 14. The next step is to subtract the mean from each score; this is done in Column C of Table 4.3, which is labelled $X - \overline{X}$. Note that scores above the mean are positive, scores at the mean are zero, and scores below the mean are negative. The differences (Column C) are then squared (multiplied by themselves); the squared differences are in Column D, labelled $(X - \overline{X})^2$. Note that all numbers in this column are positive. The squared differences are then summed; in this example, the sum of all the squared distances of scores from the mean is 900. The variance equals the sum of all the squared distances of scores from the mean divided by the number of scores; in this case, the variance equals 900/25, or 36.

The variance is very important in psychometric theory but has very limited application in score interpretation. However, its calculation is necessary to get the

TABLE 4.3		Computation of the Variance of Ms. Smith's Arithmetic Class	
Student (A)	**Test Score (B)**	$X - \overline{X}$ **(C)**	$(X - \overline{X})^2$ **(D)**
Bob	27	13	169
Lucy	26	12	144
Sam	22	8	64
Mary	20	6	36
Luis	18	4	16
Barbara	17	3	9
Carmen	16	2	4
Jane	16	2	4
Charles J.	16	2	4
Hector	14	0	0
Virginia	14	0	0
Frankie	14	0	0
Sean	14	0	0
Joanne	14	0	0
Jim	14	0	0
John	14	0	0
Charles B.	12	−2	4
Jing-Jen	12	−2	4
Ron	12	−2	4
Carole	11	−3	9
Bernice	10	−4	16
Hugh	8	−6	36
Lance	6	−8	64
Ludwig	2	−12	144
Harpo	1	−13	169
SUM	350	000	900

standard deviation, which is very important in the interpretation of test scores. The **standard deviation** is a numerical index describing the dispersion of a set of scores around the mean that is calculated as the positive square root of the variance. The symbol S is used when describing the standard deviation of a sample; the symbol σ is used when describing the standard deviation of a population.

A standard deviation is frequently used as a unit of measurement in much the same way that an inch or a ton is used. Scores on an equal-interval scale can be transformed into standard deviation units from the mean. The advantage of measuring in standard deviations is that when the distribution is normal, we know exactly what proportion of cases occurs between the mean and the particular standard deviation.

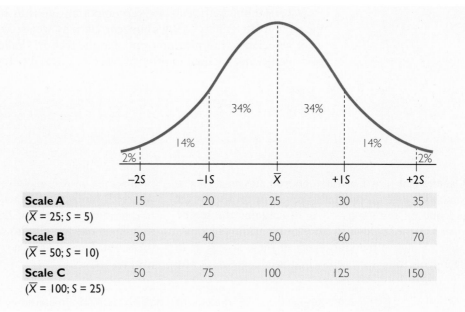

FIGURE 4.5
Scores on Three Scales,
Expressed in Standard
Deviation Units

	$-2S$	$-1S$	$\overline{X}$	$+1S$	$+2S$
Scale A ($\overline{X}$ = 25; S = 5)	15	20	25	30	35
Scale B ($\overline{X}$ = 50; S = 10)	30	40	50	60	70
Scale C ($\overline{X}$ = 100; S = 25)	50	75	100	125	150

As shown in Figure 4.5, approximately 34 percent of the cases in a normal distribution always occur between the mean and one standard deviation either above or below the mean. Thus, approximately 68 percent of all cases occur between one standard deviation below and one standard deviation above the mean (34% + 34% = 68%). Approximately 14 percent of the cases occur between one and two standard deviations below the mean or between one and two standard deviations above the mean. Thus, approximately 48 percent of all cases occur between the mean and two standard deviations either above or below the mean (34% + 14% = 48%). Approximately 96 percent of all cases occur between two standard deviations above and two standard deviations below the mean.

As shown by the positions and values for scales A, B, and C in Figure 4.5, it does not matter what the values of the mean and the standard deviation are. The relationship holds for various obtained values of the mean and the standard deviation. For scale A, where the mean is 25 and the standard deviation is 5, 34 percent of the scores occur between the mean (25) and one standard deviation below the mean (20) or between the mean and one standard deviation above the mean (30). Similarly, for scale B, where the mean is 50 and the standard deviation is 10, 34 percent of the cases occur between the mean (50) and one standard deviation below the mean (40) or between the mean and one standard deviation above the mean (60).

4-1f CORRELATION

Correlation quantifies relationships between variables. **Correlation coefficients** are numerical indexes of the relationship between two variables. (Correlations among three or more variables are called multiple correlations.) Correlations tell us the extent to which any two variables go together—that is, the extent to which changes in one variable are reflected by changes in the second variable. Correlation coefficients are expressed as a decimal value with a sign (+ or −) that indicates the direction of the relationship—whether low values with one variable are associated with high or low values on the second variable. The decimal number can range in value from .00 to either +1.00 or −1.00. and indicates the magnitude of the relationship. A correlation coefficient of either +1.00 or −1.00 indicates a perfect relationship between two variables. Thus, if you know a person's score on one variable, you can predict that person's score on the second variable without error. Correlation coefficients between .00 and 1.00 (or −1.00) allow some prediction, and the more extreme the coefficient, the greater its predictive power.

Correlation coefficients are very important in assessment. In the next chapter, the section "Reliability" shows how correlations are used to estimate the amount of error associated with measurement, and the section "Validity" shows how correlation coefficients are used to provide evidence of validity for a test.

ADVANCED INFORMATION ABOUT CORRELATION

A **scatterplot** uses Cartesian coordinates to depict a person's scores on two measures—one on the x-axis and one on the y-axis. Table 4.4 contains the scores earned by the students in Ms. Smith's arithmetic class. Figure 4.6 shows the scatterplot of these scores. It is clear from this scatterplot that students who earn high scores on test one also tend to earn high scores on test 2; students who earn low scores on test 1 tend to earn low scores on test 2. Students who score in the middle on one test tend to score in the middle on the other test. Thus, there is a strong correlation between the two tests.

TABLE 4.4	Scores Earned on Two Tests Administered by Ms. Smith to Her Arithmetic Class	
Student	**Raw Score, Test 1**	**Raw Score, Test 2**
Bob	27	26
Lucy	26	22
Sam	22	20
Mary	20	27
Luis	18	14
Barbara	17	18
Carmen	16	16
Jane	16	17
Charles J.	16	16
Hector	14	14
Virginia	14	14
Frankie	14	16
Sean	14	14
Joanne	14	12
Jim	14	14
John	14	12
Charles B.	12	14
Jing-Jen	12	11
Ron	12	12
Carole	11	10
Bernice	10	14
Hugh	8	6
Lance	6	1
Ludwig	2	2
Harpo	1	8

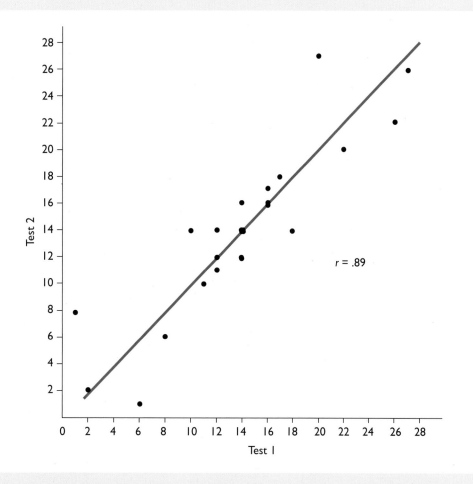

© 2017 Cengage Learning

FIGURE 4.6
Scatterplot of the Two
Tests Administered
by Ms. Smith

Figure 4.7 shows six scatterplots of three different magnitudes and two different directions. In parts a and b, all points fall on the regression line, and so the correlation between the variables is perfect. Part a has a correlation coefficient of +1.00; high scores on one test are associated with high scores on the other test. Part b has a correlation of −1.00; high scores on one test are associated with low scores on the other test (this negative correlation is sometimes called an "inverse relationship"). Parts c and d show a high degree of positive and negative relationship, respectively. Note that the departures from the best-fit lines are associated with lower degrees of relationship. Parts e and f show scatterplots with a low degree of relationship. Note the wide departures from the best-fit lines.

A correlation coefficient of .00 between two variables means that there is no linear relationship between the variables. The variables are independent; changes in one variable are not related to changes in the second variable. Zero correlation can occur in three ways, as shown in Figure 4.8. First, if the scatterplot is essentially circular (part a), the correlation is .00. In such a case, there is no relationship between the two variables; each value of the first variable

can be associated with any (and perhaps all) values of the second variable. Second, if either variable is constant (part b), the correlation is .00. For example, if a researcher tried to correlate gender and reading achievement with a sample made up entirely of boys, the correlation would be zero because gender would have only one value (male); gender would be a constant, not a variable. Third, two variables can be related in a nonlinear way (part c). For example, willingness to take risks is related to age. Younger children and adults are less willing to take risks than are teenagers. Although there is a strong curvilinear relationship, the linear regression line would parallel one of the axes. Thus, there is a curvilinear relationship, but the coefficient of linear correlation is approximately .00.

Test authors may report correlation coefficients by different names to indicate a variable's scale of measurement [for example, whether one or both variables in the relationship are dichotomous (have only two values) or continuous (have many values)]. The most commonly reported coefficients are members of the Pearson family of correlation coefficients, meaning that they are all computed by computationally equivalent formulas. When both variables to be

© 2017 Cengage Learning

FIGURE 4.7
Six Scatterplots
Illustrating Different
Degrees and Directions
of Relationship

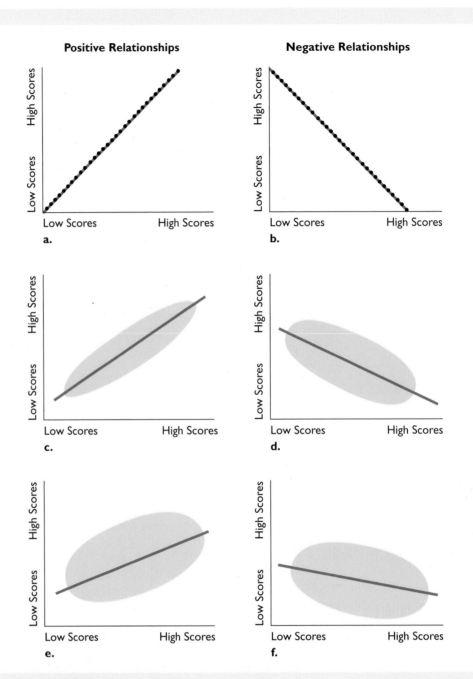

correlated are measured on an equal-interval or ratio scale (such as IQ and SAT verbal score), the correlation coefficient is called a Pearson product–moment correlation coefficient. The symbol for this statistic is ρ. When both variables to be correlated are measured on an ordinal scale (such as class standing and rank on the school's competency examination for seniors), the correlation coefficient is called a Spearman rho; the symbol for rho is ρ. Sometimes the variables to be correlated are dichotomous (for instance, male/female). When two dichotomous variables are correlated, the correlation coefficient is called a phi

coefficient; the symbol for phi is ϕ. When one of the variables is dichotomous (e.g., right or wrong on a test question) and the other variable is continuous (e.g., total number correct on the test), the correlation coefficient is called a point biserial correlation coefficient; its symbol is r_{pb}. Although there are other kinds of Pearson family coefficients (such as biserial rho) and computationally different coefficients (such as tetrachoric and biserial), they are seldom reported in test manuals.

No discussion of correlation is complete without a mention of causality. Correlation is a necessary but

FIGURE 4.8
Three Zero-Order
Linear Correlations

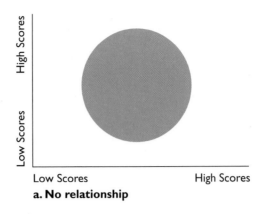

a. No relationship

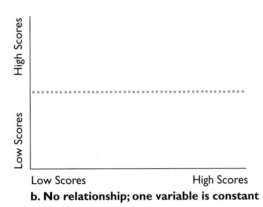

b. No relationship; one variable is constant

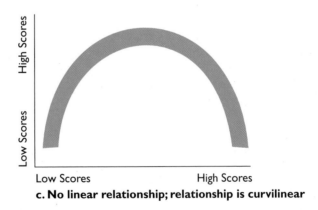

c. No linear relationship; relationship is curvilinear

not a sufficient condition for causality. Two variables cannot be causally related unless they are correlated. However, the mere presence of a correlation does not establish causality. For any correlation coefficient between variables (A and B), there are four possible interpretations (the first depends on chance; the other three do not).

First, the variables may be correlated by chance. For example, the incidence of chicken pox in Egypt (A) may be highly correlated with the sale of Purina Puppy Chow in the state of Arizona (B). There is simply no logical or reasonable explanation for the cor-

relation other than serendipity. (The probability of a correlation coefficient of a specific value occurring by chance can be determined; when a correlation coefficient is found to be "statistically significant" at the .05 level, a correlation of that magnitude occurs by chance only 5 times in 100.) Second, A can cause B; for example, burning buildings (A) cause firefighters to be present (B). Third, B can cause A; for example, Bradbury in *Fahrenheit 451* (1953) reported that firefighters (B) cause fires (A). Fourth, C can cause both A and B. For example, there actually is a positive relationship between shoe size and mental age.

Clearly, big feet do not cause mental development (A does not cause B). Moreover, mental development does not cause big feet (B does not cause A). The most satisfactory explanation of the correlation is that maturation, a third variable (C), causes both A and B: As children grow older, they develop both mentally and physically.

Although the preceding examples illustrate obvious instances of inappropriate reasoning, in testing situations the errors or potential errors are not so clear. For example, IQ scores and scores on achievement tests are correlated. Some argue that intelligence causes achievement; others argue that achievement causes intelligence. Because there are at least four possible interpretations of correlational data—and because correlational data do not tell us which interpretation is true—we must never draw causal conclusions from such data alone.

4-2 Scoring Student Performance

Tests and systematic observations occur in structured, standardized situations. Tests require the presentation of standardized materials to an individual in a predetermined manner in order to evaluate that individual's responses, using predetermined criteria. Systematic observations require the use of predetermined definitions of behavior to be observed at predetermined times and settings.

How an individual's responses are quantified depends on the materials used, the intent of the test author, and the diagnostician's intention in choosing the procedure. If we were interested only in determining whether a student had learned a specific fact or concept (for example, "What is $3 + 5$?"), we would make explicit the criteria for what constitutes a correct response and would classify the student's response as right or wrong. If we were interested in determining if a student had learned a finite set of facts (for example, the sums of all combinations of two single-digit numbers), we could classify the student's response to each fact as right or wrong. Teachers frequently use this approach for the most essential (and frequently the most basic) information that a student must master. More often we would quantify a student's performance as the number or percentage of facts known.

It is usually impractical or impossible to assess all the facts and relationships that might be tested. For example, it seems unlikely that anyone could make up a test to assess a student's knowledge of every aspect of all Shakespeare's plays; however, even if that were possible, administering all the possible questions to a student would be virtually impossible. Even when we cannot test all of the information, we may still want to know how much of the topic students have learned. To do this, testers ask a few questions and estimate students' knowledge based on their responses to those questions. In testing jargon, we use a sample of items (that is, a test) to estimate performance on the domain (all of the possible items). When we estimate a student's performance on an entire domain from the performance on a sample of items, we assume that the sample of items is a fair representation of the domain. In this situation, individual items have little importance beyond estimating performance on the domain.

4-2a SUBJECTIVE VERSUS OBJECTIVE SCORING

There are two approaches to scoring a student's response: subjective and objective. **Subjective scoring** relies on private criteria that can and do vary from tester to tester. Subjective scores have been repeatedly shown to be influenced by extraneous and irrelevant variables such as a student's race, gender, appearance, religion, or even given name (Ysseldyke, Algozzine, Regan, & McGue, 1981).

Objective scoring is based on observable public criteria. When multiple examiners or observers use objective scoring procedures to evaluate student performance, they obtain the same scores. Because objective scoring leads to systematically better decision making, the Individuals with Disabilities Education Act requires objective measurement (*Federal Register* 71(156), August 14, 2006).

TABLE 4.5	Drinking from a Cup

Level	Definition
Well	Drinks with little spilling or assistance
Acceptably	Dribbles a few drops
Learning	Requires substantial prompting or spills
Beginning	Requires manual guidance

© Cengage Learning

4-2b SUMMARIZING STUDENT PERFORMANCE

When a single behavior or skill is of interest and assessed only once, evaluators usually employ a dichotomous scoring scheme: right or wrong, present or absent, and so forth. Typically, the correct or right option of the dichotomy is defined precisely; the wrong option is defined by default. For example, a correct response to "$1 + 2 = ?$" might be defined as "3, written intelligibly, written after the $=$ sign, and written in the correct orientation"; a wrong response would be one that fails to meet one or more of the criteria for a correct response.

A single response can also be awarded partial credit that can range along a continuum from completely correct to completely incorrect. For example, a teacher might objectively score a student response and give partial credit for a response because the student used the correct procedures to solve a mathematics problem even though the student made a computational error. Partial credit can be useful when trying to document slow progress toward a goal. For example, in a life-skills curriculum, a teacher might scale the item "drinking from a cup without assistance," as shown in Table 4.5. Of course, each point on the continuum requires a definition for the partial credit to be awarded.

When an evaluation is concerned with multiple items, a tester may simply report how a student performed on each and every item. More often, however, the tester summarizes the student's performance over all the test items to provide an index of total performance. The sum of correct responses is usually the first summary index computed.

Although the number correct provides a limited amount of information about student performance, it lacks important information that provides a context for understanding that performance. Five summary scores are commonly used to provide a more meaningful context for the total score: the percent correct, percent accuracy, and the rate of correct response, fluency, and retention.

Percent correct is widely used in a variety of assessment contexts. The **percent correct** is calculated by dividing the number correct by the number possible and multiplying that quotient by 100. This index is best used with *power tests*—tests for which students have sufficient time to answer all of the questions.[1]

Percentages are given verbal labels that are intended to facilitate instruction. The two most commonly used labels are "mastery" and "instructional level." Mastery divides the percentage continuum in two: Mastery is generally set at 90 or 95 percent correct, and nonmastery is less than the level of mastery. The criterion for mastery is arbitrary, and in real life we frequently set the level for mastery too low.

Instructional level divides the percentage range into three segments: frustration, instructional, and independent levels. When material is too difficult for a student, it is said to be at the *frustration level*; this level is usually defined as material for which a student knows less than 85 percent of it. An *instructional level* provides a degree of challenge where a student is likely to be successful, but success is not guaranteed; this level is usually defined by student responses between 85 and 95 percent correct. The *independent level* is defined as the point

---

[1] A situation in which there are more opportunities to respond than time to respond is termed a *free operant*.

where a student can perform without assistance; this level is usually defined as student performance of more than 95 percent correct. For example, in reading, students who decode more than 95 percent of the words should be able to read a passage without assistance; students who decode between 85 and 95 percent of the words in a passage should be able to read and comprehend that passage with assistance; and students who cannot decode 85 percent of the words in a passage will probably have great difficulty decoding and comprehending the material, even with assistance.

Accuracy is the number of correct responses divided by the number of attempted responses multiplied by 100. Accuracy is appropriately used when an assessment precludes a student from responding to all items. For example, a teacher may ask a student to read orally for two minutes, but it should not be possible for that student (or any other student) to read the entire passage in the time allotted.[2] Thus, Benny may attempt 175 words in a 350-word passage in two minutes; if he reads 150 words correctly, his accuracy would be approximately 86 percent—that is, $100 \times (150/175)$.

Fluency is the number of correct responses per minute. Teachers often want their students to have a supply of information at their fingertips so that they can respond fluently (or automatically) without thinking. For example, teachers may want their students to recognize sight words without having to sound them out, recall addition facts without having to think about them, or supply Spanish words for their English equivalents. Criterion rates for successful performance are usually determined empirically. For example, readers with satisfactory comprehension usually read connected prose at rates of 100 or more words per minute, depending on their grade level. (See, e.g., Read Naturally, Inc., 2010; National Assessment of Educational Progress, Oral Reading Rate, 2002; Mercer & Mercer, 1985.)

Retention refers to the percentage of learned information that is recalled. Retention may also be termed recall, maintenance, or memory of what has been learned. Regardless of the label, it is calculated in the same way: Divide the number recalled by the number originally learned, and multiply that ratio by 100. For example, if Helen learned 40 sight vocabulary words and recalled 30 of them two weeks later, her retention would be 75 percent—that is, $100 \times (30/40)$. Because forgetting becomes more likely as the interval between the learning and the retention assessment increases, retention is usually qualified by the period of time between attainment of mastery and assessment of recall. Thus, Helen's retention would be stated as 75 percent over a two-week period.

4-2c INTERPRETING TEST PERFORMANCE

There are three common ways to interpret an individual student's performance in special and inclusive education: criterion-referenced, standards-referenced, and norm-referenced.

Criterion-Referenced Interpretations

When we are interested in a student's knowledge about a single fact, we compare a student's performance against an objective and absolute standard (criterion) of performance. Thus, to be considered **criterion-referenced**, there must be a clear, objective criterion for each of the correct responses to each question, or to each portion of the question if partial credit is to be awarded.

Standards-Referenced Interpretations

In large-scale assessments used for accountability purposes, school districts must ascertain the degree to which they are meeting state and national achievement standards. To do so, states specify the qualities and skills that competent learners need to demonstrate. Interpretation of an individual's performance based on comparison to

---

[2] To avoid having students practice making errors while developing basic skills, they should not be given homework (independent practice) until they are at the independent level.

the state standards is considered a **standards-referenced** interpretation. These indices consist of four components:

- Levels of performance: The entire range of possible student performances (from very poor to excellent) is divided into a number of bands or ranges. Verbal labels that are attached to each of these ranges indicate increasing levels of accomplishment. For example, a performance might be rated on a four-point scale: *poor, emerging, proficient,* and *advanced* performance.

- Objective criteria: Each level of performance is defined by precise, objective descriptions of student accomplishment relative to the task. These descriptions can be quantified.

- Examples: Examples of student work at each level are provided. These examples illustrate the range of performance within each level.

- Cut scores: These scores provide quantitative criteria that clearly delineate student performance level.

Norm-Referenced Interpretations

Sometimes testers are interested in knowing how a student's performance compares to the performances of other students—usually students of similar demographic characteristics (age, gender, grade in school, and so forth); these are considered **norm-referenced** interpretations. In order to make this type of comparison, a student's score is transformed into a derived score. **Derived scores** are of two types of norm-referenced scores: developmental scores and scores of relative standing.

Developmental Scores There are two types of developmental scores: developmental equivalents and developmental quotients. **Developmental equivalents** may be age equivalents or grade equivalents and are based on the average performance of individuals. Suppose the average performance of 10-year-old children on a test was 27 correct. Furthermore, suppose that Horace answered 27 questions correctly. Horace answered as many questions correctly as the average of 10-year-old children. He would earn an age equivalent of 10 years. An **age equivalent** means that a child's raw score is the average (the median or mean) performance for that age group. Age equivalents are expressed in years and months; a hyphen is used in age scores (for example, 7-1 for 7 years, 1 month old). If the test measured mental ability, Horace's score would be called a mental age; if the test measured language, it would be called a language age. A **grade equivalent** means that a child's raw score is the average (the median or mean) performance for a particular grade. Grade equivalents are expressed in grades and tenths of grades; a decimal point is used in grade scores (for example, 7.1). Age-equivalent and grade-equivalent scores are interpreted as a performance equal to the average of X-year-olds and the average performance of Xth graders, respectively.

The interpretation of age and grade equivalents requires great care. Five problems occur in the use of developmental scores.

1. *Systematic misinterpretation:* Students who earn an age equivalent of 12-0 have merely answered as many questions correctly as the average for children 12 years of age. They have not necessarily performed as a 12-year-old child would; they may well have attacked the problems in a different way or demonstrated a different performance pattern from many 12-year-old students. For example, a second grader and a ninth grader might both earn grade equivalents of 4.0, but they probably have not performed identically. We have known for more than 30 years that younger children perform lower-level work with greater accuracy (for instance, successfully answered 38 of the 45 problems attempted), whereas older children attempt more problems with less accuracy (for instance, successfully answered 38 of the 78 problems attempted) (Thorndike & Hagen, 1978).

2. *Need for interpolation and extrapolation:* Average age and grade scores are estimated for groups of children who are never tested. Interpolated scores are estimated for groups of students between groups actually tested. For example, students within 30 days of their eighth birthday may be tested, but age equivalents are estimated for students who are 8-1, 8-2, and so on. Extrapolated scores are estimated for students who are younger and older than the children tested. For example, a student may earn an age equivalent of 5-0 even though no child younger than 6 was tested.

3. *Promotion of typological thinking:* An average 12-0 pupil is a statistical abstraction. The average 12-year-old is in a family with 1.2 other children, 0.8 of a dog, and 2.3 automobiles; in other words, the average child does not exist. Average 12-0 children more accurately represent a range of performances, typically the middle 50 percent.

4. *Implication of a false standard of performance:* Educators expect a third grader to perform at a third-grade level and a 9-year-old to perform at a 9-year-old level. However, the way in which equivalent scores are constructed ensures that 50 percent of any age or grade group will perform below age or grade level, because half of the test takers earn scores below the median.

5. *Tendency for scales to be ordinal, not equal interval:* The line relating the number correct to the various ages is typically curved, with a flattening of the curve at higher ages or grades. Figure 4.9 is a typical developmental curve. Because the scales are ordinal and not based on equal interval units, scores on these scales should not be added or multiplied in any computation.

To interpret a developmental score (for example, a mental age), it is usually helpful to know the age of the person whose score is being interpreted. Knowing developmental age as well as chronological age (CA) allows us to judge an individual's relative

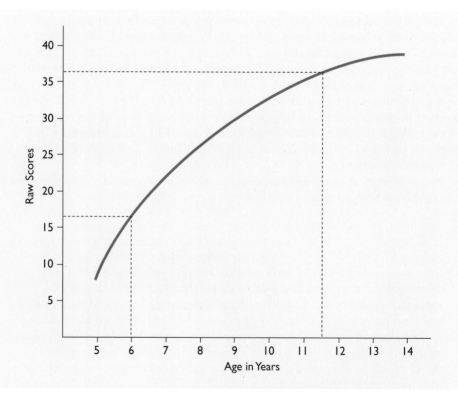

FIGURE 4.9
Mean Number Correct for 10 Age Groups: An Example of Arriving at Age-Equivalent Scores

performance. Suppose that Ana earns a mental age (MA) of 120 months. If Ana is 8 years (96 months) old, her performance is above average. If she is 35 years old, however, it is below average. The relationship between developmental age and chronological age is often quantified as a developmental quotient. For example, a *ratio IQ* is

$$IQ = MA \text{ (in months)} \times 100 \div CA \text{ (in months)}$$

All the problems that apply to developmental levels also apply to developmental quotients.

Scores of Relative Standing **Scores of relative standing** compare a student's performance to the performances of similar (in age or grade) students. In essence, these scores tell us the percentage or proportion of students who earned better or worse scores. These scores have several advantages.

1. They mean the same thing regardless of a student's age or the content being tested.

2. They allow us to compare one person's performance on several tests—for example, Jerry's scores on math, science, and language subtests.

3. They also allow us to compare several people on the same test, for example Jerry, Mary, and Tony on a math subtest.

The interpretation of test scores would be far more difficult if the scores had different means and standard deviations. Consider comparing students' heights measured on different scales. Suppose, for example, George is 70 inches tall, Bridget is 6 feet 3 inches tall, Bruce is 1.93 meters tall, and Alexandra is 177.8 centimeters tall. To compare their heights, it is necessary to transform the heights into comparable units. In feet and inches, their heights are as follows: George, 5 feet 10 inches; Bridget, 6 feet 3 inches; Bruce, 6 feet 4 inches; and Alexandra, 5 feet 10 inches. Scores of relative standing put raw scores into comparable units, such as percentiles or standard scores.

Percentile Family. **Percentile ranks (percentiles)** are derived scores that indicate the percentage of people whose scores are at or below a given raw score. Although percentiles are easily calculated, test authors usually provide tables that convert raw scores on a test to percentiles for each age or grade of test takers. Interpretation of percentiles is straightforward. If Bill earns a percentile of 48 on a test, Bill's test score is equal to or better than those of 48 percent of the test takers to whom he is being compared. (It is also correct to say that 53 percent of the test takers earned scores equal to or better than that of Bill.) Theoretically, percentiles can range from 0.1 to 99.9—that is, a performance that is equal to or better than those of one-tenth of 1 percent of the test takers to a performance that is equal to or better than those of 99.9 percent of the test takers. The 50th percentile rank is the median.

COMPUTATIONAL EXAMPLE OF CALCULATING PERCENTILE RANKS Percentile ranks (percentiles). Percentile ranks can be used when the scale of measurement is ordinal or equal-interval. They are derived scores indicating the percentage of people whose scores are at or below a given raw score. The percentage correct is not the same as the percentage of people scoring at or below a given score. Percentiles corresponding to particular scores can be computed by the following four-step sequence.

1. Arrange the scores from the highest to the lowest (that is, best to worst).

2. Compute the percentage of people with scores below the score to which you wish to assign a percentile rank.

3. Compute the percentage of people with scores at the score to which you wish to assign a percentile rank.

4. Add the percentage of people with scores below the score to one-half the percentage of people with scores at the score to obtain the percentile rank.

Mr. Greenberg gave a test to his developmental reading class, which has an enrollment of 25 children. In column 1 of Table 4.6 are the scores that could be earned by the students. Column 2 gives the number of children obtaining each score. Column 3 gives the percentage of all 25 scores that each obtained score represents. Column 4 contains the percentage of all 25 scores that were below that particular score. In the last group of columns, the percentile rank is computed. Only one child scored 24; the one score is 1/25 of the class, or 4 percent. No one scored lower than 24; so 0 percent (0/25) of the scores is below 24. The child who scored 24 received a percentile rank of 2—that is, 0 plus one half of 4. The next score obtained is 38, and again only one child received this score. Thus, 4 percent of the total (1/25) scored at 38, and 4 percent of the total scored below 38. Therefore, the percentile rank corresponding to a score of 38 is 6—that is, 4 + (1/2)(4). Two children earned a score of 40, and two children scored below 40. Therefore, the percentile rank for a score of 40 is 12—that is, 8 + (1/2)(8). The same procedure is followed for every score obtained. The best score in the class, 50, was obtained by two students. The percentile rank corresponding to the highest score in the class is 96.

The interpretation of percentile ranks is based on the percentage of people. All students who score 48 on the test have a percentile rank of 84. These four students have scored as well as or better than 84 percent of their classmates on the test. Similarly, an individual who obtains a percentile rank of 21 on an intelligence test has scored as well as or better than 21 percent of the people in the norm sample.

| TABLE 4.6 | | | Computing Percentile Ranks for a Hypothetical Class of Twenty-Five | | | | |

				Percentile Rank			
Score	Number of Students Earning This Score	Percentage of Students Earning This Score	*Percentage of Students Below the Score*	+	*Half of Percentage of Students at the Score*	=	*Percentile*
50	2	8	92	+	(1/2)(8)	=	96
49	0						
48	4	16	76	+	(1/2)(16)	=	84
47	0						
46	5	20	56	+	(1/2)(20)	=	66
45	5	20	36	+	(1/2)(20)	=	46
44	3	12	24	+	(1/2)(12)	=	30
43	2	8	16	+	(1/2)(8)	=	20
42	0	—					
41	0	—					
40	2	8	8	+	(1/2)(8)	=	12
39	0	—					
38	1	4	4	+	(1/2)(4)	=	6
.							
.							
.							
24	1	4	0	+	(1/2)(4)	=	2

Because the percentile rank is computed using one-half the percentage of those obtaining a particular score, it is not possible to have a percentile rank of either 0 or 100. Generally, percentile ranks contain decimals, so it is possible for a score to receive a percentile rank of 99.9 or 0.1. The 50th percentile rank is the median.

Occasionally, a score is reported as a percentile band. The two most common are deciles and quartiles:

- **Deciles** are bands of percentiles that are 10 percentile ranks in width; each decile contains 10 percent of the norm group. The first decile ranges from 0.1 to 9.9; the second ranges from 10 to 19.9; the tenth decile goes from 90 to 99.9.

- **Quartiles** are bands of percentiles that are 25 percentiles wide; each quartile contains 25 percent of the norm group. The first quartile ranges from the 0.1 to 24.9 percentile; the fourth quartile contains percentiles 75 to 99.9.

Standard Score Family. Standard scores are derived scores with a predetermined mean and standard deviation. Although a distribution of scores can be transformed to produce any predetermined mean and standard deviation, there are five commonly used standard-score distributions: z-scores, T-scores, deviation IQs,[3] normal-curve equivalents, and stanines.

z-scores, the most basic standard score, transform raw scores into a distribution in which the mean is always equal to 0 and the standard deviation is always equal to 1, regardless of the mean and standard deviation of the raw (obtained) scores. Any raw score can be converted to a z-score by using Equation 4.3.

$$z = (X - \bar{X}) \div S \qquad \text{Equation 4.3}$$

Positive z-scores are above the mean; negative z-scores are below the mean. The greater the magnitude of the number, the more above or below the mean is the score. Z-scores are interpreted as being X number of standard deviations above or below the mean. When the distribution of scores is bell-shaped or normal, we know the exact percentile that corresponds to any z-score.

Because signs and decimals may be awkward in practical situations, z-scores often are transformed to four other standard scores: T-scores, IQs, normal curve equivalents, and stanines. The general formula for changing a z-score into a different standard score is given by Equation 4.4, where SS and SS stand for standard score.

$$SS = \bar{X}_{ss} + (S_{ss})(z) \qquad \text{Equation 4.4}$$

- A *T-score* is a standard score with a mean of 50 and a standard deviation of 10. A person earning a T-score of 40 scored one standard deviation below the mean, whereas a person earning a T-score of 60 scored one standard deviation above the mean.

- *IQs* are standard scores with a mean of 100 and a standard deviation of usually 15. A person earning an IQ of 85 scored one standard deviation below the mean, whereas a person earning an IQ of 115 scored one standard deviation above the mean.

- *Normal curve equivalents* (NCEs) are standard scores with a mean equal to 50 and a standard deviation equal to 21.06. Although the standard deviation may at first appear strange, this scale divides the normal curve into 100 equal intervals.

[3] When it was first introduced, the IQ was defined as the ratio of mental age to chronological age, multiplied by 100. Because the standard deviation of mental ages varied by age, ratio IQs also had different percentiles at different ages. For this and other reasons, ratio IQs were largely abandoned by the 1960s.

MRS. STANLEY | Mrs. Stanley is a special education teacher. She and her family moved to the Hillsdale School District in December, and her 12-year-old daughter, Kate, enrolled in the middle school in early January. Kate had been apprehensive about making new friends in a new school so her parents were eager to hear about her first day at the new school.

At dinner that evening, Kate reported that school seemed okay except for her math class. She said they were doing things that she had learned to do years earlier. Kate's description of her math class did not change that week so Mrs. Stanley made an appointment with Kate's counselor, Mr. Norwood. Mr. Norwood confirmed what Kate had reported. She was in one of the lower math groups at the middle school. "Math is one of the only classes in which we track students. We use IQ to group our students, and Kate's IQ on her group intelligence test is the low 90s. So she is placed in a class with students of similar ability."

Mrs. Stanley was stunned. Kate had been screened for gifted placement in her previous placement. At that time, she had an IQ in the 120s on an individually administered test of intelligence. Mrs. Stanley asked if she could see the test results.

Mr. Norwood dug through Kate's file and found the report of her intelligence test. Mrs. Stanley looked at the report and slowly began to smile. "Someone here has made an error." Pointing at a number recorded on the record, Mrs. Stanley said, "The number here is 92, but it's not Kate's IQ. It's not an IQ; it is her percentile rank on that intelligence test. Her score is equal to or better than 92 percent of the students taking the test." Mr. Norwood said that he would correct the error "next semester." Mrs. Stanley suggested that the end of the week would be more acceptable.

At dinner the next week, Kate reported that she knew a lot of the kids in her new math class.

This scenario highlights the importance of understanding the meanings of different types of scores that are reported. Correct understanding and interpretation of scores is needed to protect students. Can you think of other scores that might be easily mixed up? How might such a mix-up result in inappropriate decision making?

- *Stanines* (short for standard nines) are standard-score bands that divide a distribution into nine parts. The first stanine includes all scores that are 1.75 standard deviations or more below the mean, and the ninth stanine includes all scores 1.75 or more standard deviations above the mean. The second through eighth stanines are each 0.5 standard deviation in width, with the fifth stanine ranging from 0.25 standard deviations below the mean to 0.25 standard deviations above the mean.

Standard scores are frequently more difficult to interpret than percentile scores because the concepts of means and standard deviations are not widely understood by people without some statistical knowledge. Thus, standard scores may be more difficult for students and their parents to understand. Aside from this disadvantage, standard scores offer all the advantages of percentiles plus an additional advantage: Because standard scores are equal-interval, they can be combined (for example, added or averaged).[4]

Concluding Comments on Norm-Referenced Scores   Test authors include in their test manuals tables to convert raw scores into derived scores. Thus, test users do not have to calculate derived scores. Standard scores can be transformed into other standard scores readily; they can be converted to percentiles without conversion tables only when the distribution of scores is normal. In normal distributions, the relationship between percentiles and standard scores is known. Figure 4.10 compares various standard scores and percentiles for normal distributions. When the distribution of

---

[4] Standard scores also solve another subtle problem. When scores are combined in a total or composite, the elements of that composite (for example, 18 scores from weekly spelling tests that are combined to obtain a semester average) do not count the same (that is, they do not carry the same weight) unless they have equal variances. Tests that have larger variances contribute more to the composite than tests with smaller variances. When each of the elements has been standardized into the same standard scores (for example, when each of the weekly spelling tests has been standardized as z scores), the elements (that is, the weekly scores) will carry exactly the same weight when they are combined. Moreover, the only way a teacher can weight tests differentially is to standardize all the tests and then multiply by the weight. For example, if a teacher wished to count the second test as three times the first test, the scores on both tests would have to be standardized, and the scores on the second test would then be multiplied by three before the scores were combined.

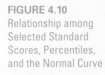

FIGURE 4.10
Relationship among
Selected Standard
Scores, Percentiles,
and the Normal Curve

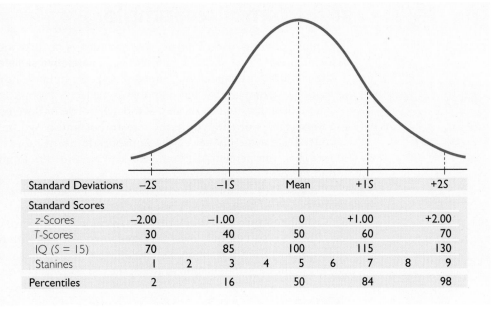

Standard Deviations	−2S		−1S		Mean		+1S		+2S
Standard Scores									
z-Scores	−2.00		−1.00		0		+1.00		+2.00
T-Scores	30		40		50		60		70
IQ (S = 15)	70		85		100		115		130
Stanines	1	2	3	4	5	6	7	8	9
Percentiles	2		16		50		84		98

scores is not normal, conversion tables are necessary in order to convert percentiles to standard scores (or vice versa). These conversion tables are test-specific, so only a test author can provide them. Moreover, conversion tables are always required in order to convert developmental scores to scores of relative standing, even when the distribution of test scores is normal. If the only derived score available for a test is an age equivalent, then there is no way for a test user to convert raw scores to percentiles. However, age or grade equivalents can be converted back to raw scores, which can be converted to standard scores if the raw score mean and standard deviation are provided.

The selection of the particular type of score to use and to report depends on the purpose of testing and the sophistication of the consumer. In our opinion, developmental scores should never be used. Both laypeople and professionals readily misinterpret these scores. In order to understand the precise meaning of developmental scores, the interpreter must generally know both the mean and the standard deviation and then convert the developmental score to a more meaningful score, a score of relative standing. Various professional organizations (for example, the International Reading Association, the American Psychological Association, the National Council on Measurement in Education, and the Council for Exceptional Children) also hold very negative official opinions about developmental scores and quotients.

Standard scores are convenient for test authors. Their use allows an author to combine subtests and to give equal weight to various test components or subtests. Their utility for the consumer is twofold. First, if the score distribution is normal, the consumer can readily convert standard scores to percentile ranks. Second, because standard scores are equal-interval scores, they are useful in analyzing strengths and weaknesses of individual students and in research.

We favor the use of percentiles. These unpretentious scores require the fewest assumptions for accurate interpretation. The scale of measurement need only be ordinal, although it is very appropriate to compute percentiles on equal-interval or ratio data. The distribution of scores need not be normal; percentiles can be computed for any shape of distribution. Professionals, parents, and students readily understand them. Most important, however, is the fact that percentiles tell us nothing more than what any norm-referenced derived score can tell us—namely, an individual's relative standing in a group. Reporting scores in percentiles may remove some of the aura surrounding test scores, but it permits test results to be presented in terms users can understand.

4-3 Normative Sample

The most obvious use of normative samples is to provide the derived scores associated with a test taker's raw scores. A **normative sample** (also referred to as a "**standardization sample**" or "**norms**") is the sample of individuals to whom an individual is compared when one obtains a derived score. In practice, testers do not actually calculate percentiles, standard scores, or developmental scores. They use norm tables developed by the test author and based on the standardization sample. Testers merely select the appropriate norm table and find the derived scores (i.e., the percentiles, standard scores, and developmental scores) corresponding to raw scores earned by the test taker.

Because they are used to interpret a test taker's score, norm tables "should refer to clearly described populations. These populations should include individuals or groups with whom test users will ordinarily wish to compare their own examinees." (AERA et al., 2014, p. 104). Not only must they contain individuals with relevant characteristics and experiences, but also those characteristics and experiences must be in the same proportion as the target population to which the test taker will be compared.

4-3a IMPORTANT CHARACTERISTICS

What makes a characteristic relevant depends on the construct being measured. Some characteristics have a clear, logical, and empirical relationship to a person's development, and several characteristics have an indirect, empirical relationship. Following are brief discussions of the most commonly considered developmental and sociocultural characteristics: gender, age, grade in school, acculturation of parents, race and ethnic identification, geography, and intelligence.

Gender

Some differences between males and females may be relevant in understanding a student's test score. For example, girls tend to develop physically at a faster rate than boys during the first year or two, and many more boys have delayed maturation than do girls during the preschool and primary school years. After puberty, men tend to be bigger and stronger than women. In addition to physical differences, gender role expectations may differ and systematically limit the types of activities in which a child participates because of modeling, peer pressure, or the responses of significant adults. Nevertheless, on most psychological and educational tests, gender differences are small, and the distributions of scores of males and females tend to overlap considerably.

Combined norms (that is, norms containing both males and females) are appropriate in two instances. First, when gender differences are minor, norm groups should contain both males and females in the appropriate proportion found in the general U.S. population (approximately 48 percent male and 52 percent female). Second, when gender differences are substantial, a combined male-female norm group may still be preferred if the purpose of testing is to select students with necessary background knowledge or skills for further training.

Separate norms for males and females are preferred when the use of combined norms leads to misinterpretations and poor decisions. For example, 3-year-old Aaron might earn a percentile of 35 on a developmental test that has both boys and girls in the norms. His score indicates that his development is behind that of other boys and girls. However, his performance would earn a score of 52 on norms for 3-year-old boys. His score indicates that he is average for a boy of his age. It is important to remember that separate gender norms equate the derived scores for males and females, but separate norms do not erase the underlying differences in performance.

Age

Chronological age is clearly related to maturation for a number of abilities and skills, and norms frequently use age groups of one year. However, we have known for 50 years or more that different psychological abilities develop at different rates.[5] Consequently, tests may use norms with narrower or wider age ranges. When an ability or skill is developing rapidly (for example, locomotion in infants and toddlers), the age range of a norm group may be much narrower than one year—e.g., 6-month norms. For mature adults whose skills and abilities have stabilized, the age range may be several years e.g., norms for persons 59 to 65 years of age, 65 to 70 years of age, etc. The months or years spanned by an age group is an empirical question. Test authors may rely on research with other similar tests or the results with their own test in deciding the range of ages in a norm group.

Grade in School

All achievement tests should measure learned facts and concepts that have been taught in school. The more grades completed by students (that is, the more schooling), the more they should have been taught. Thus, the most useful norm comparisons are usually made to students of the same grade, regardless of their ages.[6] It is also important to note that students of different ages are present in most grades; for example, some 7-year-old children may not be enrolled in school, some may be in kindergarten, some in first grade, some in second grade, and some even in third grade.

Acculturation of Parents

Acculturation is an imprecise concept that refers to an understanding of the language (including conventions and pragmatics), history, values, and social conventions of society at large. Nowhere are the complexities of acculturation more readily illustrated than in the area of language. Acculturation requires people to know more than standard American English; they must also know the appropriate contexts for various words and idioms, appropriate volume and distance between speaker and listener, appropriate posture to indicate respect, and so forth.

Because acculturation is a broad and somewhat diffuse construct, it is difficult to define or measure precisely. Typically, test authors use the socioeconomic status of the parents (usually some combination of education and occupation of the parents) as a very general indication of the level of acculturation of the home. The socioeconomic status of a student's parents is strongly related to scores on all sorts of tests, including intelligence, achievement, adaptive behavior, and social functioning. Historically the children of middle- and upper-class parents have tended to score higher on such tests (see Gottesman, 1968; Herrnstein & Murray, 1994). Whatever the reasons for such differences in child attainment, norm samples certainly must include all segments of society (in the same proportion as in the general population) in order to be representative.

Racial Identity

Race is particularly relevant to our discussion of norms for two reasons. First, the scientific and educational communities have often been insensitive and occasionally blatantly racist (for example, Down, 1866/1969). As recently as 1972, the Stanford-Binet Intelligence Scale excluded nonwhite individuals from the standardization sample. Although such overt discrimination is rare today, individuals of color still may face subtle forms of discrimination and limited opportunities.

Second, persistent racial differences in *tested* achievement and ability remain, although these differences continue to narrow. Scientists and philosophers have long tried to understand why this might be so, and they have offered a variety of explanations—genetics, environment, interactions between genes and environment,

---

[5] Guilford, 1967, pp. 417–426.

[6] In situations where students are not grouped by grade, it may be necessary to use age comparisons.

poor test construction, etc.[7] However, although trying to unravel the interactions among explanations may be interesting scientifically and politically, such an endeavor is far beyond the scope of this text. What is important for our purposes is an understanding that these differences must be considered in developing norm groups.

Geography

There are systematic differences in the attainment of individuals living in different geographic regions of the United States, and various psychoeducational tests reflect these regional differences. Most consistently, the average scores of individuals living in the southeastern United States (excluding Florida) are often lower than the average scores of individuals living in other regions of the country. Moreover, community size, population density (that is, urban, suburban, and rural communities), and gains or losses of population have also been related to academic and intellectual development.

There are several seemingly logical explanations for many of these relationships. For example, well-educated young adults tend to move away from communities with limited employment and cultural opportunities. When better educated individuals leave a community, the average intellectual ability and educational attainment in that community decline, and the average ability and attainment of the communities to which those individuals move increase. Regardless of the reasons for geographical differences, test norms should include individuals from all geographic regions, as well as from urban, suburban, and rural communities.

Intelligence

Intelligence is related to a number of variables that are considered in psychoeducational assessment. Intelligence is certainly related to achievement because most intelligence tests were actually developed to predict school success. Correlations are generally positive but decline as students age. For elementary school students, the correlation may be as high as .7, but they tend to drop for high school and college students (Atkinson, Atkinson, Smith, & Bem, 1993).

Because language development and facility are often considered an indication of intellectual development, intelligence tests are often verbally oriented. Consequently, they tend to correlate with scores on tests of linguistic or psycholinguistic ability. Various perceptual tasks are also used on intelligence tests. Items assessing perceptual abilities appeared on intelligence tests as early as Thurstone's Primary Mental Abilities test in 1941.

The full range of intellectual ability must be considered in the development of norms for perceptual and perceptual–motor tests. Historically, norms have been biased by such practices as limiting the sample to students enrolled in and attending school (usually general education classes), excluding individuals with intellectual disability, or selecting only students of *average* intelligence. Such practices inflate test means, restrict the standard deviation, and bias derived scores.

4-3b OTHER CONSIDERATIONS

Norms Are Plural

Most tests have multiple normative samples that are collectively referred to as the norm sample. For example, the norm sample of an achievement test may contain 2600 students from kindergarten through twelfth grade. However, that group consists of 200 students in thirteen norm groups (twelve grades plus kindergarten). If that achievement test also had separate norms for boys and girls at each grade, there would be 26 norm groups of 100 students each. Therefore, when we test a second-grade boy, we do not compare his performance with the performances of

---

[7] We also note that perhaps as much as 90 percent of observed racial and cultural differences can be attributed to socioeconomic differences.

2600 students in the total norm sample. Rather, we compare the boy's performance to 200 second-graders (or to 100 second-grade boys if there are separate norms for boys and girls).

The number of subjects in each norm group should be large enough to guarantee stability. If a sample is very small, another group of participants might have different means and standard deviations. Second, the number of participants should be large enough to represent infrequent characteristics. For example, if about 1 percent of the population is Native American, a sample of 25 or 50 people will be unlikely to contain even one Native American. Third, there should be enough subjects so that there can be a full range of derived scores. In practice, 100 participants in each normative group are considered the minimum.

It is crucial that various kinds of people in each normative sample be included in the same proportion as they occur in the general population. Each norm group must be representative, not just the aggregated or combined sample. Representativeness should be demonstrated for each norm group.

Age of Norms

For a norm sample to be representative, it must represent the current population. Levels of skill and ability change over time. Skilled athletes of today run faster, jump higher, and are stronger than the best athletes of a generation ago. Some of the improvement can be attributed to better training, but some also can be attributed to better nutrition and societal changes. Similarly, intellectual and educational performances have increased from generation to generation, although these increases are neither steady nor linear.

For example, on norm-referenced achievement tests, considerably more than half the students score above the average after the test has been in use for five to seven years. In such cases, the test norms are clearly dated, because only half the population can ever be above the median (Linn, Graue, & Sanders, 1990). While some increase in tested achievement can be attributed to teacher familiarity with test content (Linn et al., 1990), there is little doubt that some of the changes represent real improvement in achievement.

There are probably multiple causes for these increases. Certainly, the computer revolution forever changed the availability of information. Never before has there been so much knowledge accessible to so many people. Students of today know more than did the students in 2000. Students of today also probably know less than will the students in 2025.

The important point is that old norms tend to overestimate a student's relative standing in the population erroneously because the old norms are too easy. The point at which norms become outdated will depend in part on the ability or skill being assessed. With this caution, it seems to us that 15 years is about the maximum useful life for norm samples used in ability testing; seven years appears to be the maximum for norm life for achievement tests. Although test publishers should assure that up-to-date norms are readily available, test users ultimately are responsible for avoiding the inappropriate use of out-of-date norms (AERA et al., 2014, p. 104).

Specialized Norms

National norms are the most appropriate if we are interested in knowing how a particular student is developing intellectually, perceptually, linguistically, or physically. However, sometimes educators are interested in comparing a test taker to a particular subgroup of the national population. The term **specialized norms** refers to all comparisons that are not national. One type of specialized norm is referred to as local norms. Local norms may be based on an entire state, school district, or even a classroom. These norms are useful in ascertaining the degree to which individual students have profited from their schooling and also in retrospective interpretations of a student's performance.

Special population norms are a second type of specialized norm sample. These norms are based on personal characteristics or attainment. For example, the *American Association on Intellectual and Developmental Disabilities' Adaptive Behavior Scale* compares a student's score to those of individuals with intellectual disabilities. Other tests used in guidance are standardized on individuals in specific trades or professions.

A third type of norms are called growth norms. **Growth norms** are used to assign percentiles and standard scores to differences in scores from one test to another (e.g., the amount of gain from pretest to posttest) over a specified amount of time. Growth scores have unique issues of score reliability that are discussed in the next chapter.

ADVANCED INFORMATION ABOUT FINDING A REPRESENTATIVE SAMPLE OF PEOPLE

Finding a broadly representative sample of people requires careful planning. Therefore, test authors or publishers usually develop sampling plans to try to locate potential participants with the needed characteristics. Sampling plans involve finding communities of specific sizes within geographic regions. Cluster sampling and selection of representative communities (or some combination of the two) are two common methods of choosing these communities. In cluster sampling, urban areas and the surrounding suburban and rural communities are selected. Such sampling plans have the advantage of requiring fewer testers and less travel. When a sampling plan calls for the selection of representative communities, a representative community is usually defined as one in which the mean demographic characteristics of residents (such as educational level and income) are approximately the same as the national or regional average. For example, about 51 percent of the population was female, about 19 percent of the population lived in the northeastern region of the country, and about 25 percent of the population 25 years or older had a degree from a four-year college. A representative community in the northeastern region would be one in which about 51 percent was female, about 25 percent had earned a degree from a four-year institution, and so on.

The systematic development of representative norms is time-consuming and expensive. Samples that are convenient, such as volunteers from all the parochial schools in a big city, reduce the time needed to locate subjects and are less expensive; however, they are unlikely to be representative, even when the number of subjects is impressively large.

However, neither cluster sampling nor selection of representative communities guarantees that the participants as a group are representative of the population. Consequently, test authors may adjust norms to make them representative. One method of adjusting norms is to systematically oversample subjects (that is, to select many more subjects than are needed) and then to drop subjects until a representative sample has been achieved. Another method is to weight subjects within the normative sample differentially. Subjects with underrepresented characteristics may be counted as more than one subject, and subjects with overrepresented characteristics may be counted as fractions of persons. Both methods may be used. In such ways, norm samples can be manipulated to conform to population characteristics.

Smoothing of Norms

After the norm sample has been finalized, norm tables are prepared. Because of minor sampling fluctuations, even well-selected norm groups will show minor variations in distribution shape. Minor smoothing is believed to result in better estimates of derived scores, means, and standard deviations. For example, there might be a few outliers—scores at the extremes of a distribution that are not contiguous to the distribution of scores but are several points beyond what would be considered the highest or lowest score in a distribution. A test author might drop these outliers. Similarly, the progression of group means from age to age may not be consistent, or group variances may differ slightly from age to age for no apparent reason. As a result, test developers will often smooth these values to conform to a theoretical or empirically generated model of performance (for example, using predicted means rather than obtained means).

Smoothing is also done to remove unwanted fluctuations in the shapes of age or grade distributions by adjusting the relationship between standard scores and percentiles. Even when normal test distributions are expected on the basis of theory, the obtained distributions of scores are never completely normal. For example, several models of intelligence posit a normal distribution of scores; in practice, the distribution of test scores is skewed because of an excess of low-scoring individuals. Thus, standard scores do not correspond to the percentile ranks that are expected in a normal distribution. In such cases, a test author may force standard scores into a normal distribution by assigning them to percentile ranks on the basis of the relationship between standard scores and percentiles found in normal distributions. For example, a raw score corresponding to the eighty-fourth percentile will be assigned a *T*-score of 60, regardless of the calculated value. The process, called "area transformation," or normalizing a distribution, is discussed in detail in advanced measurement texts. When normal distributions are not expected, a test developer may remove minor inconsistencies in distribution shapes from age to age or grade to grade. To smooth out minor inconsistencies, test authors may average the percentile ranks associated with specific standard scores. For example, a *T*-score of 60 might be associated with percentile ranks of 72, 74, and 73 in 6-, 7-, and 8-year-old groups, respectively. These percentiles could be averaged, and *T*-scores of 60 in each of the age groups could be assigned a percentile rank of 73.

Normative Updates

Because the development of systematically standardized tests is so expensive, test publishers may update a test's norms more frequently than they revise the test. Normative updating can be done in two ways. First, a completely different set of norms may be systematically developed. Procedurally, this kind of update is identical to the development of any set of norms. Second, statistics based on a small representative sample can be used to adjust (or recalibrate) the old norms. The necessary statistics (for example, mean and standard deviation in classical test theory or various parameters in item-response theory) can be accurately estimated from a small sample of individuals. The old norms can be linearly transformed using the new statistics, and new tables are prepared to convert raw scores to new standard scores. Moreover, if the distribution of scores is normal, new percentiles can be calculated based on their relationship with standard scores.

The difficulty with normative updates is that the content is unchanged. This is not a problem when content is timeless. However, if the content becomes easier (as is frequently the case with achievement tests), the new norms may not discriminate among high scorers. In addition, normative updates probably will not fix problems associated with reliability or other validity considerations.

Out-of-Level Testing

When students have extremely limited abilities, tests designed for individuals of the same age may be too difficult. In such cases, tests lose their power to discriminate among test takers, and floor or ceiling effects restrict possible scores. Faced with such students, some testers may resort to out-of-level testing—using norms for a younger group of test takers. Although such a procedure may provide useful qualitative information, it cannot provide norm-referenced interpretations because the ages of the individuals in the norm group and the age of the person being tested are not the same.

A more serious error is committed when a tester uses a person's mental age rather than their chronological age to select the table to convert raw scores. We suppose the reasoning behind such practices is that if the person functions as an 8-year-old child intellectually, the use of conversion tables based on the performance of 8-year-old children can be justified. However, such practices are incorrect because the norms were not established by sampling persons by mental age. When assessing the reading skill of an adolescent or adult who performs below the first percentile, a tester has little need for further or more precise norm-referenced comparisons. The tester already knows that the person is not a good reader. If the examiner wants to ascertain which reading skills a person has or lacks, a criterion-referenced (norm-free) device will be more suitable. Sometimes the most appropriate use of norms is no use at all.

Chapter Comprehension Questions

Write your answers to each of the following questions and then compare your responses to the text.

1. Compare and contrast the two scales of measurement most commonly used in educational and psychological measurement.

2. Explain the following terms: mean, median, mode, variance, skew, and correlation coefficient.

3. Explain the statistical meaning of the following scores: percentile, *z* score, IQ, NCE, age equivalent, and grade equivalent.

4. Why is the acculturation of the parents of students in normative samples important?

TECHNICAL REQUIREMENTS

LEARNING OBJECTIVES

5-1   Understand the basic concept of reliability, what it is, how it is estimated, and the factors that affect it.

5-2   Explain the basic information used in test validation.

STANDARDS ADDRESSED IN THIS CHAPTER

CEC **CEC Initial Preparation Standards**

Standard 4: Assessment

4.0 Beginning special education professionals use multiple methods of assessment and data-sources in making educational decisions.

CEC **CEC Advanced Preparation Standards**
ADVANCED

Standard 1: Assessment

1.0 Special education specialists use valid and reliable assessment practices to minimize bias.

 National Association of School Psychologists Domains

1 Data-based Decision-making and Accountability

9 Research and Program Evaluation

5-1 Reliability

Every day, school personnel conduct assessments—mostly they test and they observe—to get information to facilitate educational decision making. For assessments to be useful they must be conducted, scored, and interpreted correctly. However, that is not enough. Assessment results must be generalizable. Except for school-specific rules (for example, no running in the halls), nothing a student learns in school would have any value unless it can be generalized to life outside of school. The very nature of schooling presumes students will generalize what they have learned. In measurement, **reliability** is the extent to which it is possible to generalize from an observation or test score made at a specific time by a specific person to a similar performance at a different time, or by a different person. When assessment results cannot be generalized, they are in error; the results are incorrect. The errors associated with each of the three dimensions (i.e., selected items, times, raters) are independent of each other (i.e., uncorrelated) and additive. Measurement error is the sum of the three kinds of error.[1]

Suppose Mr. Jeffreys wanted to know if his students could name the cursive upper case letters of the alphabet. Because there are only 26 letters, he could test every letter. Students' scores on that test would be their true scores on the domain. Suppose Mr. Jeffreys did not want to test every letter, instead preferring to test a smaller sample of letters—for example, five letters. Students' means on all of the possible five-letter tests would be their true scores for five-letter tests. Some of those tests (for example, $\mathcal{B}, C, \mathcal{D}, \mathcal{E}, O$) would be much easier than the average of all five-letter tests. Students would earn scores that were higher than their true scores—the averages of all five-letter tests. Other tests (for example, $J, \mathcal{Q}, S, Z, \mathcal{A}$) would be much harder than the average of five-letter tests. Students would earn scores that were lower than their true scores. The differences between students' true scores and their obtained scores are error. These errors are random and uncorrelated with true scores. In the long run, the average (mean) error equals zero. Across a large number of samples, the samples that raise scores are balanced by samples that lower scores.

On achievement tests dealing with beginning material and with certain types of behavioral observations, it is occasionally possible to assess an entire domain (for example, arithmetic facts). In such cases, the obtained score is a student's true score, and there is no need to estimate the reliability of the test's item sample. Usually it is not possible or feasible to assess an entire domain, even in the primary grades. In more advanced curricula, it is usually impossible to assess an entire domain—especially when that domain is a hypothetical construct (such as intelligence or visual perception). Therefore, in these cases, reliability of the item sample should always be estimated.

The same argument can be made for reliability (generalization) over times. If we are only interested in performance on one occasion, that one occasion makes up the entire domain. The student's performance at that time is the student's true score. Obviously there are very few performances that would comprise an entire domain—for example, felonies, acts of heroism.

Similarly, if we are only interested in the evaluations of one person or committee, those evaluations make up the entire domain. The performance as assessed by that one person constitutes the entire domain, and the students' scores are their true scores. Although such a situation is difficult to imagine in schools, personal evaluations are frequently all that matters outside of school. For example, your evaluation of the food at a restaurant is probably the only evaluation that is important to you in determining whether the food was good.

---

[1] Unlike measurement error that is random, **bias** is measurement error that is systematic and predictable. Bias affects a person's (or group's) score in one direction. Bias inflates people's measured abilities above their true abilities. Bias can also deflate people's measured abilities below their true abilities.

People should always be concerned about error during assessment. Read the upcoming Scenario in Assessment and associated question to think more carefully about the potential for error in typical classroom testing situations. Although there is always some degree of error, the important question is how much error is attached to a particular score. Unfortunately, a direct answer to this question is usually not available. To estimate both the amount of error attached to a score and the amount of error in general, two statistics are needed: (1) a reliability coefficient for the particular generalization and (2) the standard error of measurement.

5-1a THE RELIABILITY COEFFICIENT

The reliability coefficient is a special use of a correlation coefficient. The symbol for a correlation coefficient (r) is used with two identical subscripts (for example, r_{xx} or r_{aa}) to indicate a reliability coefficient. The **reliability coefficient** indicates the proportion of variability in a set of scores that reflects true differences among individuals. If there is relatively little error, the ratio of true score variance to obtained score variance approaches a reliability index of 1.00 (perfect reliability); if there is a relatively large amount of error, the ratio of true score variance to obtained score variance approaches .00 (total unreliability). Thus, a test with a reliability coefficient of .90 has relatively less error of measurement and is more reliable than a test with a reliability coefficient of .50. Subtracting the proportion of true-score variance from 1 yields the proportion of error variance in the distribution of scores. Thus, if the reliability coefficient is .90, 10 percent of the variability in the distribution is attributable to error.

All other things being equal, we want to use the most reliable procedures and tests that are available. Since perfectly reliable devices are quite rare, the choice of test becomes a question of minimum reliability for the specific purpose of assessment. We recommend that the standards for reliability presented in Table 5.1 be used in applied settings.

Three Types of Reliability

In educational and psychological assessment, we are concerned with three types of reliability or generalizations: generalization to other similar items, generalization to other times, and generalization to other observers. These three generalizations have different names (that is, item reliability, stability, and interobserver agreement) and are separately estimated by different procedures.

Item Reliability There are two main approaches to estimating the extent to which we can generalize to different samples of items: alternate-form reliability and internal consistency.

Alternate-form reliability represents the correlation between scores for the same individuals on two different forms of a test. These forms (1) measure the same trait

TABLE 5.1	Standards for Reliability

- If test scores are to be used for administrative purposes and are reported for groups of individuals, a reliability of .60 should be the minimum. This relatively low standard is acceptable because group means are not as affected by a test's lack of reliability.
- If weekly (or more frequent) testing is used to monitor pupil progress, a reliability of .70 should be the minimum. This relatively low standard is acceptable because random fluctuations can be taken into account when a behavior or skill is measured often.
- If the decision being made is a screening decision (for example, a recommendation for further assessment), there is a need for even higher reliability. For screening devices, we recommend a standard of .80.
- If a test score is to be used to make an important decision concerning an individual student (for example, tracking or special education placement), the minimum standard should be .90.

GEORGE AND JULES | George and Jules were going to take a test on World War II in their history class. To study, George concentrated his efforts on the causes and consequences of the war. Jules reviewed his notes and then watched the movie *Patton*. The next day, the boys took the history test, which contained three short-answer questions and one major essay question, "Discuss Patton's role leading up to and following World War II in Europe." George got a C on his test; Jules got an A. George complained that his test score was not an accurate reflection of what he knew about the war and that it was unfair because it did not specifically address the war's broader causes and consequences. On the other hand, Jules was very pleased with his score, even though it would have been considerably lower if the teacher had asked a different question. The test did not provide a reliable estimate of either's knowledge of World War II.

This scenario highlights how error is often present when using a sample of items to determine an individual's knowledge or skill in a particular area; limited representation results in greater error, and lower reliability. What might be done to improve the reliability of a test like the one George and Jules took?

© Cengage Learning

or skill to the same extent and (2) are standardized on the same population. Alternate forms offer essentially equivalent tests (but not identical items); sometimes, in fact, they are called equivalent forms. The means and variances for the alternate forms are assumed to be (or should be) the same. In the absence of error of measurement, any subject would be expected to earn the same score on both forms. To estimate the reliability of two alternate forms of a test (for example, form A and form B), a large sample of students is tested with both forms. Half the subjects receive form A and then form B; the other half receive form B and then form A. Scores from the two forms are correlated. The resulting correlation coefficient is a reliability coefficient.

Internal consistency is the second approach to estimating the extent to which we can generalize to different test items, and it is a measure of the extent to which items in a test correlate with one another. It does not require two or more test forms. Instead, after a test is given, it is split into two halves that are correlated to produce an estimate of reliability. For example, suppose we wanted to use this method to estimate the reliability of a 10-item test. The results of this hypothetical test are presented in Table 5.2. After administering the test to a group of students, we divide the test into two 5-item tests by summing the even numbered items and the odd numbered items for each student. This creates two alternate forms of the test, each containing one half of the total number of test items. We can then correlate the sums of the odd-numbered items with the sums of the even-numbered items to obtain an estimate of the reliability of each of the two halves. This procedure for estimating a test's reliability is called a *split-half reliability estimate*.

It should be apparent that there are many ways to divide a test into two equal-length tests. If the 10 items in our full test are arranged in order of increasing difficulty, both halves should contain items from the beginning of the test (that is, easier items) and items from the end of the test (that is, more difficult items). There are many other ways of dividing such a test (for example, grouping items 1, 4, 5, 8, and 9 and items 2, 3, 6, 7, and 10). The most common way to divide a test is by odd-numbered and evennumbered items (see the columns labeled "Evens Correct" and "Odds Correct" in Table 5.2).

A better method of estimating internal consistency was developed by Cronbach (1951) and is called coefficient alpha. *Coefficient alpha* is the average split-half correlation based on all possible divisions of a test into two parts. In practice, there is no need to compute all possible correlation coefficients; coefficient alpha can be computed from the variances of individual test items and the variance of the total test score.

Coefficient alpha can be used when test items are scored pass–fail or when more than one point is awarded for a correct response. An earlier, more restricted method of estimating a test's reliability, based on the average correlation between all possible split halves, was developed by Kuder and Richardson. This procedure, called *KR-20*, is coefficient alpha for dichotomously scored test items (that is, items that can only be scored right or wrong).

TABLE 5.2	Hypothetical Performance of 20 Children on a 10-Item Test

| | Items | | | | | | | | | | Totals | | |
Child	1	2	3	4	5	6	7	8	9	10	Total Test	Evens Correct	Odds Correct
1	+	+	+	−	+	−	−	−	+	−	5	1	4
2	+	+	+	+	−	+	+	+	−	+	8	5	3
3	+	+	−	+	+	+	+	−	+	+	8	4	4
4	+	+	+	+	+	+	+	+	−	+	9	5	4
5	+	+	+	+	+	+	+	+	+	−	9	4	5
6	+	+	−	+	−	+	+	+	+	+	8	5	3
7	+	+	+	+	+	−	+	−	+	+	8	3	5
8	+	+	+	−	+	+	+	+	+	+	9	4	5
9	+	+	+	+	+	+	−	+	+	+	9	5	4
10	+	+	+	+	+	−	+	+	+	+	9	4	5
11	+	+	+	+	+	−	+	−	−	−	6	2	4
12	+	+	−	+	+	+	+	+	+	+	9	5	4
13	+	+	+	−	−	+	−	+	−	−	5	3	2
14	+	+	+	+	+	+	+	−	+	+	9	4	5
15	+	+	−	+	+	−	−	−	−	−	4	2	2
16	+	+	+	+	+	+	+	+	+	+	10	5	5
17	+	−	+	−	−	−	−	−	−	−	2	0	2
18	+	−	+	+	+	+	+	+	+	+	9	4	5
19	+	+	+	+	−	+	+	+	+	+	9	5	4
20	+	−	−	−	−	+	−	+	−	−	3	2	1

© 2013 Cengage Learning

Stability **Stability** is the consistency of test scores over time. When students have learned information and behavior, we want to be confident that they can access that information and demonstrate those behaviors at times other than when they are assessed. We would like to be able to generalize today's test results to other times in the future. Educators are interested in many human traits and characteristics that, theoretically, change very little over time. For example, children diagnosed as color-blind at age 5 years are expected to be diagnosed as color-blind at any time in their lives. Color blindness is an inherited trait that cannot be corrected. Consequently, the trait should be perfectly stable. When an assessment identifies a student as color-blind on one occasion and not color-blind on a later occasion, the assessment is unreliable.

Other traits are developmental. For example, people's heights will increase from birth through adulthood. The increases are relatively slow and predictable. Consequently, we would not expect many changes in height over a two-week period. Radical changes in people's heights (especially decreases) over short periods of time would cause us to question the reliability of the measurement device. Most educational and psychological characteristics are conceptualized much as height is conceptualized. For example, we expect reading achievement to increase with length of schooling but to be relatively stable over short periods of time, such as two weeks.

Devices used to assess traits and characteristics must produce sufficiently consistent and stable results if those results are to have practical meaning for making educational decisions. When our generalizations about student performance on a domain are correctly generalized from one time to another, the test is said to be stable or have test–retest reliability. Obviously, the notion of stability excludes changes that occur as the result of systematic interventions to change the behavior. Thus, if a test indicates that a student does not know the long vowel sounds and we teach those sounds to the student, the change in the student's test performance would not be considered a lack of reliability.

The procedure for obtaining a stability coefficient is straightforward. A large number of students are tested and then retested after a short period of time (preferably two weeks later). The students' scores from the two administrations are then correlated, and the obtained correlation coefficient is the stability coefficient.

Interobserver Agreement **Interobserver agreement** is the consistency among test scorers. We would like to assume that if any other comparably qualified examiner were to give the test or make the observation, the results would be the same—we would like to be able to generalize to similarly qualified testers. Suppose Ms. Amig listened to her students say the letters of the alphabet. It would not be very useful if she assigned Barney a score of 70 percent correct, whereas another teacher (or education professional) who also listened to Barney awarded a score of 50 percent correct or 90 percent correct for the same performance. When our scoring or other observations agree with those of comparably trained observers who observe the same phenomena at the same time, the observations are said to have interobserver reliability or agreement.[2] Ms. Amig would like to assume that any other education professional would score her students' responses in the same way.

There are two very different approaches to estimating the extent to which we can generalize to different scorers: a correlational approach and a percentage of agreement approach. The correlational approach is similar to estimating reliability with alternate forms, which was previously discussed. Two testers score a set of tests independently. Scores obtained by each tester for the set are then correlated. The resulting correlation coefficient is a reliability coefficient for scorers.

Percentage of agreement is more common in classrooms and applied behavioral analysis. Instead of the correlation between two scorers' ratings, a percentage of agreement between raters is computed. Three ways of calculating percent agreement are commonly used: simple agreement, point-to-point agreement, and agreement for occurrence.[3]

Simple agreement is calculated by dividing the smaller number of occurrences by the larger number of occurrences and multiplying the quotient by 100. For example, suppose Ms. Amig and her teacher's aide, Ms. Carter, observe Sam on 20 occasions to determine how frequently he is on task during reading instruction. The results of their observations are shown in Table 5.3. Ms. Amig observes 13 occasions when Sam is on task, whereas Ms. Carter observes 11 occasions. Simple agreement is 85 percent; that is, $100 \times (11/13)$.

---

[2] Agreement among observers has several different names. Observers can be referred to as testers, scorers, or raters; it depends on the nature of their actions. Agreement can also be called reliability.

[3] There is a fourth index, Kappa, which is seldom used in classrooms. Both point-to-point agreement and agreement of occurrence indexes are affected by chance agreements. Cohen (1960) developed a coefficient of agreement, called *kappa*, that removes the proportion of agreement that would occur by chance. Kappa values range from −1.00 (total disagreement) to +1.00 (total agreement); a value of 0 indicates chance agreement. Thus, a positive index of agreement indicates agreement above what test givers would expect to find by chance. The computation of kappa is more complicated than the computation of other agreement indexes.

| TABLE 5.3 | | Observations of Sam's On-Task Behavior During Reading, Where "−" Is Off Task and "+" Is On Task | |

Observation	Ms. Amig	Ms. Carter	Observers Agree
1	+	+	Yes
2	−	−	Yes
3	−	+	No
4	+	+	Yes
5	+	+	Yes
6	+	+	Yes
7	−	−	Yes
8	−	+	No
9	+	+	Yes
10	+	−	No
11	−	−	Yes
12	+	+	Yes
13	+	+	Yes
14	+	+	Yes
15	−	−	Yes
16	+	−	No
17	+	+	Yes
18	−	−	Yes
19	+	−	No
20	+	−	No
Total No. of occurrences	13	11	14

The second type of percent agreement, **point-to-point agreement**, is a more precise way of computing percentage of agreement because each data point is considered. Point-to-point agreement is calculated by dividing the number of observations for which both observers agree (occurrence and nonoccurrence) by the total number of observations and multiplying the quotient by 100. The data from Table 5.3 are summarized in Table 5.4. There are 14 occasions when Ms. Amig's and Ms. Carter's observations agree—9 times that Sam was on task and 5 times that Sam was off task. Point-to-point agreement is 70 percent; that is, $100 \times (14/20)$.

Agreement for occurrence provides a better measure of agreement than point-to-point agreement when occurrences and nonoccurrences differ substantially, because point-to-point agreement tends to overestimate the agreement. Equation 5.1 is the formula for agreement of occurrence. The data from Table 5.3 are used to illustrate the calculation of agreement of occurrence. Of the 14 times that Ms. Amig and Ms. Carter agreed that Sam was on or off task, they agreed nine times that he was on task. The five times they agree that Sam was off task are not of interest and not considered in this calculation. Inserting the numbers into Equation 5.1, the two observers agreed on Sam being on task 60 percent of the time—$[100 \times [9 \div (20 - 5)]$.

$$\frac{(100) \left(N_{\text{agreements of occurrence}} \right)}{N_{\text{observations}} - N_{\text{agreements of nonoccurrence}}}$$ **Equation 5.1**

TABLE 5.4	Summary of Two Observers Assessment of Sam's On-Task Behavior During Reading

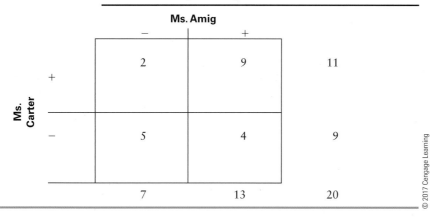

5-1b FACTORS AFFECTING RELIABILITY

Several factors affect a test's reliability and can inflate or deflate reliability estimates: test length, test–retest interval, constriction or extension of range, guessing, and variation within the testing situation.

1. *Test Length*. As a general rule, the more items there are in a test, the more reliable the test is; longer tests tend to be more reliable than short tests. This fact is especially important when considering internal-consistency estimates of reliability because split-half estimates of reliability actually estimate the reliability of half the test. Therefore, such estimates are appropriately corrected by a formula developed by Spearman and Brown. As shown in Equation 5.2, the reliability of the total test is equal to twice the reliability as estimated by internal consistency, divided by the sum of 1 plus the reliability estimate. For example, if a split-half estimate of internal consistency were computed for a test and found to be .80, the corrected estimated reliability would be .89 [i.e., (2)(.8) ÷ (1 + .8)]. A related issue is the number of effective items for each test taker. Tests are generally more reliable in the middle ranges of scores (for example, within ±1.5S). For a test to be effective at the extremes of a distribution, there must be both enough difficult items for very superior pupils and enough easy items for deficient pupils. Often, there are not enough very easy and very hard items on a test. Therefore, extremely high or extremely low scores tend to be less reliable than scores in the middle of a distribution.

$$r_{xx} = \frac{2r_{(\frac{1}{2})(\frac{1}{2})}}{1 + r_{(\frac{1}{2})(\frac{1}{2})}}$$

Equation 5.2

2. *Test–Retest Interval*. As previously noted, a person's true abilities can and do change between two administrations of a test. The greater the amount of time between the two administrations, the more likely is the possibility that true scores will change. Thus, when employing stability or alternate-form estimates of reliability, test evaluators must pay close attention to the interval between tests. Generally, the shorter the interval is, the higher the estimated reliability is.

3. *Constriction or Extension of Range*. Constriction or extension of range refers to narrowing (constriction) or widening (extension) the range of ability of the people whose performances are used to estimate a test's reliability. When the range of ability of these people is less than the range of ability in the population, a test's reliability will be underestimated. The more constricted the range of ability is, the more biased (underestimated) the reliability coefficient will be. As Figure 5.1 shows, alternative forms of a test produce a strong positive correlation when the entire range of the test

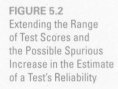

FIGURE 5.1
Constricting the Range
of Test Scores and the
Resulting Reduction
of the Estimate of a
Test's Reliability

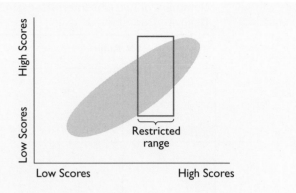

SOURCE: *Psychological Testing, 7e* by Anastasi,
©1997. Reprinted by permission of Prentice-
Hall, Upper Saddle River, NJ.

FIGURE 5.2
Extending the Range
of Test Scores and
the Possible Spurious
Increase in the Estimate
of a Test's Reliability

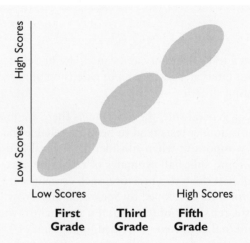

is used. However, within any restricted range of the test, as illustrated by the dark rectangular outline, the correlation may be very low. (Although it is possible to correct a correlation coefficient for restriction in range, it is generally unwise to do so.) A related problem is that extension of range overestimates a test's reliability. Figure 5.2 illustrates correlations of scores on alternate-form tests given to students in the first, third, and fifth grades. The scatterplot for each grade, considered separately, indicates poor reliability. However, spelling test scores increase as a function of schooling; students in higher grades earn higher scores. When test authors combine the scores for several grades (or from several ages), poor correlations may be combined to produce a spuriously high correlation. For this reason, tests for which scores are expected to improve as individuals age or advance in grade level should provide reliability estimates separately for age/grade groups.

4. *Guessing.* Guessing is responding randomly to items. Even if a guess results in a correct response, it introduces error into a test score and into our interpretation of that score.

5. *Variation Within the Testing Situation.* The amount of error that the testing situation introduces into the results of testing can vary considerably. Children can misread or misunderstand the directions for a test, get a headache halfway through testing, lose their place on the answer sheet, break the point of their pencil, or choose to watch a squirrel eat nuts on the windowsill of the classroom rather than take the test. All such situational variations introduce an indeterminate amount of error in testing and, in doing so, lower reliability.

5-1c DETERMINING WHICH RELIABILITY METHOD TO USE

The first consideration in choosing a method of determining a test's reliability is the type of generalization we wish to make. We must select the method that goes with the type of generalization. For example, if we were interested in generalizing about the stability of a score or observation, the appropriate method would be test–retest correlations. It would be inappropriate to use interscorer agreement as an estimate of the extent to which we can generalize to different times. Additional considerations in selecting the reliability method to be used include the following.

1. When one estimates stability, the convention is to retest after two weeks. There is nothing special about the two-week period, but if all test authors used the same interval, it would be easier to compare the relative stability of tests.

2. Many years ago, Nunnally (Nunnally & Bernstein, 1994; Nunnally, 1978) offered a hierarchy for estimating the extent to which we can generalize to similar test items. The first choice is to use alternate-form reliability with a two-week interval. (Again, there is nothing special about two weeks; it is just a convention.) If alternate forms are not available, divide the test into equivalent halves and administer the halves with a two-week interval, correcting the correlation by the Spearman-Brown formula given in Equation 5.2 on page 71. When alternate forms are not available and subjects cannot be tested more than once, use coefficient alpha.

3. When estimating the extent to which we can generalize among different scorers, we prefer computing correlation coefficients rather than percentages of agreement. Correlation coefficients bear a direct relationship to other indicators of reliability and other uses of reliability coefficients; percentages of agreement do not. We also realize that current practice is to report percentages of agreement and not to bother with the other uses of the reliability coefficient.

Concluding Comments About the Reliability Coefficient

Generalization to other items, times, and observers are independent of each other. Therefore, each index of reliability provides information about only a part of the error associated with measurement.

In school settings, item reliability is not a problem when we test students on the entire domain (for example, naming all upper- and lowercase letters of the alphabet). Item reliability should be estimated when we test students on a sample of items from the domain (for example, a 20-item test on multiplication facts that is used to infer mastery on all facts). Interscorer reliability is usually not a problem when our assessments are objective and our criteria for a correct response clear (for example, a multiple-choice test). Interscorer reliability should be assessed whenever subjective or qualitative criteria are used to score student responses (for example, using a scoring rubric to assess the quality of written responses). When students are assessed frequently with interchangeable tests or probes, stability is usually assessed directly prior to intervention by administering tests on three or more days until the student's performance has stabilized. If a test is given once, its stability should be estimated, although in practice teachers seldom estimate the stability of their tests.

5-1d STANDARD ERROR OF MEASUREMENT

The **standard error of measurement (SEM)** is another index of test error. The SEM is the average standard deviation of error distributed around people's true scores. Although we can compute standard errors of measurement for scorers, times, and item samples, SEMs for item samples are most frequently calculated.

To illustrate, suppose we wanted to assess students' emerging skill in naming letters of the alphabet and decided to estimate students' knowledge using a 10-letter test. There are many samples of 10-letter tests that could be developed. If we constructed 100 of these tests and tested just one kindergartner, we would

FIGURE 5.3
The Standard Error of Measurement: The Standard Deviation of the Error Distribution Around a True Score for One Subject

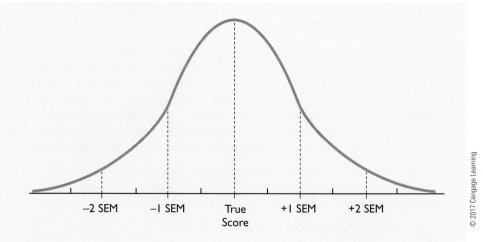

probably find that a distribution of scores for that kindergartner was approximately normal. The mean of that distribution by definition would be the student's true score. The distribution around the true score would be the result of imperfect samples of letters; some letter samples would overestimate the pupil's knowledge, and others would underestimate it. Thus, the variance around the mean would be the result of error. The standard deviation of that distribution is the standard deviation of errors attributable to sampling error, and it is called the standard error of measurement.

When students are assessed with norm-referenced tests, they are typically tested only once. Therefore, we cannot generate a distribution similar to those shown in Figure 5.3. Consequently, we do not know the test taker's true score or the variance of the measurement error that forms the distribution around that person's true score. By using what we know about the test's standard deviation and its reliability for items, we can estimate what that error distribution would be. However, when estimating the error distribution for one student, test users should understand that the SEM is an average; some standard errors will be greater than the average, and some will be less.

Equation 5.3 is the general formula for finding the SEM. The SEM equals the standard deviation of the obtained scores (S) multiplied by the square root of 1 minus the reliability coefficient. The type of unit (IQ, raw score, and so forth) in which the standard deviation is expressed is the unit in which the SEM is expressed. Thus, if the test scores have been converted to T scores, the standard deviation is in T score units and is 10; the SEM is also in T score units. From Equation 5.3, it is apparent that as the standard deviation increases, the SEM increases, and as the reliability coefficient decreases, the SEM increases. Similarly, if the reliability coefficient is based on stability, then the SEM is for times of testing. If the reliability coefficient is based on different scorers, then the SEM is for testers or scorers.

$$\text{SEM} = S\sqrt{1 - r_{xx}}$$

Equation 5.3

Because measurement error is unavoidable, there is always some uncertainty about an individual's true score. The SEM provides information about the certainty or confidence with which a test score can be interpreted. When the SEM is relatively large, the uncertainty is large; we cannot be very sure of the individual's score. When the SEM is relatively small, the uncertainty is small; we can be more certain of the score.

5-1e ESTIMATED TRUE SCORES

An obtained score on a test is not the best estimate of the true score because obtained scores and errors are correlated. Scores above the test mean have more "lucky" error (error that raises the obtained score above the true score),

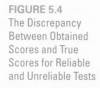

FIGURE 5.4
The Discrepancy
Between Obtained
Scores and True
Scores for Reliable
and Unreliable Tests

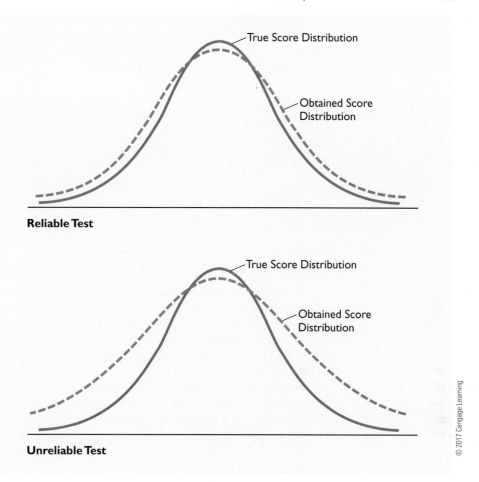

© 2017 Cengage Learning

whereas scores below the mean have more "unlucky" error (error that lowers the obtained score below the true score). An easy way to understand this effect is to think of a test on which Mike guesses on several test items. If all of Mike's guesses are correct, he has been very lucky and earns a score that is not representative of what he truly knows. However, if all his guesses are incorrect, Mike has been unlucky and earns a score that is lower than a score that represents what he truly knows.

As it turns out, obtained scores farther above or below the mean tend to be more discrepant from true scores than are obtained scores closer to the mean. Also as Figure 5.4 illustrates, the less reliable the test is, the greater is the discrepancy between obtained scores and true scores. Nunnally (Nunnally & Bernstein, 1994; Nunnally, 1978) has provided an equation (Equation 5.4) for determining the estimated true score (X'). The estimated true score equals the test mean plus the product of the reliability coefficient and the difference between the obtained score and the group mean.[4] Thus, the discrepancy between obtained scores and estimated true scores is a function of both the reliability of the obtained scores and the difference between the obtained score and the mean. It must be remembered that Equation 5.4 does not give the true score, only the estimated true score.

$$X' = \bar{X} + (r_{xx})(X - \bar{X})$$ **Equation 5.4**

[4] The particular mean that is used has been the subject of some controversy. We believe that the preferred mean is the mean of the demographic group that best represents the particular child. Thus, if the student is Asian and resides in a middle-class urban area, the most appropriate mean would be that of same-age Asian students from middle socioeconomic backgrounds who live in urban areas. In the absence of means for particular students of particular backgrounds, we are forced to use the overall mean for the student's age.

TABLE 5.5	Commonly Used z-Scores, Extreme Areas, and Area Included Between + and − z-Score Equation 5.5 values		
z-Score	**Extreme Area**	**Area Between + and −**	
.67	25.0%	50%	
1.00	16%	68%	
1.64	5%	90%	
1.96	2.5%	5%	
2.33	1.0%	98%	
2.57	0.5%	99%	

© 2017 Cengage Learning

5-1f CONFIDENCE INTERVALS

Although we can never know a person's true score, we can estimate the likelihood that a person's true score will be found within a specified range of scores. This range is called a *confidence interval*. Confidence intervals have two components. The first component is the score range within which a true score is likely to be found. For example, a range of 80 to 90 indicates that a person's true score is likely to be contained within that range. The second component is the level of confidence, generally between 50 and 95 percent. The level of confidence tells us how certain we can be that the true score will be contained within the interval. Thus, if a 90 percent confidence interval for Jo's IQ is 106 to 112, we can be 90 percent sure that Jo's true IQ is between 106 and 112. It also means that there is a 5 percent chance her true IQ is higher than 112 and a 5 percent chance her true IQ is lower than 106. To have greater confidence would require a wider confidence interval. Table 5.5 shows the extreme area for the z-scores commonly used to construct confidence intervals. The extreme area is the proportion of cases in the tail of the normal curve—that is, the area from plus or minus X number of standard deviations to the end of the curve. The general formula for a confidence interval (c.i.) is given in Equation 5.5.

$$\text{Lower limit of c.i.} = X' - (z\text{-score})(SEM)$$
$$\text{Upper limit of c.i.} = X' + (z\text{-score})(SEM)$$

Equation 5.5

Sometimes confidence intervals are implied. A score may be followed by a "±" and a number (for example, 109 ± 2). Unless otherwise noted, this notation indicates a 68 percent confidence interval with the number following the ± being the SEM. Thus, the lower limit of the confidence interval equals the score less the SEM (that is, $109 - 2$) and the upper limit equals the score plus the SEM (that is, $109 + 2$). The interpretation of this confidence interval is that we can be 68 percent sure that the student's true score is between 107 and 111.

Another confidence interval is implied when a score is given with the probable error (PE) of measurement. For example, a score might be reported as $105 \text{ PE} \pm 1$. A PE yields 50 percent confidence. Thus, $105 \text{ PE} \pm 1$ means a 50 percent confidence interval that ranges from 104 to 106. The interpretation of this confidence interval is that we can be 50 percent sure that the student's true score is between 104 and 106; 25 percent of the time the true score will be less than 104, and 25 percent of the time the true score will be greater than 106.

Constructing Confidence Intervals

Test manuals frequently table confidence intervals so testers do not have to construct them. However, if a tester needs to construct a confidence interval, the procedures are straightforward, although there is some disagreement over how to construct confidence intervals. Nunnally (Nunnally & Bernstein, 1994; Nunnally 1978) recommends using the SEM. Others (for example, Sabers, Feldt, & Reschly, 1988; Kubiszyn & Borich, 2003) prefer the standard error of estimate (that is, the average standard deviation of true scores around an obtained score.) When test reliability is high, the difference between the two procedures is negligible.

The procedures for constructing a confidence interval are as follows.

1. Select the degree of confidence—for example, 95 percent.
2. Find the z-score associated with that degree of confidence (for example, a 95 percent confidence interval is between z-scores of −1.96 and +1.96).
3. Multiply each z-score associated with the confidence interval (for example, 1.96 for 95 percent confidence) by the SEM.
4. Find the estimated true score.
5. Add the product of the z-score and the SEM to the estimated true score to obtain the upper limit of the confidence interval; subtract the product of the z-score and the SEM from the estimated true score to obtain the lower limit of the confidence interval.

For example, assume that a person's estimated true score is 75 and the SEM is 5. Further assume that you wish to be about 68 percent sure of constructing an interval that will contain the true score. Table 5.5 shows that a 68 percent degree of confidence is associated with a z-score of 1. Thus, about 68 percent of the time, the true score will be contained in the interval of 70 to 80 [that is, $75 - (1)(5)$ to $75 + (1)(5)$]; there is about a 16 percent chance that the true score is less than 70 and about a 16 percent chance that the true score is greater than 80. If you are unwilling to be wrong about 32 percent of the time, you must increase the width of the confidence interval. Thus, with the same true score (75) and SEM (5), if you wish 95 percent confidence, the size of the interval must be increased; it would have to range from 65 to 85 [that is, $75 - (1.96)(5)$ to $75 + (1.96)(5)$]. About 95 percent of the time, the true score will be contained within that interval; there is about a 2.5 percent chance that the true score is less than 65, and there is about a 2.5 percent chance that it is greater than 85.

5-1g DIFFERENCE SCORES

In many applied settings, we are interested in differences between two scores. The differences can take several forms. They can be as simple as the amount of gain from pretest to posttest. *Gap analysis* can be used to compare a student's actual growth to expected growth. Sometimes that growth is expressed in percentiles that compare the amount of growth of similar students (often students with the same pretest score). Differences can be used to compare students' academic achievement with their intellectual abilities. Some educational disorders (for example, learning disabilities) may require a "significant" discrepancy as a defining characteristic of the disorder; other disorders (for example, intellectual disability) use the absence of a significant discrepancy to rule out the disorder.

The term, significant discrepancy, can refer to three different kinds of difference (Salvia & Good, 1982): (1) reliable difference, (2) rare difference, and (3) educationally meaningful difference. Here we are concerned with reliable differences, differences that are the result of poor samples of test items, times, or observers/scorers. Two things must be remembered when dealing with difference scores. First, a difference between scores on two different tests (A and B) is a function of four things: (1) the reliability of test A, (2) the reliability of test B, (3) the correlation between tests A and B, and (4) differences in the tests' norm groups. We can estimate the reliability of difference caused by the first three factors. Second, when the two tests are correlated, the difference between a person's scores on the two tests are almost always less reliable than the scores on which the difference is based.

ADVANCED INFORMATION ABOUT DIFFERENCE SCORES

There are several approaches to calculating the reliability of a difference. The following two methods are particularly useful but rest on different assumptions and combine the data in different ways (that is, use different formulas). One method uses a regression model and was originally described by Thorndike (1963). In this model, one score is presumed to cause the second score. For example, intelligence is believed to determine achievement. Therefore, intelligence is identified as an independent (or predictor) variable, and achievement is identified as the dependent (or predicted) variable. When the predicted score (for example, the predicted achievement score) differs from the obtained achievement score, a deficit exists. The reliability of a predicted difference is given by Equation 5.6.

$$\hat{D} = \frac{r_{bb} + (r_{aa})(r_{ab}^2) - 2r_{ab}^2}{1 - r_{ab}^2} \qquad \text{Equation 5.6}$$

The reliability of a predicted difference $\hat{D}$ is equal to the reliability of the dependent variable (r_{bb}) plus the product of the reliability of the independent variable and the square of the correlation between the independent variable and the dependent variable $(r_{aa}r_{ab}^2)$, less twice the squared correlation between the independent and dependent variable $2r_{ab}^2$. This value is divided by 1 minus the squared correlation between the independent and dependent variables $(1 - r_{ab}^2)$. The standard deviation of predicted differences $(S_{\hat{D}})$, also called "standard error of the estimate" (SE_{est}), is given in Equation 5.7. The standard deviation of predicted differences $(S_{\hat{D}})$ is equal to the standard deviation of the dependent variable (S_b) multiplied by the square root of 1 minus the squared correlation between the independent and dependent variables.

$$S_{\hat{D}} = S_b \sqrt{1 - r_{ab}^2} \qquad \text{Equation 5.7}$$

The second method of evaluating the reliability of a difference was proposed by Stake and Wardrop (1971). In this method, one variable is not assumed to be the cause of the other; neither variable is identified as the independent variable. However, this method does require that both measures be in the same unit of measurement (for example, T scores or IQs). The reliability of a difference in obtained scores is given in Equation 5.8. The reliability of an obtained difference (r_{dif}) equals the average reliability of the two tests $[(1/2) (r_{aa} + r_{bb})]$ less the correlation between the two tests (r_{ab}); this difference is divided by 1 minus the correlation between the two tests $(1 - r_{ab})$.

$$r_{dif} = \frac{\frac{1}{2}(r_{aa} + r_{bb}) - r_{ab}}{1 - r_{ab}} \qquad \text{Equation 5.8}$$

The standard deviation for obtained differences is given in Equation 5.9.

$$S_{dif} = \sqrt{S_a^2 + S_b^2 - 2r_{ab}S_aS_b} \qquad \text{Equation 5.9}$$

The standard deviation of an obtained difference (S_{dif}) is equal to the square root of the sum of the variances of tests A and B $(S_a^2 + S_b^2)$ less twice the product of the correlation of A and B multiplied by the standard deviations of A and B $(2r_{ab}S_aS_b)$.

The reliability and standard deviation of an obtained difference can be combined to estimate the SEM of the obtained difference (SEM$_{dif}$) using Equation 5.3. The standard deviation of the difference (S_{dif}; see Equation 5.9) is substituted for the test's standard deviation (S) in that equation; the reliability of the difference (r_{dif}; see Equation 5.8) is substituted for the test's reliability (r_{xx}) in the equation. These substitutions generate Equation 5.10.

$$SEM_{dif} = \sqrt{S_a^2 + S_b^2 - 2r_{ab}S_aS_b}$$

$$\times \sqrt{1 - \frac{\frac{1}{2}(r_{aa} + r_{bb}) - r_{ab}}{1 - r_{ab}}} \qquad \text{Equation 5.10}$$

The standard error of measurement of a difference (SEM$_{dif}$) describes the distribution of differences between obtained scores. To evaluate difference scores, the simplest method is to establish a level of confidence (for example, 95 percent) and find the z-score associated with that level of confidence (1.96). We then divide the obtained difference by the SEM of the difference. If the quotient exceeds the z-score associated with the level of confidence selected (1.96), the obtained difference is reliable. We can also estimate the true difference in the same manner as we estimate a true score on one test. In general, we assume that the group mean difference is 0.00. Thus the formula for estimating the true difference for a particular student simplifies to Equation 5.11.

Estimated true difference = (obtained difference)(r_{dif})

Equation 5.11

5-1h DESIRABLE STANDARDS OF RELIABILLITY

It is important for test authors to present sufficient information in test manuals for test users to be able to interpret test results accurately. For a test to be valid (that is, to measure what its authors claim it measures), it must be reliable. Although reliability is not the only condition that must be met, it is a necessary condition for validity. No test can measure what it purports to measure unless it is reliable. No score is interpretable unless it is reliable.

Therefore, test authors and publishers must present sufficient reliability data to allow the user to evaluate the reliability of all test scores that are to be interpreted. Thus, reliability estimates should be presented for intermediate (for example, subtest) scores when they are to be interpreted. Moreover, reliability estimates should be reported for each age and grade. Furthermore, these indexes should be presented clearly in tabular form in one place. Test authors should not play hide-and-seek with reliability data. Test authors who recommend computing difference scores should provide, whenever possible, the reliability of the difference (r_{dif}) and the SEM of the difference (SEM_{dif}). Once test users have access to reliability data, they can judge the adequacy of the test. Refer to Table 5.1 for our suggested numeric standards for evaluating whether a test has adequate reliability for a given purpose.

5-2 Validity

> *"**Validity** refers to the degree to which evidence and theory support the interpretation of test scores for proposed uses of tests". Validity is therefore the most fundamental consideration in developing and evaluating tests. The process of validation involves accumulating relevant evidence to provide a sound scientific basis for the proposed score interpretations. It is the interpretations of test scores for proposed uses that are evaluated, not the test itself. [American Educational Research Association (AERA), American Psychological Association, & National Council on Measurement in Education, 2014, p. 11].*

In a real sense, all questions of validity are local, asking whether the testing process leads to correct inferences about a specific person in a specific situation for a specific purpose. A test that leads to valid inferences in general or about most students may not yield valid inferences about a specific student. Two circumstances illustrate this. First, unless a student has been systematically acculturated in the values, behavior, and knowledge found in the public culture of the United States, a test that assumes such acculturation is unlikely to lead to appropriate inferences about that student. Consider, for example, the inappropriateness of administering a verbally loaded intelligence test to a recent U.S. immigrant. Correct inferences about this person's intellectual ability cannot be drawn from the testing because the intelligence test requires not only proficiency in English but also proficiency in U.S. culture and mores.

Second, unless a student has been systematically instructed in the content of an achievement test, a test assuming such academic instruction is unlikely to lead to appropriate inferences about that student's ability to profit from instruction. It would be inappropriate to administer a standardized test of written language (which counts misspelled words as errors) to a student who has been encouraged to use inventive spelling and reinforced for doing so. It is unlikely that the test results would lead to correct inferences about that student's ability to profit from systematic instruction in spelling. Read the Scenario in Assessment and associated question to think more carefully about the importance of alignment within instructed and tested content.

5-2a GENERAL VALIDITY

Because it is impossible to validate all inferences that might be drawn from a test performance, test authors typically validate just the most common inferences. Thus, test users should expect some information about the degree to which each commonly

ELMWOOD AREA SCHOOL DISTRICT

The Elmwood Area School District has adopted a child-centered, conceptual mathematics investigations curriculum that stresses problem solving as well as writing and thinking about mathematics. Students are expected to discover mathematical principles and explain them in writing. In the spring, the district administered the *TerraNova* achievement test for the purpose of determining whether students were learning what the district intended for them to learn. Much to its dismay, the mean scores on the mathematics subtests were substantially below average, and many students previously thought to be doing well in school were referred to determine if they had a specific learning disability in mathematics calculation. After the school psychologists completed their initial review of student records, the problem became clear. The *TerraNova*, although generally a good test, did not measure what was being taught in the Elmwood Area School District. Because mathematical calculations were not emphasized (or even systematically taught), Elmwood students had not had the same opportunities to learn as students in other districts. *TerraNova* was not a valid test within the school district, although it was appropriately used in many others. The validity of a test is validity for the specific children being assessed.

This scenario highlights that if a test is intended to measure what has been learned by students in school, the content of the test should measure what is being taught, otherwise the test is not valid for its intended use. What steps are necessary to take to ensure that a test is valid for the purpose of determining what a particular student has learned at school?

encouraged inference has (or lacks) validity. Although the validity of each inference is based on all the information that accumulates over time, test authors are expected to provide some evidence of a test's validity for specific inferences at the time the test is offered for use. In addition, test authors should validate the inferences for groups of students with whom the test will typically be used.

5-2b EVIDENCE THAT TEST INFERENCES ARE VALID

The process of gathering information about the appropriateness of inferences is called validation. Five general types of evidence are usually considered (AERA et al., 2014, pp. 14–19).

- Evidence based on test content
- Evidence based on internal structure
- Evidence based on relations to other variables
- Evidence based on the consequences of testing
- Evidence based on response processes

These five types of evidence are not discrete. Rather, they are artificial categories that are merely intended to help organize a complex topic. Thus, one could as readily consider evidence based on internal structure to be part of a test's content, as easily as a separate type of evidence.

1. Evidence Based on Test Content

"Test content refers to the themes, wording, and format of the items, tasks, or question on a test. Administration and scoring may also be relevant to content-based evidence." (AERA et al., 2014, p. 14). Specifically, we are concerned with the extent to which a test's items actually represent the domain or universe to be measured. It is a major source of evidence for the validation for any achievement test, other education and psychological tests, and observations and ratings. Any analysis of a test's content necessarily begins with a clear definition of the domain or universe that the test's content is intended to represent. Ultimately, a test's content validity is determined by the appropriateness of the items included, the importance of items not included, and how the items assess the content.

Appropriateness of Included Items

In examining the appropriateness of the items included in a test, we must ask: Is this an appropriate test question, and does this test item really measure the domain or construct? Consider the four test items from a hypothetical primary (kindergarten through grade 2) arithmetic achievement test presented in Figure 5.5. The first item requires the student to read and add two single-digit numbers, the sum of which

FIGURE 5.5
Sample Multiple-Choice
Questions for a
Primary Grade (K–2)
Arithmetic Test

1. Three and six are _____.
    a. 4
    b. 7
    c. 8
    d. 9
2. What number follows in this series?
    1, 2.5, 6.25, _____
    a. 10
    b. 12.5
    c. 15.625
    d. 18.50

3. ¿Cuántos son tres y dos?
    a. 3
    b. 4
    c. 5
    d. 6
3. Ille puer puellas _____.
    a. amo
    b. amat
    c. amamus
    d. amant

is less than 10. This seems to be an appropriate item for an elementary arithmetic achievement test. The second item requires the student to complete a geometric progression. Although this item is mathematical, the skills and knowledge required to complete the question correctly are not taught in any elementary school curriculum by the second grade. Therefore, the question should be rejected as an invalid item for an arithmetic achievement test to be used with children from kindergarten through the second grade. The third item likewise requires the student to read and add two single-digit numbers, the sum of which is less than 10. However, the question is written in Spanish. Although the content of the question is suitable (this is an elementary addition problem), the method of presentation requires language skills that most U.S. students do not have. Failure to complete the item correctly could be attributed either to the fact that the child does not know Spanish or to the fact that the child does not know that $3 + 2 = 5$. Test givers should conclude that the item is not valid for an arithmetic test for children who do not read Spanish. The fourth item requires that the student select the correct form of the Latin verb *amare* ("to love"). Clearly, this is an inappropriate item for an arithmetic test and should be rejected as invalid.

Content Not Included

Test content must also be examined to see if important content is not included. For example, the validity of any elementary arithmetic test would be questioned if it included only problems requiring the addition of single-digit numbers with a sum less than 10. Educators would reasonably expect an arithmetic test to include a far broader sample of tasks (for example, addition of two- and three-digit numbers, subtraction, understanding of the process of addition, and so forth). Incomplete test content results in an incomplete (and usually invalid) appraisal.

How Content Is Measured

It is clear that how we assess content directly influences the results of assessment. For example, when students are tested to see if they know the sum of two single-digit numbers, their knowledge can be evaluated in a variety of ways. Children might be required to recognize the correct answer in a multiple-choice array, supply the correct answer, demonstrate the addition process with manipulatives, apply the proper addition facts in a word problem, or write an explanation of the process they followed in solving the problem. However, there is an emerging consensus that the methods used to assess student knowledge should closely parallel those used in instruction.[5]

2. Evidence Based on Internal Structure

Quite similar to evidence for a test's content is a test's internal structure. Internal structure refers to the way(s) in which test items and subtests represent a test's

[5] Current theory and research methods as they apply to trait or ability congruence under different methods of measurement are still emerging. Much of the current methodology grew out of Campbell and Fiske's (1959) early work on convergent and discriminant validity and is beyond the scope of this text.

components and/or total score. Most test domains have more than one dimension or component. For example, reading tests typically assess oral reading and comprehension; math tests typically assess computation and problem solving using whole numbers, fractions and decimals, etc.

One would rightly expect test authors to present evidence that their tests do have the structure hypothesized. When a test assesses a unidimensional skill or trait, we would expect to see evidence that the test items are homogeneous (e.g., coefficient alpha). When a test is multidimensional, we would expect to find the results of factor analytic studies that demonstrate the congruence between theoretical and obtained factor structure.[6]

3. Evidence Based on Relations to Other Variables

The relationship between a new test's results and the results obtained from other tests is of key importance. The evidence falls into two broad categories. First are the results of the new test consistent (correlated) with the results expected from other measures. The extent to which a person's performance on a criterion measure can be estimated from that person's performance on the assessment procedure being validated is an important indication that a new test is measuring what it is intended to measure. This relationship is usually expressed as a correlation between the new assessment procedure (for example, a test) and the criterion. The correlation coefficient between the new procedure and the criterion is termed a *validity coefficient*. Two types of criterion-related validity are commonly described: concurrent validity and predictive validity. These terms denote the time at which a person's performance on the criterion measure is obtained. *Concurrent criterion-related validity* refers to how accurately a person's current performance (for example, test score) estimates that person's performance on the criterion measure at the same time. Basically, does a person's performance measured with a new or experimental test allow the accurate estimation of that person's performance on a criterion measure that has been widely accepted as valid? *Predictive criterion-related validity* refers to how accurately a person's current performance (for example, test score) estimates that person's performance on the criterion measure at a later time. Thus, concurrent and predictive criterion-related validity refer to the temporal sequence by which a person's performance on some criterion measure is estimated on the basis of that person's current assessment; concurrent and predictive validity differ in the time at which scores on the criterion measure are obtained. Positive correlations between test scores and other variables can also provide evidence of a test's validity. For example, many skills and abilities are developmental. Therefore, we would expect a student's grade level or mental age would correlate positively with chronological age.

The second broad category of evidence demonstrates that the results of the new test are independent (uncorrelated) with other skills or abilities. Sometimes how one measures a skill or ability has more to do with the student's performance than the particular skill or ability being assessed. A simple example is power versus speed tests. Power tests are untimed; speed tests are timed. Some students with learning disabilities or emotional problems may perform poorly on speed tests purely as a manifestation of their disability. In such a situation, student scores in math and reading based on fluency may be similar while power tests may reveal differences in reading and math achievement.

---

[6] In addition to making judgments about how appropriately an item fits within a domain, test developers often rely on point-biserial correlations between individual test items and the total score to make decisions about item appropriateness. Items that do not correlate positively and at least moderately (.25 or .30 or more) with the total score are dropped. Retaining only items that have positive correlations with the total score ensures homogeneous test items and internally consistent (reliable) tests. Moreover, when test items are homogeneous, they are likely to be measuring the same skill or trait. Therefore, to obtain reliable tests, test developers are likely to drop items that do not statistically fit the domain.

When domains are not homogeneous, test authors can jeopardize validity by selecting items on the basis of point-biserial correlations to produce an internally consistent test. Therefore, it is generally a good idea to analyze the structure of a domain, either logically or statistically. When a domain comprises two or more homogeneous classes of test items, homogeneous subtests (representing each factor) can be developed using point-biserial correlations. In this way, the validity of the test can be heightened.

4. Evidence Based on the Consequences of Testing

"Tests are commonly administered in the expectation that some benefit will be realized from the interpretation and use of the scores intended by the test developers. A few of the many possible benefits that might be claimed are selection of efficacious therapies, placement of workers in suitable jobs, prevention of unqualified individuals from entering a profession, or improvement of classroom instructional practices. A fundamental purpose of validation is to indicate whether these specific benefits are likely to be realized. Thus, in the case of a test used in placement decisions, the validation would be informed by evidence that alternate placements, in fact, are differentially beneficial to the persons and the institution." (AERA et al., (2014, p. 19)

Although this type of evidence has been adopted by the joint testing standards committee of the American Educational Research Association, American Psychological Association, and the National Council on Measurement in Education, it is important to note that it focuses on how test scores are used, rather than on whether a test provides accurate information. If a test correctly indicates a tenth-grade student cannot read second-grade materials, how a school uses that information has nothing to do with the accuracy of that information. If the school decides nothing is to be done, the test results are accurate; if the school decides to provide the student with ineffective instruction, the test results are still accurate; if the school provides effective remediation, the test results were still correct. However, if tests are indeed used to assign students to ineffective instruction, that particular use of a test could be considered inappropriate. Therefore, this standard emphasizes the need for test users to use test results in ways that they have good reason to believe will result in positive outcomes. Because there are so many different factors apart from the accuracy of a test score that influence whether an individual actually derives benefit from its use, we find it impossible to evaluate tests according to this validity standard. Later in this book we provide reviews of various tests. In those reviews, we focus our analysis of validity on the extent to which there is good reason to believe that, for a typical individual, the associated test results can be considered generally accurate.

5. Evidence Based on Response Processes

Response process refers to the way in which students go about answering test questions as well as how examiners go about scoring student responses. In some cases, we want to assess students' skill in using the correct process to solve problems. For example, did they follow the correct mathematical algorithm in solving a long division problem? If a test is intended to measure response processes, we would expect to find evidence that test takers actually are using the desired process. Evidence of this type would include interviews with test takers, having test takers "show their work," or having test takers write essays explaining how they arrived at their answers.

5-2c FACTORS AFFECTING GENERAL VALIDITY

Whenever an assessment procedure fails to measure what it purports to measure, validity is threatened. Consequently, any factor that results in measuring "something else" affects validity. Both unsystematic error (unreliability) and systematic error (bias) threaten validity.

Reliability

Reliability sets the upper limit of a test's validity, so reliability is a necessary but not a sufficient condition for valid measurement. Thus, all valid tests are reliable, unreliable tests are not valid, and reliable tests may or may not be valid. The validity of a particular procedure can never exceed the reliability of that procedure because unreliable procedures measure error; valid procedures measure the traits they are designed to measure.

Systematic Bias

Several systematic biases can limit a test's validity. The following are among the most common.

Enabling Behaviors

Enabling behaviors and knowledge are skills and facts that a person must rely on to demonstrate a target behavior or knowledge. For example, to demonstrate knowledge of causes of the American Civil War on an essay examination, a student must be able to write. The student cannot produce the targeted behavior (the written answer) without the enabling behavior (writing). Similarly, knowledge of the language of assessment is crucial. Many of the abuses in assessment are directly attributable to examiners' failures in this area. For example, intelligence testing in English of non-English-speaking children was at one time sufficiently commonplace that a group of parents brought suit against a school district (*Diana v. State Board of Education*, 1970). Students who are deaf are routinely given the performance subtests of the Wechsler Adult Intelligence Scales (Baumgardner, 1993) even though they cannot hear the directions. Children with communication disorders are often required to respond orally to test questions. Such obvious limitations in or absences of enabling behaviors are frequently overlooked in testing situations, even though they invalidate the test's inferences for these students. Read the upcoming Scenario in Assessment and associated question to consider more carefully what may happen if attention to necessary enabling behaviors is neglected.

Differential Item Effectiveness

Test items should work the same way for various groups of students. Jensen (1980) discussed several empirical ways to assess item effectiveness for different groups of test takers. First, we should expect that the relative difficulty of items is maintained across different groups. For example, the most difficult item for males should also be the most difficult item for females, the easiest item for whites should be the easiest item for nonwhites, and so forth. We should also expect that reliabilities and validities will be the same for all groups of test takers.

The most likely explanation for items having differential effectiveness for different groups of people is differential exposure to test content. Test items may not work in the same ways for students who experience different acculturation or different academic instruction. For example, standardized achievement tests presume that the students who are taking the tests have been exposed to similar curricula. If teachers have not taught the content being tested, that content will be more difficult for their students (and inferences about the students' ability to profit from instruction will probably be incorrect).

Systematic Administration Errors

Unless a test is administered according to the standardized procedures, the inferences based on the test are invalid. Suppose Ms. Williams wishes to demonstrate how effective her teaching is by administering an intelligence test and an achievement test to her class. She allows the students five minutes less than the standardized time limits on the intelligence test and five minutes more on the standardized achievement test. The result is that the students earn higher achievement test scores (because they had too much time) and lower intelligence test scores (because they did not have enough time). The inference that less intelligent students have learned more than anticipated is not valid.

Norms

Scores based on the performance of unrepresentative norms lead to incorrect estimates of relative standing in the general population. To the extent that the normative sample is systematically unrepresentative of the general population in either central tendency or variability, the differences based on such scores are incorrect and invalid.

Responsibility for Valid Assessment

The valid use of assessment procedures is the responsibility of both the author and the user of the assessment procedure. Test authors are expected to present evidence for the major types of inferences for which the use of a test is recommended, and a rationale should be provided to support the particular mix of evidence presented for the intended uses. Test users are expected to ensure that the test is appropriate for the specific students being assessed. (AERA et al., 2014, p. 13)

CRINA | Crina was born in Eastern Europe and spent most of the first 10 years of her life in an orphanage, where she looked after younger children. She was adopted shortly before her eleventh birthday by an Ohio family. The only papers that accompanied Crina to the United States were her passport, baptismal certificate, and letter from the orphanage stating that Crina's parents were deceased.

Crina's adoptive parents learned some of Crina's language, and Crina tried to learn English in the months before she was enrolled in the local school system. When she was enrolled in the local public school, she was placed in an age-appropriate regular classroom and received additional support from an English as a second language (ESL) teacher.

Things did not go well. Crina did not adapt to the school routine, had virtually no understanding of any content area, and was viewed as essentially unteachable. She spent most of her school time trying to help the teacher by neatening up the room, passing out materials, and running errands. Within Crina's first week in school, her teacher sought additional help from the ESL teacher, the school principal, and the school psychologist. Although all offered suggestions, none of them seemed to work; the school was unable to find a native speaker of Crina's language. Within the first month of school, Crina was referred to a child study team that in turn referred her for psychological and educational assessment.

The school psychologist administered the current Wechsler Intelligence Scale for Children and the Wechsler Individual Achievement Test, although both tests are administered in English. Crina did much better on tests that did not require her to speak or understand English—for example, block designs. Her estimated IQ was in the 40s and her achievement was so low that no derived scores were available.

Given her age and the extent of her needs, the school team recommended that she be placed in a life skills class with other students with moderate intellectual disabilities. Crina's mother rejected that placement because Crina had already mastered most of the life skills she would be taught there; at the orphanage, she cleaned, cooked, bathed and tended younger children, and so forth. In addition, her mother believed more verbal students than the ones in the life skills class would be better language

models for Crina. Basically, her mother wanted a program of basic academics that would be more appropriate—a program in which Crina could learn to read and write English, learn basic computational skills, make friends, and become acculturated.

For reasons that were never entirely clear, the school refused to compromise, and the dispute went to a due process hearing. The mother obtained an independent educational evaluation. Her psychologist assessed Crina's adaptive behavior; because the test had limited validity due to Crina's unique circumstances, the psychologist estimated that Crina was functioning within the average range for a person her age. Her psychologist also administered a nonverbal test of intelligence— one that neither required her to understand verbal directions nor to make verbal responses. With the same caveats, Crina was again estimated to be functioning in the average range for a person her age. To make a long story short, the school lost; Crina and her parents won.

The Moral. One must be extremely careful when using tests for making inferences about students with unique characteristics. The district followed its policies for providing the teacher with support, for providing Crina with support, for convening a multidisciplinary team, and so on. The tests administered by the school were generally reliable, valid, and well normed. However, they were not appropriate for Crina and her unique circumstances. Obviously, she lacked the language skills, cultural knowledge, and academic background to be assessed validly by the tests given by the school. Although the tests given by the parents' psychologist were better, they still had to be considered minimum estimates of her abilities, due to the cultural considerations.

A Happy Ending. Crina learned enough English during the next several years to develop friendships, to read and write enough to be gainfully employed, and to leave school feeling positive about the experience and her accomplishments.

This scenario highlights the responsibility that test users have in selecting tests and assessment methods that result in valid inferences for any given student. In this case, those choosing which methods to use had to carefully consider how existing test content may be inappropriate for measuring Crina's ability and achievement levels given her language and cultural differences.

© Cengage Learning

Chapter Comprehension Questions

Write your answers to the following questions and then compare your responses to the text.

1. Explain the concept of measurement error.
2. What does a reliability coefficient of .75 tell you about true-score variability and error variability?
3. Compare and contrast item reliability, stability, and interobserver agreement.
4. What is the difference between simple agreement and point-to-point agreement, and when might you use each appropriately?
5. What is a standard error of measurement?
6. Explain evidence of validity based on relations to other measures.
7. Explain evidence of validity based on test content.
8. Explain three factors that can affect a test's validity.

CULTURAL AND LINGUISTIC CONSIDERATIONS

LEARNING OBJECTIVES

6-1 Ascertain the magnitude of cultural and linguistic diversity present in U.S. public schools.

6-2 Summarize various legal protections and testing requirements for students who are English language learners (ELLs).

6-3 Articulate several questions that should be used to guide the assessment process for students from culturally and linguistically diverse backgrounds.

6-4 Describe several approaches to testing students who are English language learners (ELLs), along with their merits and drawbacks.

6-5 Indicate options for making entitlement decisions for ELLs without testing.

STANDARDS ADDRESSED IN THIS CHAPTER

 CEC Initial Preparation Standards

Standard 1: Learner Development and Individual Learning Differences

1.0 Beginning special education professionals understand how exceptionalities may interact with development and learning and use this knowledge to provide meaningful and challenging learning experiences for individuals with exceptionalities.

Standard 4: Assessment

4.0 Beginning special education professionals use multiple methods of assessment and data-sources in making educational decisions.

CEC ADVANCED **CEC Advanced Preparation Standards**

Standard 1: Assessment

1.0 Special education specialists use valid and reliable assessment practices to minimize bias.

 National Association of School Psychologists Domains

1 Data-Based Decision Making and Accountability

8 Diversity in Development and Learning

Isakson/Tetra images (RF)/Jupiter Images

The assessment of students with unique cultural and linguistic backgrounds is a particularly difficult task for educators and psychologists. The overwhelming majority of classroom and commercially prepared tests are administered in English. Students who do not speak or read English cannot access the content and may not be able to respond verbally to these tests. For example, suppose Lupe does not understand English but is given an intelligence test in which she is asked, "What is a sled?" or "What is an orange?" She would not understand the questions, although she might be able to understand and define these words in her native language. Obviously, this test is not valid for Lupe; her lack of English language proficiency creates a barrier to valid testing, such that her score does not reflect her true intelligence.

Challenges in assessing students with cultural and language differences go beyond not knowing the language used for testing. They relate to a host of issues associated with acculturation and linguistic development. Students who are English language learners (sometimes called students with limited English proficiency or LEP) may speak some English. However, knowing enough English for social conversation is not the same as knowing enough English for academic instruction or for the nuances of highly abstract concepts.

Moreover, many English language learners may come from a culture that is very different from the public culture of the United States. As a result, whenever a test item relies on a student's cultural knowledge to test some other area of achievement or aptitude, the test will necessarily be invalid because it will also test the student's knowledge of American culture. In this chapter, we discuss social, political, and demographic issues that complicate the assessment process, as well as how to assess students who are English language learners.

6-1 The Diversity of English Language Learners

According to information from the U.S. Census Bureau, large numbers of individuals who live in the United States do not speak English. Table 6.1 shows the languages most frequently spoken by these individuals, the number of speakers of each of these languages, and how the numbers have changed over time. Spanish, Chinese, and French are among the most common languages other than English spoken in homes in the United States.

The number of different languages and the distribution of speakers of those languages cause problems for test makers and testers. First, because there are many languages with relatively few LEP speakers, it would be unprofitable for test publishers to develop and norm test versions in these languages. Second, even if the tests were available, it is unlikely that there would be many bilingual psychologists and teachers able to use foreign-language versions of those tests. Finally, students within the same language group may not be culturally homogeneous. For example, there are French speakers from Montreal and French speakers from Port-au-Prince; there are Russian speakers from Kazakhstan and Russian speakers from Belarus. Students speaking the same language do not necessarily share a culture or a history.

Although the number of Spanish-speaking English language learners is large enough to make it profitable for test publishers to develop Spanish-language versions of their tests, Spanish-speaking students are not a homogeneous group either. In the United States, about 63 percent of Spanish speakers are of Mexican descent, about 13 percent are of Central or South American descent, about 9 percent are of Puerto Rican descent, and about 3.5 percent are of Cuban descent (U.S. Census Bureau, 2006). Moreover, Spanish-speaking students of Mexican descent include those born in the United States and those who emigrated from Mexico; Spanish-speaking students of Puerto Rican descent include those born in the continental United States and those from the Commonwealth of Puerto Rico. Spanish speakers from Central or South America may speak a Native American language (for example, Quechua)

| TABLE 6.1.[1] | Languages Spoken at Home in Millions: 1980, 1990, 2000, and 2010[2] | | | | |

Characteristic	1980	1990	2000	2010	PCT Change 1980-2010
Population 5 years & older	210.25	230.45	262.38	289.22	37.6
Spoke only English at home	187.19	198.60	215.42	229.67	22.7
Spoke other language at home[3]	23.06	31.84	46.95	59.54	158.2
Spanish or Spanish Creole	11.12	17.35	28.10	37.00	232.8
Chinese	0.63	1.32	2.02	2.81	345.3
French[4]	1.55	1.93	2.10	2.07	33.4
Tagalog	0.47	0.84	1.22	1.57	231.9
Vietnamese	0.20	0.51	1.01	1.38	599.2
Korean	0.27	0.63	0.89	1.14	327.1
German	1.59	1.55	1.38	1.07	32.7
Russian	0.17	0.24	0.71	0.85	393.5
Italian	1.62	1.31	1.01	0.73	55.2
Portuguese[5]	0.35	0.43	0.56	0.69	95.6
Polish	0.82	0.72	0.67	0.61	25.9
Japanese	0.34	0.43	0.48	0.44	31.9
Persian	0.11	0.20	0.31	0.38	256.5
Greek	0.40	0.39	0.37	0.31	23.5
Serbo-Croatian	0.15	0.71	0.23	0.28	89.1
Armenian	0.10	0.15	0.20	0.24	0.14
Yiddish	0.32	0.21	0.18	0.15	51.0

[1] U.S. Census Bureau, 1980 and 1990 Census, Census 2000, and the 2010 American Community Survey.
[2] The languages in this table are those available for the four time periods.
[3] "Spoke other language at home" includes languages not listed in the table.
[4] Includes Patois, Cajun, and Creole.
[5] Includes Portuguese Creole.

in addition to Spanish. Thus, because students speak Spanish does not mean that they share a culture and a history with others for whom Spanish is the first and primary language.

Finally, there are political and social differences among students who are ELLs, and these differences affect their learning of English and their understanding of the culture of the United States. Regardless of the language they speak, how the students and their parents came to the United States has social and political implications. Some students are immigrants or the children of immigrants who intend to make the United States their new home. Some immigrants are seeking a better life in the United States; others are fleeing repressive governments. Some have arrived at JFK or LAX by jet; others have negotiated the Straits of Florida on a raft. Some come with or join extended families; others come alone or with one parent or sibling. Some immigrants are eager to become *American*; others prefer to maintain their own culture and remain separate from the United States and U.S. schools' cultures. All of these things may affect their acculturation and their education.

Some parents of ELL students embrace the culture and ideals of the United States, and English is likely to eventually become their primary language educationally and socially. Other parents are short-term visitors to the country. For example, they may be the children of graduate students attending U.S. colleges and universities, of business people working for foreign corporations, of diplomats, of individuals seeking political asylum—all of whom intend to return permanently to their homeland in the future. For these students, the U.S. culture is more likely to be seen as something to understand rather than something to be embraced, and assimilation into the U.S. culture may actually be disadvantageous. English is likely to be their temporary instructional language, whereas their first language is stressed in their home.

Finally, some students are the descendants of people who were neither immigrants nor visitors, but who were living on lands captured or purchased by the U.S. government—for example, many Native Americans, Pacific Islanders, and Mexican Americans. These students and their parents can have attitudes toward English and U.S. culture that run the gamut from wanting to assimilate, to having multiple national or ethnic identities, to continuing resistance to the U.S. government by rejecting English and American culture.

U.S. policy toward students who are ELLs has evolved over the last 35 years. Prior to the mid-1960s, a number of practices were accepted that today would be considered illegal and repugnant. Voter registration in some states required potential voters to pass a literacy test, and these tests were sometimes used to disfranchise minority voters. Native American students were punished for speaking their first language during recess. One particularly offensive punishment was washing their mouths out with soap—as if their language consisted of dirty words. More pertinent to this text, ELLs were routinely tested in English to ascertain whether they had an intellectual disability. When they could not pass the intelligence test in English, they were placed in segregated special education classes.

Today the United States officially celebrates the diversity of its citizens' music, dance, art, and food. Formally, the United States welcomes visitors and immigrants, but that welcome is neither all encompassing nor embraced by all citizens. Indeed some cultural practices are rejected by the vast majority of Americans—for example, practices that limit opportunities for women or that sexually mutilate girls.

In addition, although the state and federal governments champion diversity, it is the local communities that must pay for the services needed to make diversity workable. The federal government controls immigration, but local school districts must bear the added costs of educating ELLs.

In many ways, the debate about how to deal with ELLs is a debate about the very nature of who we are as a country. This debate lurks at the edges of discussions about assessing students who are ELLs. Although we acknowledge this debate, in this chapter we shall try, to the extent possible, to avoid the political and social issues surrounding the assessment of students who are ELLs. Instead, we first focus on legal considerations in testing students who are ELLs. Then we identify questions that should be considered when assessing students from culturally and linguistically diverse backgrounds. Finally, we discuss specific strategies that might be used in the assessment of such students.

6-2 Legal Considerations

Both IDEA and NCLB include specific information related to assessment of students who are ELLs. IDEA specifies certain protections for both students and parents who are involved in assessment for the purpose of determining eligibility for special education services. NCLB discusses how students with LEP are to be included in assessments for the purpose of accountability.

6-2a IDEA PROTECTIONS

Protections for Students Being Assessed

The fundamental principle when assessing students who are ELLs is to assure that the assessment materials and procedures used actually assess students' target knowledge, skill, or ability, and that they are not influenced by students' inability (or limited ability) to understand and use English. For example, suppose that Antonio, an ELL, cannot answer a word problem involving two 2-digit addends and one extraneous fact (also a two-digit number). To what does the tester attribute Antonio's failure—a lack of skill in adding numbers or an inability to understand English? Antonio must have sufficient knowledge of English in order for the tester to rule out any notion that his failure may be due to limited English proficiency rather than due to poor math skills. Clearly, the intent of the Individuals with Disabilities Education Act (IDEA) and all other pertinent court decisions is to assess students' achievement and abilities unbiased by their limited proficiency in English. The principal rationale for protecting students who are ELLs during the assessment process can be found in the IDEA. As §300.532(a)(2) states, "Materials and procedures used to assess a child with limited English proficiency [must be] selected and administered to ensure that they measure the extent to which the child has a disability and needs special education, rather than measuring the child's English language skills." To accomplish this goal, tests must be selected and administered in such a way that they are not racially or culturally discriminatory. Indeed, to the extent feasible, tests and evaluation materials must be administered in the student's native language or other mode of communication. This principle is echoed in §300.534(b) of the IDEA, which forbids a student to be identified as in need of special educational services if the determining factor is limited proficiency in English.

However, it is important to note that, if the goal of assessment is to ascertain a student's current level of functioning in English, then it is appropriate to test the student in English. If the student cannot decode the words in a passage written in English, then the student cannot decode the passage written in English. If a student cannot comprehend the meaning of the individual words in a passage written in English, then the student cannot comprehend the meaning of that passage. The assessment has provided an indication of the student's current ability to use English.

Protections for Parents in the Assessment Process

Parents are the principal advocates for their children within the educational system, and the IDEA contains a number of protections for them as well, especially in terms of notice, participation, and consent. For example, §300.503(b) requires that parents receive prior notice if the school intends to initiate or change their child's identification as a student with a disability. That notice must "be provided in the native language of the parent or other mode of communication used by the parent, unless it is clearly not feasible to do so." Although notice is usually in written form, the IDEA also provides that interpreters be used if the native language or mode of communication of the parent is not written language. Parents must be given notice of their procedural safeguards. This notice must be in the parents' native language or other mode of communication if they do not understand English [§300.504(c)]. Schools must take steps to make sure that the parents of a student with a disability have the opportunity to participate in team meetings. To that end, §300.345(e) requires the use of interpreters or other appropriate measures "for parents with deafness or whose native language is other than English." In those instances when parental consent is required (for example, to conduct an initial assessment of a student to determine special education eligibility), that consent must be given in the parents' native language or mode of communication [§300.500(b)(1)].

NCLB Requirements

In Chapter 22 ("Making Decisions About Participation in Accountability Programs"), we discuss the No Child Left Behind requirements for school accountability. According to NCLB[1], students, including students with LEP, must participate

---

[1] As noted within other chapters in this book, many states have applied for waivers to NCLB requirements, some of which include modifications to these requirements. Be sure to consult current state requirements to understand how accountability testing of ELLs is currently handled in your state.

in assessments used for the purpose of holding schools accountable. In fact, when sufficient numbers of students who are ELLs exist for results to be reliable, it is expected that scores for students who are ELLs will be both aggregated in school reports of student proficiency and disaggregated so that people can know specifically how students who are ELLs are doing. When sufficient numbers of students who are ELLs exist, the progress of these students is specifically taken into account when determining whether a school or district meets adequate yearly progress. Although they can be excluded from participation in the English/language arts tests used to hold schools accountable during their first year of public school instruction in the United States, it is expected that they will participate in all other sections of the test during their first year, and every section of the test (including English/language arts) in the years that follow. They are expected to take an additional English language proficiency test as part of NCLB. They may be provided a variety of different accommodations to assist with removing language barriers from testing in certain areas; each state provides a list of approved accommodations for students who are ELLs.

6-3 Important Questions to Consider in Assessing Students from Culturally and Linguistically Diverse Backgrounds

To assess students in a way that reduces language and cultural barriers to effective measurement of targeted skills, knowledge, and abilities among students, the answers to several important questions should be taken into consideration.

6-3a WHAT BACKGROUND EXPERIENCES DOES THE STUDENT HAVE IN ENGLISH AND IN THEIR NATIVE LANGUAGE?

Students who are ELLs vary considerably in the rate at which they learn a new language. Many different factors can affect this rate, such as the age at which they were first exposed to the new language and the extent to which they are exposed to the new language in their home, school, and community environments. They also vary in terms of the languages in which they have received instruction, with some having received considerable instruction in both their native language and English and others receiving only instruction in English. These factors should be taken into consideration during assessment, and are further described below.

English as a Second Language

It can be critical to distinguish between social/interpersonal uses of language and cognitive/academic uses. According to a theory by Dr. Jim Cummins, students learning English as a second language usually need at least two years to develop social and interpersonal communication skills, sometimes referred to as basic interpersonal communication skills (BICS). However, they may require five to six years to develop language sufficient for cognitive academic language proficiency (CALP; Cummins, 1984). In other words, after even three or four years of schooling, students who demonstrate few problems with English usage in social situations still may lack sufficient language competence to be tested in English.

At least three factors can affect the time required for students to attain cognitive and academic sufficiency in English. Related questions that should be considered when deciding how to assess students who are ELLs are provided below.

1. At what age did the student first begin to learn English? As children get older, learning another language becomes more difficult (Johnson & Newport, 1989). Thus, all things being equal, one should expect younger students to acquire English faster than older students.

2. In what contexts has the student been exposed to English? The more contexts in which English is used, the faster will be its acquisition. Thus a student's learning of English as a second language will depend in part on the language the parents speak at home. If the native language is spoken at home, progress in English will be slower. This creates a dilemma for parents who want their children to learn (or remember) their first language and also learn English.

3. To what extent is the student's native language similar to English? Languages can vary along several dimensions. The phonology may be different. The 44 speech sounds of English may be the same or different from the speech sounds of other languages. For example, Xhosa (an African language) has three different click sounds; English has none. English lacks the sound equivalent of the Spanish ñ, the Portuguese nh, and the Italian gn. The orthography may be different. English uses the Latin alphabet. Other languages may use different alphabets (for example, Cyrillic) or no alphabet (Mandarin). English does not use diacritical marks; other languages do. The letter–sound correspondences may be different. The letter h is silent in Spanish but pronounced as an English r in one Brazilian dialect. The grammar may be different. Whereas English tends to be noun dominated, other languages tend to be verb dominated. Word order varies. Adjectives precede nouns in English, but they usually follow nouns in Spanish. The more language features the second language has in common with the first language, the easier it is to learn the second language.

Bilingual Students

"Bilingual" implies equal proficiency in two languages. However, children must learn which language to use with specific people. For example, they may be able to switch between English and Spanish with their siblings; speak only Spanish with their grandparents; and use only English with their older sister's husband, who still has not learned Spanish.

Although children can switch between languages, sometimes in mid-sentence, they are seldom equally proficient in both languages. They are seldom equally competent or comfortable in using both languages, regardless of the context or situation. These students tend to prefer one language or the other for specific situations or contexts. For example, Spanish may be spoken at home and in the neighborhood, whereas English is spoken at school. Moreover, when two languages are spoken in the home, the family may develop a hybrid language borrowing a little from each. For example, in Spanish, caro means "expensive"; in English, car means "automobile." In some bilingual homes (and communities), caro may come to mean "automobile," depending on the context. These speakers may not be speaking "proper" Spanish or English, although they have no problem communicating.

These factors enormously complicate the testing of bilingual students. Some bilingual students may understand academic questions better in English, but the language in which they answer can vary. If the content was learned in English, they may be better able to answer in English. However, if the answer calls for a logical explanation or an integration of information, they may be better able to answer in their other language. Finally, it cannot be emphasized strongly enough that language dominance is not the same as language competence for testing purposes. Because a student knows more Spanish than English does not mean that the student knows enough Spanish to be tested in that language.

6-3b WHAT UNIQUE CULTURAL CHARACTERISTICS OF THE STUDENT MAY AFFECT TESTING?

Cultural factors can complicate the testing of students. In some cultures, children are expected to speak minimally to adults or authority figures; elaboration or extensive verbal output may be seen as disrespectful. In some cultures, answering questions may be seen as self-aggrandizing, competitive, and immodest. These cultural values work against students in most testing situations.

Some children who are refugees may have been traumatized by civil strife in their native countries or by a hazardous journey to the United States. Even when that is not the case, male–female relations may be subject to cultural differences. Female students may be hesitant to speak to male teachers; male students (and their fathers) may not see female teachers as authority figures. Children may be hesitant to speak to adults from other cultures. Some research suggests that it may be easier for children to work with examiners of the same race and cultural background (Fuchs & Fuchs, 1989).

Finally, some immigrant students and their families may have little experience with the types of testing done in U.S. schools. Consequently, these students may lack test-taking skills. In addition, doing well on tests may not be as valued within the cultures of some immigrant students.

6-4 Alternative Ways to Test Students Who Are ELLs

Circumstances exist in which students who are ELLs need to be tested. As noted earlier, they need to be included in testing for the purpose of school accountability. In addition, in some situations, it may be deemed necessary to administer a test to help make a decision about whether a student with LEP is eligible to receive special education services. In the following sections, we provide information about strategies that are sometimes used with regard to testing students who are ELLs. The Scenario in Assessment for this chapter provides an example of the challenges faced when interpreting test results for ELLs.

6-4a ENGAGE IN DENIAL

A common procedure is to pretend that a student has sufficient proficiency to be tested in English. Denial is frequently accompanied by self-delusion or coercion. Self-delusion manifests itself when the tester talks with the student and believes that the student's adequate social language indicates sufficient academic language to be tested in English. Coercion is present when the tester's supervisor insists that the student be tested. Sometimes denial is only denial; in this case, the tester admits that the student's language may have somewhat limited his or her ability to take the test.

6-4b USE NONVERBAL TESTS

Several nonverbal tests are available for testing intelligence. This type of test is believed to reduce the effects of language and culture on the assessment of intellectual abilities. (Nonverbal tests do not, however, completely eliminate the effects of language and culture.) Some tests (see Chapter 18, "Using Measures of Intelligence") do not require a student to speak—for example, some subtests of the fifth edition of the *Wechsler Intelligence Scale for Children*. However, these tests frequently have directions in English. Some tests (for example, the *Comprehensive Test of Nonverbal Intelligence–2* allow testers to use either oral or pantomime directions. A few tests are exclusively nonverbal (for example, the *Leiter International Performance Scale*, 3rd edition) and do not require language for directions or responses.

Because students' skills in language comprehension usually precede their skills in language production, performance tests with oral directions might be useful with some students. However, the testers should have objective evidence that a student sufficiently comprehends academic language for the test to be valid, and such evidence is generally not available. Tests that do not rely on oral directions or responses are more useful because they do not make any assumptions about students' language competence. However, other validity issues cloud the use of performance tests in schools. For example, the nature of the tasks on nonverbal intelligence tests is usually less related to success in school than are the tasks on verbal intelligence tests.

Moreover, some cultural considerations are beyond the scope of directions and responses. For example, the very nature of testing may be more familiar in U.S. culture than in the cultures of other countries. When students are familiar with the testing process, they are likely to perform better. As another example, students from other cultures may respond differently to adults in authority, and these differences may alter estimates of their ability derived from tests. Thus, although performance and nonverbal tests may be a better option than verbal tests administered in English, they are not without problems.

6-4c TEST IN THE STUDENT'S NATIVE LANGUAGE

There are several ways to test students using directions and materials in their native language. Several tests are currently available in language versions other than English—most frequently, Spanish. These tests run the gamut from tests in English that are translated, to those that are renormed, to those that are reformatted for another language and culture. The differences among these approaches are significant.

When tests are only translated, we can assume that the child understands the directions and the questions. However, the questions may be of different difficulty in U.S. culture and the English language for two reasons. First, the difficulty of the vocabulary can vary from language to language. For example, reading cat in English is different from reading gato in Spanish. Cat is a three-letter, one-syllable word containing two of the first three letters of the English alphabet; gato is a four-letter, two-syllable word with the first, seventh, fifteenth, and twentieth letters of the alphabet. The frequency of the use of the word "cat" in each language is likely different, as is the popularity of cats as house pets.

The second reason that translated questions may be of different difficulty is that the difficulty of the content can vary from culture to culture, because children from different cultures have not had the same opportunity to learn the information. For example, suppose we asked Spanish-speaking students from Venezuela, Cuba, and California who attended school in the United States to identify Simón Bolívar, Ernesto "Che" Guevara, and César Chávez. We could speculate that the three groups of students would probably identify the three men with different degrees of accuracy. The students from California would be most likely to recognize Chávez as an American labor organizer but less frequently recognize Bolívar and Guevara. Students from Venezuela would likely recognize Bolívar as a liberator of South America more often than would students from Cuba and the United States. Students from Cuba would be more likely to recognize Guevara as a revolutionary than would students from the other two countries. Thus, the difficulty of test content is embedded in culture.

Also, when tests are translated, we cannot assume that the psychological demands made by test items remain the same. For example, an intelligence test might ask a child to define peach. A child from equatorial South America may never have eaten, seen, or heard of a peach, whereas U.S. students are quite likely to have seen and eaten peaches. For U.S. students, the psychological demand of identifying a peach is to recall the biological class and essential characteristics of something they have experienced. For South American children, the item measures their knowledge of an exotic fruit. For American children, the test would measure intelligence; for South American children, the test would measure achievement.

Some of the problems associated with a simple translation of a test can be circumvented if the test is renormed on the target population and items reordered in terms of their translated difficulties. For example, to use the Wechsler Intelligence Scale for Children, fifth edition, effectively with Spanish-speaking Puerto Ricans, the test could be normed on a representative sample of Spanish-speaking Puerto Rican students. Based on the performance of the new normative sample, the items could be reordered as necessary. However, renorming and reordering do not reproduce the psychological demands made by test items in English.

6-4d DEVELOP AND VALIDATE A VERSION OF THE TEST FOR EACH CULTURAL/LINGUISTIC GROUP

Given the problems associated with translations, tests developed in the student's language and culture are clearly preferable to those that are not. For example, suppose one wished to develop a version of the Wechsler Intelligence Scale Para Los Niños de Cuba. Test items could be developed within the Cuban American culture according to the general framework of the Wechsler scale. Specific items might or might not be the same. The new test would then need to be validated. For example, factor–analytic studies could be undertaken to ascertain whether the same four factors underlie the new test (that is, verbal comprehension, perceptual organization, freedom from distractibility, and processing speed).

Although they may be preferable, culture- and language-specific tests are not economically justifiable for test publishers except in the case of the very largest minorities—for example, Spanish-speaking students with quite a bit of U.S. acculturation. The cost of standardizing a test is sizable, and the market for intelligence tests in, for example, Hmong, Ilocano, or Gujarathi is far too small to offset the development costs. For Spanish-speaking students, many publishers offer both English and Spanish versions. Some of these are translations, others are adaptations, and still others are independent tests. Test users must be careful to assess the appropriateness of the Spanish version to make sure that it is culturally appropriate for the test taker.

6-4e USE AN INTERPRETER

If the tester is fluent in the student's native language or if a qualified interpreter is available, it is possible to administer tests that are interpreted for a student who is an ELL. Interpretations can occur on an as-needed basis. For example, the tester can translate or interpret directions or test content and answer questions in the student's native language. Although interpretation is an appealing, simple approach, it has the same problems as the commercial availability of translations. In addition, the accuracy of the interpretation is unknown.

6-4f OTHER ACCOMMODATIONS

Testing in a student's native language is sometimes considered an "accommodation" (accommodations are discussed in Chapter 7). Other accommodations are sometimes used when assessing ELLs, particularly during the administration of tests used for making accountability decisions. For example, a side-by-side English/native-language version of the test might be provided. Test directions and items might use simplified English language. ELLs might be allowed to use specialized English dictionaries containing the definitions for difficult words on the test. They might be allowed access to certain accommodations that other students have (e.g., extended time, small group setting, dictating responses to a scribe). Many state accommodation policies indicate which accommodations ELLs can receive on the statewide test used for accountability purposes. However, it is important to remember that certain native language and English language accommodations would not be appropriate if the test is intended to measure English proficiency.

6-4g TEST FIRST TO SEE IF THE STUDENT IS PROFICIENT ENOUGH IN ENGLISH TO TAKE THE ENGLISH VERSION

Students are sometimes required to earn a certain level of English proficiency before taking accountability measures and tests like the *National Assessment of Educational Progress*. This practice has three potential problems. Administration of an additional test takes valuable time away from activities in which students might otherwise engage. It also singles students out as "different." Finally, there are very few reliable measures of English proficiency, especially for content areas with their own specialized vocabulary like science and social studies.

6-4h DO NOT TEST

Not all educational decisions and not all assessments require testing. For students who are ELLs from a variety of cultures, testing is usually a bad idea. Most states include language in their laws or regulations specifying that students must be in school a minimum amount of time before they can participate in the state testing program.

6-5 Making Entitlement Decisions Without Testing

Lack of progress in learning English is the most common reason students who are ELLs are referred to ascertain eligibility for special education (Figueroa, 1990). It seems that most teachers do not understand that it can take several years to acquire sufficient fluency to be fully functional academically and cognitively in English. However, the school cannot overlook the possibility that students who are ELLs may have disabilities.

Determination of disability can be made without psychological or educational testing. The determination of sensory or physical disability can be readily made with the use of interpreters. Students or their parents need little proficiency in English for professionals to determine if a student has a traumatic brain injury, other health impairments, or orthopedic, visual, or auditory disabilities. Disabilities based on impaired social function (such as emotional disturbance and autism) can be identified through direct observation of a student or interviews with family members (using interpreters if necessary), teachers, and so forth.

The appraisal of intellectual ability is required to identify students with intellectual disability. When students have moderate to severe forms of intellectual disability, it may be possible to determine that they have limited intellectual ability without ever testing. For example, direct observation may reveal that a student has not acquired language (either English or the native language), communicates only by pointing and making grunting noises, is not toilet trained, and engages in inappropriate play whether judged by standards of the primary culture or by U.S. culture. The student's parents may recognize that the student is much slower than their other children and would be judged to have an intellectual disability in their native culture. In this case, parents may want special educational services for their child. In such a situation, identification would not be impeded by the student's (or parents') lack of English. However, students with mild intellectual disabilities do not demonstrate such pronounced developmental delays; rather, their disability is relative and not easily separated from their limited proficiency in English.

The identification of students with specific learning disabilities seems very difficult. The IDEA (§300.304-§300.309) requires that failure to achieve adequately —in "oral expression, listening comprehension, written expression, basic reading skills, reading fluency, reading comprehension, math calculation or math problem-solving"—be considered indicative of a specific learning disability only if the student has been "provided with learning experiences and instruction appropriate for the child's age or State-approved grade level standards" and has either failed to respond to a scientific, research-based intervention or demonstrates a certain pattern of strengths and weaknesses. In order to find a student eligible under this category, the associated results cannot be due to cultural disadvantage or limited English proficiency. Clearly, these conditions cannot be met for students who are ELLs, especially when the students are also culturally diverse. Furthermore, limited research has been done specifically on interventions to address the needs of ELLs, and so it may be difficult to identify and implement an appropriate intervention that both meets the legal requirements and addresses the unique characteristics of students who are ELLs.

SCENARIO IN ASSESSMENT

DMETRI | Dmetri is a 12-year-old student with two elementary-age younger brothers. The family emigrated to the United States from Astana (the capital of Kazakhstan) three years ago. In Kazakhstan, Dmetri and his brothers (Yuri and Vasili) attended a Russian-language school. Dmetri's family speaks Russian at home; Dmetri's parents also both speak Kazakh. The father and children are learning English.

When the family arrived in the United States, Dmetri entered school immediately and was placed in an ESL program. His progress was slow the first year. In the spring semester, Dmitri's parents came to the parent–teacher conference accompanied by an interpreter. The parents were concerned about Dmetri's poor grades and dislike of school. They reported that Yuri and Vasili both enjoyed school and seemed to be learning English more rapidly. Dmetri's ESL teacher also expressed frustration with Dmetri's progress. He completed the minimum amount of work quickly and carelessly.

Dmetri's second year in school was academically similar to the first—poor grades, little effort, little progress. Dmetri had acquired some social English; his oral language was grammatically simple (e.g., present, future, and past tenses). His lexicon remained limited, and his main strategy for finding an appropriate word was the "that thing" strategy. For example, he would say, "that thing on wall you get water" when he didn't know "drinking fountain" or "that thing on arm [pointing to wrist] for time" when he didn't know "wristwatch." Unfortunately, Dmetri added some inappropriate behavior to his repertoire—bullying and extorting younger students. At the end of the second year, his ESL teacher suggested that the parents refer Dmetri for a psychoeducational evaluation to ascertain if he had a learning disability.

Dmetri was evaluated by both the speech and language specialist and the school psychologist. The speech and language specialist administered the Peabody Picture Vocabulary Test (IV) to assess Dmetri's vocabulary. He earned a standard score of 65, which is significantly below average. The specialist also engaged Dmetri in conversation and noted many speech problems associated with the differences between spoken Russian and English. He had difficulty with the r-controlled short vowel sound (as in fir, her, murmur); the th sound; and words beginning with w, which he pronounced as beginning with v. His speech gave the impression of being hurried and indistinct because he usually stressed only one syllable even when the word had more than one stressed syllable or weakly stressed syllables. In terms of grammar, Dmetri had not mastered the use of articles and he used gender pronouns to refer to nouns (the ship she goes fast). Finally, spelling was particularly difficult

for Dmetri. The speech and language specialist believed that Dmetri's language problems were most likely the result of the short period of time he had been in this country and the differences between the English and Russian languages. She did not believe Dmetri had a speech or language disability, although she agreed that he was not learning English as rapidly as most students.

The school psychologist administered the Test of Nonverbal Intelligence–4, the Leiter International Performance Scale–3, and the Peabody Individual Achievement Test–Revised/Normative Update.[2] On the Test of Nonverbal Intelligence–4, Dmetri earned an index score of 94. On the Leiter, Dmetri earned scaled scores (mean = 100; S = 15) ranging from 92 (Reverse Memory) to 103 (Attention Sustained). His Nonverbal IQ was 95. The psychologist chose the PIAT/NU to minimize the demands of expressive language on estimates of Dmetri's achievement. Dmetri earned the following standard scores: Oral Language 72, Mathematics 95, Math Fluency 97 Basic Reading 75, Reading Comprehension 70, Total Reading 72, and Written Expression 70. In her written report, the psychologist stated that she believed the intelligence scores to be minimum estimates of Dmetri's ability and the achievement scores to be invalid due to his limited proficiency in English, differences in schooling between Kazakhstan and the United States, and lack of cultural knowledge.

At the multidisciplinary meeting to review the assessment results and determine if Dmetri was eligible for special education and related services, the team was initially divided. The ESL teacher and the general education teacher believed Dmetri may have a learning disability; the speech and language specialist and the school psychologist stated that he could not be considered learning disabled due to cultural and language differences. The parents did not believe Dmetri was disabled, and the principal did not initially express an opinion. After some discussion, the team found Dmetri not to be eligible for special education or 504 services. However, all of the members agreed that Dmetri needed more intensive ESL services and English language instruction. While those services were not available in the district, there was a support program for Russian speakers through Dmetri's church.

This scenario highlights the difficulty faced by ELLs who may have significant educational needs. What are some pieces of information from the scenario that suggest Dmetri's difficulties are primarily due to limited English skills?

Parents, teachers, and specialists need to reconcile their differences and together reach a decision that complies with federal and state education law.

Finally, limited English proficiency should not be considered a speech or language impairment. Although it is quite possible for a student with limited English to have a speech or language impairment, that impairment would also be present in the student's native language. Speakers of the student's native language, such as the student's parents, could verify the presence of stuttering, impaired articulation, or voice impairments; the identification of a language disorder would require a fluent speaker of the child's native language.

[2] See Chapter 18 for information about the intelligence tests and Chapter 14 for information about achievement tests.

When it is not possible to determine whether a student has a disability, ELLs who are experiencing academic difficulties still need to have services besides special education available. Districts should have programs in English as a second language (ESL) that could continue to help students after they have acquired social communication skills.

Chapter Comprehension Questions

Write your answers to each of the following questions and then compare your responses to the text.

1. Describe how language and acculturation differences can affect students' progress in U.S. public schools.

2. Explain the legal protections and requirements for students who are ELLs included in IDEA and NCLB.

3. What are two questions that should be used to guide the assessment process for students from culturally and linguistically diverse backgrounds?

4. Describe the merits and limitations of three approaches to testing students who are ELLs.

5. Explain the circumstances under which tests are not appropriate for making entitlement decisions.

USING TEST ADAPTATIONS AND ACCOMMODATIONS

LEARNING OBJECTIVES

7-1 Articulate four reasons why you should care about test adaptations and accommodations.

7-2 Summarize factors to consider when deciding whether test adaptations are necessary, and if so, which test adaptations might be appropriate.

7-3 Describe two ways to categorize adaptations and accommodations.

7-4 Explain accommodation guidelines you can use in making accommodation decisions for individual students.

STANDARDS ADDRESSED IN THIS CHAPTER

 CEC Initial Preparation Standards

Standard 1: Learner Development and Individual Learning Differences

1.0 Beginning special education professionals understand how exceptionalities may interact with development and learning and use this knowledge to provide meaningful and challenging learning experiences for individuals with exceptionalities.

Standard 4: Assessment

4.0 Beginning special education professionals use multiple methods of assessment and data-sources in making educational decisions.

 CEC Advanced Preparation Standards

Standard 1: Assessment

1.0 Special education specialists use valid and reliable assessment practices to minimize bias.

Ψ **NASP Domains**

1 Data-Based Decision Making and Accountability

8 Diversity in Development and Learning

Although the use of well-designed standardized tests with strong evidence of reliability and validity can enhance assessment decision making, it does not result in optimal measurement for every student. For some students, the way in which a test is administered under standardized conditions may actually prohibit their demonstration of the target knowledge and skills. In Chapter 5, enabling behaviors and knowledge were discussed as a factor influencing the validity of an inference made based on a given test. They are the skills and knowledge that an individual must have in order to have the opportunity to demonstrate the targeted skills and knowledge on a particular test. For example, some tests require that students print their answers in a test booklet; this can make it difficult for some students with motor impairments to demonstrate their knowledge. Some tests require that students remain focused for long periods of time at a desk; this can make it difficult for some students with hyperactivity problems to demonstrate their knowledge. Clearly, changes in test conditions may be needed. **Test adaptations** refer to changes made in the presentation, setting, response, or timing/scheduling of a test that may or may not influence the construct that is measured. Some changes can have a negative impact on the validity of inferences made using test scores. Educators must attend to the kinds of adaptations that can be made without compromising the technical adequacy of tests. **Test accommodations** are changes made in the presentation, setting, response, or timing/scheduling of a test that allow for more accurate measurement of the intended skills and knowledge among the particular students to whom they are provided. **Test modifications** are changes made that alter the measurement of the intended skills and knowledge, such that it is highly questionable whether the test results accurately represent a student's skill and knowledge. It is important to note that some people use these terms interchangeably; however, we believe it is important to understand that there are differences in how test changes influence the accuracy of measurement, and therefore it is important to distinguish between them. In this chapter, we consider issues associated with adapting tests and providing accommodations for students with disabilities. In doing so, we focus on accommodations during accountability testing, when it is important to gather information about all students within a given school system. However, we acknowledge that some of the same principles may apply when making decisions about accommodations on tests used for other purposes (e.g., instructional planning, eligibility determination).

7-1 Why Care About Testing Accommodations?

There are many reasons why it is important to understand appropriate ways to adapt tests. The reasons we discuss in this chapter include the increased diversity in today's schools and legal requirements for all students to be appropriately measured toward the same standards.

7-1a INCREASED DIVERSITY

Student diversity has increased substantially in the past decade. As we discuss in Chapter 6, schools are more culturally diverse, both in terms of the numbers of students from different sociocultural backgrounds and in terms of the cultures they represent. However, in addition to racial, ethnic, and cultural differences, students enter school these days with a very diverse set of academic background experiences and opportunities. Within the same classroom, students often vary considerably in their academic skill development. Educators face two clear challenges: (1) designing instruction that will be effective with this vast range in skills and abilities and (2) using assessments that will evaluate validly the large range in student skills.

Since the mid-1970s, considerable attention has been focused on including all students in neighborhood schools and general education settings. Much attention has been focused on including students who are considered developmentally, physically, or emotionally impaired. As federal and state officials create educational policies, they are now compelled to make them for all children and youth, including those with severe disabilities. Also, as policymakers attempt to develop practices that will result in improved educational results, they rely on data from district- and state-administered tests. However, relying on assessment data presents challenges associated with deciding whom to include in the multiple kinds of assessments and the kinds of changes that can be made to include them.

Although meaningful assessment of the skills of such a diverse student population is challenging, it is clear that all students need to be included in large-scale assessment programs. If students are excluded from large-scale assessments, then the data on which policy decisions are made represent only part of the school population. If students are excluded from accountability systems, they may also be denied access to the general education curriculum. If data are going to be gathered on all students, then major decisions must be made regarding the kinds of data to be collected and how tests are to be adapted to include students with special needs. Historically, there has been widespread exclusion of students with disabilities from state and national testing (McGrew, Thurlow, Shriner, & Spiegel, 1992; Thompson & Thurlow, 2001). Participation in large-scale assessments is now recognized by many educators and parents as a critical element of equal opportunity and access to education. Thurlow and Thompson (2004) report that all states now require participation of all students. Furthermore, all states now have accommodation policies that indicate how students can participate in large-scale assessment programs with accommodations. However, many questions remain about which participation and accommodation strategies are the best for particular students. It is up to school teams to determine which accommodations are appropriate for individual students.

7-1b CHANGES IN EDUCATIONAL STANDARDS

Part of major efforts to reform or restructure schools has been a push to specify high standards for student achievement and an accompanying push to measure the extent to which students meet those high standards. It is expected that schools will include students with disabilities and ELLs in assessments, especially those completed for accountability purposes.

State education agencies in nearly every state are engaging in critical analyses of the standards, objectives, outcomes, results, skills, or behaviors that they want students to demonstrate upon completion of school. Additionally, nationwide efforts have resulted in the development of a set of common core standards in certain areas such as English language arts and mathematics. In all of these efforts, decisions must be made about the extent to which standards should be the same for students with and without disabilities. In Chapter 22 (Making Decisions about Participation in Accountability Programs), you will learn about current efforts to develop alternate achievement standards for students with significant intellectual disabilities. Development of standards is not enough. Groups that develop standards must develop ways of assessing the extent to which students are meeting the standards.

7-1c THE NEED FOR ACCURATE MEASUREMENT

It is critical that the assessment practices used for gathering information on individual students provide accurate information. Without accommodations, testing runs the risk of being unfair and inaccurate for certain students. Some test formats make it more difficult for students with disabilities to understand what they are supposed to do or what the response requirements are. Because of their disabilities, some students find it impossible to respond in a way that can be evaluated accurately unless changes are made. However, changing aspects of test presentation, setting, response, and timing/scheduling without carefully considering what the test is designed to measure can also result in poor measurement. Decisions

SCENARIO IN ASSESSMENT

AMY | Amy has a visual impairment that does not quite meet the definition of legal blindness. Her teacher provides her with accommodations during instruction. For example, Amy's seat is positioned in class directly under the large fluorescent light fixture, the spot considered by the teacher to have the brightest light. On several occasions when Amy has expressed difficulty seeing, the teacher has given her a special desk lamp that brightens her work surface. The teacher tries to arrange the daily schedule so that work that requires lots of vision (for example, reading) occurs early in the day. In doing so, her teacher hopes that Amy experiences less eyestrain. Similar accommodations are made in classroom achievement testing, and on the day of the state achievement test, the following testing accommodations are provided for Amy:

- She is tested in an individual setting, where extra bright light shines directly on her test materials.

- The test is administered on three separate mornings rather than over an entire day. This helps minimize her eyestrain.
- The test is administered with frequent breaks because of fatigue to eyes created by extra-bright light and intense strain at deciphering text.
- The teacher uses a copy machine to enlarge the print on pages requiring reading.
- A scribe records Amy's responses to avoid her spending extra time and experiencing eyestrain trying to find the appropriate location for a response and to give the response.

This scenario highlights a variety of accommodations that may be necessary for students to demonstrate their knowledge and skills on tests. Why are the changes in this scenario considered accommodations and not merely adaptations? Are there tests on which these types of test changes might be considered modifications?

---

about which adaptations facilitate more accurate measurement for a particular test, and about which students should receive the associated adaptations, can be very difficult. Read the chapter scenario and the associated questions to consider more carefully how accommodations can promote more accurate measurement for students with disabilities.

7-1d IT IS REQUIRED BY LAW

By law, students with disabilities have a right to be included in assessments used for accountability purposes, and accommodations in testing should be made to enable them to participate. This legal argument is derived largely from the Fourteenth Amendment to the U.S. Constitution (which guarantees the right to equal protection and to due process of law). The Individuals with Disabilities Education Act (IDEA) guarantees the right to education and to due process. Also, Section 504 of the Rehabilitation Act of 1973 indicates that it is illegal to exclude people from participation solely because of a disability. If a student is receiving special education services due to an educational disability, that student's instructional and testing accommodations are to be documented on an individualized education program (IEP). If a student with a disability does not necessarily need special education services but instead simply needs accommodations to allow appropriate participation in the general curriculum, then the student's accommodation needs are documented on what is commonly referred to as a 504 plan.

The Americans with Disabilities Act Amendment Act of 2008 mandates that all individuals must have access to exams used to provide credentials or licenses. Agencies administering tests must provide either auxiliary aids or modifications[1] to enable individuals with disabilities to participate in assessment, and these agencies may not charge the individual for costs incurred in making special provisions. Adaptations that may be provided include an architecturally accessible testing site, a distraction-free space, or an alternative location; a test schedule variation or extended time; the use of a scribe, sign language interpreter, reader, or adaptive equipment; and modifications of the test presentation or response format.

The 1997 and 2004 IDEA mandate that states include students with disabilities in their statewide assessment systems. The necessary accommodations are

---

[1] The ADA's use of the term "modification" is different than the definition we provide. In this case, the ADA's use of "modification" can be likened to our use of the term "accommodation."

to be provided to enable students to participate. In addition, states are to have available alternate assessments. These are to be used by students who are unable to participate in the regular assessment even with accommodations. Alternate assessments are substitute ways of gathering data, often by means of portfolios or performance measures. The No Child Left Behind Act of 2001 requires states to report annually on the performance and progress of all students, and this principle was reiterated in the 2004 reauthorization of IDEA. Furthermore, states are expected to report on the numbers of students using accommodations for state and district assessment programs.

In this chapter, we first describe factors that may contribute to a student's need for accommodations and then discuss accommodations that may address those needs. Finally, we offer recommendations for making accommodation decisions.

As you read this chapter, remember that the major objective of assessment is to benefit students. Assessment can do so either by enabling us to develop intervention and accommodation plans that help a child achieve the objectives of schooling, or by informing local, state, and national policy decisions that benefit all students, including those with diverse needs.

7-2 Considerations for Promoting Test Accessibility

The extent to which test adaptations and accommodations are needed depends in part on the way in which an assessment program is designed. When test development involves careful consideration of the unique needs of all students who may eventually participate, less "after-the-fact" changes in test conditions will be needed. Application of the principles of universal design to assessment can improve accessibility, such that appropriate testing for all students is promoted. **Universal design for assessment** involves careful consideration of the needs of all individuals who might need to participate in the test when the test is first developed. For more information on universal design for assessment, you can go to the Universally Designed Assessments section of the website of the National Center on Educational Outcomes.

Fortunately, new technologies are making it increasingly possible for students to access material in ways that best address their needs. The increasing use of computers and electronic tablets during instruction and testing makes it possible for students to customize the font size, brightness, and even language in which materials are presented to meet their individual needs. Screen-reading and speech recognition programs make it possible for students who have difficulty reading and writing to access and respond to written material. However, it is still up to test developers and users to determine which basic skills are important to teach and test, and to correspondingly monitor which changes are appropriate under various conditions. Furthermore, students may need considerable training and experience manipulating and using these features to make the most out of them during instruction and testing.

7-2a ABILITY TO UNDERSTAND ASSESSMENT STIMULI

Six factors can impede getting an accurate picture of students' abilities and skills during assessment: (1) the students' ability to understand assessment stimuli, (2) the students' ability to respond to assessment stimuli, (3) the nature of the norm group, (4) the appropriateness of the level of the items (sufficient basal and ceiling items), (5) the students' exposure to the curriculum being tested (opportunity to learn), and (6) the nature of the testing environment. Assessments are considered unfair if the test stimuli are in a format that, because of a disability, the student does not understand. For example, tests only available in print are considered unfair for students with severe visual impairments. Tests with oral directions are considered unfair for students with certain hearing impairments. In fact, because the law requires that students be assessed in their primary language and because the primary language of many deaf students is not English, written assessments in English are considered unfair and invalid for many deaf students. When students cannot understand test stimuli because of a sensory or mental limitation that is unrelated to what the test is targeted to measure, accurate measurement of the targeted skills is hindered by the sensory or mental limitation. Such a test is invalid, and failure to provide an accommodation is illegal.

7-2b ABILITY TO RESPOND TO ASSESSMENT STIMULI

Tests typically require students to produce a response. For example, intelligence tests require verbal, motor (pointing or arranging), or written (including multiple-choice) responses. To the extent that physical or sensory limitations inhibit accurate responding, these test results are invalid. For example, some students with cerebral palsy may lack sufficient motor ability to arrange blocks. Others may have sufficient motor ability but have such slowed responses that timed tests are inappropriate estimates of their abilities. Still others may be able to respond quickly but expend so much energy that they cannot sustain their efforts throughout the test. Not only are test results invalid in such instances, federal law also proscribes the use of such test results.

7-2c NORMATIVE COMPARISONS

Norm-referenced tests are standardized on groups of individuals, and the performance of the person assessed is compared with the performance of the norm group. To the extent that the test was administered to the student differently than the way it was administered to the norm group, one must be very careful interpreting the results. To allow for appropriate comparisons, these tests typically have very specific rules for how they are to be administered. Adaptations of measures require changing either stimulus presentation or response requirements. The adaptation may make the test items easier or more difficult, and it may change the construct being measured. Although qualitative or criterion-referenced interpretations of such test performances are often acceptable, norm-referenced comparisons can be flawed. The *Standards for Educational and Psychological Testing* (American Educational Research Association, American Psychological Association, & National Council on Measurement in Education, 2014) specify that when tests are adapted, it is important that there is validity evidence for the change that is made. Otherwise, it is important to describe the change when reporting the score and to use caution in score interpretation.

7-2d APPROPRIATENESS OF THE LEVEL OF THE ITEMS

Tests are often developed for students who are in specific age ranges or who have a particular range of skills. They can sometimes seem inappropriate for students who are either very high or very low functioning compared to their age-mates. Assessors are tempted to give out-of-level tests when an age-appropriate test contains either an insufficient number of easy items or not enough easy items for the student being assessed. Of course, when out-of-level tests are given and norm-referenced interpretations are made, the students are compared with a group of students who differ from them. We have no idea how same-age or same-grade students would perform on the given test. Out-of-level testing may be appropriate to identify a student's current level of educational performance or to evaluate the effectiveness of instruction with a student who is instructed out of grade level. It is inappropriate for accountability purposes.

7-2e EXPOSURE TO THE CURRICULUM BEING TESTED (OPPORTUNITY TO LEARN)

One of the issues of fairness raised by the general public is the administration of tests that contain material that students have not had an opportunity to learn. This same issue applies to the making of accommodation decisions. Students with sensory impairments have not had an opportunity to learn the content of test items that use verbal or auditory stimuli. Students receiving special education services who have not had adequate access to the general education curriculum have not had the same opportunity to master the general education curriculum.

To the extent that students have not had an opportunity to learn the content of the test (that is, they were absent when the content was taught, the content is not taught in the schools in which they were present, or the content was taught in ways that were not effective for the students), they probably will not perform well on the test. Their performance will reflect more a lack of opportunity to learn than limited ability.

7-2f ENVIRONMENTAL CONSIDERATIONS

Students should be tested in settings in which they can demonstrate maximal performance. If students cannot easily gain access to a testing setting, this may diminish their performance. Tests should always be given in settings that students with disabilities can access with ease. The settings should also be quiet enough to minimize distractibility. Also, because fatigue is an issue, tests may need to be given in multiple short sessions (broken up with breaks) so students do not become overly tired.

7-3 Categories of Testing Accommodations

There are four general types of accommodations:

- Presentation (for example, repeat directions, read aloud)
- Response (for example, mark answers in book, point to answers)
- Setting (for example, study carrel, separate room, special lighting)
- Timing/scheduling (for example, extended time, frequent breaks, multiple days)

Concerns about accommodations apply to individually administered and large-scale testing. The concerns are legal (Is an individual sufficiently disabled to require taking an accommodated test?), technical (To what extent can we adapt measures and still have technically adequate tests?), and political (Is it fair to give accommodations to some students, yet deny them to others?).

It is important to recognize that the appropriateness of an adaptation will depend on the skills targeted for measurement, as well as the types of decisions that are intended to be made. In addition, the specific needs, preferences, and experiences of the student may affect which adaptations are most appropriate. Although it may initially appear to you that it is easy to determine exactly which adaptations allow for better measurement of targeted skills and fair and appropriate assessment, people actually tend to disagree on which adaptations maintain the validity of tests, making it a more complicated issue.

Based on input from a variety of stakeholders (that is, teachers, state assessment directors, and researchers), one test publisher has created a framework for adaptations and classified many of them into one of three categories: those that have no impact on test validity, those that may affect validity, and those that are known to affect validity (CTB/McGraw-Hill, 2004). Extended descriptions of these categories, as well as adaptations that are considered to fit within these categories, are provided in Figure 7.1.

Over the past 20 years, much research on the validity of adapted test scores has been conducted. Research continues to be conducted on adaptations to refine and provide justification for how these adaptations are assigned to the various validity categories. We emphasize throughout this book the importance of considering test purpose and the decisions that assessment is intended to inform when deciding what assessment tools to use. Deciding whether a particular adaptation is appropriate for testing is no different. When deciding on adaptation appropriateness, careful attention must be paid to what the test is intended to measure and what decisions are intended to be made with the results. Furthermore, different changes are likely needed for different students.

Category 1 The adaptations listed in category 1 are not expected to influence student performance in a way that alters the interpretation of either criterion- or norm-referenced test scores. Individual student scores obtained using category 1 adaptations should be interpreted in the same way as the scores of other students who take the test under default conditions. These students' scores may be included in summaries of results without notation of adaptation(s).

Presentation

- Use visual magnifying equipment
- Use a large-print edition of the test
- Use audio amplification equipment
- Use markers to maintain place
- Have directions read aloud
- Use a tape recording of directions
- Have directions presented through sign language
- Use directions that have been marked with highlighting

Response

- Mark responses in test booklet
- Mark responses on large-print answer document
- For selected-response items, indicate responses to a scribe
- Record responses on audio tape (except for constructed-response writing tests)
- For selected-response items, use sign language to indicate response
- Use a computer, typewriter, Braille writer, or other machine (for example, communication board) to respond
- Use template to maintain place for responding
- Indicate response with other communication devices (for example, speech synthesizer)
- Use a spelling checker except with a test for which spelling will be scored

Setting

- Take the test alone or in a study carrel
- Take the test with a small group or different class
- Take the test at home or in a care facility (for example, hospital), with supervision
- Use adaptive furniture
- Use special lighting and/or acoustics

Timing/scheduling

- Take more breaks that do not result in extra time or opportunity to study information in a test already begun
- Have flexible scheduling (for example, time of day and days between sessions) that does not result in extra time or opportunity to study information in a test already begun

Category 2 Category 2 adaptations may have an effect on student performance that should be considered when interpreting individual criterion- and norm-referenced test scores. In the absence of research demonstrating otherwise, scores and any consequences or decisions associated with them should be interpreted in light of the adaptation(s) used.

Presentation

- Have stimulus material, questions, and/or answer choices read aloud, except for a reading test
- Use a tape recorder for stimulus material, questions, and/or answer choices, except for a reading test
- Have stimulus material, questions, and/or answer choices presented through sign language, except for a reading test
- Communication devices (for example, text talk converter), except for a reading test
- Use a calculator or arithmetic tables, except for a mathematics computation test

Response

- Use graph paper to align work
- For constructed-response items, indicate responses to a scribe, except for a writing test

Timing/scheduling

- Use extra time for any timed test
- Take more breaks that result in extra time for any timed test
- Extend the timed section of a test over more than one day, even if extra time does not result
- Have flexible scheduling that results in extra time

Category 3 Category 3 adaptations change what is being measured and are likely to have an effect that alters the interpretation of individual criterion- and norm-referenced scores. This occurs when the adaptation is strongly related to the knowledge, skill, or ability being measured (for example, having a reading comprehension test read aloud). In the absence of research demonstrating otherwise, criterion and norm-referenced test scores and any consequences or decisions associated with them should be interpreted not only in light of the adaptation(s) used but also in light of how the adaptation(s) may alter what is measured.

Presentation

- Use Braille or other tactile form of print
- On a reading (decoding) test, have stimulus material, questions, and/or answer choices presented through sign language
- On a reading (decoding) test, use a text-talk converter, where the reader is required to construct meaning and decode words from text
- On a reading (decoding) test, use a tape recording of stimulus material, questions, and/ or answer choices
- Have directions, stimulus material, questions, and/or answer choices paraphrased
- For a mathematics computation test, use of a calculator or arithmetic tables
- Use a dictionary, where language conventions are assessed

Response

- For a constructed-response writing test, indicate responses to a scribe
- Spelling aids, such as spelling dictionaries (without definitions) and spell/grammar checkers, provided for a test for which spelling and grammar conventions will be scored
- Use a dictionary to look up words on a writing test

Adapted from *Guidelines for Inclusive Test Administration 2005*, p. 8. Copyright ©2004 by CTB/ McGraw-Hill LLC. Reproduced with permission of The McGraw-Hill Companies, Inc.

Progress is rapid in designing and validating test accommodations. You are advised to visit the website for the National Center on Educational Outcomes at the University of Minnesota to read the latest research and publications on state and national practice in testing accommodations.

7-4 Recommendations for Making Accommodation Decisions for Individual Students

There are major debates about the kinds of adaptations that should be permitted during testing for accountability purposes. There are also major arguments about the extent to which adaptations in testing destroy the technical adequacy of tests used for determining instructional needs and eligibility for special education. We think there are some reasonable guidelines for best practice in making decisions about individuals, and we offer associated guidelines here. We first provide recommendations for making accommodation decisions on tests that are commonly used to make decisions about individuals (for example, eligibility and instructional planning for exceptional children). Then, we provide recommendations for making accommodation decisions on tests that are typically administered at the group level and used for accountability purposes.

7-4a RECOMMENDATIONS FOR MAKING ACCOMMODATION DECISIONS DURING INSTRUCTIONAL PLANNING AND ELIGIBILITY DECISIONS FOR EXCEPTIONAL STUDENTS

When making decisions about what to teach, it is important to collect information about the student's current skills in a way that the student can adequately demonstrate his or her knowledge. For example, if you want to know whether students have specific math problem-solving skills, it may be necessary to present the questions in an oral format rather than a written format to students who cannot yet accurately read. Otherwise, students may fail to answer correctly because they cannot read the item, even though they have the given math problem-solving skills. The result would unfortunately be that you continue to plan your instruction around the given math problem-solving skill, even when the student has already mastered the given skill.

However, if you are using data from tests with specific standardized administration procedures and intending to compare the data to a normative sample, it is important to follow the rules set forth in the administration manual. Published tests are increasingly providing specific rules for testing with accommodations in administration manuals. Such rules should be carefully consulted when using these tests to determine students' instructional needs and make eligibility decisions.

Some related recommendations that we suggest are provided below:

- Conduct all assessments in the student's primary language or mode of communication. The mode of communication is the one that is normally used by the person during instruction (such as sign language, Braille, or oral communication); however, note that there are additional considerations that should be made in assessing students who are English language learners (see Chapter 6, Cultural and Linguistic Considerations). Loeding and Crittenden (1993, p. 19) note that for students who are deaf, the primary communication mode is either a visual–spatial, natural sign language used by members of the American Deaf Community called American Sign Language (ASL), or a manually coded form of English, such as Signed English, Pidgin Sign English, Seeing Essential English, Signing Exact English, or Sign-Supported Speech/English. Therefore, they argue, "traditional paper-and-pencil tests are inaccessible, invalid, and inappropriate to the deaf student because the tests are written in English only."

- Make accommodations in format when the purpose of testing is not substantially impaired. For example, a student might be allowed to provide an oral response instead of a written response if the purpose is not to measure writing skills. Or a student might be given more frequent breaks when completing a task if the purpose is not to measure his or her ability to attend for long periods of time. It should be demonstrated that the accommodations assist the individual in responding but they do not provide content assistance (for example, a scribe should record the response of the person being tested—not interpret what the person says, include his or her additional knowledge, and then record a response). Personal assistants who are provided during testing, such as readers, scribes, and interpreters, should be trained in how to provide associated accommodations to ensure proper administration.

- Make normative comparisons only with groups whose membership includes students with background sets of experiences and opportunities like those of the students being tested. For example, if you provide a signed interpretation of a norm-referenced test, you should only compare the student's results with those of a group of students who also had the test signed using the same language.

7-4b RECOMMENDATIONS FOR MAKING ACCOMMODATION DECISIONS DURING ACCOUNTABILITY TESTING

Many other accommodation recommendations can be implemented when collecting assessment data to make decisions about groups of students, specifically for the purpose of making accountability decisions. Decisions about which accommodations to provide should be made separately for each individual student determined to need them; however, decisions are often guided by state accommodation policies. Thurlow, Elliott, and Ysseldyke (2003) suggest the following recommendations about accommodation decision making for the purpose of accountability:

- States and districts should have written guidelines for the use of accommodations in large-scale assessments used for accountability purposes.

- Decisions about accommodations should be made by one or more persons who know the student, including the student's strengths and weaknesses.

- Decision makers should consider the student's learning characteristics and the accommodations currently used during classroom instruction and classroom testing.

- The student's category of disability or program setting should not influence the decision.

- The goal is to ensure that accommodations have been used by the student prior to their use in an assessment—generally, in the classroom during instruction and in classroom testing situations. New accommodations should not be introduced for the district- or statewide assessment.

- The decision is made systematically, using a form that lists questions to answer or variables to consider in making the accommodation decision. Ideally, classroom data on the effects of accommodations are part of the information entered into decisions. Decisions and the reasons for them should be noted on the form.

- Decisions about accommodations should be documented on the student's individualized educational program.

- Parents and older students should be involved in the decision by either participating in the decision-making process or being given the analysis of the need for accommodations, and by signing the form that indicates accommodations that are to be used.

- Accommodation decisions made to address individual student needs should be reconsidered at least once a year, given that student needs are likely to change over time[2].

---

[2] Adapted from Thurlow, Elliott, and Ysseldyke (2003), pp. 46–47, with permission.

Chapter Comprehension Questions

Write your answers to each of the following questions and then compare your responses to the text.

1. What are four reasons why you should be concerned with test adaptations and accommodations?

2. Describe at least four factors to be considered when deciding whether test changes are necessary and what test changes may be appropriate.

3. Describe two schemes for categorizing adaptations and accommodations, and provide examples of adaptations that might fit each category within those categorization schemes.

4. What are some guidelines to use in making decisions about which accommodations to provide when making eligibility decisions?

5. What are some accommodation guidelines to use in making decisions about which accommodations to provide when making accountability decisions?

CHAPTER

8

TEACHER-MADE TESTS OF ACHIEVEMENT

LEARNING OBJECTIVES

8-1 Discuss four uses of teacher-made tests.

8-2 Explain seven considerations that are important for teachers when developing or preparing tests.

8-3 Articulate how response formats use different types of questions and have special considerations for students with disabilities.

8-4 Describe how assessment in the core achievement areas of reading, mathematics, spelling, and writing differs for beginning and advanced students.

8-5 Discuss the potential sources of difficulty in the use of teacher-made tests.

STANDARDS ADDRESSED IN THIS CHAPTER

CEC **CEC Initial Preparation Standards**

Standard 4: Assessment
4.0 Beginning special education professionals use multiple methods of assessment and data-sources in making educational decisions.

Standard 5: Instructional Planning and Strategies
5.0 Beginning Special Education Professionals select, adapt, and use a repertoire of evidence-based instructional strategies to advance learning of individuals with exceptionalities.

CEC **CEC Advanced Preparation Standards**
ADVANCED

Standard 1: Assessment
1.0 Special education specialists use valid and reliable assessment practices to minimize bias.

Ψ **National Association of School Psychologists Domains**
1 Data-Based Decision Making and Accountability
3 Interventions and Instructional Support to Develop Academic Skills

Historically, teacher-made tests have not been as highly regarded as commercially prepared, norm-referenced achievement tests. Adjectives such as "informal" or "unstandardized" have been used to describe teacher-made tests. However, neither of these adjectives is accurate. Teacher-made tests cannot be considered informal because they are seldom given haphazardly or casually. They cannot be considered unstandardized because students usually receive the same materials and directions, and the same criteria are usually used in correcting student responses. We think that teacher-made tests can be better suited to evaluation of student achievement than commercially prepared, norm-referenced achievement tests.

Achievement refers to what has been directly taught and learned by a student, whereas **attainment** refers to what has been learned anywhere. What students are expected to achieve is determined by individual states. Most states have chosen to adopt Common Core State Standards that address English language arts (that is, reading, writing, speaking and listening, language, and media and technology) and mathematics (practice and content). States prescribe their own standards for other curricular areas in their K–12 schools, but the day-to-day implementation of those standards can vary from school district to school district. Teachers are in the best position to know what has been (or at least should be) taught in their classrooms.

Most commercially prepared tests have maps showing how their items are aligned with Common Core State Standards and individual state standards, and many states have contracted with commercial vendors to develop tests to assess student achievement according to their state-specific standards. Whether or not states use standards-referenced tests prepared by one of the major consortia (that is, Smarter Balanced Assessments Consortium or Partnership for Assessment of Readiness for College and Careers) or use state-specific tests developed by a private vendor, teachers' instruction may differ. This can be true even for two teachers using the same published instructional program and trying to meet the same state standards. Although teachers may not construct tests that match the curriculum and state standards, they are the only ones capable of knowing precisely what has been taught and what level of performance is expected from students. Consequently, they are the only ones who can match testing to actual instruction.

In addition, commercially prepared, norm-referenced and standards-referenced tests are designed to assess which students know more and which students know less (that is, to discriminate among test takers on the basis of what they know). Developers of norm-referenced tests usually include the minimum number of test items that allow reliable discriminations. Teacher-made tests are usually designed to assess what students are learning or have learned. Thus, teachers include more items on their tests to make valid assessments of what students have learned. This difference between teacher-made and commercially prepared tests has four important consequences.

1. Because teacher-made tests include many more items (even all of the items of interest), they can be much more sensitive to small but important changes in student learning. For example, a teacher-made test that included all of the addition facts could show whether a student has learned single-digit addition facts with the number 9 in the past two days; norm-referenced tests usually assess all of the mathematical operations but necessarily have only a few addition problems. It is not usually possible to tell if a student has learned the single-digit addition facts with the number 9.

2. Teacher-made tests can show what content requires additional instruction and student practice; norm-referenced tests cannot.

3. Teacher-made tests can indicate when students have mastered an instructional goal, so that instruction can be provided on new objectives; norm-referenced tests cannot.

4. By examining the tests of all students, teachers can tell if their instruction has been effective. If most of the students have not learned what has been taught, it will be necessary to reteach the content (or modify instruction and reteach the content).[1]

---

[1] Class responders can serve the same function in real time. See Chapter 11.

Teachers need tests that reflect what they are teaching and are sensitive to changes in student achievement.[2] We strongly recommend that the assessments be objective—that is, based on observable phenomena and minimally affected by a variety of subjective factors. The use of objective methods is not merely a matter of personal preference. Federal regulations require that students with disabilities be evaluated using objective procedures.[3] This chapter provides a general overview of objective practices for teachers who develop their own tests for classroom assessment in the core areas of reading, mathematics, spelling, and written language.

8-1 Uses

Teachers make up tests to ascertain the extent to which their students have learned or are learning what has been taught or assigned. Student achievement is the basis on which teachers make decisions about student skill development, student progress and instructional problems, and grades. Often, an assessment can be used for more than one purpose. For example, assessments made to monitor instruction (formative assessment) can be aggregated for use in making summative assessments.

A student's level of skill development is a fundamental consideration in planning instruction. We want to know what instructional objectives our students have met in order to decide what things we should be teaching our students. Obviously, if students have met an instructional objective, we should not waste their time by continuing to teach what they have already learned. Rather, we should build on their learning by extending their learning (for example, planning for generalization of learning) or moving on to the next objective in the instructional sequence. In addition, students who meet objectives so rapidly that they are being held back by slower peers can be grouped for enrichment activities or faster-paced instruction; slower students can be grouped so that they can learn necessary concepts to the point of mastery without impeding the progress of their faster-learning peers.

Another important use of classroom tests is to monitor instruction. Students are expected to progress through the curriculum at an acceptable pace. When students fail to learn or learn at an unacceptably slow rate, it is necessary to modify instruction.[4]

Finally, classroom assessments are used to make summary judgments about student attainment and teacher effectiveness. General student attainment is generally synonymous with the grade assigned to that student for a particular marking period. How grades are determined varies considerably from school district to school district. In some districts, there are districtwide policies that define each grade (for example, to earn an A, students must average 92 percent or more on all tests). Clearly, student grades should be based on what was taught and learned; the basis of a student's grade should be carefully explained at the beginning of the year (or marking period) so that all students know how they will be graded. We also recommend that grades be as objective as possible so that they avoid any hint of bias or favoritism.

Judgments about teaching effectiveness should be made on the basis of student achievement. When many students in a classroom fail to learn material, teachers should suspect that something is wrong with their instruction. Failure to modify instruction so that students succeed is unacceptable, and in the case of students with special needs, illegal.

---

[2] Teachers assess frequently to detect changes in student achievement. However, frequent testing with exactly the same test usually produces a practice effect. Unless there are multiple forms for a test, student learning may be confused with a practice effect.

[3] Note that general educators are often trained in more subjective and holistic approaches, and the difference in approaches can cause many problems when general and special educators work together to provide an education for all students in an inclusive classroom.

[4] See Chapters 9–12 for an extensive discussion of monitoring students' response to instruction.

8-2 Dimensions of Academic Assessment

Assessments differ along several dimensions: content specificity, frequency, and response quantification. Different purposes can require different degrees of specificity, different frequency, and different formats.

8-2a CONTENT SPECIFICITY

By *content*, we mean simply the domain within which the testing will occur. When we think of teacher-made tests, we generally think of academic domains such as reading, arithmetic, spelling, and so forth. However, the domain to be tested can include supplementary curricula (for example, study skills).

By *specificity*, we mean the parts of the domain to be assessed. Any domain can be divided and subdivided into smaller and more precise chunks of content. For example, in reading we are unlikely to want to assess every possible thing within the domain of reading. Therefore, we would break down reading until we got to the part or chunk that we wanted to assess: beginning reading, one-syllable words, one-syllable words with short vowel sounds, one-syllable words with short a, consonant–short a–consonant words, consonant–short a–specific consonants (t, n, and r) words, and so forth.

The specificity of an assessment depends on the purpose of the assessment. Especially at the beginning of a school year or when a new student joins a class, educators want to know a student's level of skill development—what the student knows and does not know—in order to plan instruction. In this case, an appropriate assessment will begin with a broad sample of content to provide an estimate of student knowledge of the various topics that have been and will be covered. Similarly, to be sure that specific skills are maintained over time and that the student is appropriately generalizing their use of those skills in a coordinated fashion, it may be appropriate to include a broad sample of content. Areas in which a student lacks information or skills can be assessed with more precise procedures to identify the exact areas of deficiency so that appropriate remedial instruction can be provided.

When teachers assess to monitor instruction and document problems, their assessments are very specific. They should assess what they teach to ascertain if students have learned what was taught. If students are learning word families (for example, "bat," "cat," "fat," and "hat"), they should be tested on their proficiency with the word families they have been taught.

8-2b TESTING FREQUENCY

The time students have in school is finite, and time spent on testing is time not spent on other important activities. Therefore, the frequency of testing and the duration of tests must be balanced against the other demands on student and teacher time.

Most teacher-made tests are used to monitor instruction and assign grades. Although the frequency of assessment varies widely in practice, the research evidence is clear that more frequent assessments (two or more times a week) are associated with better learning than are less frequent assessments. When students are having difficulty learning or retaining content, teachers should measure performance and progress more frequently. Frequent measurement can provide immediate feedback about how students are doing and pinpoint the skills missing among students.[5] The more frequent the measurement, the quicker you can adapt instruction to ensure that students are making optimal progress. However, frequent measurement is only

---

[5] Many of the new measurement systems, such as those employing technology-enhanced assessments, call for continuous measurement of pupil performance and progress. They provide students with immediate feedback on how they are doing, give teachers daily status reports indicating the relative standing of all students in a class, and identify areas of skill deficits.

helpful when it can immediately direct teachers as to what to teach next or how to teach next. To the extent that teachers can use data efficiently, frequent assessment is valuable; if it consists simply of frequent measurement with no application, then it is not valuable. Student deficits in skill level and progress may dictate how frequently measurement should occur: Students with substantial deficits are monitored more frequently to ensure that instructional methods are effective. Those who want to know more about how an expected rate is set or about the specific procedures used to monitor student progress are referred to Hintze, Christ, and Methe (2005), Hosp and Hosp (2003), or Shinn (1989).

Broader assessments used for grading are given at the end of units or marking periods and cover considerable content. Thus, they must either be very general or be a limited sample of more specific content. In either case, the results of such assessments do not provide sufficiently detailed information about what a student knows and does not know for teachers to plan remediation.

8-2c TESTING FORMATS

When a teacher wants either to compare (1) the performance of several students on a skill or set of skills or (2) one pupil's performances on several occasions over time, the assessments must be the same. **Standardization** is the process of using the same materials, procedures (for example, directions and time allowed to complete a test), and scoring standards for each test taker each time the test is given. Without standardization, observed differences could be reasonably attributed to differences in testing procedures. Almost any test can be standardized if it results in observable behavior or a permanent product (for example, a student's written response).

The first step in creating a test is knowing what knowledge and skills students have been taught and how they have been taught. Thus, teachers will need to know the objectives, standards, or outcomes that they expect students to work toward mastering, and they will need to specify the level of performance that is acceptable.

Test formats can be classified along two dimensions: (1) the modality through which the item is presented—test items usually require a student to look at or listen to the question, although other modalities may be substituted, depending on the particulars of a situation or on characteristics of students—and (2) the modality through which a student responds—test items usually require an oral or written response, although pointing responses are frequently used with students who are nonverbal. Teachers may use "see–write," "see–say," "hear–write," and "hear–say" to specify the testing modality dimensions.

In addition, "write" formats can be of two types. *Selection formats* require students to indicate their choice from an array of possible answers (usually termed response options). True–false, multiple-choice, and matching are the three common selection formats. However, they are not the only ones possible; for example, students may be required to circle incorrectly spelled words or words that should be capitalized in text. Formats requiring students to select the correct answer can be used to assess much more than the recognition of information, although they are certainly useful for that purpose. They can also be used to assess students' understanding, their ability to draw inferences, and their correct application of principles. Selection response questions are not usually well suited for assessing achievement at the levels of analysis, synthesis, and evaluation.

Supply formats require a student to produce a written or oral response. The response can be a single word or number, or it can be more involved—a sentence, a paragraph, or several pages. Regardless of the length of the anticipated response, teachers should develop and use a key to score student answers. The key should specify the criteria for a correct response, how credit will be awarded, acceptable synonyms, and so forth. When students are required to write extended, complex responses, teachers usually use scoring **rubrics** that specify the criteria for awarding of points. Figure 8.1. contains possible dimensions for a generic scoring rubric.

Content	3 (pts)	2 (pts)	1 (pts)	0 (pts)
Main Ideas	all important elements present	missing an element	missing most elements	no elements
Supporting Ideas	two ideas		one idea	no ideas
Mechanics	**3 (pts)**	**2 (pts)**	**1 (pts)**	**0 (pts)**
Spelling	no spelling errors	phonetic errors	many errors	cannot decipher
Punctuation	no grade appropriate errors	few grade appropriate errors	missing sentence punctuation; run-ons	little punctuation
Capitalization	no grade appropriate errors	few grade appropriate errors	Only first letter of sentences correct	no capitals

At first glance many scoring rubrics appear to be objectively scored because they usually produce a number for each answer. However, in most rubrics the number of points assigned to cells and the basis for awarding the points to each cell are subjective.

As a general rule, supply questions can be prepared fairly quickly, but scoring them may be very time consuming. Even when one-word responses or numbers are requested, teachers may have difficulty finding the response on a student's test paper, deciphering the handwriting, or correctly applying criteria for awarding points. In contrast, selection formats usually require a considerable amount of time to prepare, but once prepared, the tests can be scored quickly and by almost anyone.

The particular formats teachers choose are influenced by the purposes for testing and the characteristics of the test takers. Testing formats are essentially bottom up or top down. Bottom-up formats assess the mastery of specific objectives to allow generalizations about student competence in a particular domain. Top-down formats survey general competence in a domain and assess in greater depth those topics for which mastery is incomplete. For day-to-day monitoring of instruction and selecting short-term instructional objectives, we favor bottom-up assessment. With this type of assessment, a teacher can be relatively sure that specific objectives have been mastered and that he or she is not spending needless instructional time teaching students what they already know. For determining starting places for instruction with new students and for assessing maintenance and generalization of previously learned material, we favor top-down assessment. Generally, this approach should be more efficient in terms of teachers' and students' time because broader survey tests can cover a lot of material in a short period of time.

For students who are able to read and write independently, see–write formats are generally more efficient for both individual students and groups. When testing individual students, teachers or teacher aides can give the testing materials to the students and can proceed with other activities while the students are completing the test. Moreover, when students write their responses, a teacher can defer correcting the examinations until a convenient time.

See–say formats are also useful. Teacher aides or other students can listen to the test takers' responses and can correct them on the spot or record them for later evaluation. Moreover, many teachers have access to electronic equipment that can greatly facilitate the use of see–say formats (for example, audio or video recorders).

The hear–write format is especially useful as a selection format for younger students and students who cannot read independently. This format can also be used for testing groups of students and is routinely used in the assessment of spelling when students are required to write words from dictation. With other content, teachers can give directions and read the test questions aloud, and students can mark their responses. The primary difficulty with a hear–write format with groups of students is the pacing of test items; teachers must allot sufficient time between items for slower-responding students to make their selections.

Hear–say formats are most suitable for assessing individual students who do not write independently or who write at such slow speeds that their written responses are unrepresentative of what they know. Even with this format, teachers need not preside over the assessment; other students or a teacher aide can administer, record, and perhaps evaluate the student's responses.

8-3 Considerations in Preparing Tests

Teachers need to build skills in developing tests that are fair, reliable, and valid. The following kinds of considerations are important in developing or preparing tests.

8-3a SELECTING SPECIFIC AREAS OF THE CURRICULUM

Tests are samples of behavior. When narrow skills are being assessed (for example, spelling words from dictation), either all the components of the domain should be tested (in this case, all the assigned spelling words) or a representative sample should be selected and assessed. The qualifier "representative" implies that an appropriate number of easy and difficult words—and of words from the beginning, middle, and end of the assignment—will be selected. When more complex domains are assessed, teachers should concentrate on the more important facts or relationships and avoid the trivial.

8-3b WRITING RELEVANT QUESTIONS

Teachers must select and use enough questions to allow valid inferences about students' mastery of short-term or long-term goals, and attainment of state standards. Nothing offends test takers quite as much as a test's failure to cover material they have studied and know, except perhaps their own failure to guess what content a teacher believes to be important enough to test. In addition, fairness demands that the way in which the question is asked be familiar and expected by the student. For example, if students were to take a test on the addition of single-digit integers, it would be a bad idea to test them using a missing-addend format (for example, "4 + ___ = 7") unless that format had been specifically taught and was expected by the students.

8-3c ORGANIZING AND SEQUENCING ITEMS

The organization of a test is a function of many factors. When a teacher wants a student to complete all the items and to indicate mastery of content (a power test), it is best to intersperse easy and difficult items. When the desire is to measure automaticity or the number of items that can be completed within a specific time period (a timed test), it is best to organize items from easy to difficult. Pages of test questions or problems to be solved should not be cluttered.

8-3d DEVELOPING FORMATS FOR PRESENTATION AND RESPONSE MODES

Different response formats can be used within the same test, although it is generally a good idea to group together questions with the same format. Regardless of the format used, the primary consideration is that the test questions be a fair sample of the material being assessed.

8-3e WRITING DIRECTIONS FOR ADMINISTRATION

Regardless of question format, the directions should indicate clearly what a student is to do—for example, "Circle the correct option," "Underline the best answer," and "Match each item in column b to one item in column a." Also, teachers should explain what materials, if any, may be used by students, and explain any time limits, any unusual scoring procedures (for example, penalties for guessing), and point values when the students are mature enough to be given questions that have different point values.

8-3f DEVELOPING SYSTEMATIC PROCEDURES FOR SCORING RESPONSES

As discussed in the opening paragraphs of this chapter, teachers must have predetermined and systematic criteria for scoring responses. However, if a teacher discovers an error or omission in criteria, the criteria should be modified. Obviously, previously scored responses must be rescored with the revised criteria.

8-3g ESTABLISHING CRITERIA TO INTERPRET STUDENT PERFORMANCE

Teachers should specify in advance the criteria they will use for assigning grades or weighting assignments. For example, they may want to specify that students who earn a certain number of points on a test will earn a specific grade, or they may want to assign grades on the basis of the class distribution of performance. In either case, they must specify what it takes to earn certain grades or how assignments will be evaluated and weighted.

8-4 Response Formats

There are two basic types of test format. Selection formats require students to recognize a correct answer that is provided on the test. Supply formats require students to produce correct answers.

8-4a SELECTION FORMATS

Three types of selection formats are commonly used: multiple-choice, matching, and true–false. Of the three, multiple-choice questions are clearly the most useful.

Multiple-Choice Questions

Multiple-choice questions are the most difficult to prepare. These questions have two parts: (1) a *stem* that contains the question and (2) a response set that contains both the correct answer, termed the *keyed response*, and one or more incorrect options, termed *distractors*. In preparing multiple-choice questions, teachers should generally follow these guidelines:

- Keep the response options short and of approximately equal length. Students quickly learn that longer options tend to be correct.
- Keep material that is common to all options in the stem. For example, if the first word in each option is "the," it should be put into the stem and removed from the options, thereby improving a poorly worded question:

  A lasting contribution of the Eisenhower presidency was the creation of (the)
    a. ~~the~~ communication satellite system
    b. ~~the~~ interstate highway system
    c. ~~the~~ cable TV infrastructure
    d. ~~the~~ Eisenhower tank

- Avoid grammatical tip-offs. Students can discard grammatically incorrect options. For example, when the correct answer must be plural, alert students will disregard singular options; when the correct answer must be a noun, students will disregard options that are verbs.

    A poorly constructed question:

    An ___ test measures what a student has learned that has been taught in school.

    a. achievement
    b. intelligence
    c. social
    d. portfolio

    A better constructed question:

    ___ tests measure what a student has learned that has been taught in school.

    a. Achievement
    b. Intelligence
    c. Social
    d. Portfolio

- Avoid implausible options. In the best questions, distractors should be attractive to students who do not know the answer. Common errors and misconceptions are often good distractors.

    A poorly constructed question:

    Who was not killed in a duel?

    a. Aaron Burr
    b. Bart Simpson
    c. Alexander Hamilton
    d. Anthony Wayne

    A better constructed question:

    Who was killed in a duel?

    a. Aaron Burr
    b. Nathan Hale
    c. Alexander Hamilton
    d. Anthony Wayne

- Make sure that one and only one option is correct. Students should not have to read their teacher's mind to guess which wrong answer is the least wrong or which right answer is the most correct.

    A poorly constructed question:

    Which of the following persons was president of the United States?

    a. John Adams
    b. John Hancock
    c. John Jay
    d. James Monroe

    A better constructed question:

    Which of the following persons was a president of the United States?

    a. John Adams
    b. John Hancock
    c. John Jay
    d. James Oglethorpe

- Avoid interdependent questions. Generally, it is bad practice to make the selection of the correct option dependent on getting a prior question correct.

    An early question:

Which of the following persons switched his allegiance from the colonial revolutionaries to the British?

   a. David Wooster

   b. Anthony Wayne

   c. Benedict Arnold

   d. Horatio Gates

A subsequent dependent question:

The traitor in the preceding question was a

   a. General in the continental army

   b. Captain of a U.S. man of war

   c. Governor of Rhode Island

   d. Ambassador to England

- Avoid options that indicate multiple correct options (for example, "all the above" or "both a and b are correct"). These options often simplify the question.

A poorly constructed question:

Which of the following persons was a general in the Union Army?

   a. George Meade

   b. J.E.B. Stuart

   c. William Sherman

   d. both a and c are correct

A better constructed question:

Which of the following persons was a general in the Union Army?

   a. George Meade

   b. J.E.B. Stuart

   c. Stonewall Jackson

   d. P. G. T. Beauregard

- Avoid similar incorrect options. Students who can eliminate one of the two similar options can readily dismiss the other one. For example, if citrus fruit is wrong, lemon must be wrong.

A poorly constructed question:

Eisenhower's inspiration for the interstate highway system was the

   a. American turnpikes

   b. modern German autobahns

   c. Pennsylvania Turnpike

   d. Alcan Highway

A better constructed question:

Eisenhower's inspiration for the interstate highway system was the

   a. ancient Roman highways

   b. modern German autobahns

   c. Pennsylvania Turnpike

   d. Alcan Highway

- Make sure that one question does not provide information that can be used to answer another question.

An early question:

A lasting contribution of the Eisenhower presidency was the creation of

   a. the communication satellite system

   b. the interstate highway system

   c. the cable TV infrastructure

   d. the Eisenhower tank

A later question that answers a prior question:
Eisenhower's inspiration for the interstate highway system was the

    a. ancient Roman highways

    b. modern German autobahns

    c. Pennsylvania Turnpike

    d. Alcan Highway

- Avoid using the same words and examples that were used in the students' texts or in class presentations.

- Vary the position of the correct response in the options. Students will recognize patterns of correct options (for example, when the correct answers to a sequence of questions are a, b, c, d, a, b, c, d) or a teacher's preference for a specific position (usually c).

When appropriate, teachers can make multiple-choice questions more challenging by asking students to recognize an instance of a rule or concept, by requiring students to recall and use material that is not present in the question, or by increasing the number of options. (For younger children, three options are generally difficult enough. Older students can be expected to answer questions with four or five options.) In no case should teachers deliberately mislead or trick students.

Matching Questions

Matching questions are a variant of multiple-choice questions in which a set of stems is simultaneously associated with a set of options. Generally, the content of matching questions is limited to simple factual associations (Gronlund, 2009). Teachers usually prepare matching questions so that there are as many options as stems, and an option can be associated only once with a stem in the set. Although we do not recommend their use, there are other possibilities: more options than stems, selection of all correct options for one stem, and multiple use of an option.[6] These additional possibilities increase the difficulty of the question set considerably.

In general, we prefer multiple-choice questions to matching questions. Almost any matching question can be written as a series of multiple-choice questions in which the same or similar options are used. Of course, the correct response will change. However, teachers wishing to use matching questions should consider the following guidelines:

- Each set of matching items should have some dimension in common (for example, explorers and dates of discovery). This makes preparation easier for the teacher and provides the student with some insight into the relationship required to select the correct option.

- Keep the length of the stems approximately the same, and keep the length and grammar used in the options equivalent. At best, mixing grammatical forms will eliminate some options for some questions; at worst, it will provide the correct answer to several questions.

- Make sure that one and only one option is correct for each stem.

- Vary the sequence of correct responses when more than one matching question is asked.

- Avoid using the same words and examples that were used in the students' texts or in class presentations.

---

[6] Scoring for these options is complicated. Generally, separate errors are counted for selecting an incorrect option and failing to select a correct option. Thus, the number of errors can be very large.

It is easier for a student when questions and options are presented in two columns. When there is a difference in the length of the items in each column, the longer item should be used as the stem. Stems should be placed on the left and options on the right, rather than stems above with options below them. Moreover, all the elements of the question should be kept on one page. Finally, teachers often allow students to draw lines to connect questions and options. Although this has the obvious advantage of helping students keep track of where their answers should be placed, erasures or scratch-outs can be a headache to the person who corrects the test. A commercially available product (Learning Wrap-Ups) has cards printed with stems and answers and a shoelace with which to "lace" stems to correct answers. The correct lacing pattern is printed on the back, so it is self-correcting. Teachers could make such cards fairly easily as an alternative to trying to correct tests with lots of erasures.

True–False Statements

In most cases, true–false statements should simply not be used. Their utility lies primarily in assessing knowledge of factual information, which can be better assessed with other formats. Effective true–false items are difficult to prepare. Because guessing the correct answer is likely—it happens 50 percent of the time—the reliability of true–false tests is generally low. As a result, they may well have limited validity. Nonetheless, if a teacher chooses to use this format, a few suggestions should be followed:

- Avoid specific determiners such as "all," "never," "always," and so on.
- Avoid sweeping generalizations. Such statements tend to be true, but students can often think of minor exceptions. Thus, there is a problem in the criterion for evaluating the truthfulness of the question. Attempts to avoid the problem by adding restrictive conditions (for example, "with minor exceptions") either render the question obviously true or leave a student trying to guess what the restrictive condition means.
- Avoid convoluted sentences. Tests should assess knowledge of content, not a student's ability to comprehend difficult prose.
- Keep true and false statements approximately the same length. As is the case with longer options on multiple-choice questions, longer true–false statements tend to be true.
- Balance the number of true and false statements. If a student recognizes that there is more of one type of statement than of the other, the odds of guessing the correct answer will exceed 50 percent.

SPECIAL CONSIDERATIONS FOR STUDENTS WITH DISABILITIES

In developing and using items that employ a selection format, teachers must pay attention to individual differences among students, particularly to disabilities that might interfere with performance. The individualized educational programs (IEPs) of students with disabilities often contain needed accommodations and adaptations. Prior to testing, it is always a good idea to double-check students' IEPs to make sure that any required accommodations and adaptations have been made. For example, students who have skill deficits in remembering things for short periods of time, or who do not attend well to verbally or visually presented information, may need multiple-choice tests with fewer distractors. Students who have difficulty with the organization of visually presented material may need to have matching questions rewritten as multiple-choice questions. Remember, it is important to assess the skills that students have in a way that is not inappropriately hindered by their disabilities. See the Scenario in Assessment example below for an example of how a special educator handles test adaptations for a teacher-made test for a student with a disability.

SCENARIO IN ASSESSMENT

BARRY | Ms. Johnson is a special education teacher in a middle school. One of her students, Barry, has an IEP that requires adapted content area tests. Mr. Blumfield, the social studies teacher, sends Ms. Johnson a test that he will be giving in eight days so that she can adapt it. The test contains both multiple-choice (five options) and true–false questions. Mr. Blumfield plans to allow students the entire period (37 minutes) to complete their tests.

Ms. Johnson has several concerns about the test. In her experience with Barry, she has found that he requires untimed and shorter tests, and that some questions must be read to him. In addition, he cannot understand true–false questions, and he has unusual difficulty when there are more than three options on multiple-choice questions. Therefore, she schedules a meeting with Mr. Blumfield to discuss her adaptation of his test.

Mr. Blumfield has 127 students, and eight of these students have IEPs. Ms. Johnson begins the meeting by reminding him that Barry's IEP provides for the adaptation of content area tests. She also tells Mr. Blumfield that she is willing to make the adaptations but will need some guidance from him. The first thing she wants to learn is what the important content is—the questions assessing the major ideas and important facts that Mr. Blumfield has stressed in his lessons. She also wants to learn which questions can be deleted.

Then Ms. Johnson explains how she will adapt the test:

- She will modify the content by deleting relatively unimportant ideas and concepts; she will retain all of the major ideas and important concepts.
- She will replace true–false questions that assess major ideas with multiple-choice questions that get at the same information.
- She will reduce the number of distractors in multiple-choice questions from five to three.
- She will reorder test items by grouping questions about related content together and ordering questions from easy to difficult whenever possible.

She also explains that she will read to Barry any part of the test that he requests, and that the test will not be timed, so he may not finish in one period. Finally, she offers to score the test for Mr. Blumfield.

This scenario highlights methods that could be used to adapt a classroom test to address the unique needs of a student with a disability. How does Ms. Johnson's modifications target Barry's unique needs?

8-4b SUPPLY FORMATS

It is useful to distinguish between items requiring a student to write one- or two-word responses (such as fill-in questions) and those requiring more extended responses (such as essay questions). Both types of items require careful delineation of what constitutes a correct response (that is, criteria for scoring). It is generally best for teachers to prepare criteria for a correct response at the time they prepare the question. In that way, they can ensure that the question is written in such a way as to elicit the correct types of answers—or at least not to mislead students—and perhaps save time when correcting exams. (If teachers change criteria for a correct response after they have scored a few questions, they should rescore all previously scored questions with the revised criteria.)

Fill-In Questions

Aside from mathematics problems that require students to calculate an answer and writing spelling words from dictation, fill-in questions require a student to complete a statement by adding a concept or fact—for example, "___ arrived in America in 1492." Fill-ins are useful in assessing knowledge and comprehension objectives; they are not useful in assessing application, analysis, synthesis, or evaluation objectives. Teachers preparing fill-in questions should follow these guidelines:

- Keep each sentence short. Generally, the less superfluous information in an item, the clearer the question will be to the student, and the less likely it will be that one question will cue another.
- If a two-word answer is required, teachers should use two blanks to indicate this in the sentence.
- Avoid sentences with multiple blanks. For example, the item "In the year ___, ___ discovered ___" is so vague that practically any date, name, and event can be inserted correctly, even ones that are irrelevant to the content; for example, "In the year 2010, Henry discovered girls."
- Keep the size of all blanks consistent and large enough to readily accommodate the longest answer. The size of the blank should not provide a clue about the length of the correct word.

The most problematic aspect of fill-in questions is the necessity of developing an appropriate response bank of acceptable answers. Often, some student errors may consist of a partially correct response; teachers must decide which answers will receive partial credit, full credit, and no credit. For example, a question may anticipate "Columbus" as the correct response, but a student might write "that Italian dude who was looking for the shortcut to India for the Spanish king and queen." In deciding how far afield to go in crediting unanticipated responses, teachers should look over test questions carefully to determine whether the student's answer comes from information presented in another question (for example, "The Spanish monarch employed an Italian sailor to find a shorter route to India").

Extended Responses

Essay questions are most useful in assessing comprehension, application, analysis, synthesis, and evaluation objectives. There are two major problems associated with extended response questions. First, teachers are generally able to sample only a limited amount of information because answers may take a long time for students to write. Second, extended-essay responses are the most difficult type of answer to score. To avoid subjectivity and inconsistency, teachers should use a scoring key that assigns specific point values for each element in the ideal or criterion answer. In most cases, spelling and grammatical errors should not be deducted from the point total. Moreover, bonus points should not be awarded for particularly detailed responses; many good students will provide a complete answer to one question and spend any extra time working on questions that are more difficult for them.

Finally, teachers should be prepared to deal with responses in which a student tries to bluff a correct answer. Rather than leave a question unanswered, some students may answer a related question that was not asked, or they may structure their response so that they can omit important information that they cannot remember or never knew. Sometimes, they will even write a poem or a treatise on why the question asked is unimportant or irrelevant. Therefore, teachers must be very specific about how they will award points, stick to their criteria unless they discover that something is wrong with them, and not give credit to creative bluffs.

Teachers should also be very precise in the directions that they give so that students will not have to guess what responses their teachers will credit. Following are a number of verbs (and their meanings) that are commonly used in essay questions. It is often worthwhile to explain these terms in the test directions to make sure that students know what kind of answer is desired.

- *Describe, define,* and *identify* mean to give the meaning, essential characteristics, or place within a taxonomy.
- *List* means to enumerate and implies that complete sentences and paragraphs are not required unless specifically requested.
- *Discuss* requires more than a description, definition, or identification; a student is expected to draw implications and elucidate relationships.
- *Explain* means to analyze and make clear or comprehensible a concept, event, principle, relationship, and so forth; thus, *explain* requires going beyond a definition to describe the hows or whys.
- *Compare* means to identify and explain similarities between two things or among more than two things.
- *Contrast* means to identify and explain differences between two things or among more than two things.
- *Evaluate* means to give the value of something and implies an enumeration and explanation of assets and liabilities, pros and cons.

Finally, unless students know the questions in advance, teachers should allow students sufficient time for planning and rereading answers. For example, if teachers believe that 10 minutes is necessary to write an extended essay to answer a question that requires original thinking, they might allow 20 minutes for the question. The less fluent the students are, the greater is the proportion of time that should be allotted.

8-5 Assessment in Core Achievement Areas

The assessment procedures used by teachers are a function of the content being taught, the criterion to which content is to be learned (such as 90 percent mastery), and the characteristics of the students. With primary-level curricula in core areas, teachers usually want more than knowledge from their students; they want the material learned so well that correct responses are automatic. For example, teachers do not want their students to think about forming the letter "a," sounding out the word "the," or using number lines to solve simple addition problems such as "3 + 5 = "; they want their students to respond immediately and correctly. Even for intermediate-level materials, teachers seek highly proficient responding from their students, whether that performance involves performing two-digit multiplication, reading short stories, writing short stories, or writing spelling words from dictation. However, teachers in all grades, but especially in secondary schools, are also interested in their students' understanding of vast amounts of information about their social, cultural, and physical worlds, as well as their acquisition and application of critical thinking skills. The assessment of skills taught to high degrees of proficiency is quite different from the assessment of understanding and critical thinking skills.

In the following sections, core achievement areas are discussed in terms of three important attributes: the skills and information to be learned within the major strands of most curricula, the assessment of skills to be learned to proficiency, and the assessment of understanding of information and concepts. Critical thinking skills are usually embedded within content areas and are assessed in the same ways as understanding of information is assessed—with written multiple-choice and extended-essay questions.

8-5a READING

Reading is usually divided into decoding skills and comprehension. The specific behaviors included in each of these subdomains will depend on the particular curriculum and its sequencing. See the Scenario in Assessment provided for examples of how a teacher created a way to measure a student's reading skills that is particularly targeted to the skills the student needs to develop.

Prereading Skills

Phonemic awareness is a prerequisite skill for reading. A phoneme is the smallest unit of sound that differentiates meaning, and the ability to analyze and manipulate sounds and syllables in words is necessary for phonics instruction to be successful (Stanovich, 2000). Instruction in phonemic awareness can include recognizing phonemes in individual words, substituting phonemes to change word meanings, segmenting words into sounds, blending sounds, and deleting sounds from words. Phonemic awareness does not require students to have any knowledge of letters or what they represent.

Beginning Skills

Instruction in beginning reading usually includes letter recognition, letter–sound correspondences, sight vocabulary, phonics, and, in some curricula, morphology. Automaticity is the goal for the skills to be learned. See–say (for example, "What letter is this?") and hear–say (for example, "What sound does the letter make?")

formats are regularly used for both instruction and assessment. During students' acquisition of specific skills, teachers should first stress the accuracy of student responses. Generally, this concern translates into allowing a moment or two for students to think about their responses. A generally accepted criterion for completion for early learning is 90 to 95 percent correct. As soon as accuracy has been attained (and sometimes before), teachers change their criteria from accurate responses to fast and accurate responses. For see–say formats, fluent students will need no thinking time for simple material; for example, they should be able to respond as rapidly as teachers can change stimuli to questions such as "What is this letter?" Once students accurately decode letters and letter combinations fluently, the emphasis shifts to fluency or the automatic retrieval of words. Fluency is a combination of speed and accuracy and is widely viewed as a fundamental prerequisite for reading comprehension (National Institute of Child Health and Human Development, 2000a, 2000b).

For beginners, reading comprehension is usually assessed in one of two ways: by assessing students' retelling or their responses to comprehension questions. The most direct method is to have students retell what they have read without access to the reading passage. Retold passages may be scored on the basis of the number of words recalled. Fuchs, Fuchs, and Maxwell (1988) have offered two relatively simple scoring procedures that appear to offer valid indications of comprehension. Retelling may be conducted orally or in writing. With students who have relatively undeveloped writing skills, retelling should be oral when it is used to assess comprehension, but it may be in writing as a practice or drill activity. Teachers can listen to students retell, or students can retell using audio recorders so that their efforts can be evaluated later.

A second common method of assessing comprehension is to ask students questions about what they have read. Questions should address main ideas, important relationships, and relevant details. Questions may be in supply or selection formats, and either hear–say or see–write formats can be used conveniently. As with retelling, teachers should concentrate their efforts on the gist of the passage.

Rate of oral reading is often used as an indirect method of assessing reading comprehension. Slower readers tend to have poor reading comprehension. The explanation offered by LaBerge and Samuels (1974) is still used to explain that relationship. Poor decoding skills create a bottleneck that impedes the flow of information, thus impeding comprehension. Slow readers must expend their energy decoding words (for example, attending to letters, remembering letter–sound associations, blending sounds, or searching for context cues) rather than concentrating on the meaning of what is written. Not only is the relationship between reading fluency and comprehension logical, but empirical research also supports this relationship (Freeland, Skinner, Jackson, McDaniel, & Smith, 2000; National Institute of Child Health and Human Development, 2000a, 2000b; Sindelar, Monda, & O'Shea, 1990).

To assess reading rate, teachers should have students read for two minutes from appropriate materials. The reading passage should include familiar vocabulary, syntax, and content; the passage must be longer than the amount any student can read in the two-minute period. Teachers have their own copy of the passage on which to note errors. The number of words read correctly and the number of errors made in two minutes are each divided by 2 to calculate the rate per minute. Mercer and Mercer (1985) suggest a rate of 80 words per minute (with two or fewer errors) as a desirable goal for reading words from lists and a rate of 100 words per minute (with two or fewer errors) for words in text. (See also, Read Naturally, Inc., 2010; National Assessment of Educational Progress, Oral Reading Rate, 2002). See Chapter 15 for a more complete discussion of errors in oral reading.

Advanced Skills

Students who have already mastered basic sight vocabulary and decoding skills generally read silently. Emphasis for these students shifts, and new demands are made. Decoding moves from oral reading to silent reading with subvocalization (that is, saying the words and phrases to themselves) to visual scanning without subvocalization; thus, the reading rates of some students may exceed 1,000 words per minute. Scanning for main ideas and information may also be taught systematically. The demands for reading comprehension may go well beyond the literal comprehension of a passage; summarizing, drawing inferences, recognizing and understanding symbolism, sarcasm, irony, and so forth may be systematically taught. For these advanced students, the gist of a passage is usually more important than the details. Teachers of more advanced students may wish to score retold passages on the basis of main ideas, important relationships, details recalled correctly, and the number of errors (that is, ideas, relationships, and details omitted plus the insertion of material not included in the passage). In such cases, the different types of information can be weighted differently, or the use of comprehension strategies (for example, summarization) can be encouraged. However, read–write assessment formats using multiple-choice and extended-essay questions are more commonly used.

Informal Reading Inventories

When making decisions about referral or initial placement in a reading curriculum, teachers often develop informal reading inventories (IRIs), which assess decoding and reading comprehension over a wide range of skill levels within the specific reading curricula used in a classroom. Thus, they are top-down assessments that span several levels of difficulty.

IRIs are given to locate the reading levels at which a student reads independently, requires instruction, or is frustrated. Techniques for developing IRIs and the criteria used to define independent, instructional, and frustration reading levels vary. Teachers should use a series of graded reading passages that range from below a student's actual placement to a year or two above the actual placement. If a reading series prepared for several grade levels is used, passages can be selected from the beginning, middle, and end of each grade. Students begin reading the easiest material and continue reading until they can decode less than 85 percent of the words. Generally, an accuracy rate of 95 percent is recommended for independent reading and 85 to 95 percent accuracy is considered the level at which a student requires instruction.

8-5b MATHEMATICS

The National Council of Teachers of Mathematics has adopted standards for pre-kindergarten through secondary education. These standards deal with both content (that is, numeracy, measurement, algebra, geometry, and data and statistics) and process (that is, reasoning, representation, problem solving, connections, and communication). Special education tends to share the goals of the National Mathematics Panel (2008), which has stressed computational proficiency and fluency in basic skills. In noninclusive special education settings, math content is generally stressed (that is, early numeracy, vocabulary and concepts, whole-number operations, fractions and decimals, ratios and percentages, measurement, and geometry).

At any grade level, the specific skills and concepts included in each of these subdomains will depend on the state standards and the particular curriculum and its sequencing. Mathematics curricula usually contain both problem sets that require only computations and word problems that require selection and application of the correct algorithm as well as computation. The difficulty of application problems goes well beyond the difficulty of the computation involved and is related to three factors: (1) the number of steps involved in the solution (for example, a student might have to add and then multiply; Caldwell & Goldin, 1979), (2) the amount of extraneous information (Englert, Cullata, & Horn, 1987), and (3) whether the mathematical operation is directly implied by the vocabulary used in the problem (for example, words such as *and* or *more* imply addition, whereas words such as *each* may imply division; see Bachor, Stacy, & Freeze, 1986). Although reading level is popularly believed to affect the difficulty of word problems, its effect has not been clearly established (see Bachor, 1990; Paul, Nibbelink, & Hoover, 1986).

SCENARIO IN ASSESSMENT

 ROBERT | Robert has learned the basic alphabetic principles, letter–sound associations, sound blending, and basic phonic rules. However, his reading fluency is very slow. This lack of fluency makes comprehension difficult and causes problems for him in completing his work in the times allotted. His IEP contains an annual goal of increasing his fluency to 100 words per minute with two or fewer errors in material written at his grade level. Mr. Williams, his special education teacher, has developed a program that relies on repeated readings. He recently read an article by Therrien (2004) that indicates the important aspects of repeated reading to follow in his program. He decides to check fluency daily using brief probes.

After Mr. Williams has determined the highest level reading materials that Robert can read with 95 percent accuracy, he prepares a series of 200-word passages at that level and one-third higher levels, up to Robert's actual grade placement. Each passage forms a logical unit and begins with a new paragraph. The vocabulary is representative of Robert's reading level, and passage comprehension does not rely on preceding material that he has not read. He prepares two copies of each passage and places each in an acetate cover. (This allows him to indicate errors directly on the passage and then to wipe both copies clean after testing for reuse at another time.)

Mr. Williams then prepares instructions for Robert: "I want to see how fast you can read material the first time and a second or third time. I want you to read as fast as you can without making errors. If you don't know a word, just skip it. I'll tell you the word when you are done. Then I'll ask you to reread the passage. When I say start, you begin reading. After one minute, I'll say stop and you stop reading. Do you have any questions?"

Mr. Williams gives Robert two practice readings that he does not score. This gives Robert some experience with the process. He then begins giving Robert daily probes; he enters Robert's rate on the first reading and connects the data points for the same passage on different days. When Robert can read three consecutive probes at the target rate the first time, Mr. Williams increases the reading level of the material (for example, days 13, 14, and 15). The intervention will end when Robert is reading grade-level materials fluently—the third level above where the intervention has started.

As shown in Figure 8.2, Robert makes steady progress, both within reading levels and between reading levels. Mr. Williams is pleased with the intervention and will continue with it until it is no longer working or when Robert achieves the goal.

This scenario highlights an approach to measuring student reading skills. How is the approach used connected to the specific skills the student needs to work on?

FIGURE 8.2
Robert's Progress in Reading

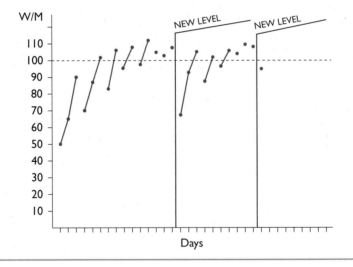

© 2013 Cengage Learning

Beginning Skills

The whole-number operations of addition, subtraction, multiplication, and division are the core of the elementary mathematics curriculum. Early numeracy skills are necessary for success in that curriculum: one-to-one correspondence, counting orally, identifying numbers, basic concepts (bigger/smaller, more/less, etc.), vocabulary (for example, "same," "equal," and "larger") and spatial concepts (for example, "left," "above," and "next to").

See–write is probably the most frequently used assessment format for mathematical skills, although see–say formats are not uncommon. For content associated with readiness, vocabulary and concepts, numeration, and applications, matching formats are commonly used. Accuracy is stressed, and 90 to 95 percent correct is commonly used as the criterion. For computation, accuracy and fluency are stressed in beginning mathematics; teachers do not stop their instruction when students respond accurately, but they continue instruction to build automaticity. Consequently, a teacher may accept somewhat lower rates of accuracy (that is, 80 percent).

When working toward fluency, teachers usually use probes. Probes are small samples of behavior. For example, in assessment of skill in addition of single-digit numbers, a student might be given only five single-digit addition problems. Perhaps the most useful criterion for math probes assessing computation is the number of correct digits (in an answer) written per minute, not the number of correct answers per minute. The actual criterion rate will depend on the operation, the type of material (for example, addition facts versus addition of two-digit numbers with regrouping), and the characteristics of the particular students. Students with motor difficulties may be held to a lower criterion or assessed with see–say formats. For see–write formats, students may be expected to write answers to addition and subtraction problems at rates between 50 and 80 digits per minute and to write answers to simple multiplication and division problems at rates between 40 and 50 digits per minute.

Advanced Skills

The more advanced mathematical skills (that is, fractions, decimals, ratios, percentages, and geometry) build on whole-number operations. These skills are taught to levels of comprehension and application. Unlike those for beginning skills, assessment formats are almost exclusively see–write, and accuracy is stressed over fluency, except for a few facts such as "half equals 0.5 equals 50 percent." Teachers must take into account the extent to which specific student disabilities will interfere with performance of advanced skills. For example, difficulties in sequencing of information and in comprehension may interfere with students' performance on items that require problem solving and comprehension of mathematical concepts.

8-5c SPELLING

Although spelling is considered by many to be a component of written language, in elementary school it is generally taught as a separate subject. Therefore, we treat it separately in this chapter.

Spelling is the production of letters in the correct sequence to form a word. The specific words that are assigned as spelling words may come from several sources: spelling curricula, word lists, content areas, or a student's own written work. In high school and college, students are expected to use dictionaries and to spell correctly any word they use. Between that point and approximately fourth grade, spelling words are typically assigned, and students are left to their own devices to learn them. In the first three grades, spelling is usually taught systematically using phonics, morphology, rote memorization, or some combination of the three approaches.

Teachers may assess mastery of the prespelling rules associated with the particular approach they are teaching. For example, when a phonics approach is used, students may have to demonstrate mastery of writing the letters associated with specific vowels, consonants, consonant blends, diphthongs, and digraphs. Teachers assess mastery of spelling in at least four ways:

1. *Recognition response:* The teacher provides students with lists of alternative spellings of words (usually three or four alternatives) and reads a word to the student. The student must select the correct spelling of the dictated word from the alternatives. Emphasis is on accuracy.

2. *Spelling dictated single words:* Teachers dictate words, and students write them down. Although teachers often give a spelling word and then use it in a sentence, students find the task easier if just the spelling word is given (Horn, 1967). Moreover, the findings from research performed in 1988 suggest that a seven-second interval between words is sufficient (Shinn, Tindal, & Stein, 1988).

3. *Spelling words in context:* Students write paragraphs using words given by the teacher. This approach is as much a measure of written expression as of spelling. The teacher can also use this approach in instruction of written language by asking students to write paragraphs and then counting the number of words spelled correctly.

4. *Students' self-monitoring of errors:* Some teachers teach students to monitor their own performance by finding and correcting spelling errors in the daily assignments they complete.

8-5d WRITTEN LANGUAGE

Written language is no doubt the most complex and difficult domain for teachers to assess. Assessment differs widely for beginners and advanced students. Once the preliminary skills of letter formation and rudimentary spelling have been mastered, written-language curricula usually stress both content and style (that is, grammar, mechanics, and diction).

Beginning Skills

The most basic instruction in written language is penmanship, in which the formation and spacing of uppercase (capital) and lowercase printed and cursive letters are taught. Early instruction stresses accuracy, and criteria are generally qualitative. After accuracy has been attained, teachers may provide extended practice to move students toward automaticity. If this is done, teachers will evaluate performance on the basis of students' rates of writing letters. Target rates are usually in the range of 80 to 100 letters per minute for students without motor handicaps.

Once students can fluently write letters and words, teachers focus on teaching students to write content. For beginners, content generation is often reduced to generation of words in meaningful sequence. Teachers may use story starters (that is, pictures or a few words that act as stimuli) to prompt student writing. When the allotted time for writing is over, teachers count the number of words or divide the number of words by the time to obtain a measure of rate. Although this sounds relatively easy, decisions as to what constitutes a word must be made. For example, one-letter words are seldom counted.

Teachers also use the percentage of correct words to assess content production. To be considered correct, the word must be spelled correctly, be capitalized if appropriate, be grammatically correct, and be followed by the correct punctuation (Isaacson, 1988). Criteria for an acceptable percentage of correct words are still the subject of discussion. For now, social comparison, by which one student's writing output is compared with the output of students whose writing is judged acceptable, can provide teachers with rough approximations. Teaching usually boils down to focusing on capitalization, simple punctuation, and basic grammar (for example, subject–verb agreement). Teachers may also use multiple-choice or fill-in tests to assess comprehension of grammatical conventions or rules.

Advanced Skills

Comprehension and application of advanced grammar and mechanics can be tested readily with multiple-choice or fill-in questions. Thus, this aspect of written language can be assessed systematically and objectively. The evaluation of content generation by advanced students is far more difficult than counting correct words. Teachers may consider the quality of ideas, the sequencing of ideas, the coherence of ideas, and consideration of the reading audience. In practice, teachers use holistic judgments of content (Cooper, 1977). In addition, they may point out errors in style or indicate topics that might benefit from greater elaboration or clarification. Objective scoring of any of these attributes is very difficult, and scoring rubrics and practice are necessary to obtain reliable judgments, if they are ever attained. More objective scoring systems for content require computer analysis and are currently beyond the resources of many classroom teachers.

SPECIAL CONSIDERATIONS FOR STUDENTS WITH DISABILITIES

In preparing IEPs for students with disabilities, it is essential to include testing adaptations and accommodations whenever necessary. Teachers must pay attention to disabilities that interfere with a student's test performance. For example, students who cannot read must have their tests read to them, as long as the test is not designed to measure reading decoding skills. Those who write very slowly can be expected to have difficulty with fill-in or essay questions. Students who have considerable difficulty organizing their thoughts will probably have difficulty completing or performing well on oral or written extended supply questions. Teachers must make sure that their tests have included the adaptations and accommodations required in student IEPs and that they have used them during their instruction.

8-6 Coping with Dilemmas in Current Practice

There are three pitfalls to be avoided: (1) relying on a single summative assessment, (2) using nonstandardized testing procedures, and (3) using technically inadequate assessment procedures. The first two are easily avoided; avoiding the third is more difficult.

First, teachers should not rely solely on a single summative assessment to evaluate student achievement after a course of instruction. Such assessments do not provide teachers with information they can use to plan and modify sequences of instruction. Moreover, minor technical inadequacies can be magnified when a single summative measure is used. Rather, teachers should use formative procedures to assess progress toward educational objectives at least two or three times a week. Frequent testing is most important when instruction is aimed at developing automatic or fluent responses in students. Although fluency is most commonly associated with primary curricula, it is not restricted to reading, writing, and arithmetic. For example, instruction in foreign languages, sports, and music is often aimed at automaticity.

Second, teachers should use standardized testing procedures. To conduct frequent assessments that are meaningful, the tests that are used to assess the same objectives must be equivalent. Therefore, the content must be equivalent from test to test; moreover, test directions, kinds of cues or hints, testing formats, criteria for correct responses, and type of score (for example, rates or percentage correct) must be the same.

Third, teachers should develop technically adequate assessment procedures. Two aspects of this adequacy are especially important: content validity and reliability. The tests must have content validity. There should seldom be problems with content validity when direct performances are used. For example, the materials used in determining a student's rate of oral reading should have content validity when they come from that student's reading materials; tests used to assess mastery of addition facts will have content validity because they assess the facts that have been taught. A problem with content validity is more likely when teachers use tests to assess achievement outside of the tool subjects (that is, other than reading, math, and language arts).

Although only teachers can develop tests that truly mirror instruction, teachers must not only know what has been taught but also prepare devices that test what has been taught. About the only way to guarantee that an assessment covers the content is to develop tables of specifications for the content of instruction and testing. However, test items geared to specific content may still be ineffective.

Careful preparation in and of itself cannot guarantee the validity of one question or set of questions. The only way a teacher can know that the questions are good is to field-test the questions and make revisions based on the field-test results. Realistically, teachers do not have time for field testing and revision prior to giving a test. Therefore, teachers must usually give a test and then delete or discount poor items. The poor items can be edited and the revised questions used the next time the examination is needed. In this way, the responses from one group of students become a field test for a subsequent group of students. When teachers use this approach, they should not return tests to students because students may pass questions down from year to year.

The tests must also be reliable. Interscorer agreement should not be a problem for tests using select or restricted fill-in formats. For select and fill-in tests, internal consistency is of primary concern. Unfortunately, very few people can prepare a set of homogeneous test questions the first time. However, at the same time that they revise poor items, teachers can delete or revise items to increase a test's homogeneity (that is, delete or revise items that have correlations with the total score of .25 or less). Additional items can also be prepared for the next test.

Interscorer agreement is a major concern for any test using a supply format but is especially important when extended responses are evaluated. Agreement can be increased by developing precise scoring guides with objective scoring criteria—and by sticking with the criteria. Interscorer agreement is a problem when subjective and holistic scoring procedures are used—especially with written language. Breland and colleagues found interscorer agreement of essays on the same topic ranged from .52 to .65 (Breland, 1983; Breland, Camp, Jones, Morris, & Rock, 1987). Consistent scoring of student writing is even more difficult when students can select topics and genres. As Dorans and Schmitt (1993, p. 135) note: "To the extent that a constructed-response item is unconstrained and examinees are free to produce any response they wish, the test scorer has a difficult and challenging task of extracting information from examinee responses." As Breland and colleagues (Breland, 1983; Breland et al., 1987) have found, interscorer agreement drops from the range of .52 to .65 to a range of .36 to .46 when the writing tasks vary.

Chapter Comprehension Questions

Write your answers to each of the following questions and then compare your responses to the text.

1. Explain how teacher-made tests can be used to ascertain skill development, monitor instruction, and document instructional problems.

2. Discuss the dimensions of content specificity, testing frequency, and testing formats.

3. What are the major considerations for teachers in preparing classroom tests?

4. What are the commonly used types of select and supply formats? What are the special considerations for students with disabilities?

5. Select one core achievement area (e.g., reading or mathematics). How does the content differ for beginning and advanced students?

6. Discuss the potential sources of difficulty in the use of teacher-made tests.

ASSESSING BEHAVIOR THROUGH OBSERVATION

LEARNING OBJECTIVES

9-1 Summarize different approaches to observation.

9-2 Describe two existing formats for documenting information collected through observation.

9-3 Describe ways in which behaviors are defined for systematic observations.

9-4 Describe how observations require careful sampling of contexts, times, and behaviors.

9-5 Explain procedures to follow in conducting systematic observations.

STANDARDS ADDRESSED IN THIS CHAPTER

CEC CEC Initial Preparation Standards

Standard 4: Assessment
4.0 Beginning special education professionals use multiple methods of assessment and data-sources in making educational decisions.

Standard 5: Instructional Planning and Strategies
5.0 Beginning special education professionals select, adapt, and use a repertoire of evidence-based instructional strategies to advance learning of individuals with exceptionalities.

CEC CEC Advanced Preparation Standards
ADVANCED

Standard 1: Assessment
1.0 Special education specialists use valid and reliable assessment practices to minimize bias.

Ψ National Association of School Psychologists Domains

1 Data-Based Decision Making and Accountability
4 Interventions and Mental Health Services to Develop Social and Life Skills

Teachers are constantly monitoring themselves and their students. Sometimes they are just keeping an eye on things to make sure that their classrooms are safe and goal oriented, to anticipate disruptive or dangerous situations, or to keep track of how things are going in a general sense. Often, teachers notice behavior or situations that seem important and require their attention: the fire alarm has sounded, Harvey has a knife, Betty is asleep, Jo is wandering around the classroom. In other situations, often as a result of their general monitoring, teachers look for very specific behaviors to observe: social behaviors that should be reinforced, attention to task, performance of particular skills, and so forth.

When assessment does not rely on permanent products (that is, written examinations and physical creations such as a table in shop or a dinner in home economics), observation is usually involved. Clearly, social behavior, learning behavior (for example, attention to task), and aberrant behavior (for example, hand flapping) are all suitable targets of observation. Obviously, behavior can be an integral part of assessing physical and mental states, physical characteristics, and educational disabilities as well as monitoring student progress and attainment. Although nonsystematic observational approaches can be helpful for gathering initial information about student behavior, we emphasize the use of systematic observation for making important decisions about whether substantial instructional changes are necessary for individual students due to their behavioral characteristics.

9-1 Approaches to Observation: Qualitative and Quantitative

There are two basic approaches to observation: qualitative and quantitative. Through **qualitative observation**, an observer monitors the situation and memorializes the observations in a narrative, the most common form being anecdotal records. **Qualitative observations** can describe behavior as well as its contexts (that is, antecedents and consequences), and usually occur without predetermining the behaviors to be observed or the times and contexts in which to observe. Good anecdotal records contain a complete description of the behavior and the context in which it occurred and can set the stage for more focused and precise *quantitative observations*. We stress systematic observation, a quantitative approach to observation. Although we note in a later section of this chapter some examples of nonsystematic observations that may be useful, we focus most of the chapter on systematic observations. Measuring behavior through **systematic observation** is distinguished by five steps that occur in advance of the actual observations: (1) The behavior is defined precisely and objectively, (2) the characteristics of the behavior (for example, frequency) are specified, (3) procedures for recording are developed, (4) the times and places for observation are selected and specified, and (5) procedures are developed to assess interobserver agreement. Behavioral observations can also vary on a number of other dimensions, which are described below.

9-1a LIVE OR AIDED OBSERVATION

Quantitative analysis of behavior can occur in real time or after the behavior has occurred by means of devices such as video or audio recorders that can replay, slow down, or speed up records of behavior. Observation can be enhanced with equipment (for example, a telescope), or it can occur with only the observer's unaided senses.

9-1b OBTRUSIVE VERSUS UNOBTRUSIVE OBSERVATION

Observations are called **obtrusive** when it is obvious to the person being observed that he or she is being observed. The presence of an observer makes observation obvious; for example, the presence of a practicum supervisor in the back of the classroom makes it obvious to student teachers that they are being observed. The presence of observation equipment makes it obvious; for example, a video camera with a red light on makes it obvious that observation is occurring. Something added to a situation can signal that someone is observing. For example, a dark, late-model, four-door sedan idling on the side of the road with a radar gun protruding from the driver's window makes it obvious to approaching motorists that they are being observed; a flickering light and noise coming from behind a mirror in a testing room indicate to test takers that there is someone or something watching from behind the mirror.

When observations are **unobtrusive**, the people being observed do not realize they are being watched. Observers may pretend that they are not observing or observe from hidden positions. They may use telescopes to watch from afar. They may use hidden cameras and microphones.

Unobtrusive observations are preferable for two reasons. First, people are reluctant to engage in certain types of behavior if another person is looking. Thus, when antisocial, offensive, or illegal behaviors are targeted for assessment, observation should be conducted surreptitiously. Behaviors of these types tend not to occur if they are overtly monitored. For example, Billy is unlikely to steal Bob's lunch money when the teacher is looking; Rosie is unlikely to bully Sandy in front of teachers; and Rodney is unlikely to spray-paint gang graffiti on the front doors of the school when other students are present.

Likewise, if people are being observed, they are reluctant to engage in highly personal behaviors in which they must expose private body parts. For example, sometimes a student with a severe disability is to be observed as he or she is learning how to properly use the toilet to determine whether the student is following appropriate procedures. In these instances, the observer should obtain the permission of the person or the person's guardian before conducting such observations. Moreover, a same-sex observer who does not know the person being observed (and whom the person being observed does not know) should conduct the observations.

The second reason that unobtrusive observations are preferable is that the presence of an observer alters the observation situation. Observation can change the behavior of those in the observation situation. For example, when a principal sits in the back of a probationary teacher's classroom to conduct an annual evaluation, both the teacher's and the students' behavior may be affected by the principal's presence. Students may be better behaved or respond more enthusiastically in the mistaken belief that the principal is there to watch them. The teacher may write on the chalkboard more frequently or give more positive reinforcement than usual in the belief that the principal values those techniques. Observation can also eliminate other types of behavior. For example, retail stores may mount circuit TV cameras and video monitors in obvious places to let potential thieves know that they are being watched constantly and to try to discourage shoplifting.

When the target behavior is not antisocial, offensive, highly personal, or undesirable, obtrusive observation may be used provided the persons being observed have been desensitized to the observers and/or equipment. It is fortunate that most people quickly become accustomed to observers in their daily environment—especially if observers make themselves part of the surroundings by avoiding eye contact, not engaging in social interactions, remaining quiet and not moving around, and so on. Observation and recording can become part of the everyday classroom routine. In any event, obtrusive observation should not begin until the persons to be observed are desensitized and are acting in their usual ways.

9-1c CONTRIVED VERSUS NATURALISTIC OBSERVATION

Contrived observations occur when a situation is set up before a student is introduced into it. For example, a playroom may be set up with toys that encourage aggressive play (such as guns or punching-bag dolls) or with items that promote other types of behavior. A child may be given a book and told to go into the room and read or may simply be told to wait in the room. Other adults or children in the situation may be confederates of the observer and may be instructed to behave in particular ways. For example, an older child may be told not to share toys with the child who is the target of the observation, or an adult may be told to initiate a conversation on a specific topic with the target child.

In contrast, **naturalistic observations** occur in settings that are not contrived. For example, specific toys are not added to or removed from a playroom; the furniture is arranged as it always is arranged.

9-2 Two Example Formats for Nonsystematic Behavioral Observation

Although the focus of this chapter is on conducting systematic observations, we think it is important to highlight two nonsystematic formats for behavioral observation that teachers and school support professionals may find useful: ABC event recording and Direct Behavior Ratings (DBR).

ABC event recording is a qualitative observational method in which the observer records descriptions of the behaviors of interest, along with the antecedents and consequences that correspond to the behaviors of interest. **Antecedents** include what is happening right before the behavior occurs, and may include things like what the student has been asked to do, or any related teacher or peer communication that occurs right before the behavior of interest. **Consequences** are what happens right after the behavior occurs, and may include things like the provision of a time-out, peer laughing/attention, teacher redirection, teacher praise. To complete an ABC event recording observation, the observer takes notes for a given time interval in a way that allows for categorization of the behaviors observed according to the ABC framework. The ABC information may be used to (a) better define the behavior of interest for more systematic observation in the future, and (b) develop some initial hypotheses about the function of a student's behavior that might later be tested and used to develop a behavioral intervention plan (see Chapter 19 for more information on conducting functional behavioral assessments). Part 1 of the scenario for this chapter provides an example of ABC event recording, and Part 2 of the scenario discusses how a systematic observation method was developed and used following the data collected through the ABC event recording approach.

Direct behavior rating (DBR) is a quantitative observational method that has become more widely recognized and used for both assessment and intervention in the area of problem behavior. It is also used to facilitate communication about a student's behavioral progress. Although it includes some aspects of systematic observation it does not require precise behavioral definitions, nor does it typically involve specifying the specific characteristic of the behavior or determining inter-observer agreement. For these reasons, we consider it a nonsystematic observation technique. The appeal of DBRs is in their simplicity and in their malleability. The overall procedure is as follows: a target behavior and observational time period are selected, an individual (typically the teacher) rates the student or groups of students on the target behavior, and the rating is communicated to someone else (typically the targeted students and parents). Target behavior(s), numbers of students to be rated, frequency of ratings, communication methods, and any associated reinforcement for behavioral improvements are determined in advance, but can be manipulated to address situational needs. For example, a teacher might decide to target an individual student's respectful behavior during transition times (e.g., gym class to academic instruction time, academic instruction time to outdoor recess). At each identified transition time, the student would be given a rating on a scale of 0 to 100 percent for the percent of time the student was showing respectful behavior during the given transition. This information could be communicated to the student as well as sent home to the parents each day. Although quantitative in nature, DBRs do not involve a highly systematic approach to data collection when compared to what is described in later sections of this chapter. Because of this, it may be the case that there is greater error evident in the ratings.

ZACK, PART 1 | Ms. Lawson notices that during sustained silent reading time, Zack is walking around the room a lot and disturbing students who are reading. When she tells him to return to his seat, he always does, but he does not seem to remain there for long. She decides to keep an eye on him and to document his behavior before developing a more systematic observation method to inform intervention development and progress monitoring.

She notes the context, antecedents, consequences, and specifics of Zack's behavior. Figure 9.1 contains the first three days of relevant notes.

This scenario highlights use of a nonsystematic observational technique (ABC event recording) as an initial approach to assessing behavior of an individual student. Why is this observation not considered systematic? See Part 2 for how Ms. Lawson decided to collect more information about Zach's behavior through a systematic observation.

FIGURE 9.1
Observations
of Zack's Behavior

Day:	Monday
Context:	Sustained Silent Reading—all students in their own seats. Zack was on task for activities other than independent seat work.
Antecedents:	I tell the class to take out their novels and begin reading where they had left off on Friday.
Behavior:	Zack takes out his novel, but does not open it. He fidgets a minute or two and then gets out of his seat, wanders around the room, talks to Cindy and Marie.
Consequences:	The girls initially ignore Zack, then tell him to go away. Zack giggles, and I scold him and tell him to return to his seat. Zack is falling behind in reading.
Day:	Tuesday
Context:	Science Activity Center—students working on time unit.
Antecedents:	I tell the class to write up their observations from their measurement experiments independently.
Behavior:	Zack requires help to find his lab book. After writing a few words, he gets up to sharpen his pencil but ends up strolling around the room. He talks to Cindy and Marie again.
Consequences:	The girls complain that Zack is bothering them again. Zack says he was just asking them about the project. I tell him to get back to work or he will get a time out. Zack is falling behind in science.
Note:	Zack was on task for activities other than independent seat work.
Day:	Wednesday
Context:	Sustained Silent Reading—all students in their own seats.
Antecedents:	I tell the class to take out their novels and begin reading where they had left off on Monday.
Behavior:	Zack puts his head down on the open pages of his novel. After about 5 minutes, he gets up and wanders around again.
Consequences:	Time out. Zack is far behind his peers in completing his novel.
Note:	Zack was again on task for activities other than independent seat work.

© 2013 Cengage Learning

9-3 Defining Behavior for Systematic Observations

Through systematic observations, behavior is usually defined in terms of its topography, its function, and its characteristics. The function that a behavior serves in the environment is not directly observable, whereas the characteristics and topography of behavior can be measured directly.

9-3a TOPOGRAPHY OF BEHAVIOR

Behavioral topography refers to the way in which a behavior is performed. For example, suppose the behavior of interest is holding a pencil to write, and we are interested in Patty's topography for that behavior. The topography is readily observable: Patty holds the pencil at a 45-degree angle to the paper, grasped between her thumb and index finger; she supports the pencil with her middle finger; and so forth. Paul's topography for holding a pencil is quite different. He holds the pencil between his great toe and second toe so that the point of the pencil is aimed toward the sole of his foot, and so forth.

9-3b FUNCTION OF BEHAVIOR

The **function of a behavior** is the reason a person behaves as he or she does, or the purpose the behavior serves. Obviously, the reason for a behavior cannot be observed; it can only be inferred. Sometimes, a person may offer an explanation of a behavior's function—for example, "I was screaming to make him stop." We can accept the explanation of the behavior's function if it is consistent with the circumstances, or we can reject the explanation of the function when it is not consistent with the circumstances or is unreasonable. Other times, we can infer a behavior's function from its consequences. For example, Johnny stands screaming at the rear door of his house until his mother opens the door, and then he runs into the backyard and stops screaming. We might infer that the function of Johnny's screaming is to have the door opened. Behavior typically serves one or more of five functions: (1) social attention/communication; (2) access to tangibles or preferred activities; (3) escape, delay, reduction, or avoidance of aversive tasks or activities; (4) escape or avoidance of other individuals; and (5) internal stimulation (Alberto & Troutman, 2006).

9-3c MEASURABLE CHARACTERISTICS OF BEHAVIOR

The measurement of behavior, whether individual behavior or a category of behavior, is based on four characteristics: duration, latency, frequency, and amplitude. These characteristics can be measured directly (Shapiro & Kratochwill, 2000).

Duration

Behaviors that have discrete beginnings and endings may be assessed in terms of their **duration**—that is, the length of time a behavior lasts. The duration of a behavior is usually standardized in two ways: average duration and total duration. For example, in computing average duration, suppose that Janice is out of her seat four times during a 30-minute activity, and the durations of the episodes are 1 minute, 3 minutes, 7 minutes, and 5 minutes. In this example, the average duration is 4 minutes—that is, $(1 + 3 + 7 + 5)/4$. To compute Janice's total duration, we add $1 + 3 + 7 + 5$ to conclude that she was out of her seat a total of 16 minutes. Often, total duration is expressed as a rate by dividing the total occurrence by the length of an observation. This proportion of duration is often called the "prevalence of the behavior." In the preceding example, Janice's prevalence is .53 (that is, 16/30).

Latency

Latency refers to the length of time between a signal to perform and the beginning of the behavior. For example, a teacher might ask students to take out their books. Sam's latency for that task is the length of time between the teacher's request and Sam's placing his book on his desk. For latency to be assessed, the behavior must have a discrete beginning.

Frequency

For behaviors with discrete beginnings and endings, we often count **frequency**—that is, the number of times the behaviors occur. When behavior is counted during variable time periods, frequencies are usually converted to rates. Using rate of behavior allows observers to compare the occurrence of behavior across different time periods and settings. For example, three episodes of out-of-seat behavior in 15 minutes may be converted to a rate of 12 per hour.

Alberto and Troutman (2005) suggest that frequency should not be used under two conditions: (1) when the behavior occurs at such a high rate that it cannot be counted accurately (for example, many stereotypic behaviors, such as foot tapping, can occur almost constantly) and (2) when the behavior occurs over a prolonged period of time (for example, cooperative play during a game of Monopoly).

Amplitude

Amplitude refers to the intensity of the behavior. In many settings, amplitude can be measured precisely (for example, with noise meters). However, in the classroom, it is usually estimated with less precision. For example, amplitude can be estimated using a rating scale that calibrates the amplitude of the behavior (for example, crying might be scaled as "whimpering," "sobbing," "crying," and "screaming"). Amplitude may also be calibrated in terms of its objective or subjective impact on others. For example, the objective impact of hitting might be scaled as "without apparent physical damage," "resulting in bruising," and "causing bleeding." More subjective behavior ratings estimate the internal impact on others; for example, a student's humming could be scaled as "does not disturb others," "disturbs students seated nearby," or "disturbs students in the adjoining classroom."

Selecting the Characteristic to Measure

The behavioral characteristic to be assessed should make sense; we should assess the most relevant aspect of behavior in a particular situation. For example, if Burl is wandering around the classroom during the reading period, observing the duration of that behavior makes more sense than observing the frequency, latency, or amplitude of the behavior. This is because it is the length of time away from his academic work that is the primary problem rather than the number of times he is away from his work. If Camilla's teacher is concerned about her loud utterances, amplitude may be the most salient characteristic to observe. If Molly is always slow to follow directions, observing her latency makes more sense than assessing the frequency or amplitude of her behavior. For most behaviors, however, frequency and duration are the characteristics measured.

9-4 Sampling Behavior

As with any assessment procedure, we can assess the entire domain if it is finite and convenient. If it is not, we can sample from the domain. Important dimensions for sampling behavior include the contexts in which the behaviors occur, the times at which the behaviors occur, and the behaviors themselves.

9-4a CONTEXTS

When specific behaviors become the targets of intervention, it is useful to measure the behavior in a variety of contexts. Usually, the sampling of contexts is purposeful rather than random. We might want to know, for example, how Jesse's behavior in the resource room differs from his behavior in the general education classroom. Consistent or inconsistent performance across settings and contexts can provide useful information about what events might set the occasion for the behavior. Differences between the settings in which a behavior does and does not occur can provide potentially useful hypotheses about **setting events** (that is, environmental events that set the occasion for the performance of an action) and **discriminative stimuli** (that is, stimuli that are consistently present when a behavior is reinforced and that come to bring out behavior even in the absence of the original reinforcer).[1] Bringing behavior under the control of a discriminative stimulus is often an effective way of modifying

---

[1] Discriminative stimuli are not conditioned stimuli in the Pavlovian sense that they elicit reflexive behavior. Discriminative stimuli provide a signal to the individual to engage in a particular behavior because that behavior has been reinforced in the presence of that signal.

it. For example, students might be taught to talk quietly (to use their "inside voice") when they are in the classroom or hallway.

Similarly, consistent or inconsistent performance across settings and contexts can provide useful information about how the consequences of a behavior are affecting that behavior. Some consequences of a behavior maintain, increase, or decrease behavior. Thus, manipulating the consequences of a behavior can increase or decrease its occurrence. For example, assume that Joey's friends usually laugh and congratulate him when he makes a sexist remark and that Joey is reinforced by his friends' behavior. If his friends could be made to stop laughing and congratulating him, Joey would probably make fewer sexist remarks.

9-4b TIMES

With the exception of some criminal acts, few behaviors are noteworthy unless they happen more than once. Behavioral recurrence over time is termed **stability** or **maintenance**. In a person's lifetime, there are almost an infinite number of times to exhibit a particular behavior. Moreover, it is probably impossible and certainly unnecessary to observe a person continuously during his or her entire life. Thus, temporal sampling is always performed, and any single observation is merely a sample from the person's behavioral domain.

Time sampling always requires the establishment of blocks of time, termed **observation sessions**, in which observations will be made. A session might consist of a continuous period of time (for example, one school day). More often, sessions are discontinuous blocks of time (for example, every Monday for a semester or during daily reading time).

Continuous Recording

Observers can record behavior continuously within sessions. They count each occurrence of a behavior in the observation session; they can time the duration or latency of each occurrence within the observation session.

When the observation session is long (for example, when it spans several days), continuous sampling can be very expensive and is often intrusive. Two options are commonly used to estimate behavior in very long observation sessions: 1) the use of rating scales to make estimates and 2) time sampling. In the first option, rating scales are used to estimate one (or more) of the four characteristics of behavior. Following are some examples of such ratings:

- *Frequency:* A parent might be asked to rate the frequency of a behavior. How often does Patsy usually pick up her toys—always, frequently, seldom, never?
- *Duration:* A parent might be asked to rate how long Bernie typically watches TV each night—more than 3 hours, 2 or 3 hours, 1 or 2 hours, or less than 1 hour?
- *Latency:* A parent might be asked to rate how quickly Marisa usually responds to requests—immediately, quickly, slowly, or not at all (ignores requests)?
- *Amplitude:* A parent might be asked to rate how much of a fuss Jessica usually makes at bedtime—screams, cries, begs to stay up, or goes to bed without fuss?

In the second observation option, duration and frequency are sampled systematically during prolonged observation intervals. Three different sampling plans have been advocated: whole-interval recording, partial-interval recording, and momentary time sampling.

Time Sampling

Continuous observation requires the expenditure of more resources than does discontinuous observation. Therefore, it is common to observe for a sample of times within an observation session.

In **interval sampling**, an observation session is subdivided into intervals during which behavior is observed. Usually, observation intervals of equal length are spaced equally through the session, although the recording and observation intervals need not be the same length. Three types of interval sampling and scoring are common.

1. In **whole-interval sampling**, a behavior is scored as having occurred only when it occurs throughout the entire interval. Thus, it is scored only if it is occurring when the interval begins and continues through the end of the interval.

2. **Partial-interval sampling** is quite similar to whole-interval recording. The difference between the two procedures is that in partial-interval recording, an occurrence is scored if it occurs during any part of the interval. Thus, if a behavior begins before the interval begins and ends within the interval, an occurrence is scored; if a behavior starts after the beginning of the interval, an occurrence is scored; if two or more episodes of behavior begin and end within the interval, one occurrence is scored.

3. **Momentary time sampling** is the most efficient sampling procedure. An observation session is subdivided into intervals. If a behavior is occurring at the last moment of the interval, an occurrence is recorded; if the behavior is not occurring at the last moment of the interval, a nonoccurrence is recorded. For example, suppose we observe Robin during her 20-minute reading period. We first select the interval length (for example, 10 seconds). At the end of the first 10-second interval, we observe if the behavior is occurring; at the end of the second 10-second interval, we again observe. We continue observing until we have observed Robin at the end of the 60th 10-second interval.[2]

Salvia and Hughes (1990) have summarized a number of studies investigating the accuracy of these time-sampling procedures. Both whole-interval and partial-interval sampling procedures provide inaccurate estimates of duration and frequency.[3] Momentary time sampling provides an unbiased estimate of the proportion of time that is very accurate when small intervals are used (that is, 10- to 15-second intervals). Continuous recording with shorter observation sessions is the better method of estimating the frequency of a behavior.

9-4c BEHAVIORS

Teachers and psychologists may be interested in measurement of a particular behavior or a constellation of behaviors thought to represent a trait (for example, cooperation). When an observer views a target behavior as important in and of itself, only that specific behavior is observed. However, when a specific behavior is thought to be one element in a constellation of behaviors, other important behaviors within the constellation must also be observed in order to establish the content validity of the behavioral constellation. For example, if taking turns on a slide were viewed as one element of cooperation, we should also observe other behaviors indicative of cooperation (such as taking turns on other equipment, following the rules of games, and working with others to attain a common goal). Each of the behaviors in a behavioral constellation can be treated separately or aggregated for the purposes of observation and reporting.

Observations are usually conducted on two types of behavior. First, we regularly observe behavior that is desirable and that we are trying to increase. Behavior of this type includes all academic performances (for example, oral reading or science knowledge) and prosocial behavior (for example, cooperative behavior or polite language). Second, we regularly observe behavior that is undesirable or may indicate a disabling condition. These behaviors are harmful, stereotypic, inappropriately infrequent, or inappropriate at the times exhibited.

---

[2] Time sampling has been made easier by various digital devices such as personal digital assistants (PDAs) and observation programs such as the Behavioral Observation of Students in Schools (Shapiro, 2003).

[3] Suen and Ary (1989) have provided procedures whereby the sampled frequencies can be adjusted to provide accurate frequency estimates, and the error associated with estimates of prevalence can be readily determined for each sampling plan.

- *Harmful behavior:* Behavior that is self-injurious or physically dangerous to others is almost always targeted for intervention. Self-injurious behavior includes such actions as head banging, eye gouging, self-biting or self-hitting, smoking, and drug abuse. Potentially harmful behavior can include leaning back in a desk or being careless with reagents in a chemistry experiment. Behaviors harmful to others are those that directly inflict injury (for example, hitting or stabbing) or are likely to injure others (for example, pushing other students on stairs or subway platforms, bullying, or verbally instigating physical altercations). Unusually aggressive behavior may also be targeted for intervention. Although most students will display aggressive behavior, some children go far beyond what can be considered typical or acceptable. These students may be described as hot-tempered, quick-tempered, or volatile. Overly aggressive behavior may be physical or verbal. In addition to the possibility of causing physical harm, high rates of aggressive behavior may isolate the aggressor socially.

- *Stereotypic behavior:* Stereotypic behaviors, or stereotypies (for example, hand flapping, rocking, and certain verbalizations such as inappropriate shrieks), are outside the realm of culturally normative behavior. Such behavior calls attention to students and marks them as abnormal to trained psychologists or unusual to untrained observers. Stereotypic behaviors are often targeted for intervention.

- *Infrequent or absent desirable behavior:* Incompletely developed behavior, especially behavior related to physiological development (for example, walking), is often targeted for intervention. Intervention usually occurs when development of these behaviors will enable desirable functional skills or social acceptance. Shaping is usually used to develop absent behavior, whereas reinforcement is used to increase the frequency of behavior that is within a student's repertoire but exhibited at rates that are too low.

- *Normal behavior exhibited in inappropriate contexts:* Many behaviors are appropriate in very specific contexts but are considered inappropriate or even abnormal when exhibited in other contexts. Usually, the problems caused by behavior in inappropriate contexts are attributed to lack of stimulus control. Behavior that is commonly called "private" falls into this category; elimination and sexual activity are two examples. The goal of intervention should be not to get rid of these behaviors but to confine them to socially appropriate conditions. Behavior that is often called "disruptive" also falls into this category. For example, running and yelling are very acceptable and normal when exhibited on the playground; they are disruptive in a classroom.

A teacher may decide on the basis of logic and experience that a particular behavior should be modified. For example, harmful behavior should not be tolerated in a classroom or school, and behavior that is a prerequisite for learning academic material must be developed. In other cases, a teacher may seek the advice of a colleague, supervisor, or parent about the desirability of intervention. For example, a teacher might not know whether certain behavior is typical of a student's culture. In yet other cases, a teacher might rely on the judgments of students or adults as to whether a particular behavior is troublesome or distracting for them. For example, are others bothered when Bob reads problems aloud during arithmetic tests? To ascertain whether a particular behavior bothers others, teachers can ask students directly, have them rate disturbing or distracting behavior, or perhaps use sociometric techniques to learn whether a student is being rejected or isolated because of his or her behavior. The sociometric technique is a method for evaluating the social acceptance of individual pupils and the social structure of a group: Students complete a form indicating their choice of companions for seating, work, or play. Teachers look at the number of times an individual student is chosen by others. They also look at who chooses whom.

For infrequent prosocial behavior or frequent disturbing behavior, a teacher may wish to get a better idea of the magnitude and pervasiveness of the problem before initiating a comprehensive observational analysis. Casual observation can provide information about the frequency and amplitude of the behavior; carefully noting the antecedents, consequences, and contexts may provide useful information about possible interventions if an intervention is warranted. If casual observations are made, anecdotal records of these casual observations should be maintained.

9-5 Conducting Systematic Observations

Systematic observations offer an approach to collecting data with greater objectivity than other observational methods. However, in order to ensure a high level of objectivity, several guidelines should be followed. In the sections that follow, we provide guidelines for preparing for observation, data gathering, summarizing the data, and setting criteria for evaluating observed performances. We also describe how technology can assist with several aspects of conducting systematic observations.

9-5a PREPARATION

Careful preparation is essential to obtaining accurate and valid observational data that are useful in decision making. Five steps should guide the preparation for systematic observation:

1. *Define target behaviors.*

   - Use definitions that describe behavior in observable terms.
   - Avoid references to internal processes (for example, understanding or appreciating).
   - Anticipate potentially difficult discriminations and provide examples of instances and noninstances of the behavior. Include subtle instances of the target behavior, and use related behaviors and behavior with similar topographies as noninstances.
   - State the characteristic of the behavior that will be measured (for example, frequency or latency).

2. *Select contexts.* Observe the target behavior systematically in at least three contexts: the context in which the behavior was noted as troublesome (for example, in reading instruction), a similar context (for example, in math instruction), and a dissimilar context (for example, in physical education or recess).

3. *Select an observation schedule.*

   - Choose the session length. In schools, session length is usually related to instructional periods or blocks of time within an instructional period (for example, 15 minutes in the middle of small-group reading instruction).
   - Decide between continuous and discontinuous observation. The choice of continuous or discontinuous observation will depend on the resources available and the specific behaviors that are to be observed. When very low-frequency behavior or behavior that must be stopped (for example, physical assaults) is observed, continuous recording is convenient and efficient. For other behavior, discontinuous observation is usually preferred, and momentary time sampling is usually the easiest and most accurate for teachers and psychologists to use. When a discontinuous observation schedule is used, the observer requires some equipment to signal exactly when observation is to occur. This can be facilitated through use of computer programs or audio recording devices. One student or several students in sequence may be observed. For example, three students can be

observed in a series of five-second intervals. A computer tablet or other audio device would signal a need to record every five seconds. On the first signal, Henry would be observed; on the second signal, Joyce would be observed; on the third signal, Bruce would be observed; on the fourth signal, Henry would be observed again; and so forth.

4. *Develop recording procedures.* The recording of observations must also be planned. When a few students are observed for the occurrence of relatively infrequent behaviors, simple procedures can be used. The behaviors can be observed continuously and counted using a tally sheet or a wrist counter. When time sampling is used, observations must be recorded for each time interval; thus, some type of recording form is required. In the simplest form, the recording sheet contains identifying information (for example, name of target student, name of observer, date and time of observation session, and observation-interval length) and two columns. The first column shows the time interval, and the second column contains space for the observer to indicate whether the behavior occurred during each interval. More complicated recording forms may be used for multiple behaviors and/or multiple students. When multiple behaviors are observed, they are often given code numbers. For example, "out of seat" might be coded as 1, "in seat but off task" might be coded as 2, "in seat and on task" might be coded as 3, and "no opportunity to observe" might be coded as 4. Such codes should be included on the observation record form. Figure 9.2 shows a simple form on which to record multiple behaviors of students. The observer writes the code number(s) in the box corresponding to the interval. Complex observational systems tend to

FIGURE 9.2
A Simple Recording Form for Three Students and Two Behaviors

Observer: *Mr. Kowalski*

Date: *2/15/11*

Times of observation: *10:15 to 11:00*

Observation interval: *10 sec*

Instructional activity: *Oral reading*

Students observed:

S1 = *Henry J.*

S2 = *Bruce H.*

S3 = *Joyce W.*

Codes:

1 = out of seat
2 = in seat but off task
3 = in seat, on task
4 = no opportunity to observe

	S1	S2	S3
1	____	____	____
2	____	____	____
3	____	____	____
4	____	____	____
5	____	____	____
.			
.			
.			
179	____	____	____
180	____	____	____

be less accurate than simple ones. Complexity increases as a function of the number of different behaviors that are assessed and the number of individuals who are observed. Moreover, both the proportion of target individuals to total individuals and the proportion of target behaviors observed to the number of target behaviors to be recorded also have an impact on accuracy. The surest way to reduce inaccuracies is to keep things relatively simple.

5. *Select the means of observation.* The choice of human observers or electronic recorders will depend on the availability of resources. If electronic recorders are available and can be used in the desired environments and contexts, they may be appropriate when continuous observation is warranted. If other personnel are available, they can be trained to observe and record the target behaviors accurately. Training should include didactic instruction in defining the target behavior, the use of time sampling (if it is to be used), and the way in which to record behavior, as well as practice in using the observation system. Training is always continued until the desired level of accuracy is reached. Observers' accuracy is evaluated by comparing each observer's responses with those of the others or with a criterion rating (usually a previously scored videotape). Generally, very high agreement is required before anyone can assume that observers are ready to conduct observations independently. Ultimately, the decision of how to collect the data should also be based on efficiency. For example, if it takes longer to desensitize students to an obtrusive video recorder than it takes to train observers, then human observers are preferred.

9-5b DATA GATHERING

Observers should prepare a checklist of equipment and materials that will be used during the observation and assemble everything that is needed, including an extra supply of recording forms, spare pens or pencils, and something to write on (for example, a clipboard or tabletop). When electronic recording (for example, a personal digital assistant or computer tablet) is used, equipment should be checked before every observation session to make sure it is in good working condition and fully charged. Also, before the observation session, the observer should check the setting to locate appropriate vantage points for equipment or furniture. During observation, care should be taken to conduct the observations as planned. Thus, the observer should make sure that he or she adheres to the definitions of behavior, the observation schedules, and recording protocols. Careful preparation can head off trouble.

As with any type of assessment information, two general sources of error can reduce the accuracy of observation. **Random error** in observational processes can result in over- or underestimates of behavior. **Systematic error** in observational processes reflects consistent errors that (once identified) can be predicted; they bias the data in a consistent direction—for example, behavior may be systematically overcounted or undercounted.

Random Error

Random errors in observation and recording usually affect observer agreement. Observers may forget behavior codes, or they may use the recording forms incorrectly. Because changes in agreement can signal that something is wrong, the accuracy of observational data should be checked periodically. The usual procedure is to have two people observe and record on the same schedule in the same session. The two records are then compared, and an index of agreement (for example, point-to-point agreement) is computed. Poor agreement suggests the need for retraining or for revision of the observation procedures. To alleviate some of these problems, we can provide periodic retraining and allow observers to keep the definitions and codes for target behaviors with them. Finally, when observers know that their accuracy is being systematically checked, they are usually more accurate. Thus, observers should not be told when they are being observed but should be told to expect their observations to be checked.

One of the most vexing factors affecting the accuracy of observations is the incorrect recording of correctly observed behavior. Even when observers have applied the criterion for the occurrence of a behavior correctly, they may record their decision incorrectly. For example, if 1 is used to indicate occurrence and 0 is used to indicate nonoccurrence, the observer might accidentally record 0 for a behavior that has occurred. Inaccuracy can be attributed to three related factors.

1. *Lack of familiarity with the recording system:* Observers definitely need practice in using a recording system when several behaviors or several students are to be observed. They also need practice when the target behaviors are difficult to define or when they are difficult to observe.

2. *Insufficient time to record:* Sufficient time must be allowed to record the occurrence of behavior. Problems can arise when using momentary time sampling if the observation intervals are spaced too closely (for example, 1- or 5-second intervals). Observers who are counting several different high-frequency behaviors may record inaccurately. Generally, inadequate opportunities for observers to record can be circumvented by electronic recording of the observation session; when observers can stop and replay segments of interest, they essentially have unlimited time to observe and record.

3. *Lack of concentration:* It may be difficult for observers to remain alert for long periods of time (for example, 1 hour), especially if the target behavior occurs infrequently and is difficult to detect. Observers can reduce the time that they must maintain vigilance by either taking turns with several observers or recording observation sessions for later evaluation. Similarly, when it is difficult to maintain vigilance because the observational context is noisy, busy, or otherwise distracting, electronic recording may be useful in focusing on target subjects and eliminating ambient noise. Inaccurate observation is sometimes attributed to lack of motivation on the part of an observer. Motivation can be increased by providing rewards and feedback, stressing the importance of the observations, reducing the length of observation sessions, and not allowing observation sessions to become routine.

Systematic Error

Systematic errors are difficult to detect through interobserver agreement procedures because they may likely influence all observers' ratings in the same direction at the same time. To minimize such error, three steps can be taken.

1. *Guard against unintended changes in the observation process.*[4] When assessment is carried out over extended periods of time, observers may talk to each other about the definitions that they are using or about how they cope with difficult discriminations. Consequently, one observer's departure from standardized procedures may spread to other observers. When the observers change together, modifications of the standard procedures and definitions will not be detected by examining interobserver agreement. Techniques for reducing changes in observers over time include keeping the scoring criteria available to observers, meeting with the observers on a regular basis to discuss difficulties encountered during observation, and providing periodic retraining.

2. *Desensitize students.* The introduction of equipment or new adults into a classroom, as well as changes in teacher routines, can signal to students that observations are going on. Overt measurement can alter the target behavior or the topography of the behavior. Usually, the pupil change is temporary. For example, when Janey knows that she is being observed, she may be more accurate, deliberate, or compliant. However, as observation becomes a part of the daily routine, students' behavior usually returns to what is typical for them.

---

[4] Technically, general changes in the observation process over time are called instrumentation problems.

This return to typical patterns of behavior functionally defines desensitization. The data generated from systematic observation should not be used until the students who are observed are no longer affected by the observation procedures and equipment or personnel. However, sometimes the change in behavior is permanent. For example, if a teacher was watching for the extortion of lunch money, Robbie might wait until no observers were present or might demand the money in more subtle ways. In such cases, valid data would not be obtained through overt observation, and either different procedures would have to be developed or the observation would have to be abandoned.

3. *Minimize observer expectancies.* Sometimes, what an observer believes will happen affects what is seen and recorded. For example, if an observer expects an intervention to increase a behavior, that observer might unconsciously alter the criteria for evaluating that behavior or might evaluate approximations of the target behavior as having occurred. The more subtle or complex the target behavior, the more susceptible it may be to expectation effects. The easiest way to avoid expectations during observations is for the observer to be blind to the purpose of the assessment. When video- or audiotapes are used to record behavior, the order in which they are evaluated can be randomized so that observers do not know what portion of an observation is being scored. When it is impossible or impractical to keep observers blind to the purpose, the importance of accurate observation should be stressed and such observation rewarded.

9-5c DATA SUMMARIZATION

Depending on the particular characteristic of behavior being measured, observational data may be summarized in different ways. When duration or frequency is the characteristic of interest, observations are usually summarized as rates (that is, the prevalence or the number of occurrences per minute or some other time interval). Latency and amplitude should be summarized statistically by the mean and the standard deviation or by the median and the range. All counts and calculations should be checked for accuracy.

9-5d CRITERIA FOR EVALUATING OBSERVED PERFORMANCES

Once accurate observational data have been collected and summarized, they must be interpreted. Behavior is interpreted in one of four ways.

1. A behavior's presence is an absolute criterion. Behaviors evaluated in this way include those that are unsafe, harmful, illegal, and taboo.

2. A behavior can be compared to the behavior of others. This comparison is generally called a normative comparison. Normative data may be available for some behaviors or, in some cases, data from behavior rating scales and tests. Social comparisons can be made using a peer whose behavior is considered appropriate. The peer's rate of behavior is then used as the standard against which to evaluate the target student's rate of behavior.

3. The social tolerance for a behavior can also be used as a criterion. For example, the degree to which different rates of out-of-seat behavior disturb a teacher or peers can be assessed. Teachers and peers could be asked to rate how disturbing is the out-of-seat behavior of students who exhibit different rates of behavior. In a somewhat different vein, the contagion of the behavior to others can be a crucial consideration in teacher judgments of unacceptable behavior. Thus, the effects of different rates of behavior can be assessed to determine whether there is a threshold above which other students initiate undesirable behavior.

4. Progress toward objectives or goals is frequently used as a standard with which to evaluate behavior. A common and useful procedure is graphing data against an aimline. As shown in Figure 9.3, an aimline connects a student's

FIGURE 9.3
Aimlines for Accelerating
and Decelerating
Behavior

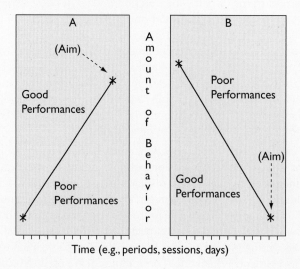

Time (e.g., periods, sessions, days)

measured behavior at the start of an intervention with the point (called an aim) representing the terminal behavior and the date by which that behavior should be attained. When the goal is to accelerate a desirable behavior (Figure 9.3A), student performances above the aimline are evaluated as good progress. When the goal is to decelerate an undesirable behavior (Figure 9.3B), student performances below the aimline are evaluated as good progress. Good progress is progress that meets or exceeds the desired rate of behavior change.

9-5e TECHNOLOGY AND OBSERVATION

Over the past few years, new technologies have been developed that can assist with systematic observations. Traditionally, systematic observations have required observers to pay close attention to both a stopwatch and the child they are observing, while at the same time recording their observations using paper and pencil. After collecting the data, the observer needed to develop a way to organize, analyze, summarize, and display the results. Handheld computer devices and associated applications help reduce several associated burdens on observers by automatically prompting observers at set time intervals to provide information and by allowing for automatic summarization and display of the information collected. For example, the Behavioral Observation of Students in Schools™ (BOSS™) is available as an application for tablet devices, and it prompts users at regular intervals to enter codes for both teacher and student behaviors. Data displays and reports can be generated automatically from the data that are entered.

Although these programs can facilitate more accurate, efficient, and less obtrusive collection and use of observational data, it remains important for users to critically examine programs they are considering for use, in order to determine if the programs will allow for appropriate data collection, analysis, and use. More specifically, it is important to ensure that a particular program will allow coding and analysis approaches that fit the nature of the behaviors intended to be observed. Unfortunately, we have encountered observational programs that involve coding of behaviors using methods that are not in alignment with the nature of the behavior to be observed. For example, they may be programmed to measure "off-task" behavior using a frequency count during an observational session rather than through use of a momentary time-sampling approach, when the latter would be more appropriate for the given behavior. It therefore remains essential for users to have solid foundational knowledge and skills associated with defining, measuring, summarizing, and evaluating behavior to make appropriate use of the associated technologies.

ZACK, PART 2 | Ms. Lawson has previously collected anecdotal information that suggests that Zack has a problem staying on task and in his seat when independent work is required, regardless of the subject matter or time of day. Before conducting systematic observations of Zack's *wanderings,* Ms. Lawson defines precisely what she means by wandering. She defines it as "walking around the classroom during seatwork assignments." She specifically excludes leaving his seat with her permission. She decides to count the frequency of both wandering and compliance during seatwork throughout the day for four days—Monday through Thursday. In addition, to have interpretive data, she decides to observe two other boys whom she considers generally well behaved but not exceptionally so.

Ms. Lawson decides to record the behavior unobtrusively by using a wrist counter and transferring the frequencies to a chart after the students have left for the day. Fortunately, she has a student teacher who can make simultaneous observations in order to check reliability. However, she must first meet with the student teacher to discuss the definition of wandering and the procedures used to record behavior. Because the target behavior was so easy to observe and the procedures so simple, reliability was not thought to be a major issue. She would like to determine the function of Zack's wandering. The likely functions seemed to be avoidance from an unpleasant task or social attention, but more information would be needed to reach a conclusion.

Each day, Ms. Lawson and her student teacher transferred the frequencies of the number of times Zack and the two comparison boys wandered the room. She calculated simple agreement and transferred her frequencies to the graph shown in Figure 9.4.

The results were as expected. Simple agreement between Ms. Lawson and her student teacher was always 100 percent. The boys who were observed for social comparison wandered an average of once per day, and Zack wandered an average of five times per day.

This scenario highlights the development and use of a systematic observation system to measure a student's problem behavior. Why would it be helpful to document in a quantitative fashion both Zack and Zack's peers' behavior? Why would it be helpful to have both Ms. Lawson and another person (in this case, her student teacher) observe at the same time and compare their results?

FIGURE 9.4
Comparison of Zack
and Peer Wanderings

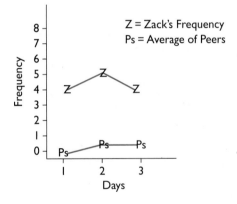

Chapter Comprehension Questions

Write your answers to each of the following questions and then compare your responses to the text.

1. What are three different dimensions on which observations can vary?
2. Describe two nonsystematic formats for conducting observations.
3. What characteristics of behavior (for example, amplitude) can be observed?
4. Explain the three ways in which behavior can be sampled.
5. What can an observer do to minimize or prevent errors in observations?

MONITORING STUDENT PROGRESS TOWARD INSTRUCTIONAL GOALS

LEARNING OBJECTIVES

10-1 Describe characteristics of effective progress monitoring.

10-2 Identify several existing progress monitoring tools.

10-3 Explain several approaches to setting instructional goals.

10-4 Explain several options for deciding when instructional changes are necessary.

10-5 Identify assessment frameworks that can be used along with progress monitoring to inform instructional changes.

STANDARDS ADDRESSED IN THIS CHAPTER

 CEC Initial Preparation Standards

Standard 4: Assessment

4.0 Beginning special education professionals use multiple methods of assessment and data-sources in making educational decisions.

Standard 5: Instructional Planning and Strategies

5.0 Beginning special education professionals select, adapt, and use a repertoire of evidence-based instructional strategies to advance learning of individuals with exceptionalities.

 CEC Advanced Preparation Standards

Standard 1: Assessment

1.0 Special education specialists use valid and reliable assessment practices to minimize bias.

 National Association of School Psychologists Domains

1 Data-Based Decision Making and Accountability

3 Interventions and Instructional Support to Develop Academic Skills

Knowing whether students have mastered a particular skill or have sufficient knowledge about a particular topic is important, but not enough. We also need to know whether students are gaining skills and knowledge at a rate that allows them to attain their instructional goals on schedule, so that ineffective instruction can be modified. We need to know when a student's rate of learning is particularly slow and then we must make instructional changes to speed up learning. We also need to know whether students are maintaining, integrating, and generalizing the skills and knowledge they have obtained in order to complete more complicated tasks. Systematic methods for monitoring progress toward both short- and long-term goals can help address these issues.

Progress monitoring is the collection of data that are used to determine the impact of instruction and intervention over a certain period of time. Not all progress monitoring is highly systematic and objective. For instance, teachers often use grades to determine whether students are making sufficient progress. Grades can be problematic for progress monitoring purposes because they often involve subjective evaluation and may or may not accurately represent a student's actual skills (consider situations in which parents actually do the homework *for* their sons and daughters!). End-of-unit tests may also be used to gauge progress, but this approach doesn't allow one to know if a student has maintained or is able to integrate their knowledge across multiple units. More systematic approaches to progress monitoring are necessary to gauge actual progress in skill development toward long-term goals, and are the focus of this chapter.

Progress monitoring can be used to measure progress toward grade-level standards and toward individual goals. Furthermore, it can be used to measure progress toward both academic and social-emotional goals. There are currently more tools available to monitor progress in the development of basic academic skills such as reading and math that meet basic levels of technical adequacy, compared to those tools available to address social-emotional development, and so we focus on those addressing academic skills in this chapter. Many of these progress monitoring tools can be effectively incorporated within a multi-tiered system of supports (MTSS) and Response-to-Intervention (RTI) models to support data-based decision making; more information on this is presented in Chapter 12 and in Chapter 21. They also can be used to help develop appropriate and specific annual individualized education program (IEP) goals for students receiving special education services, such that progress toward these goals can be appropriately monitored throughout the year and therefore instructional changes can be made as deemed necessary. More information about this is presented in Chapter 20. This chapter focuses on basic concepts associated with progress monitoring, provides examples of progress monitoring tools, and offers some helpful strategies for goal setting and decision making, in general.

Research has accumulated on the effects of systematic progress monitoring; this research indicates that systematic progress monitoring has a positive effect on student learning (Bolt, Ysseldyke & Patterson, 2010; Fuchs & Fuchs, 2002; Ysseldyke & Bolt, 2007). When these tools are used, teachers can have greater confidence in their knowledge of whether instruction and interventions are effective. They have information to know if an instructional change is needed in order for specific goals to be met.

10-1 Characteristics of Effective Progress Monitoring Tools

Although most teachers engage in some form of monitoring student progress, we argue that there are certain qualities that make some approaches better than others. In general, we consider more systematic approaches to be the most helpful. Here we highlight several qualities of effective progress monitoring tools.

1. *Involve direct measurement of basic skills.* By direct, we mean that the student is asked to demonstrate the targeted basic skill. Indirect measurement would incorporate perceptions and judgments about the student's skills rather than

asking the student to actually demonstrate the given skill. Typically, **probes** are developed and used; these involve a special testing format well suited to the direct assessment of student skills in a short amount of time. For example, a student may be asked to read a short passage out loud, or may be asked to complete a set of math computation problems.

2. *Include a representative sampling of knowledge and skills expected to be learned across the selected time period.* Instead of only measuring what has been taught, progress monitoring actually involves measurement of what has not yet been taught, so that one can detect the actual learning gains a student has made that correspond to the instruction provided. Contrary to other approaches to assessment, we expect students to earn low scores early on so that it is possible to detect learning gains over the course of a year. When only end-of-unit tests are used to examine student achievement, it is impossible to know whether a student actually learned anything. A student could earn perfect scores on every end-of-unit test across the course of one year and have actually learned nothing at all because the student already knew it all prior to receiving instruction. When only end-of-unit tests are used, it is also impossible to know whether a student has maintained knowledge of what was learned, because the student may forget what they had learned immediately after taking each end-of-unit test. By testing periodically using a representative sampling of what is expected to be learned by the end of the year, it is possible to track the extent to which a student is truly learning and maintaining new knowledge and skills that they are expected to know at the end of the year. Often, it can be helpful to monitor progress toward both short-term and long-term goals. In this case, multiple sets of probes might be developed, with one set including representation of what is expected to be learned across the entire year on each probe, and other sets including only representation of what is expected to be learned during separate units. For example, if an end-of-year goal is for a student to know both addition and subtract facts and also be able to add and subtract two-digit numbers with carrying and borrowing, and a short-term goal for the first month of the school year is for a student to know all one-digit addition facts, it would make sense to develop two sets of probes. One set would include several probes, each of which would include a representative sample of one-digit addition facts. The other set would include several probes, each of which would include a random selection of math computation problems, including some one-digit addition facts, some one-digit subtraction facts, some two-digit addition computation problems, and some two-digit subtraction problems. The first set of probes could be administered on a daily basis during the first month, to detect progress toward the end-of-month goal, and the second set of probes could be administered on a weekly basis throughout the year to detect progress toward the end-of-year goal. If, later in the year, a student was failing to maintain the earlier addition fact knowledge, it could be detected on the second set of probes, such that instruction could be altered to reteach the skill taught earlier. Read the Scenario in Assessment section for an applied example of how these different probe sets might be used.

3. *Use a probe that can be administered, scored, and interpreted quickly and frequently.* The more frequently a probe is administered, the sooner one can know when additional intervention is necessary. This can allow for highly responsive instruction and prevent students from practicing errors. In order for the measures to be administered and scored frequently, and not substantially infringe on instructional time, it is important for them to be as brief as possible, while still allowing for valid and reliable measurement. Many progress monitoring tools involve time limits to both facilitate measurement of fluency (which is often an important aspect of mastering a skill or set of knowledge) and ensure that the tool can be quickly administered.

4. *Use tools that are sensitive to change over time.* For effective progress monitoring, we need accurate measurement across the entire range of skills to be assessed, and sufficient items to detect small but important changes in knowledge. Many assessment tools are not designed with this notion in mind; instead, they are designed to be particularly good at distinguishing between satisfactory and unsatisfactory performances, and do not necessarily need to measure well across a variety of levels of achievement. Well-designed progress monitoring tools allow for accurate measurement across the range of skill levels expected for development across a given period of time.

10-2 Example Progress Monitoring Tools

Currently, there are a growing number of tools available that can be used for the purpose of progress monitoring of academic skills. Evidence for their technical adequacy has been accumulating. Several of these tools stem from the development of a set of procedures that are called "curriculum-based measurement"; others have developed out of computer-based technologies. We describe these two general types below.

10-2a CURRICULUM-BASED MEASUREMENT (CBM) APPROACHES

Developed by Dr. Stan Deno and others at the University of Minnesota Institute for Research on Learning Disabilities in the early 1980s (Deno, 1985), **curriculum-based measurement** involves a standardized set of procedures that allow one to directly measure important skills in a relatively short amount of time. CBM procedures have been developed for measuring student progress in reading, math, writing, and vocabulary.

Traditional CBMs have these characteristics:

- Direct measurement of student performance on basic skills.
- Random selection from grade-level instructional materials of things that are intended to be taught for a predetermined period of time (i.e., usually one school year).
- Common standardized, timed administration procedures.
- Common, preset objective scoring procedures.

Hosp, Hosp, & Howell (2007) describe three types of CBMs that vary in terms of the complexity of skill assessed and the purposes for which they are commonly used. These types include general outcome measures, skill-based measures, and subskill mastery measures.

General Outcome Measures (GOMs)

These tools measure important outcomes that require maintenance and coordinated use of many skills. The most commonly used general outcome measure is oral reading fluency, which requires students to read connected text that is selected to represent grade-level instructional material. Students are asked to read aloud from a passage for between one and three minutes and are scored based on the number of words they read correctly per minute. Oral reading requires students to coordinate many different foundational skills (e.g., knowledge of letter sounds, skill and automaticity with blending sounds to produce words, skill in identifying and correctly reading words that don't fit common alphabetic rules, etc.) and represents students' ability to read connected text, a skill that is fundamental to academic achievement. Several different but equivalent reading passages (sometimes referred to as "reading probes") are developed to represent the reading level that the student would be expected to attain by the end of the school year, so that the student's performance level can be assessed repeatedly to measure progress. GOMs are typically used to measure progress toward long-term goals, for example, for a student to read at a certain rate on a grade-level passage by the end of the school year.

Skill-Based Measures (SBMs)

Although similar to GOMs in that they may be created to measure progress toward an end-of-year goal, skill-based measures allow for measurement of skills in a slightly more isolated manner. They often require students to demonstrate some coordination of multiple subskills, but not to the same extent as GOMs. One commonly used SBM is math computation. CBM math computation probes are created by randomly selecting various types of problems with operational components (e.g., those including carrying and borrowing) that the student would be expected to learn and maintain by the end of the school year. The probes are created to be equivalent in difficulty level so that progress over time can be measured. Students are given a set period of time to complete the probe (this varies by grade level) and are scored in terms of the digits they write correctly in the given amount of time. An example of such a math computation probe is provided in the scenario provided with this chapter.

Subskill Mastery Measures (SMMs)

Subskill mastery measures (SMM) typically involve measurement of a subskill that is linked to SBMs or GOMs. For example, further analysis of results from an SBM may suggest that a student hasn't mastered single-digit subtraction. Several SMM probes could be developed that include just single-digit subtraction facts to measure student progress in learning that one subskill while the student receives additional instruction in single-digit subtraction. SMMs are typically used to measure progress toward short-term goals. An example of this kind of measure (a subtraction fact probe) is provided in the scenario included at the end of this chapter.

Although curriculum-based measurement tools can be used to measure a variety of important basic skills and to predict performance on other higher-level thinking tasks (i.e., reading comprehension, math problem solving), it is important to realize that they are not designed to measure higher-level thinking skills accurately. They can help us identify many students who are likely to struggle in developing these higher-level thinking skills without additional intervention; however, there are some important skills for which there are currently no CBMs available. For example, although CBM methods have been developed to monitor progress in the development of vocabulary terms associated with science, we are not aware of any common CBM methods for measuring student problem solving in science.

When CBM was first developed, educators were encouraged to develop their own equivalent passages or probes based on material that students in a particular grade were expected to cover across the course of the year. Each probe or passage would include randomly selected material that would be covered during the entire year. Using such self-generated measures could ensure appropriate alignment between the actual instructional materials being used and the materials used for the purpose of assessment. Some school professionals may continue to take this approach; however, it is very time consuming, and it is difficult to ensure that passages and probes generated in this way are of equivalent difficulty.

More recently, various off-the-shelf packages of CBM tools have been developed to help schools and teachers use CBM (e.g., AIMSweb, DIBELS Next, easyCBM, and several measures included in the Formative Assessment System for Teachers (FAST)). Descriptions of various published CBM packages and information on their associated technical characteristics can be found at the website for the National Center on Intensive Intervention.

Another option for developing CBMs is to use a program that helps generate probes that fit your particular classroom needs. The website of Intervention Central provides support for development of related materials through their CBM warehouse. Teachers can choose the types of skills they would like to measure, and the website creates probes that can allow for the measurement of progress in development of the selected skills. In the past decade, the increasing use and application of computer technology in schools has facilitated administration, scoring, management, and interpretation of data used for monitoring student progress. In fact, most published CBM packages now incorporate computer technology to assist with management and interpretation of data, in particular.

10-2b COMPUTER-ADAPTIVE APPROACHES

In addition to approaches that include CBM as their foundation, there are other technology-enhanced assessment systems that are increasingly being used to monitor student progress. Computer adaptive testing is a common feature of these systems. In **computer adaptive testing**, items are selected for administration as the student completes the test. If a student fails to correctly answer an item, an easier item is presented. If a student correctly answers an item, a more difficult item is presented. This continues until the student's pattern of performance on the test allows for an accurate estimate of his or her current level of skill. When developed to allow for progress monitoring, such tests can be administered repeatedly across the course of a year, and the student's scores compared to know whether he or she is making sufficient progress. Some examples of technology-enhanced progress monitoring tools that involve computer adaptive testing include Renaissance Learning's STAR Reading and STAR Math, Northwest Evaluation Association's Measures of Academic Progress (NWEA MAP), Curriculum Associates iReady, Scholastic Reading Inventory, several measures included in FAST, and the Smarter Balanced Assessment.

10-3 Setting Goals

Progress monitoring allows one to measure progress toward goals. In this section, we describe a variety of considerations for setting goals. In some cases the calculations and approaches are built in to the technology that is used for progress monitoring, but we believe that it is essential for school personnel to have a foundational understanding of various concepts involved in goal setting.

10-3a LEVEL VERSUS GROWTH

When using progress monitoring tools, school personnel often can examine two different dimensions of student achievement—level and growth. In the past, assessment in schools has focused primarily on examining performance levels. The notion here is that those students who meet an expected level of performance are making sufficient progress; those who are not meeting expected levels of performance are not making sufficient progress and may need additional intervention. As more technically adequate tools for progress monitoring have been developed and used, growth in achievement can be determined and used to inform decision making. This is helpful because it can allow us to know whether a student's rate of learning is higher than before, and can ultimately inform decisions about whether certain instructional techniques are more effective than others for selected students. In these situations, a **rate of improvement (ROI)**, which provides an index of growth, can be calculated. This is also sometimes described as a slope or growth rate. Although there are a variety of methods for calculating ROI, it generally can be understood as the difference between two scores obtained by a particular student at two different times, divided by the time that elapses between the two measurements. For example, if a student currently reads at 80 words correct per minute, and four weeks ago the student read at 70 words correct per minute, the student's ROI would be (80 words correct per minute—70 words correct per minute)/4 weeks = +2.5 words correct per minute per week. More advanced methods for calculating ROI can be derived using regression models and are sometimes incorporated within computer-based progress monitoring programs.

10-3b COMPARISON APPROACHES

In progress monitoring, the term benchmark is frequently used. Although benchmarks can refer to many different things, in general, a **benchmark** represents a reference standard for minimally accepted performance. Students who are described as "meeting benchmark" are often described as making adequate progress. Some existing progress monitoring tools include benchmarks that are connected to state or common core standards, such that a student's performance according to these standards can be evaluated (**standards-referenced benchmarks**). Other existing progress monitoring tools include benchmarks that are connected to information gathered on the performance and typical growth of thousands of same-grade peers from across the nation (**norm-referenced benchmarks**). Benchmarks can be very helpful in setting appropriate goals for groups of students and also individual students.

When specific benchmarks are not available, or if they are considered inappropriate for certain students, there are alternative methods for setting goals. When information on the performance and growth of similar peers is available, this information can be used. For example, for a student who is currently scoring in the 10th percentile or below, one might identify the end-of-year score associated with the 25th percentile for a given student's grade (i.e., bottom end of the "average" range) and use that to inform goal setting. Or, one might identify the typical growth rate of someone who is scoring at the 10th percentile, and set a goal for the student to have a growth rate that is higher than that growth rate.

A related term that is increasingly used in discussions of student progress, and that some publishers are providing to help with evaluating the progress of individual students, is **growth percentile**. An individual student's growth percentile is determined by comparing the target student's growth to the growth of similar peers who scored at the same initial level as the target student. A growth percentile score greater than 50 indicates above-average growth when compared to growth of the students who scored at the same level during initial testing. Growth percentiles can be helpful given that growth rates may vary substantially depending on the student's initial level of performance.

If information on peer performance is not available, or considered inappropriate for setting goals for a particular student, it may be appropriate to use the student's existing growth rate or ROI to inform goal setting. For instance, one might set a goal for an individual student's ROI to increase by a certain amount. However, it is important to recognize that in some cases, setting individual goals that are considerably higher than benchmark levels can be problematic. We have heard of situations where a teacher sets a very high oral reading fluency goal for high-achieving students, such that the goal is far beyond the threshold considered necessary for optimal comprehension. As a result of such a goal, a student might be coached to merely read faster, and not necessarily to read effectively. It is therefore important to keep in mind whether the given goal is an appropriate target for instruction or if a different focus is necessary.

10-3c MODERATE VERSUS AMBITIOUS GOALS

The above-mentioned approaches are intended to offer some guidance for goal setting, however, quite a bit of uncertainty remains. Although we know that setting goals and monitoring student progress toward those goals is important and helpful, we still are left wondering what levels are most appropriate. If goals are always set at such high levels that they are never met, this can become very frustrating for everyone involved (e.g., teachers, parents, students). However, if goals are set at levels that are not challenging, this may correspond to less effective teaching and learning in the long run. The challenge is to identify goals that are both possible to attain and high enough to stimulate the use of highly effective instruction.

Some technology-enhanced assessment programs offer goal-setting tools that allow teachers to select goals that are considered either "moderate" or "ambitious." A recent study involving such a tool showed that although most teachers selected moderate goals, those teachers who selected ambitious goals were notably more successful in terms of students meeting those goals (Ysseldyke, Stickney & Haas, 2015). Although more research in this area is needed, we think that it is likely in the best interests of students to set ambitious goals.

10-4 Knowing When to Make an Instructional Change

Because progress monitoring tools are brief, they may not have particularly strong levels of reliability. Scores often vary substantially from administration to administration, and that variation may be due to error rather than true differences in student achievement. When graphed over time (see Chapters 9 and Chapter 11 for more information on data displays), the associated student performance data may show up in the form of data points that are scattered, and it can be difficult to detect a trend. If someone were to make a decision based on only two initial data points that showed a decreasing trend, a corresponding decision to make an instructional change may be informed by estimates that are not accurate. To avoid making such mistakes, it is important to use specific guidelines for decision making that account for the high potential for error.

First, when making decisions about which progress monitoring tools to use, it is important to examine evidence that publishers provide for (a) reliability of the level scores, and (b) reliability of slope/growth or rate of improvement (ROI) scores. Higher reliability means that one can be more confident that the associated scores represent true achievement or growth differences. In addition, collecting more data can improve the reliability of the information that you have. In other words, it is often best to wait until you have administered the tool several times to make decisions about whether or not the student is making sufficient progress.

Over time, several rules of thumb have emerged for making decisions using CBM data. Similar to the approach noted in Chapter 9 for behavioral data, data from CBM administrations can be graphed over time and aimlines constructed that connect initial performance to a particular goal for level at a future point in time. When using this approach, a common rule of thumb is that one should wait until at least seven data points have been collected before examining the data to make a decision, Then, if the most recent four data points fall below the aimline, an instructional change is considered warranted. Application of these rules of thumb for CBM data are described again in Chapter 11, with a corresponding example of charted data. A slightly more sophisticated approach involves constructing a trendline, which involves calculating the equation for a best-fit line using the student performance data, and examining whether the associated trendline has a similar or greater slope than that represented by the aimline. Such a slope would suggest that the intervention is currently sufficient for helping the student meet the goal by the appointed time. If the trendline is less steep than the aimline or has a downward slope, this would indicate that an instructional change is needed.

With some technology-enhanced assessment tools, the current ROI (or growth rate or slope) may be calculated automatically within the assessment system, and so the current ROI can be compared to a desired ROI to know if an instructional change is needed. If the current ROI is lower than desired, an instructional change may be necessary. Other technology-enhanced programs may automatically prompt the teacher that an instructional change is necessary based on an internal formula that is applied to the student performance data that are collected.

10-5 Beyond Progress Monitoring

It is important to recognize that tools used for progress monitoring can provide information to indicate that an instructional change is needed, but they do not necessarily provide information on what change should be made. One mistake that we have heard some school professionals make is to focus on using a progress monitoring tool alone to make decisions about how to change instruction; for instance, some teachers who use oral reading fluency to monitor progress begin to focus entirely on interventions to develop reading fluency as opposed to doing a more careful analysis of other skills that the student might need in order to develop reading fluency (e.g., phonemic awareness, phonics, etc.). Although in some cases error analysis can be conducted using progress monitoring probes to pinpoint areas in need of additional instruction, in most cases, additional assessment is needed to identify what instructional changes are needed. Additional curriculum-based frameworks are available for diagnosing a student's difficulties in ways that can help in the design of effective interventions. Curriculum-based evaluation (Hosp, Hosp, Howell & Allison, 2014) and curriculum-based assessment (Gickling & Thompson, 1985) are broad assessment approaches that both include progress monitoring as well as additional assessment strategies that can help identify instructional targets. The Scenario in Assessment for this chapter provides an example of how progress monitoring data may prompt a teacher to collect more information to inform more targeted instruction on specific skills. Furthermore, some computer adaptive measures such as STAR Reading and STAR Math can provide statistical linkages to points in the curriculum based on learning hierarchies that may need to be the focus of instruction.

SCENARIO IN ASSESSMENT

JENNIE | Jennie is a third-grade student at Sycamore Elementary, where teachers use CBM math computation to track student progress over time. Sycamore Elementary has developed its norms based on the third-grade students who have been instructed at the school over the past three years, with norms developed for three administrations across the course of the year (fall, winter, spring). The computation probes have been developed to include math problems that address double- and triple-digit addition problems with carrying, double and triple-digit subtraction problems with borrowing, and double- and triple-digit multiplication with regrouping, given that these skills are taught during the third-grade year. Each probe contains problems representing each of these skills. Jennie's performance on the administration of the fall probe is shown below.

analysis indicates that Jennie has been attending Sycamore since kindergarten; interviews with her first- and second-grade teachers indicate that although they had taught some single- and double-digit addition and subtraction in those grades, they were not confident that Jennie had mastered those skills. An analysis of the errors Jennie made on the fall CBM probe suggests that although she has mastered her addition facts, she seems to have made a lot of mistakes on the subtraction facts. She also made many errors on the multiplication problems; however, that has not been taught yet, and so she is not expected to know those facts or how to compute using multiplication. To verify whether she knows her subtraction facts, a subskill mastery measurement is created to sample her subtraction fact fluency. Results indicate that she is not accurate with her subtraction facts (see her performance below).

12 correct digits (cd)

Jennie's Performance on a 3rd-grade Math Computation—Skill-Based Measure

```
   1
   48        53       478       676       345
 + 24      × 10     −  23     −  94     + 489
 ─────              ─────     ─────     ─────
   72                 434       692       834

   1
  934        63       933        76        15
 + 248     − 11     − 345     ×  99     +  89
 ─────     ────
  1182       42

  856        63       888       176        11
 + 124     × 14     ×  11     +  83     +  64

   34        68        90        76        11
 ×   0     − 14     −  34     −   5     +  39

  123        73       941       174        10
 −  23     − 18     − 342     ×   9     +  88

  934        33       633        76        15
 − 247     − 14     + 245     ×  39     +  69
```

7cd

```
   9        5        4        12       10
 − 2      − 1      − 2      −  2      −  4
 ───      ───      ───      ────      ───
   4        3        2        11        5

   8       13        8        17       10
 − 5      − 2      − 2      −  9      −  3
 ───      ────      ───      ────      ───
   3       10        5        16       13

   9        8        9        15        6
 − 6      − 1      − 3      −  4      −  4
          ───      ───      ────      ───
            7        5         1        2

   4        5        7        17       10
 − 2      − 3      − 2      −  2      −  6

   8        5        4        13       13
 − 1      − 5      − 2      −  2      −  9

   4        2        4        19       10
 − 4      − 1      − 2      −  9      −  4

   6       11        4        12       14
 − 2      − 1      − 2      −  4      −  7
```

Her score of 12 digits correct per minute is below the 25th percentile (15 digits correct per minute) on the norms her school has developed. She has therefore been targeted for further analysis to determine if additional support is necessary. Further

She answered only 7 digits correct per minute on this task. As a result, a subtraction fact intervention is put in place for her. Additional mastery measurement subtraction fact probes are developed to measure progress on a weekly basis toward the short-term goal of

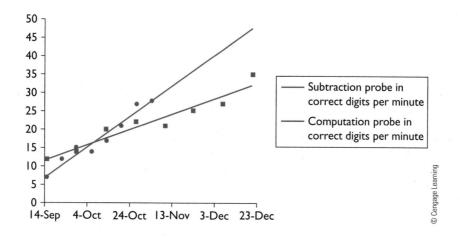

her mastering subtraction facts. Her short-term goal is for her to score 27 digits correct per minute on a single-digit subtraction fact probe by November 1 (an expected growth rate of approximately two digits correct per minute per week, which represents a growth rate that is 0.5 digits correct per minute per week higher than the typical growth rate of students at her level). A long-term goal of having her make effective use of her subtraction knowledge on math computation CBMs is also set; this is for her to score at the 25th percentile compared to the third-grade level norms on the winter CBM math computation probe, which is a score of 35 digits correct per minute. Her progress toward this goal is monitored every two weeks. With the subtraction fact intervention, Jennie is able to steadily improve in her subtraction fact fluency. The results are seen to transfer to her math computation score such that she reaches the 25th percentile mark by the winter benchmark (see the graph of her progress above).

This scenario highlights use of CBM for making decisions about the need for additional academic support, as well as to set appropriate goals and monitor progress. Why was it helpful to use both a skill-based measure and a subskill mastery measure to examine Jennie's progress?

Chapter Comprehension Questions

Write your answers to each of the following questions and then compare your responses to the text.

1. What are the defining characteristics of curriculum-based measurement (CBM)?

2. Describe three different types of CBM. For what purposes is each used?

3. Describe two ways that computers can support progress monitoring and associated data analysis efforts.

4. What are two ways to set goals using CBM? Provide an example of each.

5. What are some potential problems in using progress monitoring tools to inform the nature of instructional changes one might make?

MANAGING CLASSROOM ASSESSMENT

LEARNING OBJECTIVES

11-1 Describe three characteristics of effective testing programs.

11-2 Explain preparation guidelines associated with three different types of assessments.

11-3 Understand various ways to make decisions using charts that display progress monitoring data.

11-4 Describe how computers can assist with managing classroom assessment data.

STANDARDS ADDRESSED IN THIS CHAPTER

 CEC Initial Preparation Standards

Standard 4: Assessment
4.0 Beginning special education professionals use multiple methods of assessment and data-sources in making educational decisions.

Standard 5: Instructional Planning and Strategies
5.0 Beginning special education professionals select, adapt, and use a repertoire of evidence-based instructional strategies to advance learning of individuals with exceptionalities.

 CEC Advanced Preparation Standards

Standard 1: Assessment
1.0 Special education specialists use valid and reliable assessment practices to minimize bias.

 National Association of School Psychologists Domains
1 Data-Based Decision Making and Accountability

Hurst Photo/Shutterstock.com

Except for individual evaluations conducted by specialists such as school psychologists and speech and language pathologists, classroom teachers are responsible for most testing conducted in schools. When the state requires all students to complete standards-based assessments, teachers may be the ones who administer these tests in their classrooms. Beyond these mandated assessments, teachers routinely test to monitor student progress and ascertain the degree of student achievement on instructional units. As schools move toward implementation of Multi-Tiered System of Supports (MTSS) models, teachers become increasingly responsible for keeping track of data on student response to instruction and intervention, and this requires careful management and coordination of information. Finally, some teachers are involved in administering formal tests to individual students for the purpose of determining eligibility for special education services and need to know how to follow very specific administration rules associated with those tests.

Assessment should be an easy and natural part of classroom life. Teachers should plan their testing programs and procedures at the beginning of the year. This chapter provides basic principles and guidelines for preparation and management of assessment information collected in classrooms.

11-1 Characteristics of Effective Assessment Programs

Good testing programs have three characteristics: efficiency, ease, and integration.

- *Efficiency.* Time spent in testing (including administration, scoring, interpretation, and record keeping) is time not spent teaching and learning. Therefore, good assessment plans call for the least assessment necessary for decision making. This includes consideration of the amount of time both students and teachers must spend on assessment. Efficiency considerations are leading to greater emphasis on group testing, computer adaptive testing, and the use of technology systems to monitor and report frequently on student progress.

- *Ease.* Easy testing programs from the teacher's perspective are those that minimize teacher time and effort in all aspects of testing (that is, necessary training, preparation, administration, scoring, and record keeping). The easiest testing programs are those that can be carried out by technology devices (computers, responders, smartphones, tablets, etc.), paraprofessionals, or students. Easy testing programs from the student's perspective are those with which the student feels familiar and comfortable, and that he or she has confidence in. It is important to set expectations about how assessment works in the classroom early in the school year and reinforce those expectations periodically.

- *Integration.* Assessment activities can be integrated into the school day in two ways. First, teachers can monitor pupil performance during instructional activities. For example, basic skill drills can be structured to provide useful assessment information about accuracy and fluency, or computers can be used to manage instruction. Second, teachers can establish a regular schedule for brief assessments, such as daily one-minute oral reading probes. Making assessments frequent and part of the regular classroom routine has the added benefit of reducing student anxiety associated with higher stakes testing.

11-2 Preparing for and Managing Testing

Slightly different procedures may be needed to prepare for different types of testing (i.e., mandated testing, progress monitoring, formal individualized testing); we have highlighted suggestions according to each type below.

11-2a MANDATED TESTING

When districtwide and statewide assessments are conducted, they generally occur within classrooms. Teachers usually have advanced notice about when various mandated tests will occur, how long they will take, and how they are to be administered. Teachers should become thoroughly familiar with expectations for their role in these assessments, and they should be thoroughly prepared with backup supplies of pencils, timers, and answer sheets (if allowed). Teachers should also provide their students with advanced knowledge in such a way as to reduce anxiety about these tests without diminishing their importance. For example, it is a good idea to tell students that all students in the district or all students in their grade are taking the test, and that the tests are designed to help the district do a good job teaching all of the students.

In addition to these general considerations, teachers should check all of their students' individualized educational programs (IEPs) to verify the kinds of assessments that each student will take and what, if any, adaptations, accommodations, and alternative assessments must be provided.

Currently some mandated testing programs are implemented using computers. In these cases, it is important that the students are fluent in using the computers on which they will be tested, and know how to access and use various features that may be needed as part of the accommodations they are supposed to receive.

11-2b PROGRESS MONITORING

Even the most extensively researched curriculum and teaching techniques may not work with every student. Moreover, there is currently no way to discern the students for whom the curriculum or methods will be effective from those for whom the educational procedures will not work. The only way to know if educational procedures are effective is to determine if they were effective. That is, we can know if what we have done has worked, but we cannot know this before we do it. Thus, teachers are faced with a choice: They can either teach and hope that their instruction will work, or they can teach and measure the extent to which their instruction has worked. We advocate the latter approach.

Monitoring student achievement allows teachers the chance to reteach unlearned material, provide alternative content or methods for those students who have not learned, or get additional help for them. Moreover, student progress should be monitored frequently enough to allow early detection and error correction. Errors that are caught late in the learning process are much more difficult to correct because students have practiced the incorrect responses. Finally, the monitoring procedures must be sensitive to incremental changes in student achievement. Of all the ways in which teachers can monitor student learning, we prefer continuous (that is, daily or several times per week) and systematic monitoring rather than summative monitoring (that is, assessing student knowledge after instruction of large amounts of content or after several weeks of instruction).

Lack of time is the primary reason given by teachers for not measuring frequently or well. However, advanced planning and extra work in the beginning will save countless hours during the school year. Teachers can do five things to make assessment less time consuming for themselves and their students:

1. Establish testing routines
2. Create assessment stations
3. Prepare and organize materials
4. Maintain assessment files
5. Involve other adults, students, and technology in the assessment process when possible

An example of how these strategies could be applied in practice is provided in the Scenario in Assessment provided below.

Establish Routines

Establishing a consistent testing routine brings predictability for students. If students know that they will be taking a brief vocabulary test in Spanish class each Friday, or that a timer will be used for the two-minute quiz at the start of math class every Tuesday and Thursday, they will require progressively fewer cues and less time to get ready to take the quizzes. For younger students, it helps to use the same cues that a quiz is coming. For example, "Okay students, it's time for a math probe. Clear your desks except for a pencil." Similarly, if the test-taking rules are the same every time, student compliance becomes easier to obtain and maintain. For example, when teaching an assessment course to college students, we do not allow them to wear baseball caps (some write notes inside the bill); we allow them to use calculators (but not those with alphanumeric displays because notes can be programmed into them); students must sit in every other seat so that there is no one to their immediate left or right; and we do not return the exams to students (to allow the reuse of questions without fear of students having a file of previous questions), although we do go over the exam with students individually if they wish. After the first exam or two, students know the rules and seldom need to be reminded.

To the extent feasible, the same directions and cues should be used. For example, a teacher might always announce a quiz in the same way: "Quiz time. Get ready." Directions for specific tests and quizzes may vary by content. For example, for an oral reading probe, the teacher may say, "When I say 'start,' begin reading at the top of the page. Try to read each word. If you don't know the word, you can skip it or I'll read it for you. At the end of a minute, I'll say 'stop.'" A teacher can use similar directions for a math probe: "Write your name at the top of the paper. When I say 'start,' begin writing your answers. Write neatly. If you don't know an answer, you can skip it. At the end of a minute, I'll say 'stop.'"

Create Assessment Stations

An assessment station is a place where individual testing can occur within a classroom. An assessment station should be large enough for an adult and student to work comfortably and be free of distractions. Stations are often placed in the back of the classroom, with chairs or desks facing the back wall and portable dividers walling off the left and right sides of the workspace.

Assessment stations allow classroom testing to occur concurrently with other classroom activities. They allow a teacher or an aide to test students or students to self-test. Student responses can be corrected during or after testing.

Prepare Assessment Materials

The first consideration in preparing assessment materials is that the assessment must match the instruction. Unless there is a good match between what is taught and what is tested, test results will lack validity. The best way for assessments to match curriculum is to use the actual content and formats that are used in instruction. For example, to assess mastery of addition facts that have been taught as number sentences, one would assess using number sentences, as shown in Figure 11.1.[1]

FIGURE 11.1	**How Addition Facts Are Taught**		
Matching Math Content in Assessment	2 + 5 = _____	6 + 3 = _____	4 + 4 = _____
	How Addition Facts Should Be Tested		
	6 + 3 = _____	4 + 4 = _____	2 + 5 = _____
	How Addition Facts Should Not Be Tested		
	6 + _____ = 9	4	What are 2 and 5? _____
		+4	

© 2013 Cengage Learning

[1]Obviously, if testing is done to assess generalization or application of material, test content and perhaps formats will vary from those used during instruction.

If generic assessment devices are already available (see examples of such devices in Chapter 10, Monitoring Student Progress Toward Instructional Goals), there is no reason not to use them if they are appropriate. By appropriate, we mean that they represent measurement of the skills and knowledge that are part of the student's instruction. One advantage to using existing assessment devices is that many have been developed to ensure that the probes are of similar difficulty level across a year, such that they can truly measure student progress over time. Now that Internet access is practically universal, teachers need only to go to their favorite search engine to find reading, writing, or math probes. There are numerous sites that generate a variety of probes (for example, easy CBM and Intervention Central). Computer software can also be used to facilitate probe and quiz preparation (for example, Microsoft Word has a feature that provides summary data for print documents, including the number of words and the reading level). Any spreadsheet program allows the interchange of rows and columns so that a practically infinite number of parallel probes for word reading or math calculations can be created.

There is no need for teachers to create new assessment materials when they test the same content during subsequent semesters unless, of course, their instruction has changed enough to necessitate changing their tests. Tests, probes, projects, and other assessment devices take time to develop, and it is more efficient to use them again rather than start over. Like any other teaching material, tests may require revision. Sometimes a seemingly wonderful story starter used to measure writing skills does not work well with students. It is generally better to start the revision process while the problems or ideas are fresh—that is, immediately after a teacher has noticed that the tests are not working well. Sometimes all that is needed is a comment on the test that documents the problem. For example, "Students didn't like the story starter." Sometimes the course of action is obvious: "Words are too small—need bigger font and more space between words." If possible, teachers should make the revisions to the assessment materials as soon as they have a few moments of free time. Otherwise, the problems may be forgotten until the next time the teacher wants to use the test.

Organize Materials

When assessment materials have been developed and perhaps revised, the major management problem is retrieval—both remembering that there are materials and where those materials are located. This problem is solved by organizing materials and maintaining a filing system.

One organizational strategy is to use codes. Teachers commonly color code tests and teaching materials. For example, instructional and assessment materials for oral reading might be located in folders with red tabs, whereas those for math may have blue tabs. Within content areas or units, codes may be based on instructional goals. For example, in reading, a teacher may have 10 folders with red tabs for regular C–V–C (consonant–short vowel–consonant) words. Student materials may be kept in different locations, such as a filing cabinet for reading probes with different drawers for different goals. Once the materials have been organized, teachers need only resupply their files at the beginning of each year (or semester in secondary schools).

Involve Others or Technology

The process of assessment mainly requires professional judgment at two steps: (1) creating the assessment device and the procedures for its administration and (2) interpreting the results of the assessment. The other steps in the assessment process are routine and require only minimal training, not extensive professional expertise. Thus, although teachers must develop and interpret assessments, other adults or the students can be trained to conduct the assessments. Getting help with the actual administration of a test or probe frees teachers to perform other tasks that require professional judgment or skills, while still providing the assessment data needed to guide instruction. And, as noted, technology devices now can be used to generate tests, monitor progress, provide teachers with assessment results, and serve as data warehouses. More on computer applications is provided later in this chapter.

11-2c FORMAL TESTING

Educators are sometimes expected to administer more formalized individual testing for students to determine if they are eligible for special education services. Descriptions and reviews of tests that are sometimes used for this purpose are provided in later chapters of this book. Although we urge the selection and use of tests that are particularly easy to administer, some of these tests have very specific rules that are important to learn and follow in order to ensure that the scores obtained are accurate. Because of this, we provide guidance in this section on preparing to administer formal tests. It is important to note that although we focus this section on formal testing, there are some progress monitoring tools out there that, similarly, have very specific administration rules for which the following guidance would likely be helpful, as well.

Training

Typically, it is only possible to learn how to administer one or two formal tests during pre-service education assessment coursework. When learning to administer a new formal test or a new edition of a test, it can be wise to seek out formal training through a course or workshop on the particular test. In fact, some test authors require examiners to participate in special training workshops and seminars to be eligible to administer their test. Often you can find out about specific training opportunities in your area by contacting test publishers or visiting their websites.

Read the Administration Manual Carefully

With most formal tests, there are either sections within a comprehensive manual or a separate administration manual that provide instructions for administration. It is very important to carefully read and follow these instructions to avoid making mistakes that result in inaccurate scores (and correspondingly misinformed decisions!). Three aspects to pay particular attention to are (a) basal and ceiling rules, (b) prompting and querying instructions, and (c) scoring rules. These are often different for different tests, and may be different for different subtests on the same test, and so it is important to learn to keep them straight.

Basal and ceiling rules Many formal tests have basal and ceiling rules that are intended to promote efficient testing. They are designed to balance the need to (a) collect enough information to be sure that an accurate score can be calculated for an individual student and (b) avoid requiring students to complete items that are very easy or very difficult. Many formal tests will provide a suggested starting point for each subtest, based on the child's age or grade. A **basal rule** provides information on how many consecutive items a student must correctly answer in order for earlier items (that are consequently not administered) to be scored as correct. For example, if a test has a basal rule of "5," then the examiner will begin with the suggested starting point, and if the student answers any of the first five items incorrectly, the examiner must administer items before the start point until there are five consecutive items (according to the test order, not administration order) that the student answers correctly. A **ceiling rule** provides information on how many consecutive items a student must incorrectly answer in order for later items (that are then not administered) to be scored as incorrect. It can be tricky to accurately follow these rules when first testing, and so we advise that if test forms do not already provide reminders about basal and ceiling rules, examiners jot down reminder notes about these rules.

Timing, prompting and querying rules Formal tests often have specific directions about timing, prompting, and querying for more information that are to be used when either (a) the student doesn't respond in a timely fashion or (b) the student provides a partially correct answer but not an answer that would meet the requirements for full credit. Obviously, if these directions are not carefully followed, this may influence the student's response and corresponding score. For example, if the directions indicate a student may be given only up to 30 seconds to answer an item, and the examiner provides more time, the student may perform better, but the corresponding comparisons to the norms would be inappropriate because the student was given a timing advantage. Similarly, if an examiner decides to prompt for more information under circumstances that the manual indicates it is not appropriate to do so, the student's score may similarly be problematic. It is therefore very important to know the timing requirements, and the conditions under which various prompts and queries are expected to be given.

Scoring rules When basal and ceiling rules are applied, it is important to appropriately score those items below the obtained basal and above the obtained ceiling. A common rookie examiner mistake is forgetting to include the items below the basal in the calculation of a total score; this can result in a grossly inaccurate score! In addition to carefully attending to basal and ceiling scoring rules, it is important to pay close attention to the scoring of items for which partial credit may be available, and those that may involve somewhat more subjective criteria. For example, some subtests may provide scoring guides that show how example responses should be scored. It is very important to carefully compare the student's exact response to these example results, to determine what point value is most appropriate.

Practice administration

Prior to administering a formal test for the purpose of decision making in schools, it can be helpful to conduct practice administrations with a child or adolescent with whom the test will not be administered and used. Furthermore, it can be helpful to practice scoring mock protocols and receive feedback on your scoring from someone who knows the test well.

Observations during formal testing

During formal test administration to individual students, it is important to observe student behavior to document whether adequate effort is being expended. More specifically, the examiner should watch for student behaviors such as (a) spending a reasonable amount of time on each item or task, (b) following directions provided without needing substantial prompting, and (c) staying alert throughout the test administration session. It is helpful to provide documentation of behaviors the student exhibits that suggest he or she was putting forth adequate effort. If the student's behavior suggests the student is not putting forth a reasonable amount of effort, it may be necessary to take a break from testing and return at a later time (although note that breaks should only occur between, and not during, subtests). If repeated attempts fail to result in the student putting forth a reasonable amount of effort, it is important to document the concern and use caution in interpreting the resulting score.

11-3 Data Displays

After performances are scored, they must be recorded. Although tables and grade books are commonly used, they are not nearly as useful as charts and graphs. These displays greatly facilitate interpretation and decision making. There are two commonly used types of charts for displaying progress data on individual students: equal-interval and standard celeration charts. Both types of chart share common graphing conventions as shown in Figure 11.2.

- The vertical (y) axis indicates the amount of the variable (that is, its frequency, percent correct, rate of correct responses, and so forth). The axis is labeled (for example, correct responses per minute).

- The horizontal (x) axis indicates time, usually sessions or days. The axis is labeled (for example, school days).

- Dots represent performances on specific days; a dot's location on the chart is the intersection of the day or session in which the performance occurred and the amount (for example, rate) of performance.

SCENARIO IN ASSESSMENT

PHIL SELF-ADMINISTERS A PROBE

After instruction and guided practice, Phil knows how to take his reading probes. He goes to the assessment center and follows the steps posted on the divider.

1. He checks his probe schedule and sees that he is supposed to take the two-minute oral reading probe No. 17.
2. He goes to the file, gets a copy of the probe, and lays it face up on the desk. He inserts a blank audio cassette into the tape recorder and rewinds to the beginning of the tape.
3. After locating the three-minute timer on the desk, he starts recording.
4. He says the probe number and then sets the timer for two minutes.
5. He reads aloud into the tape recorder until the timer rings.

6. He stops the tape recorder, ejects it, and places it in the inbox on his teacher's desk.

Phil then returns to his seat and begins working. At a convenient time, his teacher or the aide gets a copy of the probe that Phil read, slides it into an acetate cover, notes errors on the cover, tallies the errors, calculates Phil's scores, and enters them on his chart. Then the teacher rewinds Phil's tape, wipes the acetate cover clean, and places the probe back into the file for reuse.

This scenario highlights the ease with which classroom progress monitoring data can be collected when appropriate procedures and routines are developed and applied. To what extent would this approach save the teacher time compared to the time necessary to administer the probe directly to the student?

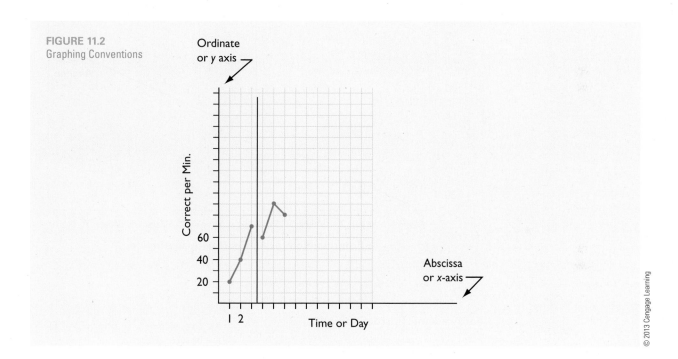

FIGURE 11.2
Graphing Conventions

© 2013 Cengage Learning

- Dots on a single graph should represent only material that is of a similar difficulty level; separate graphs are necessary to represent material of different difficulty levels (e.g., when a student switches from being monitored using first-grade passages to being monitored using second-grade passages, a new graph should be created).

- Vertical lines separate different types of performances or different intervention conditions.

- Charts contain identifying data, such as the student's name and the objective being measured.

Equal-interval charts are most likely to be familiar to beginning educators. On these charts, the differences between adjacent points are additive and equal. The difference between one and two correct is the same as the difference between 50 and 51 correct. Figures 11.3, 11.4, and 11.5 are equal-interval graphs. Figure 11.3 shows how charting student data on a graph helped a teacher know when to alter an intervention for a student. Figure 11.4 shows how a teacher was able to compare student responses to two different interventions using a graph. Figure 11.5 shows how a teacher could compare the extent to which an intervention was effective for addressing several different student behaviors.

Standard celeration charts (also called standard behavior charts, semilogarithmic charts, or seven-cycle charts) are based on the principle that changes (increases or decreases) in the frequency of behavior within a specified time (for example, number of correct responses per minute) are multiplicative, not additive. That is, the change from one correct to two correct is 100 percent and is the same as the change from 50 to 100. On daily celeration charts, the abscissa (*x*-axis) is divided into 140 days (that can be used as sessions). On the ordinate (*y*-axis), frequencies range from one per day to thousands per minute. A line from the bottom left corner of the chart to the top right corner indicates behavior that has doubled each day or session; any line parallel to that diagonal line similarly indicates behavior that has doubled each day or session. A line from the top left corner of the chart to the bottom right corner indicates that the behavior has reduced

FIGURE 11.3
Alterative Ways of
Presenting Data

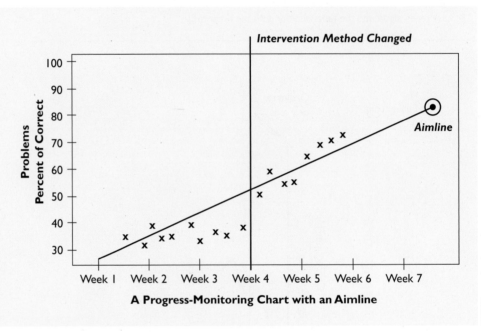

A Progress-Monitoring Chart with an Aimline

© 2013 Cengage Learning

FIGURE 11.4
Alternative Ways of
Presenting Data

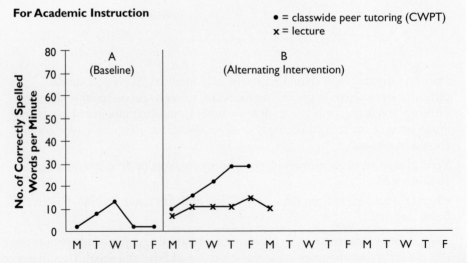

Goal: Improve Robin's spelling accuracy.

Intervention: Alternate between classwide peer tutoring and lecture formats to determine which is most effective.

© 2013 Cengage Learning

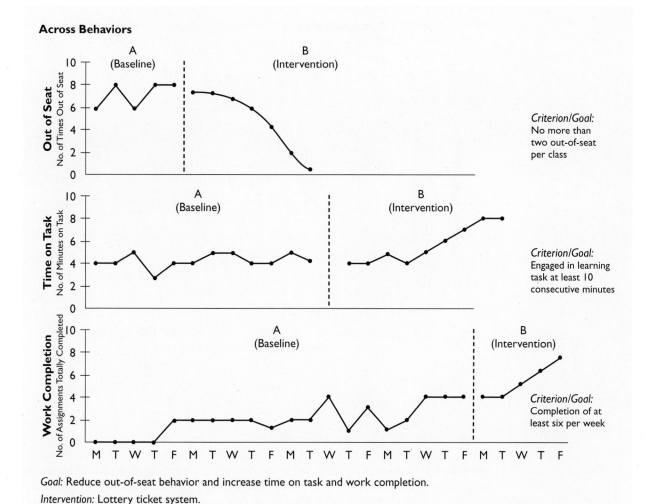

FIGURE 11.5
Alternative Ways of
Presenting Data

by half each day or session, and any diagonal line that is parallel to that line also indicates the behavior has halved each day or session. Figure 11.6 is a standard celeration day chart.

Although standard celeration charts allow one to see percentage change directly, it does not appear to matter which type of graph is used in terms of student achievement (Fuchs & Fuchs, 1987).

Graphing student performance data can help identify when instructional changes are needed. As noted in Chapter 10, results from brief tests such as those frequently used to monitor progress can fluctuate, making it difficult to know whether the student is making progress toward meeting a goal. Sometimes fluctuations in performance are due to variations in the difficulty level of the test presented, sometimes they are due to student characteristics unrelated to what the test is intended to measure (for example, interest level and concentration level), and sometimes they are due to changes in student skills and knowledge, which are what you are intending to detect.

How can we therefore truly know whether the student is failing to make progress? By charting progress monitoring data, several decision-making strategies can be applied to help make appropriate decisions.

Four-point rule: Once a goal or aimline has been drawn, each data point collected after the determination of initial performance should be plotted soon after each probe is administered. A common rule of thumb is to wait to make a decision until after at least

FIGURE 11.6
Standard Celeration
Chart

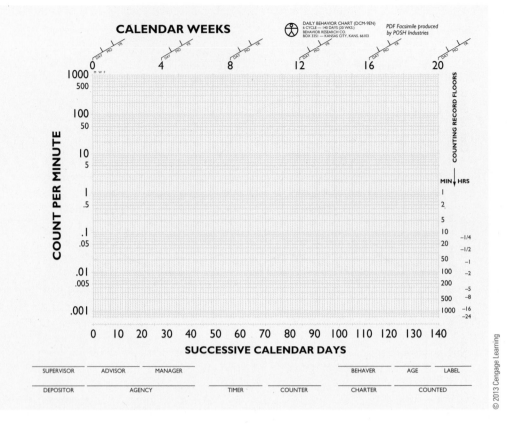

seven data points have been collected. Then, if the four most recent and consecutive data points fall below the goal line (if the goal is an increase in the behavior) or above the goal line (if the goal is a decrease in the behavior), a teaching change or intervention is considered warranted. An example of using such an approach is shown in Figure 9.3.[2]

Parallel rule: Educators can draw an aimline as previously discussed in Chapter 9. After several data points are collected, the trend (or best-fit line) for the student's actual performance can be determined and compared to the aimline. This is done by using the student's actual performance data to calculate an equation for the trendline that can then be plotted on the chart. If the instructional goal is the acquisition of a skill, the desired trendline should be parallel to, or rise more steeply than, the aimline. If the goal is decreasing a problematic behavior, the desired trendline should be parallel to, or descend more steeply than, the aimline. If the trendline does not meet the above criteria, instruction should be modified.

The benefits of charting student progress have been well documented since the 1960s. In general, students whose teachers chart pupil behavior have better achievement than students whose teachers do not chart. Students who chart their own performance have better achievement than students who do not chart their achievement. Achievement tends to be best when both teachers and students chart pupil progress (see, for example, Fuchs & Fuchs, 1986; Santangelo, 2009).

11-4 Technology and Managing Classroom Assessment Data

Computer programs and other technologies can provide substantial assistance with the collection, management, and display of data for decision making. Specific programs and software can be purchased to assist with each of these aspects of the

---

[2] Please note that the graph shows a situation in which the change was made after 7 data points were below the aimline, which is a bit delayed compared to the four-point rule. The intervention could have been changed after the fourth consecutive data point fell below the aimline, given that by that point a total of 7 data points had been collected.

assessment process. We have already mentioned some examples of related technologies that can be used to facilitate systematic observation (Chapter 9) and systematic progress monitoring in academic skill development (Chapter 10). We additionally highlight classroom response systems below, as well as some important considerations for storage of electronic data.

11-4a CLASSROOM RESPONSE SYSTEMS

The days are gone when teachers have to call on individual students one by one to check on the extent to which they understand what they are being taught. New technological advances enable teachers to ask students questions and have them enter their responses on classroom responders or small computers. Results are transmitted wirelessly to the teacher's computer, and the teacher can view a graph showing the numbers of students who answered questions correctly and incorrectly, and lists of students who have answered incorrectly. In this way, teachers obtain immediate feedback on the extent to which students comprehend lesson material, allowing teachers to reteach, adapt instruction, or move on to teaching more advanced material based on actual student performance. Although use of classroom response systems can require substantial preparation, it ultimately facilitates more active engagement of students and teaching that is particularly targeted to what the class knows and does not know. It also can minimize embarrassment that individual students may otherwise experience if the teacher calls on them to publicly answer a question to which they do not know the answer. The teacher can follow up separately with individual students who continue to answer incorrectly, using the data that are collected. Once question banks are developed and incorporated within a classroom response system, they can be used repeatedly, making the time investment all that much more worthwhile.

11-4b STORAGE OF ELECTRONIC RECORDS

With the availability to store student data electronically and via the Internet, there is an increasing need to ensure that identifiable data are kept secure. Student records are to be shared only with those who have a legitimate need to know, so it is important for related identifiable data to be made available only to current teachers and parents. Password protection procedures can be used to secure data that are only available on a particular computer. When data are to be stored via the Internet, it is important that they are de-identified. To do so, it may be helpful to create numeric keys that pair each student's name with a unique number; this key could then be stored off the Internet and could be used to connect data with student identifying information. As data storage on the Internet becomes a more common practice, it will be important for those who develop the associated technologies and school officials to work together in the development of techniques for ensuring the privacy of student assessment data.

Chapter Comprehension Questions

Write your answers to each of the following questions and then compare your responses to the text.

1. Name and describe three characteristics of effective testing programs.

2. What are three resources that you can use for setting up a plan for managing data collection and analysis in a classroom?

3. Describe two methods for charting student data for decision making.

4. Explain two advantages and one concern in using new technologies to assist with the management of student data.

RESPONSE TO INTERVENTION (RTI) AND A MULTI-TIERED SYSTEM OF SUPPORTS (MTSS)

LEARNING OBJECTIVES

12-1 List the fundamental assumptions in assessing response to instruction or response to intervention.

12-2 Describe the steps school personnel go through in assessing student needs for differing levels of support.

12-3 Indicate evidence for and against the effectiveness of response to intervention and a multi-tiered system of support.

STANDARDS ADDRESSED IN THIS CHAPTER

 CEC Initial Preparation Standards

Standard 4: Assessment

4.0 Beginning special education professionals use multiple methods of assessment and data-sources in making educational decisions.

Standard 5: Instructional Planning Strategies

5.0 Beginning special education professionals select, adapt, and use a repertoire of evidence-based instructional strategies to advance learning of individuals with exceptionalities.

CEC ADVANCED **CEC Advanced Preparation Standards**

Standard 1: Assessment

1.0 Special education specialists use valid and reliable assessment practices to minimize bias.

 National Association of School Psychologists Domains

1 Data-based Decision Making and Accountability

5 Schoolwide Practices to Promote Learning

FIGURE 12.1
Students Receive
Multiple Tiers of Support
That Increase in
Intensity If They Are Not
Successful in School

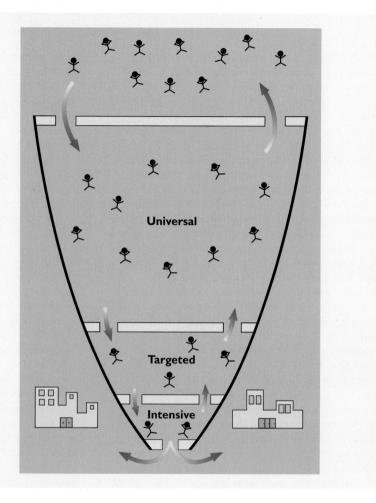

Recent federal educational policy developments have radically changed assessment and instructional practices for all students. The No Child Left Behind Act (NCLB) of 2001 established the clear expectation that schools would implement evidence-based instructional practices and engage in data-based assessment of student outcomes. The reauthorization of the Individuals with Disabilities Educational Improvement Act (IDEA) of 2004 and its accompanying regulations in 2006 brought about increased attention to two important concepts: Response to Intervention (RTI) and the development of a Multi-Tiered System of Supports (MTSS) for matching instruction/intervention to student needs.

At the heart of special and remedial education remains matching instructional content, methods, and pace to the needs and skills of students who are not making as much academic progress as expected. Students begin instruction with differing skills and needs. As shown in Figure 12.1, all students receive universal supports within general education. However, many students will require additional, more targeted supports to help them succeed. For some students, even these targeted supports are not enough; they require intensive supports to succeed. Students move up and down in the system of supports as they need more or less intensive supports to meet their needs. In this chapter we discuss the two important concepts of RTI and MTSS and describe assessment practices within each of those two sets of practices.

12-1 Response to Intervention

Good instruction is effective for most students. However, the extent to which any program or intervention will be effective with an individual student is unknown. Program or intervention effectiveness are affected by the unique characteristics of

SCENARIO IN ASSESSMENT

CHARLES | Charles, a second grader, is the oldest of three children who moved from the city into the suburban West Morgan School District over the summer. Several requests for Charles's records from the city district were never answered. By mid-September, it was clear that Charles was struggling in oral reading. Mrs. Buchanon, his teacher, noted that Charles was very inaccurate. After listening to Charles read aloud twice, she decided to tally the number of correct and incorrect words he read. The next time Charles read aloud, he read 56 percent of the words correctly and was unable to retell what he had read. Clearly, the beginning second-grade material was too difficult for Charles. Mrs. Buchanon tried material at the mid-first-grade level, but it too was too difficult. In beginning first-grade material, Charles could read with 85 percent accuracy, but his reading was very slow and he was able only to retell about 60 percent of what he had read.

Mrs. Buchanon decided to use a generally effective instructional strategy to improve Charles's reading. She paired him with Michelle, one of the better readers in the class. Charles would read beginning first-grade material aloud for five minutes, and Michelle would correct his errors. Mrs. Buchanon monitored the intervention twice a week. Although Charles seemed to enjoy working with Michelle, his reading accuracy showed no improvement after four weeks of intervention.

Mrs. Buchanon then developed a targeted intervention. She assessed Charles's knowledge of letter names and letter sounds. He could name all of the letters, all of the long vowel sounds, none of the short vowel sounds, and all of the common consonant sounds. She drilled him for two minutes daily on short vowel sounds and sent worksheets home for Charles to practice with his mother. Charles continued to read with Michelle for five minutes every day. However, instead of supplying a correct word for an incorrect one, Michelle provided the correct initial sound of the word before supplying the correct word. After a month, Charles had learned the short 'o' and improved his fluency from 35 correct sounds per minute to 45 correct sounds per minute. However, increased accuracy in letter sounds was not accompanied by increases in oral reading.

At this point, it was clear that Charles was not making the kind of gains he needed to make; he was falling farther behind his classmates. Mrs. Buchanon consulted with the school building's Student Assistance Team. The team recommended an intensive intervention of explicit instruction targeting phonemic awareness, letter–sound associations, and fluency. The team did not specifically target reading comprehension because of the likelihood that Charles's poor comprehension was the result of his lack of reading fluency. Charles received 12 minutes each day of individual instruction from the reading specialist. Data were collected weekly on Charles's reading accuracy and fluency.

Charles progressed consistently in the intensive program. The number of correct words read per minute increased steadily in progressively more difficult reading materials. By the end of the first semester, Charles was reading beginning second-grade material independently. By the end of the second grade, he had caught up to his peers; he was reading end-of-second-grade material independently. The Student Assistance Team ended instructional intervention; however, it did continue to monitor Charles in the third grade to make sure he maintained his gains. Charles continued to progress at the rate of his peers.

How are the three characteristics of response to intervention evident in this scenario?

---

the students and their teachers. A supplemental program with strong support in the research literature may not necessarily address the skills with which students at a particular school are struggling. Therefore, it is important to monitor student progress over time to know whether a program or intervention, when applied, has the intended positive impact on student learning.

Response to instruction and response to intervention (RTI) are terms that have their origins in general education, yet today both are measured in both general and special education. They are concepts with multiple meanings but without definition as yet in state or federal laws or regulations. Sometimes they are defined simply as collecting data on student performance and progress toward some goal; invariably they have to do with progress monitoring. The general notion is to monitor student progress (continuously, periodically, annually, or with some other degree of frequency) in order to spot problems, ascertain skill development, or check the efficacy of academic or behavioral interventions being used with the student. Some would say the practice is all about catching children early so that they do not get left behind. Reports of assessments of response to instruction could consist of report cards every six weeks, simple statements that a student's overall progress is satisfactory, or more formal, highly specific statements such as "In two weeks, she has increased her single-digit addition accuracy from 4 out of 10 problems correct to 8 out of 10 problems correct." Obviously, these different kinds of reports have different meanings and differ in their usefulness for instructional decision making.

The basic conceptual framework for RTI has existed in the psychological and educational literature for many years; it has its foundation in the prevention sciences (Caplan, 1964), where physicians talked about primary, secondary, and tertiary prevention or treatment. In education and psychology, the concept likely originated in the early work of Lindsley (1964) on precision teaching, and it was first implemented as an assessment model by Beck (1979) in the Sacajawea Project in Great Falls, Montana. There are many models of RTI (Jimerson, Burns, & VanDerHeyden, 2016; National Association of State Directors of Special Education, 2005; Sugai & Horner, 2009), but they all share (1) multiple tiers of effective intervention service delivery, (2) ongoing progress monitoring, and (3) data collection/assessment to inform decisions at each tier (Ysseldyke, 2008). Read the Scenario in Assessment box entitled "Charles" for an example of how a teacher used one type of response-to-intervention approach to address a student's needs.

12-1a FUNDAMENTAL ASSUMPTIONS IN ASSESSING RESPONSE TO INSTRUCTION

There are seven assumptions that underlie the practice of assessing RTI.

1. *Instruction occurs.* When we assess response to instruction, we assume that instruction actually occurs. However, some philosophies of education explicitly eschew direct or systematic instruction and instead value a student's discovering content, skills, and behavior.[1] Thus it is likely that some students could spend their time in instruction-free environments and would stand no chance of being instructed.[1]

2. *Instruction occurs as intended.* It is assumed that instruction is implemented in the way in which it is intended to be implemented and that students are actively engaged in the instruction. Over the past decade, researchers have become increasingly interested in intervention integrity (also sometimes called treatment integrity or fidelity of treatment). For example, when we assess the extent to which a student responds to phonics instruction, we are assuming that the phonics instruction is implemented as the teacher intended and that the student is actively engaged in responding to the instruction.

3. *The instruction that is assessed is known to be generally effective.* There needs to be empirical evidence that the instruction that is implemented works for students in general and, more specifically, for students who are the same age and grade as the pupil being assessed.

4. *The measurement system is adequate to detect changes in student learning as a result of instruction.* There are four subcomponents to this assumption.

   a. The measurement system reflects the curriculum or assesses the effect of instruction in that curriculum. It is axiomatic that response to instruction must reflect the content being instructed.
   b. The measurement system can be used frequently. Frequent measurement is important to avoid wasting a student's and a teacher's time when instruction is not working. It is also important to prevent a student from practicing (and mastering) errors and making them more difficult to correct.
   c. The measurement system is sensitive to small changes in student performance. If measurement is conducted frequently, it is unlikely that there will be large changes in student learning. Thus, to be effective, the measurement system must be capable of detecting small, but meaningful, changes in student learning or performance.
   d. The measurement system actually assesses pupil performance, not simply what the teacher does. Clearly, what a teacher does is important because it relates directly to treatment fidelity. However, we are interested in whether the student is learning.

5. *There are links between the assessment data and modifications in instruction.* This is the concept of data-driven decision making and reiterates our earlier point that data collected and not used to make decisions are useless.

---

[1] Most parents would prefer that this procedure not be used to teach their children to swim.

It is assumed that the data are both useful and usable for purposes of instructional planning. Student failure to respond appropriately to instruction, as determined by the formative measures used, should trigger a change in instruction. Additional data may need to be collected to determine what change has the highest probability of leading to student success; nevertheless, a change would be needed in the type of instruction, amount of instruction, or instructional delivery method.

6. *There are consequences that sustain (a) improved student outcomes and (b) continued implementation of the measurement system.* It is assumed not only that the system is good, but also that it is worth keeping in place. In our experience, we have learned that the collection of direct frequent data on student performance is considered by some teachers as both time consuming and arduous. At the same time, teachers tell us that they and their students are "better off" when data are collected. Although many teachers are motivated by their students' progress, it is sometimes necessary to provide rewards to others for data collection if we want them to engage in direct and frequent measurement. These teachers have told us that, if it does not matter to someone that they monitor student progress, they will stop doing so.

7. *Assessment of RTI is not setting-specific.* It is assumed that response to instruction can be assessed in both general and special education settings.

12-1b SPECIFICITY AND FREQUENCY OF ASSESSMENT

Assessments of student response to educational interventions vary along two dimensions: specificity and frequency. Technically adequate measures of RTI are those that are highly specific and very frequently administered. This concept is illustrated in Figure 12.2. Along the vertical axis, measures vary in their specificity from those that are global to those that are highly specific. Along the horizontal axis, measures vary in their frequency of assessment from those that are given very infrequently to those that are administered daily, hourly, or even continuously. The "best" measures, those that are most technically adequate for decision making, are in the upper right-hand quadrant (highly sensitive or specific and frequently administered).

Specificity

Assessments differ along a continuum of specificity. This is illustrated in Figure 12.3. The more specific the assessment and the more specific the information collected by

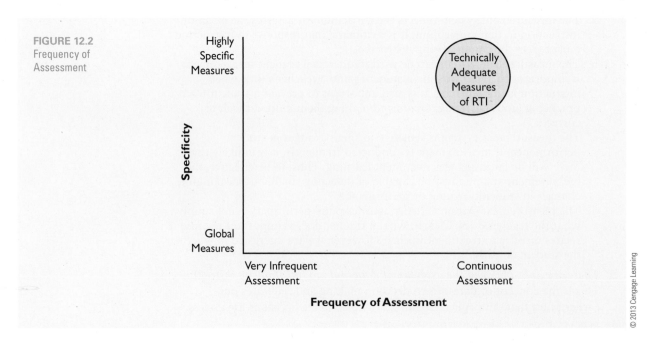

FIGURE 12.2
Frequency of Assessment

Highly Specific Measures

Specificity

Global Measures

Very Infrequent Assessment

Continuous Assessment

Technically Adequate Measures of RTI

Frequency of Assessment

FIGURE 12.3
Continuum of
Specificity

- Given 10 consonant-vowel-consonant words with the short e sound, Bill says 8 correctly.

- Bill has mastered short vowel sounds.

- Bill is at the 70th percentile in decoding skills.

- Bill passed the unit test.

- Bill earned a B in reading.

- Bill is doing fine in reading.

or reported to the teacher, the more precise the teacher can be in planning instructional interventions. Think about where you would begin teaching a student who is "doing fine in reading." Without greater specificity, you would not know what to do to improve the student's reading skills.

Frequency

Increasingly, educators are measuring performance and progress very frequently. Many of the new measurement systems, such as those employing technology-enhanced assessments, call for continuous measurement of pupil performance and progress. They provide students with immediate feedback on how they are doing, give teachers daily status reports indicating the relative standing of all students in a class, and pinpoint the skills missing among students who are experiencing difficulty. The more frequent the measurement, the quicker teachers can adapt instruction to ensure that students are making optimal progress. However, frequent measurement is only helpful when it can immediately direct teachers as to what to teach or how to teach next. To the extent that teachers can use data efficiently, frequent assessment is valuable; if it consists simply of frequent measurement with no application, then it is not valuable, and wastes students' time.

12-1c CRITERIA FOR JUDGING PROGRESS IN RTI

Determination of whether a student is responding to interventions requires specification of decision rules based on the student's level and rate of progress. School personnel should establish these rules *before* interventions are implemented. Both level of performance (i.e., third-grade level) and rate of progress (e.g., objectives mastered, periodic measures, or quizzes answered with 80 percent accuracy) should be specified. Stakeholder groups in states, districts, or individual schools often work on specification of criteria. Two concepts that may be part of the criteria used include rate of improvement and gap analysis.

Rate of Improvement

Rate of improvement (ROI) refers to trend or slope in improvement and can be calculated in a way that allows for a comparison either to grade-level peers or to individual goals or targets that are set for the student. It is used as an index of the extent to which the student is responding to instruction and intervention. It provides information about the extent to which an intervention is working or is effective and about the extent to which the student is making as much progress as would be expected or desired.

ROI Relative to Benchmark (Standard) The term **typical benchmark** represents a minimal standard for performance, and helps to indicate the growth rate required of a grade-level peer during the course of regular instruction to meet the minimal level required of all students (a specific grade-level or age-level standard). It is derived from the historical performance on CBM or CAT measures administered to large numbers of students of specific grades in the fall, winter, and spring. Most publishers of CBM measures like easyCBM, DIBELS Next, or AIMSweb or publishers of CAT measures like STAR Reading and STAR Math provide test users with benchmark targets based on the academic development of typical students in their norms. These benchmark targets can be obtained by going to the publishers' websites and then looking up the benchmark targets for the specific measures. Expected rates of improvement are calculated by producing a line connecting the score at the beginning of the year to the benchmark target at the middle and end of the year. For some measures, like AIMsweb and the STAR assessments, ROIs are calculated using student growth percentiles. A student's expected ROI is calculated relative to the ROIs of other students at the same grade and at a similar level of initial score.

ROI for Monitoring Individual Student Progress in Specific Interventions We have noted that teachers and other school personnel also develop targeted interventions for students at tiers 2 and 3 of an RTI model within an MTSS. When they do so, they measure the individual student's progress prior to the intervention and set an intervention goal or target based on the performance expected of grade-level or age-level peers. The intervention goal or target should be set with a notion that over the course of the intervention, the student will close the gap between their performance and that of their peers. Information on the level of goal to set can sometimes be obtained from test publishers. As we noted above in our discussion of benchmark approaches, individual progress monitoring approaches involve comparison of a student's attained performance and rate of improvement to the typical ROI of his/her peers and to targeted ROI based on the rate of improvement that would be necessary to close the gap between the student and the typical peers. In the scenario on Kim Jones that follows, we illustrate the use of progress monitoring information to compute rate of improvement and to compare the student's ROI to the ROI expected to attain an end-of-year benchmark.

SCENARIO IN ASSESSMENT

KIM JONES | Kim Jones is a seventh-grade student at West Middle School in a large Tennessee school district. Kim is having considerable difficulty comprehending what she reads and is receiving one-to-one Tier 2 reading instruction from her teacher, Rita Schmit. Ms. Schmit wants to monitor Kim's progress during the intervention and compare her rate of improvement to that of her grade-level peers. Further, she wants to know whether she is reducing the gap in performance between Kim and her grade-level peers. Ms. Schmit decides to use a computer adaptive test, STAR Reading Enterprise, to monitor Kim's progress during implementation of the intervention, and based on Kim's initial performance on that test, she chooses to implement an intervention she called "Comprehension Strategies" beginning in September 2014.

Progress monitoring for individual students involves setting a goal or target, establishing expected growth rates and plotting an aimline, frequent administration of a test, plotting of a trendline, and comparison of the ROI (slope) for the aimline with the ROI (slope) in the individual student's trendline. School personnel can go one step further to conduct a gap analysis by

comparing the gap between the individual student's ROI and the expected ROI.

Rita Schmit first used the resource entitled "Benchmark, Cut Scores and Growth Rates" from the Renaissance Place website for the STAR Reading Enterprise assessment to determine the benchmark expectation for seventh graders for fall (SS=696) and their benchmark expectation for spring (SS=790). The benchmark expectation is the minimum scaled score that all seventh-grade students would need to achieve at a point in time (e.g., fall or winter) in order to be on track to earn the scaled score required to meet state or local standards by the end of the year. She then set a target goal for Kim and established an aimline. In setting the target goal she again used the resource entitled "Benchmark, Cut Scores and Growth Rates" from the Renaissance Place website for the STAR Reading Enterprise assessment. She decided she wanted to see an ambitious rate of improvement, and the corresponding growth rate for that was 4.5 scaled scores per week. The corresponding target goal was 598. The ambitious rate was chosen because Rita was very interested in closing the gap between Kim's performance and that of her grade-level peers just as soon as she possibly could.

A Progress Monitoring report, showing the target goal of a scaled score of 598 as well as Kim's scores on the STAR Reading Enterprise tests administered on repeated occasions from mid-September to January, is shown in Figure 12.4. Also shown is a trendline calculated using the test publisher's software program with a scaled score growth rate of 4.5 scaled scores per week as the desired rate of growth. From the visual analysis it is readily apparent that Kim is not making progress at the expected rate, and that her performance trend is a downward (negative) slope. More detail about Kim's rate of progress is shown in Figure 12.5, a second version of the Progress Monitoring Report. In this report we see that the teacher has selected an ambitious goal and that the expected growth rate for that goal is 4.5 scaled scores per week. Inspection of the Growth Rate column shows consistent performance below the aimline with decreasing (negative) growth.

Based on Kim's lack of progress, Ms. Schmit changed her intervention to "Comprehension Success Skills." Note in the second half of Figure 12.5 that she also increased the frequency of intervention to five times per week and changed the duration of the intervention from 30 to 45 minutes per session. The target goal stayed at 598 scaled scores and the goal rate of improvement remained at 4.5 scaled scores per week. As can be seen in Figure 12.4, Kim's performance on the first test following implementation of the new intervention was above the aimline, but her performance on all subsequent tests was below the aimline. A trend in her performance was calculated using the publisher's software, and once again a decreasing (or negative) trend line was observed.

Ms Schmit then examined the relationship between Kim's rate of improvement and the typical rate of improvement for seventh graders. She calculated the "typical ROI" by subtracting the fall benchmark expectation (696) from the spring benchmark expectation (790) for seventh graders and dividing by the number of weeks in the school year (36). The

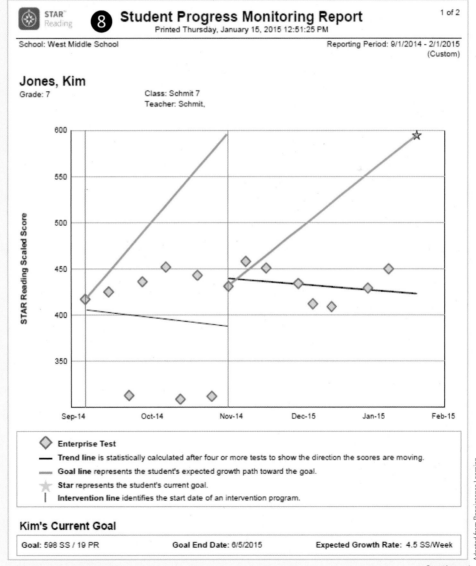

FIGURE 12.4
Progress Monitoring
Report for Kim Jones

Continued

typical ROI (slope) was 2.61. The ROI worksheet is shown in Figure 12.6. Rita Schmit calculated Kim's ROI in the same fashion, by subtracting her fall scaled score (417) from her current scaled score (450) and dividing by the number of weeks the intervention was in place (18 weeks), to get an ROI of 1.83 [(450–417)/18=1.83]. She met with the school team, who concluded that the ROI was not reasonable and that it would take Kim far too long to catch up without a change in either intervention strategy or intensity.

The school team, together with Ms. Schmit, conducted a gap analysis, a formal measure of the magnitude of the gap between the student's rate of improvement and the typical expected rate of improvement. The steps in the gap analysis are illustrated in Figure 12.7. There is a current difference of 286 scaled scores between Kim's current performance and the end-of-the-year benchmark performance. There are 18 weeks left in the school year, so Kim would have to make a rate of improvement of 15.89 scaled scores per week in order to reach the minimal benchmark score. Or, as shown conversely, it would take her 156.28 weeks (three years) to meet the goal. The school team concludes that the intervention is not working and needs to be changed to a different Tier 2 intervention, changed to a Tier 3 intervention, or perhaps that a referral needs to be made to special education.

FIGURE 12.5
Page 2 of Kim Jones's Progress Monitoring Report

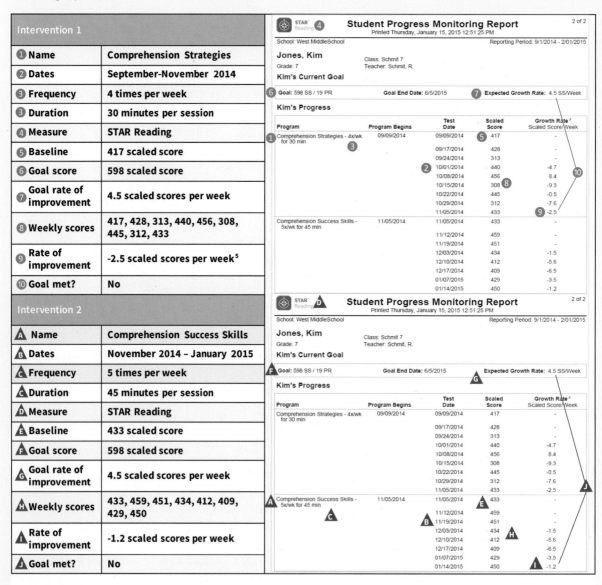

[4] This example is adapted from the National Center on Learning Disability. http://www.rtinetwork.org/images/TOOLKIT/rti-based_sld_determination_worksheet_11__16.pdf

[5] STAR uses an ordinary least squares regression equation to calculate rate of improvement.

Adapted from Renaissance Learning

Continued

FIGURE 12.6
Rate of Improvement
Worksheet for
Kim Jones

Rate of Improvement (ROI) Worksheet

Student Name: *Kim Jones*   Date: *1/15/2015*
Grade: *7*   Current Tier: *2*

Assessment Used:	*STAR Reading*
Student's score on first assessment administered:	*417*
Student's score on last assessment administered:	*450*
Fall benchmark expectation:	*696*
Spring benchmark expectation:	*790*

Step 1: Determine Typical ROI

790	-	*696*	/	36	=	*2.61*
Spring benchmark expectation		Fall benchmark expectation		Number of weeks		Typical ROI (slope)

Step 2: Determine Student ROI

450	-	*417*	/	*18*	=	*1.83*
Score on last assessment administered		Score on first assessment administered		Number of weeks		Student ROI (slope)

Step 3: Compare Student ROI to Typical ROI

2.61	x	2	=	*5.22*	**Is Student's ROI**
Typical ROI				Aggressive ROI	**<**
OR					**Aggressive/Reasonable ROI?**
2.61	x	1.5	=	*3.92*	
Typical ROI				Reasonable ROI	☒ Yes ☐ No

If the team answers "yes", consider a change in intervention:

- Increasing frequency of intervention sessions
- Changing intervention
- Changing intervention provider
- Changing time of day intervention is delivered
- Increasing intensity (Tier) of intervention

Continued

FIGURE 12.7
Gap Analysis Worksheet
for Kim Jones

Gap Analysis Worksheet

Student Name: *Kim Jones*

Grade: *7*

Date: *1/15/2015*

Current Tier: *2*

Assessment Used:	*STAR Reading*
Student's current performance:	*450*
Student's current rate of improvement (ROI):	*1.83*
Current benchmark expectation:	*736*
End-of-year benchmark expectation:	*790*
Number of weeks remaining in school year	*18*

Step 1: Determine Gap

736	/	*450*	=	*1.64*	Is gap significant?*
Current benchmark expectation		Current performance		Current gap	☒ Yes ☐ No

*Number indicating gap significance is determined by state or district. If gap is significant, complete Step 2.

Step 2: Gap Analysis

790	-	*450*	=	*286*
End-of-year benchmark		Current performance		Difference

286	/	*18*	=	*15.89*	Is this reasonable*
Difference		Weeks remaining		ROI needed	
OR					
286	/	*1.83*	=	*156.28*	☐ Yes ☒ No
Difference		Student's current ROI		Number of weeks to meet goal	

*A reasonable ROI is no more than twice (2x) the ROI of typical peers.

Step 3: Conclusion

Intervention is not working and needs to be changed to a different Tier 3 intervention or perhaps make a referral to special education.

_____

School Psychologist Signature

Gap Analysis

Gap analysis involves examining the difference between the actual rate of improvement for a student and the rate of improvement that would be necessary to attain an expected benchmark level by a particular point in time. There are no specific, legally defined guidelines or criteria for how small the gap must be to consider the student as demonstrating reasonable progress, nor are there specifications about how large the gap must be to consider a student as eligible for special education services. Some states are beginning to specify a magnitude of gap necessary to declare students eligible for special education services using the label "learning disabled." We describe gap analysis further in the chapter.

12-1d IMPORTANT CONSIDERATIONS IN RTI

Intervention Integrity

As school personnel assess response to intervention, it is critical to demonstrate that intervention is occurring and that it is occurring in ways that it was intended. Imagine assessing student response to treatment, concluding that the student did not respond to the treatment (that the treatment did not work), and then learning later that the treatment either was never put in place or was poorly implemented. Or imagine that a student starts to make substantial progress, but you are not sure what made the difference and thus are not sure what to maintain or change in a student's program. More than for other forms of assessment, RTI assessment models are dependent on effective instruction being implemented with good integrity.

There are likely a number of ways to make sure that interventions are put in place with good integrity. First, teachers need to learn the nuances of implementing an intervention. If, for example, teachers are to implement the Success for All program with their classes, it would be important that they know the specifics of doing so. They might attend specific training in Success for All, read extensively about implementation of the program, or work for a time alongside another teacher in a setting where Success for All is being implemented. Similarly, if teachers are to work with individual students on phonemic awareness, it is important that they know how to do so and that they do so with implementation integrity.

The few intervention integrity or treatment integrity measures that exist are treatment-specific, and no one method for assessing treatment integrity is widely accepted. Kovaleski has compiled a collection of treatment integrity protocols that were developed by a variety of sources (practitioners, researchers, publishers, and graduate students) for use in assessing the extent to which specific interventions are implemented with integrity. The list can be obtained at the website for the RTI Network. Kratochwill and Sanetti developed a Treatment Integrity Planning Protocol (TIPP), a comprehensive process that can be adapted to any school-based intervention. Sanetti and Kratochwill (2011) published an evaluation of the use of that protocol along with two other measures of treatment integrity.

Intervention Efficacy

When examining response to intervention for individual students, there should be good evidence that the treatment itself is generally effective with students who are at the same age and grade as the student being assessed. This is especially true in models that require normative peer comparisons (examinations of pupil progress relative to that of classmates). Under the requirements of NCLB, school personnel are expected to be putting in place evidence-based treatments. Information about the extent to which treatments are generally effective is found by reviewing the research evidence in support of the treatments.

The What Works Clearinghouse (WWC) can provide direction as to what treatments might be particularly effective. You can go to the WWC website, look up interventions for middle school math, and find a topic report listing the kinds of interventions that the clearinghouse reviewed on middle school math. Information on the extent to which there is good empirical support for a particular intervention can be obtained from the WWC website.

However, always remember that efficacy is local. It is highly recommended that you consider the characteristics of the student and teachers when selecting an intervention rather than relying solely on what has been shown to be most effective in the research literature. If an intervention is not targeted appropriately to an individual child's or school's needs, it may not be effective. What works in general might not work for Billy. That is why we monitor Billy's performance to see if the treatment is efficacious for him, too.

Response Stability

In assessing response to intervention, it is important to document the extent to which the student's response varies over content and over time. We expect that in nearly all instances it will. Few students respond to the content of different subject matter in the same way, and their responses are seldom consistent over time. We are interested in the usual response to instruction, not response to instruction on a bad day.

It is said that we all "get sick of too much of a good thing." It is often the case that an intervention that "works" and is effective in moving a student toward an instructional goal will work for only a limited period of time. Students get satiated with specific instructional approaches or interventions and also reinforcers. Indeed, one of the evidence-based principles of effective instruction is that variety in instructional presentation and in response demand enhances instructional outcomes. This presents significant challenges for those who teach students with learning and behavior problems. They must not only identify instructional approaches that work, they must also identify multiple instructional approaches that work. You may need to work to identify several different approaches to achieve the same instructional goals.

Frequency of Progress Monitoring

As noted earlier, school personnel decide how often to monitor progress, and typically do so either periodically (e.g., twice a week or three times a month) or continuously. Periodic progress monitoring approaches are the most commonly used. Continuous progress monitoring approaches are the most effective (Ysseldyke & Bolt, 1997; Bolt, Ysseldyke, & Patterson, 2010).

12-2 The Concept of a Multi-Tiered System of Supports and Differentiated Student Needs

In Chapter 1 we noted that in the past decade many districts and schools have begun using Multi-Tiered System of Supports (MTSS) models to match more effectively the content, methods, and intensity of instruction to individual student needs. Low-functioning students and/or those who are not making as much academic progress as expected are identified for more intensive instruction and intervention. In Chapter 1 we talked briefly about how instruction was differentiated for Kim, Bill, Sally, Kamryn, Rosa, Mohammed, and others based on review of their records, interviews, observation, and testing. We indicated that a major purpose of assessment has been to monitor pupil progress; this means assessing and documenting a student's achievement—that is, responses to or responsiveness to instruction. Standardized norm-referenced tests (which are the focus of Chapters 14–19) often are not satisfactory instruments for monitoring response to instruction. They are time consuming, insensitive to small but important changes, expensive, not suitable for repeated administrations, and fail to match a student's curriculum and instruction. Over time, demands to develop new ways to monitor student progress and response to instruction have increased. These have gone under the titles problem-solving model, response to intervention (RTI), response to instruction, and now most recently multi-tiered system of supports (MTSS).

A **multi-tiered system of supports (MTSS)** is "a coherent continuum of evidence-based, system-wide practices to support a rapid response to academic and behavior needs with frequent data-based monitoring for instructional decision

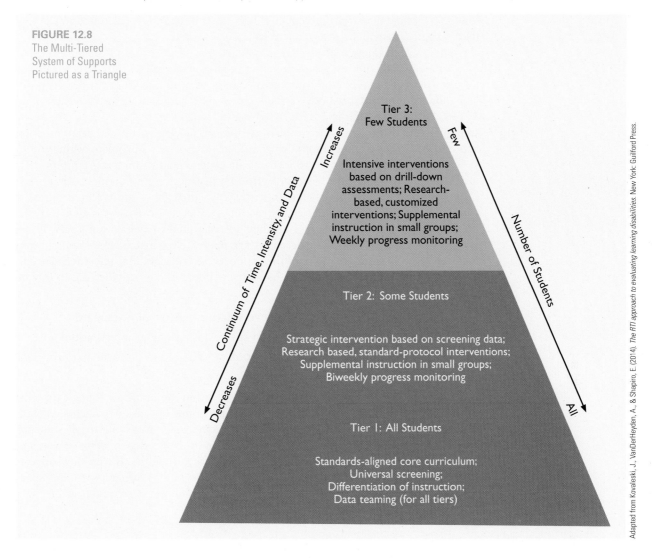

Adapted from Kovaleski, J., VanDerHeyden, A., & Shapiro, E. (2014). *The RTI approach to evaluating learning disabilities.* New York: Guilford Press.

FIGURE 12.8
The Multi-Tiered
System of Supports
Pictured as a Triangle

making to empower each student to achieve to high standards" (as defined by the Kansas Multi-Tier System of Supports). In Figure 12.1 we depicted the MTSS as a funnel, with students filtering downward in the funnel as they need increasing levels of support.

Some educators depict the multi-tiered system of supports as a triangle, as shown in Figure 12.8. A multi-tiered system is illustrated in which students receive increasingly intensive levels of service and supports until interventions are identified that result in a positive response to intervention. Whether a funnel, triangle, or pyramid is used to illustrate the concept, what is communicated by these drawings is that (1) there are individual differences in the intensity of supports that students need in order to be successful, and (2) the numbers of students served decreases as more intensive supports are needed and provided. Assessment helps you figure out what skills and skill deficits students have, the intensity of supports that students need, whether good instruction is happening with students, the extent to which they are profiting from it, and the extent to which teachers and schools are "effective."

The development of the concept of a multi-tiered system of supports came about in response to legal mandates or permissions. In the 2002 No Child Left Behind Act, Congress called for renewed and intensified focus on assessment and accountability. In the 2004 revision of the Individuals with Disabilities Education Improvement Act (IDEA), Congress added the assessment requirements of universal screening and progress monitoring. The law also indicated that decisions about eligibility for some kinds of special education services could be made based on the examination of student response to evidence-based effective instruction (RTI).

The MTSS framework is designed to address the academic and behavioral needs of *all* students, whether they are struggling or have advanced learning needs. The key assessment question is, "What supports do students need to be successful?" A "problem-solving" model (Christ & Aranas, 2014) is used throughout the provision of an MTSS. Problem solving is a data-based decision-making process that includes the steps illustrated in Figure 12.9: problem definition, problem analysis, deciding what action to take, intervening, monitoring student progress, and problem evaluation.

The foundation of an MTSS begins in general education programming that includes a focus on the provision of effective instruction and supports that assist in preventing academic and behavior problems. Throughout an MTSS, progress is closely monitored at each stage of instruction or intervention to verify that students are making appropriate progress on their instructional or behavioral goals. When progress is less than adequate, decisions are made about instructional content and methods as well as the intensity of the supports and services that the student needs. Within an MTSS, the collection of assessment information provides the following information about a student:

- An indication of the student's skill level relative to peers or a standard
- An indication of the success or lack of success of particular interventions
- A sense of the intensity of supports a student will need to perform at a proficient level

Think of an MTSS as a **series of tiers**. Tiers within the funnel or triangle describe the intensity of instruction, not specific places, programs or types of students, or staff. The **first tier** is the core instructional programming made available to all students. Screening tests (e.g., formative assessments) given in the classroom show which students are at risk for reading, math, and other learning difficulties. Brief follow-up tests for those who are at risk may show that a student who has difficulty reading needs additional instruction in word fluency. In the **second tier**, the classroom teacher might

FIGURE 12.9
Assessment Is a Problem-Solving Process That Takes Place at All Tiers or Levels

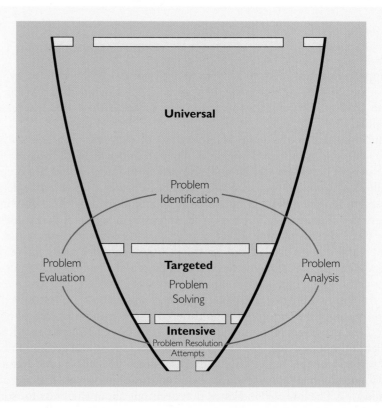

Universal

Problem Identification

Problem Evaluation

Targeted
Problem Solving

Problem Analysis

Intensive
Problem Resolution Attempts

provide corrective feedback and extra instruction. In other cases, another educator who has expertise in reading and fluency might instruct the student along with other students who are having the same difficulty. Or specific instructional programs like *Read Naturally* or *Read Well* may be implemented. Students who fail to respond to specific targeted interventions may then be considered for more specialized instruction in the **third tier**, where instruction may occur with increased intensity—that is, instructional sessions of longer duration, more targeted to the student's needs, and/or increased frequency. If difficulties persist, a team of educators may complete a comprehensive evaluation to determine eligibility for special education and related services.

Regardless of the intervention within a tier, the goal is to use student performance data to inform ways to provide the type of instruction and educational assistance that the student needs to be successful. Typical assessments in tier 1 include universal screening and continuous or periodic (e.g., three times per year) progress monitoring to identify students at risk. At tier 2, typical assessments include diagnostic assessment in academic content areas to inform instruction and intervention and also progress monitoring designed to help in making instructional decisions. At tier 3, assessment consists primarily of continuous or very frequent collection of information, consideration of referral to a multidisciplinary child study team, and assessment designed to determine eligibility for special education services. When correctly implemented, an MTSS results in:

- All students receiving high-quality instruction in the general education setting
- A reduction of referrals for special education eligibility consideration
- The use of assessment information to make decisions about all students as they are screened for academic and behavior problems
- Ongoing monitoring of individual student progress and analysis of the data to pinpoint specific difficulties experienced by individual students
- At-risk students receiving immediate individual attention without having to wait to be identified as eligible for special education services
- Consistent, rigorous implementation of progress monitoring and effective interventions
- All students receiving appropriate instruction prior to consideration for special education placement

12-3 The Effectiveness of RTI/MTSS

Tindal and others (2012) describe three "pieces" necessary for RTI to work well. These include:

1. Measurement Sufficiency. There must a selection of good measurement tools that provide sufficient information to decide whether or not the instructional intervention is working.
2. Instructional Adequacy. Educators must ask themselves what instructional strategies they will use and how they will decide if they are using those strategies with integrity.
3. Decision-Making Rules. There must be predetermined rules for making decisions about when to change instruction or alter tiers.

If RTI is being implemented well, one would see teachers engaged in evidence-based instruction, monitoring student progress toward intended goals, and adjusting instruction based on student response to instruction. Teachers would meet regularly in study groups to review and discuss students' progress and there would be clear criteria, specified ahead of time, indicating desired levels of performance and rates of progress. There would be lots of communication with those parents whose children may be at risk, and the use of short, efficient assessments to monitor progress.

Students who failed to make reasonable progress would receive increasingly intensive supports in the form of extra resources or more intensive interventions. Special education services would be reserved for students with disabilities who demonstrate the need for intensive instruction in order to meet their instructional goals.

It remains unclear about whether RTI is being implemented well in schools. Like many new educational practices, implementation integrity is highly varied, and many questionable practices are going on under the name of "RTI." Many of the measurement tools that some school districts and educators select do not meet Tindal's requirement of measurement sufficiency. They do not provide sufficient data for the purpose of making instructional decisions. Many of the instructional interventions going on are not evidence-based. For example, people are using perceptual training or modality training interventions with known lack of empirical support (Fletcher, 2015). And, there is not widespread agreement on decision rules like the number of assessments that need to be below aimline before a change should be made in instruction. Readers should follow the professional literature for research findings that add clarity to appropriate and effective RTI/MTSS practices.

There is increasing evidence that the implementation of an RTI/MTSS Model is not only effective but is more effective than the use of a standard refer–test–serve model of services for students with disabilities. For example, VanDerHeyden and her colleagues (VanDerHeyden & Burns, 2005; VanDerHeyden, Witt, & Gilbertson, 2007) reported that when MTSS was implemented in grades 1–8 in the Vail, Arizona, Unified School District and then replicated with fidelity in three districts:

- Intervention was successful for about 95 to 98 percent of children screened
- Referrals to special education were reduced by more than half
- The percent of students identified as having "learning disabilities" went from 6 percent of all students to 3.5 percent
- There were corresponding gains on state reading and math assessments

Hughes and Dexter (2012) reviewed all field studies of RTI programs for the RTI Action Network. They reported that "All of the studies examining the impact of an RTI program on academic achievement or performance resulted in some level of improvement" (p. 4), and they attributed the changes to the RTI approach. They concluded there was emerging evidence that a tiered early intervention approach can improve the academic performance of at-risk students. However it is important to note that research on the implementation of RTI and MTSS is ongoing, and that these models should continue to be examined as applied in practice. Hughes et al. (2015) caution that there are limitations of RTI field studies as shown by Burns, Appleton & Stehouwer (2005) and VanDerHeyden, Witt & Gilbertson (2007), and that most of the research is limited to studies of reading outcomes. Despite some conflicting evidence in existing research on implementation, MTSS does provide a framework for implementing many of the assessment practices that show great promise for improving student outcomes, particularly for those students who are at-risk for poor academic outcomes.

Chapter Comprehension Questions

Write your answers to each of the following questions and then compare your responses to the text.

1. List the fundamental assumptions in assessing response to instruction or response to intervention.

2. Describe the steps school personnel go through in assessing student needs for differing levels of support.

3. Indicate evidence for and against the effectiveness of response to intervention and a multi-tiered system of supports.

CHAPTER

13

How to Evaluate a Test

LEARNING OBJECTIVES

13-1 Explain a step-by-step process for evaluating a test.

STANDARDS ADDRESSED IN THIS CHAPTER

 CEC Initial Preparation Standards

Standard 4: Assessment

4.0 Beginning special education professionals use multiple methods of assessment and data-sources in making educational decisions.

 CEC Advanced Preparation Standards

Standard 1: Assessment

1.0 Special education specialists use valid and reliable assessment practices to minimize bias.

 National Association of School Psychologists Domains

1 Data-Based Decision Making and Accountability

9 Research and Program Evaluation

Teachers, psychologists, counselors, and other educators often need to evaluate a test to decide if they should put their faith in the test's results. In some instances, educators will want to evaluate a specific test that has already been used, such as an unfamiliar test reported in a multidisciplinary evaluation. In other instances, educators may be looking for a test that can be used to evaluate a specific student or group of students. Various reference books provide information about specific tests: *The Nineteenth Mental Measurements Yearbook* (Carlson, Geisinger, & Jonson, 2014); *Tests, Sixth Edition—A Comprehensive Reference for Assessments in Psychology, Education, and Business* (Maddox, 2008); and *Tests in Print VIII* (Murphy, Geisinger, Carlson, & Spies, 2011). Publishers provide general information about their tests in their catalogs and on their websites. Finally, critical reviews of tests can be found at the *Buros Online Shop* (Buros Center for Testing) and by Internet searches (for example, using phrases like "tests of oral reading").

13-1 Evaluating Tests

It is essential that testers understand that they—not test authors or publishers—are ultimately responsible for accurate and appropriate inferences about the specific students whom they test. Whether evaluating a test that has already been administered or looking for a test to use, educators deal with the same questions.

13-1a IS THE TEST'S CONTENT APPROPRIATE?

Making sure that a test's content is relevant involves more than the names of its subtests. Valid testing of student achievement requires that test content match instructional content. Test and instruction match when what is taught is tested in the same way that it is taught. It also requires testing only content that has been taught. The content of ability tests are a somewhat different matter. These tests usually require test takers to perform some sort of mental or physical manipulation of content. If they are not familiar with the content, failure to manipulate the content does not indicate lack of ability. For example, test takers may be asked to identify the similarity among atlas, dictionary, and thesaurus. If they do not know what a thesaurus and atlas are, they cannot identify the common attribute (a reference book).

The age of the test is also important. Generally, tests that were published 15 or more years ago should not be used unless absolutely necessary (for example, if it is the only test available to assess a specific domain, or newer tests lack adequate norms, reliability, or validity). When dealing with older tests, it is a good idea to contact the publisher to make sure that you are considering the most recent version of a test. It is a waste of time to evaluate a test that is not the latest edition or one that will be replaced soon by a newer version.

13-1b IS THE TEST APPROPRIATE FOR THE STUDENTS TO BE TESTED?

Content that is generally appropriate may still not be appropriate for all students of the same age or grade. Students with physical and sensory handicaps often require extensive test accommodations. However, students who are not identified as disabled may also need test accommodations. These include students from different language and cultural backgrounds, students who are very anxious or distractible, or students who read or process information slowly.

Some tests can be administered to groups while others must be administered individually. While group tests can be appropriately administered to an individual student, the converse is not true. Individual tests cannot be used with groups of students.

13-1c ARE THE TESTING PROCEDURES APPROPRIATE?

Some tests require special training to administer. Other tests may require a specific license or credential to inspect or purchase. In addition to having the necessary credentials to use a test, testers must also be thoroughly familiar with it. First-time users should practice administering and scoring the test.

13-1d IS THE TEST TECHNICALLY ADEQUATE?

In Chapters 4 and 5, we discussed the major technical considerations in test development and use. When evaluating a specific test, it is necessary to understand that each piece of information is probably not of equal importance. For example, while there are several types of information that bear on an achievement test's validity, content validity is usually the most important. It is also important to understand that some types of information are seldom provided by test authors and publishers. For example, test authors seldom provide information about the curriculum in which the students in the norm group were instructed.

An examination of the technical aspects of a test goes beyond checking to determine if specific information relating to important standards is provided; we also consider the quality of the evidence presented. Evaluating the evidence presented in test materials requires a "prove or show me" mind-set. One should expect that test authors will tend to put the best face on their tests. Test authors must demonstrate to potential users that their tests provide accurate educational and psychological information that can be properly used to draw inferences about students.

13-1e THE EVALUATION PROCESS

1. Acquire All Relevant Materials

Usually, this means contacting a test publisher and obtaining a specimen kit and any supplementary manuals that are available. Sometimes publishers will give or lend specimen kits; sometimes they must be purchased. Tests are not just sold by the company that owns the copyright; the same test kit may be sold by different publishing companies. In our experience, the company that owns a test's copyright is often more willing to provide a specimen kit.

It is also helpful to have a copy of the *Standards for Educational and Psychological Testing* (American Educational Research Association, American Psychological Association, and the National Council on Measurement in Education, 2014). This monograph provides brief explanations of the various criteria and the evidence to demonstrate that the criteria have been met.

2. Specify the Test's Most Important Characteristics

Generally speaking, what makes some types of evidence more important than others is a function of the students being tested, the domain being assessed, and the purpose of testing. For example, evidence of content validity is usually more important for achievement tests than for ability tests; evidence of internal consistency is more important than stability when tests are given frequently. It's a good idea to make a list of the important characteristics to indicate your rating of the evidence provided.

3. Review the Test

We begin our review by locating the evidence presented by the author. Often, we find neatly organized test manuals that have useful chapter titles, subsections, and indexes so that we can readily find the sections we seek (for example, reliability). Even when a test manual is organized carefully, we often must extract the evidence we are seeking from large tables or appendices.

When test materials are not well organized or use idiosyncratic terminology, locating the evidence is more difficult. In such instances, we need to assemble all materials. (Because we often need to have all of them open at once, we will need a large workspace.) Then we begin reading and making notes on the important types of evidence for our purpose, content, testing procedures, scores, norms, reliability, and validity. It does not matter where one starts; however, validity and usefulness of inferences based on test scores are better left for last.

Test's Purposes

We generally begin our reviews by finding the uses that the author recommends for a test. For example, the authors of the *Gray Oral Reading Test, fifth edition* (Wiederholt & Bryant, 2012, p. 4) state that their test is intended to (1) identify students with reading difficulties, (2) aid in the diagnosis of reading disabilities, (3) aid in determining particular kinds of reading strengths and weaknesses, (4) document students' progress in reading as a consequence of special intervention programs, and (5) be used in research of the abilities of school children. Thus, if one of the test's intended purposes is the reason we are giving the test, we would look for evidence that the test can be used effectively for that purpose.

Test Content and Assessment Procedures

We first look for a definition of the domain being assessed and then examine the test's content to see if it represents that domain. Some test manuals contain extensive descriptions of the domains they assess. Other manuals merely name the domains, and those names can imply a far broader assessment than the test content actually provides. For example, the *Wide Range Achievement Test 4* (Wilkinson & Robertson, 2006) claims to measure reading. However, cursory examination of the test's content reveals that it only assesses letter identification, word recognition, and comprehension of sentences using a modified cloze[1] procedure.

We also examine testing procedures. Some tests use very tight testing procedures; the test specifies exactly how test materials are to be presented, how test questions are to be asked, if and when questions can be restated or rephrased, and how and when students can be asked to explain or elaborate on their answers. Other tests use loose testing procedures—that is, flexible directions and procedures. In either case, the directions and procedures should contain sufficient detail so that test takers can respond to a task in the manner that the author intended. When test authors provide adaptations and accommodations for students who lack the enabling skills to take the test in the usual manner, the author should provide evidence that the adaptations and accommodations produce scores with the same meaning as those produced by nonadapted, nonaccommodated procedures. Generally, the more flexible the materials and directions, the more valid the test results will be for students with severe disabilities. For example, the *Scales of Independent Behavior–Revised* (Bruininks, Woodcock, & Hill, 1984) can be administered to any respondent who is thoroughly familiar with the person being assessed.

It is also necessary to examine how test content is tested. Specifically, we look for evidence that the test's content and scoring procedures represent the domain. Evidence may include any of the following, alone or in combination:

- Comparisons of tested content with some external standard. For example, the National Council of Teachers of Mathematics has explicated extensive standards for what and how mathematical knowledge should be tested.

- Comparisons of tested content with the content tested by other accepted tests.

- Expert opinion.

- Reasoned rationale for the inclusion and exclusion of test content as well as assessment procedures.

---

[1] In a cloze procedure, one or more words are removed from a sentence, and the test taker is asked to replace the missing word with a contextually appropriate one.

Scores

The types of derived scores available on a test should be the most straightforward piece of evidence about a test. Information about the types of scores might be found in several places: in a section on scoring the test, in a section on norms, in a separate section on scores, in a section on interpreting scores, or on a scoring form.

We must consider if the types of scores lead to correct inferences about students. For example, norm-referenced scores lead to inferences about a student's relative standing on the skills or abilities tested. Such scores are appropriate when a student is being compared to other students, for example, when trying to determine if a student is lagging behind peers significantly. Such scores are not appropriate when trying to determine if a student has acquired specific information (for example, knows the meaning of various traffic signs) or skills (for example, can read fluently material at grade level). On the other hand, knowing that a student can perform accurately and fluently with grade-level material provides no information about how that performance compares to the performances of other similarly situated students.[2] If test authors use unique kinds of scores (or even scores that they create), it is their responsibility to define the scores. For example, the Woodcock-Johnson Psychoeducational Battery IV (Shrank, McGrew, & Mather, 2014) includes a "W-Score" as one unit of analysis.

Norms

Whenever a student's score is interpreted by comparing it to scores earned by a reference population (that is, scores earned by other test takers who comprise the normative sample), the reference population must be clearly described (AERA et al., 2014, p. 104). For example, whenever a student's performance is converted to a percentile or some other derived score, it is essential that the normative sample be composed of a sufficient number of test takers to whom we would ordinarily want to compare our student's performance.

A word of caution is warranted. In developing test norms, several thousand students may actually be tested, but not all of those students' scores may be used. Scores might be dropped for any one of several reasons:

- Demographic data are missing (for example, a student's gender or age might not be noted).
- A student failed to complete the test or an examiner inadvertently failed to administer all items.
- A student failed to conform to criteria for inclusion in the norm group (for example, he or she may be too old or too young).
- A score may be an outlier (for example, a fifth grader may correctly answer all of the questions that could be given to an adult).

Thus, the number of students initially tested will not be the same as the number of students in the norm group.[3]

Good norms are based on far more than just the age (or grade) and gender of students. Norms must be generally representative of all students of that age or grade. Thus, we would expect students from major racial and ethnic groups (that is, Caucasian Americans, African Americans, Asian Americans, and Hispanic Americans) to be included. We would also expect students from throughout the United States as well as students from urban, suburban, and rural communities to be included. Finally, we would expect students from all socioeconomic classes to be included. Moreover, we would expect that the proportions of students from each

[2] We repeat the warning that grade equivalents do not indicate the level of materials at which a student is instructional. A grade equivalent of 3.0 does not indicate that a student is accurate or fluent in 3.0 materials. More likely, 3.0 materials are far too difficult for a person with a grade equivalent of 3.0.

[3] The difference between the number of students tested and the number of students actually used in the norms is of relevance only when a number of students are dropped, and the validity of the norming process is therefore called into question.

of these groups would be approximately the same as the proportions found in the general population. Therefore, we look for a systematic comparison of the proportion of students with each characteristic to the general population for each separate norm group. For example, when the score of a 9-year-old girl is compared to those of 9-year-old girls in general, we look for evidence that the norm group of 9-year-old girls (1) consists of the correct proportions of Caucasian Americans, African Americans, and Asian Americans, (2) contains the correct proportion of Hispanic students, (3) contains the correct proportion of students from each region of the country and each type of community, and so forth. Because some authors do not use weighting procedures, we do not expect perfect congruence with the population proportions. However, when the majority group's proportion differs by 5 percent or more from its proportion in the general population, we believe the norms may have problems. (We recognize that this is an arbitrary criterion; but it seems generally reasonable to us.)

Reliability

For every score that is recommended for interpretation, a test author must provide evidence of reliability. First, every score means all domain and norm comparison scores. Domain scores are scores for each area or subarea that can be interpreted appropriately. For example, an author of an achievement test might recommend interpreting scores for reading, written language, and mathematics; an author might recommend interpreting scores for oral reading and reading comprehension, whereas another author might use oral reading and reading comprehension as intermediate calculations that should not be interpreted. Next, norm comparison means each normative group to which a person's score could be compared (for example, a reading score for third-grade girls, for second-grade boys, or for fifth graders). Thus, if an author provides whole-year norms for students (boys and girls combined) in the first through third grades in reading and mathematics, there should be reliability information for 6 scores—that is, 3 (grades) multiplied by 2 (subject matter areas). If there were whole-year norms for students in the first through the twelfth grades in 3 subject matter areas, there would be 36 recommended scores— that is, 12 grades multiplied by 3 subject matter areas. In practice, it is not unusual to see reliability information for 100 or more domain-by-age (or grade) scores.[4]

As we have already learned, reliability is not a unitary concept. It refers to the consistency with which a test samples items from a domain (that is, item reliability), to the stability of scores over time, and to the consistency that testers score responses. Information about a test's item reliability, as well as its stability estimates, must be presented; these indices are necessary for all tests. Information about interscorer reliability is only required when scoring is difficult or not highly objective. Thus, we expect to see estimates of item reliability and stability (and perhaps interscorer agreement) for each domain or subdomain by norm–group combination. If there are normative comparisons for reading and mathematics for students in the first through third grades, and item reliability and stability were estimated, there would be 12 reliability estimates: 6 estimates of item reliability for reading and mathematics at each grade and 6 estimates of stability for reading and mathematics at each grade.

Given modern computer technology, there is really no excuse for failing to provide all estimates of internal consistency. Collecting evidence of a test's stability is far more expensive and time consuming. Thus, we often find incomplete stability data. This can occur in a couple of ways. One way is for authors to report an average stability by using standard scores from a sample that represents the entire age or grade range of the test.[5] Although this procedure gives an idea of the test's stability

---

[4] Note that information about reliability coefficients applies to any type of score (for example, standard scores, raw scores, and so forth). Information about standard errors of measurement is specific to each type of score.

[5] Using raw scores would overestimate the test's stability if raw scores were correlated with age or grade.

in general, it provides no information about the stability of scores at a particular age or grade. Another way authors incompletely report stability data is by providing data for selected ages (or age ranges) that span a test's age range. For example, if a test was intended for students in kindergarten through sixth grade, an author might report stability for first, third, and fifth grades.

It is not enough, however, for a test merely to contain the necessary reliability estimates. Every reliability estimate should be sufficient for every purpose for which the test was intended. Thus, tests (or subtests) used in making important educational decisions for students should have reliability estimates of .90 or higher. Also, each test (and subtest) must have sufficient reliability for each age or grade at which it is used. For example, if a reading test was highly reliable for all grades except second grade, it would not be suitable for use with second graders.

Finally, when test scoring is subjective, evidence of interscorer agreement must be provided. Failure to report this type of evidence severely limits the utility of a test.

Validity

The evaluation of a test's general validity can be the most complicated aspect of test evaluation. Strictly speaking, a test found lacking in its content, procedures, scores, norms, or reliability cannot yield valid inferences. Regardless of the domains they assess, all tests should present convincing evidence of general validity. General validity refers to evidence that a test measures what its authors claim it measures. Thus, we would expect some evidence for content validity, criterion-related validity, and construct validity.

However, we expect more. Test authors should also present evidence that their test leads to valid inferences for each recommended purpose of the test. For example, if test authors claim their test can be used to identify students with learning disabilities, we would expect to see evidence that use of the test leads to correct inferences about the presence of a disability. When these inferences rely on the use of cutoff scores, there should be evidence that a specific cutoff score is valid. Similarly, if test authors claim their test is useful in planning instruction, evidence is needed. Evidence for a standardized test's utility in planning instruction would consist of data showing how a test score or profile can be used to find instructional starting points—and the accuracy of those starting points.

Making a Summative Evaluation

In reaching an overall evaluation of a test, it is a good idea to remember that it is the test authors' responsibility to convince potential test users of the usefulness of their test. However, once you, the tester, use a test, you—not the test author—become responsible for test-based inferences.

Test-based inferences can only be correct when a test is properly normed, yields reliable scores, and has evidence for its general validity. If evidence for any one of these components is lacking or insufficient (for example, the norms are inadequate or the scores are unreliable), then the inferences cannot be trusted. Having found that a test is generally useful, it is still necessary to determine if it is appropriately used with the specific students you intend to test, for the purpose you are testing. Of course, a test that is not generally useful will not be useful with a specific student.

4. Make a Summative Decision

The summative decision answers the questions we asked in Table 2.1 on page 16. Are the results of this test accurate enough to use in making decisions about screening, student progress, instructional planning, resource allocation, eligibility for special education services, evaluating pupil programs, and overall accountability? The criteria for each of these decisions are different because the consequences of each decision are different. Making long-term life altering decisions about individual students requires the highest quality of evidence. When making decisions about groups of students, individual errors tend to balance out, so a somewhat lower quality of evidence can be used. Regardless of the decision, testers must be transparent about the quality of the data they present.

Chapter Comprehension Questions

Write your answers to each of the following questions and then compare your responses to the text.

1. What are the four steps involved in reviewing a test?

2. What are the specific qualities one examines when reviewing a test?

CHAPTER
14

ASSESSMENT OF ACADEMIC ACHIEVEMENT WITH MULTIPLE-SKILL DEVICES

LEARNING OBJECTIVES

14-1 Describe factors to consider in selecting an achievement test.

14-2 Explain the reasons why we assess academic achievement.

14-3 Describe and compare representative individually administered achievement tests.

14-4 Explain how to get the most out of an achievement test.

STANDARDS ADDRESSED IN THIS CHAPTER

 CEC Initial Preparation Standards
Standard 4: Assessment
4.0 Beginning special education professionals use multiple methods of assessment and data-sources in making educational decisions.

 CEC Advanced Preparation Standards
Standard 1: Assessment
1.0 Special education specialists use valid and reliable assessment practices to minimize bias.

National Association of School Psychologists Domains
1 Data-Based Decision Making and Accountability
3 Interventions and Instructional Support to Develop Academic Skills

Until very recently school personnel gave group-administered, norm-referenced achievement tests that assessed student skills in multiple domains (e.g. Reading Vocabulary, Reading Comprehension, Reading Rate, Mathematics Computation, Mathematics Concepts and Problem Solving, Language, Spelling, Writing, Listening Comprehension, Science and Social Studies) for purposes of screening and student progress evaluation. The tests used included measures like the Stanford Achievement Test, Metropolitan Achievement Tests, Iowa Tests of Basic Skills, and the Terra Nova. Administration of these tests took extensive classroom time (6 to 8 hours spread over several days), took long to score and to provide feedback to teachers and parents, and provided teachers with limited information to direct instructional planning. With the development and increased use of curriculum-based and computer adaptive measures of specific skills, the use of group achievement tests diminished significantly. And, with federal accountability requirements as part of the No Child Left Behind Education Act, states were required to report annually on the performance and progress of all students relative to specific state standards, and later, toward common core state standards. States and their schools now use standards-referenced tests that are either part of specific assessment consortia like the Smarter Balanced Assessment Consortium (SBAC) or the Partnership for Assessment of Readiness for College and Careers (PARCC), or are custom-made for them by specific test publishers.[1]

In this chapter we concentrate on description and review of the individually administered tests of multiple skills that are used in making screening, eligibility, instructional, and program evaluation decisions. They are among the measures most frequently used by IEP teams in making such decisions. **Multiple-skill achievement tests** evaluate knowledge and understanding in several curricular areas, such as reading, spelling, math, and/or language. These tests are intended to assess the extent to which students have profited from schooling and other life experiences, compared with other students of the same age or grade.

14-1 Considerations for Selecting a Test

In selecting an individually administered multiple-skill achievement test, teachers must consider four factors: content validity, stimulus response modes, opportunity to learn, and relevant norms.

First, teachers must evaluate evidence for content validity, the most important kind of validity for achievement tests. Many multiple-skill tests have general content validity—the tests measure important concepts and skills that are generally part of most curricula. This validity makes their content suitable for assessing general attainment.[2] However, if a test is to be used to assess the extent to which students have profited from school instruction—that is, to measure student achievement, more than general content—validity is required: The test must match the instruction provided. *Tests that do not match instruction lack content validity, and decisions based on such tests should be restricted.* Read the upcoming Dilemmas in Current Practice section within this chapter for more information on this issue. When making

---

[1] SBAC is a group of states working together to develop a system of computer adaptive assessments aligned with the Common Core State Standards (CCSS) in English Language Art/Literacy (ELA) and Mathematics for grades 3–8 and 11. The measures consist of a summative measure to be used for accountability purposes and interim measures to be used for instructional planning (see the website of SBAC for more information). PARCC is a group of states (the states involved in SBAC and PARCC are mutually exclusive) working together to develop a set of assessments that measure whether students are on track to be successful in college and their careers. The measures are computer-based math and English Language Arts/Literacy (ELA) tests that help teachers design learning to meet students' needs. The set of measures include diagnostic tests, mid-year tests and end-of-year (summative) tests (see the website of PARCC for more information). We also cover more information on the use of the SBAC and PARCC measures in Chapter 22. In Chapter 10 we have described CBM and CAT measures that are used in progress monitoring for the purpose of making instructional planning and evaluation decisions.

[2] Achievement generally refers to content that has been learned as a product of schooling. Attainment is a broader term referring to what individuals have learned as a result of both schooling and other life experiences.

decisions about content validity for students with disabilities, educators must consider the extent to which the student has had an opportunity to learn the content of the test. In some situations, student with disabilities have not had adequate access to instruction in the skills measured on multiple-skill achievement tests. In these cases, a low score on such a test may reflect lack of instruction rather than the influence the school has had on the student's development of academic skills.

Second, educators who use achievement tests for students with disabilities need to consider whether the stimulus–response modes of subtests may be exceptionally difficult for students with physical or motor problems. Tests that are timed may be inappropriately difficult for students whose reading or motor difficulties cause them to take more time on specific tasks. (Many of these issues are described in greater detail in Chapter 7 on accommodations).

Third, educators must consider the common core standards and the state education standards for the state in which they work. In doing so, they should examine the extent to which the achievement test they select measures the content of their state standards.

Fourth, educational professionals must evaluate the adequacy of each test's norms by asking whether the normative group is composed of the kinds of individuals to whom they wish to compare their students. If a test is used to estimate general attainment, a representative sample of students from throughout the nation is preferred. However, if a test is used to estimate achievement compared to other students within a school system, local norms are probably better. Finally, teachers should examine the extent to which a total test and its components have the reliability necessary for making decisions about what students have learned.

14-2 Why Do We Assess Academic Achievement?

Achievement tests are used most often as a broad assessment of academic skill development in making universal screening or accountability decisions. They also may be used to identify individual students for whom educational intervention is necessary, either in the form of remediation (for those who demonstrate relatively low-level skill development) or in the form of academic enrichment (for those who exhibit exceptionally high-level skill development). However, screening tests have limited behavior samples. They are necessarily broad samples of behavior. Therefore, students who are identified with screening tests should be further assessed with diagnostic tests in specific content areas like reading or math to verify their need for specific educational intervention. Specific diagnostic tests are described and evaluated in the chapters on diagnostic testing in reading, math, and written language.

14-3 Specific Individually Administered Tests of Academic Achievement

This section of the chapter addresses four individually administered multiple-skill devices (the Diagnostic Achievement Battery–4, the Peabody Individual Achievement Test [PIAT-R/NU], the Wechsler Individual Achievement Test 3 [WIAT-III], and the Wide Range Achievement Test 4 [WRAT4]). Later chapters discuss both screening and diagnostic tests that are devoted to specific content areas, such as reading and mathematics. In Chapter 18, we review the Woodcock–Johnson IV Tests of Achievement, a very comprehensive individually administered achievement test that is part of a larger battery of intelligence, achievement, and oral language tests.

14-3a DIAGNOSTIC ACHIEVEMENT BATTERY–4 (DAB-4)

The most recent edition of the Diagnostic Achievement Battery–4 (Newcomer, 2014) is the fourth in a series of measures that was originally published in 1984. The DAB–4 is widely used to (1) identify student standing in basic academic content areas with a focus on identification of those who are significantly below their peers, (2) identify academic strengths and weaknesses, (3) document academic progress or growth, and (4) conduct research on academic achievement. With this fourth edition of the test the number of subtests was reduced from 14 to eight. There are no set time limits for this test; all eight subtests can be given in approximately 60 to 90 minutes. Testing time can be shortened by administering three of the subtests (Spelling, Punctuation/Capitalization, and Mathematics Calculation) to small groups. Test materials consist of an examiner's manual, examiner's response booklets, student booklets, assessment probes, and an audio CD.

Subtests

Listening Comprehension The examiner plays the audio CD or reads aloud brief stories and asks the student to respond to questions about them. The subtest has 35 items.

Synonyms A 28-item subtest requiring the student to say a word that has the same meaning as a word read by the examiner.

Alphabet/Phonics/Word Identification A 67-item subtest requiring students to identify letters of the alphabet, sounds of letters, and words in isolation.

Reading Comprehension This 45-item subtest involves two kinds of tasks. One is a Word–Picture Relationship Task in which the student must read a word silently and then point to the picture that matches the word. The second is a Story Comprehension Task in which students read short stories silently and answer a series of questions about the stories.

Punctuation/Capitalization This is a paper-and-pencil task in which students must add capitalization and punctuation to a series of sentences that range in difficulty from simple two-word structures to complex structures.

Spelling Students must write a series of words dictated by the examiner.

Mathematics Reasoning This is a 28-item subtest ranging in difficulty from lower-level items, in which students respond to orally presented mathematics questions about pictures, to higher-level word problems.

Mathematics Calculation The student must solve 36 math problems arranged in order of difficulty, including basic facts, decimal usage, fractions, and some algebraic concepts.

The subtests of the DAB–4 are combined to form five academic composites, including Spoken Language, Reading, Writing, Mathematics, and Total Basic Academic Skills. Specific rules regarding where to start administration of each subtest and rules for establishing basals and ceilings are provided. These help limit the number of items that must be administered to students and shorten the administration of the subtests.

Scores

Several kinds of scores are obtained for DAB–4. These include Age Equivalents, Grade Equivalents, Percentile Ranks, Scaled Scores for each subtest (M = 10, SD = 3), and Standard Scores (called Index Scores) for the composites (M = 100, SD = 15). The author provides a set of tables in the test manual indicating the magnitude of difference between DAB–4 subtest scores or between DAB–4 composite scores to be statistically significant. This helps users interpret whether differences represent reliable strengths and weaknesses.

The DAB–4 manual provides the user with specific points to start each subtest. And, specific rules for establishing **basals** (that point in the subtest below which it is assumed the student would get all items correct) and **ceilings** (that point in the subtest above which it is assumed the student would fail all items) are provided. This shortens administration time.

Norms

The DAB–4 was standardized between summer 2011 and fall 2013 on a sample of 1,310 students from 25 states. There were between 114 and 166 students at each age level, ages 6 to 14. As such, the normative sample is limited in size. The author contends that the norm sample is representative in demographic characteristics and provides evidence that the sample characteristics match those of the U.S. school-age population on geographic region, gender, race, Hispanic status, exceptionality status, parental education, and household income. However, no cross-tabs are provided. That is, there is no indication of whether the African American students came primarily from the Southeast, whether the males were predominantly Hispanic, and so forth. Such evidence would help school personnel make judgments about the extent to which the students they are assessing are like those in the norm group.

Reliability

Internal consistency reliability coefficients for subtests of the DAB–4 range from .73 to .96, with only the listening comprehension subtest having reliabilities below .80. Internal consistency for the composite scores ranges from .89 to .97. Internal consistency coefficients are also provided for gender, ethnicity, and selected exceptionality subgroups, and these are again in excess of .80.

A test–retest reliability study was conducted on two groups of students ages 6–10 and 11–14. All but one of the reliability coefficients for the combined samples exceeded .80 for the subtests and all but one exceeded .90 for the composite scores. The internal consistency and test–retest reliabilities are sufficiently high to use the test in making important educational decisions about students.

Validity

Extensive material is included in the DAB–4 manual on the rationale for the specific test items and formats included in the test, and there is evidence provided that the subtests measure content areas usually included on other individually administered achievement tests. The author provides detail on item analysis procedures used to select test items and on the results of statistical analyses used to examine item bias. There is reasonable evidence for the content validity of DAB–4.

The author provides evidence of criterion-predictive validity of the DAB–4 by showing that scores on DAB–4 are closely related to scores on other achievement tests and to eight measures of school achievement from two tests. Correlations with other tests range from .56 to .76. There is reasonable evidence for the content and predictive validity of the DAB–4.

Summary

The DAB–4 is an individually administered achievement test that has eight subtests that assess basic skills in four academic composite areas: spoken language, reading, writing, and mathematics. The test is standardized on a limited sample, but has adequate reliability and validity for use in making important educational decisions.

14-3b PEABODY INDIVIDUAL ACHIEVEMENT TEST–REVISED/ NORMATIVE UPDATE

The most recent edition of the Peabody Individual Achievement Test (PIAT-R/NU; Markwardt, 1998) is not a new edition of the test but a normative update of the 1989 edition of the PIAT-R. The test is an individually administered, norm-referenced instrument designed to provide a wide-ranging screening measure of academic achievement in six content areas. It can be used with students in kindergarten through grade 12. PIAT-R/NU test materials are contained in four easel kits, one for each volume of the test. Easel kit volumes present stimulus materials to the student at eye level; the examiner's instructions are placed on the reverse side. The student can see one side of the response plate, whereas the examiner can see both sides. The test is recommended by the author for use in individual evaluation, guidance, admissions and transfers, grouping of students, progress evaluation, and personnel selection. This test was once one of the most popular individually administered tests used to assess students' academic achievement. The items and norms for the test are now so out-of-date that the test is no longer useful in making important decisions about students.

The original PIAT (Dunn & Markwardt, 1970) included five subtests. The PIAT-R added a written expression subtest. The 1989 edition updated the content of the test. The 1998 edition is identical to the 1989 edition. Behaviors sampled by the six subtests of the PIAT-R/NU follow.

Subtests

Mathematics This subtest contains 100 multiple-choice items, ranging from items that assess such early skills as matching, discriminating, and recognizing numerals, to items that assess advanced concepts in geometry and trigonometry. The test is a measure of the student's knowledge and application of math concepts and facts.

Reading Recognition This subtest contains 100 items, ranging in difficulty from preschool level through high school level. Items assess skill development in matching letters, naming capital and lowercase letters, and recognizing words in isolation.

Reading Comprehension This subtest contains 81 multiple-choice items assessing skill development in understanding what is read. After reading a sentence, the student must indicate comprehension by choosing the correct picture out of a group of four.

Spelling This subtest consists of 100 items sampling behaviors from kindergarten level through high school level. Initial items assess the student's ability to distinguish a printed letter of the alphabet from pictured objects and to associate letter symbols with speech sounds. More difficult items assess the student's ability to identify, from a response bank of four words, the correct spelling of a word read aloud by the examiner.

General Information This subtest consists of 100 questions presented orally, which the student must answer orally. Items assess the extent to which the student has learned facts in social studies, science, sports, and the fine arts.

Written Expression This subtest assesses written-language skills at two levels. Level I, appropriate for students in kindergarten and first grade, is a measure of prewriting skills, such as skill in copying and writing letters, words, and sentences from dictation. At Level II, the student writes a story in response to a picture prompt.

Scores

All but one of the PIAT-R/NU subtests are scored in the same way: The student's response to each item is rated pass–fail. On these five subtests, raw scores are converted to grade and age equivalents, grade- and age-based standard scores, percentile ranks, normal-curve equivalents, and stanines. The Written Expression subtest is scored differently from the other subtests. The examiner uses a set of scoring criteria included in an appendix in the test manual. At Level I, the examiner scores the student's writing of his or her name and then scores 18 items pass–fail. For the more difficult items at Level I, the student must earn a specified number of subcredits to pass the item. Methods for assigning subcredits are specified clearly in the manual. At Level II, the student generates a free response, and the assessor examines the response for certain specified characteristics. For example, the student is given credit for each letter correctly capitalized, each correct punctuation, and the absence of inappropriate words. Scores earned on the Written Expression subtest include grade-based stanines and developmental scaled scores (with mean –8 and standard deviation –3).

Three composite scores are used to summarize student performance on the PIAT-R/NU: total reading, total test, and written language. Total reading is described as an overall measure of "reading ability" and is obtained by combining scores on Reading Recognition and Reading Comprehension. The total test score is obtained by combining performance on the General Information, Reading Recognition, Reading Comprehension, Mathematics, and Spelling subtests. A third composite score, the written-language composite score, is optional and is obtained by combining performance on the Spelling and Written Expression subtests.

Norms

The 1989 edition of the PIAT-R/NU was standardized on 1,563 students in kindergarten through grade 12. The 1998 normative update was completed in conjunction with normative updating of the Kaufman Test of Educational Achievement, the Key Math–Revised, and the Woodcock Reading Mastery Tests–Revised. The sample for the normative updates was 3,184 students in kindergarten through grade 12. A stratified multistage sampling procedure was used to ensure selection of a nationally representative group at each grade level. Students in the norm group did not all take each of the five tests. Rather, one-fifth of the students took each test, along with portions of each of the other tests. Thus, the norm groups for the brief and comprehensive forms consist of approximately 600 students. There are as few as 91 students at three-year age ranges. Because multiple measures were given to each student, the authors could use linking and equating to increase the size of the norm sample.

Approximately 10 years separate the data-collection periods for the original PIAT norms and the updated norms. Changes during that time in curriculum and educational practice, in population demographics, and in the general cultural environment may have affected levels of academic achievement. Now the content of this test is more than 35 years old and the norm sample is more than 25 years dated. The relatively small size of the norm sample at each age and grade level, as well as the fact that the content and

norms are very seriously outdated, make the PIAT-R/NU virtually useless as a measure of current academic achievement.

Reliability

All data on the reliability of the PIAT-R/NU are for the original PIAT-R. The performance of students on the two measures has changed, and so the authors should have conducted a few reliability studies on students in the late 1990s. Generalizations from the reliability of the original PIAT-R to reliability of the PIAT-R/NU are suspect.

Validity

All data on the validity of the PIAT-R/NU are for the original PIAT-R. The performance of students on the two measures has changed, and so the authors should have conducted a few validity studies on students in the late 1990s. Generalizations from the validity of the original PIAT-R to validity of PIAT-R/NU are suspect. This is especially true for measures of validity based on relations with external measures, where the measures (for example, the Wide Range Achievement Test or the Peabody Picture Vocabulary Test) have been revised.

Summary

The PIAT-R/NU is an individually administered achievement test that was renormed in 1998. Reliability and validity information is based on studies of the 1989 edition of the test. As with any achievement test, the most crucial concern is content validity. Users must be sensitive to the correspondence of the content of the PIAT-R/NU to a student's curriculum. The test is essentially a 1970 test that was revised and renormed in 1989 and then renormed again in 1998. Data on reliability and validity are based on the earlier version of the scale, which of course has gone unchanged. The practice of updating norms without gathering data on continued technical adequacy is dubious. The norm sample is both very small and very dated. This test now should be considered very dated and of questionable relevance to current curricula. It is a good example of a test that should not be used in today's schools. School personnel should measure academic achievement using other tests.

14-3c WECHSLER INDIVIDUAL ACHIEVEMENT TEST–THIRD EDITION[3]

The Wechsler Individual Achievement Test–Third Edition (WIAT-III; Psychological Corporation, 2009) is a diagnostic, norm-referenced achievement test designed to assess reading, mathematics, written

[3] Written by Jill Fortain, Kristen S. Girard, Nathan von der Embse.

expression, listening, and speaking of individuals ages 4 years, 0 months, to 19 years, 11 months (or pre-kindergarten through grade 12). In this third edition, the authors contend that the WIAT-III better captures and aligns with recent federal legislation and state regulation changes in the identification of learning disabilities. They further argue that the WIAT-III, which includes 16 subtests (organized into seven domain composite scores and one total achievement composite; see Table 14.1), fully assesses each of the eight achievement areas in which specific learning disabilities can be identified under the Individuals with Disabilities Education Improvement Act of 2004 (IDEA, 2004; basic read-

ing skills, reading fluency, reading comprehension, written expression, oral expression, listening comprehension, mathematics calculation, mathematics problem solving) in greater depth than previous versions of the test. New subtests on the WIAT-III that were not included on the WIAT-II include the oral reading fluency and mathematics fluency subtests. For children in pre-kindergarten or kindergarten, the length of administration is approximately 45 to 50 minutes; administration to students in grades 1 through 6 lasts approximately 1.5 hours and for grades 7 through 12 is approximately 1.5 to 2 hours.

TABLE 14.1	Description of the WIAT-III Composites and Subtests

Composite	Subtest	Description
Total Reading		
Basic Reading	Word Reading	Assess word recognition, word reading, and decoding skills ■ Fluently pronounce or read aloud individual words presented in isolation
	Pseudoword Decoding	Assess the ability to apply phonetic decoding skills ■ Read aloud nonsense, made-up words that conform to typical English language phonetic structures
Reading Comprehension and Fluency	Reading Comprehension	Assess skills in drawing meaning from text. ■ Reading passages (out loud or silently) and providing oral responses to content questions
	Oral Reading Fluency	Assess the ability to read text quickly, accurately, and with comprehension ■ Read a series of grade-level passages aloud ■ Answer a question pertaining to the passage's content
	Early Reading Skills*	Assess decoding and prereading skills ■ Identify letters by name and by sound ■ Identify words that begin/end with the same sound(s) ■ Word rhyming and letter blending activities ■ Match printed words to the appropriate picture
Mathematics	Math Problem Solving	Assess mathematical reasoning skills ■ Count ■ Identify shapes ■ Solve single- and multiple-step story problems ■ Interpret graphs and charts ■ Solve problems using geometry, statistics and probability
	Numerical Operations	Assess the ability to identify and write numbers; perform mathematical computations ■ Solve written computation problems ■ Solve basic equations involving addition, subtraction, multiplication, or division of whole numbers, decimals, and/or fractions
Math Fluency	Math Fluency – Addition	Evaluate computational fluency ■ Solve basic addition problems quickly and accurately
	Math Fluency – Subtraction	Evaluate computational fluency ■ Solve basic subtraction problems quickly and accurately

(Continues)

TABLE 14.1		Description of the WIAT-III Composites and Subtests *Continued*
Composite	**Subtest**	**Description**
	Math Fluency – Multiplication	Evaluate computational fluency ▪ Solve basic multiplication problems quickly and accurately
Written Expression	Alphabet Writing Fluency	Assess automatic letter writing skills ▪ Write the letters of the alphabet in any order, in print or cursive, lower- or uppercase
	Spelling	Assess spelling skills ▪ Write dictated letters, letter blends, and whole words
	Sentence Composition	Evaluate the ability to write well-formulated sentences ▪ Combine multiple sentences into single sentences while preserving meaning and using correct spelling, capitalization, and punctuation ▪ Build sentences using target words
	Essay Composition	▪ Measure writing skills, including theme development text organization, and grammar and mechanics ▪ Construct a narrative essay based on the given prompt
Oral Language	Listening Comprehension	Measure comprehension of single sentences and extended orally presented discourse ▪ Pointing to objects upon request ▪ Orally responding to questions about passages presented aloud
	Oral Expression	Measure expressive vocabulary and word retrieval skills ▪ Providing words orally to match described constructs ▪ Repeating orally presented sentences verbatim

*NOTE: Although the Early Reading Skills subtest does measure students' prereading skills, it is not included in the calculation of the Total Reading Composite score or any of the other two reading-related composites. It is only included in the calculation of students' Total Achievement Score.

© 2013 Cengage Learning

Scores

Seven types of scores are available on the WIAT-III, including standard scores, percentile ranks, normal curve equivalents, stanines, age and grade equivalents, and growth scale value scores. In order to obtain these scores, examiners must first obtain the students' raw subtest scores following the appropriate basal and ceiling rules or item-set guidelines for each subtest. Additionally, two subtests (Reading Comprehension and Oral Reading Fluency) require raw scores be converted to weighted raw scores prior to obtaining the corresponding standard scores.

Norms

The WIAT-III was standardized on a national sample of 2,775 students. A stratified sampling procedure was used to ensure that the normative samples for both grade and age were representative of students in grades pre-kindergarten through grade 12 on each of the following demographic variables (based on the U.S. Bureau of the Census data from October 2005): grade, age, race/ethnicity, sex, parent education level, and geographic region. The grade-based normative sample included 1,400 and 1,375 students (a fall and a spring sample, respectively), reflecting 14 grade-level groups. With the exception of a pre-kindergarten sample in the spring, which had only 75 participants, all grade groups had 100 participants in both fall and spring samples. The age-based normative sample included 1,826 students, which, like the grade-based groups, were divided into 14 groups based on age. The racial-ethnic makeups of each age and grade sample, as well as the geographic representation within each age and grade sample, were reported to reflect those of the U.S. population. Cross-tabs are not provided, so we do not know which racial groups came from which regions, whether males were overrepresented in specific regions, and such. Such information would assist users in deciding the extent to which their students were similar to the norm group.

Reliability

Split-half reliability coefficients were calculated with the exception of timed subtests and those subtests that do not provide data at the individual item-level (i.e., Alphabet Writing Fluency, Math Fluency, Alphabet Writing Fluency, Sentence Composition, Essay Composition, Oral Expression, and Oral Reading Fluency). All eight composites across all school ages and grades had split-half reliabilities higher than .90 except for the Oral Language and Written Expression composites, which were equal to or higher than .85 across all school ages and grades.

Test–retest reliability was also calculated in order to demonstrate the stability of the WIAT-III using a sample of 131 students. The reported average test–retest interval for pre-kindergarten through fifth grades was 13 days, and 14 days for grades six through twelve. Correlations suggested generally adequate stability for both grade-level groups. Specifically, the average correlation coefficients for the Reading Comprehension, Word Reading, Pseudoword Decoding, Oral Reading Fluency, Oral Reading Rate, and Spelling subtests were the highest, ranging from .90 to .94. Early Reading Skills, Math Problem Solving, Essay Composition, Essay Composition: Grammar and Mechanics, Numerical Operations, Oral Expression, Oral Reading Accuracy, and Math Fluency (Addition, Subtraction, and Multiplication subtests) also demonstrated strong levels of stability with average correlation coefficients ranging from .82 to .89. Two subtests, Listening Comprehension and Sentence Composition, demonstrated lower, yet still acceptable, levels of stability with average correlation coefficients of .75 and .79.

Finally, interrater agreement was calculated for subtests with objective and more subjective scoring criteria. For the objective subtests, agreement was reported to range from 98 percent to 99 percent. Intraclass correlation procedures were used to obtain interrater reliability coefficients for those subtests or subtest components in which scoring is more subjective (i.e., Reading Comprehension, Alphabet Writing Fluency, Sentence Composition, Essay Composition, Oral Expression). The authors report that the interrater reliability coefficients for these subtests ranged from .92 to .99. Thus, it appears that the more subjective subtests are still quite reliable, despite the need for professional judgment in scoring.

Validity

Several methods were used to establish validity for the WIAT-III. In order to establish content validity, both the content of the previous test version and the suggested new subtests and specific items for the WIAT-III were subjected to exhaustive literature and expert reviews. Evidence for construct validity was established by examining the relationships among composites, subtests, and items scores (i.e., by examining the internal structure) of the WIAT-III. Students' response processes were also examined to

demonstrate that the subtest items elicit the expected cognitive processes. Empirical and descriptive examinations of students' common errors and response patterns suggesting misunderstanding of questions, as well as comprehensive literature reviews and expert consultation, are included in the technical manual to provide evidence for validity of the response processes required by subtest items.

Criterion-related validity was established by examining the relationships between the WIAT-III and several other measures (i.e., WIAT-II, WPPSI–III, WISC-IV, WAIS-IV, WNV, and DAS-II). For example, the corrected correlation coefficients between WIAT-III and WIAT-II composites ranged from .65 for Math Fluency—Math to .93 for Total Achievement—Total. In addition, the correlation coefficient for the WIAT-III Total Achievement and the WPPSI-III Full Scale IQ (FSIQ) was .78, and the correlation between the WIAT-III Total Achievement and the WISC-IV FSIQ was .82. The WISC-IV FSIQ and WIAT-III Composites correlation coefficients ranged from .53 to .75.

Finally, the authors of the WIAT-III also sought to determine the clinical utility of the WIAT-III by conducting special group studies with nonrandomly selected subsamples of students with disabilities (i.e., mild intellectual disability, reading disorder, mathematics disorder, disorder of written expression, and individuals with expressive language disorder). In order to achieve this end, the average composite and subtest scores obtained by the special group and by a matched control group were compared. Participants were matched based on gender, race/ethnicity, parent education level, geographic region, grade, and semester. Students with mild intellectual impairment, on average, scored significantly lower on all WIAT-III composites and subtests than their matched counterparts (at the $p < .01$ level) with the mean standard score differences ranging from 22.08 on Alphabet Writing Fluency to 41.55 on Reading Comprehension.

Summary

The WIAT-III is an individually administered, norm-referenced diagnostic assessment tool. Made up of 16 subtests, it allows one to measure skills related to the eight learning disability categories defined by federal law. Overall, the WIAT-III demonstrates adequate evidence for being a reliable and valid tool for use with school-age populations.

14-3d WIDE RANGE ACHIEVEMENT TEST 4

The Wide Range Achievement Test 4 (WRAT4; Wilkinson & Robertson, 2007) is an individually administered norm-referenced test designed to measure word recognition, spelling, and math computation skills in individuals 5 to 94 years of age. The test takes approximately 15 to 25 minutes to administer to students ages 5 to 7 years and approximately 35 to 45 minutes for older students. There are two alternate forms of the WRAT4. The test contains four subtests.

Subtests

Word Reading The student is required to name letters and read words.

Sentence Comprehension The student is shown sentences and is to indicate understanding of the sentences by filling in missing words.

Spelling The examiner dictates words and the student must write these down, earning credit for each word spelled correctly.

Math Computation The student is required to solve basic computation problems through counting, identifying numbers, solving simple oral problems, and calculating written math problems.

Scores

The raw scores that students earn on the WRAT4 can be converted to standard scores, confidence intervals (85, 90, and 95 percent), percentiles, grade equivalents, normal curve equivalents, and stanines. Separate scores are available for each subtest and for a reading composite (made up of Word Recognition and Sentence Comprehension).

Norms

The WRAT4 was standardized on a national sample of more than 3,000 individuals, ages 5 to 94 years. The sample was stratified on the basis of age, gender, ethnicity, geographic region, and parental education. Although tables in the manual report the relationship between the standardization sample and the composition of the U.S. population, cross-tabs (indicating, for example, the number of boys of each ethnicity from each geographic region) are not provided.

Reliability

Two kinds of reliability information are provided for the WRAT4: internal consistency and alternate-form reliability. Internal consistency coefficients range from .81 to .99, with median internal consistency coefficients ranging from .87 to .96. Alternate-form reliabilities range from .78 to .89 for an age-based sample and from .86 to .90 for a grade-based sample. The reliabilities of the Math Computation subtest are noticeably lower than those for other subtests. Test–retest reliabilities are sufficient, again with the exception of the Math Computation subtest. With the exception of the Math Computation subtest, the test is reliable enough for use in making screening decisions.

Validity

The WRAT4 is a screening test that covers a broad range of behaviors, so there are few items of each specific type. This results in a relatively limited behavior sample. The authors provide evidence of validity by demonstrating that test scores increase with age, that intercorrelations among the various subtests are theoretically as would be expected, and that correlations are high among performance on WRAT4 and previous versions of the test. Validity is also demonstrated by high correlations among subtests of the WRAT4 and comparable samples of behavior from the WIAT-II, Kaufman Test of Educational Achievement–II (KTEA-II), and the Woodcock–Johnson III Tests of Achievement (note: all of these measures have now been revised).

Summary

The WRAT4 provides a very limited sample of behaviors in four content areas. Evidence for reliability is good, but evidence for validity is based on correlations to forms of other tests that since have been updated. Its use is limited to making screening decisions.

14-4 Getting the Most out of an Achievement Test

The achievement tests described in this chapter provide the teacher with global scores in areas such as word meaning and math computation skills. Although global standards can help in screening children, they generally lack the specificity to help in planning individualized instructional programs. The fact that Emily earned a standard score of 85 on the Mathematics Problem Solving subtest of the WIAT-IV does not tell us what math skills Emily has. In addition, a teacher cannot rely on test names as an indication of what is measured by a specific test. For example, a reading standard score of 115 on the WRAT4 tells a teacher nothing about reading comprehension or rate of oral reading. Teachers typically have other information, such as scores from cumulative records or their own observations of student performance that they can use along with test scores, to make judgments about the reasonable level at which to instruct students and the specific skills that need to be taught. Read the upcoming Scenario in Assessment and associated question to consider how an achievement test that addresses multiple skills might be used in a school setting.

A teacher must look at any screening test (or any test, for that matter) in terms of the behaviors sampled by that test. Here is a case in point. Suppose Richard earned a standard score of 70 on a spelling subtest. What do we know about Richard? We know that Richard earned enough raw score points to place him two standard deviations below the mean of students in his grade. That is all we know without going beyond the score and examining the kinds of behaviors sampled by the test. The test title tells us only that the test measures skill development in spelling. However, we still do not know what Richard did to earn a score of 70.

First, we need to ask, "What is the nature of the behaviors sampled by the test?" Spelling tests can be of several kinds. Richard may have been asked to write a word read by his teacher, as is the case in the Spelling subtest of the WRAT4. Such a behavior sampling demands that he recall the correct spelling of a word and actually produce that correct spelling in writing. On the other hand, Richard's score of 70 may have been earned on a spelling test that asked him just to recognize the correct spelling of a word. For example, the Spelling subtest of the PIAT-R/NU presents the student with four alternative spellings of a word (for example, "empti," "empty," "impty," and "emity"), and the teacher asks a child to point to the word "empty." Such an item demands recognition and pointing, rather than recall and production. Thus, we need to look first at the nature of the behaviors sampled by the test.

Second, we must look at the specific items a student passes or fails. This requires going back to the original test protocol to analyze the specific nature of skill development in a given area. We need to ask, "What kinds of items did the child fail?" and then look for consistent patterns among the failures. In trying to identify the nature of spelling errors, we need to know, "Does the student consistently demonstrate errors in spelling words with long vowels? With silent *e*'s? With specific consonant blends?" and so on. The search is for specific patterns of errors, and we try to ascertain the student's relative degree of consistency in making certain errors. Of course, finding error patterns requires that the test content be sufficiently dense to allow a student to make the same error at least two times.

Similar procedures are followed with any screening device. Obviously, the information achieved is not nearly as specific as the information obtained from diagnostic tests. Administration of an achievement test that is a screening test gives the classroom teacher a general idea of where to start with any additional diagnostic assessment.

Dilemmas in Current Practice

Unless the content assessed by an achievement test reflects the content of the curriculum, the results are meaningless. Students will not have had a formal opportunity to learn the material tested. When students are tested on material they have not been taught, or tested in ways other than those by which they are taught, the test results will not measure what they may have learned. Jenkins and Pany (1978) compared the contents of four reading achievement tests with the contents of five commercial reading series at grades 1 and 2. Their major concern was the extent to which students might earn different scores on different tests of reading achievement simply as a function of the degree of overlap in content between tests and curricula. Jenkins and Pany calculated the grade scores that would be earned by students who had mastered the words taught in the respective curricula and who had correctly read those words on the four tests. Grade scores are shown in Table 14.2. It is clear that different curricula result in different performances on different tests.

The data produced by Jenkins and Pany are now more than 30 years old. Yet the table is still the best visual illustration of issues with limited test–curriculum overlap. Shapiro and Derr (1987) showed that the degree of overlap between what is taught and what is tested varied considerably across tests and curricula. Also, Good and Salvia (1988) demonstrated significant differences in test performance for the same students on different reading tests. They indicate the significance of the test curriculum overlap issue, stating,

> Curriculum bias is undesirable because it severely limits the interpretation of a student's test score. For example, it is unclear whether a student's reading score of 78 reflects deficient reading skills or the selection of a test with poor content validity for the pupil's curriculum. (p. 56)

| TABLE 14.2 | Grade-Equivalent Scores Obtained by Matching Specific Reading Test Words to Standardized Reading Test Words |

		MAT			
Curriculum	PIAT	Word Knowledge	Word Analysis	SDRT	WRAT
Bank Street Reading Series					
Grade 1	1.5	1.0	1.1	1.8	2.0
Grade 2	2.8	2.5	1.2	2.9	2.7
Keys to Reading					
Grade 1	2.0	1.4	1.2	2.2	2.2
Grade 2	3.3	1.9	1.0	3.0	3.0
Reading 360					
Grade 1	1.5	1.0	1.0	1.4	1.7
Grade 2	2.2	2.1	1.0	2.7	2.3
SRA Reading Program					
Grade 1	1.5	1.2	1.3	1.0	2.1
Grade 2	3.1	2.5	1.4	2.9	3.5
Sullivan Associates Programmed Reading					
Grade 1	1.8	1.4	1.2	1.1	2.0
Grade 2	2.2	2.4	1.1	2.5	2.5

SOURCE: From "Standardized Achievement Tests: How Useful for Special Education?" by J. Jenkins & D. Pany, *Exceptional Children*, 44 (1978), 450. Copyright 1978 by The Council for Exceptional Children. Reprinted with permission.

SCENARIO IN ASSESSMENT

JOSH | In January, Josh, a sixth-grade student in the local middle school, was referred for a psychoeducational evaluation because of his deteriorating achievement in language arts and social studies. A multidisciplinary team met to formulate an assessment plan. Attending this meeting were Josh's mother; his language arts teacher, who represented the other teachers on his team (i.e., social studies, science, and math); the school principal, Josh's counselor, and the building's school psychologist.

Josh's teachers began the discussion by expressing their concern that Josh was not completing his homework and was earning poor scores on tests and quizzes in language arts and social studies; depending on his performance on the last tests in the marking period, he might pass those courses. In contrast, Josh was earning an A in science. In his mathematics class, Josh was a contradiction. He could do all of the calculations with speed and accuracy. He solved word problems accurately, but slowly. He was going to earn a C in math for the semester because he did not complete the homework and because his written explanations about how he solved the problems were

incomplete. All of his teachers felt Josh was a bright student, but some worried that he was becoming discouraged.

Josh's mother reported that he is the youngest of three children. Josh's older brother and sister had not experienced any difficulties in school. The mother reported that Josh spent several hours every day working on his homework and studying for tests. Although he wanted to go to college to become an engineer and build bridges, he was doubting his ability to even pass sixth grade.

Josh's counselor summarized his elementary school records. Josh earned an IQ of 128 on the group intelligence test administered in the third grade. Yet his records indicated that he had had more difficulty than other students in reading. He was consistently evaluated as outstanding in math and science. Last year, his fifth-grade teacher had noted upon each report card that Josh was a slow reader.

The team felt that the school psychologist should complete a formal assessment of Josh's intelligence and achievement to see if he had a learning disability in reading that was affecting his school performance. The school psychologist administered the fifth edition of the Wechsler Intelligence Scale for Children (WISC-V). The psychologist also administered the third edition of the Wechsler Individual Achievement Test (WIAT-III) because it corresponded nicely to the district's curriculum and instruction.

Josh earned the following standard scores (mean = 100; S = 15) on the WISC-V.

Verbal Comprehension	127
Visual Spatial	126
Working Memory	100
Fluid Reasoning	105
Processing Speed	100

He earned the following standard scores (mean = 100, S = 15) on the WIAT-III subtests, supplemental subtests, and composites.

Subtests

Listening Comprehension	121
Reading Comprehension	102
Math Problem Solving	115
Sentence Composition	91
Word Reading	88
Essay Composition	97
Pseudoword Decoding	84
Numerical Operations	123
Oral Expression	119
Oral Reading Fluency	77
Spelling	100
Math Fluency–Addition	125
Math Fluency–Subtraction	123
Math Fluency–Multiplication	130

Supplemental Subtests

Oral Reading Accuracy	91
Oral Reading Rate	79

Composites

Oral Language	120
Reading	88
Written Expression	96
Mathematics	123

The psychologist also reported that Josh was quite forthcoming about how school was going and why he was having trouble in language arts and social studies. He said that the reading was really hard to understand and that he had to read the same passage a few times to get it. He also said that by the time he had finished his reading assignments, he was so tired that he just rushed through his written homework. He said that he did not like to write "that stuff in math class" and that it should be enough to get the right answer by doing the problem in the right way.

The team concluded that Josh clearly had difficulty with reading decoding. He was slow and inaccurate. Lack of reading fluency in and of itself reduces reading comprehension, and Josh was clearly below that threshold of reading fluency. His lack of fluency combined with his poor performances in word reading and pseudoword decoding strongly suggested that Josh was having a major problem in decoding. Given the nature of the school's curriculum in middle school, where reading is a primary way in which students acquire information, Josh's limited reading skills necessarily were causing achievement problems in language arts and social studies, where reading is stressed. His reading skills were also having an impact on science, but to a lesser degree. The team concluded that Josh was eligible for special education in the area of reading. However, given that the multiple-skill test of achievement (WIAT-III) only provided initial information suggesting that Josh was struggling with decoding, additional information was collected using a diagnostic reading test, which provided a greater sampling of Josh's specific skills, and lack thereof, in the area of reading decoding. Furthermore, more detailed information was collected on the nature of reading instruction he had been provided. This information could better inform instructional planning to address his difficulties.

An IEP team was formed, and the team met and developed a plan whereby Josh received intensive instruction in phonics, starting with a focus on vowel digraphs, with additional emphases on both accuracy and fluency. By the end of the spring semester, Josh's reading accuracy and fluency had improved significantly. His grades had improved, although he still saw little relevance to the required writing in his mathematics class. Josh was again talking about becoming an engineer and building bridges.

This scenario highlights how when multiple-skill tests of achievement appropriately match the curriculum and instruction a student is receiving, they can be used to provide initial information on student achievement. However, additional diagnostic testing is often needed to provide more specific guidance for instruction. If the test that was used did not match the instruction Josh had received, how might this have led to inappropriate decision making?

Chapter Comprehension Questions

Write your answers to each of the following questions and then compare your responses to the text.

1. Identify at least four important considerations in selecting a specific achievement test for use with the third graders in your local school system.

2. Describe the major advantages and disadvantages of using individually administered, multiple-skill achievement tests.

3. A new student is assessed in September using the WRAT4. Her achievement test scores (using the PIAT-R/NU) are forwarded from her previous school and place her in the 90th percentile overall. However, the latest assessment places her only in the 77th percentile. Give three possible explanations for this discrepancy.

USING DIAGNOSTIC READING MEASURES

15

LEARNING OBJECTIVES

15-1 Explain why we assess reading.

15-2 Explain the ways in which reading is taught.

15-3 Identify the areas assessed by diagnostic reading tests, including oral reading, comprehension, word-attack, reading recognition, and reading-related behaviors.

15-4 Identify the strengths and weaknesses of three diagnostic reading tests.

STANDARDS ADDRESSED IN THIS CHAPTER

 CEC Initial Preparation Standards

Standard 4: Assessment

4.0 Beginning special education professionals use multiple methods of assessment and data-sources in making educational decisions.

 CEC Advanced Preparation Standards

Standard 1: Assessment

1.0 Special education specialists use valid and reliable assessment practices to minimize bias.

 National Association of School Psychologists Domains

1 Data-Based Decision Making and Accountability

3 Interventions and Instructional Support to Develop Academic Skills

Tim Hall/Cultura/Getty Images

15-1 Why Do We Assess Reading?

Reading is one of the most fundamental skills that students learn. For poor readers, life in school is likely to be difficult even with appropriate curricular and testing accommodations and adaptations, and life after school is likely to have constrained opportunities and less personal independence and satisfaction. Moreover, students who have not learned to read fluently by the end of third grade are unlikely ever to read fluently (Adams, 1990). For these reasons, students' development of reading skills is closely monitored in order to identify those with problems early enough to enable remediation. Fortunately, there is strong evidence that intensive systematic intervention involving instruction in several foundational reading skills is effective for students who are struggling (Gersten et al., 2009).

Diagnostic tests are most often used at tiers 2 and 3 (targeted and intensive) levels in the Multi-Tiered System of Supports (MTSS) model; they are used primarily to improve two educational decisions. First, they are administered to children who are experiencing difficulty in learning to read. In this case, tests identify a student's strengths and weaknesses so that educators can plan appropriate interventions. Second, they are given to ascertain a student's initial or continuing eligibility for special services. Tests given for this purpose are used to compare a student's achievement with the achievement of other students. Diagnostic reading tests may also be administered to evaluate the effects of instruction; however, the use of diagnostic reading tests for this purpose is generally unwise. This is because lengthy individually administered tests tend to be an inefficient way to evaluate instructional effectiveness for large groups of students; brief individually administered and group survey tests are generally more appropriate for this purpose. Furthermore, diagnostic tests are generally too insensitive to identify small but important gains by individual students. Teachers should monitor students' daily or weekly progress with direct performance measures (such as having a student read aloud currently used materials to ascertain accuracy [percentage correct] and fluency [rate of correct words per minute]) to know whether instruction is effective.

Because reading skills are fundamental to success in our society, their development should be closely monitored. When necessary, diagnostic tests should be administered and results used to inform instructional adjustments that can be made to address specific aspects of reading with which the student struggles. When used appropriately, diagnostic reading tests can help to ensure that all students have an opportunity to learn to read, and to learn to do so quickly. However, there may be some students who, even with the most effective instruction, never manage to develop adequate reading skills. Fortunately, technologies such as text-to-speech converters and computer screen-readers are making it increasingly possible for such students to access printed information without the prerequisite reading skills. At the same time, this brings up a new dilemma: Under what conditions should we reduce reading intervention efforts in order to focus more on teaching a student to use reading accommodations (e.g., computer screen-readers, text-to-speech (TTS) software)? We unfortunately don't have a good answer to this right now. But we do know that some of these accommodations can actually facilitate reading development, and so we believe that their use should be encouraged, particularly for those students with the most severe reading difficulties. Overall, we can't predict who will and who will not learn to read, so it is essential that we operate under the assumption that each student will learn to read when we assess and intervene appropriately.

15-2 The Ways in Which Reading Is Taught

For approximately 150 years, educators have been divided (sometimes acrimoniously) over the issue of teaching the language code (letters and sounds). Some educators favor a "look–say" (or whole-word) approach, in which students learn whole words and practice them by reading appropriate stories and other passages. Proponents of this approach stress the meaning of the words and usually believe that students learn the code incidentally (or with a little coaching). Finally, proponents of this approach offer the opinion (contradicted by empirical research) that drilling children in letters and sounds destroys their motivation to read. Other educators favor systematically teaching the language code: how letters represent sounds and how sounds and letters are combined to form words—both spoken and written. Proponents of this approach argue that specifically and systematically teaching phonics produces more skillful readers more easily; they also argue that reading failure destroys motivation to read.

For the first 100 years or so of the debate, observations of reading were too crude to indicate more than that the reader looked at print and said the printed words (or answered questions about the content conveyed by those printed words). Consequently, theoreticians speculated about the processes occurring inside the reader, and the speculations of advocates of whole-word instruction dominated the debate until the 1950s. Thereafter, **phonics instruction** (systematically teaching beginning readers the relationships among the alphabetic code, phonemes, and words) increasingly became part of prereading and reading instruction. Some of that increased emphasis on phonics may be attributable to *Why Johnny Can't Read* (Flesch, 1955), a book vigorously advocating phonics instruction; what's more important, the growing body of empirical evidence increasingly showed phonics instruction's effectiveness. By 1967, there was substantial evidence that systematic instruction in phonics produced better readers and that the effect of phonics instruction was greater for children of low ability or from disadvantaged backgrounds. With phonics instruction, beginning readers had better word recognition, better reading comprehension, and better reading vocabulary (Bond & Dykstra, 1967; Chall, 1967). Subsequent empirical evidence leads to the same conclusions (Adams, 1990; Foorman, Francis, Fletcher, Schatschneider, & Mehta, 1998; National Institute of Child Health and Human Development, 2000a, 2000b; Pflaum, Walberg, Karegianes, & Rasher, 1980; Rayner, Foorman, Perfetti, Pesetsky, & Seidenberg, 2001; Stanovich, 1986).

While learning more about how students begin to read, scholars also learned that some long-held beliefs were not valid. For example, it is incorrect to say that poor readers read letter by letter, but skilled readers read entire words and phrases as a unit. Actually, skilled readers read letter by letter and word by word, but they do it so quickly that they appear to be reading words and phrases (see, for example, Snow, Burns, & Griffin, 1998). It is also incorrect to say that good readers rely heavily on context cues to identify words (Share & Stanovich, 1995). Good readers do use context cues to verify their decoding accuracy. Poor readers rely on them heavily, however, probably because they lack skill in more appropriate word-attack skills (see, for example, Briggs & Underwood, 1984).

Today, despite clear evidence indicating the essential role of phonics in reading and strong indications of the superiority of reading programs with direct instruction in phonics (Foorman et al., 1998), some professionals continue to reject phonics instruction. Perhaps this may explain why most students who are referred for psychological assessment are referred because of reading problems, and why most of these students have problems changing the symbols (that is, alphabet letters) into sounds and words. The obvious connection between phonics instruction and beginning reading has not escaped the notice of many parents, however. They have become eager consumers of educational materials (such as "Hooked on Phonics" and "The Phonics Game") and private tutoring (for example, instruction at a Sylvan Learning Center, Huntington Learning Center, or online tutoring services such as Smart Tutor and Kaplan). The Scenario in Assessment for this chapter describes a situation in which a student benefited from an approach to reading involving explicit phonics instruction that was carefully informed by a diagnostic reading test; however, parents had to enroll the student in private tutoring in order for the student to be instructed according to this approach.

Educators' views of how students learn to read and how students should be taught will determine their beliefs about reading assessment. Thus, diagnostic testing

LLOYD | The Springfield School District uses a child-centered whole-language approach to teaching reading. Near the end of the school year, the district screened all first-grade students to identify students who would require supplementary services in reading the following year. Lloyd earned a score that was at the seventh percentile on the district's norms, and the district notified his parents that he would be receiving additional help the next year so that he could improve his skills. Lloyd's parents were upset by the news because until the notification, they thought that Lloyd was progressing well in all school subjects.

The parents requested a meeting with Lloyd's teacher, who also invited the reading specialist. At that meeting, the reading specialist told the parents that a fairly large percentage of first graders were in the same predicament as Lloyd, but not to worry, because many students matured into readers. She said that Lloyd only needed time. She urged the parents to let Lloyd enjoy his summer, and the district would retest him at the beginning of the second grade to determine if he still needed the extra help.

Lloyd's parents ignored the district's advice and enrolled him in a reading course at a local tutoring program. Lloyd was first tested to identify the exact nature of his problem. The test results indicated that he had excellent phonemic awareness, could print and name all upper- and lowercase letters, knew all the consonant sounds, knew the sounds of all long vowels, did not know any of the short vowel sounds, could not blend sounds, and had a sight vocabulary of approximately 50 words. Lloyd's tutor taught him the short vowel sounds rather quickly. However, he had trouble with sound blending until his tutor used his interest and skill in math to explain the principles. She wrote: c + a + t = cat, and then said each of the three sounds and "cat." As she explained to Lloyd's parents, it was like a light going on in his head. He got it. The tutor spent a few more sessions using phonics to help Lloyd increase his sight vocabulary.

In September, the district retested Lloyd as it had promised. The district sent home a form letter in which it explained that Lloyd was now at the 99th percentile in reading and no longer needed supplementary services. At the bottom was a handwritten note from the reading specialist: "Lloyd just needed a little time to become a reader. We're so glad you let him just enjoy his summer!"

Epigram Lloyd did enjoy his summer as well as the second grade. And he won an award as the best second-grade reader in the district.

This scenario highlights how important it can be to identify and teach specific reading skills that students need to read successfully. What do you think would have happened if the tutoring program did not carefully assess Lloyd's early reading skills?

in reading is caught between the opposing camps. If the test includes an assessment of the skills needed to decode text, it is attacked by those who reject analytic approaches to reading. If the test does not include an assessment of decoding skills, it is attacked by those who know the importance of those skills in beginning reading.

15-3 Skills Assessed by Diagnostic Reading Tests

Reading is a complex process that changes as readers develop. The ultimate goal of reading is to comprehend written material with efficiency, but students need to develop and learn to integrate many subskills to reach that end. Beginning readers rely heavily on a complex set of decoding skills that can be assessed holistically by having a student read orally and assessing his or her accuracy and fluency. Decoding skills may also be measured analytically by having students apply these skills in isolation (for example, using phonics to read nonsense words). Once fluency in decoding has been attained, readers are expected to go beyond the comprehension of simple language and simple ideas to the process of understanding and evaluating what is written. Advanced readers rely on different skills (that is, linguistic competence and abstract reasoning) and different facts (that is, vocabulary, prior knowledge and experience, and beliefs). Comprehension may be assessed by having a student read a passage that deals with an esoteric topic and is filled with abstract concepts and difficult vocabulary; moreover, the sentences in that passage may have complicated grammar with minimal redundancy.

15-3a ASSESSMENT OF WORD-ATTACK SKILLS

Word-attack, or word analysis, skills are those used to derive the pronunciation or meaning of a word through phonic analysis, structural analysis, or context cues. Phonic analysis is the use of letter–sound correspondences and sound blending to identify words. Structural analysis is a process of breaking words into morphemes, or meaningful units. Words contain free morphemes (such as *farm*, *book*, and *land*) and bound morphemes (such as *-ed*, *-s*, and *-er*).

Because lack of word-attack skills is the principal reason why students have trouble reading, a variety of subtests of commonly used diagnostic reading tests specifically assess these skills. Subtests that assess word-attack skills range from such basic assessments as analysis of skill in associating letters with sounds to tests of syllabication and blending. Generally, for subtests that assess skill in associating letters with sounds, the examiner reads a word aloud and the student must identify the consonant–vowel–consonant cluster or digraph that has the same sound as the beginning, middle, or ending letters of the word. Syllabication subtests present polysyllabic words, and the student must either divide the word orally into syllables or circle specific syllables.

Blending subtests, on the other hand, are of three types. In the first method, the examiner may read syllables out loud (for example, "wa-ter-mel-on") and ask the student to pronounce the word. In the second type of subtest, the student may be asked to read word parts and to pronounce whole words. In the third method, the student may be presented with alternative beginning, middle, and ending sounds and asked to produce a word.

15-3b ASSESSMENT OF WORD RECOGNITION SKILLS

Subtests of diagnostic reading tests that assess a pupil's word recognition skills are designed to ascertain what many educators call "sight vocabulary." A student learns the correct pronunciation of letters and words through a variety of experiences. The more a student is exposed to specific words and the more familiar those words become, the more readily he or she recognizes those words and is able to pronounce them correctly. Well-known words require very little reliance on word-attack skills. Most readers of this book immediately recognize the word *hemorrhage* and do not have to employ phonetic skills to pronounce it. On the other hand, a word such as *nephrocystanastomosis* is not a part of the sight vocabulary for most of us. Such words slow us down; we must use phonetics to analyze them.

Word recognition subtests form a major part of most diagnostic reading tests. Some tests expose words for brief periods of time (usually one-half second) to determine whether students can process words quickly. Students who recognize many words are said to have good sight vocabularies or good word recognition skills. Other subtests assess letter recognition, recognition of words in isolation, and recognition of words in context.

15-3c ORAL READING

A number of tests and subtests are designed to assess the accuracy and/or fluency of a student's oral reading. Oral reading tests consist of a series of graded paragraphs that are read sequentially by a student. The examiner notes reading errors and behaviors that characterize the student's oral reading.

Rate of Reading

Good readers are fluent; they recognize words quickly (without having to rely on phonetic analysis) and are in a good position to construct meaning of sentences and paragraphs. Readers who are not fluent have problems comprehending what they read, and the problems become more severe as the complexity of the reading material increases. Indeed, reading fluency is an excellent general indicator of reading achievement. Consequently, more and more states are including reading fluency as part of their comprehensive reading assessment systems.

Nonetheless, many commercially available reading tests do not assess reading fluency. However, there are some exceptions. For example, the Gray Oral Reading Test–Fifth Edition (GORT-5) is timed. A pupil who reads a passage on the GORT-5 slowly but makes no errors in reading may earn a lower score than a rapid reader who makes one or two errors in reading.

Oral Reading Errors

Oral reading requires that students say the word that is printed on the page correctly. However, all errors made by a student are not equal. It is important to carefully read the scoring directions for a test to know how specific errors are handled; each test handles these a bit differently. Some errors are relatively unimportant to the extent that they do not affect the student's comprehension of the material. Other errors are ignored. Examiners may note characteristics of a student's oral reading that are not counted as errors. Self-corrections are not counted as errors. Disregarded punctuation marks (for example, failing to pause for a comma or to inflect vocally to indicate a question mark) are not counted as errors. Repetitions and hesitations due to speech handicaps (for example, stuttering or stammering) are not counted as errors. Dialectic accents are not counted as mispronunciations.[1]

The following types of errors typically count against the student:

Teacher Pronunciation or Aid If a student either hesitates for a time without making an audible effort to pronounce a word or appears to be attempting for three seconds to pronounce the word, the examiner pronounces the word and records an error.

Hesitation The student hesitates for three or more seconds before pronouncing a word.

Gross Mispronunciation of a Word A gross mispronunciation is recorded when the pupil's pronunciation of a word bears so little resemblance to the proper pronunciation that the examiner must look at the word to recognize it. An example of gross mispronunciation is reading "encounter" as "actors."

Partial Mispronunciation of a Word A partial mispronunciation can be one of several different kinds of errors. The examiner may have to pronounce part of a word for the student (an aid); the student may phonetically mispronounce specific letters (for example, by reading "red" as "reed"); or the student may omit part of a word, insert elements of words, or make errors in syllabication, accent, or inversion.

Omission of a Word or Group of Words Omissions consist of skipping individual words or groups of words.

Insertion of a Word or Group of Words. Insertions consist of the student putting one or more words into the sentence being read. The student may, for example, read "the dog" as "the mean dog." However, it is important to note that for some assessment instruments this counts against the student, but for others it does not.

Substitution of One Meaningful Word for Another Substitutions consist of the replacement of one or more words in the passage by one or more different meaningful words. The student might read "dense" as "depress." Students often replace entire sequences of words with others, as illustrated by the replacement of "he is his own mechanic" with "he sat on his own machine." Some oral reading tests require that examiners record the specific kind of substitution error. Substitutions are classified as meaning similarity (the words have similar meanings), function similarity (the two words have syntactically similar functions), graphic/phoneme similarity (the words look or sound alike), or a combination of the preceding.

Repetition Repetition occurs when students repeat words or groups of words while attempting to read sentences or paragraphs. In some cases, if a student repeats a group of words to correct an error, the original error is not recorded, but a repetition error is. In other cases, such behaviors are recorded simply as spontaneous self-corrections.

Inversion, or Changing of Word Order Errors of inversion are recorded when the child changes the order of words appearing in a sentence; for example, "house the" is an inversion.

---

[1] Other characteristics of a student's oral reading are problematic (although not errors): poor posture, inappropriate head movement, finger pointing, loss of place, lack of expression (for example, word-by-word reading, lack of phrasing, or monotone voice), and strained voice.

15-3d ASSESSMENT OF READING COMPREHENSION

Diagnostic tests assess five different types of reading comprehension:

1. *Literal comprehension* entails understanding the information that is explicit in the reading material.
2. *Inferential comprehension* means interpreting, synthesizing, or extending the information that is explicit in the reading material.
3. *Critical comprehension* requires analyzing, evaluating, and making judgments about the material read.
4. *Affective comprehension* involves a reader's personal and emotional responses to the reading material.
5. *Lexical comprehension* means knowing the meaning of key vocabulary words.

In our opinion, the best way to assess reading comprehension is to give readers access to the material and have them restate or paraphrase what they have read.

Poor comprehension has many causes. The most common is poor decoding, which affects comprehension in two ways. First, if a student cannot convert the symbols to words, he or she cannot comprehend the message conveyed by those words. The second issue is more subtle. If a student expends all of his or her mental resources on sounding out the words, he or she will have no resources left to process their meaning. For that reason, increasing reading fluency frequently eliminates problems in comprehension.

Another problem is that students may not know how to read for comprehension (Taylor, Harris, Pearson, & Garcia, 1995). They may not actively focus on the meaning of what they read or know how to monitor their comprehension (for example, by asking themselves questions about what they have read or whether they understand what they have read). Students may not know how to foster comprehension (for example, by summarizing material, determining the main ideas and supporting facts, and integrating material with previous knowledge). Finally, individual characteristics can interact with the assessment of reading comprehension. For example, in an assessment of literal comprehension, a reader's memory capacity can affect comprehension scores unless the reader has access to the passage while answering questions about it or retelling its gist. In addition, the extent to which a student has background information and interest in the topic area may affect the student's score. For instance, if a student has substantial prior knowledge about basketball and a passage on which the student is tested is about basketball, the student's score may reflect existing knowledge rather than current reading comprehension skills. Inferential comprehension depends on more than reading; it also depends on a reader's ability to see relationships (a defining element of intelligence) and on background information and experiences.

Although many of the same processes are involved in comprehending different types of texts, it is important to recognize that the skills necessary can vary slightly depending on genre or *type* of reading material. For instance, effective comprehension of narrative text may require one to read from beginning to end, and understand concepts such as characters, plot, and setting, whereas effective comprehension of informational text may involve use of navigational tools such as the table of contents and index and an understanding of how to comprehend information presented in diagrams. It is possible for a student to have strong comprehension skills for one type of genre and not for another, and so it can be important to assess student skills across a wide variety of genres.

15-3e ASSESSMENT OF OTHER READING AND READING-RELATED BEHAVIORS

A variety of subtests that fit none of the aforementioned categories are included in diagnostic reading tests as either major or supplementary subtests. Examples of such tests include oral vocabulary, spelling, handwriting, and auditory discrimination. In most cases, such subtests are included simply to provide the examiner with additional diagnostic information.

15-4 Specific Diagnostic Reading Tests

In Table 15.1, we list a variety of diagnostic reading tests. Then we provide a detailed review of the Gray Oral Reading Test–Fifth Edition (GORT-5); the Group Reading Assessment and Diagnostic Evaluation (GRADE); and the Test of Phonological Awareness–Second Edition: Plus (TOPA-2+).

15-4a GRAY ORAL READING TEST–FIFTH EDITION (GORT-5)

The Gray Oral Reading Test–Fifth Edition (GORT-5) is the fourth revision of the Gray Oral Reading Test by Wiederholt and Bryant (2012). The GORT-5 remains an individually administered, norm-referenced measure of oral reading and comprehension. Each of the two forms (A and B) of the GORT-5 contains 16 reading passages of increasing difficulty. Students are required to read paragraphs orally and to respond to five comprehension questions for each passage that are read by the examiner. The test is intended for use with students between the ages of 6–0 and 23–11. Specific basal and ceiling rules are used to limit time, which typically ranges from 15 to 45 minutes.

The authors of the GORT-5 state four purposes of the test: "(a) to help identify those students who are significantly below their peers in oral reading and determine the degree of the problem; (b) to discover oral reading strengths and weaknesses within individual students; (c) to monitor students' progress in special intervention programs; and (d) to be used in research studying reading in school-aged students" (Wiederholt & Bryant, 2012, p. 3).

In the manual, the authors go into considerable detail in describing the development of the oral reading passages for GORT-5. However, except for two higher-level passages written for the GORT-5, and one reading passage added to each form of GORT-4, the most recent version of the GORT is identical in every way to the GORT-3 and to the Gray Oral Reading Test–Revised (GORT-R), which are in turn identical to Forms B and D of the Formal Reading Inventory (Wiederholt, 1986). Modifications to the previous edition of the test (GORT-4) include the addition of two higher-level passages on each form, an open-ended comprehension question format to increase passage dependence for the associated items, an updated norm sample that includes more advanced and older students, and new reliability and validity information.

TABLE 15.1	Commonly Used Diagnostic Reading Tests		
Test	**Authors**	**Year of Publication**	**Publisher**
Comprehensive Test of Phonological Processing – Second Edition (CTOPP-2)	Wagner, Togeson & Raschotte	2013	Pro-Ed
Gray Oral Reading Test–Fifth Edition (GORT-5)	Wiederholt & Bryant	2012	Pro-Ed
Group Reading Assessment and Diagnostic Evaluation	Williams	2001	Pearson
Test of Early Reading Ability–Third Edition (TERA-3)	Reid, Hresko & Hammill	2001	Pearson
The Test of Phonological Awareness–Second Edition: Plus (TOPA-2+)	Torgeson & Bryant	2004	Pro-Ed
Test of Reading Comprehension–Fourth Edition (TORC-4)	Brown, Wiederholt & Hammill	2008	Pro-Ed
Test of Silent Contextual Reading Fluency	Hammill, Wiederholt & Allen	2014	Pro-Ed
Test of Silent Word Reading Fluency–Second Edition (TOSWRF-2)	Mather, Hammill, Allen & Roberts	2014	Pro-Ed
Test of Word Reading Efficiency–2 (TOWRE-2)	Torgeson, Wagner & Raschotte	2012	Pro-Ed
Woodcock Diagnostic Reading Battery–Third Edition	Woodcock, Mather & Schrank	2004	Riverside

Scores

The examiner (a) records the number of seconds that the student needed to read the passage aloud and (b) tallies the number of deviations from the text (that is, any deviation from print is scored as an oral-reading miscue, unless the deviation is the result of normal speech variations). At the bottom of the test protocol is a matrix. The top row of the matrix has a six-point scale (0–5); the next row of the matrix has six time ranges corresponding to the six-point scale. The examiner awards points (0–5) for the speed and accuracy with which the passage is read. For each passage, the sum of the rate and accuracy scores is called the "fluency score." A comprehension score is determined from the number of multiple-choice comprehension questions answered correctly (0–5). The rate, accuracy, passage, and comprehension scores for the stories read are then summed to yield total scores for rate, accuracy, fluency, and comprehension. From these total scores, corresponding age and grade equivalents, percentiles, and standard scores (mean = 10; standard deviation = 3) can be found in various tables in the manual. The passage and comprehension standard scores are added and then transformed into a standard score called the "oral reading index," which has a mean of 100 and a standard deviation of 15. The examiner can also record both the number and kinds of miscues using a separate worksheet. Then the number can be converted into a percentage.

Norms

The GORT-5 was standardized on 2,556 students from 33 states. The norms appear to be representative of the school-age population as reported by various publications of the U.S. Bureau of the Census between 2006 and 2010 in terms of gender, race, geographical region, various disability statuses, family income and education level; however, slightly higher proportions of white students and slightly lower proportions of students from the South were identified in the sample. Furthermore, students with parents who had less than a bachelor's degree were slightly overrepresented in the sample. The sample was additionally stratified according to 12 age intervals for all of the aforementioned variables, with the exception of disability status. No further cross-tabulations are provided in the manual.

Reliability

The internal consistency for five scores (rate, accuracy, passage, comprehension, and oral reading index) at 14 age levels were estimated from the performances of all students in the normative sample by form. The 112 alphas for subtests ranged from .86 to .98; 89 of the 93 coefficients equaled or exceeded .90. Alpha for the oral reading quotient equaled or exceeded .94 at all ages. Average test–retest reliability correlation coefficients were determined according to various grade levels using information from students taking both test forms; these correlations ranged from .79 to .95. In addition, reliability between the alternate forms allows the estimation of both error due to content sampling and error due to instability. These coefficients, again determined by various grade levels and averaged across forms, ranged from .74 to .95. Overall, the oral reading quotient of the GORT-5 appears sufficiently reliable for making important decisions for individual students; use of other scores for this purpose will depend on the grade of the student and the particular subtest.

Validity

The authors argue that the test has good content validity because of the procedures used in test construction. Specifically, they argue that the reading passages were written with "close attention to sentence structure, the logical connections between sentences and clauses, and the coherence of topics" (Wiederholt & Bryant, 2012, p. 56). They also describe item-level analyses that were conducted in order to eliminate biased items. Results indicated that there were no items demonstrating substantial gender, race, or ethnic bias.

To provide evidence of criterion-related validity of the GORT-5, the authors provide information on correlations between the GORT-5 and four other published reading tests (i.e., Nelson-Denny Reading Test, Test of Silent Contextual Reading Fluency, Test of Silent Reading Efficiency and Comprehension, Test of Silent Word Reading Fluency), as well as with the Reading Observation Scale, using four different samples of students. Correlations for all of these studies for the rate, accuracy, fluency, and comprehension scores ranged from .54 (i.e., GORT-5 Accuracy score correlated with the Reading Observation Scale) to .85 (i.e., GORT-5 correlated with the Vocabulary score of the Nelson-Denny Reading Test). Correlations for the oral reading index among these studies ranged from .64 (i.e., Test of Silent Word Reading Fluency) to .85 (Vocabulary score of the Nelson-Denny Reading Test).

The authors provide evidence for the construct validity of the GORT-5 by showing that GORT-4 scores increase with age and grade, and are appropriately correlated with measures of school achievement and intelligence. Evidence is also provided that students with reading deficits identified prior to GORT-5 test administration performed relatively low (i.e., Oral Reading Index standard score of 81 and 80 on Form A and Form B, respectively).

Summary

The GORT-5 is an individually administered, norm-referenced measure of oral reading and comprehension for use with students between the ages of 6–0 and 23–11. Multiple scores are derived from a student's reading (rate, accuracy, and rate plus accuracy); a single score is derived for comprehension; and a composite score based on rate, accuracy, and comprehension can be calculated. The standardization sample used for the GORT-5 appears to be generally representative of the U.S. population in terms of gender, race, geographic region, and socioeconomic status (SES). Overall, the oral reading quotient of the GORT-5 appears sufficiently reliable for making important decisions for individual students; use of other scores for this purpose will depend on the age of the student and the particular score. The GORT-5 appears to have satisfactory validity.

15-4b GROUP READING ASSESSMENT AND DIAGNOSTIC EVALUATION (GRADE)

The Group Reading Assessment and Diagnostic Evaluation (GRADE; Williams, 2001) is a norm-referenced test of reading achievement that can be administered individually or in a group. It is designed to be used for students between the ages of 4 years (preschool) and 18 years (12th grade). There are 11 test levels, each with two forms (A and B). These include separate levels across each grade for pre-kindergarten through sixth grade, a middle school level (M), and two high school levels (H and A). Although the test is untimed, the author estimates that older students should be able to complete the assessment in one hour, whereas younger children may require up to 90 minutes. The manual provides both fall and spring norms to help in tracking progress over a school year. The following five test applications are discussed by the author: (1) placement and planning, (2) understanding the reading skills of students, (3) testing on level and out of level (which may allow more appropriate information on a child's strengths and weaknesses to be obtained among children at the margins), (4) monitoring growth, and (5) research.

Subtests

Five components of reading are assessed: prereading, reading readiness, vocabulary, comprehension, and oral language. Different subtests are used to assess these components at different levels.

Prereading Component

Picture Matching For each of the 10 items in this subtest, a student must mark the one picture in the four-picture array that is the same as the stimulus picture.

Picture Differences For each of the eight items in this subtest, a student must mark the one picture in the four-picture array that is different from the other pictures.

Verbal Concepts For each of the 10 items in this subtest, a student must mark the one picture in the four-picture array that is described by the examiner.

Picture Categories For each of the 10 items in this subtest, a student must mark the one picture in the four-picture array that does not belong with the other pictures.

Reading Readiness

Sound Matching For each of the 12 items in this subtest, a student must mark the one picture in the four-picture array that has the same beginning (or ending) sound as a stimulus word. Students are told what words the pictures represent.

Rhyming For each of the 14 items in this subtest, a student must mark the one picture in the four-picture array that rhymes with a stimulus word. Students are again told what words the pictures represent.

Print Awareness For each of the four items in this subtest, a student must mark the one picture in the four-picture array that has the following print elements: letters, words, sentences, capital letters, and punctuation.

Letter Recognition For each of the 11 items in this subtest, a student is given a five-letter array and must mark the capital or lowercase letter read by the examiner.

Same and Different Words For each of the nine items in this subtest, a student must mark the one word in the four-word array that is either the same as or different from the stimulus word.

Phoneme–Grapheme Correspondence For each of the 16 items in this subtest, a student must mark the one letter in the four-word array that is the same as the beginning (or ending) sound of a word read by the examiner.

Vocabulary

Word Reading The subtest contains 10 to 30 items, depending on the level. For each item in this subtest, a student is given a four-word array and must mark the word read by the examiner.

Word Meaning For each of the 27 items in this subtest, a student must mark the one picture in the four-picture array that represents a written stimulus word.

Vocabulary This subtest contains 30 to 40 items, depending on the test level. Students are presented a short written phrase or sentence that has one word bolded. A student must mark the one word in the four- or five-word array that has the same meaning as the bolded word.

Comprehension

Sentence Comprehension For each of the 19 cloze items in this subtest, a student must choose the one word in the four- or five-word array that best fits in the blank.

Passage Comprehension The number of reading passages and items for this subtest varies by test level. A student must read a passage and answer several multiple-choice questions about the passage. Questions are of four types: questioning, clarifying, summarizing, and predicting.

Oral Language

Listening Comprehension In this 17- or 18-item subtest, the test administrator reads aloud a sentence. A student must choose which of four pictures represents what was read. Items require students to comprehend basic words, understand grammar structure, make inferences, understand idioms, and comprehend other nonliteral statements.

Scores

Subtest raw scores can be converted into stanines. Depending on the level administered, certain subtest raw scores can be added to produce composite scores. Similarly, each level has a different set of subtest raw scores that are added in computing the total test raw score. Composite and total test raw scores can be converted to unweighted standard scores (mean of 100 and standard deviation of 15), stanines, percentiles, normal-curve equivalents, grade equivalents, and growth scale values.[2] Conversion tables provide both fall and spring normative scores. For students who are very skilled or very unskilled readers in comparison to their same-grade peers, out-of-level tests may be administered. Appropriate normative tables are available for some out-of-level tests in the teacher's scoring and interpretative manuals. Other out-of-level normative scores are reported only in the scoring and reporting software.

Norms

The GRADE standardization sample included 16,408 students in the spring sample and 17,024 in the fall sample. Numbers of students tested in each grade ranged from 808 (seventh grade, spring) to 2,995 (kindergarten, spring). Gender characteristics of the sample were presented by grade level, and roughly equal numbers of males and females were represented in each grade and season level (fall and spring). Geographic region characteristics were presented without disaggregating results by grade and were compared to the population data as reported by the U.S. Census Bureau (1998). Southern states were slightly overrepresented, whereas Western states were slightly underrepresented in both the fall and the spring norm samples. Information on community type was also presented for the entire fall and spring norm samples; the samples are appropriately representative of urban, suburban, and rural communities. Information on students receiving free lunch was also provided. Information on race was also compared to the percentages reported by the U.S. Census Bureau (1998) and appeared to be representative of the population. It is important to note, again, that this information was not reported by grade level. Finally, the authors report that special education students were included in the sample but do not provide the number included.

Reliability

Total test coefficient alphas were calculated as measures of internal consistency for each form of the test, for each season of administration (fall and spring). These ranged from .89 to .98. Coefficient alphas were also computed for various subtests and subtest combinations (for example, Picture Matching and Picture Differences were combined into a Visual Skills category at the preschool and kindergarten levels). These were calculated for each GRADE level, form, and season of administration; several reliabilities were calculated for out-of-level tests (for example, separate alpha coefficients were computed for preschoolers and kindergartners taking the kindergarten-level test). These subtest–subtest combination coefficients ranged from .45 (Listening Comprehension, Form B, eleventh grade, spring administration) to .97 (Listening Comprehension, Form A, preschool, fall administration). Of the 350 coefficients calculated, 99 met or exceeded .90. The Comprehension Composite was found to be the most reliable composite score across levels. Listening Comprehension had consistently low coefficients from the first grade level tested to the highest level (Level A); thus, these are not included in calculating the total test raw scores for these levels. Alternate-forms reliability was determined across a sample of 696 students (students were included at each grade level). Average time between testing ranged from eight to 32.2 days. Correlation

---

[2] Because growth scale values include all levels on the same scale, these scores make it possible to track a student's reading growth when the student has been given different GRADE levels throughout the years. It is important to note, however, that particular skills measured on the test vary from level to level, so growth scale values may not represent the same skills at different years.

coefficients ranged from .81 (11th grade) to .94 (preschool and third grade). Test–retest reliability was determined from a sample of 816 students. The average interval between testing ranged from 3.5 days (eighth-grade students taking Form A of Level M) to 42 days (fifth-grade students taking Form A of Level 5). Test–retest correlation coefficients ranged from .77 (fifth-grade students taking Form A of Level 5) to .98 (fourth-grade students taking Form A of Level 4). Reliability data were not provided on growth scale values.

Validity

The author presents three types of validity: content, criterion-related, and construct validity. A rationale is provided for why particular item formats and subtests were included at particular ages and what skills each subtest is intended to measure. Also, a comprehensive item tryout was conducted on a sample of children throughout the nation. Information from this tryout informed item revision procedures. Statistical tests and qualitative investigations of item bias were also conducted during the tryout. Finally, teachers were surveyed, and this information was used in modifying content and administration procedures (although specific information on this survey is not provided). Criterion-related validity provided by the author included correlations of the GRADE total test standard score with five other measures of reading achievement: the total reading standard score of the Iowa Test of Basic Skills, the California Achievement Test total reading score, the Gates–MacGinitie Reading Tests total score, the Peabody Individual Achievement Test–Revised (PIAT-R) scores (General Information, Reading Recognition, Reading Comprehension, and Total Reading subtests), and the TerraNova. Each of these correlation studies was conducted with somewhat limited samples of elementary and middle school students. Coefficients ranged from .61 (GRADE total test score correlated with PIAT-R General Information among 30 fifth-grade students) to .90 (GRADE total test score correlated with Gates total reading score for 177 first-, second- and sixth-grade students). Finally, construct validity was addressed by showing that the GRADE scores were correlated with age. Also, scores for students with dyslexia ($N = 242$) and learning disabilities in reading ($N = 191$) were compared with scores for students included in the standardization sample that were matched on GRADE level, form taken, gender, and race/ethnicity but who were not receiving special education services. As a group, students with dyslexia performed significantly below the matched control group. Similarly, students with learning disabilities in reading performed significantly below the matched control group.

Summary

The GRADE is a standardized, norm-referenced test of reading achievement that can be group administered. It can be used with children of a variety of ages (4 to 18 years) and provides a "growth scale value" score that can be used to track growth in reading achievement over several years. Different subtests and skills are tested, depending on the grade level tested; 11 forms corresponding to 11 GRADE levels are included. Although the norm sample is large, certain demographic information on the students in the sample is not provided, and in some cases, groups of students are over- or underrepresented. Total test score reliability data are strong. However, other subtest–subtest composite reliability data do not support the use of these particular scores for decision-making purposes, although the validity data provided in the manual suggest that this test is a useful measure of reading skills.

15-4c THE TEST OF PHONOLOGICAL AWARENESS, SECOND EDITION: PLUS (TOPA 2+)

The Test of Phonological Awareness, Second Edition: Plus (TOPA 2+; Torgesen & Bryant, 2004) is a norm-referenced device intended to identify students who need supplemental services in phonemic awareness and letter–sound correspondence. The TOPA 2+ can be administered individually or to groups of students between the ages of 5 and 8 years to assess phonological awareness and letter–sound correspondences.

Two forms are available: the Kindergarten form and the Early Elementary form for students in first or second grades. The Kindergarten form has two subtests. The first, Phonological Awareness, has two parts, each consisting of 10 items. In the first part, students must select from a three-choice array the word that begins with the same sound as the stimulus word read by the examiner. In the second part, students must select from a three-choice array the word that begins with a different sound. The second subtest, Letter Sounds, consists of 15 items requiring students to mark the letter in a letter array that corresponds to a specific phoneme. The Early Elementary form also has two subtests. The first, Phonological Awareness, also has two parts, each consisting of 10 items. In the first part, students must select from a three-choice array the word that ends with the same sound as the stimulus word read by the examiner. In the second part, students must select from a three-choice array the word that ends with a different sound. The second subtest, Letter Sounds, requires students to spell 18 nonsense words that vary in length from two to five phonemes.

Scores

The number correct on each subtest is summed, and sums can be converted to percentiles and a variety of standard scores.

Norms

Separate norms for the Kindergarten form are in four 6-month age intervals (that is, 5–0 through 5–5, 5–6 through 5–11, 6–0 through 6–5, and 6–6 through 6–11). Separate norms for the Early Elementary form are in 12-month age groups (that is, 6–0 through 6–11, 7–0 through 7–11, and 8–0 through 8–11).

The TOPA 2+ was standardized on a total of 2,085 students: 1,035 of whom were in the Kindergarten form and 1,050 of whom were in the Early Elementary form. Norms for each form at each age are representative of the U.S. population in 2001 in terms of geographic regions, gender, race, ethnicity, and family income. Parents without a college education are slightly underrepresented.

Reliability

Coefficient alpha was calculated for each subtest at each age. For the Kindergarten form, only Letter Sounds for 6-year-olds fell below .90; that subtest reliability was .88. For the Early Elementary form, all alphas were between .80 and .87. In addition, alphas were calculated separately for males and females, whites, blacks, Hispanics, and students with language or learning disabilities. These alphas ranged from .82 to .91.

Test–retest correlations were used to estimate stabilities. For the Kindergarten form, 51 students were retested within approximately a two-week interval. Stability for Phonological Awareness was .87, and stability for Letter Sounds was .85. For the Early Elementary form, 88 students were retested within approximately a two-week interval. Stability for Phonological Awareness was .81, and stability for Letter Sounds was .84.

Finally, interscorer agreement was evaluated by having two trained examiners each score 50 tests. On the Kindergarten form, interscorer agreement for Phonological Awareness was .98 and for Letter Sounds was .99. On the Early Elementary form, interscorer agreement for Phonological Awareness was .98 and for Letter Sounds was .98.

Overall, care should be taken when interpreting the results of the TOPA 2+. The internal consistency is sufficient for screening and in some cases for use in making important educational decisions for students.

Validity

Evidence for the general validity of the TOPA 2+ comes from several sources. First, the contents of scales were carefully developed to represent phonemic awareness and knowledge of letter–sound correspondence. For example, the words in the Phonological Awareness subscales come from the 2,500 most frequently used words in first graders' oral language, and all consonant phonemes had a median age of customary articulation no later than 3.5 years of age. Next, the TOPA 2+ correlates well with another scale measuring similar skills and abilities (Dynamic Indicators of Basic Early Literacy Skills) and with teacher judgments of students' reading abilities. Evidence for differentiated validity comes from the scales' ability to distinguish students with language and learning disabilities from those without such problems. Other indices of validity include the absence of bias against males or females, whites, African Americans, and Hispanics.

Summary

The TOPA 2+ assesses phonemic awareness using beginning and ending sounds and letter–sound correspondence at the kindergarten and early elementary levels. The norms appear representative and are well described. Coefficient alpha for phonemic awareness is generally good for kindergartners but only suitable for screening students in the early elementary grades and for letter–sound correspondence for all students. Stability was estimated in the .80s, but interscorer agreement was excellent. Overall, care should be taken when interpreting the results of the TOPA 2+. Evidence for validity is adequate.

Dilemmas in Current Practice

There are three major problems in the diagnostic assessment of reading strengths and weaknesses. The first is the problem of curriculum match. Students enrolled in different reading curricula or whose teachers use different instructional programs have different opportunities to learn specific skills. Although many districts are now using the common core to guide English/language arts instruction, important variation remains in how curriculum and instruction occur. Reading instruction programs differ in the skills that are taught, in the emphasis placed on different skills, in the sequence in which skills are taught, and in the time at which skills are taught. Tests differ in the skills they assess. Thus, it can be expected that pupils studying different curricula and experiencing different instructional programs will perform differently on the same reading test. It can also be expected that pupils studying the same curriculum and experiencing the same instructional programs will perform differently on different reading tests. Diagnostic personnel must be very careful to examine the match between skills taught in the students' curriculum and instructional program and skills tested. Most teachers' manuals for reading instructional programs include a listing of the skills taught at each level in the series. Many authors of diagnostic reading tests now include in test manuals a list of the objectives measured by the test. At the very least, assessors should carefully examine the extent to which the test measures what has been taught. Ideally, assessors would select specific parts of tests to measure exactly what has been taught. To the extent that there is a difference between what has been taught and what is tested, the test is not a valid measure.

A second problem is the selection of tests that are appropriate for making different kinds of educational decisions. We noted that there are different types of diagnostic reading tests. In making classification decisions, educators must administer tests individually. They may either use an individually administered test or give a group test to one individual. For making instructional planning decisions, the most precise and helpful information will be obtained by giving individually administered criterion-referenced measures. Educators can, of course, systematically analyze pupil performance on a norm-referenced test, but the approach is difficult and time consuming. It may also be futile because norm-referenced tests usually do not contain enough items on which to base a diagnosis. When evaluating individual pupil progress, assessors must consider carefully the kinds of comparisons they want to make. If they want to compare pupils with same-age peers, norm-referenced measures are useful. If, on the other hand, they want to know the extent to which individual pupils are mastering curriculum objectives, criterion-referenced measures are the tests of choice.

The third problem is one of generalization. Assessors are faced with the difficult task of describing or predicting pupil performance in reading. Yet reading itself is difficult to describe, being a complex behavior composed of numerous subskills. Those who engage in reading diagnosis will do well to describe pupil performance in terms of specific skills or subskills (such as recognition of words in isolation, listening comprehension, and specific word-attack skills). They should also limit their predictions to making statements about probable performance of specific reading behaviors, not probable performance in reading.

Chapter Comprehension Questions

Write your answers to each of the following questions and then compare your responses to the text.

1. Why is reading important to assess?
2. Explain the two approaches traditionally used to teach reading.
3. Explain what is assessed in word-attack, reading recognition, oral reading, and reading comprehension.
4. Explain two potential problems in diagnostic testing of reading.

USING DIAGNOSTIC MATHEMATICS MEASURES

LEARNING OBJECTIVES

16-1 Ascertain why we administer and use diagnostic math tests.

16-2 Explain the ways in which mathematics is taught.

16-3 Identify the distinction between assessment of mathematics content and assessment of mathematics processes.

16-4 Identify the strengths and weaknesses of two diagnostic math tests.

STANDARDS ADDRESSED IN THIS CHAPTER

 CEC Initial Preparation Standards

Standard 4: Assessment

4.0 Beginning special education professionals use multiple methods of assessment and data-sources in making educational decisions.

 CEC Advanced Preparation Standards

Standard 1: Assessment

1.0 Special education specialists use valid and reliable assessment practices to minimize bias.

 National Association of School Psychologists Domains

1 Data-Based Decision Making and Accountability

3 Interventions and Instructional Support to Develop Academic Skills

Diagnostic testing in mathematics is designed to identify specific strengths and weaknesses in skill development. We have seen that all major achievement tests designed to assess multiple skills include subtests that measure mathematics competence. These tests are necessarily global; they most often are used at tier 1 in the multi-tiered system of supports and they attempt to assess a wide range of skills. However, in most cases these multiple-skills tests include only a small number of items assessing specific math skills, and the sample of math behaviors is insufficient for diagnostic purposes. Diagnostic testing in mathematics is more specific, providing more depth and a detailed assessment of skill development within specific areas. It is typically used at tiers 2 and 3 (targeted and intensive) levels in the multi-tiered system of supports model (see the discussion of the model in Chapter 12).

There are fewer diagnostic math tests than diagnostic reading tests, but math assessment is more clear-cut. Because the successful performance of some mathematical operations clearly depends on the successful performance of other operations (for example, multiplication depends on addition), it is easier to sequence skill development and assessment in math than in reading. Diagnostic math tests generally sample similar behaviors. They sample various mathematical contents, concepts, and operations as well as applications of mathematical facts and principles. Some now also include assessment of students' attitudes toward math.

16-1 Why Do We Assess Mathematics?

There are several reasons to assess mathematics skills. First, diagnostic math tests are intended to provide sufficiently detailed information so that teachers and intervention-assistance teams can ascertain a student's mastery of specific math skills and plan individualized math instruction. Second, some diagnostic math tests provide teachers with specific information on the kinds of items students in their classes pass and fail. This gives them information about the extent to which the curriculum and instruction in their class are working, and it provides opportunities to modify instruction to better promote student learning of important math skills. Third, all public school programs teach math facts and concepts. Teachers need to know whether pupils have mastered those facts and concepts. Finally, diagnostic math tests are occasionally used to make exceptionality and eligibility decisions. Individually administered tests are usually required for eligibility and placement decisions. Therefore, diagnostic math tests are often used to establish special learning needs and determine eligibility for programs for children with learning disabilities in mathematics.

16-2 The Ways to Teach Mathematics

There are major differences in the ways in which math is taught, and these influence how we assess performance and progress. Traditionally, mathematics emphasized the mastery of basic facts and algorithms, deductive reasoning, and proofs; teachers explained, modeled, and gave corrective feedback. With the launch of Sputnik in 1957 and the Soviet lead in space exploration, some reacted by blaming the way in which science and mathematics were taught in American schools. The old way was thought to stifle creativity and understanding.

In the 1960s, *new math* became popular in teacher-education programs in colleges and universities. Set theory; number bases; and the commutative, associative, and distributive properties became part of the curriculum. However, it soon became clear that the new math curricula were not improving student performances. In the mid-1970s, *Why Johnny Can't Add* convincingly criticized the many shortcomings of new math and advocated a return to more traditional mathematics curricula.

New math was replaced by a child-centered, constructivist approach, usually referred to as *standards-based math*. This approach provided students with the free-dom to select activities that fit their interests and prior experiences. Using concrete

ALFRED | Alfred is a fifth-grade student who is having particular difficulty solving mathematics problems. Alfred's school uses an instructional program in which students must discover and explain the process they use to solve problems. Now, near the end of the year, he is not fluent in any of the basic whole number processes (i.e., addition, subtraction, multiplication, and simple division). Fractions and decimals are a mystery to him. His teacher has provided Alfred with extra time and encouragement as well as peer models; she followed all of the suggestions for students who are having difficulty learning that were included in the teacher's edition of the instructional program. None of these additional interventions brought about noticeable improvement.

Alfred's parents met with the teacher to express their concern about his lack of progress and to find out what they can do at home to help their son. The teacher explained that Alfred needs to learn how to solve the problems on his own and that the parents should do no more than encourage him to try hard. Alfred's parents were not persuaded by the teacher, so they met with the school principal to request an evaluation to determine if Alfred had a learning disability in mathematics.

As a first step, the principal referred Alfred to the school's student assistance team for a tier 2 intervention. A review of Alfred's records (including previous report cards, teacher comments, and the results of the G•MADE administered at the end of third grade) indicated that Alfred's problems in math were not new; math had been a problem for him since at least the third grade. The team decided first to conduct a systematic assessment of Alfred's knowledge of the basic facts in whole number operations. A learning specialist conducted the evaluation that required both oral and written responses. Alfred responded fluently to some of the addition facts (i.e., those that included 1, 2, and 5); he could calculate the remaining addition facts accurately using his fingers. He knew all subtraction facts where the subtrahend was 1 and could calculate subtraction facts with minuends of 10 or less accurately. He did not know or did not correctly calculate other subtraction facts nor multiplication and division facts.

The team decided to provide direct instruction (relying on the commutative property, for example, teaching 3 + 4 and 4 + 3 together) in the memorization of paired addition facts. Alfred would be seen by the learning specialist twice a day for 10 minutes per session. In addition, Alfred's parents reviewed the addition facts with him nightly. Alfred made good progress and was proud of himself. He mastered the basic addition facts in two weeks. The instructional goal was then changed to basic subtraction facts. (Periodic reviews were also made of the addition facts.) Alfred made progress, but even though his retention of previously learned addition and subtraction facts was excellent, his progress was not deemed sufficient. Alfred's classroom performance was not showing improvement.

At this point, the team was faced with a decision. Should Alfred continue in tier 2 intervention or move to more intensive intervention? The answer depended on the school district's policies. In some districts, Alfred would remain in tier 2; in others, he would progress to tier 3 interventions; in still others, he would be evaluated for special education.

This scenario highlights how some students need systematic and explicit instruction in basic math concepts in order to succeed. Why might Alfred continue to struggle in the classroom?

materials, students created their own subjective mathematical understandings using their own feelings, thoughts, and intuition. Teachers played a major role in structuring the situations in which their students constructed knowledge with little or no help from the teacher.

By the 1990s, advocates of the child-centered approach were pitted against parents and mathematicians who wanted a return to more traditional mathematics curriculum and ways of teaching. Both sides had their experts, and the debate was often rancorous. However, it was becoming clear that the child-centered, standards approach was not producing the improvements envisioned. The results of the *Third International Mathematics and Science Study* (1995) provided some early indications: U.S. twelfth graders outperformed only two countries in math.

Today the evidence is unequivocal. Explicit systematic instruction improves the performance of low-achieving students and those with learning disabilities in a variety of mathematical components: computation, word problems, and problem solving (National Mathematics Advisory Panel, 2008, p. 48). Thus, students learn better when their teachers demonstrate algorithms, highlight critical features, provide opportunities to ask and answer questions, and sequence content precisely. The panel also stresses that struggling students require some explicit instruction regularly to ensure that they acquire the foundational skills and conceptual knowledge necessary for understanding their grade-level material.

The National Mathematics Advisory Panel also observed that there is clear evidence that math achievement is enhanced significantly when teachers monitor student progress. They recommended that all mathematics instruction be accompanied by ongoing monitoring of student progress toward objectives.

Read the Scenario in Assessment for this chapter, which illustrates what can happen to some students when there is little explicit instruction provided and they are therefore expected to learn without systematic instruction provided by the teacher.

16-3 Behaviors Sampled by Diagnostic Mathematics Tests

The National Council of Teachers of Mathematics (NCTM) has specified a set of standards for learning and teaching in mathematics. The most recent specification of those standards was in a document titled *Principles and Standards for School Mathematics,* issued in 2000. The NCTM specified five content standards and five process standards. Diagnostic math tests now typically assess knowledge and skill in some subset of those 10 standards, or they specify how what they assess relates to the NCTM standards. The standards are listed in Table 16.1, and for each of the standards we list the kinds of behaviors or skills identified by NCTM as important.

In 2006, NCTM published Curriculum Focal Points for pre-kindergarten through Grade Eight mathematics. Focus points are a small number of mathematical topics or areas that teachers should focus on at each grade level. More recently, the common core state standards in math have been published. Although there are a few slight differences in the ordering of specific topics by grade level across the NCTM Curriculum Focal Points and the common core state standards, generally the coverage and timing of specific topics is similar across these two sets of standards. The common core state standards tend to be more specific. We anticipate that diagnostic math tests will become more aligned with the common core state standards over time.

TABLE 16.1	NCTM Standards for Learning and Teaching in Mathematics

Content Standards

Number and Operations   Instructional programs from pre-kindergarten through grade 12 should enable all students to

- understand numbers, ways of representing numbers, relationships among numbers, and number systems;
- understand meanings of operations and how they relate to one another; and
- compute fluently and make reasonable estimates.

Algebra   Instructional programs from pre-kindergarten through grade 12 should enable all students to

- understand patterns, relations, and functions;
- represent and analyze mathematical situations and structures using algebraic symbols;
- use mathematical models to represent and understand quantitative relationships; and
- analyze change in various contexts.

Geometry   Instructional programs from pre-kindergarten through grade 12 should enable all students to

- analyze characteristics and properties of two- and three-dimensional geometric shapes and develop mathematical arguments about geometric relationships;
- specify locations and describe spatial relationships using coordinate geometry and other representational systems;
- apply transformations and use symmetry to analyze mathematical situations; and
- use visualization, spatial reasoning, and geometric modeling to solve problems.

Measurement   Instructional programs from pre-kindergarten through grade 12 should enable all students to

- understand measurable attributes of objects and the units, systems, and processes of measurement; and
- apply appropriate techniques, tools, and formulas to determine measurements.

Data Analysis and Probability   Instructional programs from pre-kindergarten through grade 12 should enable all students to

- formulate questions that can be addressed with data and collect, organize, and display relevant data to answer them;
- select and use appropriate statistical methods to analyze data;
- develop and evaluate inferences and predictions that are based on data; and
- understand and apply basic concepts of probability.

(Continued)

TABLE 16.1	NCTM Standards for Learning and Teaching in Mathematics *Continued*

Process Standards

Problem Solving Instructional programs from pre-kindergarten through grade 12 should enable all students to

- build new mathematical knowledge through problem solving;
- solve problems that arise in mathematics and in other contexts;
- apply and adapt a variety of appropriate strategies to solve problems; and
- monitor and reflect on the process of mathematical problem solving.

Reasoning and Proof Instructional programs from pre-kindergarten through grade 12 should enable all students to

- recognize reasoning and proof as fundamental aspects of mathematics;
- make and investigate mathematical conjectures;
- develop and evaluate mathematical arguments and proofs; and
- select and use various types of reasoning and methods of proof.

Communication Instructional programs from pre-kindergarten through grade 12 should enable all students to

- organize and consolidate their mathematical thinking through communication;
- communicate their mathematical thinking coherently and clearly to peers, teachers, and others;
- analyze and evaluate the mathematical thinking and strategies of others; and
- use the language of mathematics to express mathematical ideas precisely.

Connections Instructional programs from pre-kindergarten through grade 12 should enable all students to

- recognize and use connections among mathematical ideas;
- understand how mathematical ideas interconnect and build on one another to produce a coherent whole; and
- recognize and apply mathematics in contexts outside of mathematics.

Representation Instructional programs from pre-kindergarten through grade 12 should enable all students to

- create and use representations to organize, record, and communicate mathematical ideas;
- select, apply, and translate among mathematical representations to solve problems; and
- use representations to model and interpret physical, social, and mathematical phenomena.

Some math tests include survey questions that ask students about their attitudes toward math. Students are asked the extent to which they enjoy math, the extent to which their friends like math more than they do, and so on.

16-4 Specific Diagnostic Math Tests

Commonly used diagnostic mathematics tests are listed in Table 16.2. Two of the tests (Group Mathematics Assessment and Diagnostic Evaluation [G•MADE] and KeyMath-3 Diagnostic Assessment [KeyMath-3 DA]) are reviewed in detail in this chapter.

16-4a GROUP MATHEMATICS ASSESSMENT AND DIAGNOSTIC EVALUATION (G•MADE)

The Group Mathematics Assessment and Diagnostic Evaluation (G•MADE; Williams, 2004) is a group-administered, norm-referenced, standards-based test for assessing the math skills of students in grades K–12. It is norm referenced in that it is standardized on a nationally representative group. It is standards based in that the content assessed is based on the standards of NCTM.

G•MADE is a diagnostic test designed to identify specific math skill development strengths and weaknesses, and the test is designed to lead to teaching strategies. The test provides information about math skills and error patterns of each student, using the efficiencies of group administration. Test materials include a CD that provides a cross-reference between specific math skills and math teaching resources. Teaching resources are also available in print.

TABLE 16.2	Commonly Used Diagnostic Mathematics Tests		
Test	**Authors**	**Year of Publication**	**Publisher**
KeyMath-3	Connolly	2007	Pearson
Comprehensive Mathematical Abilities Test (CMAT)	Hresko, Schlieve, Herron, Swain & Sherbenou	2003	Pro-Ed
Group Mathematics Assessment and Diagnostic Evaluation (G•MADE)	Williams	2004	Pearson
Test of Early Mathematics Abilities–Third Edition (TEMA-3)	Ginsburg & Baroody	2003	Pro-Ed
Test of Mathematical Abilities–Third Edition (TOMA-3)	Brown, Cronin & D. Bryant	2012	Pro-Ed

There are nine levels, each with two parallel forms. Eight of the nine levels have three subtests (the lowest level has two). The three subtests are Concepts and Communication, Operations and Computation, and Process and Applications. The items in each subtest fit the content of the following categories: numeration, quantity, geometry, measurement, time/sequence, money, comparison, statistics, and algebra. Diagnosis of skill development strengths and needs is fairly broad. For example, teachers learn that an individual student has difficulty with concepts and communication in the area of geometry.

Subtests

Concepts and Communication This subtest measures students' knowledge of the language, vocabulary, and representations of math. A symbol, word, or short phrase is presented with four choices (pictures, symbols, or numbers). It is permissible for teachers to read words to students, but they may not define or explain the words. Figure 16.1 is a representation of the kinds of items used to measure concepts and communication skills.

Operations and Computation This subtest measures students' skills in using the basic operations of addition,

FIGURE 16.1
Concepts and Communication Example from Levels M and H

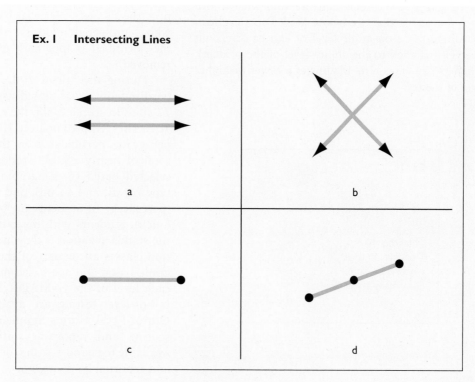

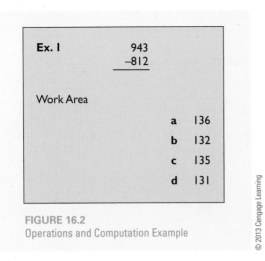

FIGURE 16.2
Operations and Computation Example

subtraction, multiplication, and division. This subtest is not included at Level R (the readiness level and lowest level of the test). There are 24 items on this subtest at each level, and each consists of an incomplete equation with four answer choices. An example is shown in Figure 16.2.

Process and Applications This subtest measures students' skill in taking the language and concepts of math and applying the appropriate operations and computations to solve a word problem. Each item consists of a short passage of one or more sentences and four response choices. An example is shown in Figure 16.3. At lower levels of the test, the problems are one-step problems, whereas at higher levels they require application of multiple steps.

The G•MADE levels each contain items that are on grade level, items that are somewhat above level, and items that are below level. Each level can be administered on grade level or can be given out of level (matched to the ability level of the student). Teachers can choose to administer a lower or higher level of the test.

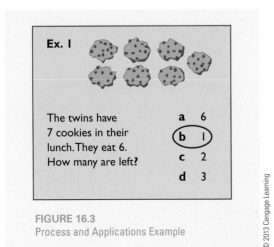

FIGURE 16.3
Process and Applications Example

Scores

Raw scores for the G•MADE can be converted to standard scores (with a mean of 100 and a standard deviation of 15) using fall or spring norms. Grade scores, stanines, percentiles, and normal curve equivalents are also available. Growth scale values are provided for the purpose of tracking growth in math skills for students who are given different levels of the test over the years. G•MADE can be used to track growth over the course of a year or from year to year.

The publisher provides diagnostic worksheets that consist of cross-tabulations of the subtests with the content areas. The worksheets are used to identify areas in which individual students or whole classes did or did not demonstrate skills. The worksheets are used to prepare reports identifying specific areas of need. For example, the objective assessed by item 28 in Level 1, Form B is skill in solving a one-step sequence problem that requires the ability to recognize a pattern. When reporting on performance on this item, the teacher might report that "Joe did not solve one-step sequence problems that require the ability to recognize a pattern." He might also indicate that "two-thirds of the class did not solve one-step problems that require the ability to recognize a pattern."

Norms

There were two phases to standardization of the G•MADE. First, a study of bias by gender, race/ethnicity, and region was conducted on more than 10,000 students during a national tryout. In addition, the test was reviewed by a panel of educators who represented minority perspectives, and items they identified as apparently biased were modified or removed.

During the fall of 2002, G•MADE was standardized on a nationwide sample of students at 72 sites. In spring 2003, the sampling was repeated at 71 sites. Approximately 1,000 students per level per grade participated in the standardization (a total of nearly 28,000 students). The sample was selected based on geographic region, community type (rural, and so on), and socioeconomic status (percentage of students on free and reduced-price lunch). Students with disabilities were included in the standardization if they attended regular education classes all or part of the day. Fall and spring grade-based and age-based norms are provided for each level of the G•MADE. Norms that allow for out-of-level testing are available in a G•MADE Out-of-Level Norms Supplement and through the scoring and reporting software. Templates are available for hand-scoring, or the test can be scored and reported by computer.

Reliability

Data on internal consistency and stability over time are presented in the G•MADE manual. Internal consistency reliabilities were computed for each G•MADE subtest and the total test score for each level and form using the split-half method. All reliabilities exceed .74, with more than 90 percent exceeding .80. The only low reliabilities are at seventh grade for Concepts and Communications and for Process and Applications at all grades beyond grade 4. Thus, the only really questionable subtest is Process and Applications beyond grade 4. Internal consistency reliability coefficients are above .90 for the total score at all levels of the test.

Alternate-form reliability was established on a sample of 651 students, and all reliabilities exceeded .80. Stability of the test was established by giving it twice to a sample of 761 students. The test–retest reliability coefficients for this group of students exceeded .80, with the exception only of .78 for Level 4, Form A. Overall, there is good support for the reliability of the grade. Internal consistency and stability are sufficient for using the test to make decisions about individuals. The two forms of the test are comparable.

Validity

The content of the G•MADE is based on the NCTM Math Standards, though the test was developed following a year-long research study of state standards, curriculum benchmarks, the score and sequence plans of commonly used math textbooks, and review of research on best practices for teaching math concepts and skills. The author provides a strong argument for the validity of the content of the G•MADE.

Several studies support the criterion-related validity of the test. Correlations with subtests of the Iowa Tests of Basic Skills (ITBS), the TerraNova, and the Iowa Tests of Educational Development are reported. Surprisingly, correlations between G•MADE subtests and reading subtests of the ITBS are as high as they are between G•MADE subtests and math subtests of the G•MADE. This was not the case for correlations with the TerraNova, in which those with the math subtests exceeded by far correlations with the reading subtests. In a comparison of performance on KeyMath and the G•MADE, all correlations were in excess of .80. The two tests measure highly comparable skills.

Summary

The G•MADE is a group-administered, norm-referenced, standards-based, and diagnostic measure of student skill development in three separate areas. There is good evidence for the content validity of the test, and the test was appropriately and adequately standardized. Evidence for reliability and validity of the G•MADE is good. The lone exception to this is the finding that performance on the test is as highly correlated with the reading subtests of some other criterion measures as it is with the math subtests of those measures.

16-4b KEYMATH-3 DIAGNOSTIC ASSESSMENT (KEYMATH-3 DA)

KeyMath-3 Diagnostic Assessment (KeyMath-3 DA; Connolly, 2007) is the third revision of the test originally published in 1971. Over the three editions of the test, a number of "normative updates" have been published. KeyMath-3 DA is an untimed, individually administered, norm-referenced test designed to provide a comprehensive assessment of essential math concepts and skills in individuals aged 4 years, 6 months through 21 years. The test takes 30 to 40 minutes for students in the lower elementary grades and 75 to 90 minutes for older students. Four uses are suggested for the test: (1) assess math proficiency by providing comprehensive coverage of the concepts and skills taught in regular math instruction, (2) assess student progress in math, (3) support instructional planning, and (4) support educational placement decisions. The author designed this revision of the test to reflect the NCTM content and process standards described previously in this chapter.

KeyMath-3 DA includes a manual, two freestanding easels for either Form A or Form B, and 25 record forms with detachable Written Computation Examinee Booklets. Two ancillary products are available for KeyMath-3 DA: an ASSIST Scoring and Reporting Software program and a KeyMath-3 Essential Resources instructional program. There are two parallel forms of the test (A and B), and each has 372 items divided into the following subtests: Numeration, Algebra, Geometry, Measurement, Data Analysis and Probability, Mental Computation and Estimation, Addition and Subtraction, Multiplication and Division, Foundations of Problem Solving, and Applied Problem Solving.

Scores

The test can be hand-scored or scored by using the KeyMath-3 DA ASSIST Scoring and Reporting Software. Users can obtain three indices of relative standing (scale scores, standard scores, and percentile ranks) and three developmental scores (grade and age equivalents and growth scale values). Users also obtain three composite scores: Basic Concepts (conceptual knowledge), Operations (computational skills), and Application (problem solving). In addition, tools are available to help users analyze students' functional range in math, and they provide an analysis of students' performance specific to focus items and behavioral objectives. The scoring software can be used to create progress reports across multiple administrations of the test, produce a narrative summary report, export derived scores to Excel spreadsheets for statistical analysis, and generate reports for parents.

Dilemmas in Current Practice

There are three major problems in the diagnostic assessment of math skills. The first problem is the recurring issue of instructional match. Despite recent initiatives such as the common core state standards in math, considerable variation in math instructional programming remains. This variation means that diagnostic math tests will not be equally representative of all instructional programs or even appropriate for some commonly used ones. As a result, great care must be exercised in using diagnostic math tests to make various educational decisions. Assessment personnel must be extremely careful to note the match between test content and instructional programming. This should involve far more than a quick inspection of test items by someone unfamiliar with the specific classroom instructional programming. For example, a professional could inspect the teacher's manual to ensure that the teacher assesses only material that has been taught and that there is reasonable correspondence between the relative emphasis placed on teaching the material and testing the material. To do this, the professional might have to develop a table of specifications for the math instructional programming and compare test items with that table. However, once a table of specifications has been developed, a better procedure would be to select items from a standards-referenced system to fit the cells in the table exactly.

The second problem is selecting an appropriate test for the type of decision to be made. School personnel are usually required to use individually administered norm-referenced devices in eligibility decisions. Decisions about a pupil's eligibility for special services, however, need not be based on detailed information about the pupil's strengths and weaknesses, as provided by diagnostic tests; instead, information on a pupil's relative standing may be more appropriate. In our opinion, the best mathematical achievement survey tests are subtests of group-administered tests. A practical solution is not to use a diagnostic math test for eligibility decisions but to administer individually a subtest from one of the better group-administered achievement tests.

The third problem is that most of the diagnostic tests in mathematics do not test a sufficiently detailed sample of facts and concepts. Consequently, assessors must generalize from a student's performance on the items tested to his or her performance on the items that are not tested. The reliabilities of the subtests of diagnostic math tests often are not high enough for educators to make such a generalization with any great degree of confidence. As a result, these tests are not very useful in assessing readiness or strengths and weaknesses in order to plan instructional programs. We believe that the preferred practice in diagnostic testing in mathematics is for teachers to develop achievement tests that exactly parallel the instruction being provided.

Norms

KeyMath-3 DA was standardized on 3,630 individuals, ages 4 years, 6 months to 21 years. The test was standardized by contacting examiners and having them get permission to assess students, sending the permissions to the publisher, and then randomly selecting students to participate in the norming. The sample closely approximates the distributions reported in the 2004 census, and cross-tabs (i.e., how many males were from the Northeast) are reported in the manual. In addition, the test was standardized on representative proportions of students with specific learning disability, speech/language impairment, intellectual disability, emotional/behavioral disturbance, and developmental delays. The test appears adequately standardized.

Reliability

The author reports data on internal consistency, alternate-form, and test–retest reliability. Internal consistency reliabilities for students in kindergarten and first grade are low. At other ages, internal consistency reliability coefficients generally exceed .80. Internal consistency coefficients for the composite scores exceed .90 except in grades K–2. Alternate-form reliabilities exceed .80 with the exception of the reliabilities for different forms of the Geometry and the Data Analysis and Probability subtests. Adjusted test–retest reliabilities based on the performance of 103 students (approximately half on each form) in grades K–12 generally exceed .80 with the exception

of the Foundations of Problem Solving subtest (.70) and the Geometry subtest (.78). The reliability of all subtests and composites is adequate for screening purposes and good for diagnostic purposes.

Validity

The authors report extensive validity information in the manual. All validity data are for composite scores. KeyMath-3 DA composites correlate very highly with scores on the KeyMath-Revised normative update and math scores on the Kaufman Test of Educational Achievement (with the exception of the Applications and Mathematics Composite), ITBS, Measures of Academic Progress, and the G•MADE (with the exception of the operations composite [.63]). Evidence for content validity is good, based on alignment with state and NCTM standards. The authors provide data on how representatives of special populations perform relative to the general population, and scores are within expected ranges.

Summary

KeyMath-3 DA is a norm-referenced, individually administered comprehensive assessment of skills and problem solving in math appropriate for use with students 4 years, 6 months to 21 years of age. The test is adequately standardized, and there is good evidence for reliability and validity. Comparative data are provided on the performance of students with disabilities.

Chapter Comprehension Questions

Write your answers to each of the following questions and then compare your responses to the text.

1. Why do we administer and use diagnostic math tests?

2. Provide two examples each of content and processes sampled by diagnostic mathematics tests.

3. What is the distinction between assessment of mathematics content and assessment of mathematics process?

4. Identify two differences in the kinds of behaviors sampled by two commonly used diagnostic mathematics tests: G•MADE and KeyMath-3 DA.

5. Briefly describe three major dilemmas in diagnostic testing in mathematics:

   a. Instructional match

   b. Selecting the correct tests for making specific decisions

   c. Adequate and sufficient behavior sampling

Using Measures of Written Language

LEARNING OBJECTIVES

17-1 Understand why we assess written language.

17-2 Explain ways in which written language is taught.

17-3 Identify what behaviors are sampled by diagnostic written language tests.

17-4 Describe the strengths and weaknesses of two written language tests.

STANDARDS ADDRESSED IN THIS CHAPTER

 CEC Initial Preparation Standards

Standard 4: Assessment

4.0 Beginning special education professionals use multiple methods of assessment and data-sources in making educational decisions.

 CEC Advanced Preparation Standards

Standard 1: Assessment

1.0 Special education specialists use valid and reliable assessment practices to minimize bias.

 National Association of School Psychologists Domains

1 Data-Based Decision Making and Accountability

3 Interventions and Instructional Support to Develop Academic Skills

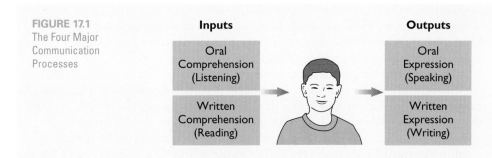

FIGURE 17.1
The Four Major
Communication
Processes

Written expression involves coordination of a variety of skills to produce a coherent product to be read and understood by others. It is just one of four major communication processes, but is often considered the most challenging. The four major communication processes are: oral comprehension (listening and comprehending speech), written comprehension (reading), oral expression (speaking), and written expression (writing). These are illustrated in Figure 17.1. Because many skills involved in written expression build on those involved in the other three communication processes, comprehensive language assessment involving consideration of all four processes is often undertaken. Typically, school personnel with specialized training in speech and language development focus on assessment of oral comprehension and oral expression, and those with specialized training in academic development focus on written comprehension (reading) and written expression. Although students who struggle with written expression often have difficulty with one or more of the other three processes, that is not necessarily the case. For example, a student who has normal comprehension does not necessarily have normal production skills. Also, a student with relatively normal expressive skills may have problems with receptive language. When educators and speech language pathologists work together on language concerns, they can more carefully identify specific language areas of concern for individual students. We focus this chapter on assessment of written expression.

17-1 Why Assess Written Language?

There are two primary reasons for assessing written language abilities. First, well-developed written language abilities are desirable in and of themselves. The ability to express thoughts and feelings through writing is a goal of most individuals. Second, written language is regularly taught in school, and this area is singled out for assessment in the Individuals with Disabilities Education Act. Written and oral language tests are administered for purposes of screening, instructional planning and modification, eligibility, and progress monitoring. Those who have difficulties with various aspects of written language are often eligible for special services from special education teachers and related services personnel.

17-2 The Ways in Which Written Expression Is Taught

There is tremendous variability in the methods used to teach skills for written expression—perhaps even more so than is the case for instruction in the basic skills discussed in prior chapters (i.e., reading and math). Although more attention is now being placed on writing instruction than in prior decades, the research base for writing instruction is not nearly as solid as it is for reading and math instruction. Given the strong connections to basic reading skills, many classrooms include instruction in written expression in a block of time dedicated broadly to English/language arts. However, the sequencing and emphasis of particular written expression skills within instruction can vary considerably from district to district, school to school, and even classroom to classroom. Although the common core state standards may provide some greater consistency within states that adopt the associated standards, it is likely that substantial variation will continue.

There are two major components of written language that provide a foundation for instruction: content and form. The **content of written expression** is the product of considerable intellectual and linguistic activity: formulating, elaborating, sequencing, and then clarifying and revising ideas; choosing the precise word to convey meaning; and so forth. Moreover, much of what we consider to be content is the result of a creative endeavor. Our ability to use words to excite, to depict vividly, to imply, and to describe complex ideas is far more involved than simply putting symbols on paper.

The **form of written language** refers to the conventions or rules that are evident in writing output; it is far more mechanistic than its content. For writer and reader to communicate, three sets of conventions or rules are used: penmanship, spelling, and style rules. The most fundamental rules deal with *penmanship*, the formation of individual letters and letter sequences that make up words. Although letter formation tends to become more individualistic with age, there are a limited number of ways, for example, that the letter *A* can be written and still be recognized as an *A*. Moreover, there are conventions about the relative spacing of letters between and within words.

Spelling is also rule governed. Although American English is more irregular phonetically than other languages, it remains largely regular, and students should be able to spell most words by applying a few phonetic rules. For example, we have known since the mid-1960s that approximately 80 percent of all consonants have a single spelling (Hanna, Hanna, Hodges, & Rudoff, 1966). Short vowels are the major source of difficulty for most writers. The third set of conventions involves style. *Style* is a catchall term for rule-governed writing, which includes grammar (such as parts of speech, pronoun use, agreement, and verb voice and mood) and mechanics (such as punctuation, capitalization, abbreviations, and referencing).

Just as with reading and writing, explicit instruction in characteristics of form have been supported as helpful for students with writing difficulties. For instance, teaching letter formation to those with handwriting difficulties has been found to be effective (Berninger and Graham, 1998). Providing explicit instruction on spelling patterns has similarly been effective (Berninger et al., 1998). Furthermore, explicit instruction in strategies for planning, revising, and editing written work is important (Graham, 2006).

However, districts, schools, and classrooms vary considerably in the extent of explicit instruction provided, and in the ordering of specific skills taught. In some schools, spelling is not addressed until after students have become somewhat fluent in expression of their ideas; such schools may be proponents of "inventive spelling" in which students are encouraged to simply produce content without concern for whether they are spelling any of it correctly. Others focus on having students spell words correctly from the very beginning. This has very important implications for how to best assess student achievement in written language. Read the Scenario in Assessment for this chapter for an illustration of how this may influence assessment.

17-3 Behaviors Sampled by Diagnostic Written Language Tests

Because of the rules associated with the form of written language, aspects of form are the easiest to assess objectively, and they are the predominant skills assessed on diagnostic tests of written expression. To assess skills related to form, students are often expected to dictate various words, phrases, and sentences, and scores are based on whether they spell correctly and use appropriate grammar, capitalization, and punctuation.

Because the associated skills may be taught at different grade levels, the results from standardized diagnostic written expression tests may not be accurate indicators

SCENARIO IN ASSESSMENT

JOSÉ | In the Fairfield School District, students are encouraged to use inventive spelling from kindergarten to second grade. In other words, they are encouraged to come up with their own spelling for words that they do not yet know how to spell. When completing independent writing assignments, Fairfield teachers simply encourage students to focus on getting their thoughts on paper. Although spelling is taught in Fairfield, it is not expected that students know how to correctly spell the words that they choose to use in their independent writing assignments. Students are provided feedback on the quality of description and organization evident in their writing. As long as the spelling makes sense, they are not corrected.

In the Lakewood School District, just to the north of Fairfield, the focus of writing instruction and feedback is on the form of writing (that is, handwriting, spelling, punctuation, and so on). Students are encouraged to use those words that have been taught as weekly spelling words in their weekly independent writing assignments. Teachers spend a substantial amount of time teaching letter formation, word spacing, capitalization, and spelling during writing instruction. Students' grades on their independent writing assignments are based on the percentage of words spelled correctly.

José is a first grader who just moved into the Lakewood School District after attending Fairfield for kindergarten and part of first grade. His new teacher is appalled when José turns in the following independent writing assignment:

Mi trip to flourda

I went to flourda on brake and it was rely wrm and i wint swemmin in a pul. I jummd of a dyving bord and mad a big splaz that mad evrywon wet. I wood like to go thare agin neckst yeer.

The teacher views this writing sample to be far below the quality of Meika's writing assignment, which is much shorter but includes correct spelling and capitalization. Meika's writing sample is as follows:

My Winter Break

I had fun with my sister. We played games. We watched T.V.

The teacher is very concerned that José will not be successful in her class and requests the assistance of the school psychologist to help determine whether he may have a writing disability and need additional services. Although José performs similarly to Meika on a standardized measure of written language in which scores are based on both spelling achievement and total words written, greater differences in their achievement are evident when applying the different writing standards associated with the two different districts. In Fairfield, where total words written in three minutes is the measure used, he scored at the 85th percentile. In Lakewood, where total words spelled correctly in three minutes is the measure used, he scored at the 9th percentile.

Instead of considering a full-blown special education evaluation, the school psychologist recommends that José be specifically instructed to use only the words he knows how to spell in his independent writing. As José receives more consistent feedback on his mechanics, he begins to increase his performance according to his new school district's standards and eventually is performing above average according to both total words written and words spelled correctly on the three-minute writing task.

This scenario highlights how measures of student achievement should be aligned with instruction. For students who have not had exposure to the associated instruction, it is important to be patient and provide opportunities to learn accordingly. How do you think Meika's performance would have faired in Fairfield?

---

of what students have learned. The spelling words that students learn vary considerably across instructional programs. For example, Ames (1965) examined seven spelling series and found that they introduced an average of 3,200 words between the second and eighth grades. However, only approximately 1,300 words were common to all the series; approximately 1,700 words were taught in only one series. Moreover, those words that were taught in several series varied considerably in their grade placement, sometimes by as many as five grades. The grade level at which various capitalization and punctuation rules are taught varies considerably, as well. To be valid, the measurement of achievement in these areas must be closely tied to what is being taught. For example, pupils may learn in kindergarten, first grade, second grade, or later that a sentence always begins with a capital letter. They may learn in the sixth grade or several grades earlier that commercial brand names are capitalized. Students may be taught in the second or third grade that the apostrophe in "it's" makes the word a contraction of "it is" or they may still be studying "it's" in high school. Finally, in assessing word usage, organization, and penmanship, we must take into account the emphasis that individual teachers place on these components of written language and when and how students are taught.

Objective assessment of the content of writing can be particularly difficult. To assess writing content, a student may be provided a story starter or writing prompt that they must then write about for a given period of time. Their output can be quantified in terms of the total number of words written or total correct word sequences. In addition, a rubric may be applied to determine a score for various aspects of the writing output, such as organization, supporting details, sentence complexity, and so forth. However, scoring with rubrics often fails to meet expected thresholds for reliability, and unless they are aligned with the nature of instruction provided to the student, they are not likely to provide adequate information about what the student has learned.

The more usual way to assess written language is to evaluate a student's written work and to develop vocabulary and spelling tests, as well as written expression rubrics that parallel the curriculum. In this way, teachers can be sure that they are measuring precisely what has been taught. Most teacher's editions of language arts textbook series contain scope-and-sequence charts that specify fairly clearly the objectives that are taught in each unit. From these charts, teachers can develop appropriate criterion-referenced and curriculum-based assessments. There are also some rubrics available in the research literature that may be used by teachers to guide their instruction toward important components of writing content (Tindal & Hasbrouck, 1991).

17-4 Specific Diagnostic Writing Tests

Table 17.1 provides a list of commonly administered tests of written language. Reviews of two of these tests (that is, the Test of Written Language–Fourth Edition and the Oral and Written Language Scales–Second Edition) are provided in the following section.

17-4a TEST OF WRITTEN LANGUAGE–FOURTH EDITION (TOWL-4)

The Test of Written Language–4 (TOWL-4; Hammill & Larsen, 2008) is a norm-referenced device designed to assess the written language competence of students between the ages of 9–0 and 17–11. Although the TOWL-4 was designed to be individually administered, the authors provide a series of modifications to allow group administration, with follow-up testing of individual students to ensure valid testing. The recommended uses of the TOWL-4 include identifying students who have substantial difficulty in writing, determining strengths and weaknesses of individual students, documenting student progress, and conducting research. Two alternative forms (A and B) are available.

The TOWL-4 uses two writing formats (contrived and spontaneous) to evaluate written language. In a contrived format, students' linguistic options are purposely constrained to force the students to use specific words or conventions. The TOWL-4 uses these two formats to assess three components of written language (conventional, linguistic, and cognitive). The conventional component deals with using widely accepted rules in punctuation and spelling. The linguistic component deals with syntactic and semantic structures. The cognitive component deals with producing "logical, coherent, and contextual written material" (Hammill & Larsen, 2008, p. 25).

Subtests

The first five subtests, eliciting writing in contrived contexts, are briefly described here.

TABLE 17.1	Commonly Used Diagnostic Writing Tests		
Test	**Authors**	**Year of Publication**	**Publisher**
Oral and Written Language Scales–Second Edition (OWLS-2)	Carrow-Woolfolk	2011	Western Psychological Services
Test of Early Written Language–Third Edition (TEWL-3)	Hresko, Herron, Peak & Hicks	2012	Pro-Ed
Test of Written Language–Fourth Edition (TOWL-4)	Hammill & Larsen	2009	Pro-Ed
Test of Written Spelling–Fifth Edition (TWS-5)	Larsen, Hammill & Moats	2013	Pro-Ed

Vocabulary This area is assessed by having a student write correct sentences containing stimulus words.

Spelling The TOWL-4 assesses spelling by having a student write sentences from dictation.

Punctuation Competence in this aspect of writing is assessed by evaluating the punctuation and capitalization in sentences written by a student from dictation.

Logical Sentences Competence in this area is assessed by having a student rewrite illogical sentences so that they make sense.

Sentence Combining The TOWL-4 requires a student to write one grammatically correct sentence based on the information in several short sentences.

The last two subtests elicit more spontaneous, contextual writing from the student in response to a picture used as a story starter. After the story has been written (and the other five subtests administered), the story is scored on two dimensions. Each dimension is treated as a subtest. Following are brief descriptions of these subtests:

Contextual Conventions A student's ability to use appropriate grammatical rules and conventions of mechanics in context (such as punctuation and spelling) is assessed using the student's story.

Story Composition As described by Hammill and Larsen (2008, p. 29), this subtest evaluates a student's story on the basis of the "quality of its composition (e.g., vocabulary, plot, prose, development of characters, and interest to the reader)."

Scores

Raw scores for each subtest can be converted to percentiles or standard scores. The standard scores have a mean of 10 and a standard deviation of 3. Various combinations of subtests result in three composites: contrived writing (Vocabulary, Spelling, Punctuation, Logical Sentences, and Sentence Combining), spontaneous writing (Contextual Conventions and Story Composition), and overall writing (all subtests). Subtest standard scores can be summed and converted to standard scores (that is, "index scores") and percentiles for each composite. The composite index scores have a mean of 100 and a standard deviation of 15. Both age and grade equivalents are available; however, the authors appropriately warn against reporting these scores.

Norms

Two different sampling techniques were used to establish norms for the TOWL-4. First, sites in each of the four geographic regions of the United States were selected, and 977 students were tested. Second, an additional 1,229 students were tested by volunteers who had previously purchased materials from the publisher. The total sample is distributed such that there are at least 200 students represented at each age level; however, at some age levels there are very few students represented in either the fall or the spring sample. The total sample varies no more than 5 percent from information provided by the U.S. Census Bureau for the 2005 school-age population on various demographic variables (that is, gender, geographic region, ethnicity, family income, educational attainment of parents, and disability), with the exception that those with a very high household income are overrepresented (that is, 35 percent of the sample has a household income of more than $75,000, whereas just 27 percent of the population has this level of household income). The authors also present data for three age ranges (that is, 9 to 11, 12 to 14, and 15 to 17), showing that each age range also approximates information on the nationwide school-age population for 2005. However, the comparisons of interest (that is, the degree to which each normative group approximates the census) are absent.

Reliability

Three types of reliability are discussed in the TOWL-4 manual: internal consistencies (both coefficient alpha and alternate-form reliability), stability, and interscorer agreement.

Two procedures were used to estimate the internal consistency of the TOWL-4. First, a series of coefficient alphas was computed. Using the entire normative sample, coefficient alpha was used to estimate the internal consistency of each score (age and grade) and composite on each form at each age. Of the 238 alphas reported, 85 are in the .90s, 80 are in the .80s, 62 are in the .70s, 10 are in the .60s, and 1 is below .60. Alphas are consistently higher on the Vocabulary, Punctuation, and Spelling subtests and lowest on the Logical Sentences and Story Composition subtests. As is typical, coefficient alpha was substantially higher for the composites. For Contrived Writing and Overall Writing, all coefficients equaled or exceeded .95. For Spontaneous Writing, they were substantially lower, with all in the .70s and .80s. Thus, two of the composites are sufficiently reliable for making important educational decisions about students.

The authors are to be commended for also reporting subtest internal consistencies for several demographic subgroups (that is, males and females, Caucasian Americans, African Americans, Hispanic Americans, and Asian Americans), as well as students with disabilities (that is, learning disabled, speech impaired, and attention deficit hyperactive). The obtained coefficients for the various demographic subgroups are comparable to those for the entire normative sample.

Second, alternate-form reliability was also computed for each subtest and each composite at each age and grade, using the entire normative sample. These coefficients were distributed in approximately the same way as the alphas were.

The two-week stability of each subtest and each composite on both forms was estimated with 84 students ranging in age from 9 to 17 years; results were examined according to two age and grade ranges. Of the 80 associated coefficients, 30 coefficients equaled or exceeded .90, 34 were in the .80s, 15 were in the .70s, and 1 was in the .60s. These followed the pattern of other reliability indices, with higher coefficients identified for the contrived writing and overall writing composites than for the spontaneous writing composite.

To estimate interscorer agreement, 41 TOWL-4 protocols were selected at random and scored. The correlations between scorers were remarkably consistent. Of the 40 coefficients associated with subtest and composite scoring agreement, 36 were in the .90s, 2 were in the .80s, and 2 were in the .70s. The scoring of written language samples is quite difficult, and unacceptably low levels of interscorer agreement appear to be the rule rather than the exception. It appears that the scoring criteria contained in the TOWL-4 manual are sufficiently precise and clear to allow for consistent scoring. The only subtest with interscorer reliability below .90 was Story Composition.

Validity

Support for content validity comes from the way in which the test was developed, the many dimensions of written language assessed, and the methods by which competence in written language is assessed. The evidence for criterion-related validity comes from a study in which three measures—the Written Language Observation Scale (Hammill & Larsen, 2009), the Reading Observation Scale (Hammill & Larsen, 2009), and the Test of Reading Comprehension–Fourth Edition (TORC-4; Brown, Wiederholt, & Hammill, 2009)—were correlated with each score on the TOWL-4. Correlations ranging from .34 (Story Composition correlated with the Written Language Observation Scale) to .80 (Spelling correlated with the TORC-4) provide somewhat limited support for the TOWL-4's validity; teacher ratings for reading correlated as well as or better than those for writing. The authors also conducted positive predictive analyses using these data on the three literacy measures. Based on the results, which indicate levels of sensitivity and specificity exist meeting the .70 threshold, the authors suggest that the TOWL-4 can be used to identify those students who have literacy difficulties.

Construct validity is considered at some length in the TOWL-4 manual. First, the authors present evidence to show that TOWL-4 scores increase with age and grade. The correlations with age are substantially stronger for students between the ages of 9 and

12 years than for students 13 to 17 years old, for whom correlations are small. Second, in examining the subtest intercorrelations and conducting a factor analysis, the TOWL-4 appears to assess a single factor for the sample as a whole. Thus, although individual subtests (or the contrived and spontaneous composites) may be of interest, they are not independent of the other skills measured on the test. Third, scores on the TOWL-4 for students with learning disabilities and speech/language impairments, who are anticipated to struggle in the area of written language, were generally lower than those for other subgroups. However, it is important to note that score differences for these exceptionality groups tended to be no more than one standard deviation below the average.

The authors were careful to examine the possibility of racial or ethnic bias in their assessment tool. They conducted reliability analyses separately by gender, race/ethnicity, and exceptionality grouping. They also conducted an analysis of differential item functioning in which they examined whether item characteristics varied by gender and ethnicity, which would suggest the possibility of item bias. Although two items were identified with differences in item characteristics across groups, these represented less than 5 percent of the test items.

Summary

The TOWL-4 is designed to assess written language competence of students aged 9–0 to 17–11. Contrived and spontaneous formats are used to evaluate the conventional, linguistic, and cognitive components of written language. The content and structure of the TOWL-4 appear appropriate.

Although the TOWL-4's norms appear representative in general, the fall and spring samples tend to be uneven by age group, with some of these seasonal samples including very few students at certain grade levels. Interscorer reliability is quite good for this type of test. The internal consistencies of one composite (that is, Contrived Writing) and the total composite are high enough for use in making individual decisions; the stabilities of subtests and the remaining composite (that is, Spontaneous Writing) are lower.

Although the test's content appears appropriate and well conceived, the validity of the inferences to be drawn from the scores is unclear. Specifically, group means are the only data to suggest that the TOWL-4 is useful in identifying students with disabilities or in determining strengths and weaknesses of individual students. Students with learning disabilities and speech/language disorders earn TOWL-4 subtest scores that are only one standard deviation (or less) below the mean; they earn composite scores that are no more than 1.2 standard deviations below the mean. However, because we do not know whether these students had disabilities in written language, their scores tell us little about the TOWL-4's ability to identify students with specific written language needs. Although positive predictive analyses were conducted to determine whether the TOWL-4 could identify students with literacy difficulties, these similarly do not provide evidence that the test is particularly helpful in identifying specific written language difficulties. Given that the TOWL-4 has only two forms and relatively low stability, its usefulness in evaluating pupil progress is also limited.

17-4b ORAL AND WRITTEN LANGUAGE SCALES–SECOND EDITION (OWLS-2)

The Oral and Written Language Scales–Second Edition (OWLS-2; Carrow-Woolfolk, 2011) are an individually administered test of receptive and expressive language for children and young adults ages 3 through 21 years, although portions of the test are only administered to students five years and older. The test includes four scales: Listening Comprehension, Oral Expression, Reading Comprehension, and Written Expression. Additional composite scales include Oral Language Composite, Written Language Composite, Receptive Language Composite, Expressive Language Composite, and Overall Language Composite. Test results are used to determine broad levels of language skills and specific performance in listening, speaking, reading, and writing. The OWLS-2 is designed to be used in identification of students with language difficulties and disorders, in intervention planning, and in monitoring student progress.

Subtests

Listening Comprehension This scale is designed to measure understanding of spoken language. It consists of 130 items. The examiner reads aloud a verbal stimulus, and the student has to identify which of four pictures is the best response to the stimulus. The scale takes 10 to 20 minutes to administer.

Oral Expression This scale is a measure of understanding and use of spoken language. It consists of 106 items. The examiner reads aloud a verbal stimulus and shows a picture. The student responds orally by answering a question, completing a sentence, or generating one or more sentences. The scale takes 10 to 30 minutes to administer.

Reading Comprehension This scale is a measure of semantic, syntactic, and supralinguistic understanding of printed text for students aged 3 to 21 years. It consists of 140 items. The examinee is presented with either a picture or some written text, along with a question or direction presented orally, and must select one of four options that best answers the question. The scale takes 10 to 30 minutes to administer.

Written Expression This scale is an assessment of written language for students 5 to 21 years old. It is designed to measure ability to use conventions (spelling, punctuation, and so on), and quality of text organization and cohesion. It includes 50 items. The student responds to direct writing prompts provided by the examiner. The scale takes 15 to 30 minutes to administer.

Norms

The OWLS standardization sample consisted of 2,123 students chosen to match data from the U.S. Census Bureau published in 2009. Tables in the manual show the comparison of the sample to the U.S. population according to gender, race/ethnicity, parents' education level, and geographic region. Anywhere from 39 (at age 20) to 226 (at age 5) individuals are included at each age level by year (3 years to 21 years). Cross-tabulations are not provided. The sample appears slightly overrepresentative of students who have parents with an educational level of four-year college and beyond and underrepresentative of those with just some college.

Scores

The OWLS produces raw scores, which may be transformed to standard scores with a mean of 100 and a standard deviation of 15. In addition, test age and test grade equivalents and percentiles can be obtained. Scores are obtained for each of the four subtests and for each of the five composites.

Reliability

Internal consistency reliability was calculated using students in the standardization sample, with results stratified by two- to five-year age groups. Reliability coefficients range from .93 to .98 for Listening Comprehension, from .93 to .97 for Oral Expression, from .97 to .99 for Reading Comprehension, and from .94 to .99 for Written Expression. They range from .96 to .99 for the Oral Language composite, from .97 to .99 for the Written Language composite, from .97 to .99 for the Receptive Language composite, from .96 to .99 for the Expressive Language composite, and from .98 to .99 for the Overall Language composite. Test–retest reliabilities were computed on a sample of 117 students from the standardization sample. The coefficients range from .73 to .94 for the subtests and from .85 to .95 for the composites. The low test–retest reliabilities, even for the composite scores (apart from the overall language composite, for which both forms were above .90 in terms of test–retest reliability), are a bit concerning for use in making important decisions about individual students.

Validity

The authors describe the connection between the OWLS-2 subtests and Integrative Language Theory,

Dilemmas in Current Practice

ISSUES IN THE ASSESSMENT OF WRITTEN LANGUAGE

There are two serious problems in the assessment of written language.

PROBLEM 1

The first problem involves assessing the content of written expression. The content of written language is usually scored holistically and subjectively. Holistic evaluations tend to be unreliable. When content on the same topic and of the same genre (such as narratives) is scored, interscorer agreement varies from the .50 to .65 range (as in Breland, 1983; Breland, Camp, Jones, Morris, & Rock, 1987) to the .75 to .90 range, immediately following intensive training (such as in Educational Testing Service, 1990). Consistent scoring is even more difficult when topics and genres vary. Interscorer agreement can decrease to a range of .35 to .45 when the writing tasks vary (as in Breland, 1983; Breland et al., 1987). Subjective scoring and decision making are susceptible to the biasing effects associated with racial, ethnic, social class, gender, and disability stereotypes.

We believe the best alternative to holistic and subjective scoring schemes is to use a measure of writing fluency as an indicator of content generation. Two options have received some support in the research literature: (1) the number of words written (Mather, Roberts, Hammill, & Allen, 2009; Shinn, Tindall, &

Stein, 1988) and (2) the percentage of correctly written words (Isaacson, 1988).

PROBLEM 2

The second problem is in identifying a match between what is taught according to school instructional programming and what is tested. The great variation in the time at which various skills are taught renders a general test of achievement inappropriate. Commercially prepared tests have doubtful validity for planning individual programs and evaluating the progress of individual pupils.

We recommend that teachers and diagnosticians construct criterion-referenced achievement tests that closely parallel the instructional programming followed by the students being tested. In cases in which normative data are required, there are three choices. Diagnosticians can (1) select the devices that most closely parallel the instructional program, (2) develop local norms, or (3) select individual students for comparative purposes. Care should be exercised in selecting methods of assessing written language skills. For example, it is probably better to test pupils in ways that are familiar to them. Thus, if the teacher's weekly spelling test is from dictation, then spelling tests using dictation are probably preferable to tests requiring the students to identify incorrectly spelled words.

---

on which the test is based, and indicate how factor analyses support the notion that the test aligns with the theory. They also report the results of a set of criterion-related validity studies, each consisting of a comparison of performance on the OWLS-2 to performance on other measures, including the original OWLS, and the Clinical Evaluation of Language Fundamentals–Fourth Edition. These validity studies were conducted using clinical samples of students with identified difficulties. Correlations with subtests from the original OWLS ranged from .56 to .79. Correlations with the CELF-4 were relatively low (.45 and .59) when comparing receptive and expressive scales of the CELF-4 with the corresponding composites from the OWLS-2. An additional study was conducted, comparing the OWLS-2 Reading Comprehension subtest with the WJ-III Broad Reading Comprehension and the OWLS-2 Written Expression subtest with the WJ-III

Broad Writing Composite. Correlations were .86 for the reading comprehension subtest and .79 for the written expression subtest.

Summary

The OWLS-2 is a language test combining assessment of oral and written language. The test was standardized on the same population, so comparisons of student performance on oral and written measures are enhanced. The manual includes data showing that the standardization sample is generally representative of the U.S. population as a whole, however demographic breakdowns by age group are not available. Apart from the Broad Language composite, reliabilities may be too low to permit use of this measure in making important decisions for individuals. Evidence for validity is good, although it is based on a set of studies with special samples of students.

Chapter Comprehension Questions

Write your answers to each of the following questions and then compare your responses to the text.

1. Describe four processes associated with communication.

2. What are the two major components of written language that are typically addressed through instruction?

3. How can behaviors associated with the two major components of written language be measured?

4. What are some of the dilemmas associated with assessment of written language?

CHAPTER

18

USING MEASURES OF INTELLIGENCE

LEARNING OBJECTIVES

18-1 Ascertain why we assess intelligence.

18-2 Explain how student characteristics can affect student performance on intelligence tests.

18-3 Identify behaviors commonly sampled on intelligence tests.

18-4 Summarize theories that form the foundation of many intelligence tests used today.

18-5 Identify factors that are commonly interpreted using intelligence tests.

18-6 Describe the legal foundation for assessment of cognitive strengths and weaknesses in the identification of learning disabilities.

18-7 Identify the various types of intelligence tests.

18-8 Describe the strengths and weaknesses of three intelligence tests.

STANDARDS ADDRESSED IN THIS CHAPTER

 CEC Initial Preparation Standards

Standard 4: Assessment

4.0 Beginning special education professionals use multiple methods of assessment and data-sources in making educational decisions.

 CEC Advanced Preparation Standards

Standard 1: Assessment

1.0 Special education specialists use valid and reliable assessment practices to minimize bias.

 National Association of School Psychologists Domains

1 Data-Based Decision Making and Accountability

No other area of assessment has generated as much attention, controversy, and debate as the testing of what we call "intelligence." For centuries, philosophers, psychologists, educators, and laypeople have debated the meaning of intelligence. Numerous definitions of the term *intelligence* have been proposed, with each definition serving as a stimulus for counterdefinitions and counterproposals. Several theories have been advanced to describe and explain intelligence and its development. Some theorists argue that intelligence is a general ability that enables people to do many different things, whereas other theorists contend that there are multiple intelligences and that people are better at some things than others. Some argue that, for the most part, intelligence is genetically determined (hereditary), inborn, and something you get from your parents. Others contend that intelligence is, for the most part, learned—that it is acquired through experience. Most theorists today recognize the importance of both heredity and experience, including the impact of parental education, parental experience, maternal nutrition, maternal substance abuse, and many other factors. However, most theorists take positions on the relative importance of these factors.

Both the interpretation of group differences in performance on intelligence tests and the practice of testing the intelligence of schoolchildren have been topics of recurrent controversy and debate. In some instances, the courts have acted to curtail or halt intelligence testing in the public schools; in other cases, the courts have defined what composes intelligence testing. Debate and controversy have flourished about whether intelligence tests should be given, what they measure, and how different levels of performance attained by different populations are to be explained.

During the past 25 years, there has been a significant decline in the use of intelligence tests in schools, as a result of several factors. Teachers and related services personnel have found that knowing the score a student earns on an intelligence test (IQ or mental age) has not been especially helpful in making decisions about specific instructional interventions or teaching approaches to use. It has only provided them with general information about how rapidly to pace instruction. Also, it is argued that scores on intelligence tests too often are used to set low expectations for students, resulting in diminished effort to teach students who earn low scores. This has been the case especially with students who were labeled intellectually disabled on the basis of low scores on intelligence tests. In cases where specific groups of students (such as African American or Hispanic students) have earned lower scores on tests, and this has resulted in disproportionate placement of these groups of students in special education or in diminished expectations for performance, the courts have found intelligence tests discriminatory and mandated an end to their use.

No one has seen a specific thing called "intelligence." Rather, we observe differences in the ways people behave—either differences in everyday behavior in a variety of situations or differences in responses to standard stimuli or sets of stimuli; then we attribute those differences to something we describe as intelligence. In this sense, intelligence is an inferred entity—a term or construct we use to explain differences in present behavior and to predict differences in future behavior.

We have repeatedly stressed the fact that all tests, including intelligence tests, assess samples of behavior. Regardless of how an individual's performance on any given test is viewed and interpreted, intelligence tests—and the items on those tests—simply sample behaviors. A variety of different kinds of behavior samplings are used to assess intelligence; in most cases the kinds of behaviors sampled reflect a test author's conception of intelligence. The behavior samples are combined in different ways by different authors based on how they conceive of intelligence. In this chapter, we review the kinds of behaviors sampled by intelligence tests, with emphasis on the psychological demands of different item types, as a function of pupil characteristics. We also describe several ways in which intelligence theorists and test authors have conceptualized the structure of intelligence.

In evaluating the performance of individuals on intelligence tests, teachers, administrators, counselors, and diagnostic specialists must go beyond test names and scores to examine the kinds of behaviors sampled on the test. They must be willing to question the ways in which test stimuli are presented, to question the response requirements, and to evaluate the psychological demands placed on the individual.

18-1 Why Do We Assess Intelligence?

Given the controversy surrounding the measurement of intelligence, and the many important questions that remain about whether scores on intelligence tests can meaningfully inform instructional decisions, you might wonder why they are used in schools today. We do know that in some places, including several school districts located in central Iowa, they are not ever administered. However, in the majority of other school districts across the United States, they are used to inform special education eligibility decision making, particularly those decisions about whether a student qualifies for special education services as (a) a student with an intellectual disability or (b) a student with a learning disability. In many districts, students with particularly low scores on intelligence tests, for which there is additional corroborating information suggesting both limited intelligence and limited adaptive behavior, can qualify for special education services as a student with an intellectual disability. Using intelligence test scores to inform decisions about whether students have learning disabilities is much more controversial; however, it is still quite a common practice in schools today.

18-2 The Effect of Student Characteristics on Assessment of Intelligence

Acculturation is the most important characteristic to consider in evaluating performance on intelligence tests. **Acculturation** refers to a process an individual goes through in adapting to a new culture, and often depends on an individual's particular set of background experiences and opportunities to learn in both formal and informal educational settings. These, in turn, depend on the person's initial culture and the culture to which the person is now exposed, the experiences available in the person's environment, and the length of time the person has had to assimilate those experiences. The culture in which an individual lives and the length of time the person has lived in that culture may influence the psychological demands presented by a test item. Simply knowing the kind of behavior sampled by a test is not enough, because the same test item may create different psychological demands for people undergoing different experiences and acculturation.

Suppose, for example, that we assess intelligence by asking children to tell how hail and sleet are alike. Children may fail the item for very different reasons. Consider Juan (a student who recently moved to the United States from Mexico) and Marcie (a student from Michigan). Juan does not know what hail and sleet are, so he stands little chance of telling how hail and sleet are alike; he will fail the item simply because he does not know the meanings of the words. Marcie may know what hail is and what sleet is, but she fails the item because she is unable to integrate these two words into a conceptual category (precipitation). The psychological demand of the item changes as a function of the children's knowledge. For the child who has not learned the meanings of the words, the item assesses vocabulary. For the child who knows the meanings of the words, the item is a generalization task.

In considering how individuals perform on intelligence tests, we need to know how acculturation affects test performance. Items on intelligence tests range along a continuum from items that sample fundamental psychological behaviors that are relatively unaffected by the test taker's learning history, to items that sample primarily learned behavior. To determine exactly what is being assessed, we need to know the essential background of the student. Consider the following item:

> *Jeff went walking in the forest. He saw a porcupine that he tried to take home for a pet. It got away from him, but when he got home, his father took him to the doctor. Why?*

For a student who knows what a porcupine is, that a porcupine has quills, and that quills are sharp, the item can assess comprehension, abstract reasoning, and problem-solving skill. The student who does not know any of this information may very well fail the item. In this case, failure is due not to an inability to comprehend or solve the problem but to a deficiency in background experience.

Similarly, we could ask a child to identify the seasons of the year. The experiences available in children's environments are reflected in the way they respond to this item. Children from central Illinois, who experience four discernibly different climatic conditions, may well respond "summer, fall, winter, and spring." Children from central Pennsylvania, who also experience four discernibly different climatic conditions but who live in an environment in which hunting is prevalent, might respond "buck season, doe season, small game, and fishing." Within specific cultures, both responses are logical and appropriate; only one is scored as correct.

Items on intelligence tests also sample different behaviors as a function of the age of the child assessed. Age and acculturation are positively related: Older children in general have had more opportunities to acquire the skills and cultural knowledge assessed by intelligence tests. The performances of 5-year-old children on an item requiring them to tell how a cardinal, a blue jay, and a swallow are alike are almost entirely a function of their knowledge of the word meanings. Most college students know the meanings of the three words; for them, the item assesses primarily their ability to identify similarities and to integrate words or objects into a conceptual category. As children get older, they have increasing opportunities to acquire the elements of the collective intelligence of a culture.

The interaction between acculturation and the behavior sampled determines the psychological demands of an intelligence test item. For this reason, it is impossible to define exactly what any one intelligence test would assess for any one student. Identical test items place different psychological demands on different children. Thirteen kinds of behaviors sampled by intelligence tests are described later in this chapter. These types of behavior will vary in their psychological demands based on the test taker's experience and acculturation. Given the great number of potential questions that could be asked for each type of question, as well as the number of combinations of question types, the number of questions is practically infinite.

In order to limit the effect of linguistic differences on students' scores on intelligence tests, nonverbal tests of intelligence are frequently administered. However, nonverbal tests really only reduce concerns as far as linguistic differences go; the influence of cultural differences remain.

The Scenario in Assessment for this chapter highlights how intelligence testing must be undertaken carefully, with due consideration of a student's cultural and linguistic background. Used appropriately, intelligence tests can provide information that can lead to the enhancement of both individual opportunity and protection of the rights of students. Used inappropriately, they can restrict opportunity and rights.

INTELLIGENCE TESTING CAN HELP STUDENTS | Daraswan was born in Laos. Eventually,

she and her family were brought to a suburb of Minneapolis by a church group. Daraswan and her sister were enrolled immediately in an elementary school. She was placed in the second grade with her younger sister although there was no indication that either child had ever attended school. The two girls were placed in an English language learner program option for part of the day and in classrooms with English-speaking teachers and students for nonacademic material. As the year went by, Daraswan's regular education teacher became increasingly concerned about her lack of progress in picking up appropriate English and school routines. In her English language learner program, Daraswan's progress was slow. Her younger sister was making more rapid progress: she could count, identify letters, and write her first name. Finally, the regular education teacher referred Daraswan for evaluation to determine if she was eligible for service as a student with an intellectual disability.

Several evaluations were conducted. The speech and language specialist declined to assess Daraswan for a language disorder because she had had so little exposure to the English language and the family continued to speak their native language at home. Reluctantly, the school psychologist agreed to attempt some assessments, in part because Daraswan's progress was notably slower than that of her sister. Due process procedures were followed. An interpreter discussed parental rights with Daraswan's mother and had her sign for permission to assess.

During the assessment process, the psychologist felt challenged in attempting to do a good assessment. She tried using an interpreter, but verbal items were outside of Daraswan's cultural experience. She tried using nonverbal subtests, but they still were not culturally appropriate. The psychologist also administered the Leiter International Performance Scale–Third Edition, a test requiring no verbal directions or response, and Daraswan earned a score that was somewhat above average. Adaptive behavior scales were administered to both Daraswan's teacher and mother. Although there were cultural factors that could bias the scores against Daraswan, the psychologist reported her somewhat-below-average scores.

A multidisciplinary individualized educational program (IEP) team met to consider the assessment data. The IEP conference complied with all state and federal guidelines and appropriate procedures were followed (that is, an interpreter was present, introductions were made, and assessment data were shared). The school psychologist was adamant that the testing data clearly ruled out the possibility that Daraswan was intellectually disabled. Moreover, because of Daraswan's cultural and educational history, she would not agree to a diagnosis of learning disability. The team recommended that Daraswan receive more intensive instruction in English and remedial instruction in both reading and mathematics. Finally, a speech and language evaluation was conducted to ascertain if Daraswan might profit from individual therapy.

This scenario highlights how a carefully conducted assessment of intelligence can help ensure a student is not inappropriately labeled as having a disability. What might have happened had the assessor not taken Daraswan's limited English language proficiency and cultural background into account?

18-3 Behaviors Sampled by Intelligence Tests

Regardless of the interpretation of measured intelligence, it is a fact that intelligence tests simply sample behaviors. This section describes the kinds of behaviors sampled, including discrimination, generalization, motor behavior, general knowledge, vocabulary, induction, comprehension, sequencing, detail recognition, analogical reasoning, pattern completion, abstract reasoning, and memory.

18-3a DISCRIMINATION

Intelligence test items that sample skill in discrimination usually present a variety of stimuli and ask the student to find the one that differs from all the others. Figure 18.1 illustrates items assessing discrimination: Items a and b assess discrimination of figures, items c and d assess symbolic discrimination, and items e and f assess semantic discrimination. In each case, the student must identify the item that differs from the others.

18-3b GENERALIZATION

Items assessing generalization present a stimulus and ask the student to identify which of several response possibilities goes with the stimulus. Figure 18.2 illustrates several items assessing generalization. In each case, the student is given a stimulus element and is required to identify the one that is like it or that goes with it.

FIGURE 18.1
Items That Assess
Figural, Symbolic, and
Semantic Discrimination

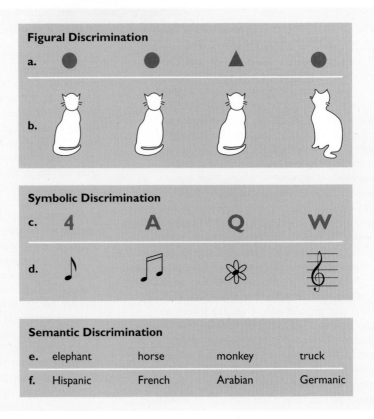

© 2013 Cengage Learning

FIGURE 18.2
Items That Assess
Figural, Symbolic, and
Semantic Generalization

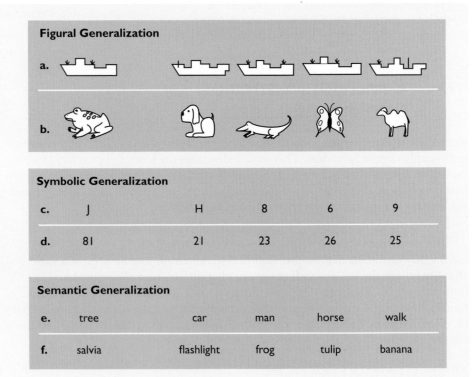

© 2013 Cengage Learning

18-3c MOTOR BEHAVIOR

Many items on intelligence tests require a motor response. The intellectual level of very young children, for example, is often assessed by items requiring them to throw objects, walk, follow moving objects with their eyes, demonstrate a pincer grasp in picking up objects, build block towers, and place geometric forms in a recessed-form board. Most motor items at higher age levels are actually visual–motor items. The student may be required to copy geometric designs, trace paths through a maze, or reconstruct designs from memory.

18-3d GENERAL KNOWLEDGE

Items on intelligence tests sometimes require a student to answer specific factual questions, such as "In what direction would you travel if you were to go from Poland to Argentina?" and "What is the cube root of 8?" Essentially, such items are like the kinds of items in achievement tests; they assess primarily what has been learned.

18-3e VOCABULARY

Many different kinds of test items are used to assess vocabulary. In some cases, the student must name pictures, and in others he or she must point to objects in response to words read by the examiner. Some vocabulary items require the student to produce oral definitions of words, whereas others call for reading a definition and selecting one of several words to match the definition.

18-3f INDUCTION

Induction items present a series of examples and require the student to induce a governing principle. For example, the student is given a magnet and several different cloth, wooden, and metal objects and is asked to try to pick up the objects with the magnet. After several trials, the student is asked to state a rule or principle about the kinds of objects that magnets can pick up.

18-3g COMPREHENSION

There are three kinds of items used to assess comprehension: items related to directions, to printed material, and to societal customs and mores. In some instances, the examiner presents a specific situation and asks what actions the student would take (for example, "What would you do if you saw a train approaching a washed-out bridge?"). In other cases, the examiner reads paragraphs to a student and then asks specific questions about the content of the paragraphs. In still other instances, the student is asked questions about social mores, such as "Why should we keep promises?"

18-3h SEQUENCING

Items assessing sequencing consist of a series of stimuli that have a progressive relationship among them. The student must identify a response that continues the relationship. Four sequencing items are illustrated in Figure 18.3.

FIGURE 18.3
Items That Assess
Sequencing Skill

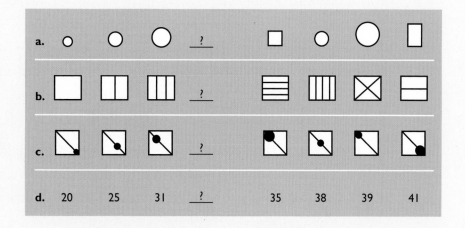

FIGURE 18.4
Analogy Items

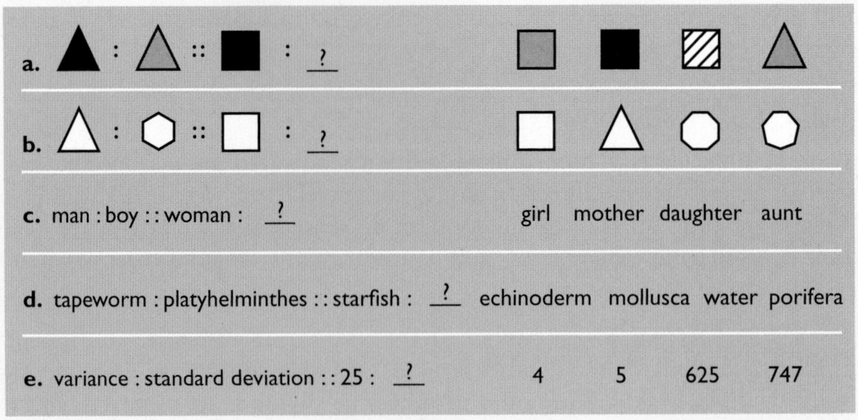

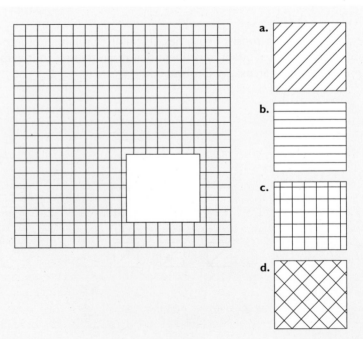

18-3l DETAIL RECOGNITION

In general, not many tests or test items assess detail recognition. Those that do evaluate the completeness and detail with which a student solves problems. For instance, items may require a student to count the blocks in pictured piles of blocks in which some of the blocks are not directly visible, to copy geometric designs, or to identify missing parts in pictures. To do so correctly, the student must attend to detail in the stimulus drawings and must reflect this attention to detail in making responses.

18-3j ANALOGICAL REASONING

"A is to B as C is to ___" is the usual form for analogies. Element A is related to element B. The student must identify the response having the same relationship to element C as B has to A. Figure 18.4 illustrates several different analogy items.

18-3k PATTERN COMPLETION

Some tests and test items require a student to select from several possibilities the missing part of a pattern or matrix. Figures 18.5 and 18.6 illustrate two different completion items. The item in Figure 18.5 requires identification of a missing part in a pattern. The item in

FIGURE 18.5
A Pattern Completion Item

FIGURE 18.6
A Matrix Completion Item

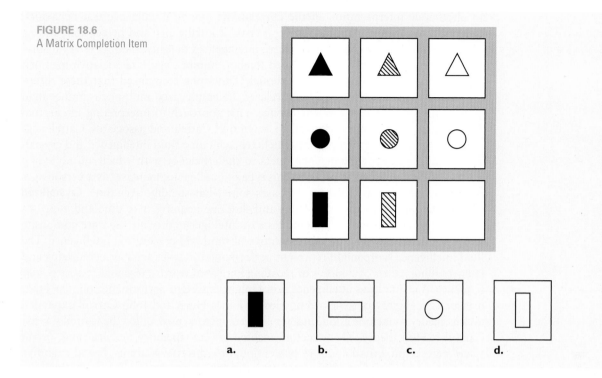

a.   b.   c.   d.

Figure 18.6 calls for identification of the response that completes the matrix by continuing both the triangle, circle, rectangle sequence, and the solid, striped, and clear sequence.

18-3l ABSTRACT REASONING

A variety of items on intelligence tests sample abstract reasoning ability. The Stanford–Binet Intelligence Scale, for example, presents absurd verbal statements and pictures and asks the student to identify the absurdity. In the Stanford–Binet and other scales, arithmetic reasoning problems are often thought to assess abstract reasoning.

18-3m MEMORY

Several different kinds of tasks assess memory: repetition of sequences of digits presented orally, reproduction of geometric designs from memory, verbatim repetition of sentences, and reconstruction of the essential meaning of paragraphs or stories. Simply saying that an item assesses memory is too simplistic. We need to ask: Memory for what? The psychological demand of a memory task changes in relation to both the method of assessment and the meaningfulness of the material to be recalled.

18-4 Theories that have Informed Intelligence Testing

Early in the study of intelligence, it became apparent that the behaviors used to assess intelligence were highly related to one another. Charles Spearman, an early twentieth-century psychologist, demonstrated that a single statistical factor could explain the high degree of intercorrelation among the behaviors. He named this single factor *general intelligence* (g). Although he noted that performance on different tasks was influenced by other specific intelligence factors, he argued that knowing a person's level of g could greatly improve predictions of performance on a variety of tasks. Today, nearly every intelligence test allows for the calculation of an overall test score that is frequently considered indicative of an individual's level of g in comparison to same-age peers.

Later, it became clear that different factor structures would emerge depending on the variables analyzed and the statistical procedures used. Thurstone (1941) proposed an alternative interpretation of the correlations among intelligence test behaviors. He conducted factor analyses of several tests of intelligence and perception, and he concluded that there exist seven different intelligences that he called "primary mental abilities": verbal comprehension, word fluency, number, space, associative memory, perceptual speed, and reasoning. Although Thurstone recognized that these different abilities were often positively correlated, he emphasized multiplicity rather than unity within the construct of intelligence. This approach to interpreting intellectual performance was further expanded by Raymond Cattell and associates. Cattell suggested the existence of two primary intelligence factors: fluid intelligence and crystallized intelligence. **Fluid intelligence** refers to the efficiency with which an individual learns and completes various tasks. This type of intelligence increases as a person ages until early adulthood and then decreases somewhat steadily over time. **Crystallized intelligence** represents the knowledge and skill one acquires over time and increases steadily throughout one's life. Some tests of intelligence provide separate composite scores for behaviors that are representative of fluid and crystallized intelligence. The fluid intelligence score might represent performance on tasks such as memorizing and later recalling names of symbols or recalling unrelated words presented in a particular sequence. A crystallized intelligence score might represent performance on items that measure vocabulary or general knowledge. James Horn and John Carroll expanded on this theory to include additional intelligence factors, now called the Cattell–Horn–Carroll (CHC) theory. These factors include general memory and learning, broad visual perception, broad auditory perception, broad retrieval ability, broad cognitive speediness, and decision/reaction time/speed. CHC theory is the theory on which the Woodcock–Johnson IV Tests of Cognitive Abilities is based.

18-5 Commonly Interpreted Factors on Intelligence Tests

Educational professionals will encounter many different terms that describe various intelligence test factors, clusters, indexes, and processes. We describe several common (and overlapping) terms in Table 18.1.

TABLE 18.1   Common Intelligence Test Terms, Associated Theorists and Tests, and Examples of Associated Behaviors Sampled

Term	Definition	Theorists[a]	Tests	Example of a Behavior Sampled
Attention	Alertness	Das, Naglieri	CAS2	When given a target figure and many distracting stimuli, the individual must quickly select those that are identical to the target figure.
Auditory perception/ processing	Ability to analyze, manipulate, and discriminate sounds	Cattell, Horn, Carroll	WJ-IV	When given a sound, the examinee must name words that begin with that sound.
Cognitive efficiency/ speediness	Ability to process information quickly and automatically	Cattell, Horn, Carroll	WJ-IV	When given a worksheet with rows of letter patterns, the examinee must circle the two sets of letter patterns that match in each row.
Comprehension knowledge	Communication and use of acquired knowledge	Cattell, Horn, Carroll	WJ-IV	When provided a word, the examinee must provide a word that has the same meaning.

(Continued)

| TABLE 18.1 | Common Intelligence Test Terms, Associated Theorists and Tests, and Examples of Associated Behaviors Sampled *Continued* | | | |

Term	Definition	Theorists[a]	Tests	Example of a Behavior Sampled
Fluid reasoning/ intelligence	Efficiency with which an individual learns and completes various tasks	Cattell, Horn, Carroll	WJ-IV	When given a set of information, examinee must determine and apply a rule for the information.
Long-term retrieval/delayed recall	Ability to store and easily recall information at a much later point in time	Cattell, Horn, Carroll	WJ-IV	After listening to a story, examinee must recall details from the story.
Perceptual speed	Ability to identify patterns		WJ-IV	When given a worksheet with rows of number patterns, examinee must circle the two sets of numbers that match in each row.
Planning	Ability to identify effective strategies to reach a particular goal	Das, Naglieri	CAS2	When given a legend that pairs numbers with a set of symbols, and a series of numbered boxes, the examinee must write the corresponding symbols in the appropriate boxes.
Processing speed	Ability to quickly complete tasks that require limited complex thought	Cattell, Horn, Carroll	WJ-IV, WISC-V	The individual is presented with a key for converting numbers to symbols and must quickly write down the associated symbols for numbers that are presented.
Quantitative reasoning	Ability to reason with numbers	Cattell, Horn, Carroll	WJ-IV	When given a series of numbers that fit a pattern, but one number is missing, the examinee must provide the missing number.
Short-term memory or working memory	Ability to quickly store and then immediately retrieve information within a short period of time	Cattell, Horn, Carroll	WISC-V, WJ-IV	The examiner says several numbers, and the individual must repeat them accurately in backward order.
Simultaneous processing	Extent to which one can integrate pieces of information into a complete pattern	Das, Naglieri	CAS2	When asked a question verbally and presented with figures, the individual must pick the figure that answers the question.
Successive processing	Extent to which one can recall things presented in a particular order	Das, Naglieri	CAS2	When given a set of words, the individual must repeat them back in the same order.
Verbal comprehension	"Verbal abilities utilizing reasoning, comprehension, and conceptualization" (p. 6, WISC-V Examiner's Manual)		WISC-V	The individual must verbally express how two things are similar.
Visual perception/ processing	Integrating and interpreting visual information	Cattell, Horn, Carroll	WJ-IV	When given various shapes and a corresponding set of pieces, the examinee must identify which pieces make up the shape.

[a]There are often many theorists, researchers, and tests associated with a given intelligence term; we provide here just one or two individuals who were key in defining these terms and tests that involve measurement of behaviors associated with these terms.

18-6 Assessment of Cognitive Strengths and Weaknesses

According to the most recent reauthorization of IDEA, one way that students can be identified as having a learning disability is if they "exhibit a pattern of strengths and weaknesses in performance, achievement, or both, relative to age, State-approved grade-level standards, or intellectual development," as long as other potential reasons for the associated patterns are ruled out (e.g., cultural factors, limited English proficiency, intellectual disability, etc.) [34 CFR 300.309(a) (2)]. There are some districts that are currently using this approach to guide their approach to the identification of learning disability, and consequently are using student performance on intelligence tests to make related eligibility decisions. Although specific criteria for considering something as a "strength" or "weakness" vary from district to district, school personnel generally look for a pattern in subtest performance that suggests at least one strength and at least one weakness. In addition to the concerns with measuring intelligence noted earlier in this chapter, there are two more specific problems that we see with this approach. First, subtest reliabilities tend to be very low, and so such decisions may be made on test scores that are fraught with error. Second, just about any student's profile of performances on various subtests will include variation, with some high scores and some low scores. Unless very strict criteria are used for what constitutes a strength or a weakness, it is likely that every individual will display both strengths and weaknesses in intellectual functioning. To address this concern, an approach to intelligence testing that takes into consideration issues with low subtest reliabilities has been developed, namely, the **cross-battery assessment** approach (XBA; Flanagan, Ortiz, & Alfonso, 2013). Using this approach, an examiner may use multiple test batteries to measure student intelligence according to CHC theory. Although this may lead to greater reliability, it also complicates one's understanding of student performance, given that different tests involve the sampling of slightly different behaviors. Furthermore, questions remain about the extent to which the associated information can meaningfully inform instruction beyond the information that could be provided through more direct measurement of the student's academic skills.

18-7 Types of Intelligence Tests

Depending on what types of decisions are being made, as well as the specific characteristics of the student, different types of intelligence tests might be selected for administration. We describe three different types in the following sections.

18-7a INDIVIDUAL TESTS

Individually administered intelligence tests are most frequently used for making exceptionality, eligibility, and educational placement decisions. State special education eligibility guidelines and criteria typically specify that the collection of data about intellectual functioning must be included in the decision-making process for eligibility and placement decisions, and that these data must come from individual intellectual evaluation by a certified school psychologist. Districts may have more specific guidelines than those provided by the state.

18-7b GROUP TESTS

Group-administered intelligence tests are used for one of two purposes: as screening devices for individual students or as sources of descriptive information about groups of students. Most often, they are administered as screening devices to identify those students who differ enough from average to warrant further assessment. In these cases, the tests' merit is that teachers can administer them relatively quickly to large numbers of students. The tests suffer from the same limitations as any group test: They can be made to yield qualitative information only with difficulty, and they require students to sit still for approximately 20 minutes, to mark with a pencil, and, often, to read. During the past 25 years, it has become increasingly common for school districts to eliminate the practice of group intelligence testing. When administrators are asked why they are doing so, they cite (1) the limited relevance of knowing about students' capability, as opposed to knowing about the subject matter skills (such as for reading and math) that students do and do not have; (2) the difficulty teachers experience in trying to use the test results for instructional purposes; and (3) the cost of a schoolwide intellectual screening program.

18-7c NONVERBAL INTELLIGENCE TESTS

A number of nonverbal tests are among the most widely used tests for assessment of intelligence, particularly when there are questions about the intelligence of a child who is not proficient in English or who is deaf. Some nonverbal tests are designed to measure intelligence broadly; others are called "picture–vocabulary tests." The latter are not measures of intelligence per se; rather, they measure only one aspect of intelligence—receptive vocabulary. In picture–vocabulary tests, pictures are presented to the test taker, who is asked to identify those pictures that correspond to words read by the examiner. Some authors of picture–vocabulary measures state that the tests measure receptive vocabulary; others equate receptive vocabulary with intelligence and claim that their tests assess intelligence. Because the tests measure only one aspect of intelligence, they should not be used to make eligibility decisions.

18-8 Assessment of Intelligence: Commonly Used Tests

In this section, we provide information on some of the most commonly used intelligence tests. Table 18.2 provides a list of intelligence tests that you may come across in educational settings. We also provide more detailed reviews of several intelligence tests, with special reference to the kinds of behaviors they sample and to their technical adequacy. Although some individual intelligence tests may be appropriately administered by teachers, counselors, or other specialists, the intelligence tests on which school personnel rely most heavily must be given by psychologists.

18-8a WECHSLER INTELLIGENCE SCALE FOR CHILDREN–FIFTH EDITION (WISC-V)

The Wechsler Intelligence Scale for Children–V (WISC-V; Wechsler, 2014) is the latest version of the WISC and is designed to assess the cognitive ability and problem-solving processes of individuals ranging in age from 6 years, 0 months to 16 years, 11 months.

Developed by David Wechsler in 1949, the WISC adapted the 11 subtests found in the original Wechsler Scale, the Wechsler–Bellevue Intelligence Scale (1939), for use with children, and added the Mazes subtest. In 1974, the Wechsler Intelligence Scale for Children–Revised (WISC-R) was developed. This revision retained the 12 subtests found in the original WISC but altered the age range from 5 to 15 years to 6 to 16 years. The Wechsler Intelligence Scale for Children–III (WISC-III) was developed in 1991. This scale retained the 12 subtests and added a new subtest, Symbol Search. Previous editions of the WISC provided verbal IQ, performance IQ, and full-scale IQ scores. The WISC-III maintained this tradition but introduced four new index scores: Verbal Comprehension Index (VCI), Perceptual Organization Index (POI), Freedom from Distractibility Index (FDI), and Processing Speed Index (PSI). For the WISC-IV, new terminology was provided for several of the four indexes, which were then called the Verbal Comprehension Index, Perceptual Reasoning Index, Working Memory Index, and the Processing Speed Index, and the verbal and performance IQ scores were eliminated.

The WISC-V provides a new scoring framework while maintaining the theory of intelligence underlying the previous scales. This theory was summarized by Wechsler when he stated that "intelligence is the overall capacity of an individual to understand and cope with the world around him" (Wechsler, 1974, p. 5). The definition is consistent with his original one, in which he stated that intelligence is "the capacity of the individual to act purposefully, to think rationally, and to deal effectively with his or her environment" (Wechsler, 1974, p. 3).

Based on the premise that intelligence is both global (characterizing an individual's behavior as a whole) and specific (composed of distinct elements) (Wechsler, 2014, p. 2), the WISC-V measures overall

TABLE 18.2	Commonly Used Tests of Intelligence		
Test	**Authors**	**Year of Publication**	**Publisher**
Cognitive Abilities Test (CogAT)	Lohman & Hagan	2001	Riverside
Cognitive Assessment System–Second Edition (CAS2)	Das & Naglieri	1997	Riverside
Comprehensive Test of Nonverbal Intelligence–Second Edition (CTONI-2)	Hammill, Pearson, & Wiederholt	2009	Pro-Ed
Detroit Tests of Learning Aptitude–Fourth Edition (DTLA-4)	Hammill	1998	Pro-Ed
Kaufman Assessment Battery for Children–Second Edition (KABC-2)	Kaufman & Kaufman	2004	Pearson
Leiter International Performance Scale–Third Edition (Leiter-3)	Roid, Miller, Pomplun, & Koch	2013	Stoelting
Otis–Lennon School Ability Test–Eighth Edition (OSAT-8)	Pearson	2003	Pearson
Peabody Picture Vocabulary Test–Fourth Edition (PPVT-4)	Dunn & Dunn	2007	Pearson
Test of Nonverbal Intelligence–Fourth Edition (TONI-4)	Brown, Sherbenou, & Johnsen	2010	Pro-Ed
Stanford–Binet Intelligence Scale, Fifth Edition (SB-5)	Roid	2003	Riverside
Universal Nonverbal Intelligence Test–Second Edition (UNIT-2)	Bracken & McCallum	2016	Riverside
Wechsler Intelligence Scale for Children–Fifth Edition (WISC-V)	Wechsler	2014	Pearson
Wechsler Preschool and Primary Scale of Intelligence–4th Edition (WPPSI-IV)	Wechsler	2012	Pearson
Woodcock–Johnson IV Tests of Cognitive Abilities (WJ-IV)	Schrank, Mather, & McGrew	2014	Riverside

global intelligence, as well as discrete domains of cognitive functioning.

The WISC-V presents a new scoring framework. Similar to the WISC-IV, it does not provide verbal and performance IQ scores. However, it maintains the full-scale IQ (FSIQ) as a measure of general intellectual functioning and includes five index scores as measures of specific cognitive domains. The five indexes were proposed based on analyses of prior WISC-IV data and the development of three new subtests intended to provide better measurement of the following three indexes: Visual Spatial, Fluid Reasoning, and Working Memory. The five primary indexes that are part of the WISC-V include the Verbal Comprehension Index, the Visual Spatial Index, the Fluid Reasoning Index, the Working Memory Index, and the Processing Speed Index. A description of the subtests that comprise each index is provided next. Those familiar with the WISC-IV will note that in the revisions, two subtests have been dropped, 13 subtests have been retained, and eight subtests have been added. Instead of core and supplemental subtests, the WISC-V categorizes subtests as primary, secondary, and complementary. Seven primary subtests are

necessary to obtain the overall score (FSIQ), and secondary subtests can be used in certain cases as substitutes to primary subtests to obtain index scores. Complementary subtests can be administered for additional information.

Subtests

Verbal Comprehension Subtests

Similarities (Primary). This subtest requires identification of similarities or commonalities in superficially unrelated verbal stimuli.

Vocabulary (Primary). Items on this subtest assess ability to define words. Beginning items require individuals to name picture objects. Later items require individuals to verbally define words that are read aloud by the examiner.

Comprehension (Secondary). This subtest assesses ability to comprehend verbal directions or to understand specific customs and mores. The examinee is asked questions such as "Why is it important to wear boots after a large snowfall?"

Information (Secondary). This subtest assesses ability to answer specific factual questions. The content is learned; it consists of information that a person is expected to have acquired in both formal and informal educational settings. The examinee is asked questions such as "Which fast-food franchise is represented by the symbol of golden arches?"

Visual Spatial Subtests

Block Design (Primary). In this subtest, individuals are given a specified amount of time to manipulate blocks in order to reproduce a stimulus design that is presented visually.

Visual Puzzles (Primary). In this subtest, individuals are shown a completed puzzle, and must select from a variety of response options the three responses that when put together will make the completed puzzle. There is a time limit for each item.

Fluid Reasoning Subtests

Picture Concepts (Secondary). In this subtest, an individual is shown two or three rows of pictures and must choose one picture from each row in order to form a group that shares a common characteristic. For example, an individual would choose the picture of the horse in row 1 and the picture of the mouse in row 2 because they are both animals. This is basically a picture classification task.

Matrix Reasoning (Primary). In this subtest, individuals must select the missing portion of an incomplete matrix given five response options. Matrices range from 2×2 to 3×3. The last item differs from this general form, requiring individuals to identify the fifth square in a row of six.

Figure Weights (Primary). Within a given time limit, the examinee must select a weight value that will keep a scale that is presented balanced.

Arithmetic (Secondary). This subtest assesses ability to solve problems requiring the application of arithmetic operations. In this subtest, individuals must mentally solve problems presented orally within a specified time limit.

Working Memory Subtests

Digit Span (Primary). This subtest assesses immediate recall of orally presented digits. In Digit Span Forward, individuals repeat numbers in the same order that they were presented aloud by the examiner. In Digit Span Backward, individuals repeat numbers in the reverse of the order that they were presented by the examiner. In Digit Span Sequencing, individuals must mentally manipulate numbers presented aloud by the examiner so that they provide the numbers in an ascending order.

Picture Span (Primary). In this subtest, the individual views a page with a variety of pictures for a prespecified time, and then is shown a response page in which the individual must select pictures (in order, if possible) that were on the original page.

Letter–Number Sequencing (Secondary). This subtest assesses an individual's ability to recall and mentally manipulate a series of numbers and letters that are orally presented to them. After hearing a random sequence of numbers and letters, individuals must first repeat the numbers in ascending order and then repeat the letters in alphabetical order.

Processing Speed Subtests

Coding (Primary). This subtest assesses the ability to associate symbols with either geometric shapes or numbers and to copy these symbols onto paper within a specified time limit.

Symbol Search (Primary). This subtest consists of a series of paired groups of symbols, with each pair including a target group and a search group. The child scans the two groups and indicates whether the target symbols appear in the search group within a specified time limit.

Cancellation (Secondary). In this subtest, individuals are presented with first a random and then a structured arrangement of pictures. For both arrangements, individuals must mark the target pictures within the specified time limit.

Complementary Subtests

Naming Speed Literacy. In this subtest, the individual is presented with a variety of colored objects or letters and numbers, and must correctly name them as fast as possible.

Naming Speed Quantity. In this subtest the individual is presented with a variety of large boxes that contain varying numbers of boxes. The examinee must state the number of boxes in each large box as quickly as possible.

Immediate Symbol Translation. In this subtest, the individual is presented symbols and told what word each symbol represents. Then, the individual is presented with long strands of symbols and must state the corresponding words in order.

Delayed Symbol Translation. The examinee is presented the same symbols as in the Immediate Symbol Translation subtest, but after approximately 20 to 30 minutes have elapsed since completing the Immediate Symbol Translation subtest. The examinee must recall as many of the symbols as possible.

Recognition Symbol Translation. The examinee is presented the same symbols as before, and must select the correct response from several presented options for what each symbol means. This must be administered after Delayed Symbol Translation.

Scores

Subtest raw scores obtained on the WISC-V are transformed to scaled scores with a mean of 10 and a standard deviation of 3. The scaled scores for 2 Verbal

Comprehension (VC) subtests, 1 Visual Spatial (VS) subtests, 1 Working Memory (WM) subtests, 2 Fluid Reasoning (FR) subtest, and 1 Processing Speed (PS) subtest are added and then transformed to obtain the composite FSIQ score. The scaled scores for two of the corresponding subtests are used to make up the corresponding indexes (VC, VS, WM, FR, PS). IQs for Wechsler scales are deviation IQs with a mean of 100 and a standard deviation of 15. Tables are provided for converting the subtest scaled scores and composite scores to percentile ranks and confidence intervals. Raw scores may also be transformed to age equivalents. Additional indexes can be derived through sums of scaled scores for various subtests; these indexes include Quantitative Reasoning, Auditory Working Memory, Nonverbal, General Ability, and Cognitive Proficiency. Ten process scores can also be derived. Process scores are "designed to provide more detailed information on the cognitive abilities that contribute to a child's subtest performance" (Wechsler, 2004, p. 107). The WISC-V provides for various subtest, index, and process score discrepancy comparisons. Tables provide the difference scores needed in order to be considered statistically significant at the .15, .10, .05, and .01 confidence level for each age group, and they also provide information on the percentage of children in the standardization sample who obtained the same or a greater discrepancy between scores.

The WISC-V employs a differential scoring system for some of the primary and secondary subtests. Responses for the Digit Span, Coding, Figure Weights, Visual Puzzles, Picture Concepts, Letter–Number Sequencing, Matrix Reasoning, Cancellation, Arithmetic, and Information subtests are scored pass–fail. A weighted scoring system is used for the Similarities, Vocabulary, Picture Span, and Comprehension subtests. Incorrect responses receive a score of 0, lower-level or lower-quality responses are assigned a score of 1, and more abstract responses are assigned a score of 2. Block Design and Symbol Search are timed, and individuals who complete the tasks in shorter periods of time receive more credit. These differential weightings of responses must be given special consideration, especially when the timed tests are used with children who demonstrate motor impairments that interfere with the speed of response.

Norms

The WISC-V was standardized on 2,200 children ages 6–0 to 16–11 years. This age range was divided into 11 whole-year groups (for example, 6–0 to 6–11). All groups had 200 participants. The standardization group was stratified on the basis of age, sex, race/ethnicity (whites, African Americans, Hispanics, Asians, and others), parent education level (based on number of years and degree held), and geographic region (Northeast, South, Midwest, and West),

according to 2012 U.S. Census Bureau information. A sample of children from special groups (such as children with a specific learning disability, children identified as gifted and talented, children with attention deficit hyperactivity disorder, and so on) were included in the normative sample at each age group in order to accurately represent the population of children enrolled in school. Extensive tables in the manual are used to compare sample data with census data. These tables are stratified across the following characteristics: (1) age, race/ethnicity, and parent education level; (2) age, sex, and parent education level; (3) age, sex, and race/ethnicity; and (4) age, race/ethnicity, and geographic region. Overall, the samples appear representative of the U.S. population of children across the stratified variables.

Reliability

Because the Coding, Symbol Search, Naming Speed, Symbol Translation, and Cancellation subtests are timed, reliability estimates for these subtests are based on test–retest coefficients. However, split-half reliability coefficient alphas corrected by the Spearman–Brown formula are reported for all the remaining subtest and composite scores. Moreover, standard errors of measurement (SEMs) are reported for all scores. Scores are reported for each age group and as an average across all age groups. As would be expected, subtest reliabilities for the 16 primary and secondary subtests (overall averages range from .81 to .94; age levels range from .67 to .96) are lower than index reliabilities (overall averages range from .88 to .96; age level reliabilities range from .86 to .97). Reliabilities for the full-scale IQ are excellent, with age-level coefficient alphas ranging from .96 to .97.

Test–retest stability data were collected on a sample of 218 children. These data were calculated for five age groups (6 to 7, 8 to 9, 10 to 11, 12 to 13, and 14 to 16) using Pearson's product–moment correlation. Subtest correlations range from .53 to .93, and index scores range from .68 to .96, with the full-scale IQ stability coefficient ranging from .90 to .94. Stability coefficients[1] that represent results across all age levels are provided for each subtest, index, and the FSIQ. The stability coefficient for the FSIQ was .92. Index stabilities ranged from .81 (Quantitative Reasoning Index) to .94 (Verbal Comprehension), and subtest stability correlations ranged from .71 (Picture Concepts) to .90 (Vocabulary).

The full-scale IQ and a few of the index scores are reliable enough to be used to make important educational decisions. The subtests and many of the index scores are not sufficiently reliable to be used in making these important decisions.

---

[1]Stability coefficients provided are based on corrected correlations.

Validity

The authors present evidence for validity based on four areas: test content, response processes, internal structure, and relationship to other variables. In terms of test content, they emphasize the extensive revision process, based on comprehensive literature and expert reviews, which was used to select items and subtests that would adequately sample the domains of intellectual functioning they sought to measure.

Evidence for appropriate response processes (child's cognitive process during subtest task) is based on (1) prior research that supports retained subtests and (2) literature reviews, expert opinion, and empirical examinations that support the new subtests. Furthermore, during development, the authors engaged in empirical (for instance, response frequencies conducted to identify incorrect answers that occurred frequently) and qualitative (for instance, they directly questioned students regarding their use of problem-solving strategies) examination of response processes and made adjustments accordingly.

In terms of internal structure, evidence of convergent and discriminant validity is provided based on the correlations between subtests for each age group, and across age groups, using Fisher's z-transformation. Subtests were found to significantly correlate with one another, as would be expected considering that they all presumably measure g (general intelligence). Moreover, subtests that contribute to the same index score were generally found to highly correlate with one another. Further evidence of internal structure is presented through confirmatory factor analysis. Confirmatory factor analysis using structural equation modeling and five goodness-of-fit measures confirmed that a five-factor model provided the best fit for the data.

In terms of relationships with other variables, evidence is provided based on correlations between WISC-V and other Wechsler measures. The WISC-V FSIQ score was correlated with the full-scale IQ or total achievement measures from other Wechsler scales. The correlations are as follows: WISC-IV, $r = .86$; WPPSI-IV, $r = .83$; Wechsler Adult Intelligence Scale–III (WAIS-III), $r = .89$; and Wechsler Individual Achievement Test–III (WIAT-III), $r = .81$. Correlations were made with a set of specific intellectual measures, including the Kaufman Assessment Battery for Children–2nd edition (KABC-II), and the Kaufman Test of Educational Achievement–3rd edition (KTEA-3). Correlations of the FSIQ with composite indexes from these measures ranged from .44 to .82. They also provide information on correlations with the Vineland–II; the FSIQ correlated .01 with the Adaptive Behavior Composite from the Vineland–II.

The authors conclude by presenting special group studies that they conducted during standardization in order to examine the clinical utility of the WISC-V. They note the following four limitations to these studies: (1) Random selection was not used, (2) diagnoses might have been based on different criteria due to the various clinical settings from which participants were selected, (3) small sample sizes that covered only a portion of the WISC-V age range were used, and (4) only group performance is reported. The authors caution that these studies provide examples but are not fully representative of the diagnostic categories. The studies were conducted on children identified as intellectually gifted and children with mild-to-moderate intellectual disability, borderline intellectual functioning, specific learning disorders, attention deficit hyperactivity disorder (ADHD), disruptive behavior, English language learners (ELLs), traumatic brain injury, and autism spectrum disorder.

Summary

The WISC-V is a widely used individually administered intelligence test that assesses individuals ranging in age from 6 years, 0 months to 16 years, 11 months. Evidence for the reliability of the scales is generally good. Reliabilities are high for the full-scale intelligence quotient and for some of the index scores, but somewhat lower for other index scores—and much lower for subtests, so subtest scores should not be used in making placement or instructional planning decisions. Evidence for validity, as presented in the manual, is based on four areas: test content, response processes, internal structure, and relationship to other variables. Evidence for validity is somewhat limited.

The WISC-V is of limited usefulness in making educational decisions. Those who use the WISC-V in educational settings would do well not to go beyond using the full-scale score in making decisions about students.

18-8b WOODCOCK–JOHNSON IV: TESTS OF COGNITIVE ABILITIES AND TESTS OF ACHIEVEMENT

The fourth edition of the Woodcock–Johnson Psychoeducational Battery (WJ-IV) was developed in 2014 (Schrank, McGrew, & Mather, 2014). The WJ-IV is an individually administered, norm-referenced assessment system for the measurement of general intellectual ability, specific cognitive abilities, oral language, and academic achievement. We review here only the tests of cognitive abilities and the tests of achievement, but not the tests of oral language. The battery is intended for use from ages 2 to 90+ years. The complete set of WJ-IV test materials for the cognitive (COG) and achievement (ACH) batteries includes four easels for presenting the stimulus items: One for the standard battery cognitive tests, one for the extended battery cognitive tests, one for the standard achievement battery, and one for the extended achievement battery. Other materials include examiner's manuals for the cognitive and achievement tests, one technical manual provided on a DVD, an audio recording on a DVD that is used for the administration of several cognitive subtests, test records, scoring frames, and subject response booklets.

The WJ-IV contains several modifications to the previous version of the battery (that is, WJ-III). The Tests of Cognitive Abilities were revised to focus on the specific broad and narrow abilities considered most important; several subtests have been modified. Several additional clusters are available, along with a Gf-Gc composite. New subtests were added to the Tests of Achievement, along with several new clusters. Several subtests from both the cognitive and achievement batteries have been removed and placed in the oral language battery. The procedures developed to examine intra-ability and ability/achievement comparisons have been altered slightly for simplicity. Given that this is a new edition of the tests, all new norms have been constructed, and new information on reliability and validity of the fourth edition is available.

WJ-IV Tests of Cognitive Abilities

The 18 subtests of WJ-IV-COG are based on the CHC theory of cognitive abilities. The General Intellectual Ability (GIA) score is intended to represent the common ability underlying all intellectual performance, and is determined based on performance on seven standard battery subtests (i.e., Oral Vocabulary, Number Series, Verbal Attention, Letter-Pattern Matching, Phonological Processing, Story Recall, and Visualization). A Brief Intellectual Ability (BIA) score is also available for screening purposes, and is determined based on performance on three standard battery subtests (i.e., Oral Vocabulary, Number Series, and Verbal Attention). A Gf-Gc Composite is also available, and is composed of Oral Vocabulary, Number Series, General Information, and Concept Formation.

Other interpretive scores on the WJ-IV-COG are based on the broad CHC abilities. In addition, scores associated with several narrow ability and other clinical clusters can be derived. We describe the CHC factor clusters, as well as the subtests that correspond with those clusters below.

Comprehension–Knowledge (Gc) Assesses one's acquired knowledge and ability to communicate that knowledge, as well as the ability to reason using acquired knowledge and processes. The following two subtests are included: Oral Vocabulary (measuring vocabulary knowledge through synonym and antonym items) and General Information (measuring knowledge of where certain items can be found and what they do).

Fluid Reasoning (Gf) Assesses a person's reasoning and problem-solving abilities as applied to novel situations. The following two subtests are included: Number Series (measuring ability to identify number patterns) and Concept Formation (measuring ability to identify a rule that corresponds with presentation of a set of information).

Long-Term Retrieval (Glr) Assesses ability to store and retrieve information at a later point in time. The following two subtests are included: Story Recall (measuring ability to recall details presented in stories) and Visual–Auditory Learning (measuring ability to learn and recall symbols representing words).

Visual Processing (Gv) Assesses a person's ability to think with visual patterns with two subtests: Visualization (measuring the ability to identify pieces and patterns that match a target shape or pattern when rotated and/or flipped) and Picture Recognition (a visual memory task).

Auditory Processing (Ga) Assesses a person's ability to synthesize and discriminate auditory information that is presented with two subtests: Phonological Processing (measuring ability to recall and name words with specific phonetic elements) and Nonword Repetition (measuring one's ability to repeat a set of increasingly complex nonsense words).

Cognitive Processing Speed (Gs) Assesses a person's ability to quickly perform cognitive tasks. Two subtests are included: Letter-Pattern Matching and Pair Cancellation (both measures of fluency with identifying patterns).

Short-Term Working Memory (Gwm) Assesses a person's ability to maintain information in immediate awareness to carry out a particularly task. The two subtests that measure this cluster are: Verbal Attention (measuring one's ability to remember a sequence of presented information and answer specific questions about the sequence) and Numbers Reversed (measuring one's ability to listen to and manipulate series of numbers that are presented).

WJ-IV Tests of Achievement

The WJ-IV-ACH now contains 20 tests that can be combined to form several clusters. A Brief Achievement cluster is derived from performance on Letter-Word Identification, Applied Problems, and Spelling. To obtain the Broad Achievement cluster, an additional six subtests are administered (Passage Comprehension, Calculation, Writing Samples, Sentence Reading Fluency, Math Fact Fluency, and Sentence Writing Fluency). Each of the reading, math, and writing clusters is described below, with associated subtests listed.

Reading Assesses a person's ability to decode and comprehend text. It is composed of *Letter-Word Identification* and *Passage Comprehension*.

Broad Reading In addition to what is measured as part of the Reading cluster, it also assesses reading speed. It is composed of the two subtests making up the reading cluster (*Letter-Word Identification* and *Passage Comprehension*), as well as *Sentence Reading Fluency*.

Basic Reading Skills Assesses phonics and word analysis skills, and includes *Letter-Word Identification* and *Word Attack*.

Reading Comprehension Assesses comprehension, reasoning, and long-term retrieval, and includes *Passage Comprehension* and *Reading Recall*.

Reading Comprehension–Extended In addition to what is measured as part of the Reading Comprehension cluster, it also includes the *Reading Vocabulary* subtest, and therefore also measures vocabulary.

Reading Fluency Assesses reading fluency, including accuracy, prosody (rhythm pattern in oral reading), and automaticity. It includes *Oral Reading* and *Sentence Reading Fluency*.

Mathematics Assesses both computation and problem solving, and includes *Applied Problems* and *Calculation*.

Broad Mathematics In addition to what is measured as part of the Mathematics cluster, it also assesses fluency. It includes the same subtests as the Mathematics cluster (*Applied Problems* and *Calculation*), as well as *Math Facts Fluency*.

Math Calculation Skills Assesses computation and basic math fact automaticity. It includes *Calculation* and *Math Facts Fluency*.

Math Problem Solving Assesses math knowledge and reasoning. It includes *Applied Problems* and *Number Matrices*.

Written Language Assesses spelling and quality of written expression. It includes *Spelling* and *Writing Samples*.

Broad Written Language In addition to what is measured as part of the Written Language cluster, it assesses production fluency. It includes the two subtests of the written language cluster (*Spelling* and *Writing Samples*) as well as *Sentence Writing Fluency*.

Basic Writing Skills Assesses spelling and punctuation knowledge. It includes *Spelling* and *Editing*.

Written Expression Assesses fluency and quality of written expression. It is composed of *Writing Samples* and *Sentence Writing Fluency*.

Scores

As with the WJ-III NU, the WJ-IV must be scored by a computer program—which eliminates complex hand-scoring procedures. Age norms (ages 2 to 90+ years) and grade norms (from kindergarten to first-year graduate school) are included. Although WJ-IV age and grade equivalents are not extrapolated, they still imply a false standard and promote typological thinking. (See Chapter 4 for a discussion of these issues.) A variety of other derived scores are also available: percentile ranks, standard scores, and Relative Proficiency Indexes (RPIs). RPIs can be used to identify instructional zones, or tasks that will likely be perceived as particularly easy or particularly difficult depending on the student's score. In addition, raw scores can be computed into W scores, which represent performance irrespective of age or grade level; a W score of 500 is intended to approximate the average performance of a 10-year-old on the given task. Finally, each Test Record contains a seven-category Test Session Observation Checklist to rate a student's conversational proficiency, cooperation, activity, attention and concentration, self-confidence, care in responding, and response to difficult tasks.

Norms

WJ-IV calculations are based on the performances of 7,416 individuals living in more than 46 states and the District of Columbia within the United States. Individuals were randomly selected within a stratified sampling design that controlled for 12 specific community and individual variables. The preschool sample includes 664 children from 2 to 5 years of age (not enrolled in kindergarten). The K–12 sample is composed of 3,891 students. The college/university sample is based on 775 students. The adult sample includes 2,086 individuals. Demographic information is provided by sample (i.e., preschool, K–12, college/university, adult) for geographic region, gender, race/ethnicity, country of birth (U.S. vs. other). Additional demographic information is available for some of the samples (e.g., community type for all but college/university sample; parent education for preschool and K–12 sample). Within the K–12 sample, there are several categories in which discrepancies between the sample demographics and population demographics are noted; for example, there appears to be underrepresentation of individuals from the South and an overrepresentation of individuals whose parents' highest level of education is high school. Weighting was applied so that the actual norms could be considered more representative of the U.S. population. A multiple-matrix sampling design, in which all norm sample participants are administered several key subtests, with the remaining subtests administered to certain subsamples from the norm group, was applied.

Reliability

The *WJ-IV Technical Manual* contains extensive information on the reliability of the WJ-IV. The precision of each test and cluster score is reported in terms of the SEM. SEMs are provided for the W and standard scores at each age level. The precision with which relative standing in a group can be indicated (rather than the precision of the underlying scores) is reported for each test and cluster by the reliability coefficient. Odd–even correlations, corrected by the Spearman–Brown formulas, were used to estimate reliability for each untimed test.

Some human traits are more stable than others; consequently, some WJ-IV tests that precisely measure important, but less stable, human traits show reliabilities in the .70s and .80s for certain age groups. However, in the WJ-IV, individual tests are combined to provide clusters for educational decision making. Median reliabilities (across age groups) for the standard broad cognitive and achievement clusters are primarily .90 and above, with a few exceptions.

Validity

Careful item selection is consistent with claims for the content validity of both the Tests of Cognitive Ability and the Tests of Achievement. Multidimensional scaling techniques were also applied to examine and provide support for the content validity of the tests. Developmental patterns based on cross-sectional data are presented, and they align generally with what one would expect in terms of development of performance on the clusters over time. All items retained had to fit the Rasch measurement model as well as other criteria related to bias and sensitivity.

Factor-analytic studies support the presence of seven CHC factors of cognitive ability and two domains of academic achievement (reading/writing and quantitative knowledge). To augment evidence of validity based on internal structure, the authors examined the intercorrelations among tests within each battery. As expected, tests assessing the same broad cognitive ability or achievement area usually correlated more highly with each other than with tests assessing different cognitive abilities or areas of achievement.

For the Tests of Cognitive Ability, evidence of validity based on relations with other measures is provided. Scores were compared with performances on other intellectual measures appropriate for individuals at the ages tested. The criterion measures included the Wechsler Intelligence Scale for Children–Fourth Edition, the Differential Ability Scales–Second Edition, the Kaufman Assessment Battery for Children–Second Edition, and the Stanford–Binet Intelligence Scales–Fifth Edition. The correlation between the WJ-IV General Intellectual Ability score and the WISC-IV Full-Scale IQ was .86.

For the Tests of Achievement, scores were compared with other appropriate achievement measures (for example, the Wechsler Individual Achievement Test–Third Edition, Kaufman Tests of Educational Achievement–Second Edition, and the Oral and Written Language Scales—Written Expression). The pattern and magnitude of correlations suggest that the WJ-IV-ACH is measuring skills similar to those measured by other achievement tests.

Summary

The WJ-IV consists of three batteries—the WJ-IV Tests of Cognitive Abilities, the WJ-IV Tests of Achievement, and the WJ-IV Tests of Oral Language. The first two batteries are the focus of the current review. These batteries provide a comprehensive system for measuring general intellectual ability, specific cognitive abilities, scholastic aptitude, and achievement over a broad age range. There are 18 cognitive tests and 20 achievement tests. A variety of scores are available for the tests and are combined to form clusters for interpretive purposes. A wide variety of derived scores are available. The WJ-IV's norms, reliability, and validity appear adequate.

18-8c PEABODY PICTURE VOCABULARY TEST–FOURTH EDITION (PPVT-4)

The Peabody Picture Vocabulary Test–4 (PPVT-4; Dunn & Dunn, 2007) is an individually administered, norm-referenced, nontimed test assessing the receptive (hearing) vocabulary of children and adults. The authors identify additional uses for the test results: "It is useful (perhaps as part of a broader assessment) when evaluating language competence, selecting the level and content of instruction, and measuring learning. In individuals whose primary language is English, vocabulary correlates highly with general verbal ability" (Dunn & Dunn, 2007, p. 1). The assessment of vocabulary can also be useful when evaluating the effects of injury or disease and is a key component of reading comprehension.

The PPVT-4 is a revised version of the PPVT, PPVT-R, and PPVT III, which were written and revised in 1959, 1981 and 1997, respectively. The new version contains many of the features of its predecessors, such as individual administration, efficient scoring, and the fact that it is untimed. The test continues to offer two parallel forms, broad samples of stimulus words, and it can be used to assess a wide range of examinees. The PPVT-4 has a streamlined administration and contains larger, full-color pictures; new stimulus words; expanded interpretive options to analyze items by parts of speech; a new growth scale value scale for measuring change; and a report to parents and letter to parents (available in Spanish and English). Other conveniences include a carrying tote and optional computerized scoring.

The PPVT-4 is administered using an easel. The examinee is shown a series of plates, each containing a set of four colored pictures. The examiner states a word and the examinee selects the picture that best represents the stimulus word. The PPVT-4 is an untimed power test, usually finished in 20 minutes or less. It consists of stimuli sets of 12 and examinees are tested at their ability or age level; therefore, test items that are either too difficult or too easy are not administered. The authors provide recommended starting points by age.

Scores

Examinees earn a raw score based on the number of pictures correctly identified between basal and ceiling items. A basal is defined as the lowest set administered that contains one or no errors. A ceiling is defined as the highest set administered that contains eight or more error responses. Once a ceiling is established, testing is discontinued. The raw score is determined by subtracting the total number of errors from the ceiling item. The PPVT-4 has two types of normative scores: deviation (standard scores, percentiles, normal curve equivalents, and stanines) and developmental (age equivalent and grade equivalent). The test also produces a nonnormative score called a growth scale value that measures change in PPVT-4 performance over time. It is a nonnormative score because it does not involve comparison with a norm group.

Norms

Two national tryouts were conducted in 2004 and 2005 to determine stimulus items for the test. Both classical and Rasch item analysis methods were applied to determine item difficulty, discrimination, bias, distracter performance, reliability, and the range of raw score by age. Some items from the previous versions of the PPVT were maintained in the development of the PPVT-4. The PPVT-4 contains two parallel forms with a total of 456 items, 340 of which were adapted from the third edition and 116 were created for the fourth edition.

The PPVT-4 was standardized on a representative national sample of 3,540 people ages 2 years, 6 months to 90 years or older (for age norms) and a subsample of 2,003 individuals from kindergarten through grade 12 (for grade norms). The goal was to have approximately 100 to 200 cases in each age group, with the exception of the oldest two age groups, for which the target was 60. Due to rapid vocabulary growth in young children, the samples were divided into six-month age intervals at ages 2 years, 6 months through 6 years. Whole-year intervals were used for ages 7 through 14 years. The adult age groups use multiyear age intervals.

The manual includes a table showing the number of individuals at each age level included in the standardization.

The standardization sample for the PPVT-4 was composed of more than 450 examiners tested at 320 sites in four geographical areas of the United States. Background information, including birth date, sex, race/ethnicity, number of years of education completed, school enrollment status, special education status, and English language proficiency, was gathered either from the examinee (those older than 18 years) or from parents (for children 17 years old or younger). All potential examinee information was entered, a stratified random sampling was made from the pool, and testing assignments for each site were determined. More cases were collected than planned, allowing the opportunity to choose final age and grade samples that closely matched the U.S. population characteristics. The test appears to adequately represent the population at each age and grade level.

Reliability

There are multiple kinds of reliability reported for the PPVT-4. The manual contains detailed information on reliability data. The PPVT-4 reports split-half reliability and coefficient alpha as indicators of internal consistency reliability; also included are alternate-form reliability and test–retest reliability. The split-half reliabilities average .94 or .95 for each form across the entire age and grade ranges. Coefficient alpha is also consistently high across all ages and grades, averaging .97 for Form A and .96 for Form B. During the standardization, a total of 508 examinees took both Form A and Form B (most during the same testing session, but some as many as seven days apart). The alternate-form reliability is very high, falling between .87 and .93 with a mean of .89. The average test–retest correlation, reported on 349 examinees retested with the same form an average of four weeks after initial trial, is .93. The information on reliability indicates that the PPVT-4 scores are very precise and users can depend on consistent scores from the PPVT-4.

Validity

The manual discusses validity information in detail. Five studies were conducted comparing the PPVT-4 with the Expressive Vocabulary Test, second edition; the Comprehensive Assessment of Spoken Language; the Clinical Evaluation of Language Fundamentals, fourth edition; the PPVT-III; and the Group Reading Assessment and Diagnostic Evaluation. The PPVT-4 scores correlate highly with those of the previously mentioned assessments. Note that slightly lower correlations were found on assessments that measured broader areas of language than primarily vocabulary.

Dilemmas in Current Practice

The practice of assessing children's intelligence is currently marked by controversy. Intelligence tests simply assess samples of behavior, and different intelligence tests sample different behaviors. For that reason, it is wrong to speak of a person's IQ. Instead, we can refer only to a person's IQ on a specific test. An IQ on the Stanford–Binet Intelligence Scale, Fifth Edition, is not derived from the same samples of behavior as an IQ on any other intelligence test. Because the behavior samples are different for different tests, educators and others must always ask, "IQ on what test?"

This should also be considered when interpreting factor scores for different intelligence tests. Just as the measurement of overall intelligence varies across tests, factor structures and the behaviors that comprise factors differ across tests. Although authors of intelligence tests may include similar factor names, these factors may represent different behaviors across different tests. It is helpful to understand that, for the most part, the particular kinds of items and subtests found on an intelligence test are a matter of the way in which a test author defines intelligence and thinks about the kinds of behaviors that represent it.

When interpreting intelligence test scores, it is best to avoid making judgments that involve a high level of inference (judgments that suggest that the score represents much more than the specific behaviors sampled). Always remember that these factor, index, and cluster scores represent merely student performance on certain sampled behaviors, and that the quality of measurement can be affected by a host of unique student characteristics that need to be taken into consideration.

Interpreting a student's performance on intelligence tests must be done with great caution. First, it is important to note that factor scores tend to be less reliable than total scores because they have fewer items. Second, the same test may make different psychological demands on various test takers, depending on their ages and acculturation. Test results mean different things for different students. It is imperative that we be especially aware of the relationship between a person's acculturation and the acculturation of the norm group to which that person is compared.

We think it is also important to note that many of the behaviors sampled on intelligence tests are more indicative of actual achievement than ability to achieve. For instance, quantitative reasoning (a factor commonly included in intelligence tests) typically involves measuring a student's math knowledge and skill. Students who have had more opportunities to learn and achieve are likely to perform better on intelligence tests than those who have had less exposure to information, even if they both have the same overall potential to learn. Intelligence tests, as they are currently available, are by no means a pure representation of a student's ability to learn.

It is important to recognize that using subtests from intelligence tests to identify students as having learning disabilities has the potential to be fraught with error, and appears to provide limited guidance for how to instruct a student. As a result, we caution against this practice until there is further evidence to show that such information can be helpful.

The authors provide data on how representatives of special populations (speech and language impairment, hearing impairment, specific learning disability, intellectual disability, giftedness, emotional/behavioral disturbances, and ADHD) perform in relation to the general population. The results indicate the value of the PPVT-4 in assessing special populations.

Summary

The PPVT-4 is an individually administered, norm-referenced, nontimed test assessing the receptive vocabulary of children and adults. The test is adequately standardized, and there is good evidence for reliability and validity. Data are also included on the testing and performance of students with disabilities.

Chapter Comprehension Questions

Write your answers to each of the following questions and then compare your responses to the text.

1. Provide two reasons why intelligence tests are used in schools today.

2. Explain the possible impact of acculturation on intelligence test performance.

3. Describe four behaviors that are commonly sampled on intelligence tests.

4. Describe the theoretical contributions of three individuals to the development of intelligence tests.

5. Describe four commonly interpreted factors in intelligence testing.

6. How are intelligence tests sometimes used to identify learning disabilities?

7. What are three types of intelligence testing, and for what purposes might you use each of them?

8. Compare and contrast three commonly used tests of intelligence.

9. Describe two dilemmas in using scores from intelligence tests in school settings.

CHAPTER

19

USING MEASURES OF SOCIAL AND EMOTIONAL BEHAVIOR

LEARNING OBJECTIVES

19-1 Ascertain why we assess social–emotional functioning and adaptive behavior.

19-2 Identify key considerations in the assessment of social–emotional and adaptive behavior.

19-3 Identify four methods for assessing social–emotional functioning and one common method for assessing adaptive behavior.

19-4 Explain the steps of a functional behavioral assessment.

19-5 Describe the strengths and weaknesses of scales for assessing social–emotional functioning and adaptive behavior.

STANDARDS ADDRESSED IN THIS CHAPTER

 CEC Initial Preparation Standards

Standard 4: Assessment

4.0 Beginning special education professionals use multiple methods of assessment and data-sources in making educational decisions.

 CEC Advanced Preparation Standards

Standard 1: Assessment

1.0 Special education specialists use valid and reliable assessment practices to minimize bias.

 National Association of School Psychologists Domains

1 Data-Based Decision Making and Accountability

4 Interventions and Mental Health Services to Develop Social and Life Skills

Social and emotional functioning often plays an important role in the development of student academic skills. When students either lack or fail to demonstrate a certain repertoire of expected behavioral, coping, and social skills, their academic learning can be hindered. The reverse is also true: School experiences can impact student social–emotional well-being and related behaviors. To be successful in school, students frequently need to engage in certain positive social behaviors, such as turn taking and responding appropriately to criticism. Other behaviors, such as name calling and uttering self-deprecating remarks, may cause concern and can denote underlying social and emotional problems. In Chapter 9, we noted that teachers, psychologists, and other diagnosticians systematically observe a variety of student behaviors. In this chapter, we discuss additional methods and considerations for the assessment of behaviors variously called social, emotional, and problem behaviors.

In addition, it is important for students to adapt to their physical and social environments, to stay safe, and avoid danger. This is often referred to as **adaptive behavior**. For instance, looking both ways before crossing a road, selecting appropriate attire for a cold day, and being able to navigate your way home from a reasonable distance away, are all examples of adaptive behaviors. In addition to appropriate responses to the demands of the immediate environment, adaptive behavior requires preparation for responses to probable future environments. Certain current behaviors (for example, smoking or high-risk sexual activity) can have life-threatening future consequences. Similarly, acquiring more education or job training and saving money increase the likelihood of thriving in later years. Adaptive behavior varies by age; adults are typically expected to take reasonable care of themselves (by managing their own health, dressing, eating, and so on), to work, and to engage in socially acceptable recreational or leisure activities. In children and adolescents, the behaviors of interest are of two kinds. We assess behaviors that demonstrate age-appropriate independence and responsibility. We assess those behaviors that are believed to enable the development or acquisition of desired adult behaviors.

19-1 Why Do We Assess Social–Emotional and Adaptive Behavior?

There are two major reasons for assessing social emotional and adaptive behavior: (1) identification and classification and (2) intervention planning. First, some disabilities are defined, in part, by inappropriate behavior. For example, the regulations for implementing the Individuals with Disabilities Education Act (IDEA) describe in general terms the types of inappropriate behavior that are indicative of emotional disturbance and autism. Thus, to classify a pupil as having one of these disabilities and in need of special education, educators need to assess social and emotional behavior. IDEA also requires that in order to be eligible for special education services under the category of intellectual disability, there must be evidence of both low intelligence and limited adaptive behavior, and so adaptive behavior must be assessed as part of the assessment of students suspected of having an intellectual disability. See the Scenario in Assessment section titled "Crina" for an example of when an assessment of adaptive behavior was necessary and important.

Second, assessment of social–emotional and adaptive behavior may lead to appropriate intervention. For students whose disabilities are defined by behavior problems, the need for intervention is obvious. However, the development and demonstration of social and coping skills, and the reduction of problem behavior, are worthwhile goals for any student. Both during and after intervention, behaviors are monitored and assessed to learn whether the treatment has been successful and the desired behavior has generalized.

CRINA | Remember Crina from Chapter 5? She was the girl from Eastern Europe who was adopted by an American family when she was 10 years old. Crina was evaluated by a district multidisciplinary team that recommended placement in a life skills class because her scores on the English language intelligence test and achievement tests were very low. Crina's mother disagreed with the school's diagnosis and obtained an independent educational evaluation that included an assessment of her adaptive behavior. That assessment indicated that Crina was functioning within the average range for a person her age. Nonetheless, the district remained adamant about the recommended placement, and the dispute was eventually settled at a due process hearing that was won by the parents.

In her opinion, the hearing officer wrote the following:

The IDEA is clear with respect to the definition of intellectual disability. It is "significantly subaverage general intellectual functioning, existing concurrently

with deficits in adaptive behavior and manifested during the developmental period, that adversely affects a child's educational performance" (§300.7(c)(6)). The evidence in this case is overwhelming: Crina, while having severe academic problems, does not have deficits in adaptive behavior. Therefore, she cannot be classified as a student with an intellectual disability. The District has erred in its classification and this order will prohibit her classification as such a student.

Not only did Crina's parents prevail at the hearing, the district was severely reprimanded for its failure to follow both state and federal law.

This scenario highlights the role that assessment of adaptive behavior can play in determining eligibility for special education due to an intellectual disability. In Crina's situation, if such an assessment were not conducted, how would this have affected the associated decisions?

19-2 Important Considerations in the Assessment of Social–Emotional Functioning and Adaptive Behavior

The appropriateness of social and emotional behavior, as well as adaptive behavior, is somewhat dependent on societal expectations, which may vary according to the age of a child, the setting in which the behavior occurs, the frequency or duration of the behavior, and the intensity of the behavior. For example, it is not uncommon for preschool students to cry in front of other children when their parents send them off on the first day of school. However, the same behavior would be considered atypical if exhibited by an eleventh grader. It would be even more problematic if the eleventh grader cried every day in front of her peers at school. Some behaviors are of concern even when they occur infrequently, if they are very intense. For example, setting fire to an animal is significant even if it occurs rarely—only every year or so.

Although some social and emotional problems that students experience are clearly apparent, others may be much less easily observed, even though they have a similar negative impact on overall student functioning. Externalizing problems, particularly those that contribute to disruption in classroom routines, are typically quite easily detected. Excessive shouting, hitting or pushing of classmates, and talking back to the teacher are behaviors that are not easily overlooked. Internalizing problems, such as anxiety and depression, are often less readily identified. These problems might be manifested in the form of social isolation, excessive fatigue, or self-destructive behavior. In assessing both externalizing and internalizing problems, it can be helpful to identify both behavioral excesses (for instance, out-of-seat behavior or interrupting) and deficits (such as sharing, positive self-talk, and other coping skills) that can then become targets for intervention.

Sometimes students fail to behave in expected ways because they do not have the requisite coping or social skills; in other cases, students may actually have the necessary skills but fail to demonstrate them under certain conditions. Bandura (1969) points to the importance of distinguishing between such acquisition and performance deficits in the assessment of social behavior. If students never demonstrate certain expected social behaviors, they may need to be instructed how to do so, or it may be necessary for someone to more frequently model the expected behavior for them. If the behavior is expected to be demonstrated across all contexts and is restricted to one or few contexts, there may be discriminative stimuli unique to the few environments that occasion the behavior, or there may be specific contingencies in those environments that increase or at least maintain the behavior. An analysis of associated environmental variables can help determine how best to intervene. When problematic behavior is generalized across a variety of settings, it can be particularly difficult to modify and may have multiple determinants, including biological underpinnings.

19-3 Ways of Assessing Social–Emotional and Adaptive Behavior

Four methods are commonly used, singly or in combination, to gather information about social and emotional functioning: observational procedures, interview techniques, situational measures, and rating scales. Direct observation of social and emotional behavior is often preferred, given that the results using this method are generally quite accurate. However, obtaining useful observational data across multiple settings can be time consuming, particularly when the behavior is very limited in frequency or duration. Furthermore, internalizing problems can go undetected unless specific questions are posited, given that the associated behaviors may be less readily detected. The use of rating scales and interviews can often allow for more efficient collection of data across multiple settings and informants, which is particularly important in the assessment of social–emotional behavior. The use of rating scales with adult respondents is the most common way adaptive behavior is measured. Observational procedures were discussed in Chapter 9; the remaining methods are described in the following sections.

19-3a INTERVIEW TECHNIQUES

Interviews are most often used by experienced professionals to gain information about the perspectives of various knowledgeable individuals, as well as to gain further insight into a student's overall patterns of thinking and behaving. Martin (1988) maintains that self-reports of "aspirations, anxieties, feelings of self-worth, attributions about the causes of behavior, and attitudes about school are [important] regardless of the theoretical orientation of the psychologist" (p. 230). There are many variations on the interview method—most distinctions are made along a continuum from structured to unstructured or from formal to informal. Regardless of the format, Merrell (1994) suggests that most interviews probe for information in one or more of the following areas of functioning and development: medical/developmental history, social–emotional functioning, educational progress, and community involvement. Increasingly, the family as a unit (or individual family members) is the focus of interviews that seek to identify salient home environment factors that may be having an impact on the student (Broderick, 1993).

19-3b SITUATIONAL MEASURES

Situational measures of social–emotional behavior can include nearly any reasonable activity (D. K. Walker, 1973), but two well-known methods are peer-acceptance nomination scales and sociometric ranking techniques. Both types of measures provide an indication of an individual's social status and may help describe the attitude of a particular group (such as the class) toward the target student. **Peer nomination techniques** require that students identify other students whom they prefer on some set of criteria (such as students they would like to have as study partners). From these measurements, sociograms, pictorial representations of the results, can be created. **Sociometric ranking techniques** involve asking parents to rank students on various social dimensions. Overall, sociometric techniques provide a contemporary point of reference for comparisons of a student's status among members of a specified group.

19-3c RATING SCALES

There are several types of rating scales; generally a parent, teacher, peer, or "significant other" in a student's environment must rate the extent to which that student demonstrates certain desirable or undesirable behaviors. Raters are often asked to determine the presence or absence of a particular behavior and may be asked to quantify the amount, intensity, or frequency of the behavior. Rating scales are popular because they are easy to administer and useful in providing basic information about a student's level of functioning. They bring structure to an assessment or evaluation and can be used in almost any environment to gather data from almost any source. The important concept to remember is that rating scales provide an index of someone's perception of a student's behavior. Different raters will probably have different perceptions of the same student's behavior and are likely to provide different ratings of the student; each is likely to have different views of acceptable and unacceptable expectations or standards. Chafouleus et al. (2010) suggest that training for raters should occur if results from multiple raters are going to be used for decision making. A self-report is also often a part of rating scale systems. Gresham and Elliott (1990) point out that rating scales are inexact and should be supplemented by other data collection methods.

Just as is the case for academic skills (e.g., reading, math, etc.), assessment of social–emotional behavior occurs at each tier within an educational system, with increasing comprehensiveness and frequency of assessment occurring at higher tiers. One procedure that has been developed to incorporate multiple methods in the assessment of social and emotional behavior, and that resembles a multi-tiered approach to assessment, is multiple gating (Walker & Severson, 1992). This procedure is evident in the Systematic Screening for Behavior Disorders, which involves the systematic screening of all students using brief rating scales. The screening is followed by the use of more extensive rating scales, interviews, and observations for those students who are identified as likely to have social–emotional problems. Multiple gating may help limit the number of undetected problems, as well as target time-consuming assessment methods toward the most severe problems.

19-4 Functional Behavioral Assessment and Analysis

An assessment strategy that has become more commonly used to address problem behavior is **functional behavioral assessment (FBA)**. An **FBA** represents a set of assessment procedures used to identify the function of a student's problematic behavior, as well as the various conditions under which it tends to occur. It involves the integration of data from a variety of methods to meaningfully inform intervention efforts. Those who conduct FBAs may use a variety of different assessment methods and tools (for example, interviews, observations, and rating scales), depending on the nature of the student's behavioral difficulties. Once an FBA has been conducted, a behavior intervention plan can be developed that has a high likelihood of reducing the problem behavior. According to IDEA 2004, an FBA must be conducted for any student undergoing special education eligibility evaluation in which problem behavior is of concern. An FBA must also be conducted (or reviewed) following a manifestation determination review[1] in which the associated suspensions from school were determined to be due to the child's disability. FBAs are to be conducted by those who have been appropriately trained.

19-4a STEPS FOR COMPLETING A FUNCTIONAL BEHAVIOR ASSESSMENT

Although a variety of different tools and measures might be used to conduct an FBA, certain steps are essential to the process. These include the following:

Defining the behavior. Although a student may display a variety of problematic behaviors, for the purpose of conducting a functional behavioral assessment, it is important to narrow in on just one or two of the most problematic behaviors. For

---

[1] A manifestation determination review must be conducted when a student receiving special education services has been the recipient of disciplinary action that constitutes a change of placement for more than 10 days within a school year.

example, although Annie may exhibit a variety of problematic behaviors, including excessive crying, self-mutilation (that is, repeatedly banging her head against her desk until she develops bruises), and noncompliance with teacher directions, a support team may decide to focus on her self-mutilation behavior, given that it is particularly intense and harmful to her body. It is important to define the behavior such that it is observable, measurable, and specific (see Chapter 9 for ways in which behaviors can be measured). A review of records, interviews with teachers and caregivers, and direct observations may help in defining the behavior of primary concern.

Identifying the conditions under which behavior is manifested. Once the behavior has been carefully defined, it is necessary to identify any patterns associated with occurrences of the behavior. In doing so, it is important to identify the following:

- Antecedents: These represent events that occur immediately before the problem behavior. They may include such things as being asked to complete a particular task, having a particularly disliked person enter the room, or receiving a bad grade.

- Setting events: These represent events that make it such that the student is particularly sensitive to the antecedents and consequences associated with the problem behavior. For example, a setting event might include not having gotten enough sleep the night before school, such that the student is particularly sensitive to a teacher's request for her to finish work quickly and subsequently acts out in response to the teacher's request.

- Consequences: These represent what happens as a result of the behavior. For example, the consequence for a student tearing up a paper that he or she does not want to work on may be that the student does not have to complete the difficult task presented on the paper. Or, if a student hits another student in the arm, the consequence may be that he is sent to the office and his parents are called to pick him up and take him home.

Developing a hypothesis about the function of the behavior. Using information that is collected about antecedents, setting events, and consequences through record review, interview, and observation, one can begin to develop hypotheses about the function of the behavior. In Chapter 9, we described several different functions of behavior, including (1) social attention/communication; (2) access to tangibles or preferred activities; (3) escape, delay, reduction, or avoidance of aversive tasks or activities; (4) escape or avoidance of other individuals; and (5) internal stimulation (Carr, 1994).

Testing the hypothesized function of the behavior. Although this step is typically considered part of a functional behavioral *analysis* (as opposed to a functional behavioral *assessment*), it is important to verify that your hypothesis about the function of the behavior is correct. Otherwise, the associated intervention plan may not work. By manipulating the antecedents and consequences, one can determine whether the function is correct. For example, if it is assumed that escape from difficult tasks is a function of the student's problematic behavior of tearing up assignments, one could provide tasks that the student finds easy, and enjoys, and examine whether he or she tears up the paper. If the student correspondingly stops tearing up assignments, this would provide evidence that the function of the behavior is to escape from a difficult task. If the behavior continues at the same rate, even when provided easy tasks, one might test out a different hypothesis. For example, if the student commonly is reprimanded for tearing up the paper and put on a time-out with a teacher assistant present, another hypothesis might be that receiving attention from the teacher or teacher assistant is a function of the student's problematic behavior. To test this out, the teacher and teacher assistant could provide special attention to the student more frequently when the student is behaving in an appropriate manner, and provide no reprimand and have the student complete time-outs without the teacher assistant present. If this corresponds with a reduction in the problem behavior, attention is likely the function of the behavior. An example of a situation in which the function of a behavior was initially incorrectly identified is provided in the Scenario in Assessment for this chapter titled "Joseph."

Developing a behavioral intervention plan. Although this comes after the actual FBA, it is important to know how to use the assessment data that are collected to inform the development of an intervention plan. Ideally, a behavior intervention plan will involve the following:

- Identifying, teaching, and reinforcing a replacement behavior. As part of the behavior intervention plan, the support team needs to identify a behavior that the student can use to address the identified function in an appropriate manner. For example, if the function of a problematic behavior (such as tearing up work) is escape from a difficult task, the student might be taught how to request a break from the difficult task, such that the same function (escape) would be met when the student engaged in a more appropriate behavior. Although some might initially think that teaching replacement behaviors (that is, to ask for a break and have it granted) results in a lowering of standards, it is important to highlight that having the student ask for a break is certainly more socially appropriate behavior than tearing up an assignment, and it is a step in the right direction. In order to ensure that the student makes use of newly taught replacement behaviors, the intervention plan might include a reward for when the student initially makes appropriate use of the replacement behavior.

SCENARIO IN ASSESSMENT

JOSEPH | Joseph was a kindergarten student who, within the first three weeks of school, had been sent to the office more than 15 times for his inappropriate behavior, which included hitting and shouting at his peers. Joseph's teacher used a time-out procedure to discipline students in her classroom. Joseph frequently received multiple time-outs in a single morning. The teacher would then decide that he needed to receive a more substantial consequence. This typically included being sent to the principal's office.

After a very brief consultation with one of the school's special education teachers and another kindergarten teacher, Joseph's teacher decided to keep track of the antecedents and consequences associated with his behavior for a few days, using the following recording device. This is what Joseph's teacher recorded:

Antecedents	Behavior	Consequence
Morning large-group time, students sitting on the floor while the teacher was pointing to the calendar	Hit the peer sitting next to him in the arm	Reprimanded, sent to the time-out corner
Morning group time, while the teacher was reading a story	Kicked the peer sitting next to him	Reprimanded, sent to the time-out corner
Afternoon group time, while watching a video	Shouted "I hate this; I hate this video!"	Peers laugh, Joseph is reprimanded and sent to the office
Morning group time, when a student was describing the weather	Kicked the peer sitting next to him	Reprimanded, sent to the time-out corner
Morning group time, when the teacher was asking questions about the story that was just read	Hit the peer sitting next to him	Reprimanded, sent to the office

Joseph's teacher brought this information to the other two teachers and sought their guidance. Based on the information, they thought that Joseph's behavior served an attention function. Joseph seemed to get quite a bit of negative attention from his teacher and peers following his behavior; he also likely got some attention from the principal when he was sent to her office. They suggested that Joseph be provided with more attention when he was behaving appropriately; they also suggested developing a very brief signal (rather than using words) to send him to the time-out area when he behaved inappropriately. This way the teacher would not have to verbally reprimand and call attention to his inappropriate behavior.

Unfortunately, this did not seem to help decrease Joseph's behavior. The other teachers suggested that they bring this to the attention of the district behavior consultant. After analyzing the data that had been collected and asking a few questions, the consultant decided to observe Joseph in the classroom environment. She made a couple of interesting observations that were pertinent to the situation: (1) The area where the teacher held group time was very crowded, (2) Joseph tended to engage in the problem behavior toward the end of group times, and (3) he had a very difficult time sitting still during group time. This led her to believe that the function of the behavior was to escape from having to do something he had not yet developed the skill to do (that is, sit and listen for long periods of time). If this was the case, the teacher's consequence of time-out would only serve to reinforce the problem behavior. The consultant suggested developing an intervention that involved initially reducing the length of time spent in group activity and reinforcing Joseph for his appropriate behavior. Once Joseph's appropriate behavior had been established, the teacher told the students that the group activity would be increased by three additional minutes. Joseph's appropriate behavior continued to be reinforced. The teacher continued to increase the length of time in group activity as Joseph's behavior allowed. Using this intervention plan, Joseph's behavioral problems decreased dramatically.

This scenario highlights the importance of correct identification of the function of a behavior. Why was the correct identification of function so important?

• Appropriately addressing setting events, antecedents, and consequences. Behavior intervention plans may include an alteration of the conditions surrounding antecedents and/or a change in consequences. For example, if escape from difficult items presented on a worksheet is the function of a behavior, and the antecedent is presentation of those difficult items, the teacher might set up an activity to begin with a few very easy tasks, followed by a medium task, some more easy tasks, and perhaps one difficult task toward the end. If peer attention is the function of a behavior, the teacher might train the entire class how to ignore the target student's problematic behavior.

Once a behavior intervention plan is developed, it is important to also create a method for measuring implementation integrity as well as a monitoring strategy to determine whether the behavioral intervention plan is appropriately addressing the student's problem behavior.

19-5 Specific Rating Scales of Social-Emotional Behavior

In Table 19.1, we provide information on several commonly used scales of social–emotional behavior. In the following section, we provide full reviews of the Behavior Assessment System for Children, Third Edition, and the Vineland Adaptive Behavior Scales, Second Edition (VABS II), which is an instrument commonly used to measure adaptive behavior.

19-5a BEHAVIOR ASSESSMENT SYSTEM FOR CHILDREN, THIRD EDITION (BASC-3)

The Behavior Assessment System for Children, Third Edition (BASC-3; Reynolds & Kamphaus, 2015) is a "multimethod, multidimensional system

TABLE 19.1		Commonly Used Measures of Social–Emotional Behavior	
Test	**Year of Publication**	**Author(s)**	**Publisher**
Achenbach System of Empirically Based Assessment (ASEBA)	2001	Achenbach & Rescorla	Research Center for Children, Youth, & Families at the University of Vermont
Asperger Syndrome Diagnostic Scale (ASDS)	2001	Myles, Bock, & Simpson	Pro-Ed
Behavioral and Emotional Rating Scale, Second Edition (BERS-2)	2004	Epstein	Pro-Ed
Behavior Assessment System for Children, Third Edition (BASC-3)	2015	Reynolds & Kamphaus	Pearson
Behavior Rating Profile, Second Edition	2007	L. Brown & Hammill	Pro-Ed
Gilliam Asperger's Disorder Scale (GADS)	2001	Gilliam	Pro-Ed
Gilliam Autism Rating Scale–Third Edition (GARS-3)	2014	Gilliam	Pro-Ed
Social Skills Improvement System Rating Scales (SSIS)	2010	Gresham & Elliott	Pearson
Temperament and Aytpical Behavior Scale (TABS)	1999	Neisworth, Bagnato, Salvia & Hunt	Brookes

used to evaluate the behavior and self-perceptions of children and young adults aged 2 through 25 years" (p. 1). This comprehensive assessment system is designed to assess numerous aspects of an individual's adaptive and maladaptive behavior. The BASC-3 is composed of eleven components, including five main measures of behavior that are reviewed here: (1) Teacher Rating Scale (TRS), (2) Parent Rating Scale (PRS), (3) Self-Report of Personality (SRP), (4) Structured Developmental History (SDH), and (5) Student Observation System (SOS). The rating scale authors indicate that the BASC-3 can be used for clinical diagnosis, educational classification, and program evaluation. The authors indicate that it can facilitate treatment planning and describe how it may be used in forensic evaluation and research, as well as in making manifestation determination decisions.

Behaviors Sampled

The Teacher Rating Scale (TRS) is a comprehensive measure of both adaptive and maladaptive behaviors that a child exhibits in school and caregiving settings. Three different forms are available—preschool (2 to 5 years), child (6 to 11 years), and adolescent (12 to 21 years)—with the behavior items tailored for each age range. Teachers, school personnel, or caregivers rate children on a list of behavioral descriptions using a four-point scale of frequency ("never," "sometimes," "often," or "almost always"). Estimated time to complete the TRS is 10 to 15 minutes. Items consist of ratings of behaviors similar to the following: "Has the flu," "Displays fear in new settings," "Speeds through assignments without careful thought," and "Works well with others." It can be completed using either a paper-and-pencil or online format.

The Parent Rating Scale (PRS) is a comprehensive measure of a child's adaptive and problem behavior exhibited in community and home settings. The PRS uses the same four-point rating scale as the TRS. In addition, three forms are provided by age groups, as defined previously. Estimated time to complete this measure is 10 to 20 minutes. Like the TRS, it can be completed using either a paper-and-pencil or online format.

The Self-Report of Personality (SRP) has four different versions depending on age level of the student. The first version, intended for 6- to 7-year-olds, is administered in interview format (SRP-I), during which time the student responds to a variety of yes/no questions and to a set of corresponding follow-up questions. The other three versions are rating scales and correspond to age/schooling level of the student: child (8 to 11 years), adolescent (12 to 21 years), and young adult/college (for 18- to 25-year-old students in a postsecondary educational setting). Each contains short statements that a student is expected to mark as either true or false or to provide a rating ranging from "never" to "almost always." Estimated

administration time is 20 to 30 minutes, and can be completed online or with paper and pencil. Spanish translations of the PRS and SRP are available.

The Structured Developmental History (SDH) is a broad-based developmental history instrument developed to obtain information on the following areas: social, psychological, developmental, educational, and medical history. The SDH may be used either as an interview or as a questionnaire. The organization of the SDH may help in conducting interviews and obtaining important historical information that may be beneficial in the diagnostic process.

The Student Observation System (SOS) is an observation tool developed to facilitate diagnosis and monitoring of intervention programs. Both adaptive and maladaptive behaviors are coded during a 15-minute classroom observation. An electronic version of the SOS is available for use on a laptop computer or personal digital assistant.

The SOS is divided into three parts. The first section, the Behavior Key and Checklist, is a list of 71 specific behaviors organized into 14 categories (four categories of positive behavior and 10 categories of problem behavior). Following the 15-minute observation, the coder rates the child on the 71 items according to a three-point frequency gradation ("never observed," "sometimes observed," and "frequently observed"). The rater can separately indicate whether the behavior is disruptive.

The second part, Time Sampling of Behavior, requires the informant to decide whether a behavior is present during a three-second period following each 30-second interval of the 15-minute observation. Observers place a check mark in separate time columns next to any of the 14 categories of behavior that occur during any one interval. The third section, Teacher's Interaction, is completed following the 15-minute observation. The observer scores the teacher's interactions with the students on three aspects of classroom interactions: (1) teacher position during the observation, (2) teacher techniques to respond to student behavior, and (3) additional observations that are relevant to the assessment process.

Scores

The BASC-3 can be either hand- or computer-scored. Digital administrations are computer-scored, and paper-and-pencil administrations can be either hand-scored or tabulated by a computer. Hand-scoring requires use of a hand-scoring worksheet that is used in addition to the response form to calculate scores. Validity scores are tabulated to evaluate the quality of completed forms and to guard against response patterns that may skew the data profiles positively or negatively. Detailed scoring procedures that use a nine-step procedure for each of the rating scales are described in the administration manual, along with directions for scoring the SRP-I.

When hand-scoring, raw scores for each scale are transferred to a summary table for each individual measure. T-scores (mean $= 50$, standard deviation $= 10$), 90 percent confidence intervals, and percentile ranks are obtained after selecting appropriate norm tables for comparisons. In addition, a high/low column is provided to give the assessor a quick and efficient method for evaluating whether differences among composite scores for the individual are statistically significant.

The TRS produces four composite scores of clinical problems: Externalizing Problems, Internalizing Problems, Adaptive Skills, and School Problems. Clinical scales for the Externalizing Problems composite include Aggression, Hyperactivity, and Conduct Problems. Clinical scales for the Internalizing Problems composite include Anxiety, Depression, and Somatization. Clinical scales for the School Problems composite include Attention and Learning Problems. Positive skills included in the Adaptive Skills composite include Leadership, Social Skills, Study Skills, Adaptability, and Functional Communication subscales. A broad composite score of overall problem behaviors is provided on the Behavioral Symptoms Index, which includes subscales listed previously, in addition to Atypicality and Withdrawal. An optional content scale can also be used, which provides information according to the following subscales: Anger Control, Bullying, Developmental Social Disorders, Emotional Self-Control, Executive Functioning, Negative Emotionality, and Resiliency. The PRS provides the same scoring categories and subscales, with the exception that the School Problems composite scores, composed of subscales for learning problems and study skills, are omitted, and Activities of Daily Living is added. Additional clinical indexes and executive functioning indexes are also available on the TRS and PRS.

The SRP produces four composite scores— Inattention/Hyperactivity, Internalizing Problems, Personal Adjustment, and School Problems—and an overall composite score referred to as an Emotion Symptoms Index (ESI). The composite ESI score includes both negative and adaptive scales. Inattention/ Hyperactivity includes the Attention Problems and Hyperactivity subscales. The Internalizing Problems composite includes Atypicality, Locus of Control, Social Stress, Anxiety, Depression, and Sense of Inadequacy. Personal Adjustment groupings include Relations with Parents, Interpersonal Relations, Self-esteem, and Self-reliance. The School Problems composite includes Attitude to School and Attitude to Teachers. Additional subscales, including Sensation Seeking, Alcohol Abuse, School Maladjustment, and Somatization, are included in the ESI. An optional content scale is also available that includes the following subscales: Anger Control, Ego Strength, Mania, and Test Anxiety. The SRP-I includes simply a total score without subscales.

Three validity scores are provided. To detect either consistently negative bias or consistently positive bias in the responses provided by the student, there is an F index ("fakes bad") and an L index ("fakes good"). The V index incorporates nonsensical items (similar to "Spiderman is a real person"), such that a child who consistently marks these items "true" may be exhibiting poor reading skills, may be uncooperative, or may have poor contact with reality.

The SDH and SOS are not norm-referenced measures and do not provide individual scores of comparison. Rather, these instruments provide additional information about a child, which may be used to describe his or her strengths and weaknesses.

Norms

Standardization and norm development for the general and clinical norms on the TRS, PRS, and SRP took place between April 2013 and November 2014. The number of children who received or provided behavioral ratings across the different measures were, for the TRS, $N = 1700$; for the PRS, $N = 1,800$; and for the SRP, $N = 900$. Efforts were made to ensure that the standardization sample was representative of the U.S. population of children ages 2 to 18 years, including exceptional children. The standardization sample was compared by age group with 2013 census data for geographic region, parent education level, gender, and race/ethnicity. Some of the data collected through Spanish versions of the PRS and SRP are included in the standardization sample. The authors present data to support mostly balanced norms; however, the 2- to 3-year-old sample tends to vary somewhat in representativeness of parental education categories when compared to the population. Information on children with emotional and behavioral disturbances included in the norm sample is provided; however, this information is collapsed across large age ranges (6 years to 11 years; 12 years to 18 years).

Clinical population sample norms consist of data collected on children receiving school or clinical services for emotional, behavioral, or learning problems. Sample sizes were, for the TRS, $N = 611$ for the PRS, $N = 755$; and for the SRP, $N = 519$. The authors state that the clinical sample was not controlled demographically because this subgroup is not a random set of children, but they do provide considerable demographic information on the associated samples.

Reliability

The manual has three chapters devoted to the technical information supporting reliability and validity for each normed scale (TRS, PRS, and SRP), as well as an additional chapter that describes research that has been conducted across the three forms to provide further evidence of validity. For each scale, three types of reliability are provided within the technical manual: internal consistency, test–retest, and interrater agreement.

Internal Consistency Coefficient alpha reliabilities are provided for the TRS and PRS by gender according to the following six age levels: ages 2 to 3, ages 4 to 5, ages 6 to 7, ages 8 to 11, ages 12 to 14, and ages 15 to 18. Reliabilities for the TRS subscales for these age/gender groups range from .73 to .96. Lower reliabilities are evident for subscales associated with the Internalizing Problems scale (including Anxiety, Depression, and Somatization) than for those associated with the Externalizing Problems scale, and for those at lower ages. Composite reliabilities are all greater than .90, except for the Internalizing Problems composite for the 2- to 3-year-old age range. The TRS Behavioral Symptoms Index is .95 or higher for all age/gender groups. Reliabilities for the PRS subscales range from .71 to .96 across these age/gender groups; reliabilities tend to be lower at the preschool-and-below ages. PRS composite reliabilities are .88 and above. The PRS Behavioral Symptoms Index is .95 or higher for all age/gender groups except for the male 2- to 3-year-old sample. SRP coefficient alpha reliabilities are provided by gender according to the following age levels: ages 8 to 11, ages 12 to 14, ages 15 to 18, and ages 18 to 25. Subscale reliabilities for the SRP range from .69 to .95 across age/gender groups. Internal consistency reliabilities for the composite scales exceeded .90 for just about all age/gender groups. The SRP-I Total Score has a coefficient alpha of .71 for boys and .74 for girls. TRS, PRS, and SRP coefficient alphas are also provided for ADHD in the clinical sample by gender, for an "all clinical" group by gender), and for those taking the Spanish version of the SRP and the PRS. However, they are not broken down by age/gender groups in the same way as indicated for the general norm sample.

Test–Retest Reliability TRS test–retest reliability was computed by having teachers rate the same child twice, with seven to 70 days intervening between rating periods; this was done for a total of 249 students. Results are presented by age level (preschool, child, adolescent) for each subscale and composite. Adjusted reliabilities ranged from .77 to .94 for composites and from .65 to .95 for the subscales. PRS test–retest reliability was determined based on parent ratings of 266 students, with an intervening time period of seven to 70 days. Adjusted reliabilities for the PRS composites ranged from .87 to .94; those for the subscales ranged from .80 to .93. Test–retest reliabilities for the SRP were based on ratings provided by 281 students. Adjusted composite reliabilities ranged from .77 to .93; adjusted subscale reliabilities ranged from .59 to .91.

SRP-I test–retest reliability was determined based on 102 students, with a reliability of .72.

Interrater Reliability A total of 267 students were rated according to the TRS by two teachers to determine interrater reliability of the TRS. Adjusted reliabilities ranged from .37 to .83 for the composite scales and from .32 to .84 for the subscales. Parents and caregivers completed the PRS for 356 students, such that two rating scales were completed for each student by different individuals. Adjusted reliabilities for the PRS composite scales ranged from .59 to .87; associated reliabilities for the PRS subscales ranged from .47 to .85. No interrater reliability study was conducted for the SRP, given that the scale is a self-report instrument.

Validity

The authors describe the procedures used to develop and select items for inclusion in the BASC-3. Many of the items included on the BASC-3 are taken directly from the BASC-2, which were correspondingly taken from the original BASC. In the development of the original items, alternate-behavior rating scales and related instruments were examined, and clinicians provided consultation in the selection of items to measure both problem and adaptive behaviors. Teacher and student surveys were also administered to help in the development of original items, which went through several cycles of testing via expert and statistical review for inclusion in the original BASC. Based on additional surveys administered to teachers, students, and parents to develop the BASC-3, several new items were developed and tested; however, the majority of BASC-3 items are similar to those from the original BASC and BASC-2. Correlations between items and their corresponding scales, along with loadings identified via confirmatory factor analyses, were used to determine which items to keep and which to reject. Differential item-functioning analyses were conducted to examine whether items were measuring appropriately across various student demographic groups (for instance, females versus males, African Americans versus white, and Hispanics versus white). A small number of items were eliminated based on bias reviews. Both exploratory and confirmatory factor-analytic procedures were used to examine the appropriateness of the composite scale structure for the TRS, PRS, and SRP. These analyses supported the factor structures evident for the BASC-3.

Criterion-Related Validity The TRS was compared with several related behavior rating scales, including various portions of the Achenbach System of Empirically Based Assessment (ASEBA; Achenbach & Rescorla, 2000), the Conners Teacher Rating Scale–Third Edition (Conners, 2008), and the BASC-2 TRS. Ratings from the preschool form of the TRS were compared to an associated form of the ASEBA among

90 children ages 2 to 5 years. Forty-five children ages 6 to 11 years and 70 adolescents ages 12 to 18 years similarly had corresponding rating forms from the BASC-3 and the ASEBA compared. Correlations for related subscales were primarily in the .60 to .90 range, with the exception of Somatization subscales, which tended to be very weakly correlated across rating scales. Correlations across corresponding composite scales were generally in the .70s; however, Internalizing Problems composite correlations tended to be lower than the other composite scale correlations.

Correlations with the Conners Teacher Rating Scale–Third Edition were based on teacher ratings for 65 children ages 6 to 11 years and 44 adolescents ages 12 to 18 years. Associated subscale correlations ranged from .68 (Executive Functioning scales for children) to .89 (Aggression scales for adolescents). Composite behavior scale correlations (Conners Global Index and the BASC Behavioral Symptoms Index) were .70 at the child level and .80 at the adolescent level. Information is presented on the correlations with ratings from the BASC-2 for the standardization samples. The authors report very high correlations for these two instruments, which is to be expected.

The PRS was also compared to a variety of similar rating scales, including the following: related forms of the ASEBA, the Conners Parent Rating Scale–Third Edition, and the BASC-2 PRS. The associated parent rating forms for the ASEBA and the BASC-3 were completed for 66 young children, 61 school-age children, and 91 adolescents. Correlations for associated subscales ranged from .40 to .67; adjusted correlations for associated composites ranged from .50 to .70. Internalizing Problems composites tend to have weaker correlations than Externalizing Problems composites.

Correlations with the Conners Parent Rating Scale were determined based on 103 children ages 6 to 11 years and 70 adolescents ages 12 to 18 years. The Conners Global Index and the BASC-3 Behavioral Symptoms Index correlated .81 at the child level and .41 at the adolescent level. Corresponding subscale correlations ranged from .64 to .79 at the child level and .37 to .76 at the adolescent level. Finally, correlations with the original BASC PRS were very high, as expected.

Criterion-related validity of the SRP was evidenced through correlations with the associated forms of the ASEBA, the Conners-3 Self-Report Scale (Conners, 2008), the Children's Depression Inventory–Second Edition (Kovacs, 2011), and the Children's Manifest Anxiety Scale–Second Edition (Reynolds & Richmond, 2008). The associated scales of the ASEBA were administered concurrently with the SRP among 60 adolescents. Associated composite correlations were in the .76 to .84 range. All associated subscales of the Conners-3 Self-Report correlated positively (.48 to .77) with the BASC-3 scales among 41 children and 56 adolescents, with an exception being the negative correlations showing up as expected for the relationship between "family problems" and "relations with parents" across these scales. The associated scales of the Children's Depression Inventory–Second Edition and the Children's Manifest Anxiety Scale–Second edition correlated positively with the Depression and Anxiety scales on the BASC-3 SRP. These two instruments also correlated positively with the Total Score from the BASC-3 SRP-I.

Although there appears to be evidence of validity for using the BASC-3 in making diagnostic decisions, no evidence of validity for the purposes of program evaluation and treatment planning is provided.

Summary

The BASC-3 is a comprehensive instrument that may be used to evaluate the behavior and self-perception of children ages 2 to 25 years. The integrated system comprises five separate measures of behavior: (1) Teacher Rating Scale, (2) Parent Rating Scale, (3) Self-Report of Personality, (4) Structured Developmental History Inventory, and (5) Student Observation Scale. Although the multimethod and multidimensional approach should be commended, the TRS, PRS, and SRP are the only scales for which normative data are provided on which any classification statements can be made. Norms for the BASC are more than adequate, with general and clinical norm data provided. Reliability of the composite scales is good, although the internalizing composites tend to have lower reliability coefficients, along with lower reliability coefficients evident for very young children. The BASC-3, like the ASEBA, provides one of the most comprehensive assessment tools on the market today. Good evidence of reliability and validity is presented via analysis of standardization sample data and correlations with additional behavior rating scales; however, validity evidence is not present for all of the possible uses described by the authors.

19-5b VINELAND ADAPTIVE BEHAVIOR SCALES, SECOND EDITION (VABS II)

The Vineland Adaptive Behavior Scales, Second Edition (VABS II; Sparrow, Cicchetti, & Balla, 2005), is an individually administered adaptive behavior scale for use with individuals from birth through 90 years of age. The VABS II is intended for use in diagnostic evaluations, monitoring a student's progress, planning educational and treatment plans, and research. The scale is completed by respondents who are familiar with the target individual's behavior. Respondents can either complete a rating form or participate in a structured third-party interview. The VABS II authors recommend using the interview form for diagnostic decisions and the rating form for program planning and evaluation. A Spanish translation and a teacher form are available, and available computer software can convert raw scores to derived scores and generate score reports.

The Survey Interview Form consists of 413 questions distributed among five domains:

- *Communication.* This domain has two subdomains. Expressive Communication consists of 54 items, such as crying when wet or hungry and saying one's complete home address when asked. Written Communication consists of 25 items, such as recognizing one's own name and writing business letters.

- *Daily Living Skills* (DLS). This domain has three subdomains. Personal DLS has 41 items, such as opening the mouth when food is offered and making appointments for regular medical and dental checkups. Domestic DLS consists of 24 items, such as being careful with hot objects and planning and preparing the main meal of the day. Community DLS consists of 44 items, such as talking to familiar people on the telephone and budgeting for monthly expenses.

- *Socialization.* This domain has three subdomains. Interpersonal Relationships has 38 items, such as looking at a parent's (caregiver's) face and going on single dates. Play and Leisure Time has 31 items, such as responding to playfulness of a parent (or caregiver) and going to places in the evening with friends. Coping Skills consists of 30 items, such as apologizing for unintended mistakes and showing respect for coworkers.

- *Motor Skills.* This domain has two subdomains. Gross Motor consists of 40 items, such as holding the head up for 15 seconds and pedaling a tricycle for 6 feet. Fine Motor consists of 36 items, such as reaching for a toy and using a keyboard to type 10 lines.

- *Maladaptive Behavior.* This domain has three subdomains. Internalizing consists of 11 items, such as being overly dependent and avoiding social interaction. Externalizing consists of 10 items, such as being impulsive and behaving inappropriately. Other Maladaptive Behavior consists of 15 items, such as sucking one's thumb, being truant, and using alcohol or illegal drugs during the school or work day. Critical Items consists of 14 items, such as engaging in inappropriate sexual behavior, causing injury to self,

and being unable to complete a normal school or work day because of psychological symptoms.

The Parent/Caregiver Rating Form consists of 433 questions distributed among six domains.

- *Communication.* This domain has three subdomains. Listening and Understanding consists of 20 items, such as responding to one's spoken name and listening to informational talk for 30 minutes. Talking consists of 54 items, such as crying or fussing when hungry or wet and using possessives in phrases or sentences to describe long-range goals. Reading and Writing consists of 25 items, such as recognizing one's name when printed and editing or correcting one's written work before handing it in.

- *Daily Living.* This domain has three subdomains. Caring for Self has 41 items, such as eating solid foods and keeping track of medications and refilling them as needed. Caring for Home has 24 items, such as cleaning up play or work area at the end of an activity and performing routine maintenance tasks. Living in the Community consists of 44 items, such as being aware and demonstrating appropriate behavior when riding in a car and holding a full-time job for a year.

- *Social Skills and Relationships.* This domain has three subdomains. Relating to Others consists of 38 items, such as showing two or more emotions, recognizing the likes and dislikes of others, and starting conversations about things that interest others. Playing and Using Leisure Time consists of 31 items, such as playing simple interaction games (for example, peekaboo), showing good sportsmanship, and planning fun activities requiring arrangements for two or more things. Adapting has 30 items, such as saying thank you and controlling anger or hurt feelings when not getting one's way.

- *Physical Activity.* This domain has two subdomains. Using Large Muscles has 40 items, such as climbing on and off an adult-sized chair and catching a tennis ball from 10 feet. Using Small Muscles has 36 items, such as picking up small objects, holding a pencil in proper position for writing or drawing, and tying a bow.

- *Maladaptive Behavior Part 1.* This domain contains 36 items divided into three parts: Internalizing, Externalizing, and Other Behaviors. Maladaptive behaviors include both states (for example, being overly anxious or nervous) and behaviors (for example, tantruming and being truant).

- *Problem Behaviors Part 2.* This domain has 14 "critical" items, such as obsessing with objects or activities and being unaware of things happening around oneself.

Scores

Individual items are scored on a four-point scale: 2 = usually, 1 = sometimes or partially, 0 = never, and DK = don't know.[2] To speed administration of the VABS II, basal and ceiling rules are used in all subtests except those assessing maladaptive behavior.

Raw scores are converted to v-scale scores, a standard score with a mean of 10 and a standard deviation of 3. Summed v-scale scores can be converted to normalized standard scores (mean = 100, standard deviation = 15) and stanines for subdomains; subdomain scores can be summed and converted to domain indexes and to an Adaptive Behavior Composite. Raw scores can also be converted to age equivalents.[3] Percentiles are available for domain scores and the Adaptive Behavior Composite. Percentiles are based on the relationship between standard scores and percentiles in normal distributions.

Norms

Regardless of the method of assessment (that is, interview or rating scale), one set of norms is used to interpret VABS II scores. The decision to use a single set of norms was based on the results of a study comparing the results from both interviews and rating scales for 760 individuals. Three of the four analyses performed by the authors support the decision to use a single set of norms. However, the analysis of correlations between the two methods of assessment does not support that conclusion. For individuals 6 years of age or older, less than 10 percent of the correlations between the two assessment methods equal or exceed .90; almost half are less than .80. Clearly, the scores are not interchangeable.

The normative sample consists of 3,695 individuals selected to represent the U.S. population. The manual offers only the most cursory explanation of how these individuals were selected from a larger pool of potential subjects: Selections were made electronically "in a way that matched the demographic variable targets within each age group" (Sparrow et al., 2005, p. 93).

The number of persons within each age group varies considerably from age to age. Samples of children younger than 2 years of age, the sample of children 4 to 4.5 years old, the sample of individuals between 19 and 21 years, and samples of adults older than 31 years of age each contain fewer than 100 individuals. The norms are generally representative in terms of ethnicity (African American, Hispanic, and Caucasian), educational level of the respondents, and geographic region.

Reliability

Split-half estimates of internal consistency for adaptive behavior are provided for 19 age groups: one-year age groups from 0 through 11 years, two-year groups from 12 to 21 years, and four multiyear ranges from 22 through 90 years. The reliability of 18 of the 19 Adaptive Behavior Composites equals or exceeds .90; the exception is the 32- to 51-year-old age group. Domain scores are generally less reliable. In six of the 19 age groups, the reliability of the Communication domain is less than .90; in nine of the 19 age groups, the reliability of the Daily Living Skills domain is less than .90; in seven of the 19 age groups, the reliability of the Socialization domain is less than .90; and in five of the 19 age groups, the reliability of the Motor Skills domain is less than .90. Coefficient alpha is also reported for Part 1 Maladaptive Behavior for five age groups: 3 to 5, 6 to 11, 12 to 18, 19 to 30, and 40 to 90 years. No alpha for the Internalizing composite reaches .90, and only one (for 12- to 18-year-olds) equals .90. Only the alphas for the Maladaptive Behavior index for individuals 6 to 11 years old (.90) and for individuals 12 to 18 years old (.91) are large enough to use in making important individual decisions.

Test–retest estimates of reliability for adaptive behavior are provided for six age ranges.[4] Except for the 14- to 21-year-old age group, the obtained stability[5] of the Adaptive Behavior Composite equals or exceeds .90; stability for the same group is .81. Stabilities of domains are lower; 11 of the 18 reported stability coefficients are less than .90. Stabilities of subdomain scores are generally less than those for the domains; 45 of the 50 subdomain stabilities reported are less than .90. Test–retest estimates are also provided for Part 1 Maladaptive Behavior for five age groups: 3 to 5, 6 to 11, 12 to 18, 19 to 39, and 40 to 71 years. Only the Externalizing and Maladaptive indexes for individuals between 40 and 71 years old reach the .90 level. All estimates of internalizing behavior and all other estimates of Externalizing and Maladaptive Behavior indexes are between .72 and .89.

Interinterviewer reliability was also evaluated for the interview form. Two interviewers interviewed the same respondent at different times. For adaptive behavior, two age ranges were used: 0 to 6 and 7 to 18 years. No VABS II score had an estimated reliability of .90 or higher, and most estimates were in the .40 to .60 range. For Part 1 Maladaptive Behavior, three age ranges were used: 3 to 11, 12 to 18, and 19 to 70 years. Estimated interinterviewer reliabilities ranged from .44 to .83.

---

[2] If the number of items scored DK is greater than two, the subdomain should not be scored.

[3] Age equivalents are defined on the VABS II as representing "the age at which that score is average." It is unclear whether the average refers to the mean, the median, or the mode.

[4] Although it appears that standard scores were used to estimate the stability of domain scores, it is unclear what scores were used to estimate the stability of subdomain scores. We note that the use of raw scores would inflate stability estimates.

[5] The authors report both obtained and adjusted stability estimates. We prefer interpreting the reliability estimates that were actually obtained and therefore do not discuss adjusted estimates.

Interrespondent reliability was evaluated by having two respondents rate the same individual. For adaptive behavior, two age ranges were again used: 0 to 6 and 7 to 18 years. In neither age group did the Adaptive Behavior Composite, nor any domain score, reach an estimated reliability of .90. Most estimates were in the .60 to .80 range. For Part 1 Maladaptive Behavior, three age ranges were again used: 3 to 11, 12 to 18, and 19 to 70 years. Estimated interrater reliabilities ranged from .32 to .81.

Validity

Five types of information about the VABS II validity are included in the manual: test content, response process, test structure, clinical groups, and relationship with other measures. The description of content development lacks sufficient detail to allow a systematic analysis of that process. Similarly, the description of how items were selected is vague. In contrast, factor-analytic studies support the existence of separate domains and subdomains, whereas the examination of test content for sex bias, socioeconomic status bias, and ethnic bias indicates a lack of bias. Also, VABS II raw scores show a consistent developmental pattern, as would be expected with any measure of adaptive behavior.

Previously identified groups of individuals with intellectual disability, autism, attention deficit hyperactivity disorder, emotional disturbance, learning disability, and vision and hearing impairments each earned the types of scores that would be expected for persons with those disabilities. For example, individuals with intellectual disability all showed significant deficits on the Adaptive Behavior Composite and domain scores.

The VABS II correlates well with the previous edition of the scale. Correlations vary by age and domain, ranging from .65 (Communication for children 0 to 2 years of age) to .94 (Socialization for children 3 to 6 years of age). The VABS II correlates moderately with the Adaptive Behavior Assessment System, Second Edition, and the Behavior Assessment System for Children, Second Edition.

Summary

The VABS II is an individually administered, norm-referenced scale for evaluating the adaptive behavior of individuals from birth to 90 years of age. The scale can be administered as a structured interview or as a rating scale, but these two methods appear to yield somewhat different results (that is, they are not so highly correlated that they can be used interchangeably). Despite the differences in the results of the two administrations, one set of norms is used to convert raw scores to derived scores. Thus, although norms appear representative, their use for both methods of administration is problematic.

Reliability is generally inadequate for making important individual decisions about students, especially adolescents. Both interinterviewer and interrespondent reliability are too low to use the VABS II with confidence. The internal consistency of the Adaptive Behavior Composite is generally reliable enough to use in making important educational decisions for students. Domain, subdomain, and maladaptive reliabilities are not. Except for adolescents, the stability of the Adaptive Behavior Composite is adequate; the domain, subdomain, and maladaptive items stabilities are usually too low for making important individual decisions.

General indications of validity are adequate. However, no data are presented to indicate that the VABS II is valid for monitoring a student's progress or planning educational and treatment plans.

Chapter Comprehension Questions

Write your answers to each of the following questions and then compare your responses to the text.

1. Why do we assess social–emotional functioning? Why do we assess adaptive behavior?

2. What are two important considerations in the assessment of social–emotional functioning and adaptive behavior?

3. What are four methods for assessing social–emotional functioning?

4. Describe the steps that you would follow in conducting a functional behavioral assessment.

5. Name and describe one commonly used measure of social–emotional functioning and one commonly used measure of adaptive behavior. What evidence of reliability and validity is available for these measures?

CHAPTER

20

MAKING INSTRUCTIONAL DECISIONS

LEARNING OBJECTIVES

20-1 Articulate a set of questions that should be addressed when individual students struggle in school, along with various sources of information that can inform targeted instructional changes.

20-2 Describe the questions that need to be addressed for students receiving special education services, and how an individualized education program (IEP) is designed to provide the necessary instruction and services.

STANDARDS ADDRESSED IN THIS CHAPTER

 CEC Initial Preparation Standards

Standard 4: Assessment

4.0 Beginning special education professionals use multiple methods of assessment and data-sources in making educational decisions.

5.0 Beginning special educators select, adapt, and use a repertoire of evidence-based instructional strategies to advance learning of individuals with exceptionalities.

 CEC Advanced Preparation Standards

Standard 1: Assessment

1.0 Special education specialists use valid and reliable assessment practices to minimize bias.

 National Association of School Psychologists Domains

1 Data-Based Decision Making and Accountability

3 Interventions and Instructional Support to Develop Academic Skills

4 Interventions and Mental Health Services to Develop Social and Life Skills

Image Source/Jupiter Images

Each regular and special education teacher makes literally hundreds of professional decisions every day. The assessment tools and strategies discussed in earlier chapters can be used to assist in making many of these decisions. In this chapter, we are primarily concerned with the decisions that teachers make about the effectiveness of instruction for students who are at risk, and students who have disabilities, and the procedures that can be used in making these decisions.

Both general and special educators share responsibility for students who are disabled. General educators are largely responsible for identifying general education students who are experiencing sensory, learning, or behavior problems. They are also responsible for addressing those problems with or without the assistance of other educators. Both general and special educators share responsibility for the education of students with disabilities who are instructed in general education classrooms. Special educators are additionally responsible for students whose disabilities are so severe that they cannot be educated in general education settings even with a full complement of related services and classroom adaptations and accommodations.

Throughout the chapter you will follow the stories of three struggling students, who are described in the scenario boxes located throughout the chapter. Two students experience academic difficulties (Jenna and Alex), and one experiences behavioral difficulties (Nick). The needs of one of these students are met with general education services alone; the other two are identified as needing special education supports for which IEPs are developed, implemented, and evaluated. It is important to realize that in many cases, it is nearly impossible to know ahead of time who will require special education services. Interventions must be implemented, and data collected to understand the needs of each student who is struggling.

20-1 Decisions About Students Who Are Not Receiving Special Education Services

Children with moderate or severe disabilities usually are identified before the age of 3 or 4 years and enroll in school as students with disabilities. Approximately 40 percent of all students will experience difficulty during their school career. Most of these problems will be successfully addressed in general education by regular educators. When students' problems are not addressed successfully by regular educators, those students are often referred to multidisciplinary teams to ascertain if they have a disability and are in need of special education (that is, eligible for special education). In this part of the chapter, we deal with those decisions that precede entitlement to special education. If there is a strong RTI or MTSS model in place within a school for the area in which a student struggles (e.g., reading, math, behavior), many of the instructional decision-making processes and procedures described in this section may be highly systematized.

20-1a DOES A STUDENT HAVE A HIDDEN DISABILITY?

The overwhelming majority of children enter school under the presumption that they do not have disabilities. However, educators know that some of these students have less severe disabilities that may not be apparent to parents and that some students will develop disabilities during their education. Because disabilities are likely to be less severe if special services are provided early, federal regulations (§300.125) require states to have policies and procedures to ensure all children with disabilities who need special education and related services are located, evaluated, and identified. This requirement, generally referred to as *child find*, means that local school districts and other agencies must inform parents of available services through strategically placed flyers, notices in local newspapers, and so forth.

Universal screening by school districts may uncover additional disabilities. Some children may have undiagnosed sensory difficulties (i.e., vision or hearing difficulties) that are not apparent to parents, physicians, or teachers. Therefore, schools routinely screen all children to identify undetected hearing and vision problems and to provide services for those who need them. Sensory screening is usually conducted by a school nurse with the intention of finding children who require diagnosis by a health care professional—a hearing specialist such as an audiologist or a vision specialist such as an optometrist or ophthalmologist. The critical point is that screening, by itself, cannot be used to identify a student as disabled. There must be follow-up.

20-1b IS A STUDENT HAVING ACADEMIC DIFFICULTIES?

Some of the students in general education will not make adequate progress toward individual, classroom, or state goals. In academic areas for which universal screening is in place, these students can be identified early on for further assessment to determine if additional academic supports are warranted. In areas in which such screening is not in place at a particular school, teachers must recognize when a student is struggling and not making appropriate progress. The threshold of recognition varies from teacher to teacher and may be a function of several factors: teacher skill and experience, class size, availability of alternative materials and curriculum, ability and behavior of other students in the class, and the teacher's tolerance for atypical progress or behavior. Generally, when a student is performing academically at a rate that is between 20 and 50 percent of the rate of other students, a teacher has reason to be concerned. Certain student behaviors are also red flags for teachers:

- asks questions that indicate that he or she does not understand new material.
- does not know material that was previously taught and presumed to be mastered.
- makes numerous errors and few correct responses.
- does not keep up with peers in general, or in his or her instructional groups.
- is so far behind peers that he or she cannot be maintained in the lowest instructional group in a class—that is, the student becomes instructionally isolated.
- changes from doing good or acceptable work to doing poor or unacceptable work.
- performs adequately in most academic areas but has extreme difficulty in one or more important core skill areas.

The cause of a student's academic difficulty is seldom clear at this point in the decision-making process. There are two broad categories of reasons for student difficulties: ineffective instruction or individual differences. It can be particularly helpful to focus on identifying reasons for a student's academic difficulties that can be addressed through intervention rather than reasons that may be "dead ends" and not facilitate targeted intervention within the school environment. For example, finding out that a student had tubes put in her ears when she was an 11-month-old may have in some way contributed to her difficulties in developing phonemic awareness; however, that doesn't help one to know how to intervene now. On the contrary, knowing that the student's instruction is currently focused on teaching blending at the sound level, when the student hasn't yet mastered blending at the syllable level and needs more instruction and practice with this prerequisite skill, can better inform intervention efforts. You can read Jenna Part 1 and Alex Part 1 for examples of students experiencing academic difficulties.

SCENARIO IN ASSESSMENT

JENNA PART 1 | Jenna is a fourth grader whose teacher is concerned about her writing skills. Assessment information is of two types, qualitative and quantitative. First, her teacher notes that Jenna has been placed in the classroom's highest instructional group for arithmetic, reading, social science, and music, where her performance is among the best in the class. However, her teacher notices that she struggles in her written work. Her writing is messy and often indecipherable. Her written work is like that of the least able students in the class. Second, her teacher assesses Jenna and some of her peers using timed writings with story starters. Jenna's writings contain relatively few words (7 words per minute), whereas peers judged to be progressing satisfactorily write almost twice as many (13) words per minute. Jenna has frequent misspellings (approximately 30 percent of her words), whereas peers progressing satisfactorily misspell approximately 10 percent of their words. Although not quantified, Jenna's writing demonstrates poor graphomotor skills (for example, letter formation, spacing within and between words, and text lines that move up and down as they go across the page), whereas her peers' writing is much neater and more legible.

What is the quantitative discrepancy between Jenna's writing behavior and that of her peers?

SCENARIO IN ASSESSMENT

ALEX PART 1 | Alex is a third grader whose teacher is worried that he is falling behind his peers. Assessment information is of two types, qualitative and quantitative. First, his teacher notices that he has not kept up with the slowest students in the class nor acquired reading skills as quickly as those students. Second, his teacher assesses Alex and some of his peers and finds that the students in the lowest reading group are reading preprimer materials orally at a rate of 50 words per minute or more, with no more than two errors per minute. Alex reads the same materials at a rate of 20 words per minute with four errors per minute. The reading materials used by the lowest group are too difficult for Alex; easier reading materials are needed for effective instruction.

What is the quantitative discrepancy between Alex's reading behavior and that of his peers?

Ineffective Instruction

Some students make progress under almost any instructional conditions. When students with emerging skills and a wealth of information enter a learning situation, they merely need the opportunity to continue learning and developing their skills. These students often learn despite ineffective instructional methodology. However, some students enter a learning situation with poorly developed skills and require effective instruction. Without good instruction, these students are in danger of becoming casualties of the educational system. This situation can occur in at least five ways.

1. *Students' lack of prerequisite knowledge or skill.* Some students may lack the prerequisites for learning specific content. In such cases, the content to be learned may be too difficult because the student must learn the prerequisites and the new content simultaneously. For example, Mr. Santos may give Alex a reader in which he knows only 70 percent of the words. Alex will be forced to learn sight vocabulary that he lacks while trying to comprehend what he is reading. The chances are that he will not comprehend the material because he must read too many unknown words.

2. *Insufficient instructional time.* The school curriculum may be so cluttered with special events and extras that sufficient time cannot be devoted to core content areas. Students who need more extensive and intensive instruction in order to learn may suffer from the discrepancy between the amounts of instruction (or time) they need and the time allocated to teaching them.

3. *Teachers' lack of subject matter knowledge.* The teacher may lack the skills to teach specific subject matter. For example, in some rural areas, it may not be possible to attract physics teachers, so the biology teacher may have to teach the physics course and try to stay one or two lectures ahead of the students.

4. *Teachers' lack of pedagogical knowledge.* A teacher may lack sufficient pedagogical knowledge to teach students who are not independent learners. Although educators have known for a very long time about teaching

methods that promote student learning (see Stevens & Rosenshine, 1981), this information is not as widely known to teachers and supervisors as one would hope. Thus, some educators may not know how to present new material, structure learning opportunities, provide opportunities for guided and independent practice, or give effective feedback. Also, given the number of families in which all adults work, there is less opportunity for parents to provide supplementary instruction at home to overcome ineffective instruction at school.

5. *Teachers' commitment to ineffective methods.* A teacher may be committed to ineffective instructional methods. A considerable amount of effort has gone into the empirical evaluation of various instructional approaches. Yet much of this research fails to find its way into the classroom. For example, a number of school districts have rejected systematic instruction in phonics. However, the empirical research has been clear for a long time that early and systematic phonics instruction leads to better reading (Adams, 1990; Foorman, Francis, Fletcher, Shatschneider, & Mehta, 1998; Pflaum, Walberg, Karegianes, & Rasher, 1980).

Individual Differences

A few students make little progress despite systematic application of sound instructional principles that have been shown to be generally effective. There are at least three reasons for this.

1. Student abilities affect learning. Obviously, instruction that relies heavily on visual or auditory presentation will be less effective with students who have severe visual or auditory impairments.[1] Just as obviously, slow learners require more practice to acquire various skills and knowledge.

2. Some students may find a particular subject inherently interesting and be motivated to learn, whereas other students may find the content to be boring and require additional incentives to learn.

3. Cultural differences can affect academic learning and behavior. For example, reading is an interactive process in which an author's writing is interpreted on the basis of a reader's experience and knowledge. To the extent that students from different cultures have different experiences, their comprehension of some written materials may differ. Thus, students from different cultural groups may have different understandings of, for example, "all men are created equal." Similarly, cultural norms for instructional dialogues between teacher and student may also vary, especially when the teacher and student are of different genders. Boys and girls may be raised differently, with different expectations, in some cultures. Thus, it may be culturally appropriate for women and girls to be reticent in their responses to male teachers. Similarly, teachers may feel ill equipped to teach students from different cultures. For example, teachers may be hesitant to discipline students from another culture, or they may not have culturally relevant examples to illustrate concepts and ideas.

20-1c IS A STUDENT HAVING BEHAVIORAL DIFFICULTIES?

Some students may fail to meet behavioral expectations. As discussed in Chapter 9, any behavior that falls outside the range typically expected—for example, too much or too little compliance, too much or too little assertiveness—can be problematic in and of itself. In other cases, a behavior may be problematic because

---

[1] The instructional importance of other abilities has been asserted; however, there is scant evidence to support such assertions. There is limited and dated support for the notion that intelligence interacts with teaching methods in mathematics. Maynard and Strickland (1969) found that students with high IQs tended to learn mathematics somewhat better when discovery methods were used, although more direct methods were equally effective with students with lower IQs.

it interferes with learning, either of the students themselves or their peers. Finally, behavior that is dangerous to the student or the student's classmates cannot be ignored.

As is true with academic learning problems, why a student is having behavioral difficulty may be unclear. The problem may lie in the teacher's inability to manage classroom behavior, the individual student's distinctive behavior, or a combination of both.

A teacher may lack sufficient knowledge, skill, or willingness to structure and manage a classroom effectively. Many students come to school with well-developed interpersonal and intrapersonal skills, and such students are well behaved and easily directed or coached in almost any setting. Other students enter the classroom with far less developed skills. For these students, a teacher needs much better management skills. In a classroom in which the teacher lacks these skills, the behavior of such students may interfere with their own learning and the learning of their peers. Thus, a teacher must know how to manage classroom behavior and be willing to do so. Classroom management is one of the more emotional topics in education, and often teachers' personal values and beliefs affect their willingness to control their classrooms. Although for some time there has been extensive empirical research supporting the effectiveness of various management techniques (see Alberto & Troutman, 2005; Sulzer-Azaroff & Mayer, 1986), these techniques may be rejected by some teachers on philosophical grounds. Occasionally, teachers may know how to manage behavior and be willing to do so generally but might be unwilling to deal with specific students for some reason. For example, some teachers may be hesitant to discipline minority students. You can read the scenario Nick Part 1 for an example of a student experiencing behavioral difficulties.

Even when teachers use generally effective management strategies, they may be unable to control some students effectively. For example, some students may be difficult to manage because they have never had to control their behavior before, because they reject women as authority figures, or because they seek any kind of attention—positive or negative. Other students may not get enough sleep or nutritious food to be alert and ready to participate and learn in school. Thus, generally effective management strategies may be ill suited to a particular student. Because there is seldom a one-to-one relationship between undesirable behavior and its cause, it is impossible to know *a priori* whether a student's difficulties are the result of different values, lack of learning, or flawed management techniques, without modifying some of the management strategies and observing the effect of the modifications. If a student begins to behave better with the modifications, the reasons for the initial difficulties are not particularly important (and no one should assume that the teacher has found the cause of the difficulty).

SCENARIO IN ASSESSMENT

NICK PART 1 | Nick is a fifth grader who is earning unsatisfactory grades in all instructional areas. His teacher notices that Nick frequently does not understand new material and seldom turns in homework. His teacher also notices that Nick frequently stares into space or watches the tropical fish in the class aquarium at inappropriate times. He occasionally seems startled when his teacher calls on him. Although he usually begins seatwork, he usually fails to complete his assignments, unlike the other students in class. He seldom brings his homework to school even when his mother says that he has done it.

Nick's teacher systematically observes Nick and two of his peers who are progressing satisfactorily for their attention to task. Specifically, once each minute during language arts and arithmetic seatwork, the teacher notes if the boys are on task (that is, looking at their work, writing, or appearing to be reading). After a week of observation, the teacher summarizes the data and finds that Nick is off task in both language arts and arithmetic approximately 60 percent of the time. His peers are off task less than 5 percent of the time. It is not surprising, given Nick's lack of attention, that he is doing poorly in school.

What is the quantitative discrepancy between Nick's behavior and that of his peers?

20-1d CAN WE INCREASE TEACHER COMPETENCE AND SCHOOL CAPACITY?

Many academic and behavioral problems can be remediated or eliminated when classroom teachers intervene quickly and effectively. When teachers recognize that students are experiencing difficulties, they usually provide those students with a little extra help.

However, when teachers are unable to remediate or eliminate the problem, they need help. Help can come in two basic forms: (1) increasing teachers' competence so that they can handle the problem themselves or (2) bring additional resources to bear on the problem. This may take the form of informal consultation with other teachers or building specialists, and it may involve the provision of Title I services or tier 2 and tier 3 services within an MTSS model.

20-1e CAN AN INTERVENTION ASSISTANCE TEAM HELP?

A team can provide more intensive interventions; short-term consultation; continuous support; or information, resources, or training for teachers who request its help. By providing problem-specific support and assistance to teachers, those teachers become more skillful in their work with students. Although the team's makeup and job titles vary by state, team members should be skilled in areas of learning, assessment, behavior management, curriculum modification, and interpersonal communication.

Intervention assistance teams provide tiers of intervention between what was available in a regular classroom teacher and what is provided in special education. Obviously, students do not need, and should not receive, special education when better teaching or behavioral management would allow them to make satisfactory progress in regular education. Thus, when a teacher seeks more intensive help for students, the first form of help offered should be providing additional strategies and materials. The goals of intervention assistance are (1) to remediate, if possible, student difficulties before they become disabling; (2) to provide remediation in the least restrictive environment; and (3) to verify that if the problems cannot be resolved effectively, they are not caused by the school (that is, to establish that the problems are unique to the individual student). Typically, there are four (Bergen & Kratchowill, 1990) or five (Graden, Casey, & Bonstrom, 1983) stages of prereferral activities, depending on how making a formal request for service is counted: (1) making a formal request for services, (2) clarifying the problem, (3) designing the interventions, (4) implementing the interventions, and (5) evaluating the interventions' effects.

Making the Request

Because prereferral intervention is a formalized process, a formal request for services may be required and might be made on a form similar to that shown in Figure 20.1. When a prereferral[2] form is used, it should contain identifying information (such as teacher and student names), the specific problems for which the teacher is seeking consultation, the interventions that have already been attempted in the classroom, the effectiveness of those interventions, and current academic instructional levels. This information allows those responsible for providing consultation to decide whether the problem warrants their further attention.

Typically, at this stage it is expected that data are presented indicating that a student is struggling. When universal screening for academic difficulties and behavioral difficulties is in place, this can provide the information necessary for the request. Universal screening can also help ensure that all students potentially in need of intervention assistance are identified and brought forward for additional assessment.

---

[2] Early on, special educators adopted the term *referral* to designate a request that a student be evaluated for special education eligibility and entitlement. Subsequently, an additional step was inserted into the process. Because referral had already gained widespread acceptance, the new step was called "prereferral," although this step clearly involves referral, too. We use the term *prereferral* to describe assessment and intervention activities that occur prior to formal referral to determine eligibility for special education.

FIGURE 20.1
Request for Prereferral Consultation

Request for Prereferral Consultation

Student _____ Gender _____ Date of Birth _____

Referring Teacher _____ Grade _____ School _____

Specific Educational/Behavioral Problems:

_____

_____

_____

_____

Current Level or Materials in Deficit Areas:

_____

_____

_____

Specific Interventions to Improve Performance in Deficit Areas and
Their Effectiveness:

_____

_____

_____

_____

What Special Services Does the Student Receive
(e.g., Title I Reading, Speech Therapy)?

_____

_____

Most Convenient Days and Times for Consultation:

_____

_____

Clarifying the Problem

In the initial consultation, the team works with the classroom teacher to specify the nature of a problem or the specific areas of difficulty. These difficulties should be stated in terms of observable behavior, not hypothesized causes of the problem. For example, the teacher may specify a problem by saying that "Jenna does not write legibly" or that "Nick does not complete homework assignments as regularly as other students in his class." The focus is on the discrepancy between actual and desired performance. When the discrepancy can be quantified, this can help establish a baseline performance level to allow for monitoring whether an intervention that is designed and implemented is associated with improvement.

The team may seek additional information. For example, the referring teacher may be asked to describe in detail the contexts in which problems occur, the student's curriculum, the way in which the teacher interacts with or responds to the student, the student's interactions with the teacher and with classmates, the student's instructional groupings and seating arrangements, and antecedents and consequences of the student's behaviors. The referring teacher may also be asked to specify the ways in which the student's behavior affects the teacher or other students and the extent to which the behavior is incongruent with the teacher's expectations. When multiple problems are identified, they may be ranked in order of importance for action.

Finally, as part of the consultation, a member of the staff support team may observe the pupil in the classroom to verify the nature and extent of the problem. In relevant school settings, a designated member of the team observes the student, notes the frequency and duration of behaviors of concern, and ascertains the extent to which the student's behavior differs from that of classmates. At this point (or later in the process), the perceptions of the student and the student's parents may also be sought.

Designing the Interventions

Next, the team and the referring teacher design interventions to remediate the most pressing problems. The team may need to coach the referring teacher on how to implement the interventions. Initially, the interventions should be based on empirically validated procedures that are known to be generally effective. In addition, parents, other school personnel, and the student may be involved in the intervention.

A major factor determining whether an intervention will be tried or implemented by teachers is feasibility. Those who conduct assessments and make recommendations about teaching must consider the extent to which the interventions they recommend are doable. (Unfortunately, too often feasibility is determined on the basis of how much of a hassle the intervention planning will be or how much work it will take to implement a given program.) Phillips (1990) identifies eight major considerations in making decisions about feasibility, which we suggest that assessors address.

1. *Degree of disruption.* How much will the intervention the teacher recommends disrupt school procedures or teacher routines?

2. *Side effects.* To what extent are there undesirable side effects for the student (for example, social ostracism), peers, home and family, and faculty?

3. *Support services required.* How readily available are the support services required, and are the costs reasonable?

4. *Prerequisite competencies.* Does the teacher have the necessary knowledge, motivation, and experience to be able to implement the intervention? Does the teacher have a philosophical bias against the recommended intervention?

5. *Control.* Does the teacher have control of the necessary variables to ensure the success of the intervention?

6. *Immediacy of results.* Will the student's behavioral change be quick enough for the teacher to be reinforced for implementing the intervention?

7. *Consequences of nonintervention.* What are the short- and long-term prognoses for the student if the behaviors are left uncorrected?

8. *Potential for transition.* Is it reasonable to expect that the intervention will lead to student self-regulation and generalize to other settings, curriculum areas, or even to other students who are experiencing similar difficulties?

The intervention plan should include a clear delineation of the skills to be developed or the behavior to be changed, the methods to be used to effect the change, the duration of the intervention, the location of the intervention, and the names of the individuals responsible for each aspect of the intervention. Moreover, the criteria for a successful intervention should be clear. As noted in Chapter 10, the use of systematic progress monitoring tools can help with goal setting. At a minimum, the intervention should bring a student's performance to an acceptable or tolerable level. For academic difficulties, this usually means accelerating the rate of acquisition. For an instructional isolate, achievement must improve sufficiently to allow placement in an instructional group. For example, if Bernie currently cannot read the material used in the lowest reading group, the team would need to know the level of the materials used by the lowest instructional group. In addition, the team would need to know the probable level of materials that the group will be using when Bernie's intervention has been completed.

For students with more variable patterns of achievement, intervention is directed toward improving performance in areas of weakness to a level that approximates performance in areas of strength.

Setting the criterion for a behavioral intervention involves much the same process as setting targets for academic problems. When the goal is to change behavior, the teacher should select two or three students who are behaving appropriately. These students should not be the best behaved students but, rather, those in the middle of the range of acceptable behavior. The frequency, duration, latency, or amplitude of their behavior should be used as the criterion. Usually, the behavior of the appropriate students is stable, so the team does not have to predict where they will be at the end of the intervention.

Implicit in this discussion is the idea that the interventions will reach the criterion for success within the time allotted. Thus, the team not only desires progress toward the criterion but also wants that progress to occur at a specific rate—or faster. Finally, it is generally a good idea to maintain a written record of these details. This record might be as informal as a set of notes from the team meeting, or it might be a formal document such as the Prereferral Intervention Plan shown in Figure 20.2.

FIGURE 20.2
Prereferral
Intervention Plan

Prereferral Intervention Plan

Complete one form for each targeted problem.

Student _____ Gender _____ Date of Birth _____

Referring Teacher _____ Grade _____ School _____

Intervention Objectives

Behavior to be changed:

Criterion for success/termination of intervention:

Duration of intervention:

Location of intervention:

Person responsible for implementing the intervention:

Strategies

Instructional methods:

Instructional materials:

Special equipment:

Signatures

_____   _____
(Referring Teacher)   (Date)

_____   _____
(Member, Teacher Assistance Team)   (Date)

Implementing the Interventions

The interventions should then be conducted as planned. To ensure that the intervention is being carried out faithfully, a member of the team may observe the teacher using the planned strategy or special materials, or careful records may be kept and reviewed in order to document that the intervention occurred as planned.

Evaluating the Effects of the Interventions

The effects of the interventions should be evaluated frequently enough to allow fine-tuning of the teaching methods and materials. Frequently, student performance is graphed to make pictures of progress. Effective programs designed to increase desired behavior produce results like those shown in Figure 20.3: The student usually shows an increase in the desired behavior (correct responses) and a decrease in the number of errors (incorrect responses). It is also possible for successful programs to produce only increasingly correct responses or only a decrease in errors. Ineffective programs show no increase in the desired correct responses, no decrease in the unwanted errors, or both. Although frequent data collection is important, it is also important to realize that in some cases, substantial intervention time may be needed before intervention effects will be detected. It is therefore important to balance the desire for immediate effects with an understanding that it may take time for a student to respond to an intervention. The team should determine ahead of time how much intervention time should elapse and how much data should be collected before they evaluate the effectiveness of the intervention.

To assess a student's rate of behavior change, we graph the acceleration of a desired behavior (or the deceleration of an undesired behavior) with an aimline (see Chapter 9), as shown in Figure 20.4. The aimline connects the student's current level of performance with the point that represents both the desired level of behavior and the time at which the behavior is to be attained. When behavior is targeted for increase, we expect the student's progress to be at or above the aimline (as shown in Figure 20.4); when behavior is targeted for decrease, we expect the student's progress to be at or below the aimline (not shown). Thus, a teacher, the intervention assistance team, and the student can look at the graph and make a decision about the adequacy of progress.

When adequate progress is being made, the intervention should obviously be continued until the criterion is reached. When better-than-anticipated progress is being made, the teacher or team can decide to set a more ambitious goal (that is, raise the level of desired performance) without changing the aim date, or they can

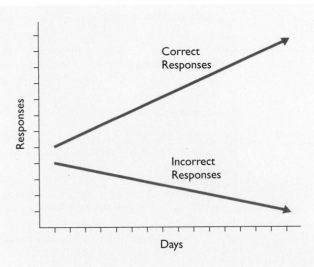

FIGURE 20.3
A Successful Learning Intervention

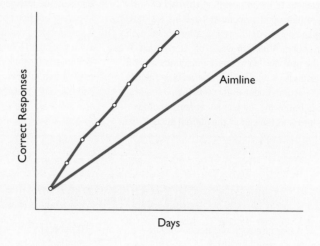

FIGURE 20.4
Student Progress
with an Aimline

set an earlier target for achieving the criterion without changing the level of performance. When inadequate progress is being made, teachers can take several steps to fine-tune the student's program.

20-1f SHOULD THE STUDENT BE REFERRED FOR MULTIDISCIPLINARY EVALUATION?

When several attempted interventions at each level of a multi-tiered system of supports (MTSS) have not led to sufficient success, the student is likely to be referred for psychoeducational evaluation to ascertain eligibility for special education.

Read Part 2 for each of the student scenarios to understand the decisions made within the prereferral process for Jenna, Alex, and Nick.

SCENARIO IN ASSESSMENT

JENNA PART 2 | Jenna's teacher meets individually with Jenna to try and gather more information about her difficulty writing. Jenna tells her teacher that her hand hurts when she writes, and that she broke two fingers over the summer and although they are generally healed, she experiences pain if she is asked to write for long periods of time. Jenna, her teacher, and her parents meet to discuss this and decide to accommodate her difficulty by allowing her to use the computer for writing tasks, with the spell-checking feature turned off when it is important for her to demonstrate her spelling achievement. Jenna's parents also take her to the doctor to review whether her fingers are truly healing appropriately; the doctor indicates that Jenna indeed needs more time to heal and that using the computer for writing tasks for up to six weeks would likely allow

the time needed to heal. Using the computer, Jenna's writing fluency is similar to that of her peers, although her spelling remains discrepant from peers. The teacher consults the building assistance team about the spelling concern, who encourage use of the "Cover, Copy, Compare" intervention strategy for Jenna using her weekly spelling words. Her end-of-week spelling performance is monitored throughout the semester, as is her spelling in context, based on her writing on the computer (with no spell-check features enabled). At the end of the semester, Jenna's fingers are in much better physical shape, and she begins transitioning back to writing with paper without a problem. Also, her spelling shows marked improvement such that the intervention can be discontinued. *How are the various steps of the prereferral process evident in how Jenna's situation was handled?*

SCENARIO IN ASSESSMENT

ALEX PART 2 | Alex's teacher finds an easier reader for him and reads individually with him for 15 minutes each day. During this time, the teacher corrects his errors and shows him how to sound out words. Although Alex can read the lower-level materials more fluently, he is unable to advance to more grade-appropriate reading materials (that is, his fluency and error rate are below an instructional level). The building assistance team

recommends that the teacher assess Alex's knowledge of letter–sound associations. Alex is found to know all long vowel sounds, the short *a* sound, and hard consonant sounds. Consequently, the team develops a program that targets the sounds of the consonants and vowels that he has not yet mastered. One of the district's reading specialists administers the intervention daily and evaluates his progress every other day. Assessment data to

continued on the next page

ascertain the effectiveness of the intervention consists of Alex's progress in learning letter–sound associations and his oral reading fluency. The reading specialist administers a letter–sound probe after each day's instruction. After four weeks of intervention, Alex has learned half of the unknown soft consonant sounds as well as the short *e* and *i* sounds. A retest of his oral reading fluency indicates that he has become fluent in the next-higher reading level. At the rate he is improving, he will fall at least another half-year behind his peers at the end of the current school year.

Because the intervention selected has support in the research literature but has not proved sufficiently effective with Alex, he is referred for multidisciplinary evaluation to ascertain if there are nonschool factors that could be impeding his learning (for example, a disability). Determination of eligibility requires further assessment by specialists, such as school psychologists, who use commercially prepared instruments.

How are the various steps of the prereferral process evident in how Alex's situation was handled?

SCENARIO IN ASSESSMENT

NICK PART 2 | Because Nick has trouble paying attention, his teacher moves him to the front of class and away from the class aquarium. When his attention seems to wander, she taps his desk unobtrusively with her index finger; this usually brings him back to task. The teacher also has a conference with Nick's mother, and they agree that the teacher will send the parents each homework assignment via e-mail. The mother agrees to check Nick's book bag each morning to make sure that his completed homework is taken to school. It is important that the teacher monitors the effect of these interventions on Nick's attention and learning—that is, determine if the intervention improves Nick's behavior. The assessment data used by the teacher consist of the frequency of homework turned in before and after the homework intervention is introduced. The teacher also notes the duration of Nick's redirected attention.

The data on the effectiveness of the interventions on Nick's on-task behavior showed mixed results. Nick's rate of homework completion immediately jumped to 100 percent. Thus, Nick's completion problem was solved by providing the parents with each homework assignment and having them make sure that Nick actually brought his homework to school. Moving Nick to the front of the class, nearer to the teacher, stopped him from staring at the aquarium but had little effect on his staring into space in general. The tapping cue to redirect Nick's attention worked 100 percent of the time, but the duration of his redirected attention was short, averaging approximately 30 seconds. Moreover, the teacher found that increasingly harder tapping was required, and that this intervention had become intrusive and distracting to the students seated next to Nick. Because the teacher's classroom interventions had met with little success and because Nick's lack of attention was still affecting his learning, the teacher decided to consult with the school building's child study team to find out if they had other suggestions.

The team suggested using direct behavior ratings (DBRs) with Nick, and Nick's teacher and parents agreed to try out this strategy. At the end of each class period, Nick's teacher would rate his on-task behavior on a scale of 1 (10% or less of time on task) to 5 (90% or more of time on task), record it on a behavior recording sheet, and briefly discuss the rating with Nick. At the end of the day, the scores would be emailed to Nick's parents. Initially, he was earning an average of three "5"s each day. His parents planned to provide him a special movie night when he earned all 4 or 5 ratings for an entire day. Although he did earn a movie night for a particularly good day in the first week of the intervention, Nick never again met the "all 4 or 5 ratings for an entire day" criteria during the next three weeks that the intervention was in place.

How are the various steps of the prereferral process evident in how Nick's situation was handled?

20-2 Decisions Made in Special Education

Approximately 10 to 12 percent of all students who enter school will experience sufficient difficulty to be identified as having a disability at some time during their school career. Most of these students will receive special education services because they need special instruction. Some students with disabilities (such as students with certain chronic health impairments) will not need special education but will require special related services that must be provided under Section 504 of the Rehabilitation Act of 1973.

After students have been determined to be eligible for special education, special education decisions revolve around design and implementation of their individualized education plans (IEPs). An IEP is a blueprint for instruction and specifies the goals, procedures, and related services for an individual eligible student. Assessment data are important for such planning. Numerous books and hundreds of articles in professional and scientific journals discuss the importance of using assessment data to plan instructional programs for students. The Individuals with Disabilities

Education Act (IDEA) requires a thorough assessment that results in an IEP. Pupils are treated differentially on the basis of their IEPs. Moreover, most educators would agree that it is desirable to individualize programs for students in special and remedial education because the general education programs have not proved beneficial to them.

20-2a WHAT SHOULD BE INCLUDED IN A STUDENT'S IEP?

The Individuals with Disabilities Education Act of 1997 and subsequent revisions to the act and its regulations set forth the requirements for IEPs. Instructionally, an IEP is a road map of a student's one-year trip from point A to point B. This road map is prepared collaboratively by an IEP team composed of the parents and student (when appropriate), at least one general education teacher, at least one of the student's special education teachers, a representative of the school administration, an individual who can interpret the instructional implications of evaluation results, and other individuals who have knowledge or special expertise regarding the student.

Development and implementation of an IEP involves all of the processes involved in **program planning** more generally, which includes defining a problem, goal setting, development and implementation of intervention strategies, and evaluation, but in this case they are targeted to address the needs of an individual child. The IEP begins with a description of the student's current educational levels—the starting point of the metaphoric trip. Next, the IEP specifies measurable, annual, academic, and functional goals (the student's destination). The IEP must include a description of how progress toward meeting annual goals will be measured and when progress reports will be provided to parents. The IEP must identify the special education and related services that are based on peer-reviewed research (to the extent practicable) needed by the student in order to reach the goals (the method of transportation and provisions that make the trip possible). Finally, the IEP requires measurement, evaluation, and reporting of the student's progress toward the annual goals (periodic checks to make sure the student is on the correct road and traveling fast enough).

Current Levels

A student's current level of performance is not specifically defined in the regulations. However, because current levels are the starting points for instruction, a current level must be instructionally relevant and expressed quantitatively. Although legally permissible, scores from standardized achievement are not particularly useful. Even if there is adequate correspondence between test and curricular content, the fact that a student is reading less well than 90 percent of students in the grade is not useful information about where the teacher should begin instruction. If a student is physically aggressive in the third-grade classroom, that alone is too vague to allow a teacher, parents, and the student to tell whether progress toward acceptable behavior is being made. Although not defined in the IDEA, we think a current educational level in an academic area should be the level at which a student is appropriately instructed. For example, knowing that Sam is at an *instructional* reading level in third-grade materials (i.e., reads that material with between 90 and 95 percent accuracy) is directly related to where his instruction should begin.

The current educational level in behavioral areas should also be quantified. Frequency, duration, latency, and amplitude can be quantified, and the results can be compared to those of a peer who is performing satisfactorily on the target skill or behavior. Read Alex Part 3 and Nick Part 3 for information on how each student's current level was determined once they were each found eligible for special education services.

SCENARIO IN ASSESSMENT

ALEX PART 3 | Alex is found eligible for special education services as a student with a learning disability in reading. To ascertain Alex's current level of performance in oral reading, he is again assessed by having him read from the materials actually used in his school. Two passages of 300 to 400 words that are representative of the beginning, middle, and end of each grade-level reading text are selected. Because Alex is already known to be reading only slightly above the preprimer level, he is asked to start reading at that level. He

reads passages of increasing difficulty until he is no longer reading at an instructional level (that is, reading with 85 to 95 percent accuracy).[3] Alex reads beginning first-grade material with 95 percent accuracy, but he reads middle first-grade material with only 87 percent accuracy. Thus, his current instructional level in oral reading is determined to be middle first grade.

Why might it be particularly helpful to use materials currently used at his school for assessing Alex's current level?

SCENARIO IN ASSESSMENT

NICK PART 3 | Nick has also been found eligible for special education services as a student with other health impairments. To ascertain the duration of Nick's attention to task during academic instruction, the school counselor systematically observes Nick and another student who is not reported as having attention problems. Observations occurred between 10:00 and 10:45 for a week during reading and arithmetic instruction. Nick's teacher does not use the tapping

cue during this time period. The counselor sits behind and to Nick's side and uses an audio signal tape with beeps at a fixed interval of 30 seconds. The counselor calculates that Nick is on task 35 percent of the time, whereas his peer is on task 95 percent of the time. Nick's current level of attention to academic tasks is 35 percent.

Why is it helpful to include a peer comparison when defining Nick's current level of attention to academic tasks?

Annual Goals

IEPs must contain a statement of measurable annual goals, which meet each educational need arising from the student's disability and ensure the student's access to the general education curriculum (or appropriate activities, if a preschooler). Thus, for each area of need, parents and schools must agree on what should be a student's level of achievement after one year of instruction.

In part, the selection of long-term goals is based on the aspirations and prognosis for a student's post-school outcomes. Although these are not formally required by federal law until a special education student reaches 16 years of age, the expected or desired post-school outcomes shape the special education a student receives. For students with pervasive and severe cognitive disabilities, the prognosis may be assisted living with supported employment. With this prognosis, educational goals are likely to center on daily living, social skills, and leisure rather than academic areas. For students with moderate disabilities, the prognosis may be independent living and unskilled or semiskilled employment. With this prognosis, educational goals are likely to be basic academics and vocational skills. For students with mild disabilities, the prognosis may be professional or skilled employment. For these students, educational goals can prepare students for college or technical schools.

Annual goals are derived directly from a student's curriculum and a student's current instructional levels. When continued academic integration is the desired educational outcome, a student's goals are mastery of the same content at the same rate as nondisabled peers. Thus, after one year, the student would be expected to be instructional in the same materials as his or her peers. When reintegration is the desired educational outcome, a student's goal depends on where the regular class peers will be in one year. For students pursuing alternative programming, the IEP

---

[3] To calculate accuracy, first identify the total number of words read (either incorrectly or correctly). Then count the number of errors; for example, words a reader did not decode correctly and words a reader hesitates on for a given period of time. Accuracy is (total words read minus errors)/total words read. See Chapter 15 for a discussion of errors in oral reading.

ALEX PART 4 | Alex is finishing third grade, so his annual goal specifies his desired performance near the end of fourth grade. If he were to be completely caught up with his peers, Alex would read independently in his fourth-grade materials. However, the lowest group will use reading materials written at the middle fourth-grade level at the end of fourth grade. Thus, for Alex to be "caught up" with his peers, he would need to complete approximately three years in one year. Both Alex's parents and teachers are concerned that it will be too difficult for him to gain three years in one. Because this much growth in reading could not likely be attained without omitting instruction in other key curricular areas (such as science and written language), the IEP team decides to take two years to try to catch Alex up to his age peers. Thus, his annual goal becomes "At the end of one year of instruction in oral reading Alex will read material written at the end of second-grade difficulty level with 95 percent accuracy."

---

team makes an educated guess about where the student should be after one year of instruction. Increasingly, goal setting can be meaningfully informed by information supplied by publishers of progress monitoring instruments. Read Alex Part 4 for an example of how an annual goal was set for Alex.

Specially Designed Instruction

IDEA defines special education, in part, as specially designed instruction that is provided in classrooms, the home, or other settings (see 34 CFR §300.26). It includes the adaptation of instructional content, methods, or delivery to meet the needs of a student with disabilities.

Currently, the best way to teach handicapped learners appears to rely on generally effective procedures.[4] Teachers can do several things to make it easier for their pupils to learn facts and concepts, skills, or behavior. They can model the desired behavior. They can break down the terminal goal into its component parts and teach each of the steps and their integration. They can teach the objective in a variety of contexts with a variety of materials to facilitate generalization. They can provide time for practice, and they can choose the schedule on which practice is done (in other words, they can offer distributed or massed practice). Several techniques that are under the direct control of the teacher can be employed to instruct any learner effectively. To help pupils recall information that has been taught, teachers may organize the material that a pupil is to learn, provide rehearsal strategies, or employ overlearning or distributed practice. There are also a number of things that teachers can do to elicit responses that have already been acquired: Various reinforcers and punishers have been shown to be effective in the control of behavior.

Assessment personnel can help teachers identify specific areas in which instructional difficulties exist, and they can help teachers plan interventions in light of information gained from assessments. Procedures such as the Functional Assessment of Academic Behavior (Ysseldyke & Christenson, 2002) may be used both to pinpoint the extent to which a student's academic or behavioral problems are a function of factors in the instructional environment, and to identify likely starting points for designing appropriate interventions for individual students. Yet there is no way to know for certain ahead of time how best to teach a specific student.

---

[4] Historically, some psychologists and educators have believed that students learn better when instruction is matched to test-identified abilities. This approach led to the development of instructional procedures that capitalized on areas of strength or avoided weaker abilities. For example, test scores from the first edition of the Developmental Test of Visual Perception (Frostig, Maslow, Lefever, & Whittlesey, 1964), the Illinois Test of Psycholinguistic Abilities (Kirk, McCarthy, & Kirk, 1968), and the Purdue Perceptual–Motor Survey (Roach & Kephart, 1966) were at one time believed to be instructionally useful. In part because test-identified abilities were frequently unreliable and in part because special instructional methods did not result in better learning, this approach to instruction gradually lost favor, although some educators today still cling to a belief in it. In the 1980s, attempts to match instruction to specific student attributes resurfaced. However, hypothetical cognitive structures and learning processes replaced the hypothetical abilities of the 1960s (for example, see Resnick, 1987). This approach is interesting but has yet to be validated.

There should be good evidence that the instructional interventions are generally effective with students who are at the same age and grade as the student being assessed. Under the requirements of No Child Left Behind, school personnel are expected to be putting in place evidence-based treatments. Information about the extent to which treatments are generally effective is found by reviewing the research evidence in support of the treatments. The What Works Clearinghouse (WWC) can provide direction as to what treatments might be particularly effective. At the WWC website, you can look up interventions for middle-school math and find a topic report listing the kinds of interventions that WWC reviewed on middle-school math. Information on the extent to which there is good empirical support for a particular intervention can be obtained from that website. Read Alex Part 5 and Nick Part 4 for information on the specially designed instruction each student was determined to need.

However, always remember that efficacy is local. We recommend that teachers first rely on general principles that are known and demonstrated to be effective in facilitating learning for students with disabilities. However, even when we find studies that demonstrate that a particular application of a learning principle worked for a research sample, we still cannot be certain that it will work for specific students in a specific classroom. The odds are that it will, but we cannot be sure. Consequently, we must treat our translation of these principles, known to be effective, as tentative. In a real sense, we hypothesize that our treatment will work, but we need to verify that it has worked. The point was made years ago by Deno and Mirkin (1977) and remains true today:

> At the present time we are unable to prescribe specific and effective changes in instruction for individual pupils with certainty. Therefore, changes in instructional programs that are arranged for an individual child can be treated only as hypotheses that must be empirically tested before a decision can be made about whether they are effective for that child. (p. 11)

Teaching is often experimental in nature. When there is no database to guide our selection of specific tasks or materials, decisions must be tentative. The decision maker makes some good guesses about what will work and then implements an instructional program. We do not know whether a decision is correct until we gather data on the extent to which the instructional program actually works. We never know if the program will work until we have tried it and monitored whether a student makes subsequent gains in performance.

SCENARIO IN ASSESSMENT

ALEX PART 5 | The assessment data also indicated that Alex needs specially designed instruction in reading. Although he has now mastered all of the sounds of consonants and vowels, he is slow and inaccurate in reading grade-appropriate materials. To improve Alex's accuracy, the IEP team decides that Alex should be taught the basic sight vocabulary needed to read the words in his language arts text as well as content-area curricula. To improve Alex's reading fluency, the IEP team decides to use the strategy of rereading.

How is the instruction uniquely tied to Alex's difficulties?

SCENARIO IN ASSESSMENT

NICK PART 4 | The assessment data pointed to areas where Nick needs specially designed instruction. Although Nick's physician prescribes Ritalin, Nick also needs systematic behavioral intervention to minimize the effects of his attention deficit hyperactivity disorder on school functioning.[5] The team develops a program of specially designed instruction that includes systematic reinforcement for appropriate attention and systematic instruction in self-monitoring his attention. The district behavior management specialist will be responsible for training Nick to self-monitor accurately, and Nick's teacher will be trained to implement the plan developed by the district specialist.

How is the instruction uniquely tied to Nick's difficulties?

---

[5] Assume that Nick's psychoeducational evaluation does not reveal other intellectual, physical, or cognitive problems beyond his lack of attention.

Tests do provide some very limited information about how to teach. Tests of intelligence, for example, yield information that gives a teacher some hints about teaching. Generally, the lower a pupil's intelligence, the more practice the student will require for mastery. A score of 55 on the Wechsler Intelligence Scale for Children–IV does not tell the teacher whether a pupil needs 25 percent or 250 percent more practice, but it does alert the teacher to the likelihood that the pupil will need more practice than the average student will need. Other tenuous hints can be derived, but we believe that it is better to rely on direct observation of how a student learns in order to make adjustments in the learning program. Thus, to determine whether we had provided enough practice, we would observe Sally's recall of information rather than looking at Sally's IQ. We cannot do anything about Sally's IQ, but we can do something about the amount of practice she gets.

Related Services

In addition to special instruction, eligible students are entitled to developmental, corrective, and other supportive services, if such services are needed in order for the students to benefit from special education; federal legislation uses the term *related services*, which has been widely adopted by states and school districts. Related services include both those not typically provided by schools and those typically provided (34 CFR §300.24).

Schools must provide to students with disabilities a variety of services to which nondisabled students are seldom entitled. Services described in 34 CFR §300.24 include, but are not limited to, the following types:

1. *Audiology.* Allowable services include evaluation of hearing, habilitation (for example, programs in auditory training, speech reading, and speech conservation), amplification (including the fitting of hearing aids), and hearing conservation programs.

2. *Psychological services.* Psychological services allowed include testing, observation, and consultation.

3. *Physical and occupational therapy.* These therapies can be used to (a) improve, develop, or restore functional impairments caused by illness, injury, or deprivation; and (b) improve independent functioning. These therapies may also be used with preschool populations to prevent impairment or further loss of function.

4. *Recreation.* Allowable programs include those located in the schools and community agencies that provide general recreation programs, therapeutic recreation, and assessment of leisure functioning.

5. *Counseling services.* Either group or individual counseling may be provided for students and their parents. Student counseling includes rehabilitation counseling that focuses on career development, employment preparation, achievement of independence, and integration in the workplace and community; it also includes psychological counseling. Parental counseling includes therapies addressing problems in the student's living situation (that is, home, school, and community) that affect the student's schooling. Parental counseling also includes assistance to help parents understand their child's special needs, as well as information about child development.

6. *Medical services.* Diagnostic and evaluative services required to determine medically related disabilities are allowed.

The schools must also provide to students with disabilities the services they typically provide to all children. Thus, schools must provide to students with disabilities, as needed, speech and language services, school health and school social work services, and transportation. School-provided transportation includes whatever is needed to get students to and from school, as well as between schools or among school buildings, including any required special equipment such as ramps. Although these related services are mandatory for students who need them to profit from their special education, there is nothing to prohibit a school from offering other services. Thus, schools may offer additional services free of charge to eligible students.

Although federal law is very clear about the need to provide related services to students with disabilities, how that need should be established remains unclear. In practice, most schools or parents seek an evaluation by a specialist. The specialist notes a problem and expresses a belief that a specific therapy could be successful and benefit the student. Thus, need is frequently based on professional opinion. We must also note that related services can be very costly, and some school districts try to avoid providing them. We have heard of districts maintaining that they do not offer a particular service, even though federal law mandates that service should be provided to students who need it.

Least Restrictive Environment

Federal law expresses a clear preference for educating students with disabilities as close as possible to their home and with their nondisabled peers to the maximum extent appropriate. Education in "special classes, separate schooling or other removal of children with disabilities from the regular educational environment occurs only if the nature or severity of the disability is such that education in regular classes with the use of supplementary aids and services cannot be achieved satisfactorily" (34 CFR §300.550). The IEP must include an explanation of the extent to which a student will not participate with students in regular programming.

Placement Options

A hierarchy of placements ranges from the least restrictive (educating students with disabilities in a general education classroom with a general education teacher who receives consultative services from a special education teacher) to the most restrictive (educating students with disabilities in segregated residential facilities that provide services only to students with disabilities). Between these two extremes are at least five other options:

1. *Instructional support from a special education teacher in the general education classroom.* In this arrangement, eligible students remain in the general education classroom in their neighborhood schools, and the special education teacher comes to the student to provide whatever specialized instruction is necessary.

2. *Instructional support from a special education teacher in a resource room.* In this arrangement, eligible students remain in a general education classroom for most of the day. When they need specialized instruction, they go to a special education resource room to receive services from a special education teacher. Because districts may not have enough students with disabilities in each school to warrant establishing a resource room program at each school, a student may be assigned to a general education classroom that is not in the student's neighborhood school.

3. *Part-time instruction in a special education classroom.* In this arrangement, eligible students have some classes or subject matter taught by the special education teacher and the rest taught in the general education classroom. As is the case with resource rooms, the general education classroom may not be in the student's neighborhood school.

4. *Full-time instruction in a special education classroom, with limited integration.* In this arrangement, eligible students receive all academic instruction from a special education teacher in a special classroom. Eligible students may be integrated with nondisabled peers for special events or activities (such as lunch, recess, and assemblies) and nonacademic classes (such as art and music).

5. *Full-time instruction in a special education classroom, without integration.* In this arrangement, eligible students have no interaction with their nondisabled peers, and their classrooms may be in a special day school that serves only students with disabilities.

Factors Affecting the Placement Choice The selection of a particular option should be based on the intensity of education needed by the eligible student: The less intensive the intervention needed by the student, the less restrictive the environment; the more intensive the intervention needed by the student, the more restrictive the environment. The procedure for determining the intensity of an intervention is less than scientific. Frequently, there is some correspondence between the severity of disability and the intensity of service needed, but that correspondence is not perfect. Therefore, special education teachers and parents should consider the frequency and duration of the needed interventions. The more frequent an intervention is (for instance, every morning versus one morning per week) and the longer its duration (for example, 30 minutes versus 15 minutes per morning), the more likely it is that the intervention will be provided in more, rather than less, restrictive settings. When frequent and long interventions are needed, the student will have less opportunity to participate with nondisabled peers, no matter what the student's placement. Obviously, if students require round-the-clock intervention, they cannot get what they need from a resource room program.

In addition to the nature of needed interventions, parents and teachers may also reasonably consider the following factors when deciding on the type of placement:

1. *Disruption.* Bringing a special education teacher into or pulling a student out of a general education classroom may be disruptive. For example, some students with disabilities cannot handle transitions: They get lost between classrooms, or they forget to go to their resource rooms. When eligible students have a lot of difficulty changing schedules or making transitions between events, less restrictive options may not be appropriate.

2. *Well-being of nondisabled individuals.* Eligible students will seldom be integrated when they present a clear danger to the welfare of nondisabled peers or teachers. For example, assaultive and disruptive students are likely to be placed in more restrictive environments.

3. *Well-being of the student who has a disability.* Many students with disabilities require some degree of protection—in some cases, from nondisabled peers who may tease or physically abuse a student who is different; in other cases, from other students with disabilities. For example, the parents of a seriously withdrawn student may decide not to place their child in a classroom for students with emotional disabilities when those students are assaultive.

4. *Labeling.* Many parents, especially those of students with milder handicaps, reject disability labels. They desire special education services, but they want these services without having their child labeled. Such parents often prefer consultative or itinerant services for their children.

5. *Inclusion.* Some parents are willing to forgo the instructional benefits of special education for the potential social benefits of having their children educated exclusively with nondisabled peers. For such parents, full inclusion is the only option.

There are also pragmatic considerations in selecting the educational setting. One very real consideration is that a school district may not be able, for economic reasons, to provide a full range of options. In such districts, parents are offered a choice among existing options unless they are willing to go through a due process hearing or a court trial. A second consideration is instructional efficiency. When several students require the same intervention, the special education teacher can often form an instructional group. Thus, it will probably cost less to provide the special education services. A third consideration is the specific teachers. Some teachers are better than others, and parents may well opt for a more restrictive setting because the teacher there is highly regarded.

SCENARIO IN ASSESSMENT

ALEX PART 6 | Because the reading interventions designed by the IEP team are not being used in Alex's classroom and because Alex requires more instruction in reading than can be provided in his regular classroom, the IEP team recommends placement in a special education resource room for one hour per day. The team decides that Alex will go to the resource room when the rest of his class is being instructed in social studies and art.

How does this reflect the Least Restrictive Environment for Alex?

SCENARIO IN ASSESSMENT

NICK PART 5 | Although Nick's behavior is not disruptive or detrimental to the learning of his peers, the interventions that his regular class teacher has used are distracting to the other students. However, the team believes that the specially designed instruction that has been approved by the team (systematic reinforcement for appropriate attention and self-monitoring) will be much less intrusive. Therefore, the team believes that the impact of the intervention on Nick's peers will not be a consideration.

The classroom teacher, once properly trained by the behavior management specialist, can administer the positive reinforcement correctly. Although the behavior management specialist will remove Nick from class when teaching him to self-monitor, the special education teacher and the behavior specialist will evaluate Nick's use of the self-monitoring system in his classroom. Thus, Nick's needs can readily be met in the regular classroom; he will not be instructed in a special education setting.

How does this reflect the Least Restrictive Environment for Nick?

Parents and special education teachers must realize that selecting a placement option is an imprecise endeavor. Thus, although federal regulations are clear in their preference for less restrictive placements, the criteria that guide the selection of one option over another are unclear. Choices among placement options should be regarded as best guesses. Read Alex Part 6 and Nick Part 5 for information on how placement was determined for each of these students.

Is the Instructional Program Effective?

IEPs are supposed to result in effective instruction for students with disabilities. IDEA requires that each student's IEP contain a statement detailing the way in which progress toward annual goals will be measured and how parents will be informed of their child's progress (34 CFR §300.347). In addition, IDEA requires IEP teams to review each student's IEP "periodically, but not less than annually, to determine whether the annual goals for the child are being achieved" (34 CFR §300.343). If adequate progress is not being made, IEP teams are required to revise the IEPs of students who are not making expected progress toward their annual goals. An exception to this rule is that, according to IDEA 2004, some states may put in place comprehensive multiyear IEPs for those students who have milder disabilities and for whom parents agree a multiyear IEP is sufficient. Read Alex Part 7 and Nick Part 6 for information on the effectiveness of these students' programs.

Throughout this book, we have discussed procedures that are useful in collecting information about students' achievement and behavior. We have also discussed how that information can be systematized using graphs and charts. We have offered guidelines about how to reach decisions about a student's progress. All of these discussions are relevant to the decision about the effectiveness of each component of a student's instructional program. Judgments about the simultaneous effectiveness of all of the components of an instructional program are geometrically more complicated. Based on our personal experience, a program is effective if the most important goals are achieved. What makes a goal important varies by student. For an aggressive, acting-out student, self-control may be more important than quadratic equations. For a bright student with a learning disability, learning to read may be more important than improvement in spelling.

SCENARIO IN ASSESSMENT

ALEX PART 7 | Alex's special education teacher provides quarterly updates on how Alex is progressing in reading, with each indicating progress that suggests he is on his way toward the two-year goal of catching up to his peers. After one year of receiving special education services, the IEP team meets to more formally review his progress. The special education teacher presents information showing that Alex has surpassed his annual goal, and is well on his way to meeting the two-year goal of performing at the level of his peers. The team decides that if Alex continues at his current rate of progress, they will meet at the end of the school year, prior to when his next annual IEP meeting would be necessary, and plan for a transition out of receiving special education services so that he will start fifth grade without **any** additional support necessary.

Why is it essential to follow up on how Alex's program is working?

SCENARIO IN ASSESSMENT

NICK PART 6 | The special educator that has been assigned to Nick's case regularly checks in with the regular classroom teacher about the self-monitoring system. In addition, a video camera is permanently set up in the classroom to record Nick's behavior; the special educator selects random sections of tape to observe and code Nick's on-task behavior in comparison to peers each week. A video is used instead of a human observer to avoid Nick's identification of when his behavior is being observed, which may bias the results. Although Nick's on-task behavior improves during independent seatwork activities for approximately three months, it fluctuates considerably thereafter, with only slight improvement noted in comparsion to peers at the IEP meeting held at the end of the first year of services being provided. The IEP team decides that some additional information should be collected to identify specific self-monitoring and reinforcement techniques that may be more effective for Nick at the current time.

Why is it essential to follow up on how Nick's program is working?

Chapter Comprehension Questions

Write your answers to each of the following questions and then compare your responses to the text.

1. List and explain three instructional decisions that are made prior to a student being found eligible for special education.

2. List and explain three instructional decisions that are made after a student has been found eligible for special education.

MAKING SPECIAL EDUCATION ELIGIBILITY DECISIONS

LEARNING OBJECTIVES

21-1 Identify and define the disabilities recognized by the Individuals with Disabilities Education Improvement Act.

21-2 Articulate the difference between an RTI approach and a discrepancy approach to identifying a learning disability.

21-3 Explain how the need for special education is established.

21-4 Describe the composition and responsibilities of multidisciplinary teams.

21-5 Describe the process for determining eligibility (including procedural safeguards, the requirements for valid assessment, and the team process).

21-6 Discuss common problems in determining eligibility.

STANDARDS ADDRESSED IN THIS CHAPTER

CEC CEC Initial Preparation Standards

Standard 1: Learner Development and Individual Learning Differences

1.0 Beginning special education professionals understand how exceptionalities may interact with development and learning and use this knowledge to provide meaningful and challenging learning experiences for individuals with exceptionalities.

Standard 4: Assessment

4.0 Beginning special education professionals use multiple methods of assessment and data-sources in making educational decisions.

Standard 6: Professional Learning and Ethical Practice

6.0 Beginning Special Education Professionals use foundational knowledge of the field and their Professional Ethical Principles and Practice Standards to inform special education practice, to engage in lifelong learning, and to advance the profession.

CEC ADVANCED CEC Advanced Preparation Standards

Standard 1: Assessment

1.0 Special education specialists use valid and reliable assessment practices to minimize bias.

Standard 6: Professional and Ethical Practice
6.0 Special Education Specialists use foundational knowledge of the field and Professional Ethical Principles and Practice Standards to inform special education practice, engage in lifelong learning, advance the profession, and perform leadership responsibilities to promote the success of professional colleagues and individual with exceptionalities.

 National Association of School Psychologists Domains
1 Data-Based Decision Making and Accountability
8 Diversity in Development and Learning
10 Legal, Ethical and Professional Practice

The issue of eligibility for special education hinges on two questions: (1) Does the student have a disability? and (2) If so, does the student need special education? Both questions must be answered in the affirmative to be eligible for special education and related services. Students who have disabilities but do not need special education are not eligible (although they may well be eligible for services under Section 504 of the Rehabilitation Act of 1973). Students who do not have disabilities but need (or would benefit from) special education services are not eligible. Once students have been determined to be eligible for special education, they are automatically entitled to procedural safeguards, special services, and special fiscal arrangements, as discussed in Chapter 3. Furthermore, some students with disabilities who receive special education services experience altered outcome expectations as explained in Chapter 22.

21-1 Official Student Disabilities

Students are classified as having a disability under several laws; three are particularly important: The Americans with Disabilities Act (Public Law 101-336), Section 504 of the Rehabilitation Act of 1973, and the Individuals with Disabilities Education Improvement Act (IDEA; 34 CFR §300.7). In the schools and other educational settings, the following disabilities, enumerated in regulations of the IDEA (34 CFR §300.7), are the most frequently used: autism, intellectual disability, specific learning disability, emotional disturbance, traumatic brain injury, speech or language impairment, visual impairment, deafness and hearing impairment, orthopedic impairments, other health impairments, deaf–blindness, multiple disabilities, and developmental delay.[1] Identification under §300.306 of the IDEA requires that

- a team (i.e., group of qualified professionals and the parent(s) of the student) determines whether the student has a disability and the student's educational needs.

- a student cannot be determined to have a disability if that determination is based on (1) a lack of appropriate instruction in reading or math, (2) limited English proficiency, or (3) if the child does not otherwise meet the eligibility criteria.

- the team draws upon information from a variety of sources, which may include aptitude and achievement tests, input from parents, and teachers, as well as information about the child's physical condition, social or cultural background, and adaptive behavior; and

- the team ensures that information obtained from all of these sources is documented and carefully considered.

§300.8 of the IDEA regulations defines the specific disabilities. These definitions are described below.

21-1a AUTISM

Students with autism are those who demonstrate "developmental disability significantly affecting verbal and nonverbal communication and social interaction, generally evident before age 3 that adversely affects a child's educational performance. Other

---

[1] The definitions in IDEA (excluding the need for special education) are generally used for entitlements under Section 504.

characteristics often associated with autism are engagement in repetitive activities and stereotyped movements, resistance to environmental change or change in daily routines, and unusual responses to sensory experiences. Autism does not apply if a child's educational performance is adversely affected primarily because the child has an emotional disturbance."

Students with suspected autism are usually evaluated by speech and language specialists and psychologists after it has been determined that some aspects of their educational performance fall outside the normal range and various attempts to remedy the educational problems have failed. Frequently, a speech and language specialist would look for impaired verbal and nonverbal communication. A proportion of autistic children are mute, an impairment that is readily apparent. Autism in students with speech and language might manifest itself as overly concrete thinking. For example, a student with autism might react to a statement such as "don't cry over spilled milk" quite literally ("I didn't spill any milk"). Another manifestation would be a lack of conversational reciprocity (usually long, often tedious, orations about a favorite subject) and failure to recognize a listener's waning interest. Moreover, this impaired social communication would be a consistent feature of the student's behavior rather than an occasional overexuberance. A psychologist looks for behavior that defines the condition: repetitive activities (for example, self-stimulating behavior, spinning objects, aligning objects, and smelling objects), stereotyped movements (for example, hand flapping, rocking, and head banging), resistance to change (for example, eating only certain foods or tantruming when activities are ended). A psychologist may also administer a behavior rating scale (for example, the Gilliam Autism Rating Scale) as an aid to diagnosis. Finally, a psychologist rules out emotional disturbance as a cause of the student's behavior and impairments.

21-1b INTELLECTUAL DISABILITY

Students with intellectual disabilities are those who demonstrate "significantly subaverage general intellectual functioning, existing concurrently with deficits in adaptive behavior and manifested during the developmental period that adversely affects a child's educational performance." Students who are eventually labeled "intellectually disabled" are often referred because of generalized slowness: They lag behind their age-mates in most areas of academic achievement, social and emotional development, language ability, and, perhaps, physical development.

Usually, a psychologist will administer a test of intelligence that is appropriate in terms of the student's age, acculturation, and physical and sensory capabilities. In most states, students must have an IQ that is two standard deviations or more below the mean (usually 70 or less) on a validly administered test. However, a test of intelligence is not enough. The pupil must also demonstrate impairments in adaptive behavior. There is no federal requirement that a test or rating scale be used to assess adaptive behavior psychometrically. In practice, most school psychologists will administer an adaptive behavior scale (for example, the Vineland Adaptive Behavior Scales, Second Edition). However, when it is not possible to do so appropriately, a psychologist will interview parents or guardians and make a clinical judgment about a student's adaptive behavior.

21-1c EMOTIONAL DISTURBANCE

Emotional disturbance means "a condition exhibiting one or more of the following characteristics over a long period of time and to a marked degree that adversely affects a child's educational performance: (1) an inability to learn that cannot be explained by intellectual, sensory, or health factors; (2) an inability to build or maintain satisfactory interpersonal relationships with peers and teachers; (3) inappropriate types of behavior or feelings under normal circumstances; (4) a general pervasive mood of unhappiness or depression; (5) a tendency to develop physical symptoms or fears associated with personal or school problems" [§300.8(c)(4)]. This disability includes schizophrenia but excludes "children who are socially maladjusted, unless it is determined that they have an emotional disturbance." Students who are eventually labeled as having an emotional disorder are often referred for problems in interpersonal relations (for example, fighting or extreme noncompliance) or unusual behavior (for example, unexplained episodes of crying or extreme mood swings).

Students suspected of being emotionally disturbed are evaluated by a psychologist after it has been determined that some of their school performance falls outside the normal range and various attempts to remedy the school problems have failed. Requirements for establishing a pupil's eligibility as a student with emotional disturbance vary among the states. However, multidisciplinary teams usually obtain a developmental and health history from a student's parent or guardian to rule out sensory and health factors as causes of a student's inability to learn. A parent or guardian is usually interviewed about the student's relationships with peers, feelings (for example, anger, alienation, depression, and fears), and physical symptoms (for example, headaches or nausea). Parents or guardians may also be asked to complete a behavior rating scale such as Achenbach's Child Behavior Checklist to obtain normative data on the student's behavior. Teachers will likely be interviewed about their relationships with the student and the student's relationships with peers at school. They may also be asked to complete a rating scale (for example, the Behavior Assessment System for Children–3) to obtain normative data for in-school behavior. In addition, a psychologist might be asked to administer a norm-referenced achievement battery to verify that the student's educational performance has been negatively affected by the student's emotional problems.

21-1d TRAUMATIC BRAIN INJURY

Students with traumatic brain injury have "an acquired injury to the brain caused by an external physical force, resulting in total or partial functional disability or psychosocial impairment, or both, that adversely affects a child's educational performance. Traumatic brain injury applies to open or closed head injuries resulting in impairments in one or more areas, such as cognition; language; memory; attention; reasoning; abstract thinking; judgment; problem solving; sensory, perceptual, and motor abilities; psychosocial behavior; physical functions; information processing; and speech. Traumatic brain injury does not apply to brain injuries that are congenital or degenerative, or to brain injuries induced by birth trauma" [§300.8(c)(12)]. Students with traumatic brain injury have normal development until they sustain a severe head injury. As a result of this injury, they have a disability. Most head injuries are the result of an accident (frequently an automobile accident), but they may also occur as a result of physical abuse or intentional harm (for example, being shot).

Traumatic brain injury will be diagnosed by a physician, who is usually a specialist (a neurologist). The need of a student with brain injury for special education will be based first on a determination that the student's school performance falls outside the normal range and various attempts to remedy the educational problems have failed. Next, a school psychologist will likely administer a standardized achievement battery to verify that the student's achievement has been adversely affected.

21-1e SPEECH OR LANGUAGE IMPAIRMENT

A student with a speech or language impairment has "a communication disorder, such as stuttering, impaired articulation, a language impairment, or a voice impairment, that adversely affects a child's educational performance." [§300.8(c)(11)] Many children will experience some developmental problems in their speech and language. For example, children frequently have difficulty with the *r* sound and say "wabbit" instead of "rabbit." Similarly, many children will use incorrect grammar, especially with internal plurals; for example, children may say, "My dog has four foots." Such difficulties are so common as to be considered a part of normal speech development. However, when such speech and language errors continue to occur beyond the age when most children have developed correct speech or language, there is cause for concern. Not all students who require intervention for speech or language problems are eligible for special education. A student may be eligible for speech or language services but not have a problem that adversely affects his or her school performance. Thus, for a student to be eligible for special education as a person with a speech or language impairment, that student must not only have a speech/language impairment but also need special education.

The identification of students with speech and language impairments proceeds along two separate paths. School personnel identify the educational disability in the same way that other educational disabilities are identified. When extra help from a teacher does not solve the problem, the student is referred to a child study team for prereferral intervention. If those interventions fail to remedy the achievement problem, the student is referred for multidisciplinary evaluation. A psychologist or educational diagnostician will likely administer a norm-referenced achievement test to verify the achievement problem. At the same time, speech and language specialists will use a variety of assessment procedures (norm-referenced tests, systematic observation, and criterion-referenced tests) to identify the speech and language disability. If the student has both need and disability, the student will be eligible for special education and related services.

21-1f VISUAL IMPAIRMENT

A student with a visual impairment has "an impairment in vision that, even with correction, adversely affects a child's educational performance. The term includes both partial sight and blindness" [§300.8(c)(13)]. Students with severe visual impairments are usually identified by an ophthalmologist before they enter school. Many students who are partially sighted will be identified by routine vision screening that usually takes place in the primary grades; others will be identified when visual demands increase (for example, when the font size is reduced from the larger print used in beginning reading materials). Severe visual impairment is always presumed to adversely affect their educational development, and students with this disability are presumed to require special education services and curricular adaptations (for example, mobility training, instruction in Braille, and talking books). A vision specialist usually assesses functional vision through systematic observation of a student's responses to various types of paper, print sizes, lighting conditions, and so forth.

21-1g DEAFNESS AND HEARING IMPAIRMENT

Deafness is an impairment in hearing "that is so severe that the child is impaired in processing linguistic information through hearing, with or without amplification, and that adversely affects a child's educational performance" [§300.8(c)(3)]. A student with a hearing impairment has a permanent or fluctuating impairment "that adversely affects educational performance but that is not included under the definition of deafness."

Most students classified as deaf will be identified as such before they enter school. Deafness will be presumed to adversely affect a student's educational development, and students with this disability are presumed to require special education services and curricular adaptations. However, even severe hearing impairments may be difficult to identify in the first years of life, and students with milder hearing impairments may not be identified until school age. Referrals for undiagnosed hearing-impaired students may indicate expressive and receptive language problems, variable hearing performance, problems in attending to aural tasks, and perhaps problems in peer relationships. Diagnosis of hearing impairment is usually made by audiologists, who identify the auditory disability, in conjunction with school personnel, who identify the educational disability.

21-1h ORTHOPEDIC IMPAIRMENTS

An orthopedic impairment is "a severe impairment that adversely affects a child's educational performance. The term includes impairments caused by a congenital anomaly, impairments caused by disease (such as poliomyelitis and bone tuberculosis), and impairments from other causes (such as cerebral palsy, amputations, and fractures or burns that cause contractures)" [§300.8(c)(8)].

Physical disabilities are generally identified prior to entering school. However, accidents and disease may impair a student who previously did not have a disability. Medical diagnosis establishes the presence of the condition. The severity of the condition may be established in part by medical opinion and in part by systematic observation of the particular student. For many students with physical disabilities, the ability to learn is not affected. These students may not require special education classes, but they will need accommodations and modifications to the curriculum—and perhaps the school building—that can be managed through a 504 plan. For example, a student may require a personal care aide to help with positioning, braces, and catheterization; educational technology (for example, a voice-activated computer); and transportation to and from school that can accommodate a wheelchair. When such adaptations and accommodations are insufficient to allow adequate school progress, special education is indicated. The specially designed instruction can include alternate assignments, alternative curricula, alternative testing procedures, and special instruction.

21-1i OTHER HEALTH IMPAIRMENTS

Other health impairment "means having limited strength, vitality, or alertness, including a heightened alertness to environmental stimuli, that results in limited alertness with respect to the educational environment that (i) is due to chronic or acute health problems such as asthma, attention deficit hyperactivity disorder, diabetes, epilepsy, a heart condition, hemophilia, lead poisoning, leukemia, nephritis, rheumatic fever, sickle cell anemia, and Tourette syndrome; and (ii) adversely affects a child's educational performance" [§300.8(c)(9)]. Diagnosis of health impairments is usually made by physicians, who identify the health problems, and school personnel, who identify the educational disability. For some students with other health impairments, the ability to learn is not affected. These students may not require special education classes, but they will need accommodations and modifications to the curriculum that can be managed through a 504 plan. For example, a student may require nursing services to administer medication, times and places to rest during the day, and provisions for instruction in the home. When health impairments adversely affect educational progress even with the curricular adaptations and modifications, special education is indicated.

21-1j DEAF–BLINDNESS

Deaf–blindness means "concomitant hearing and visual impairments, the combination of which causes such severe communication and other developmental and educational needs that they cannot be accommodated in special education programs solely for children with deafness or children with blindness" [§300.8(c)(2)].

Only a small number of students are deaf–blind, and their assessment is typically complex. Tests that compensate for loss of vision usually rely on auditory processes; tests that compensate for loss of hearing usually rely on visual processes. Psychological and educational evaluations of students who are both deaf and blind rely on observations as well as interviews of and ratings by individuals sufficiently familiar with the student to provide useful information.

21-1k MULTIPLE DISABILITIES

Multiple disabilities "means concomitant impairments (such as intellectual disability–blindness or intellectual disability–orthopedic impairment), the combination of which causes such severe educational needs that they cannot be accommodated in special education programs solely for one of the impairments. The term does not include deaf–blindness" [§300.8(c)(7)].

21-1l DEVELOPMENTAL DELAY

Although not mandated by IDEA, states may use the category of developmental delay for children between the ages of 3 and 9 years who are "(1) experiencing developmental delays, as defined by the state and as measured by appropriate diagnostic instruments and procedures, in one or more of the following areas: physical development, cognitive development, communication development, social or emotional development, or adaptive development; and (2) . . . need special education and related services" [§300.8(b)]. Diagnosis of developmental delay is usually made by school personnel, who identify the educational disability, and other professionals (such as speech and language specialists, physicians, and psychologists), who identify the delays in the developmental domains.

21-1m SPECIFIC LEARNING DISABILITY (SLD)

A student with a learning disability is one who "does not achieve adequately for the child's age or . . . meet state-approved grade-level standards in one or more of the following areas, when provided with learning experiences and instruction appropriate for the child's age or state-approved grade-level standards: oral expression, listening comprehension, written expression, basic reading skills, reading fluency skills, reading comprehension, mathematics calculation, [or] mathematics problem solving" (34 CFR 300.306). In addition, the student's failure to meet age or state standards cannot be due to: a visual, hearing, or motor disability; intellectual disability; emotional disturbance; cultural factors; environmental or economic disadvantage; or limited English proficiency.

To ensure that the lack of progress is not due to lack of appropriate instruction in reading or math, there must be data to demonstrate that the student received appropriate instruction in regular education settings from qualified personnel, that there were repeated assessments of student progress at reasonable intervals, and that reports of progress were provided to the child's parents (Office of Special Education, undated).

Therefore, initial evaluations to ascertain if a student has a learning disability have four components: rule outs, verification of achievement difficulties, documentation of unsuccessful attempts to remediate the achievement difficulties, and evidence of a disorder in a basic psychological process.

1. Rule-Outs

Those responsible for making the actual determination that a student has a learning disability must rule out various potential causes for poor achievement. IDEA specifically forbids that the student's achievement problem be the result of a visual, hearing, or motor impairment; intellectual disability; emotional disturbance; or environmental, cultural, or economic disadvantage. The presence of various medical conditions may also be used to rule out a diagnosis of learning disability.

2. Verification of Achievement Difficulties

It is expected that all students will meet age or grade and local and state achievement standards; however, students with high IQs may fail to meet expectations when their performance is only average. Only students who fail to meet expected grade-level academic standards can be considered for a diagnosis of learning disability. Academic difficulties must be verified by direct observation during classroom instruction. In addition, school personnel will likely perform a records review to ascertain the intensity and duration of the problems. Previous grades, teacher comments, and the results of standardized achievement tests (e.g., from tier 1 screening) are useful. Finally, individual achievement tests may be administered by a school psychologist or learning specialist. The student may also be evaluated by a speech and language specialist who would look for manifestations of a disorder in producing or understanding language. This specialist may conduct an assessment of a student's spontaneous or elicited language during an interview or play situation; the specialist may administer a formal test.[2] There are no quantitative guidelines in the regulations to indicate a language disorder, but a child with a disability in language would be expected to earn scores that are substantially below average.

3. Unsuccessful Attempts at Remediation

Before it can be assumed that a student is unable to learn, educators must demonstrate that the student has had the opportunity to learn—that the teacher has used effective and appropriate teaching methods and curricula. Normally, this means that there have been numerous, documented attempts to remediate the educational problems using at least tier 2 (targeted) interventions and that these attempts have failed.

4. Evidence of a Learning Disability

Either of two approaches can be used to infer that a student has a disorder in a basic psychological process—response to intervention or severe discrepancy. Either approach can be used singly or in combination with the other approach.

Response to intervention[3] In this approach, students receive targeted (i.e., tier 2) interventions. The academic problem is verified, alternative hypotheses about how to remediate the problem are generated, interventions are developed and applied, and assessment data are collected and interpreted. If a student fails to progress or if a student makes insufficient progress after several interventions, there is *prima facie* evidence of a learning disability. However, the rule-outs still apply. The student cannot have an intellectual disability, and so forth. Thus, in this approach, students are thought to have a learning disability when they fail to progress sufficiently after receiving intensive instruction using methods of proven effectiveness (that is, validated by objective, empirical research). We describe more about this approach later in this chapter.

Severe discrepancy In this approach, students must exhibit a pattern of strengths and weaknesses in performance, achievement, or both, relative to age, state-approved grade-level standards or intellectual development [34 CFR 300.309(a)(2)]. In this approach, a psychologist typically looks for large differences between a student's measured intelligence (i.e., scores on a test of intelligence)[4] and measured achievement (i.e., scores on a standardized test of achievement). A significant difference between ability and achievement is taken as a demonstration of a learning disability when the previously enumerated criteria are present. Schools may also consider a pattern of strengths and weaknesses within a student's achievement (for example, large differences between reading and mathematics scores on a standardized achievement test). An analysis of strengths and weaknesses is based on differences between scores. Such differences are almost always less reliable than the individual scores on which the differences are based. For example, the difference between reading and math achievement will almost always be less reliable than either the reading or the math achievement score. Difference scores are discussed in more detail in the chapter on technical requirements.

Finally, psychologists may also administer tests to assess specific psychological processes such as visual perception (for example, the Developmental Test of Visual Perception). Low scores may also be used to support a diagnosis of a learning disability.

21-2 The RTI Approach to Identifying Students with Learning Disabilities

When Congress passed the IDEA in 2004 and the U.S. Department of Education published regulations that accompany that law in 2006, school personnel were given permission to use Response to Intervention (RTI) as an alternative approach to the identification

---

[2] For example, the Test of Written Language—Fourth Edition or the Oral and Written Language Scales—Second Edition.

[3] Chapter 12 [Multi-Tiered System of Supports (MTSS) and Response to Intervention (RTI)] deals extensively with response to intervention.

[4] Scores from an intelligence test can also be used to rule out an intellectual disability.

of students with learning disabilities. Within RTI models, evidence-based instructional interventions are implemented over relatively long periods of time (usually for more than 8 to 12 weeks) and decisions are made about whether or not a student's rate of progress is indicative of responding or not responding to the intervention. Students are considered eligible for special education services if, after exposure to multiple evidence-based interventions, they continue to show inadequate progress. In addition to showing slow growth, it must be demonstrated that the students are performing at a low level relative to their age-level or grade-level peers and that they do not show evidence of another disability condition (e.g., intellectual disability, emotional disturbance, or visual impairment). There is no federal guidance on how low is low and how slow is slow (Kovaleski, VanDerHeyden & Shapiro, 2013).

Within RTI models there may be reliance on norm-referenced tests, though this typically is not the case. Rather, the assessment procedures used are those more closely aligned with the process of teaching and learning: curriculum-based measurement and computer-adaptive measures linked closely to classroom instruction.

The use of the RTI approach requires systematic monitoring of student progress over time, careful analysis of Rate of Improvement (ROI), and analysis of the gap between observed and expected performance over time. We discussed procedures for calculating ROI and for conducting a gap analysis in Chapter 12. Kovaleski, VanDerHeyden & Shapiro (2013) also provide a very nice description of the steps involved in calculating ROI and in conducting a gap analysis (pp. 61–77 of their book *The RTI Approach to Evaluating Learning Disabilities)*. They identify the following steps involved in using an RTI approach to making decisions about eligibility for special education under the label Specific Learning Disability (SLD).

Step 1 Determine Present Level of Performance (PLOP). Universal screening measures typically are used to determine the student's current level of academic performance in specific content areas. Scores are expressed as standard scores for computer-adaptive tests or in units like "words correct per minute" for curriculum-based measures. The evaluation team must demonstrate that the student "does not achieve adequately for the child's age or to meet State-approved grade-level standards" across a variety of sources of data.

Step 2 Document Deficiency in the Student's Rate of Improvement (ROI). To accomplish this the team must do the following:

1. Calculate the Typical Rate of Improvement (ROI) for students at that level. Publishers of some curriculum-based measures (like DIBELS Next or Easy CBM) and some computer-adaptive measures (like STAR Reading and STAR Math) maintain large databases of student performance that are used to develop norms on typical rates of growth for students at specific age and grade levels. These norms can be used to identify typical ROIs for students who are at the level of performance for the student assessed.

2. Set the Instructional Goal or Target. School personnel must decide what outcomes they want students to achieve. If they want students to maintain performance as is, then they set moderate goals. If they want to close the gap between low-level performance and average (age-level or grade-level) performance, they may set ambitious goals. Some publishers provide tools for goal setting. For example, Renaissance Learning, publisher of the STAR Enterprise measures (STAR Reading, STAR Math, and STAR Early Literacy) provides users with a Goal Setting Tool that can be used to set moderate, ambitious, or custom goals for student improvement.

3. Monitor Student Progress. Computer-adaptive tests or curriculum-based measures are administered periodically to ascertain the student's rate of improvement (ROI).

4. Conduct a Progress Monitoring ROI and Benchmark ROI Gap Analysis. In Chapter 12, we described the procedures one uses to calculate ROI. One

can also look up the relationship between the student's actual ROI and the expected ROI on publishers' websites (for example the websites for DIBELS Next and Renaissance Learning, publisher of the STAR Enterprise measures).

The team can use this information to compute the magnitude of the gap between actual and expected performance, and also to reach an indication of the number of weeks it would take the student to reach his/her goal. Armed with this information, the team can make a decision about whether there is a reasonable gap or significant gap between the student's ROI and the ROI for typical students. If the gap is considered significant or unreasonable, then the student may be declared eligible for special education services. The difficulty here is that there are no rules, guidelines, or published empirical criteria on how large the gap must be to consider the student eligible for special education services. As a "rule of thumb," educators operate under the general consideration that "a student would be sufficiently deficient in level of performance and sufficiently deficient in ROI such that the student would not attain acceptable performance in a reasonable amount of time" (Kovaleski et al. 2013, p. 150). And, of course, the two terms debated are "acceptable performance" and "reasonable amount of time." Generally speaking, educators do not expect students with SLD to catch up to grade level within a period of one year. Rather, they show that given the student's rate of improvement the student will not catch up to the target that is set for him or her in a selected period of time (e.g. one year, two years).

Hauerwas, Brown and Scott (2013) conducted an analysis of state-level special education regulations, SLD criteria, and guidance documents used to define responsiveness to intervention. They found that some states (Colorado, Connecticut, Pennsylvania, and Oregon, as of 2013) provide best practice descriptions about RTI data collection and processes for determining LD eligibility. However, they report that there is no national consensus on how to use RTI data as part of SLD identification.

Step 3 Rule Out Other Disability Conditions. The evaluation team always must rule out other disability conditions like visual, hearing, or physical disability; emotional disturbance; intellectual disability; or autism. The team must also rule out that the student's poor academic performance and growth is due to cultural factors, environmental disadvantage, or limited English proficiency.

Step 4 Document That Low Level Performance Is Not the Result of Lack of Instruction. The evaluation team must rule out the possibility that lack of instruction is the cause of the student's academic problems. In so doing, the team must demonstrate that the student has been receiving evidence-based core instruction in the general education curriculum and that the instruction has been delivered by a qualified teacher. In addition to this, the team should document the interventions that were implemented at tiers 2 and 3 and the extent to which the student responded to those interventions.

Step 5 Determine That the Student Needs Special Education. Recall that we have pointed out on several occasions in this textbook that eligibility for special education requires that students (1) meet the criteria for a federally identified disability condition, and (2) need special education services to be successful in school. The previous steps above were focused on demonstrating that the student meets the criteria for the condition of specific learning disability. Determining the "need" for special education services is difficult. Typically such decisions are made based on the intensity of interventions the student needs. Kovaleski et al. (2013) cite Barnett, Daly, Jones, and Lenz (2004) as providing the best definition of intervention intensity as "qualities of time, effort, or resources that make intervention support in typical environments difficult as intensity increases, establishing a clear role for specialized services" (p. 68). Special education services are those that require enhancements to management and planning, modifications to typical classroom routines, and types of intervention episodes, materials, and change agents not available in the general education classroom.

Kovaleski et al. (2013) further describe distinctions of special education when they state that:

> *Enhancements to management and planning in special education would include more frequent monitoring of student responding, more frequent progress monitoring, more explicit teacher prompting, and more frequent and detailed communication with parents and professionals. Modifications to typical classroom routines would involve different instructional tasks and assessments, increased assistance to students during instruction, additional practice opportunities, enhanced feedback to students about performance, and unique contingencies for meeting expectations....providing special education presupposes that teaching staff are specially trained to deliver highly explicit instruction and make instructional adjustments based on students' responding (p. 159).*

21-3 Establishing Educational Need for Special Education

In addition to having one (or more) of the disabilities specified in IDEA, a student must experience a lack of academic success. This criterion is either implicit or explicit in the IDEA definitions of disabilities. Autism, hearing impairment, intellectual disability, and six other disabling conditions are defined as "adversely affecting a child's educational performance." Multiple disabilities (such as deaf–blindness) cause "severe educational needs." Learning disability results in an "imperfect ability" to learn basic academic skills.

Most students without obvious sensory or motor disabilities are presumed to not have disabilities when they enter school. However, during their education, it becomes clear to school personnel that these students have significant problems. They fail to behave appropriately or to meet state-approved grade-level standards in one or more core achievement areas when provided with appropriate instruction. In short, they demonstrate marked discrepancies from mainstream expectations or from the achievement and behavior of typical peers. The magnitude of the discrepancy necessary to consider a student for special education is not codified, and there are many opinions on this issue.

The presence of a discrepancy alone does not establish need, because there are many causes for a discrepancy. Thus, school personnel usually should engage in a number of remedial and compensatory activities designed to reduce or eliminate the discrepancy. As discussed in Chapter 20, interventions initially may be designed and implemented by the classroom teacher. If the teacher's interventions are unsuccessful, the student is referred to a teacher assistance team that designs and may help implement further interventions. Need for special educational services for students is established when one of two conditions is met. As we noted in the discussion of RTI approaches in section 2, if a student fails to respond to validated and carefully implemented interventions, need for special education is indicated. Second, as we also noted, successful interventions may be too intensive or extensive for use in regular education. That is, the interventions needed to remediate the student's academic or behavioral deficits are so intrusive, labor-intensive, or specialized, that a general education classroom teacher cannot implement them without the assistance of a special education teacher or without seriously detracting from the education of other students in the classroom.

Some students have such obvious sensory or motor problems that they are identified as having a disability before they enter school. From accumulated research and professional experience, educators know that students with certain disabilities (for example, blindness, deafness, and severe intellectual disabilities) will not succeed in school without special education. Thus, educators (and relevant regulations) assume that the presence of a severe disability is sufficient to demonstrate the need for special educational services.

21-4 The Multidisciplinary Team

The determination that a student has a disability is made by a team of professionals called a multidisciplinary team (MDT). The team conducts a multidisciplinary evaluation (MDE) by collecting, assembling, and evaluating information to determine whether a student meets the conditions that define a disability as set forth in IDEA and state law.[5]

21-4a COMPOSITION OF THE MDT

IDEA requires that the team have members with the same qualifications as those who must serve on IEP teams and "other qualified professionals, as appropriate" (34 CFR §300.533). Thus, the team must include the student's parents (and the student, if appropriate), a general education teacher, a special education teacher, a representative of the school administration, and an individual who can interpret the instructional implications of evaluation results. If the student is suspected of having a learning disability, the team must also include "at least one person qualified to conduct individual diagnostic examinations of children, such as a school psychologist, speech–language pathologist, or remedial reading teacher" (34 CFR §300.540). In practice, school psychologists are usually members of most MDTs.

21-4b RESPONSIBILITIES OF THE MDT

The team is responsible for gathering information and determining if a student has a disability. In theory, the decision-making process is straightforward. Members of the MDT assess the student to determine whether he or she meets the criteria for a specific disability. Thus, the MDT must collect, at a minimum, information required by the definition of the disability being considered. Moreover, federal regulations (34 CFR §300.532) require that a student be "assessed in all areas related to the suspected disability, including, if appropriate, health, vision, hearing, social and emotional status, general intelligence, academic performance, communicative status, and motor abilities."

In reaching its decision about eligibility, the team must do two things. First, it must draw upon information from a variety of sources, including aptitude and achievement tests, parent input, information about response to evidence-based intervention attempts, and teacher recommendations, as well as information about the child's physical condition, social or cultural background, and adaptive behavior. Second, it must ensure that information obtained from all of these sources is documented and carefully considered [§300.306(c)].

21-5 The Process of Determining Eligibility

IDEA has established rules that MDTs must follow in determining whether a student is eligible for special education and related services. The first set of rules provides a variety of procedural safeguards intended to provide students and their parents the right to full and meaningful participation in the evaluation process.

21-5a PROCEDURAL SAFEGUARDS

As specified in §300.504, school districts and other public agencies must give parents a copy of the procedural safeguards relating to

- independent educational evaluation;
- prior written notice in the native language of the parent or other mode of communication used by the parent;

[5] Note that there are two types of teams required under special education law, and the same people may or may not serve on the two types of teams: evaluation teams (usually called MDTs) and individualized educational program (IEP) teams (always called IEP teams). In addition, many schools have teacher teams (often called child study teams) that deal with student difficulties before a student is referred for evaluation.

- parental consent;
- access to educational records;
- opportunity to present complaints to initiate due process hearings;
- the child's placement during pendency of due process proceedings;
- procedures for students who are subject to placement in an interim alternative educational setting;
- requirements for unilateral placement by parents of children in private schools at public expense;
- mediation;
- due process hearings, including requirements for disclosure of evaluation results and recommendations;
- state-level appeals (if applicable in that state);
- civil actions;
- attorneys' fees; and
- the state's complaint procedures.

21-5b VALID ASSESSMENTS

The next set of rules requires valid and meaningful assessments. School districts and other public agencies must ensure that students are assessed in all areas related to their suspected disabilities, including, if appropriate, health, vision, hearing, social and emotional status, general intelligence, academic performance, communicative status, and motor abilities. The evaluations must be sufficiently comprehensive to identify all of the child's special education and related services needs, whether or not they are commonly linked to the disability category in which the child has been classified.

School districts and other public agencies must ensure that the assessment includes a variety of techniques, including information provided by the parent, that provide relevant information about

- whether the student is a student with a disability; and
- the student's involvement and progress in the general curriculum.

The assessments must be conducted by trained and knowledgeable personnel in accordance with any instructions provided by the producer of the tests (and if an assessment is not conducted under standard conditions, a description of the extent to which it varied from standard conditions must be provided in the evaluation report). As specified in §300.304(c), only tests or other evaluation materials may be used that are

- "not racially or culturally discriminatory";
- "administered in the child's native language or other mode of communication" (in addition, for students with limited English proficiency, districts and other public agencies must select and use materials and procedures that measure the extent to which the child has a disability and needs special education, rather than measuring the child's English language skills);
- "selected and administered so as best to ensure that if a test is administered to a child with impaired sensory, manual, or speaking skills, the test results accurately reflect the child's aptitude or achievement level or whatever other factors the test purports to measure, rather than reflecting the child's impaired sensory, manual, or speaking skills (unless those skills are the factors that the test purports to measure)";
- technically sound instruments that may assess the relative contribution of cognitive and behavioral factors, in addition to physical or developmental factors;

- "tailored to assess specific areas of educational need and not merely designed to provide a single general intelligence quotient"; and
- relevant in assisting persons determining the educational needs of the student.

21-5c TEAM PROCESS

The final set of requirements sets forth the process for determining a student's eligibility for special education and related services. The MDT team follows four basic steps as specified in §§300.305/306:

1. The team reviews existing evaluation data to determine if additional data are needed.
2. The team gathers any additional data that are needed, ensuring that information obtained from all sources is documented.
3. The team determines if the student is a child with a disability by considering information from a variety of sources—that is, aptitude and achievement tests, parent input, teacher recommendations (including response to intervention), physical condition, social or cultural background, and adaptive behavior—and comparing this information to the state and federal standards for the suspected disability.
4. The team prepares an evaluation report.

In practice, deciding whether a student is entitled to special education can be complex. Sometimes, the problems a student is experiencing can suggest a specific disability to team members. For example, having problems maintaining attention, being fidgety, and being disorganized may suggest the possibility of attention deficit hyperactivity disorder; persistent and major difficulties learning letter–sound correspondences despite many interventions may suggest a learning disability. MDTs should do more than simply confirm a disability. MDTs should adopt a point of view that is, in part, disconfirmatory—a point of view that seeks to disprove the working hypothesis.

Many behaviors are indicative of specific disabilities. For example, stereotypic hand flapping is associated with autism, intellectual disabilities, and some emotional disturbances. Assessors must be open to alternative explanations for the behavior and, when appropriate, collect information that will allow them to reject a working hypothesis of a particular disability. For example, if Tom was referred for inconsistent performance in expressive language, even though his other skills— especially math and science—were average, an MDT might suspect that he could have a learning disability. What would it take to reject the hypothesis that he has such a disability? He would not be considered to have a learning disability if it could be shown that his problem was caused by a sensorineural hearing loss, if his problem arose because his primary language is a dialect of English, if he suffered from recurrent bouts of otitis media (middle ear infections), and so forth. Therefore, the MDT would have to consider other possible causes of his behavior. Moreover, when there is evidence that something other than the hypothesized disability is the cause of the educational problems, the MDT would need to collect additional data that would allow it to evaluate these other explanations. Thus, MDT evaluations frequently (and correctly) go beyond the information required by the entitlement criteria to rule out other possible disabling conditions or to arrive at a different diagnosis.

Finally, in attempting to establish that a student should be classified with a disability, we often must choose among competing procedures and tests. However, as indicated in Chapter 18, individual tests of intelligence are not interchangeable. They differ significantly in the behaviors they sample and in the adequacy of their norms and reliability, and slightly in their standard deviations. A dull, but normal, person may earn an IQ of less than 70 on one or two tests of intelligence but earn scores greater than 70 on two others. Thus, if we had to assess such a student, we could be caught in a dilemma of conflicting information.

CHERYL | Cheryl was the youngest of Jack and Melinda Stenman's three children. She was a full-term baby but weighed only 1,800 grams (4 pounds) at birth. In addition to her significantly low birth weight, she was placed in the neonatal intensive care unit for almost three days and was not released from the hospital until she was 10 days old. Although her health during her early years was unremarkable, she was slower to attain the common developmental milestones (walking and talking) than her older siblings.

Cheryl entered a local daycare center at age 3. Little information is available from the center except the general perception that Cheryl did not engage in developmentally appropriate play activities. The daycare center provided no interventions because its philosophy was that each child developed uniquely and there was plenty of time for intervention.

Mrs. Stenman enrolled Cheryl in the local school district's half-day kindergarten the September when she was 5 years and 8 months of age. Cheryl was slow compared to her peers. She still had toileting accidents, had immature speech and language, and did not engage in cooperative play, preferring parallel play instead. At the end of the first semester of kindergarten, she had not learned her colors, whereas her peers had mastered the primary and additive colors (that is, red, green, blue, yellow, violet, blue-green, brown, black, and white); she recognized only five capital letters (A, B C, D, and S), whereas most of her peers recognized and could write all upper- and lowercase letters. Her teacher characterized her as following other children around but not joining in the various activities.

The teacher implemented several interventions known to be effective in teaching students to recognize and write letters, and several social interaction interventions. She monitored Cheryl's progress and showed that there was a consistent lack of progress. In January, Cheryl's teacher sought the help of the school's student assistance team. The teacher met with Mr. and Mrs. Stenman and agreed that some interventions would be appropriate to try to accelerate her academic progress. They agreed that Cheryl should attend all-day kindergarten and developed a program in which the teachers or the reading specialist provided individual direct instruction in the recognition and writing of all letters of the alphabet; they also developed a behavior plan that reinforced Cheryl for successive approximations of cooperative play.

From the very beginning, the classroom interventions did not work. Cheryl seemed to learn one or two new letters but forget them the next day. The team met with the teacher several times and modified the instructional program, but Cheryl's progress was slow. She did not master more than two letters per week, and that rate of progress was simply not enough to get her ready for first grade. The results of the behavioral interventions were similarly unsuccessful. At the end of the year, all kindergartners received a district screening test. Cheryl scored at or below the first percentile in all academic areas.

The teacher and the student assistance team (which included the parents) weighed various options for Cheryl's next year: retention, promotion with help from the student assistance team, and referral for an MDE to determine if Cheryl had a disability that required special education and related services. After some discussion, the team was unanimous in its recommendation that Cheryl should be evaluated for eligibility for special education.

An MDT was appointed and consisted of Cheryl's kindergarten teacher, a special education teacher who worked with children of Cheryl's age, the school principal (who chaired the meetings), and the school psychologist assigned to Cheryl's school. At the first team meeting, the principal gave the parents a copy of a document listing the procedural safeguards guaranteed by IDEA and the state. The principal also explained each element carefully and answered all of the parents' questions to their satisfaction. Next, the team reviewed all relevant documents: attendance records, data from the interventions developed by the student assistance team, the results of the district's routine hearing and vision screening (which indicated Cheryl was normal), and the results from the district's first-grade readiness assessment. After reviewing the data and discussing Cheryl's strengths and weaknesses, the MDT decided that additional data would be necessary to determine if Cheryl was eligible for special education and related services. The team discussed the possibility of special language or cultural considerations and concluded there were none. The team then decided that it needed (1) the results of a valid, individually administered test of intelligence; (2) the results of a valid, individually administered test of achievement; (3) ratings from a validly administered scale of social and emotional development; and (4) the ratings from a valid evaluation of adaptive behavior. The principal would be responsible for distributing and collecting the results from the social–emotional rating scale; the school psychologist would be responsible for administering and scoring the test of intelligence and the adaptive behavior scale, and also for scoring and interpreting the social–emotional ratings provided by the teachers.

The testing went smoothly. Teachers completed the Behavior Assessment System for Children, Third Edition; the parents completed the Vineland Adaptive Behavior Scales, Second Edition; and the school psychologist administered the Wechsler Intelligence Scale for Children–Fifth Edition and the Stanford–Binet Intelligence Scale, Fifth Edition. The school psychologist drafted an evaluation report and distributed copies to each team member. The MDT then met to consider the results of their evaluation and to decide if additional data might be needed to make sure that their evaluation examined all areas of potential disability. If the evaluation results were complete and sufficient, the team would decide if Cheryl was a student with a disability under IDEA and state law. The school psychologist affirmed that all of the instruments were administered under standard conditions and that she believed the results to be valid. She next interpreted the evaluation results and answered all of the questions posed by the parents and educators. The results indicated that Cheryl's level of general intellectual functioning was 59 ± 4 points. Her achievement in Reading, Mathematics, and Written Language was at the second percentile. Her parent's ratings of adaptive behavior resulted in a composite (total) score of 64, with Daily Living her area of highest functioning and Communication her lowest area. Although the evaluation results suggested that Cheryl was a student with an intellectual disability, the parents believed that Cheryl was too young to be diagnosed with such a stigmatizing diagnosis. After some discussion, the team unanimously agreed that a diagnosis of developmental delay would be appropriate at that time. Cheryl met the criteria for that disability, and she would not be 9 years of age for almost three years.

continued on the next page

The MDT next turned to the question of need for special education. The team relied heavily on Cheryl's lack of progress when she was given the maximum amount of intervention services within the regular education classroom. Clearly, she needed more services. The MDT added recommendations for special education and related services to the evaluation report. The team noted that Cheryl needed direct instruction in the core academic areas of reading, writing, and mathematics. The team recommended that Cheryl's social interactions be monitored for possible intervention later in the first semester. The MDT also recommended that Cheryl be evaluated by a speech and language therapist to determine if the teacher should have ongoing consultations with the therapist about curriculum or methods and/or if Cheryl would benefit from direct speech and language services. The team also recommended that Cheryl should be included in all nonacademic activities with her same-age peers. Finally, it recommended that Cheryl receive her special education services from an itinerant special education teacher in the general education classroom who would also consult with the regular education teacher, who would also be implementing portions of Cheryl's educational program.

This scenario depicts the processes and procedures used to determine whether Cheryl is eligible to receive special education services. What assessment instruments were used to determine if she had a disability? What assessment information was used to determine that she needed special education services?

The routes around and through the eligibility process are many and varied, but they must be guided by key principles. First, we should choose (and put the most faith in) objective, technically adequate (reliable and well-normed) procedures that have demonstrated validity for the particular purpose of classification. Second, we must consider the specific validity. For example, we must consider the culture in which the student grew up and how that culture interacts with the content of the test. A test's technical manuals may contain information about the wisdom of using the test with individuals of various cultures, or the research literature may have information for the particular cultural group to which a student belongs. Often, theory can guide us in the absence of research. Sometimes it is just not possible to test validly, and we must also recognize that fact. Read the Scenario in Assessment on pages 316–317 to follow the process used to evaluate whether Cheryl was eligible to receive special education services.

21-6 Problems in Determining Special Education Eligibility

Four problems with the criteria used to determine eligibility for special services are especially noteworthy. First, we find the prevalent (but mistaken) belief that special educational services are for students who could benefit from them. Thus, in many circles, educational need is believed to be sufficient for entitlement. Clearly, this belief is contradicted by pertinent law, regulations, and litigation. Students must need the services *and* meet the criteria for a specific disability. Nonetheless, some educators have such strong humanitarian beliefs that when they see students with problems, they want to get those students the services that they believe are needed. Too often, the regulations may be bent so that students fit entitlement criteria.

Second, the definitions that appear in state and federal regulations are frequently very imprecise. The imprecision of federal regulations creates variability in definitional criteria and regulations among states, and the imprecision of state regulations creates variability in application of definitional criteria and regulations among districts within states. Thus, students who are eligible in one state or district may not be eligible in other states or districts. For example, some states and school districts may define a learning disability as a severe discrepancy between measured intellectual ability and actual school achievement. However, there is no consensus about the meaning of "severe discrepancy"; certainly, there is no widely accepted mathematical formula to ascertain severe discrepancy. To some extent, discrepancies between achievement and intelligence are determined by the specific tests used. Thus, one test battery might produce a significant discrepancy, whereas another battery would not produce such a discrepancy for the same student. Other states and school districts may define a learning disability by an inadequate response to intervention. Yet, what constitutes an inadequate response is ambiguous.

Third, the definitions treat disabilities as though they were discrete categories. However, most diagnosticians are hard-pressed to distinguish between primary and secondary intellectual disability or between primary and secondary emotional disturbance. Also, for example, distinctions between individuals with autism and individuals with severe intellectual disabilities and autistic-like behaviors are practically impossible to make with any certainty.

Fourth, parents may often prefer the label associated with one disability (for example, autism or learning disability) over the label associated with another (for example, intellectual disability). Because of the procedural safeguards afforded students with special needs and their parents, school districts may become embroiled in lengthy and unnecessarily adversarial hearings in which each side has an expert testifying that a particular label is correct, even though those labels are contradictory and sometimes mutually exclusive. School personnel find themselves in a no-win situation because the definitions and their operationalizations are so imprecise. As a result, school districts sometimes give parents the label they want rather than what educators, in their best professional judgments, believe to be correct. Districts may be reluctant to risk litigation because parents can frequently find an expert to contradict the district staff members. In some states, special educational services are noncategorical. In these states, a label qualifies a student for special education but does not determine the nature of the special education; that is determined by the individual student's needs, not label, and students with different labels are grouped together for instructional purposes.

Chapter Comprehension Questions

Write your answers to each of the following questions and then compare your responses to the text.

1. List and define each disability recognized by IDEA.

2. Distinguish between RTI and discrepancy-based approaches to identification of learning disabilities.

3. How is the need for special education established?

4. What are the responsibilities of the MDT?

5. What procedural safeguards are guaranteed by IDEA?

6. State three important issues encountered in making eligibility decisions.

CHAPTER

22

MAKING DECISIONS ABOUT PARTICIPATION IN ACCOUNTABILITY PROGRAMS

LEARNING OBJECTIVES

22-1 Describe the legal requirements for state and school district assessment and accountability systems specified in the No Child Left Behind Act and the Individuals with Disabilities Education Improvement Act.

22-2 Explain the two different types of accountability.

22-3 Define the important terms associated with assessment for the purpose of making accountability decisions.

22-4 Describe the role that standards play in accountability systems.

22-5 Explain the purpose of the alternate assessment.

22-6 Articulate the important considerations for making decisions about how students participate in accountability systems.

22-7 Describe important considerations for interpreting assessment information from accountability testing.

STANDARDS ADDRESSED IN THIS CHAPTER

 CEC Initial Preparation Standards

Standard 4: Assessment
4.0 Beginning special education professionals use multiple methods of assessment and data-sources in making educational decisions.

Standard 6: Professional Learning and Ethical Practice
6.0 Beginning Special Education Professionals use foundational knowledge of the field and their Professional Ethical Principles and Practice Standards to inform special education practice, to engage in lifelong learning, and to advance the profession.

 CEC Advanced Preparation Standards

Standard 1: Assessment
1.0 Special education specialists use valid and reliable assessment practices to minimize bias.

E.D. Torial/Alamy

319

Standard 6: Professional Learning and Ethical Practice

6.0 Special Education Specialists use foundational knowledge of the field and Professional Ethical Principles and Practice Standards to inform special education practice, engage in lifelong learning, advance the profession, and perform leadership responsibilities to promote the success of professional colleagues and individual with exceptionalities.

 National Association of School Psychologists Domains
1 Data-Based Decision Making and Accountability
10 Legal, Ethical and Professional Practice

Are our schools producing the results we want? To what extent are individual students meeting the goals, standards, or outcomes that their schools have set for them? What goals or standards should we expect students and schools to meet? How should we assess progress toward meeting educational standards? During the past 20 years, there has been an increased focus on the results of education for all students, including students with disabilities. In this chapter, we examine the collection and use of assessment information for the purpose of making decisions about how students should participate in school, district, and state accountability systems.

A powerful idea dominates policy discussions about schools: the notion that "students should be held to high, common standards for academic performance and that schools and the people who work in them should be held accountable for ensuring that students—all students—are able to meet those standards" (Elmore, 2002, p. 3). It has not always been that way. Until the early to mid-1990s, school personnel focused on the *process* of providing services to students. They provided evidence that they were teaching students, and often evidence that they were teaching specific types of students (for example, Title I, intellectually disabled, deaf, or disadvantaged students). When administrators were asked about special education students or services, typically they described the numbers and kinds of students who were tested or taught, the settings in which they were taught, or the numbers of special education teachers who tested and taught them (for example, "We have 2,321 students with disabilities in our district; 1,620 are educated in general education classes with special education supports, and the remainder are in resource rooms, self-contained classes, and out-of-school settings; the students are served by 118 special education teachers and 19 related services personnel"). Few administrators could provide evidence for the results or outcomes of the services being provided. Since the early 1990s, there has been a dramatic shift in focus from serving students with disabilities to measuring the results of the services provided. This shift has paralleled the total quality management (TQM; Deming, 1994, 2000), results-based management, and management by objectives (Olson, 1964) movements in business and, more recently, in federal and state government.

Much of the impetus for this shift to a focus on results was the publication of *A Nation at Risk: The Imperative for Educational Reform* (National Commission of Excellence in Education, 1983). In this document, the then-secretary of education revealed the low status of U.S. schoolchildren relative to their counterparts in other nations and reported that "the educational foundations of our society are presently being eroded by a rising tide of mediocrity that threatens our very future as a nation and a people" (p. 5). In this report, the secretary argued that the nation was at risk because mediocrity, not excellence, was the norm in education. Recommendations included more time for learning; better textbooks and other materials; more homework; higher expectations; stricter attendance policies; and improved standards, salaries, rewards, and incentives for teachers. The entire nation began to focus on raising educational standards, measuring performance, and achieving results. Policymakers and bureaucrats, who had been spending a great deal of money to fund special education, began demanding evidence of its effectiveness. In essence, they employed the old saying, "The proof of the pudding is in the eating"—arguing that it matters little what you do if it does not produce what you want.

In 1994, the Clinton administration specified a set of national education goals. Called "Goals 2000," these were a list of goals that students should achieve by the year 2000. The 1994 reauthorization of the Elementary and Secondary Education Act, known as the Improving American Schools Act, included a requirement that in Title I schools, disadvantaged students should be expected to attain the same challenging standards as all other students. Additional requirements for large-scale assessment and accountability systems designed to measure the performance and progress of all students toward high standards were included in the general and special education legislation that followed (i.e., No Child Left Behind (NCLB) Act of 2001 and the 1997 and 2004 reauthorizations of the Individuals with Disabilities Education Act), and represented a continued emphasis on promoting high achievement across all students. The status of related legislation as we write this chapter is provided in the following section; however, you are encouraged to consult the web for more recent updates.

22-1 Legal Requirements

During the 1990s, state educational agencies put forth great efforts in the development of educational standards and large-scale assessment programs to measure student progress toward those standards. However, the extent to which students with disabilities were included in those efforts was questionable. The 1997 reauthorization of the Individuals with Disabilities Education Act (IDEA) included provisions specifying that students with disabilities should participate in states' assessment systems, and that statewide assessment program reports would include information on the extent to which *all* students, including students with disabilities, met state-specified standards. Recognizing that some students with disabilities had unique assessment needs, and that the regular assessment programs might not allow for appropriate measurement of their achievement toward state standards, IDEA 1997 introduced the requirement for IEP teams to determine which accommodations (if any) were needed for individual students to effectively participate in the statewide assessment program. It also required the development of alternate assessments for those students who could not effectively participate in the regular assessment even with accommodations. The 2004 reauthorization of IDEA contains those same requirements.

NCLB included the requirement that states have assessment and accountability systems, and report annually on the performance and progress of all students in reading, math, and science. In 2003, the U.S. Department of Education issued a set of guidelines for alternate assessments that included the concept of alternate achievement standards. The law requires that school systems consider not only how their students are doing as a whole but also how particular groups of students are doing, with a focus on the following groups: economically disadvantaged, students with limited English proficiency, students receiving special education services, and students from major racial/ethnic groups. To be considered successful, schools must succeed with all students. States, school districts, and individual schools are required by law to measure the performance and progress of all students. Schools that don't make adequate yearly progress are subjected to certain sanctions (see the Types of Accountability section below for more information on NCLB accountability requirements). School personnel need to know much about how assessment information is used by state education agency personnel to make accountability decisions. Many states have applied for waivers or exemptions from NCLB assessment and accountability requirements, and it could be helpful to go to the website for your state education agency to know the current status of accountability programs in your state. The National Center on Educational Outcomes (NCEO) maintains a website where they report the states who have been granted waivers. It may be helpful to get a picture of nationwide accountability practices relative to those in your state by examining the NCEO website.

Reauthorization of the NCLB is expected to occur in the very near future. Given the impact of federal legislation on statewide assessment and accountability systems, we anticipate that many things that we write about in this chapter will change by the time it goes to print. We certainly do not expect accountability to go away; in fact, most believe that legislative changes will have an even greater emphasis on holding schools accountable for the achievement of all students. You can find more information about recent legislative changes related to accountability systems and related assessment information by tracking information at the websites for No Child Left Behind, the National Center on Educational Outcomes, and the National Center for Research on Evaluation, Standards and Student Testing. Information on the progress of the major assessment consortia can be found at websites for Smarter Balanced Assessment Consortium (SBAC), Partnership for Assessment of Readiness for College and Careers (PARCC), Dynamic Learning Maps (DLM), and National Center and State Collaborative (NCSC).

22-2 Types of Accountability

Accountability systems hold schools responsible for helping all students reach high, challenging standards, and they provide rewards to schools that reach those standards and sanctions to schools that do not. Today, the consequences of accountability systems are becoming more significant, often referred to as "high stakes." As we write this chapter, federal accountability requirements are in the midst of being updated as the ESEA reauthorization process has been initiated, but not completed. Many states have sought out and received waivers to NCLB in recent years, and so there is variation in practices across states. States may choose to add additional features to their accountability system. Although all states include system accountability, some also include accountability for students.

System accountability is accountability designed to improve educational programs, and is the focus of federal education reform efforts. NCLB required that states develop adequate yearly progress (AYP) targets for schools that are based primarily on student progress as measured by statewide assessment programs, assessment participation rates, and student attendance/graduation rates. Schools that did not make AYP in consecutive years experienced the following:

- After two years of not making AYP, the school had to allow students to attend a higher performing school in the district.
- After three years of not making AYP, the school had to provide supplemental supports to low-achieving disadvantaged students.
- After four years of not making AYP, the school had to take corrective action that may include replacing school staff or restructuring the organizational structure of the school.
- After six years of not making AYP, the school had to develop and implement an alternative governance plan.

All states are expected to publicly report on the performance of their students and school systems. States may additionally decide to incorporate additional school rewards and sanctions for schools based on student performance. Among the sanctions that states commonly use are assigning negative labels to schools, removing staff, and firing principals. Rewards include assigning positive labels to schools and giving extra funding to schools or cash awards to staff. **Student accountability** is accountability designed to motivate students to do their best. Nothing in NCLB required that states attach rewards or sanctions to individual student performance; however, some states chose to do so. The most common high-stakes use of assessment evidence for individual students is to determine whether a student receives a standard high school diploma or some other type of document. Another type of student accountability that has appeared is the use of test scores to determine whether a student will move from one grade to another.

22-3 Important Terminology

The standards-based assessment and accountability movement and the federal laws that accompany it have brought a new assessment vocabulary that includes terms such as "alternate achievement standards," "adequate yearly progress," and "schools in need of improvement." Some of these terms are used in many different ways in the professional and popular literature. In fact, the multiple uses of the terms cause confusion. The Council of Chief State School Officers publishes a *Glossary of Assessment Terms and Acronyms Used in Assessing Special Education*, which is a good source of definitions for terms used in assessment and accountability systems. We include an adapted version of this glossary in Table 22.1.

TABLE 22.1   Glossary of Assessment Terms Used Within Accountability Systems

---

Academic standards. There are two types of standards: content and achievement.

- *Content standards.* Statements of the subject-specific knowledge and skills that schools are expected to teach students, indicating what students should know and be able to do in reading/language arts, math, and science. Many states have content standards in other academic areas as well. These standards must be the same for all schools and all students within a state.
- *Achievement (performance) standards.* Specifications of how well students need to know the academic content standards. They must have the following components:

    1. Specific levels of achievement: States are required to have at least three levels of achievement—basic, proficient, and advanced. Many states have more than three levels and may use different names for the levels.
    2. Descriptions of what students at each particular level must demonstrate relative to the task.
    3. Examples of student work at each level illustrating the range of performance within each level.
    4. Cut scores clearly separating each performance level.

Accommodations. Changes made in the presentation, setting, response, or timing/scheduling of a test that allow for more accurate measurement of the intended skills and knowledge among the particular students to whom they are provided.

Accountability. The use of assessment results and other data to ensure that schools are moving in desired directions. Common elements include standards, indicators of progress toward meeting those standards, analysis of data, reporting procedures, and rewards or sanctions.

Accountability system. A plan that uses assessment results and other data outlining the goals and expectations for students, teachers, schools, districts, and states to demonstrate the established components or requirements of accountability. An accountability system typically includes rewards for those who exceed the goals and sanctions for those who fail to meet the goals.

Adaptations. A generalized term that describes a change made in the presentation, setting, response, or timing or scheduling of an assessment that may or may not change the construct of the assessment.

Adequate yearly progress (AYP). The annual improvement that school districts and schools were expected to make each year in order to reach the NCLB goal of having every student proficient by the year 2014. In order to meet AYP requirements, schools had to test at least 95 percent of their students in each of the subgroups, and schools had to demonstrate sufficient progress for students in each of eight subgroups (for example, students with disabilities, students with limited English proficiency, and students who are members of specific racial/ethnic groups). Nontest indicators, such as attendance or high school graduation rate, were also used as indicators of AYP.

Alignment. The similarity or match between or among content standards, performance standards, curriculum, instruction, and assessments, in terms of knowledge and skill expectations.

Alternate achievement standards. Expectations for performance that differ in complexity from a grade-level achievement standard but that are linked to the content standards.

Alternate assessment based on alternate achievement standards (AA-AAS). An alternate assessment for which the expectation of performance differs in complexity from grade-level achievement standards and that is designed for use with students whose significant cognitive disabilities preclude their participation in the regular grade-level assessment.

Alternate assessment based on grade-level academic achievement standards (AA-GLAS). An instrument in a different format than the regular test, but it defines for students with disabilities a level of "proficient" performance as equivalent to grade-level achievement and of the same difficulty as on the state's regular grade-level assessment.

Benchmark. A minimum level of performance required of all students at a specific point in time; usually the end of a specific grade.

Body of evidence. Information or data that establish that a student can perform a particular skill or has mastered a specific content standard and that was either produced by the student or collected by someone who is knowledgeable about the student.

(Continues)

TABLE 22.1	Glossary of Assessment Terms Used Within Accountability Systems *Continued*

Cut score. A specified point on a score scale. Scores at or above that point are interpreted differently from scores below that point.

Disaggregation. The collection and reporting of student achievement results by particular subgroups (e.g., students with disabilities and limited English-proficient students) to ascertain a subgroup's academic progress. Disaggregation makes it possible to compare subgroups or cohorts.

Norm-referenced test. A standardized test designed, validated, and implemented to rank a student's performance by comparing that performance to the performance of the student's peers.

Opportunity to learn. The provision of learning conditions, including suitable adjustments, to maximize a student's chances of attaining the desired learning outcomes, such as the mastery of content standards.

Out-of-level testing (off-grade or off-level). Administration of a test at a level above or below a student's present grade level to enable the student to be assessed at the level of instruction rather than the level of enrollment. According to federal education law, this practice is not allowed for accountability purposes.

Standards-referenced test (sometimes called a criterion-referenced test). A standardized test designed, validated, and implemented to rank a student's performance by comparing that performance to the specific standards for the state in which the student resides. Students are said to have met or not met the state standards.

Student accountability. Consequences exist for individual students and are based on their individual assessment performance. For example, students might not be promoted to the next grade or graduate if their assessment results do not meet a prespecified level.

System or school accountability. Consequences exist for school systems and are based on the assessment performance of a group of individuals (for example, the school building, district, or state education agency). For example, a school might receive a financial award or special recognition for having a large percentage of students meeting a particular assessment performance level.

SOURCE: Adapted from the Council of Chief State School Officers (CCSSO) (2006). "Assessing Students with Disabilities: A Glossary of Assessment Terms in Everyday Language." Washington, DC: Author; and Cortiella, C. (2006). *NCLB and IDEA: What Parents of Students with Disabilities Need to Know and Do.* Minneapolis, MN: University of Minnesota, National Center on Educational Outcomes.

22-4 It's All About Meeting Standards

Assessments completed for accountability purposes involve measuring the extent to which students are learning what we want them to learn, or the extent to which school systems are accomplishing what we want them to accomplish. To do this, state education agency personnel must specify the standards that schools and students will work toward. They typically do so by specifying a set of *content standards*, which are statements of the subject-specific knowledge and skills that schools are expected to teach students, indicating what students should know and be able to do. States are required by law to specify academic content standards in reading, math, and science. For quite some time, each state educational agency was expected to develop its own academic content and achievement standards. As a result, standards, and the focus of grade-level instruction, varied across states. Alicia might be taught multiplication in third grade in Michigan, while her cousin, Dennis, who lives in Missouri, might not be taught multiplication until fourth grade. This could cause substantial problems for students who move from state to state and consequently miss out on important instruction. Furthermore, statewide assessments designed to hold schools and students accountable for achieving state standards also varied, making comparisons across states inappropriate. Arizona might report having 76 percent of students proficient on the statewide assessment, and Alaska might report 90 percent of students proficient. Does this mean Alaskans have higher achievement? Not necessarily—the differences in content and achievement standards (and consequent difference in statewide assessments) might be such that one test is much more difficult than another. Given these and related concerns, the Council of Chief State School Officers (CCSSO) and the National Governors Association Center for Best Practices (NGA Center) led efforts in the development and implementation of common core standards through the Common Core State Standards Initiative. Forty-eight states were involved in the development of these standards in math and English/language arts, and forty-two states have adopted the final standards that were released in June of 2010. In addition, two consortia have been formed and have been involved in developing assessments to measure progress toward the common core standards: the PARCC Race to the Top Assessment Consortium and the Smarter Balanced Assessment Consortium.

The Common Core State Standards (CCSS) are quantifiable benchmarks in English language arts (ELA) and math at each grade level from kindergarten through high school. The ELA standards mandate the teaching of reading, writing, speaking and listening, language and media and technology, and keyboarding. States can also choose cursive writing as a sixth standard. Math standards mandate the teaching of eight principles. Students are to:

- Make sense of problems and persevere in solving them
- Reason abstractly and quantitatively
- Construct viable arguments and critique the reasoning of others
- Model with mathematics
- Use appropriate tools strategically
- Attend to precision
- Look for and make use of structure
- Look for and express regularity in repeated reasoning

The standards for kindergarten through sixth grade include operations and algebraic thinking, numbers and operations in base 10, measurement and data, and geometry. In grades 6 through 8, students are to learn the number system, expressions and equations, geometry, and statistics and probability. The six conceptual categories for high school students to understand are number and quantity, algebra, functions, modeling, geometry, and statistics and probability. During the development process the standards were divided into two categories: (1) college and career readiness standards, which specify what students were to know when they graduated, and (2) K–12 standards, which specify what students are to know at specific grade levels from elementary through high school.

If you go to the Common Core website you can find an up-to-date list of which states have adopted the Common Core State Standards. Many states have decided to build their own set of state-specific standards rather than to go along with those specified by the Common Core. The Smarter Balance assessment consortium is building a computer-adaptive test, while the PARCC consortium is building a computer-administered test for states to use in assessing the extent to which students are making progress toward the Common Core standards.

In order for students with disabilities to meet high academic standards and to fully demonstrate their conceptual and procedural knowledge and skills in mathematics, reading, writing, and speaking and listening (English language arts), their instruction must incorporate supports and accommodations, including:

- Supports and related services designed to meet the unique needs of these students and to enable their access to the general education curriculum (IDEA 34 CFR §300.34, 2004).

- An individualized education program (IEP), which includes annual goals aligned with and chosen to facilitate their attainment of grade-level academic standards.

- Teachers and specialized instructional support personnel who are prepared and qualified to deliver high-quality, evidence-based, individualized instruction and support services.

Promoting a culture of high expectations for all students is a fundamental goal of the Common Core State Standards. In order to participate with success in the general curriculum, students with disabilities, as appropriate, may be provided additional supports and services, such as instructional supports for learning—based on the principles of universal design for learning (UDL)—which foster student engagement by presenting information in multiple ways and allowing for diverse avenues of action and expression.

Many states specify academic content standards in other areas. States must also specify **achievement standards** (sometimes called **performance standards**), which are statements of the levels at which, or the proficiency with which, students will show that they have mastered the academic content standards. Academic achievement standards use language drawn directly from the NCLB law, and they have the force of law. States are required to define at least three levels of proficiency (usually called basic, proficient, and advanced). Some states specify more than three levels of proficiency (for example, they may choose to indicate that a student's level of performance is below basic). The law requires that all students be assessed related to the state content and achievement standards. The state must provide for students with disabilities reasonable adaptations and accommodations necessary to measure their academic achievement relative to state academic content and state student academic achievement standards. It is important to know that all students, including students with disabilities, must have access to the same content standards. However, it is possible for students with disabilities to be instructed and assessed according to different achievement standards.

The other kind of standards that apply specifically to students with disabilities are alternate achievement standards. Although most students with disabilities are expected to be instructed and assessed according to the grade-level achievement standards, it can be determined that some will work toward alternate achievement standards. **Alternate achievement standards** are expectations for performance that differ in complexity from grade-level achievement standards, but they are linked to those general education standards. States are permitted to define alternate achievement standards to evaluate the achievement of students with the most significant cognitive disabilities.

Standards-based assessment is characterized by specifying what all students can be expected to learn, and then expecting that time will vary, but that all will achieve the standards. States are required to have in place assessments of student proficiency relative to academic content standards. The following are reasons why school personnel would want to assess student performance and progress relative to standards:

- To ascertain the extent to which individual students are meeting state standards—that is, accomplishing what it is that society wants them to accomplish
- To identify student strengths and weaknesses for instructional planning
- To allocate supports and resources
- To ascertain the extent to which specific schools within states are providing the kinds of educational opportunities and experiences that enable their students to achieve state-specified standards
- To provide data on student or school performance that can be helpful in making instructional policy decisions (curricula or instructional methodologies to use)
- To decide who should receive a diploma as indicated by performance on tests that measure whether standards are met
- To inform the public on the performance of schools or school districts
- To know the extent to which specific subgroups of students are meeting specified standards

22-5 Alternate Assessment

Regardless of where students receive instruction, all students with disabilities should have access to, participate in, and make progress in the general curriculum. Thus, all students with disabilities must be included in state assessment systems and in state reporting of AYP toward meeting the state's standards. We have noted that states must specify academic content standards and academic achievement standards, and they must have assessments aligned to those standards. To address the needs of students with substantial concerns, states may choose to develop alternate achievement standards that are based on the expectations for all students.

States must include all students in their assessment and accountability systems. However, not all students can participate in the general state assessments, even with assessment accommodations designed to compensate for their specific needs. IDEA 1997 included a provision that by the year 2000 states would have in place alternate assessments intended for use with those students who evidenced severe cognitive impairments. In August 2002, the U.S. Secretary of Education proposed a regulation to allow states to develop and use alternate achievement standards for students with the most significant cognitive disabilities for the purpose of determining the AYP of states, local education agencies, and schools. In August 2003, the secretary specified that the number of students considered proficient using alternate assessments toward alternate achievement standards could not exceed 1 percent of all students.

An **alternate assessment** is defined in the NCLB federal regulations as "an assessment designed for the small number of students with disabilities who are unable to participate in the regular state assessment, even with appropriate accommodations." It is further indicated that "an alternate assessment may include materials collected under several circumstances, including (1) teacher observation of the student, (2) samples of student work produced during regular classroom instruction that demonstrate mastery of specific instructional strategies ..., or (3) standardized performance tasks produced in an 'on demand' setting, such as completion of an assigned task on test day" (p. 68699). The assessments must yield results separately in both reading/language arts and mathematics, and they must be designed and implemented in a manner that supports use of the results as an indicator of AYP.

Alternate assessments are not simply compilations of student work, sometimes referred to as box or folder stuffing. Rather, they must have a clearly defined structure, specific participation guidelines, and clearly defined scoring criteria and procedures; must meet requirements for technical adequacy; and must have a reporting format that clearly communicates student performance in terms of the academic achievement standards specified by the state. They must meet the same standards for technical adequacy as does the general assessment. It has been a struggle for some states to satisfy this requirement. Alternate assessments may be needed for students with a broad array of disabling conditions, so a state may use more than one alternate assessment.

Alternate assessments can be designed to measure student performance toward grade-level standards or alternate achievement standards. Recall that an alternate achievement standard is an expectation of performance that differs in complexity from a grade-level standard. For example, the Massachusetts Curriculum Frameworks include the following content standard: "Students will identify, analyze, and apply knowledge of the purpose, structure, and elements of nonfiction or informational materials and provide evidence from the text to support their understanding." A less complex demonstration of this standard is "to gain information from signs, symbols, and pictures in the environment"; a more complex demonstration is to "gain information from captions, titles, and table of contents in an informational text" (Massachusetts Department of Education, 2001).

There currently are two federally funded assessment consortia that are designing alternate assessments for use across states: the Dynamic Learning Maps consortium and the National Center and State Collaborative consortium. The states involved in these consortia efforts change over time. You may gain information about current state membership and the latest activities of the consortia by going to their respective websites.

22-6 Important Considerations in Making Participation Decisions for Individual Students

All *students*, including all students with disabilities, need to be included in accountability systems. Federal law requires that states and districts report annually on the performance and progress of <u>all</u> students, including students with disabilities. Teachers, related services personnel, and IEP teams need to make decisions about how individual students will participate. Students with disabilities can participate either by (a) regular assessment, (b) regular assessment with accommodations, or (c) alternate assessment. It is up to the IEP team to decide how to include each student. In making these decisions, the team should answer each of the following questions:

1. What standards is the student working toward? If the student is working toward the regular content and achievement standards, then he or she should participate in the regular assessment. If the student is working toward alternate achievement standards, then he or she should participate in the alternate assessment.

2. Are there specific characteristics of the individual student and/or of the test that may represent barriers to optimal measurement of the targeted skills/knowledge? The student may have a specific disability that is such that low test performance would be a result of the disability rather than the student's actual achievement on the skills targeted for measurement. For example, if the student is visually impaired and the reading comprehension test requires reading of printed material, a low score on the printed test may indeed be due to a visual impairment rather than low reading comprehension skills. If such characteristics are present, an accommodation should be considered. For example, if the student is instructed in Braille, a Braille version of the test may be necessary and appropriate. States typically provide lists of accommodations that may be provided and considered standard for the accountability test, as well as guidelines for making accommodation decisions. In some cases, the list the state provides is not all-inclusive, and it is possible to request permission to use other unique accommodations that are deemed necessary for individual students.

3. Does the student receive accommodations during instruction? Assessment accommodations should be provided only if and when students have had exposure to and experience with those accommodations prior to testing. The accommodation should not be a new, first-time experience during assessment.

School personnel should always monitor the effects of provision of an accommodation to ensure that it does not adversely affect student performance. And parents (and to the extent possible, students themselves) should be involved in making decisions about the kind of assessment in which the student participates and the accommodations provided.

Read the Scenario in Assessment to follow how participation decisions were made for a student with a disability.

STEVEN | Steven is a third-grade student diagnosed with autism. Steven receives instruction in the general education setting for most of his day, although he needs a teacher assistant to assist with implementation of his comprehensive behavior plan. This plan involves providing him with a variety of cues and reminders about the daily classroom schedule and how he is expected to behave during various activities. He has a very difficult time behaving appropriately when there are changes in the classroom schedule; in such cases, he often becomes very anxious, sometimes throws tantrums, and rarely completes his work.

This is the first year that Steven is expected to complete the statewide assessment used for accountability purposes, and his individualized education program team must determine how he can best participate. At first, Steven's parents are very concerned that he will have an anxious reaction to testing, and they do not want him to participate. His general education teacher is also fearful that he will not be able to focus and complete the test.

Steven's school district has been warned by the state that it needs to increase its rates of participation of students with disabilities in the statewide assessment; in the past, many students with disabilities were excluded from statewide testing. Steven's school is under considerable pressure to show that it is including all students, particularly those with disabilities, in the accountability program. At the meeting, the administrator, special educator, and school psychologist explain how important it is for Steven to participate—in order for the education that he and students like him receive to be of concern to those who help in determining how resources will be allocated throughout the district. They also point out how he is working toward all the same grade-level achievement standards as other students, and

that his participation may help them determine what he can and cannot do. They explain the variety of ways in which Steven can be accommodated during testing. For instance, they can continue to have the teacher assistant implement his behavior management plan. They can role-play in the days prior to the test what the test will be like. Also, they can develop a picture schedule that is similar to the one he uses in the classroom to go along with the testing schedule.

After presenting the underlying rationale for having Steven participate, as well as the ways in which he could be accommodated during testing, the team agrees that it is appropriate to have Steven attempt the statewide assessment toward grade-level achievement standards. His teacher assistant is provided specific training on how she can and cannot assist Steven during testing in order to ensure that his results are as accurate as possible.

The day of the test is considerably draining for Steven and his teacher assistant, but Steven manages to complete the test. Although his total score ends up falling below the proficiency standard, and his teachers question whether it is an optimal measure of his skills and knowledge, his teachers and parents are impressed with the fact that he did not score in the lowest proficiency category. In fact, Steven was able to correctly answer many of the items on the test; he was able to demonstrate some of what he knew when provided appropriate accommodations during testing.

This scenario highlights the decision-making process for including a student with a disability in an accountability test. Why is it so important for students like Steven to be effectively included in accountability programs?

22-7 Important Considerations in Understanding Assessment Information Used to Make Accountability Decisions

As a result of accountability system implementation, student assessment data have become much more readily available to the public. Although this public reporting is intended to promote better student instruction and learning, it is important that those who have access to the data know how to appropriately interpret the information. Without these skills, poor judgments and decisions may be made that are harmful to students. For instance, it is important for consumers of accountability information to understand that most tests used for accountability purposes are intended to measure performance of an entire group of students, and that the tests do not necessarily provide reliable data on the skills of individual students. Without this knowledge, consumers may make unwarranted judgments and decisions about individual students based on their test scores.

In addition, it is important for people to recognize that not all students need to be tested in the same way; it is often important for students to be tested using different formats. Some students have special characteristics that make it difficult for them to demonstrate their knowledge on content standards in a traditional paper-and-pencil format. These students may need accommodations to demonstrate their true knowledge. What is most important is that students' knowledge and skill toward the identified achievement standards are measured. Those with assessment expertise can help determine what accommodations or alternate assessments might be necessary for students to best demonstrate their skills and knowledge.

Chapter Comprehension Questions

Write your answers to each of the following questions and then compare your responses to the text.

1. What legal requirements for state and school district assessment and accountability systems are specified in NCLB and IDEA 2004?

2. What is the difference between system and student accountability?

3. Name and define five important terms used to describe accountability systems.

4. What is the difference between content and achievement standards? Why has there been a movement toward the development of Common Core State Standards?

5. What is an alternate assessment, who is it intended for, and why is it important?

6. What are some important considerations in making participation decisions for students with disabilities?

7. State two important considerations in understanding assessment information that is used for making accountability decisions.

CHAPTER

23

COLLABORATIVE TEAM DECISION MAKING

LEARNING OBJECTIVES

23-1 Articulate characteristics of effective school teams.

23-2 Describe the types of collaborative teams that are commonly formed in school settings.

23-3 Describe strategies for effectively communicating assessment information to parents.

23-4 Depict the variety of ways in which assessment information is communicated and maintained in written formats, and various related rules about data collection and record keeping.

STANDARDS ADDRESSED IN THIS CHAPTER

 CEC Initial Preparation Standards

Standard 4: Assessment

4.0 Beginning special education professionals use multiple methods of assessment and data-sources in making educational decisions.

Standard 7: Collaboration

7.0 Beginning special education professionals collaborate with families, other educators, related service providers, individuals with exceptionalities, and personnel from community agencies in culturally responsive ways to address the needs of individuals with exceptionalities across a range of learning experiences.

CEC **CEC Advanced Preparation Standards**
ADVANCED
Standard 1: Assessment

1.0 Special education specialists use valid and reliable assessment practices to minimize bias.

Standard 7: Collaboration

7.0 Special education specialists collaborate with stakeholders to improve programs, services, and outcomes for individuals with exceptionalities and their families.

Ableimages/Jupiterimages Corporation

331

National Association of School Psychologists Domains
1 Data-Based Decision Making and Accountability
2 Consultation and Collaboration
7 Family-School Collaboration Services

Many important decisions are not made individually but by groups of people. In schools, important decisions are made by teams of individuals. Some team members may be well versed in assessment concepts; however, research conducted through the Center for Research on Evaluation, Standards, and Student Testing suggests that many educational professionals do not know how to carefully examine and use assessment data (Baker, Bewley, Herman, Lee, & Mitchell, 2001; Baker & Linn, 2002). Parents may need considerable support to understand and make appropriate use of assessment information that is collected. Some professional associations (for example, the American Psychological Association, the Council for Exceptional Children, and the National Association of School Psychologists) specify in their ethical standards or principles that their members are responsible for accurate and sensitive communication of assessment information.

In this chapter, we provide information on the many different teams that may be formed to examine assessment data and also suggestions for making appropriate team decisions. We offer guidelines for communicating assessment information in both oral and written formats, as well as regulations governing record keeping and the dissemination of information collected in school settings.

23-1 Characteristics of Effective School Teams

Many individuals play important roles in promoting student learning; each brings unique expertise that can be useful in the process of decision making. In using assessment data to make decisions, you will work with special and general educators, administrators, speech/language pathologists, school psychologists, social workers, nurses, physicians, physical therapists, occupational therapists, audiologists, counselors, curriculum directors, attorneys, child advocates, and probably many others. Effective communication and collaboration are essential to promoting positive student outcomes. Although the expertise each individual offers can be an asset to decision making, it is important to recognize that group decision making does not necessarily result in better decisions than individual decision making. Unfortunately, there are many ways in which group dynamics can hinder appropriate decision making. Gutkin and Nemeth (1997) summarize ways in which group decision making can go awry, including (1) the tendency for groups to concede to the majority opinion regardless of its accuracy, and (2) **group polarization**, in which groups tend to become more extreme in their decision making than what any individual originally intended (which could either hinder or promote best practice). In order to avoid making poor decisions, it is important to adhere to several principles when working as a team. Although the goals and purposes of school teams may vary, certain principles of effective teaming appear to be universal.

- *Have shared goals and purpose.* Unnecessary conflict and inefficiencies in decision making occur when team members do not understand the team's purpose and when their activities do not reflect that purpose. For example, some members of prereferral intervention teams may view the team's purpose as "just one more hoop to jump through" before a referral for evaluation to determine special education eligibility is made, whereas others may view it as an opportunity to identify the conditions under which a student learns best. Those holding the former perspective may be less inclined to put forth substantial effort in associated team activities, which may reduce team effectiveness. It is important for the team's purpose and function to be clearly articulated when the team is formed, and for all team members to be committed to working toward that goal.

- *Clearly articulate the roles and functions of team members.* Team composition needs to be determined carefully, balancing the need for unique expertise and the need for a team to efficiently complete commissioned tasks. Those team members who are selected for participation need to be fully aware of the unique expertise that they bring and also be aware of their knowledge limitations. More team members is not always better; managing large teams can be overwhelming and may intimidate important members of the team (for example, some parents may be intimidated when they walk into a team meeting that includes many school professionals). In addition, large teams may lead to decisions that are informed by just one or two particularly dominant team members (Moore, Fifield, Spira, & Scarlato, 1989). The appointment of a team meeting facilitator can be helpful in assisting the team in following appropriate organizational procedures and ensure that all team members are fully able to share their expertise and knowledge in ways that facilitate progress toward the team's goal.

- *Listen to and respect each team member's contributions.* Teams sometimes gravitate toward **groupthink** (that is, agreeing with the majority opinion), despite the fact that group decisions can be inaccurate (Gutkin & Nemeth, 1997). It is important for those with minority opinions to be given the opportunity to express their positions and for their ideas to be respected and considered within the group's functioning. Effective problem solving can occur when all individuals are encouraged to contribute.

- *Balance structure and flexibility within team meetings.* It can often be helpful for teams to develop and implement systematic procedures for operation. In many cases, teams may have forms that facilitators use to guide team meetings (see Figure 23.1 for an example of such a form). The facilitator might create a written agenda for team meetings, in which there is time for those who have collected information to present their findings, time for additional input from team members, and time for group decision making. Such procedures and structures can help teams maintain attention to task and promote efficiency toward addressing the team's goals. When team members want to discuss important issues that are not associated with the specific decisions to be made, it is important to know how to tactfully address those concerns. We have found the following statement to be helpful in such circumstances: "That's an important issue, but it will take us away from the decision that we are trying to make now. Can we discuss it later or at another meeting?" Some decisions that school teams make are associated with a substantial amount of conflicting opinion and emotionality. For example, discussing certain disability labels such as "student with an emotional disturbance" can be very troubling to parents. It is important that team meeting facilitators be willing to shuffle the agenda or even stop and reschedule meetings when the emotional nature of the meeting is such that progress toward the team's goals cannot be made.

- *Use objective data to guide decision making.* Often, educational decisions are made without appropriate attention to relevant student data (Ysseldyke, 1987). Without the appropriate collection of and adherence to using data to guide team decision making, the subjective preferences of team members may take precedence over what is truly in the best interest of the student being served. To obtain and interpret data in an objective manner requires one to pay attention to and be on the lookout for both data that confirm and disconfirm a hypothesis. **Confirmation bias** describes the tendency to primarily pay attention to data that confirm one's original hypothesis while disregarding or underemphasizing data that conflict with the original hypothesis (see Nickerson 1998 for a review). It is therefore important for teams to carefully attend to all collected data, and be sure to carefully consider information that is collected, but which is not aligned with the original hypothesis. The appropriate use of data to inform decision making can (1) ensure that appropriate practices are put into place and (2) help eliminate conflicting viewpoints on how to proceed.

FIGURE 23.1
Completed Example
Form to Guide Initial
Problem Solving
Team Meeting

Date of meeting: 01/30/11
Student name: Jesse Johansen
Student's grade: 3
Teacher's name: Darcy Dunlap
School: Eastern Elementary
Name and title of those attending the meeting (note facilitator and recorder):
Carrie Court (3rd grade lead teacher), Darcy Dunlap (recorder), Greg Gorter
(guidance counselor), Jackie Johansen (mother), Eric Enright (principal, facilitator)

A. Student Strengths (Provide brief summary of student strengths; 2–3 minutes)
Jesse has many friends and gets along really well with all the other students. He likes
to play soccer, and is very good at math.

B. Nature of Difficulties (In 2 minutes, circle all that apply)

<u>Academic</u>

(Reading)   Writing   Spelling   Math   Social Studies   History   Other:_____

<u>Behavioral</u>

Aggression Attention Task Completion Homework Attendance Tardiness   Other:_____

<u>Social/Emotional</u>

Depression   (Anxiety)   Peer Relationships   Social Skills   Other:_____

<u>Physical</u>

Body Odor   Headaches   Nausea   Fatigue/Sleeping in Class   Other:_____

C. Summary of Data Collected to Support Difficulties Circled Above (2–3 minutes
per area)
Jesse performed in the at-risk range on the Fall and Winter DIBELS benchmarking
tasks during third grade. When asked to read in class, his voice becomes shaky, and
he shuts down, and he refuses to read. His mother reports that he is beginning to not
like going to school, and doesn't eat his breakfast (most likely due to his nervousness
about having to go to school).

D. Prioritization of Difficulties (2–3 minutes)
#1 Most Problematic of the Above Listed Difficulties: Reading (the team believes
that his poor skills in reading are what are contributing to his anxiety).

#2 Most Problematic of the Above Listed Difficulties: Anxiety

#3 Most Problematic of the Above Listed Difficulties: _____

E. Problem Definition in Observable and Measurable Terms (2 minutes)
Currently when presented with a third grade DIBELS benchmark passage, Jesse
reads a median of 60 words correctly in one minute.

F. Goal (2 minutes)
Eight weeks from now when presented with a third grade DIBELS benchmark passage,
Jesse will read a median of 75 words correctly in one minute.

(Continues)

FIGURE 23.1
(Continued)

G. Suggested Intervention Ideas for Addressing #1 of Prioritized Difficulties (15 minutes)

Intervention Idea #1: After school tutoring with an eighth-grade student.

Intervention Idea #2: Flashcards of phonics patterns that Jesse's teacher would administer after school two days per week, and Jesse's mom would administer at home the other three days each week.

Intervention Idea #3: Read Naturally® program that would be administered after school.

H. Description of Final Intervention Selected (10 minutes)

i. What will the student do? Jesse will be taught how to use the Read Naturally® program, and will practice listening to and reading aloud with the tapes.

ii. How often and when will this occur? Two times a week for 45 minutes after school (Tues./Thurs.).

iii. Who is responsible for implementing the intervention? Jesse's mom and teacher

iv. How will progress be measured? DIBELS progress monitoring probes will be administered once a week.

v. Who is responsible for measuring progress? Jesse's teacher

vi. How, when, and to whom will progress be reported? Progress will be reported at the follow-up meeting, unless four consecutive data points fall below the aim line, in which case an earlier meeting will be convened.

I. Date and Time of Follow-Up Meeting (2 minutes): April 9, 2011

- *Ensure confidentiality—it's the law!* Those who study team decision making find that confidentiality can break down. Ultimately, it is against the law to break confidentiality rules, and such breaches can be grounds for termination. When confidentiality rules are not followed and a member learns that someone betrayed confidentiality, the team ceases to function well. It is suggested that regular reminders are provided by an administrator, school psychologist, or other team leader that meeting discussions are confidential. We suggest that the leader tell members at the very first meeting that confidentiality is critical and that he or she will be reminding members of this regularly. Then the reminders do not raise questions of "I wonder who talked inappropriately about what we are discussing."

- *Regularly evaluate team outcomes and processes to promote continuous improvement in team functioning.* Team processes and procedures can always be improved. It is important for the team to engage in periodic self-evaluation in order to ensure that it is meeting identified goals and objectives, and that it is respectful of all team members' contributions. In some cases, it may be helpful to ask someone uninvolved in the team functioning to do an anonymous evaluation of a team's functioning. This can help to ensure that all team members are able to contribute their skills and knowledge in a way that is most beneficial to students.

23-2 Types of School Teams

There are many different teams created to examine assessment data and inform decision making in schools. These teams may have very different names and be composed of professionals with varying expertise. Although all the teams described here are typically involved in examination of data for the purpose of decision making, the teams vary considerably in the types of decisions made and, therefore, the nature of data collected, analyzed, and interpreted. Although we provide titles for these teams, it is important to recognize that there may be a variety of different terms used to describe similarly functioning teams in the schools and districts you encounter.

23-2a SCHOOLWIDE ASSISTANCE TEAMS

With the development of technology for managing large amounts of student data, as well as increased attention to accountability for student outcomes, teams of educational professionals are more frequently being formed to collect, analyze, and interpret data on students across the entire school or district. The ultimate purpose of these teams is to inform instructional planning and resource allocation at school and district levels such that student achievement is optimized. They can be thought of as teams intended to ensure that the fundamental level of support within MTSS (core instruction) is effective. Sometimes these teams are referred to as "resource teams." Team members may consist of those with special expertise in data analysis, curriculum, and instruction. These individuals come together to examine statewide assessment data, results from schoolwide screening efforts, and information on existing educational programming, with the purpose of identifying strategies for improving student achievement. In some cases, such teams may be created by grade level, such that all teachers from a particular grade meet on a regular basis with the administrator and someone with expertise in assessment in order to identify areas for instructional improvement. Following a systematic analysis of data, the team may make recommendations for professional development and changes in school programming.

Participants on these teams who have specialized expertise in assessment can contribute to the team by (1) helping the school identify methods for collecting relevant data on all students effectively and efficiently, (2) creating and interpreting visual displays of assessment data for the purpose of decision making, (3) recognizing areas where additional assessment is needed prior to making substantial changes in school programming, and (4) identifying methods for monitoring the effectiveness of any associated changes in school programming.

23-2b INTERVENTION ASSISTANCE TEAMS

Intervention assistance teams are formed to address difficulties that small groups of students or individual students experience within general education classrooms. The purpose of the team is to define the specific problem, analyze the problem in order to develop a targeted intervention plan, implement the intervention plan, monitor the plan implementation and student progress, and evaluate the effectiveness of the plan. Initially, the team may simply consist of a general education teacher and parents of the child involved. However, if the problem is not solved, additional school professionals may be added to the team in order to more systematically define and analyze the problem and to inform the development of interventions that are of increasing intensity. The parent–teacher team might be expanded to include other teachers or the school guidance counselor; these individuals could help conduct a more in-depth problem analysis and brainstorm additional ideas for intervention. If that plan does not lead to progress, other personnel, such as the school psychologist, social worker, or special education teacher, might be added to the intervention assistance team to provide additional support for assessment and intervention. In other words, as a student is determined to need a higher level of support through the MTSS, additional expertise is sought to assist with development of a more intensive intervention. Names for teams with a function similar to that of an intervention assistance team described previously include "teacher assistance teams," "student assistance teams," "building assistance teams," "problem solving teams," "child study teams," and "instructional consultation teams."

Those with expertise in assessment can assist these teams by helping select and administer assessment tools to define and analyze the problem, as well as to monitor intervention integrity and student progress.

23-2c MULTIDISCIPLINARY TEAMS

These teams are convened when a child has not made appropriate progress following support provided through multiple levels of MTSS and is being considered for special education evaluation; the function and activities of these teams are more fully discussed in Chapter 21. They are charged with the responsibility of determining whether a student has a disability and is in need of special education services according to the Individuals with Disabilities Education Act (IDEA).

23-2d INDIVIDUAL EDUCATION PLAN TEAMS

After a student is found eligible for special education services under IDEA, the individualized education program is developed by a team of individuals who have specialized knowledge in the specific areas of the child's disability, those who will be responsible for carrying out the plan, and the child's parents. These teams typically meet on an annual basis to review the progress and programming for each student receiving special education services individually.

23-3 Communicating Assessment Information to Parents and Students

Parents and guardians usually have more information about certain aspects of their child's life than any other person involved in the assessment process. However, many parents have limited knowledge and skill in understanding assessment and can find it challenging to take in all of the information presented by different individuals and understand what it means in terms of what is best for their child. Given the influential role that they play in the lives of their children, it is crucial that they understand the assessment results; this will allow them to participate fully in the decision-making process. Many parents (as well as other team members) may lack the knowledge to understand assessment results without substantial explanation. Some parents may themselves have disabilities. However, not all parents will lack knowledge or technical expertise; some parents are professionals themselves—psychologists, special educators, attorneys, therapists, and so forth. Other parents will have educated themselves about their child's needs. Regardless of their backgrounds, all parents may need to be empowered to be active and helpful members of school decision-making teams.

A variety of things can limit parent understanding of assessment information and participation in team decision making. Language barriers can clearly hinder effective communication. Many parents may not have a schedule that permits participation in meetings scheduled by school professionals. They may feel intimidated by various school professionals. They may not recognize the important knowledge that they can bring to the team or not understand how to effectively communicate that knowledge to the team. They may have strong emotional reactions to data that are presented about their child's academic successes and failures, which may hinder rational decision making. They may have strong feelings and opinions about the quality of educational services provided to their child and about how their child's needs might best be met by educational professionals. Unfortunately, parents' unique knowledge about their child is often disregarded or ignored by school professionals, who often make decisions prior to team meetings.

Students can also be important contributors to team decision making, and assessment information needs to be communicated to them in developmentally appropriate ways. Older students are required by law to be included in aspects of IEP decision making; participation in associated meetings can help to ensure that their perspectives and desires are appropriately considered. With advanced information about meeting purposes and procedures, students from a variety of age groups can participate in important and meaningful ways (Martin, VanDycke, Christensen, Greene, Gardneer, & Lovett, 2006).

Schools can take several steps to make communication with parents and students more effective. Better communication should result in more effective parental and student participation in associated team decision making.

- *Communicate with parents frequently.* In the past, it was often the case that parents were not made aware of difficulties that their child was having until the child was being considered for special education evaluation. When this happens, it can lead to strong emotional reactions and frustration among parents. It can also lead to unnecessary conflict if parents do not think that special education services would be in the best interest of their child. It is important that parents are provided frequent and accurate information on the progress of their child from the very beginning of their child's enrollment in school. When provided this information, parents of those students who are consistently low-performing may become more involved in helping to develop intervention plans that may reduce their child's difficulties. Furthermore, when parents receive frequent communication about their child's progress (or lack thereof), they may more readily understand why a referral for a special education eligibility evaluation is made. In schools where MTSS is used, communication with parents often occurs more frequently, given that student instruction may shift as students begin receiving different levels of support.

- *Communicate both the child's strengths and the child's weaknesses.* Many parents of students with special needs are often reminded of their child's weaknesses and difficulties in school and may rarely be alerted to their child's successes and strengths. Alternatively, some parents may overvalue their child's relative strengths and ignore or minimize their child's weaknesses. In order to work effectively with parents, and to facilitate creative problem solving as a part of a team, it is important to recognize and communicate about a child's specific strengths and weaknesses. An emphasis on strengths can be particularly helpful when the student is present or will have access to the associated report.

- *Translate assessment information and team communications as needed.* Assessment data that are reported to all parents (for example, statewide assessment results and screening results) should be made available in the parent's primary language or mode of communication. To facilitate participation in team meetings, interpreters should be provided. In order to interpret well, they may need special training in how to communicate the pertinent information to parents, and in how to ensure that parents' questions, concerns, and contributions have a voice within team meanings. For all parents, even those who have English as their primary language, it is important to avoid jargon and acronyms, and to use figures and graphs to show assessment results as much as possible to facilitate their understanding. When students are present, it is important to promote their understanding of assessment information and results, as well.

- *Be aware of how cultural differences may impact the understanding of assessment information.* It is also suggested that when cultural differences exist, a person who understands both the student's culture and educational matters be present. This may be necessary even when language differences are nonexistent (for example, the student is Amish and the culture of the school is not Amish). This can help a team identify issues that may be cultural in nature. Sometimes communication modes that are a normal part of school functioning (e.g., email) are not part of the home environment, and it is important to be aware of these differences.

- *Schedule meetings to facilitate parent attendance.* Efforts should be made to schedule meetings at a time when parents can be present. Challenges associated with transportation should be addressed. In certain circumstances, it may be necessary for school professionals to meet at a location that is more convenient for parents than the school setting. It may also be necessary for school personnel to communicate directly with an employer, encouraging the employer to allow the parent to be excused from work. This is especially true in communities where one company (for example, a paper mill, an automobile factory, or a meat packing plant) is the employer of many parents. In this case, a blanket arrangement could be made in which the company agrees to release the parent for school meetings if a request is made by the school.

- *Clearly explain the purpose of any assessment activities, and also the potential outcomes.* Whereas school professionals may be very familiar with assessment-related processes and procedures, and the associated decisions that are made, parents often are new to the process. It is important to prepare them for what to expect as it relates to administration of assessment instruments, and using the results of assessment data that are collected. It is important to let the parents know up-front what will be involved in assessing the child (e.g., when it will occur, what assessment materials are used, etc.), and how the assessment process will be explained to the child. Sometimes, it can be helpful for school professionals to contact parents before a meeting to explain the purpose of the meeting and what they can expect to happen at the meeting. Parents should be informed of all potential outcomes of a particular meeting (for example, development of an intervention plan, decision to collect more data, and decision that the student is eligible to receive special education services) so that they are not caught off guard.

- *Communicate using nontechnical language as much as possible.* By now, you have most certainly recognized that language used in educational circles is full of acronyms. It is important to explain these, as well as all of the other technical terms that may be used, to parents so that they can be in dialog with team members. Whereas some parents may understand technical terms associated with assessment data, others may not. It is more appropriate to err on the side of using language that is easier to understand than to assume that parents understand terminology that is used by school professionals. Figures and graphs can often help to convey student progress in an understandable way.

- *Maintain a solution-focused orientation and avoid pointing blame.* Just about every school team meeting is intended to promote student achievement, whether directly or indirectly. Making this goal happen requires that individual team members focus on alterable rather than unalterable variables, and on what can be changed in the future to promote student learning rather than dwelling on what has happened in the past. Unfortunately, there can be a tendency to focus on what people may have done or failed to do in the past rather than making plans for the future. Although it is important to learn from past mistakes, team members should focus on what can be done in the future to improve student learning. Focusing on past failure can decrease morale and contribute to unnecessary conflict and blame among team members.

- *Prepare students for active engagement in meetings.* Although in some cases it may make sense to hold a meeting without the student present, in many cases it can be helpful to have the student present in order for the student's interests and desires to be considered. If a student will attend, it is important to prepare him or her for what the meeting will entail, and when possible, provide training to facilitate effective participation of the student in team decision making.

Read the Scenario in Assessment for this chapter for an illustration of both ineffective and effective methods of communicating assessment information to parents.

AMELIA

Ineffective Communication of Assessment Information with Parents

In early November, Mr. and Mrs. Martinez were notified that a meeting was being scheduled to discuss their third-grade daughter Amelia's failure to make progress in reading. The meeting was scheduled as part of a series of intervention assistance team meetings, in which a total of seven children from her elementary school would be discussed by a team of individuals who included the principal, guidance counselor, and the students' general education teachers. General educators were rotated into the meeting at 10-minute intervals, as each child was being discussed. Although Mr. and Mrs. Martinez were notified by Amelia's teacher that the meeting would be held, they were told that it was not important for them to attend, and that it would probably be better for them to plan to attend the meeting that would likely be held in mid-December to discuss Amelia's need for special education services. A few days later, Amelia's parents received a letter and consent form in the mail asking them to sign for permission to conduct an evaluation to determine whether Amelia was eligible to receive special education services. Amelia's parents, although discouraged and confused about what this meant, promptly signed and returned the form, assuming that the school knew what was in Amelia's best academic interests.

On December 15, a multidisciplinary team meeting was held. Mr. Martinez could not make it to the early afternoon meeting, given his work schedule. Mrs. Martinez was able to catch a bus and arrive at the school with her two young children 30 minutes prior to the meeting. At the meeting, several different professionals shuffled into the room at different times, with each presenting results from speech/language testing, intelligence testing, achievement testing, and classroom observations of Amelia. Toward the end of the meeting, a special education teacher asked Mrs. Martinez to sign some forms, which she was told would allow Amelia to get the services she needed, given that Amelia was in the words of her teacher "clearly a student with a learning disability."

Effective Communication of Assessment Information with Parents

In January of Amelia Martinez's first-grade year, Mr. and Mrs. Martinez received a phone call from her teacher. The teacher indicated that although Amelia was making many friends in first grade and seemed to get along very well with her classmates, she was performing below expectations in her development of early literacy skills as measured by the early literacy screening measures administered to all students in the fall and winter. The teacher invited Amelia's parents to attend a meeting in which they would discuss strategies for targeting instruction to Amelia's needs and discuss the possibility of implementing strategies at home for helping her develop early literacy skills.

At the meeting, Mr. and Mrs. Martinez, along with the classroom teacher and a more experienced first-grade teacher, discussed the fact that Amelia did not demonstrate adequate letter–sound correspondence. They developed a plan that allowed her to receive additional instruction and practice in this area at both home and school (with the teacher assistant) each day for six weeks, after which they would reconvene as a team to examine the progress that she had made. After six weeks, the two teachers and Amelia's parents met, and an additional person (that is, an intervention specialist) was added to the team to help identify any additional assessment and intervention that might be applied, given that Amelia had not made the progress needed to put her on track for learning how to read by the end of third grade. After reviewing Amelia's progress together, and recognizing that she had made small gains as a result of the intervention, they decided to intensify the support she was receiving by providing her more intervention time during the school day, and they continued to monitor her progress. Her mother was provided simple phonemic awareness development activities to practice with Amelia at home in the evening.

Soon after spring break of her first-grade year, the team reconvened to examine Amelia's progress, which continued to be below expectations. Together, the team decided that an evaluation for special education services was warranted. Mr. and Mrs. Martinez were provided information on their rights as parents of a child undergoing evaluation to determine special education eligibility. They were briefly told about the types of testing that would occur and how this would help determine whether Amelia might be in need of and benefit from special education services. At the end of her first-grade year, the team was brought together to examine the assessment results. Based on the information collected, it was clear that Amelia met the state criteria for having a specific learning disability in reading, and the team identified instructional strategies that were beneficial to include as part of an individualized education program for her.

This scenario depicts some important differences in effective versus ineffective communication with parents through the prereferral and eligibility determination processes. What are some of key differences in communication across the two scenarios presented?

23-4 Communicating Assessment Information Through Written and Electronic Records

Although presentation of assessment information and related decision making is frequently done verbally and in team meetings, assessment data are also collected, summarized, and interpreted in written form. Policies and standards for the collection, maintenance, and dissemination of information in written formats must balance two sometimes conflicting needs. Parents and children have a basic right to privacy;

schools need to collect and use information about children (and sometimes parents) in order to plan appropriate educational programs. Schools and parents have a common goal: to promote the welfare of children. In theory, schools and parents should agree on what constitutes and promotes a child's welfare, and in practice, schools and parents generally do work cooperatively.

In 1974, many of these recommended guidelines became federal law when the Family Educational Rights and Privacy Act (Public Law 93-380, commonly called FERPA) was enacted. Now these are incorporated within IDEA (IDEA §300.560–300.577). The basic provisions of the act are quite simple. All educational agencies that accept federal money (preschools, elementary and secondary schools, community colleges, and colleges and universities) must grant parents the opportunity to inspect and challenge student records; however, parents typically lose this right when their child turns 18. Regardless of whether the school decides to change the records according to parent input, parents have the right to supplement the records with what they understand to be true or with an explanation as to why they believe the file to be inaccurate. The only records to which parental access may be denied are the personal notes of teachers, supervisors, administrators, and other educational personnel that are kept in the sole possession of the maker of the records. Also, educational agencies must not release identifiable data without the parents' written consent. However, at age 18, the student becomes the individual who has the authority to provide consent for his or her data to be released to others. Violators of the provisions of FERPA are subject to sanctions; federal funds may be withheld from agencies found to be in violation of the law.

The following section discusses specific issues and principles in the collection, maintenance, and dissemination of pupil information through written records and electronic reports.

23-4a COLLECTION OF PUPIL INFORMATION

Schools routinely collect massive amounts of information about individual pupils and their parents, and not all of this information requires parental permission to collect or maintain. As discussed in Chapter 2, information can be used for a number of legitimate educational decisions: screening, progress monitoring, instructional planning and modification, resource allocation, special education eligibility determination, program evaluation, and accountability. Considerable data must be collected if a school system is to function effectively, both in delivering educational services to children and in reporting the results of its educational programs to the various community, state, and federal agencies to which it may be responsible.

Schoolwide Screening

Many schools systematically collect and keep written records of hearing, vision, and basic skill development across all students. The associated screening measures are intended to identify very early all students who have the potential for additional difficulties, and the screening measures are purposely developed to overidentify students. This can help to ensure that true difficulties are not missed, and that difficulties can be addressed earlier rather than later. When students fail to meet minimum thresholds of performance on screening measures, they may be referred for additional assessment to determine whether true difficulties exist. Vision and hearing screening records are typically maintained at the school for a substantial amount of time; review of this information can help determine that basic abilities such as hearing and vision are not contributing to difficulties that a student may experience.

In addition to hearing and vision information, individual student academic records may also contain results from group-administered district- and statewide assessment programs. With the increasing application of MTSS, schools are implementing additional screening and monitoring programs in order to ensure early identification of academic problems. Programs such as DIBELS, AIMSweb, and others described in Chapter 10 may be used to screen for academic problems and monitor student progress. Some screening is done schoolwide; however, other screening may occur for individual students who are initially identified as having difficulties. Students who do not meet benchmark levels on screening measures and who fail to make expected levels of progress toward meeting proficiency may be identified for additional assessment and referred to an intervention assistance team. Although it is best practice to remain in frequent communication with parents about data that are collected about their children, it is not always necessary to get their explicit permission for data collection. For example, prior to holding an intervention assistance team meeting, a school professional may collect data to inform the selection of an intervention that would target a student's individual academic deficits. Such assessment would not necessarily require explicit parent permission.

Consent for Additional Data Collection

Although it is best practice to communicate with parents frequently about student progress, and to alert them to any academic difficulties that the student is having as soon as possible, schools are not required to have parental consent for additional data collection unless a change in educational placement or the provision of a free and appropriate public education according to the Individuals with Disabilities Education Act (IDEA) is being considered.[1] In the section on procedural safeguards, IDEA mandates that prior written notice be given to the parents or guardians of a child whenever an educational agency proposes to initiate or change (or refuses to initiate or change) either the identification, evaluation, or educational placement of the child or the provision of a free and appropriate education to the child. It further requires that the notice fully inform the parent, in the parent's native language, regarding all appeal procedures available. Thus, schools must inform parents of their right to present any and all complaints regarding the identification, evaluation, or placement of their child; their right to an impartial due process hearing; and their right to appeal decisions reached at a due process hearing, if necessary, by bringing civil action against a school district.

Verification

Verifying information means ascertaining or confirming the information's truth, accuracy, or correctness. Depending on the type of information, verification may take several forms. For observations or ratings, verification means confirmation by another individual. For standardized test data, verification means conducting a reliable and valid assessment. (The concepts of reliability and validity are defined and discussed in detail in Chapter 5.)

Unverified information can be collected, but every attempt should be made to verify such information before it is retained in a student's records. For example, serious misconduct or extremely withdrawn behavior is of direct concern to the schools. Initial reports of such behavior by a teacher or counselor are typically based on observations that can be corroborated by other witnesses. Behavior that cannot be verified can still provide useful hints, hypotheses, and starting points for diagnosis. Ultimately, when the data are not confirmable, they should not be collected and must not be retained. We believe that this requirement should also apply to unreliable or invalid test data that cannot otherwise be substantiated.

Summarization and Interpretation

When additional assessment data are collected as part of an evaluation to determine whether a student is eligible to receive special education services under IDEA, a written report is typically developed prior to the multidisciplinary team meeting that will be held to determine whether a student is eligible for services. The purpose of the report is to summarize the assessment data collected. Written reports communicate information

---

[1] This is also the case if data are to be collected for the purpose of research. The collection of research data requires the individual informed consent of parents. Various professional groups, such as the American Psychological Association and the National Association of School Psychologists, consider the collection of data without informed consent to be unethical; according to the Buckley amendment, it is illegal to experiment with children without prior informed consent. Typically, informed consent for research-related data collection requires that the pupil or parents understand (1) the purpose of and procedures involved in the investigations, (2) any risks inherent in participation in the research, (3) the fact that all participants will remain anonymous, and (4) the participants' option to withdraw from the research at any time.

to both existing team members and those who may review the child's file in the future. Although the content of these reports will vary depending on the nature of data needed to determine eligibility, certain principles should be used to promote effective written communication about the data that are collected. These are discussed here.

- *Organize the report.* In general, an eligibility evaluation report will include the following information: a reason for referral, identifying and background information about the student, a description of the assessment methods and instruments used, documentation of interventions used and the associated results, information on observations conducted while assessment data were being collected (that is, to substantiate that test results represent accurate measures of typical student behavior), assessment results, recommendations, and an overall summary. In order for readers to easily access the information presented, it can be helpful to present assessment results in tables and figures.

- *Use language that is easily understood by team members.* As when communicating assessment information orally, it is important that your language is accessible to parents and other school professionals. Avoid jargon, and carefully explain all terminology that may be unfamiliar to any members of your audience. When reporting scores, it is important to use scores (like percentiles) that are easily interpreted by those who will read your report. When you are not sure whether readers will understand reported scores, explain them clearly. It is always best to err on the side of "overexplaining" than "underexplaining."

- *Focus on the reporting of observed behaviors.* In report writing, it is important to be transparent in how you describe assessment tasks and results. In your writing, clearly communicate that scores represent performance on particular tasks rather than innate student qualities or characteristics. In doing so, you will reflect more accurately the nature of the data collected and will help to avoid misinterpretations and high-level inferences based on collected data.

  Poor example of a report statement: John is average in his short-term memory capabilities.

  Better example of a report statement: On tasks that required John to listen to and recall numbers in the order that were verbally communicated to him by the examiner, John performed in the average range in comparison to his same-grade peers.

  However, it is important to ensure that the specific content of test items remains secure. When offering example items in written reports, avoid providing the exact content of test items and/or paraphrasing or revising an item in such a way that the item is essentially the same as the original.

- *Focus on relevant information.* You will likely sift through and collect a large amount of information in the process of conducting a special education eligibility evaluation. Instead of reporting on all information examined and collected, it is important to report only the most relevant information. In order to determine whether the information is relevant, ask yourself the following: (1) To what extent is the given information needed to answer the specific referral question? and (2) To what extent will the given information promote the provision of better educational services to the student? Include only those data that address these questions.

- *Clearly convey your level of certainty.* The potential for error is always present. When reporting the results of tests, it is important to convey this potential. In the presentation of test scores, we suggest explaining and providing confidence intervals for reported scores in order to appropriately communicate the existence of error in testing.

- *Make data-based recommendations.* The assessment summary and recommendations sections are by far the most frequently read sections of assessment reports. Recommendations are perhaps the most important aspect of reports; it is important that they are made very carefully and are clearly supported by the data collected. Although it is expected that the recommendation section will document what students need in order to ensure that they receive a free and appropriate public education, recommendations that are made carelessly and without adequate support can result in inefficient use of educational resources.

23-4b MAINTENANCE OF PUPIL INFORMATION

The decision to keep test results and other information should be governed by three principles: (1) retention of pupil information for limited periods of time, (2) parental rights of inspection and amendment, and (3) assurance of protection against inappropriate snooping. First, the information should be retained only as long as there is a continuing need for it. Only verified data of clear educational value should be retained. A pupil's school records should be periodically examined, and information that is no longer educationally relevant or no longer accurate should be removed. Natural transition points (for example, promotion from elementary school to junior high) should always be used to remove material from students' files.

The second major principle in the maintenance of pupil information is that parents have the right to inspect, challenge, and supplement student records. Parents of children with disabilities or with special gifts and talents have had the right to inspect, challenge, and supplement their children's school records for some time. Parents or guardians must be given the opportunity to examine all relevant records with respect to the identification, evaluation, and educational placement of the child and the free and appropriate public education of the child, and they must be given the opportunity to obtain an independent evaluation of the child. Again, if parents have complaints, they may request an impartial due process hearing to challenge either the records or the school's decision regarding their child.

The third major principle in the maintenance of pupil records is that the records should be protected from snoopers, both inside and outside the school system. In the past, secretaries, custodians, and even other students have had access, at least potentially, to pupil records. Curious teachers and administrators who had no legitimate educational interest had access. Individuals outside the schools, such as credit bureaus, have often found it easy to obtain information about former or current students. To ensure that only individuals with a legitimate need have access to the information contained in a pupil's records, it is recommended that pupil records be kept under lock and key. Adequate security mechanisms are necessary to ensure that the information in a pupil's records is not available to unauthorized personnel. With increasing electronic and Internet storage of records, it becomes increasingly important for appropriate security measures to be taken in order to avoid unauthorized access of information.

23-4c DISSEMINATION OF PUPIL INFORMATION

Educators need to consider both access to information by officials and dissemination of information to individuals and agencies outside the school. In both cases, the guiding principles are (1) the protection of pupils' and parents' rights to privacy and (2) the legitimate need to know particular information, as demonstrated by the person or agency to whom the information is disseminated.

Access Within the Schools

Those school professionals desiring access to pupil records must sign a form stating why they need to inspect the records. A list of people who have had access to their child's files and the reasons that access was sought should be available to parents. The provisions of both FERPA and IDEA state that all persons, agencies, or organizations desiring access to the records of a student shall be required to sign a written form that shall be kept permanently with the file of the student, but only for inspection by the parents or student, indicating specifically the legitimate educational or other interest that each person, agency, or organization has in seeking this information (§438, 4A; §300.563).

When a pupil transfers from one school district to another, the pupil's records are also transferred. FERPA is very specific with regard to the conditions of transfer. When a pupil's file is transferred to another school or school system in which the pupil plans to enroll, the school must (1) notify the pupil's parents that the records have been transferred, (2) send the parents a copy of the transferred records if the parents so desire, and (3) provide the parents with an opportunity to challenge the content of the transferred data.

Access for Individuals and Agencies Outside the Schools

School personnel collect information about pupils enrolled in the school system for educationally relevant purposes. There is an implicit agreement between the schools and the parents that the only justification for collecting and keeping any pupil data is educational relevance. However, because the schools have so much information about pupils, they are often asked for pupil data by potential employers, credit agencies, insurance companies, police, the armed services, the courts, and various social agencies. To divulge information to any of these sources is a violation of this implicit trust unless the pupil (if older than 18 years) or the parents request that the information be released. However, many schools create forms that parents can sign to indicate their willingness for information to be exchanged about their child between the school and certain outside agencies. Note that the courts and various administrative agencies have the power to subpoena pupil records from schools. In such cases, FERPA requires that the parents be notified that the records will be turned over in compliance with the subpoena.

Except in the case of the subpoena of records or the transfer of records to another school district, no school personnel should release any pupil information without the written consent of the parents. FERPA states that no educational agency may release pupil information unless "there is written consent from the student's parents specifying records to be released, the reasons for such release, and to whom, and with a copy of the records to be released to the student's parents and the student if desired by the parents" (§438, b2A).

Electronic Communication

The increasing use of technology in schools has strong potential to promote student learning, as noted in several chapters throughout this book. Large files containing student performance data can be maintained on computers and allow for more efficient analysis of student data. The use of email can also greatly enhance the speed with which information is disseminated. However, with these advances also comes a need for guidelines to prevent misuse and mishandling of this information, given that such information can be more easily transmitted to those who do not have a right or a need to have the given information. Password-protection systems should be developed and used to ensure that only those who have a legitimate need can access specific student information electronically (this includes password-protecting flash drives or CDs). Separate identification codes should be developed and used rather than actual student names and identification numbers within large datasets that include sensitive information. Also, email messages should be encrypted or worded in a way that avoids use of actual student names in order to prevent accidental transmission or forwarding to those who do not need the given information.

Chapter Comprehension Questions

Write your answers to each of the following questions and then compare your responses to the text.

1. Describe four characteristics of effective school teams.

2. Name and describe the functions of three types of teams commonly formed in school settings.

3. What are some potential barriers to communicating effectively about assessment with parents? What are some ways to overcome these barriers?

4. What are some ways in which assessment information is communicated in written form in schools? What are the rules governing who has access to this information?

GLOSSARY

ABC event recording A qualitative observational method in which the observer records descriptions of the behaviors of interest, along with the antecedents and consequences that correspond to the behaviors of interest

accountability decisions Decisions in which assessment information is used to decide the extent to which school districts, schools, and individual teachers are making adequate progress with the students they teach

accountability systems Systems that hold schools responsible for helping all students reach high, challenging standards, and that provide rewards to schools that reach those standards and sanctions to schools that do not

acculturation A process an individual goes through in adapting to a new culture

accuracy The number of correct responses divided by the number of attempted responses multiplied by 100; expressed in terms of percent (e.g., 90% accurate)

achievement What has been directly taught and learned by a student

achievement standards (sometimes called *performance standards*) Statements of the levels at which, or the proficiency with which, students show that they have mastered the academic content standards

adaptive behavior The process of students adapting to their physical and social environments, to stay safe, and avoid danger

age equivalent This means that a child's raw score is the average (the median or mean) performance for that age group. Age equivalents are expressed in years and months

agreement for occurrence An indication of percent agreement for two observers that is given by the following formula: 100 × (Number of agreed occurrences)/(number of observations – number of agreed nonoccurrences); it is considered a better measure of agreement than point-to-point agreement when occurrences and nonoccurrences differ substantially, because point-to-point agreement tends to overestimate the agreement

alternate achievement standards Expectations for performance that differ in complexity from grade-level achievement standards, but which are linked to those general education standards

alternate assessment An assessment designed for the small number of students with disabilities who are unable to participate in the regular state assessment, even with appropriate accommodations

alternate-form reliability The correlation between scores for the same individuals on two different forms of a test. These forms (1) measure the same trait or skill to the same extent and (2) are standardized on the same population

American Psychological Association's (2002) Ethical Principles of Psychologists and Code of Conduct A document that explains ethical principles psychologists are expected to use to guide their professional practice

Americans with Disabilities Act (ADA) The law that requires agencies receiving federal funding to provide appropriate access to their activities for individuals with disabilities

Americans with Disabilities Act Amendments of 2008 (ADAA) Reauthorization and revision of ADA

amplitude The intensity of a behavior

antecedents Events that include what is happening right before the behavior occurs, and which may include things like what the student has been asked to do, or any related teacher or peer communication that occurs right before the behavior of interest

assessment The process of collecting information (data) for the purpose of making decisions for or about individuals

attainment What has been learned anywhere

basal rule A rule that provides information on how many consecutive items a student must correctly answer in order for earlier items (that are consequently not administered) to be scored as correct

basals The point in a subtest at which it can be assumed the student would get all prior items correct

behavioral topography The way in which a behavior is performed

benchmark A reference standard for minimally accepted performance

beneficence Responsible caring

bias Measurement error that is systematic and predictable

ceiling rule A rule that provides information on how many consecutive items a student must incorrectly answer in order for later items (that are then not administered) to be scored as incorrect

Common Core State Standards Quantifiable benchmarks in English language arts (ELA) and math at each grade level from kindergarten through high school

competency-based assessment Assessment of very specific knowledge and skills using authentic or simulated situations in which the knowledge and skill can be demonstrated

computer adaptive testing An assessment method whereby items are selected for administration based on the student's performance on earlier items within the test

confirmation bias The tendency to primarily pay attention to data that confirm one's original hypothesis while disregarding or underemphasizing data that conflict with the original hypothesis

consequences Events that happen right after a behavior occurs, and which may include things like the provision of a time-out, peer laughing/attention, teacher redirection, teacher praise

content of written expression   The product of considerable intellectual and linguistic activity: formulating, elaborating, sequencing, and then clarifying and revising ideas; choosing the precise word to convey meaning; and so forth

contrived observations   Observations of student behavior that occur when a situation is set up before a student is introduced into it

correlation coefficients   Numerical indexes of the relationship between two variables

criterion-referenced   Interpretation of an individual's performance where there must be a clear, objective criterion for each of the correct responses to each question, or to each portion of the question if partial credit is to be awarded

cross-battery assessment   An approach to intelligence testing that takes into consideration issues with low subtest reliabilities

crystallized intelligence   The knowledge and skill one acquires over time, which increases steadily throughout one's life

curriculum-based measurement   A standardized set of procedures that allow one to directly measure important skills in a relatively short amount of time

deciles   Bands of percentiles that are 10 percentile ranks in width; each decile contains 10 percent of the norm group. The first decile ranges from 0.1 to 9.9; the second ranges from 10 to 19.9; the tenth decile goes from 90 to 99.9

derived scores   Two types of norm-referenced scores: developmental scores and scores of relative standing

developmental equivalents   A type of developmental score that may be age equivalents or grade equivalents and are based on the average performance of individuals

differentiated instruction   A process that involves matching the content and instructional approach to individual students' learning needs in order to accelerate the learning of all students

direct behavior rating (DBR)   A quantitative observational method that involves selection of a target behavior and observation time, provision of a rating for the selected behavior at the selected time, and communication of that rating to various individuals; it is increasingly used as a part of assessment and intervention of problematic behavior in schools

discriminative stimuli   Stimuli that are consistently present when a behavior is reinforced and that come to bring out the behavior even in the absence of the original reinforcer

distribution's shape   A two-dimensional plot of scores by the number of people earning each score

due process   A constitutional guarantee that the various procedures specified in federal and state regulations will be followed in legal and quasi-legal proceedings

duration   The length of time a behavior lasts

Education for All Handicapped Children Act (Public Law 94-142)   A law that included many instructional and assessment requirements for serving and identifying students with disabilities in need of specially designed instruction. The law was reauthorized, amended, and updated in 1986, 1990, 1997, and 2004

eligibility decisions   Decisions that involve the collection and use of assessment information to decide whether a student meets the state criteria for a disability condition and needs special education services to be successful in school

equal-interval scales   Ratio scales that do not have an absolute and logical zero

evidence-based instructional methods   Teaching methods proven to work

first tier within a multi-tiered system of supports (MTSS)   The core instructional programming made available to all students

fluency   The number of correct responses per minute

fluid intelligence   The efficiency with which an individual learns and completes various tasks. This type of intelligence increases as a person ages until early adulthood and then decreases somewhat steadily over time

form of written language   The conventions or rules that are evident in writing output; it is far more mechanistic than its content

frequency   The number of times a behavior occurs

functional behavioral assessment (FBA)   A set of assessment procedures used to identify the function of a student's problematic behavior, as well as the various conditions under which it tends to occur. It involves the integration of data from a variety of methods to meaningfully inform intervention efforts

function of a behavior   The reason a person behaves as he or she does, or the purpose a behavior serves

gap analysis   Examining the difference between the actual rate of improvement for a student and the rate of improvement that would be necessary to attain an expected benchmark level by a particular point in time

grade equivalent   This means that a child's raw score is the average (the median or mean) performance for a particular grade. Grade equivalents are expressed in grades and tenths of grades

group polarization   A condition where groups tend to become more extreme in their decision making than what any individual originally intended (which could either hinder or promote best practice)

groupthink   The tendency in group decision making to agree with the majority opinion

growth norms   Norms that are used to assign percentiles and standard scores to differences in scores from one test to another (e.g., the amount of gain from pretest to posttest) over a specified amount of time

growth percentile   A measurement determined by comparing the target student's growth to the growth of similar peers who scored at the same initial level as the target student

inclusive education   Educational approaches that facilitate learning of all students, including those with and without disabilities, within the same environment

individualized education program (IEP)   A legal document that describes the services that are to be provided to a student with a disability who qualifies for special education services

Individuals with Disabilities Education Act (IDEA)   A reauthorization of the Education for All Handicapped Children Act that included updated provisions for identifying and serving students with disabilities. To reflect contemporary practices, Congress replaced references to "handicapped children" with "children with disabilities"

instructional planning and modification decisions   The collection of assessment information for the purpose of planning individualized instruction or making changes in the instruction students are receiving

internal consistency   An approach to estimating the extent to which we can generalize to different test items; it is a measure of the extent to which items in a test correlate with one another

interobserver agreement   The consistency among test scorers

interval sampling   An observation session that is subdivided into intervals during which behavior is observed

interview   An assessment method involving a conversation between two or more people where questions are asked by the interviewer to elicit facts or statements from the interviewee

kurtosis   The peakedness of a curve—that is, the rate at which a curve rises and falls

latency   The length of time between a signal to perform and the beginning of the behavior

least restrictive environment (LRE)   The specification in IDEA that, to the maximum extent appropriate, students with disabilities are to be educated with children who are not disabled, and that they should be removed to separate classes, schools, or elsewhere only when the nature or severity of their disability is such that education in regular classes with the use of supplementary aids and services cannot be achieved satisfactorily

leptokurtic   Fast-rising distributions with strong peaks

maintenance   Behavioral recurrence over time

mean   The arithmetic average of the scores in the distribution; the most important average for use in assessment

median   The point in a distribution above which are 50 percent of test takers (not test scores) and below which are 50 percent of test takers (not test scores)

mode   The score most frequently obtained. A mode (if there is one) can be found for data on nominal, ordinal, ratio, or equal-interval scales

momentary time sampling   The most efficient sampling procedure. An observation session is subdivided into intervals. If a behavior is occurring at the last moment of the interval, an occurrence is recorded; if the behavior is not occurring at the last moment of the interval, a nonoccurrence is recorded

multiple-skill achievement tests   Tests that evaluate knowledge and understanding in several curricular areas, such as reading, spelling, math, and/or language. These tests are intended to assess the extent to which students have profited from schooling and other life experiences, compared with other students of the same age or grade

multi-tiered system of supports (MTSS)   "A coherent continuum of evidence-based, system-wide practices to support a rapid response to academic and behavior needs with frequent data-based monitoring for instructional decision making to empower each student to achieve to high standards" (taken directly from the website of the Kansas Multi-Tier System of Supports)

National Association of School Psychologists' (2010) Principles for Professional Ethics   A document that explains ethical principles school psychologists are expected to use to guide their professional practice

National Education Association's Code of Ethics of the Education Profession   A document that explains ethical principles educators are expected to use to guide their professional practice

naturalistic observations   Observations that occur in settings that are not contrived

negatively skewed   A distribution that occurs when a test is too easy, and many students earn high scores and fewer students earn low scores. There will be more scores above the mean that are balanced by fewer but more extreme scores below the mean

No Child Left Behind Act of 2001   is the reform of the federal Elementary and Secondary Education Act, signed into law on January 8, 2002, and it has several major provisions that affect assessment and instruction of students with disabilities and disadvantaged students

nominal scales   Scales that name the values of the scale, but adjacent values have no inherent relationship

normative sample   (also referred to as a "**standardization sample**" or "**norms**") The sample of individuals to whom an individual is compared when one obtains a derived score

nonsystematic, or informal, observation   Process wherein an observer simply watches an individual in his or her environment and notes the behaviors, characteristics, and personal interactions that seem significant

normative sample   (also referred to as a "**standardization sample**" or "**norms**") The sample of individuals to whom an individual is compared when one obtains a derived score

norm-referenced   Interpretations of a student's performance compared to the performances of other students—usually students of similar demographic characteristics (age, gender, grade in school, and so forth). In order to make this type of comparison, a student's score is transformed into a derived score

norm-referenced benchmarks   Progress monitoring tools that are connected to information gathered on the performance and typical growth of thousands of same-grade peers from across the nation

objective scoring   Scoring that is based on observable public criteria

observation sessions   Blocks of time in which observations will be made

obtrusive   Observations are obtrusive when it is obvious to the person being observed that he or she is being observed

ordinal scales   Scales that order values from worse to better (for example, pass-fail, or poor-OK-good-better-best), and there is a relationship among adjacent scores

partial-interval sampling   Sampling wherein an occurrence is scored if it occurs during any part of the interval

peer nomination techniques   Techniques that require that students identify other students whom they prefer on some set of criteria (such as students they would like to have as study partners)

percent correct   A calculation made by dividing the number correct by the number possible and multiplying that quotient by 100

percentile ranks (percentiles)   Derived scores that indicate the percentage of people whose scores are at or below a given raw score

performance standards   (see *achievement standards*)

phonics instruction   Systematically teaching beginning readers the relationships among the alphabetic code, phonemes, and words; increasingly becoming a part of prereading and reading instruction

platykurtic   Distributions that are relatively flat

point-to-point agreement   A relatively precise way of computing percentage of agreement because each data point is considered. Point-to-point agreement is calculated by dividing the number of observations for which both observers agree (occurrence and nonoccurrence) by the total number of observations and multiplying the quotient by 100

positively skewed   Distributions that occur when a test is difficult, and many students earn low scores while a few students earn high scores. There are more scores below the mean that are balanced by fewer but more extreme scores above the mean

probe   A special testing format well suited to the direct assessment of student skills in a short amount of time

program evaluation decisions   Decisions in which the emphasis is on gauging the effectiveness of the curriculum in meeting the goals and objectives of the school

program planning   Includes defining a problem, goal setting, development and implementation of intervention strategies, and evaluation

progress monitoring decisions   Decisions that answer the following questions: (1) Is the student making adequate progress toward individual goals? and (2) Is the student making adequate progress toward common core standards or specified state standards?

qualitative data   Pieces of information collected based on nonsystematic and unquantified observations

qualitative observations   Observations that can describe behavior as well as its contexts (that is, antecedents and consequences), and usually occur without predetermining the behaviors to be observed or the times and contexts in which to observe

quantitative data   Observations that have been tabulated or otherwise given numerical values

quartiles   Bands of percentiles that are 25 percentiles wide; each quartile contains 25 percent of the norm group. The first quartile ranges from the 0.1 to 24.9 percentile; the fourth quartile contains percentiles 75 to 99.9

Race to the Top   A federal program that has granted funds to two consortia of states for the development of common assessments that measure student achievement against standards that represent what is needed to be successful in the workplace and college

random error   In measurement, sources of variation in scores that make it impossible to generalize from an observation of a specific behavior observed at a specific time by a specific person to observations conducted on similar behavior, at different times, or by different observers

range   The distance between the extremes of a distribution; it is usually defined as the highest score less the lowest score

rate of improvement (ROI)   A trend or slope in improvement, used as an index of the extent to which the student is responding to instruction and intervention

ratio scales   Scales that not only order values but also have two very important characteristics: (1) the magnitude of the difference between adjacent values is known and is equal, and (2) each scale has an absolute and logical zero

record review   An assessment method involving review of student cumulative records or medical records

reliability   The extent to which it is possible to generalize from an observation or test score made at a specific time by a specific person to a similar performance at a different time, or by a different person

reliability coefficient   The proportion of variability in a set of scores that reflects true differences among individuals

resource allocation decisions   The collection and use of assessment information for the purpose of deciding what kinds of resources and supports individual students need in order to be successful in school

retention   The percentage of learned information that is recalled. Retention may also be termed recall, maintenance, or memory of what has been learned

rubrics   A scoring method that specifies the criteria for awarding of points

scatterplot   A graph that uses Cartesian coordinates to depict a person's scores on two measures—one on the x-axis and one on the y-axis

scores of relative standing   Scores that compare a student's performance to the performances of similar (in age or grade) students

screening decisions   Involve the collection of assessment information for the purpose of deciding whether students have unrecognized problems

second tier   Within a multi-tiered system of supports (MTSS), the set of services provided to those students who are not meeting benchmark with first-tier services alone, but who are not determined eligible for third-tier services; second services are of greater intensity and frequency, and are more targeted to students' identified needs than first-tier services

Section 504 of the Rehabilitation Act of 1973   A federal law that gave individuals with disabilities equal access to programs and services funded by federal monies

series of tiers   Tiers within the funnel or triangle of a Multi-Tiered System of Supports (MTSS) that describe the intensity of instruction, not specific places, programs or types of students, or staff

setting events   Environmental events that set the occasion for the performance of an action

simple agreement   Agreement that is calculated by dividing the smaller number of occurrences by the larger number of occurrences and multiplying the quotient by 100

skew   The asymmetry of a distribution of scores

sociometric ranking techniques   Techniques that involve asking students to rank other students on various social dimensions

special education   A set of unique educational services and supports provided to students with disabilities who meet particular disability criteria; these may include services provided in separate settings or services provided in settings comprising both students with and without disabilities

specialized norms   All comparisons that are not national. One type of specialized norm is referred to as local norms. Local norms may be based on an entire state, school district, or even a classroom

stability or maintenance   Behavioral recurrence over time

standard deviation   A numerical index describing the dispersion of a set of scores around the mean that is calculated as the positive square root of the variance

standardization   The process of using the same materials, procedures (for example, directions and time allowed to complete a test), and scoring standards for each test taker each time the test is given

standardization sample   See *normative* sample

standard scores   Derived scores with a predetermined mean and standard deviation

Standards for Educational and Psychological Testing   Standards that specify a set of requirements for test development and use

standards-referenced   Interpretation of an individual's performance based on comparison to the state standards

standards-referenced benchmarks   Progress monitoring tools that are connected to state or common core standards, such that a student's performance according to these standards can be evaluated

student accountability   Accountability designed to motivate students to do their best

subjective scoring   Scoring that relies on private criteria that can and do vary from tester to tester

symmetrical distribution   Distribution where the scores above the mean mirror the scores below the mean

system accountability   Accountability designed to improve educational programs; the focus of federal education reform efforts

systematic error   A consistent error that can be predicted; bias

systematic observation   Observation that is distinguished by five steps that occur in advance of the actual observations: (1) The behavior is defined precisely and objectively, (2) the characteristics of the behavior (for example, frequency) are specified, (3) procedures for recording are developed, (4) the times and places for observation are selected and specified, and (5) procedures are developed to assess interobserver agreement

test   A predetermined set of questions or tasks for which predetermined types of behavioral responses are sought

test accommodations   Changes made in the presentation, setting, response, or timing/scheduling of a test that allow for more accurate measurement of the intended skills and knowledge among the particular students to whom they are provided

test adaptations   Changes made in the presentation, setting, response, or timing/scheduling of a test that may or may not influence the construct that is measured

testing   Administering a predetermined set of questions or tasks, for which predetermined types of behavioral responses are sought, to an individual or group of individuals in order to obtain a score

test modifications   Changes made that alter the measurement of the intended skills and knowledge, such that it is highly questionable whether the test results accurately represent a student's skill and knowledge

third tier   Within a multi-tiered system of supports (MTSS), the set of services provided to those students who are not meeting benchmark with first- and second-tier services alone, and are determined to be eligible for third-tier services; third-tier services are of greater intensity and frequency, and are more targeted to students' identified needs than first- and second-tier services

typical benchmark   A minimal standard for performance, helping to indicate the growth rate required of a grade-level peer during the course of regular instruction to meet the minimal level required of all students (a specific grade-level or age-level standard)

universal design for assessment   Concept that involves careful consideration of the needs of all individuals who might need to participate in the test when the test is first developed

unobtrusive   Observations wherein the people being observed do not realize they are being watched

validity   The degree to which evidence and theory support the interpretation of test scores for proposed uses of tests, therefore the most fundamental consideration in developing and evaluating tests

variance   A numerical index describing the dispersion of a set of scores around the mean of the distribution

whole-interval sampling   Sampling in which a behavior is scored as having occurred only when it occurs throughout the entire interval

z-scores   The most basic standard score; transform raw scores into a distribution in which the mean is always equal to 0 and the standard deviation is always equal to 1, regardless of the mean and standard deviation of the raw (obtained) scores

REFERENCES

Achenbach, T. M. (1986). *The Direct Observation Form (DOF)*. Burlington: University of Vermont, Department of Psychiatry.

Achenbach, T. M., & Rescorla, L. A. (2000). *Manual for the ASEBA Preschool Forms and Profiles*. Burlington: University of Vermont, Department of Psychiatry.

Achenbach, T. M., & Rescorla, L. A. (2001). *Manual for the ASEBA School-Age Forms and Profiles*. Burlington: University of Vermont, Department of Psychiatry.

Adams, M. (1990). *Beginning to Read: Thinking and Learning About Print*. Cambridge, MA: MIT Press.

Alberto, P. A., & Troutman, A. C. (2005). *Applied Behavior Analysis for Teachers* (7th ed.). Upper Saddle River, NJ: Prentice-Hall.

American Association for the Advancement of Science. (1987). *Science for All Americans*. New York: Oxford University Press.

American Association for the Advancement of Science. (1993). *Benchmarks for Science Literacy*. New York: Oxford University Press.

American Educational Research Association (AERA), American Psychological Association, & National Council on Measurement in Education. (2014). *Standards for Educational and Psychological Testing*. Washington, DC: American Educational Research Association.

American Psychological Association. (2010). *Ethical Principles of Psychologists and Code of Conduct*. Washington, DC: Author.

Ames, W. (1965). A comparison of spelling textbooks. *Elementary English, 42*, 146–150, 214.

Ardoin, S. P., & Christ, T. J. (2009). Curriculum based measurement of oral reading: Estimates of standard error when monitoring progress using alternate passage sets. *School Psychology Review, 38*, 266–283.

Armbruster, B., & Osborn, J. (2001). *Put Reading First: The Research Building Blocks for Teaching Children to Read*. Jessup, MD: Partnership for Reading. Available from the National Institute for Literacy website: https://lincs.ed.gov/publications/pdf/PRFbooklet.pdf.

Ayers, A. (1981). *Sensory Integration and the Child*. Los Angeles, CA: Western Psychological Services.

Bachor, D. (1990). The importance of shifts in language level and extraneous information in determining word-problem difficulty: Steps toward individual assessment. *Diagnostique, 14*, 94–111.

Bachor, D., Stacy, N., & Freeze, D. (1986). *A Conceptual Framework for Word Problems: Some Preliminary Results*. Paper presented at the conference of the Canadian Society for Studies in Education, Winnipeg, Manitoba.

Bailey, D. B., & Rouse, T. L. (1989). Procedural considerations in assessing infants and preschoolers with handicaps. In D. B. Bailey & M. Wolery (Eds.), *Assessing Infants and Preschoolers with Handicaps*. Columbus, OH: Merrill.

Baker, E. L., Bewley, W. L., Herman, J. L., Lee, J. J., & Mitchell, D. S. (2001). *Upgrading America's Use of Information to Improve Student Performance* (Proposal to the U.S. Secretary of Education). Los Angeles: University of California, National Center for Research on Evaluation, Standards, and Student Testing.

Baker, E. L., & Linn, R. L. (2002). *Validity Issues for Accountability Systems*. Los Angeles, CA: University of California, National Center for Research on Evaluation, Standards, and Student Testing.

Bandura, A. (1969). *Principles of Behavior Modification*. Oxford: Holt, Rinehart, & Winston.

Barnett, D. W., Daly, E. J., Jones, K. M., & Lentz, F. E. (2004). Response to intervention: Empirically based special service decisions from single-case designs of increasing and decreasing intensity. *Journal of Special Education, 38*, 66–79.

Barsch, R. (1966). Teacher needs motor training. In W. Cruickshank (Ed.), *The Teacher of Brain-Injured Children*. Syracuse, NY: Syracuse University Press.

Baumgardner, J. C. (1993). *An Empirical Analysis of School Psychological Assessments: Practice with Students who are Deaf and Bilingual*. Unpublished doctoral dissertation, University of Minnesota, Minneapolis.

Bayley, N. (2006). *Bayley Scales of Infant and Toddler Development*. San Antonio, TX: Psychological Corporation.

Beck. R. (1979). *Great Falls Precision Teaching Project: Report for Joint Dissemination and Review Panel*. Great Falls, MT: Great Falls Public Schools.

Beery, K. E. (1982). *Revised Administration, Scoring, and Teaching Manual for the Developmental Test of Visual-Motor Integration*. Cleveland, OH: Modern Curriculum Press.

Beery, K. E. (1989). *The Developmental Test of Visual-Motor Integration*. Cleveland, OH: Modern Curriculum Press.

Beery, K. E., & Beery, N. (2004). *Beery VMI*. Minneapolis, MN: NCS Pearson.

Bell, P. (1992). Effects of curriculum-test overlap on standardized achievement test scores: Identifying systematic confounds in educational decision-making. *School Psychology Review, 21*(4), 644–655.

Bender, L. (1938). *Bender Visual-Motor Gestalt Test*. New York: Grune & Stratton.

Bergen, J. R. & Kratochwill, T. R. (1990). *Behavioral Consultation*. Columbus, OH: Merrill.

Berninger, V. W., Vaughn, K., Abbott, R. D., Brooks, A., Abbott, S., Reed, E., et al. (1998). Early intervention for spelling problems: Teaching spelling units of various size within a multiple connections framework. *Journal of Educational Psychology, 90,* 587–605.

Bess, F. H., & Hall, J. W. (1992). *Screening Children for Auditory Function.* Nashville, TN: Bill Wilkerson Center Press.

Betebenner, D. (2008). Towards a normative understanding of student growth. In K. E. Ryan & L. A. Shepard (Eds.), *The Future of Test-Based Educational Accountability* (pp. 155–170). New York: Taylor & Francis.

Betebenner, D. (2009). Norm- and criterion-referenced student growth. *Educational Measurement: Issues and Practice, 28,* 42–51.

Betebenner, D. & Linn, R. L. (2010). *Growth in Student Achievement: Issues of Measurement, Longitudinal Data Analysis and Accountability.* Princeton, NJ: Educational Testing Service.

Betts, J. (2005). *Evaluating Different Methods for Making Value-Added Decisions Across Classrooms.* Minneapolis, MN: Minnesota Public Schools: Research, Evaluation and Assessment.

Betts, J. (April, 2010). *Measuring Academic Growth with Growth Norms: A Method for RTI Models.* Paper presented at the annual meeting of the National Council on Measurement in Education conference. Denver, CO.

Blake, J., Austin, W., Cannon, M., Lisius, A., & Vaughn, A. (1994). The relationship between memory span and measures of imitative and spontaneous language complexity in preschool children. *International Journal of Behavioral Development, 17*(1), 91–107.

Boehm, A. E. (2001). *Boehm Test of Basic Concepts—Third Edition.* Bloomington, MN: Pearson.

Bolt, D. M, Ysseldyke, J. E. & Patterson, M. J. (2010). Students, teachers, and schools as sources of variability, integrity, and sustainability in implementing progress monitoring. *School Psychology Review, 39*(4), 612–630.

Bond, G., & Dykstra, R. (1967). The cooperative research program in first-grade reading instruction (1967). *Reading Research Quarterly, 2,* 5–142.

Bracken, B., & McCallum, R. S. (1998). *Universal Nonverbal Intelligence Test.* Itasca, IL: Riverside Publishing Company.

Brannigan, G., & Decker, S. (2003). *Bender Visual-Motor Gestalt Test* (2nd ed.). Itasca, IL: Riverside Publishing.

Breland, H. (1983). *The Direct Assessment of Writing Skill: A Measurement Review* (College Board Report No. 83-6). New York: College Entrance Examination Board.

Breland, H., Camp, R., Jones, R., Morris, M. M., & Rock, D. (1987). *Assessing Writing Skill.* New York: The College Board.

Briggs, A., & Underwood, G. (1984). Phonological coding in good and poor readers. *Reading Research Quarterly, 20,* 54–66.

Broderick, C. B. (1993). *Understanding Family Process: Basics of Family Systems Theory.* Newbury Park, CA: Sage.

Brown, L., & Hammill, D. (1990). *Behavior Rating Profile* (2nd ed.). Austin, TX: Pro-Ed.

Brown, L., Hammill, D., & Wiederholt, J. L. (1995). *Test of Reading Comprehension–3.* Austin, TX: Pro-Ed.

Brown, L., Sherbenou, R., & Johnsen, S. (1997). *Test of Nonverbal Intelligence–3.* Austin, TX: Pro-Ed.

Brown, V., Wiederholt, J. L., & Hammill, D. D. (2009). *Test of Reading Comprehension* (4th ed.). Austin, TX: PRO-ED.

Bruininks, R., Woodcock, R., Weatherman, R., & Hill, B. (1996). *Scales of Independent Behavior, Revised, Comprehensive Manual.* Chicago: Riverside Publishing Company.

Butcher, N. N., Graham, J. R., Ben-Porath, Y. S., Tellegen, Y. S., Dahlstrom, W. G., & Kaemmer, B. (2001). *Minnesota Multiphasic Personality Inventory-2.* Minneapolis, MN: University of Minnesota Press.

Caldwell, J., & Goldin, J. (1979). Variables affecting word problem difficulty in elementary school mathematics. *Journal of Research in Mathematics Education, 10,* 323–335.

Camarata, S. M., & Nelson, K. E. (1994). Comparison of conversational recasting and imitative procedures for training grammatical structures in children with specific language impairment. *Journal of Speech, Language and Hearing Research, 37,* 1414–1423.

Campbell, D., & Fiske, D. (1959). Convergent and discriminate validation by the multitrait-multimethod matrix. *Psychological Bulletin, 56*(2), 81–105.

Caplan, G. (1964). *The Principles of Preventive Psychiatry.* New York, NY: Basic Books.

Carrow-Woolfolk, E. (1995). *Manual for the Listening Comprehension and Oral Language Subtests of the Oral and Written Language Scales.* Circle Pines, MN: American Guidance Service.

Carrow-Woolfolk, E. (1999a). *Comprehensive Assessment of Spoken Language.* Circle Pines, MN: American Guidance Service.

Carrow-Woolfolk, E. (1999b). *Test for Auditory Comprehension of Language* (3rd ed.). San Antonio, TX: Harcourt.

Center for Universal Design. (1997). *The Principles of Universal Design, Version 2.0.* Raleigh: North Carolina State University.

Chafouleas, S. M., Riley-Tillman, T. C. & Christ, T. J. (2009). Direct Behavior Rating (DBR): An emerging method for assessing social behavior within a tiered intervention system. *Assessment for Effective Intervention, 34,* 195–200.

Chafouleas, S., Briesch, A., Riley-Tillman, T. C., Christ, T. J., Black, A. C., & Kilgus, S. P. (2010). An investigation of the generalizability and dependability of Direct Behavior Rating Single Item Scales (DBR-SIS) to measure academic engagement and disruptive behavior of middle school students. *Journal of School Psychology, 48,* 219–246.

Chall, J. (1967). *Learning to Read: The Great Debate.* New York: McGraw-Hill.

Chase, J. B. (1985). Assessment of the visually impaired. *Diagnostique, 10,* 144–160.

Christ, T. J., & Aranas, Y. A. (2014). Best practices in problem analysis. In P. L Harrison & A. Thomas (Eds.),

Best Practices in School Psychology: Data Based and Collaborative Decision Making. Bethesda, MD: NASP Publications, 87–98.

Christ, T. J., & Ardoin, S. P. (2009). Curriculum-based measurement of oral reading: Passage equivalence and probe-set development. *Journal of School Psychology, 47,* 55–75.

Conners, C. K. (1997). *Conners Parent Rating Scale-Revised.* New York: Psychological Corporation.

Connolly, J. (2007). *KeyMath 3 Diagnostic Assessment (KeyMath 3 DA).* Minneapolis, MN: Pearson.

Cooper, C. (1977). Holistic evaluation of writing. In C. Cooper & L. Odell (Eds.), *Evaluating Writing: Describing, Measuring, Judging.* Buffalo, NY: National Council of Teachers of English.

Crocker, L. M., Miller, M. D., & Franks, E. A. (1989). Quantitative methods for assessing the fit between test and curriculum. *Applied Measurement in Education, 2*(2), 179–194.

Cronbach, L. (1951). Coefficient alpha and the internal structure of tests. *Psychometrika, 16,* 297–334.

CTB McGraw-Hill (undated). *Yearly Progress Pro.* Monterey, CA: author.

CTB/McGraw-Hill. (2004). *Guidelines for Inclusive Test Administration 2005.* Monterey, CA: Author.

CTB/McGraw-Hill. (2008). *TerraNova—Third Edition.* Monterey, CA: Author.

Cummins, J. (1984). *Bilingual Special Education: Issues in Assessment and Pedagogy.* San Diego, CA: College Hill.

Das, J., & Naglieri, J. (1997). *Cognitive Assessment System.* Itasca, IL: Riverside Publishing.

Deming, W. E. (1994). *The New Economics for Industry, Government and Education.* Cambridge, MA: MIT, Center for Advanced Educational Services.

Deming, W. E. (2000). *The New Economics for Industry, Government and Education* (2nd ed.). Cambridge, MA: MIT Press.

Deno, S. L. (1985). Curriculum-based assessment: The emerging alternative. *Exceptional Children, 52,* 219–232.

Deno, S. L., & Fuchs, L. S. (1987). Developing curriculum-based measurement systems for data-based special education problem solving. *Focus on Exceptional Children, 19,* 1–16.

Deno, S. L., & Mirkin, P. (1977). *Data-Based Program Modification: A Manual.* Reston, VA: Council for Exceptional Children.

Derogatis, L. R. (1993). *Brief Symptom Inventory.* Minneapolis, MN: National Computer Systems.

Diana v. State Board of Education, 1970 (*Diana v. State Board of Education,* C-70: 37RFT) (N.D. Cal., 1970).

Doman, R., Spitz, E., Zuckerman, E., Delacato, C., & Doman, G. (1967). Children with severe brain injuries: Neurological organization in terms of mobility. In E. C. Frierson & W. B. Barbe (Eds.), *Educating Children with Learning Disabilities.* New York: Appleton-Century-Crofts.

Dunn, L. M., & Dunn, M. (2007). *Peabody Picture Vocabulary Test* (4th ed.). San Antonio, TX: Pearson Assessment.

Dunn, L. M., & Markwardt, F. C. (1970). *Peabody Individual Achievement Test.* Circle Pines: MN: American Guidance Service.

Dunn, L. M., & Markwardt, F. C. (1998). *Peabody Individual Achievement Test—Revised/Normative Update.* Circle Pines, MN: American Guidance Service.

Educational Testing Service. (1990). *Exploring New Methods for Collecting Students' School-Based Writing: NAEP's 1990 Portfolio Study* (ED 343154). Washington, DC: U.S. Department of Education.

Elmore, R. (2002). *Bridging the Gap Between Standards and Achievement.* Washington, DC: The Albert Shanker Institute.

Englemann, S., Granzin, A., & Severson, H. (1979). Diagnosing instruction. *Journal of Special Education, 13,* 355–365.

Englert, C., Cullata, B., & Horn, D. (1987). Influence of irrelevant information in addition word problems on problem solving. *Learning Disabilities Quarterly, 10,* 29–36.

Epstein, M. H. (2004). *Examiner's Manual for the Behavioral and Emotional Rating Scale* (2nd ed.). Austin, TX: Pro-Ed.

Fernsten, L., & Fernsten, J. (2005). Portfolio assessment and reflection: Enhancing learning through effective practice. *Reflective Practice 6,* 303–309.

Figueroa, R. (1990). Assessment of linguistic minority group children. In C. R. Reynolds & R. W. Kamphaus (Eds.), *Handbook of Psychological Assessment of Children.* New York: Guilford Press.

Flanagan, D. P., Ortiz, S. O., & Alfonso, V. C. (2013). *Essentials of Cross-Battery Assessment with C/D ROM* (3rd ed.). New York: Wiley.

Flesch, R. (1955). *Why Johnny Can't Read.* New York: Harper & Row.

Foorman, B., Francis, D., Fletcher, J., Schatschneider, C., & Mehta, P. (1998). The role of instruction in learning to read: Preventing reading failure in at-risk children. *Journal of Educational Psychology, 90,* 1–13.

Freeland, J., Skinner, C., Jackson, B., McDaniel, C., & Smith, S. (2000). Measuring and increasing silent reading comprehension rates: Empirically validating a related reading intervention. *Psychology in the Schools, 37*(5), 415–429.

Frostig, M. (1968). Education for children with learning disabilities. In H. Myklebust (Ed.), *Progress in Learning Disabilities.* New York: Grune & Stratton.

Frostig, M., Maslow, P., Lefever, D. W., & Whittlesey, J. R. (1964). *The Marianne Frostig Developmental Test of Visual Perception: 1963 Standardization.* Palo Alto, CA: Consulting Psychologists Press.

Fuchs, D., & Fuchs, L. S. (1989). Effects of examiner familiarity on black, Caucasian, and Hispanic children: A meta-analysis. *Exceptional Children, 55*(4), 303–308.

Fuchs, L. S., Deno, S. L., & Mirkin, P. (1984). The effects of frequent curriculum based measurement and evaluation on pedagogy, student achievement and student awareness of learning. *American Educational Research Journal, 21,* 449–460.

Fuchs, L. S., & Fuchs, D. (1986). Effects of systematic formative evaluation: A meta-analysis. *Exceptional Children, 53,* 199–208.

Fuchs, L. S., & Fuchs, D. (1987). The relation between methods of graphing student performance data and achievement: A meta-analysis. *Journal of Special Education Technology, 8*(3), 5–13.

Fuchs, L. S., Fuchs, D., Hamlett, C. L., Walz, L., & Germann, G. (1993). Formative evaluation of academic progress: How much growth can we expect? *School Psychology Review, 22,* 27–48.

Fuchs, L. S., Fuchs, D., & Maxwell, L. (1988). The validity of informal reading comprehension measures. *Remedial and Special Education, 9*(2), 20–28.

Gersten, R., Compton, D., Connor, C.M., Dimino, J., Santoro, L., Linan-Thompson, S., and Tilly, W.D. (2008). *Assisting Students Struggling with Reading: Response to Intervention and Multi-Tier Intervention for Reading in the Primary Grades. A Practice Guide.* (NCEE 2009-4045). Washington, DC: National Center for Education Evaluation and Regional Assistance, Institute of Education Sciences, U.S. Department of Education. Retrieved from http://ies.ed.gov/ncdee/wwc/publications/practiceguides/.

Gickling, E. E., & Thompson, V. P. (1985). A personal view of curriculum-based assessment. *Exceptional Children, 52*(3), 205–218.

Gilliam, J. E. (2001). *Manual for the Gilliam Asperger Disorder Scale.* Circle Pines, MN: American Guidance Service.

Ginsburg, H., & Baroody, A. (2003). *Test of Early Mathematics Ability* (3rd ed.). Austin, TX: Pro-Ed.

Gioia, G. A., Isquith, P. K., Guy, S. C., & Kenworthy, L. (2000). *Behavior Rating Inventory of Executive Functioning (BRIEF).* Lutz, FL: Psychological Assessment Resources.

Goldman, R., & Fristoe, M. (2000). *Goldman-Fristoe Test of Articulation* (2nd ed.). Circle Pines, MN: American Guidance Service.

Good, R. H., & Kaminski, R. A. (Eds.). (2002). *Dynamic Indicators of Basic Early Literacy Skills* (6th ed.). Eugene, OR: Institute for the Development of Educational Achievement. Available at dibels.uoregon.edu. Also available in print form from Sopris West Educational Publishers (sopriswest.com).

Good, R. H., & Salvia, J. A. (1988). Curriculum bias in published norm-referenced reading tests: Demonstrable effects. *School Psychology Review, 17*(1), 51–60.

Gottesman, I. (1968). Biogenics of race and class. In M. Deutsch, I. Katz, & A. Jensen (Eds.), *Social Class, Race, and Psychological Development.* New York: Holt, Rinehart, & Winston.

Graden, J., Casey, A., & Bonstrom, O. (1983). *Prereferral Interventions: Effects on Referral Rates and Teacher attitudes* (Research Report No. 140). Minneapolis: Minnesota Institute for Research on Learning Disabilities.

Graham, S. (2006). Strategy instruction and the teaching of writing: A meta-analysis. In C. A. MacArthur, S. Graham, & J. Fitzgerald (Eds.), *Handbook of Writing Research* (pp. 187–207). New York: Guilford Press.

Greenspan, S. I. (2004). *Greenspan Social Emotional Growth Chart: A Screening Questionnaire for Infants and Young Children.* San Antonio, TX: Harcourt Educational Measurement.

Greenspan, S. I. (2006). *Bayley Scales of Infant and Toddler Development: Socio-Emotional Subtest.* San Antonio, TX: Harcourt Educational Measurement.

Gresham, F., & Elliott, S. N. (1990). *Social Skills Rating System.* Circle Pines, MN: American Guidance Service.

Grimes, J., & Kurns, S. (2003, December). *Response to Intervention: Heartland's Model of Prevention and Intervention.* National Research Center on Learning Disabilities Responsiveness to Intervention Symposium, Kansas City.

Gronlund, N. E., & Waugh, C. K. (2008). *Assessment of Student Achievement* (9th ed.). New York: Allyn & Bacon.

Guilford, J. P. (1967). *The Nature of Human Intelligence.* New York: McGraw-Hill.

Gutkin, T. B., & Nemeth, C. (1997). Selected factors impacting decision making in prereferral intervention and other school-based teams: Exploring the intersection between school and social psychology. *Journal of School Psychology, 35,* 195–216.

Hammill, D. (1998). *Examiner's Manual: Detroit Tests of Learning Aptitude.* Austin, TX: Pro-Ed.

Hammill, D., & Larsen, S. (2008). *Examiner's Manual for the Test of Written Language, Fourth Edition.* Austin, TX: Pro-Ed.

Hammill, D. D., & Larsen, S. C. (2009). *Written Language Observation Scale.* Austin, TX: Hammill Institute on Disabilities.

Hammill, D., Mather, H., & Roberts, R. (2001). *Illinois Test of Psycholinguistic Abilities* (3rd ed.). Austin, TX: Pro-Ed.

Hammill, D., & Newcomer, P. (2008). *Test of Language Development–Intermediate* (4th ed.). Austin, TX: PRO-ED.

Hammill, D., Pearson, N., & Voress, J. (1993). *Examiner's Manual: Developmental Test of Visual Perception* (2nd ed.). Austin, TX: Pro-Ed.

Hammill, D., Pearson, N., & Voress, J. (1996). *Test of Visual-Motor Integration.* Austin, TX: Pro-Ed.

Hammill, D., Pearson, N., & Wiederholt, L. (1997). *Comprehensive Test of Nonverbal Intelligence.* Austin, TX: Pro-Ed.

Hanna, P., Hanna, J., Hodges, R., & Rudoff, E. (1966). *Phoneme-Grapheme Correspondence as Cues to Spelling Improvement.* Washington, DC: U.S. Department of Health, Education, and Welfare.

Harcourt Assessment, Inc. (2004). *Stanford Achievement Test Series, Tenth Edition Technical Data Report.* San Antonio, TX: Author.

Harcourt Brace Educational Measurement. (1996). *Stanford Diagnostic Mathematics Test 4.* San Antonio, TX: Psychological Corporation.

Harcourt Educational Measurement. (2002). *Metropolitan Achievement Test* (8th ed.). San Antonio, TX: Author.

Harcourt Educational Measurement. (2003). *Otis Lennon School Ability Test* (8th ed.). San Antonio, TX: Author.

Harrison, P. (2006). *Bayley Scales of Infant and Toddler Development: Adaptive Behavior Subtest.* San Antonio, TX: Harcourt Educational Measurement.

Harrison, P., & Oakland, T. (2003). *Adaptive Behavior System, Second Edition.* San Antonio, TX: Harcourt Educational Measurement.

Hasbrouck, J., & Tindal, G. (2006). Oral reading fluency norms: A valuable assessment tool for reading teachers. *The Reading Teacher, 59*(7), 636–644.

Hauerwas, L. B., Brown, R., & Scott, A. N. (2013). Specific learning disability and response to intervention: State level guidance. *Exceptional Children, 80*(1), 101–120.

Herrnstein, R., & Murray, C. (1994). *The Bell Curve: Intelligence and Class Structure in American Life.* New York: The Free Press.

Hintze, J., Christ, T., & Methe, S. (2005). Curriculum-based assessment. *Psychology in the Schools, 43*(1), 45–56.

Horn, E. (1967). *What Research Says to the Teacher: Teaching Spelling.* Washington, DC: National Education Association.

Hosp, J. L., Hosp, M. K., Howell, K. W., & Allison, R. (2014). *The ABCs of Curriculum-Based Evaluation: A Practical Guide for Decision Making.* New York: Guilford Press.

Hosp, M. K., & Hosp, J. L. (2003). Curriculum-based measurement for reading, spelling, and math: How to do it and why. *Preventing School Failure, 48*(1), 10–17.

Hosp, M., Hosp, J., & Howell, K. (2007). *The ABCs of CBM: A Practical Guide to Curriculum-Based Measurement.* New York: Guilford.

Howell, K. W. & Morehead, M. K. (1987). *Curriculum-Based Evaluation for Special and Remedial Education: A Handbook for Deciding What to Teach.* Columbus, OH: Merrill.

Howell, K. W., & Nolet, V. (2000). *Curriculum-Based Evaluation* (3rd ed.). Atlanta, GA: Wadsworth.

Hresko, W., Peak, P., Herron, S., & Bridges, D. L. (2000). *Young Children's Achievement Test.* Austin, TX: Pro-Ed.

Hresko, W. P., Schlieve, P. L., Herron, S. R., Swain, C., & Sherbenou, R. J. (2003). *Comprehensive Mathematical Abilities Test.* Austin, TX: Pro-Ed.

Hughes, C., & Dexter, D. D. (2007). Field studies of RTI programs, Revised. Retrieved from the website for the RTI Action Network, January 26, 2015.

Isaacson, S. (1988). Assessing the writing product: Qualitative and quantitative measures. *Exceptional Children, 54,* 528–534.

Jacob, S., Decker, D. M. & Hartshorne, T. S. (2011). *Ethics and Law for School Psychologists.* New York: Wiley.

Jenkins, J., & Pany, D. (1978). Standardized achievement tests: How useful for special education? *Exceptional Children, 44,* 448–453.

Jensen, A. R. (1980). *Bias in Mental Testing.* New York: The Free Press.

Jimerson, S. R., Burns, M. K. & VanDerHeyden, A. M. (Eds.) (2007). *Handbook of Response to Intervention: The Science and Practice of Assessment and Intervention.* New York, NY: Springer.

Johnson, D., & Myklebust, H. (1967). *Learning Disabilities: Educational Principles and Practices.* New York: Grune & Stratton.

Johnson, J. S., & Newport, E. L. (1989). Critical period effects in second language learning: The influence of maturational state on the acquisition of English as a second language. *Cognitive Psychology, 21*(1), 60–99.

Kaplan, E., Fein, D., Kramer, J., Morris, R., Delis, D., & Maerlender, A. (2004). *Wechsler Intelligence Scale for Children* (4th ed., Integrated). San Antonio, TX: Psychological Corporation.

Kaufman, A. S. (2009). *IQ Testing 101.* New York, NY: Springer.

Kaufman, A. S. & Kaufman, N. L. (1998). *Kaufman Test of Educational Achievement—Second Edition.* Circle Pines, MN: American Guidance Service.

Kaufman, A., & Kaufman, N. (2004). *Kaufman Assessment Battery for Children, Second Edition.* Bloomington, MN: Pearson.

Kephart, N. (1971). *The Slow Learner in the Classroom.* Columbus, OH: Merrill.

Kirk, S., & Kirk, W. (1971). *Psycholinguistic Disabilities.* Urbana: University of Illinois Press.

Kirk, S., McCarthy, J., & Kirk, W. (1968). *Illinois Test of Psycholinguistic Abilities.* Urbana: University of Illinois Press.

Kline, M. (1973). *Why Johnny Can't Add: The Failure of the New Math.* New York: St. Martin's Press.

Koppitz, E. M. (1963). *The Bender Gestalt Test for Young Children.* New York: Grune & Stratton.

Kovacs, M. (1992). *Children's Depression Inventory: Manual.* North Tonawanda, NY: Multi-Health Systems.

Kovaleski, J., & Glew, M. (2006). Bringing instructional support teams to scale: Implications of the Pennsylvania experience. *Remedial and Special Education, 27,* 16–25.

Kovaleski, J. F., VanDerHeyden, A. M., & Shapiro, E. S. (2013). *The RTI Approach to Evaluating Learning Disabilities.* New York: Guilford Press.

LaBerge, D., & Samuels, S. (1974). Toward a theory of automatic information processing in reading. *Cognitive Psychology, 6,* 293–323.

Larsen, S., Hammill, D. D., & Moats, L. (1999). *Test of Written Spelling-4.* Austin, TX: Pro-Ed.

Lindsley, O. R. (1964). Direct measurement and prosthesis of retarded behavior. *Journal of Education, 147,* 68–81.

Linn, R., Graue, E., & Sanders, N. (1990). Comparing state and district test results to national norms: The validity of claims that "everyone is above average." *Educational Measurement: Issues and Practice, 9*(3), 5–14.

Loeding, B. L., & Crittenden, J. B. (1993). Inclusion of children and youth who are hearing impaired and deaf in outcomes assessment. In J. E. Ysseldyke & M. L. Thurlow (Eds.), *Views on Inclusion and Testing Accommodations for Students with Disabilities.* Minneapolis: University of Minnesota, National Center on Educational Outcomes.

Lohman, D., & Hagan, E. (2001). *Cognitive Abilities Test.* Chicago: Riverside Publishing.

Maddox, T. (Ed.). (2008). *Tests, Sixth Edition—A Comprehensive Reference for Assessments in Psychology, Education, and Business.* Austin, TX: PRO-ED.

Mardell-Czudnowski, C., & Goldenberg, D. (1998). *Manual: Developmental Indicators for The Assessment of Learning* (3rd ed.). Circle Pines, MN: American Guidance Service.

Markwardt, F. (1998). *Peabody Individual Achievement Test–Revised–Normative Update.* Circle Pines, MN: American Guidance Service.

Marston, D., & Magnusson, D. (1985). Implementing curriculum-based measurement in special and regular education settings. *Exceptional Children, 52,* 266–276.

Marston, D., Muyskens, P., Lau, M., & Canter, A. (2003). Problem-solving model for decision making with high-incidence disabilities: The Minneapolis experience. *Learning Disabilities Research and Practice, 18*(3), 187–200.

Martin, J. E., Van Dycke, J. L., Christensen, W. R., Greene, B. A., Gardner, J. E., & Lovett, D. L. (2006). Increasing student participation in their transition IEP meetings: Establishing the self-directed IEP as an evidenced-based practice. *Exceptional Children, 72,* 299–316.

Martin, R. P. (1988). *Assessment of Personality and Behavior Problems: Infancy Through Adolescence.* New York: Guilford Press.

Massachusetts Department of Education. (2001). *Resource Guide to the Massachusetts Curriculum Frameworks for Students with Significant Disabilities–English Language Arts Section.* [Retrieved April 5, 2005, at www.doe.mass.edu/mcas/alt/rg/ela.pdf].

Mather, N., Roberts, R., Hammill, D. D., & Allen, E. A. (2009). *Test of Orthographic Competence.* Austin, TX: Pro-Ed.

Mather, N., Hammill, D., Allen, E., & Roberts, R. (2004). *Test of Silent Word Reading Fluency.* Austin, TX: Pro-Ed.

Maynard, F., & Strickland, J. (1969). *A Comparison of Three Methods of Teaching Selected Mathematical Content in Eighth and Ninth Grade General Mathematics Courses* (ED 041763). Athens, GA: University of Georgia.

McBride, J. & Martin, J. T. (1983). Reliability and validity of adaptive ability tests. In D. J. Weiss (Ed.), *New Horizons in Testing: Latent Trait Test Theory and Computerized Adaptive Testing* (Chapter 11, pp. 224–225), New York: Academic Press.

McCarney, S. B. (1992a). *Early Childhood Behavior Scale: Technical Manual.* Columbia, MO: Hawthorne Educational Services.

McCarney, S. B. (1992b). *Preschool Evaluation Scale.* Columbia, MO: Hawthorne Educational Services.

McGraw-Hill Digital Learning. (2004). *Yearly Progress Pro.* Columbus, OH: Author.

McGrew, K., Thurlow, M. L., Shriner, J., & Spiegel, A. N. (1992). *Inclusion of Students with Disabilities in National and State Data Collection Programs* (Technical Report 2). Minneapolis: University of Minnesota, National Center on Educational Outcomes.

McGrew, K. S., LaForte, E. M., & Schrank, F. A. (2014). *Technical Manual. Woodcock-Johnson IV.* Rolling Meadows, IL: Riverside.

McGrew, K. S., & Woodcock, R. W. (2001). *Woodcock-Johnson III: Technical Manual.* Itasca, IL: Riverside Publishing Company.

McNamara, K. (1998). Adoption of intervention-based assessment for special education: Trends in case management variables. *School Psychology International, 19,* 251–266.

Meller, P. J., Ohr, P. S., & Marcus, R. A. (2001). Family-oriented, culturally sensitive (FOCUS) assessment of young children. In L. A. Suzuki, J. G. Ponterotto, & P. J. Meller (Eds.), *Handbook of Multicultural Assessment: Clinical, Psychological, and Educational Applications* (2nd ed., pp. 461–496). San Francisco: Jossey-Bass.

Mercer, C., & Mercer, A. (1985). *Teaching Students with Learning Problems* (2nd ed.). Columbus, OH: Merrill.

Merrell, K. W. (1994). *Assessment of Behavioral, Social, and Emotional Problems.* New York: Longman.

Miller, J. (1981). *Assessing Language Production in Children.* Austin, TX: Pro-Ed.

Moore, K. J., Fifield, M. B., Spira, D. A., & Scarlato, M. (1989). Child study team decision making in special education: Improving the process. *Remedial and Special Education, 10,* 50–58.

Mullen, E. (1995). *Mullen Scales of Early Learning: AGS Edition.* Circle Pines, MN: American Guidance Service.

Myles, B., Bock, S., & Simpson, R. (2001). *Examiner's Manual for the Asperger Syndrome Diagnostic Scale.* Circle Pines, MN: American Guidance Service.

Naglieri, J. (2008). *Naglieri Nonverbal Ability Test* (2nd ed.). San Antonio, TX: Pearson Assessment.

National Association for the Education of Young Children. (2003). *Position Statement on Early Childhood Curriculum, Assessment, and Program Evaluation.* Washington, DC: Author. [Retrieved June 14, 2008, at www.naeyc.org/about/positions/pdf/pscape.pdf].

National Association of School Psychologists. (2002). *Principles for Professional Ethics.* Bethesda, MD: Author.

National Association of State Directors of Special Education (2005). *Response to Intervention: Policy Considerations and Implementation.* Alexandria, VA: National Association of State Directors of Special Education.

National Center for Educational Statistics. (1995). *Trends in International Mathematics and Science Study.* Washington, DC: Institute of Educational Sciences.

National Center for Educational Statistics (2002). *Fourth Grade Students Reading Aloud: NAEP 2002 Special Study on Oral Reading.* Washington, DC: U.S. Department of Education, Institute of Education Sciences.

National Center on Response to Intervention Technical Review Committee. (2010, April 19). *Progress Monitoring Tool Chart: Reading and Math.* [Retrieved at http://www.rti4success.org/tools_charts/supplemental Content/progress/ProgressMonitoring.pdf].

National Commission of Excellence in Education. (1983). *A Nation at Risk: The Imperative for Educational Reform.* Washington, DC: U.S. Government Printing Office.

National Council of Teachers of Mathematics. (2000). *Principles and Standards for School Mathematics.* Reston, VA: Author.

National Institute of Child Health and Human Development. (2000). Report of the National Reading Panel. *Teaching Children to Read: An Evidence-Based Assessment of the Scientific Research Literature on Reading and Its Implication for Reading Instruction* (NIH Publication 00-4). Washington, DC: U.S. Government Printing Office.

National Institute of Child Health and Human Development. (2008). Report of the National Mathematics Advisory Panel. (2008). *Foundations for Success: The Final Report of the National Mathematics Advisory Panel*. Washington, DC: U.S. Department of Education.

National Reading Panel. *Teaching Children to Read: An Evidence-Based Assessment of the Scientific Research Literature on Reading and Its Implication for Reading Instruction: Reports of the Subgroups* (Chapter 2, Part II). Available at www.nichd.hih.gov/publications/nrp/ch2-II .pdf.

Neisworth, J., Bagnato, S., Salvia, J. A., & Hunt, F. (1999). *Temperament and Atypical Behavior Scale*. Baltimore, MD: Paul H. Brookes.

Newcomer, P. (2014). *Diagnostic Achievement Battery–4*. Austin, TX: ProEd.

Newcomer, P. (2001). *Diagnostic Achievement Battery* (3rd ed.). Austin, TX: Pro-Ed.

Newcomer, P., & Hammill, D. (2008). *Test of Language Development–Primary* (4th ed.). Austin, TX: Pro-Ed.

Nickerson, R. S. (1998). Confirmation bias: A ubiquitous phenomenon in many guises. *Review in General Psychology, 2,* 175–220.

Nihira, K., Leland, H., & Lambert, N. (1993a). *AAMR Adaptive Behavior Scale–School* (2nd ed.). Austin, TX: Pro-Ed.

Nihira, K., Leland, H., & Lambert, N. (1993b). *Examiner's Manual, AAMR Adaptive Behavior Scale–Residential and Community* (2nd ed.). Austin, TX: Pro-Ed.

Northern, J. L., & Downs, M. P. (1991). *Hearing in Children* (4th ed). Baltimore, MD: Williams & Wilkens.

Nunnally, J. (1967). *Psychometric Theory*. New York: McGraw-Hill.

Nurss, J., & McGauvran, M. (1995). *The Metropolitan Readiness Tests: Norms Book* (6th ed.). San Antonio, TX: Harcourt Brace.

Olson, D. (1964). *Management by Objectives*. Auckland, NZ: Pacific Book Publishers.

Otis, A. S., & Lennon, R. T. (2003). *Otis-Lennon School Ability Test* (8th ed.). San Antonio, TX: Harcourt Educational Measurement.

Paul, D., Nibbelink, W., & Hoover, H. (1986). The effects of adjusting readability on the difficulty of mathematics story problems. *Journal of Research in Mathematics Education, 17,* 163–171.

Pearson. (2001). *AIMSweb*. San Antonio, TX: Author.

Pflaum, S., Walberg, H., Karegianes, M., & Rasher, S. (1980). Reading instruction: A quantitative analysis. *Educational Researcher, 9,* 12–18.

Phillips, K. (1990). *Factors That Affect the Feasibility of Interventions*. Workshop presented at Mounds View Schools, unpublished.

Prutting, C., & Kirshner, D. (1987). A clinical appraisal of the pragmatic aspects of language. *Journal of Speech and Hearing Disorders, 52,* 105–119.

Psychological Corporation. (2009). *Wechsler Individual Achievement Test* (3rd ed.). San Antonio, TX: Author.

Rayner, K., Foorman, B., Perfetti, C., Pesetsky, D., & Seidenberg, M. (2001). How psychological science informs the teacher of reading. *Psychological Science in the Public Interest, 2,* 31–73.

Reid, D., Hresko, W., & Hammill, D. (2001). *Test of Early Reading Ability* (3rd ed.). Austin, TX: Pro-Ed.

Renaissance Learning. (1997). *Standardized Test for the Assessment of Reading*. Wisconsin Rapids, WI: Author.

Renaissance Learning. (1998). *STAR Math*. Wisconsin Rapids, WI: Author.

Renaissance Learning. (2006). NEO-2. Wisconsin Rapids, WI: Author.

Renaissance Learning. (2007). DANA. Wisconsin Rapids, WI: Author.

Renaissance Learning (2009). *STAR Math Technical Manual*. Wisconsin Rapids, WI: Author.

Renaissance Learning (2009). *STAR Reading Technical Manual*. Wisconsin Rapids, WI: Author.

Resnick, L. (1987). *Education and Learning to Think*. Washington, DC: National Academy Press.

Reynolds, C. R. (2007). *Koppitz Developmental Scoring System for the Bender Gestalt Test–Second Edition (Koppitz-2)*. Austin, TX: Pro-Ed.

Reynolds, C. R., & Kamphaus, R. W. (2004). *Behavior Assessment System for Children–Second Edition–Manual*. Circle Pines, MN: American Guidance Service.

Reynolds, C. R., & Richmond, B. O. (2000). *Revised Children's Manifest Anxiety Scale*. Los Angeles: Wester Psychological Services.

Roach, E. F., & Kephart, N. C. (1966). *The Purdue Perceptual-Motor Survey*. Columbus, OH: Merrill.

Roid, G. (2003). *Stanford-Binet Intelligence Scale* (5th ed.). Chicago, IL: Riverside Publishing.

Roid, G., & Miller, N. (1997). *Leiter International Performance Scale–Revised*. Chicago: Stoelting.

Salvia, J. A., Neisworth, J., & Schmidt, M. (1990). *Examiner's Manual: Responsibility and Independence Scale for Adolescents*. Allen, TX: DLM.

Sanetti, L. M. Hagermoser, & Kratochwill, T. R. (2011). An evaluation of the treatment integrity planning protocol and two schedules of treatment integrity self-report: Impact on implementation and report accuracy. *Journal of Educational and Psychological Consulting, 21*(4), 284–308.

Santangelo, T. (2009). Collaborative problem solving effectively implemented, but not sustained: A case for aligning the sun, the moon, and the stars. *Exceptional Children, 75,* 185–209.

Schmidt, M., & Salvia, J. A. (1984). Adaptive behavior: A conceptual analysis. *Diagnostique, 9*(2), 117–125.

Shapiro, E. S. (2003). *BOSS—Behavioral Observation of Students in Schools*. San Antonio, TX: Psychological Corporation. [Software for PDA platform]

Shapiro, E. S. (2004). *Academic Skills Problems Workbook*. New York: Guilford Press.

Shapiro, E. S., & Derr, T. (1987). An examination of overlap between reading curricula and standardized reading tests. *Journal of Special Education, 21*(2), 59–67.

Shapiro, E. S., & Kratochwill, T. (Eds.). (2000). *Behavioral Assessment in Schools: Theory, Research, and Clinical Foundations* (2nd ed.). New York: Guilford Press.

Share, D., & Stanovich, K. (1995). Cognitive processes in early reading development: A model of acquisition and individual differences. *Issues in Education: Contributions from Educational Psychology, 1,* 1–57.

Sharpe, M., McNear, D., & McGrew, K. (1996). *Braille Assessment Inventory.* Columbia, MO: Hawthorne Educational Services.

Shinn, M. (1998). *Advanced Applications of Curriculum-Based Measurement.* New York: Guilford Press.

Shinn, M. R. (Ed.). (1989). *Curriculum-Based Measurement: Assessing Special Children.* New York: Guilford.

Shinn, M., Tindal, G., & Stein, S. (1988). Curriculum-based measurement and the identification of mildly handicapped students: A review of research. *Professional School Psychology, 3*(1), 69–85.

Shriner, J., & Salvia, J. A. (1988). Content validity of two tests with two math curricula over three years: Another instance of chronic noncorrespondence. *Exceptional Children, 55,* 240–248.

Sindelar, P., Monda., L., & O'Shea, L. (1990). Effects of repeated readings on instructional- and mastery-level readers. *Journal of Educational Research, 83*(4), 220–226.

Snow, C., Burns, M., & Griffin, P. (1998). *Preventing Reading Difficulties in Young Children.* Washington, DC: National Academy Press.

Sparrow, S., Cicchetti, D., & Balla, D. (2005). *Vineland Adaptive Behavior Scales* (2nd ed.). Circle Pines, MN: American Guidance Service.

Stanovich, K. (1986). Matthew effects in reading: Some consequences of individual differences in the acquisition of literacy. *Reading Research Quarterly, 21,* 360–406.

Stanovich, K. (2000). *Progress in Understanding Reading: Scientific Foundations and New Frontiers.* New York: Guilford Press.

Stevens, R., & Rosenshine, B. (1981). Advances in research on teaching. *Exceptional Education Quarterly, 2*(1), 1–9.

Stevens, S. S. (1951). Mathematics, measurement, and psychophysics. In S. S. Stevens (Ed.), *Handbook of Experimental Psychology* (p. 23). New York: Wiley.

Suen, H., & Ary, D. (1989). *Analyzing Quantitative Behavioral Observation Data.* Hillsdale, NJ: Lawrence Erlbaum Associates.

Sugai, G., & Horner, R. (2009). Responsiveness-to-intervention and school-wide positive behavior supports: Integration of multi-tiered systems approaches. *Exceptionality, 17,* 223–237.

Sulzer-Azaroff, B., & Mayer, G. Roy (1986). *Achieving Educational Excellence: Using Behavior Strategies.* New York: Holt, Rinehart, and Winston.

Taylor, B., Harris, L., Pearson, P. D., & Garcia, G. (1995). *Reading Difficulties: Instruction and Assessment* (2nd ed.). New York: McGraw-Hill.

Tharp, R. G., & Wetzel, R. J. (1969). *Behavior Modification in the Natural Environment.* New York: Academic Press.

Therrien, W. (2004). Fluency and comprehension gains as a result of repeated reading: A meta-analysis. *Remedial and Special Education, 25*(4), 252–261.

Thompson, S., & Thurlow, M. (2001). *State Special Education Outcomes: A Report on State Activities at the Beginning of the New Decade.* Minneapolis: University of Minnesota, National Center on Educational Outcomes.

Thompson, S. J., Johnstone, C. J., & Thurlow, M. L. (2002). *Universal Design Applied to Large Scale Assessments* (Synthesis Report 44). Minneapolis: University of Minnesota, National Center on Educational Outcomes. [Retrieved April 9, 2008, at http://cehd.umn.edu/NCEO /OnlinePubs/Synthesis44.html].

Thorndike, R. L., & Hagen, E. (1978). *Measurement and Evaluation in Psychology and Education.* New York: Wiley.

Thurlow, M. L., Elliott, J. L., & Ysseldyke, J. E. (2003). *Testing Students with Disabilities: Practical Strategies for Complying with District and State Requirements* (2nd ed.). Thousand Oaks, CA: Corwin Press.

Thurlow, M. L., Elliott, J. L., & Ysseldyke, J. E. (2003). *Testing Students with Disabilities: Procedures for Complying with District and State Requirements.* Thousand Oaks, CA: Corwin Press.

Thurlow, M. L., Quenemoen, R., Thompson, S., & Lehr, C. (2001). *Principles and Characteristics of Inclusive Assessment and Accountability Systems* (Synthesis Report 40). Minneapolis, MN: National Center on Educational Outcomes, University of Minnesota.

Thurlow, M. L., & Thompson, S. (2004). *2003 State Special Education Outcomes.* Minneapolis: University of Minnesota, National Center on Educational Outcomes.

Thurstone, T. G. (1941). Primary mental abilities in children. *Educational and Psychological Measurement, 1,* 105–116.

Tindal, G., & Hasbrouck, J. (1991). Analyzing student writing to develop instructional strategies. *Learning Disabilities: Research and Practice, 6,* 237–245.

Tindal, G., Nese, J., Saez, L., & Alonzo, J. (2012, February). *Validating Progress Monitoring in the Context of RTI.* Paper presented at the Pacific Coast Research Conference, Coronado, CA.

Torgesen, J., & Bryant, B. (2004). *The Test of Phonological Awareness, Second Edition: Plus, Examiner's Manual.* Austin, TX: Pro-Ed.

U.S. Census Bureau. (1998). *Current Population Survey.* Washington, DC: Author.

U.S. Census Bureau. (2006). *American Community Survey.* Washington, DC: Author.

U.S. Census Bureau. (2010). *Language Use in the United States 2007: American Community Survey Reports.* Washington, DC: Author.

VanDerHeyden, A. M., & Burns, M. K. (2005). Using curriculum-based assessment and curriculum-based measurement to guide elementary mathematics instruction: Effect on individual and group accountability scores. *Assessment for Effective Intervention, 30,* 15–31.

VanDerHeyden, A. M., Witt, J. C., & Gilbertson, D. A (2007). Multi-year evaluation of the effects of a response to intervention (RTI) model on identification of children for special education. *Journal of School Psychology, 45,* 225–256.

Venn, J. J. (2000). *Assessing Students with Special Needs* (2nd ed.). Upper Saddle River, NJ: Merrill.

Voress, J., & Maddox, T. (1998). *Developmental Assessment of Young Children.* Austin, TX: Pro-Ed.

Wagner, R., Torgesen, J., & Rashotte, C. (1999). *Comprehensive Test of Phonological Processing*. Austin, TX: Pro-Ed.

Walker, D. K. (1973). *Socioemotional Measures for Preschool and Kindergarten Children*. San Francisco: Jossey-Bass.

Walker, H. M., & McConnell, S. R. (1988). *Walker-McConnell Scale of Social Competence*. Austin, TX: Pro-Ed.

Walker, H. M., & Severson, H. H. (1992). *Systematic Screening for Behavior Disorders* (2nd ed.). Longmont, CO: Sopris West.

Wallace, G., & Hammill, D. (2002). *Comprehensive Receptive and Expressive Vocabulary Test* (2nd ed.). Austin, TX: Pro-Ed.

Warren, C. (2005). Creating portfolios of schools. *Education Week, 24*(41), 47, 56.

Wechsler, D. (2014). *WISC-V Technical and Interpretive Manual*. Bloomington, MN: NCS Pearson.

Wechsler, D. (1939). *Wechsler-Bellevue Intelligence Scale*. New York: Psychological Corporation.

Wechsler, D. (1974). *Manual for the Wechsler Intelligence Scale for Children–Revised*. Cleveland, OH: Psychological Corporation.

Wechsler, D. (2001). *Wechsler Individual Achievement Test—Second Edition*. San Antonio, TX: Psychological Corporation.

Wechsler, D. (2002). *Wechsler Preschool and Primary Scale of Intelligence* (3rd ed.). San Antonio, TX: Pearson Assessment.

Wechsler, D. (2003). *Wechsler Intelligence Scale for Children* (4th ed.). San Antonio, TX: Psychological Corporation.

Wechsler, D. (2004). *Wechsler Intelligence Scale for Children, Fourth Edition–Integrated: Technical and Interpretive Manual*. San Antonio, TX: Psychological Corporation.

Wechsler, D. (2008). *Wechsler Adult Intelligence Scale* (4th ed.). San Antonio, TX: Pearson Assessment.

White, O., & Haring, N. (1980). *Exceptional Teaching* (2nd ed.). Columbus, OH: Merrill.

Wiederholt, L., & Bryant, B. (2001). *Gray Oral Reading Tests–4*. Austin, TX: Pro-Ed.

Wiederholt, L., & Bryant, B. (2001b). *Examiner's Manual: Gray Oral Reading Tests–3*. Austin, TX: Pro-Ed.

Wilkinson, G. S., & Robertson, G. J. (2007). *Wide Range Achievement Test 4 (WRAT 4)*. Lutz, FL: Psychological Assessment Resources.

Williams, K. (2001). *Group Reading Assessment and Diagnostic Evaluation*. Circle Pines, MN: American Guidance Service.

Williams, K. T. (2004). *Group Mathematics Assessment and Diagnostic Evaluation*. Circle Pines, MN: AGS Publishing.

Woodcock, R. W. (1998). *Woodcock Reading Mastery Tests–Revised: Normative Update*. Circle Pines, MN: American Guidance Service.

Woodcock, R. W., Mather, N., & Schrank, F. A. (2004). *Woodcock-Johnson III Diagnostic Reading Battery*. Itasca, IL: Riverside Publishing.

Woodcock, R. W., McGrew, K. S., & Mather, N. (2001). *WJ-III Tests of Cognitive Abilities and Tests of Achievement*. Itasca, IL: Riverside Publishing.

Woodcock, R. W., McGrew, K. S., & Mather, N. (2003). *Woodcock-Johnson III Tests of Cognitive Abilities*. Itasca, IL: Riverside Publishing.

Woodcock, R. W., Schrank, F. A., McGrew, K. S., & Mather, N. (2007). *Woodcock–Johnson III Normative Update*. Itasca, IL: Riverside.

Ysseldyke, J., & Bolt, D. (2007). Effect of technology-enhanced continuous progress monitoring on math achievement. *School Psychology Review, 36*(3), 453–467.

Ysseldyke, J. E. (1987). Classification of handicapped students. In M. C. Wang, M. Reynolds, & H. J. Walberg (Eds.), *Handbook of Special Education: Research & Practice* (vol. 1, pp. 253–271). New York: Pergamon.

Ysseldyke, J. E., Algozzine, R. F., Regan, R., & McGue, M. (1981). The influences of test scores and naturally occurring pupil characteristics on psychoeducational decision making with children. *Journal of School Psychology, 19*, 167–177.

Ysseldyke, J. E., & Christenson, S. L. (1987). *The Instructional Environment Scale*. Austin, TX: Pro-Ed.

Ysseldyke, J. E., & Christenson, S. L. (2002). *Functional Assessment of Academic Behavior: Creating Successful Learning Environments*. Longmont, CO: Sopris West.

Ysseldyke, J. E., Christenson, S. L., & Kovaleski, J. F. (1994). Identifying students' instructional needs in the context of classroom and home environments. *Teaching Exceptional Children, 26*(3), 37–41.

Ysseldyke, J. E., & McLeod, S. (2007). Using technology tools to monitor response to intervention. In S. R. Jimerson, M. K. Burns, and A. M. VanDerHeyden (Eds.), *Handbook of Response to Intervention*. New York: Springer.

Ysseldyke, J. E., & Salvia, J. A. (1974). Diagnostic-prescriptive teaching: Two models. *Exceptional Children, 41*, 181–186.

Ysseldyke, J. E., Stickney, E., & Haas, A. (2015). *Using Growth Norms to Set Instructional Goals for Struggling Students*. Paper presented at the Annual Meeting of the National Association of School Psychologists, Orlando, FL, February.

Ysseldyke, J. E., & Thurlow, M. L. (1993). *Self-Study Guide to the Development of Educational Outcomes and Indicators*. Minneapolis: University of Minnesota, National Center on Educational Outcomes.

INDEX

Chapter	CEC CEC Initial Preparation Standards	CEC ADVANCED CEC Advanced Preparation Standards	Ψ National Association of School Psychologists Domains
Chapter 6 Cultural and Linguistic Considerations	**Standard 1: Learner Development and Individual Learning Differences** 1.0 Beginning special education professionals understand how exceptionalities may interact with development and learning and use this knowledge to provide meaningful and challenging learning experiences for individuals with exceptionalities. **Standard 4: Assessment** 4.0 Beginning special education professionals use multiple methods of assessment and data-sources in making educational decisions.	**Standard 1: Assessment** 1.0 Special education specialists use valid and reliable assessment practices to minimize bias.	**1** Data-Based Decision Making and Accountability **8** Diversity in Development and Learning
Chapter 7 Using Test Adaptations and Accommodations	**Standard 1: Learner Development and Individual Learning Differences** 1.0 Beginning special education professionals understand how exceptionalities may interact with development and learning and use this knowledge to provide meaningful and challenging learning experiences for individuals with exceptionalities. **Standard 4: Assessment** 4.0 Beginning special education professionals use multiple methods of assessment and data-sources in making educational decisions.	**Standard 1: Assessment** 1.0 Special education specialists use valid and reliable assessment practices to minimize bias.	**1** Data-Based Decision Making and Accountability **8** Diversity in Development and Learning
Chapter 8 Teacher-Made Tests of Achievement	**Standard 4: Assessment** 4.0 Beginning special education professionals use multiple methods of assessment and data-sources in making educational decisions. **Standard 5: Instructional Planning and Strategies** 5.0 Beginning special education professionals select, adapt, and use a repertoire of evidence-based instructional strategies to advance learning of individuals with exceptionalities.	**Standard 1: Assessment** 1.0 Special education specialists use valid and reliable assessment practices to minimize bias.	**1** Data-Based Decision Making and Accountability **3** Interventions and Instructional Support to Develop Academic Skills
Chapter 9 Assessing Behavior through Observation	**Standard 4: Assessment** 4.0 Beginning special education professionals use multiple methods of assessment and data-sources in making educational decisions. **Standard 5: Instructional Planning and Strategies** 5.0 Beginning special education professionals select, adapt, and use a repertoire of evidence-based instructional strategies to advance learning of individuals with exceptionalities.	**Standard 1: Assessment** 1.0 Special education specialists use valid and reliable assessment practices to minimize bias.	**1** Data-Based Decision Making and Accountability **4** Interventions and Mental Health Services to Develop Social and Life Skills
Chapter 10 Monitoring Student Progress Toward Instructional Goals	**Standard 4: Assessment** 4.0 Beginning special education professionals use multiple methods of assessment and data-sources in making educational decisions. **Standard 5: Instructional Planning and Strategies** 5.0 Beginning special education professionals select, adapt, and use a repertoire of evidence-based instructional strategies to advance learning of individuals with exceptionalities.	**Standard 1: Assessment** 1.0 Special education specialists use valid and reliable assessment practices to minimize bias.	**1** Data-Based Decision Making and Accountability **3** Interventions and Instructional Support to Develop Academic Skills

Chapter	CEC Initial Preparation Standards	CEC Advanced Preparation Standards	National Association of School Psychologists Domains
Chapter 11 Managing Classroom Assessment	**Standard 4: Assessment** 4.0 Beginning special education professionals use multiple methods of assessment and data-sources in making educational decisions. **Standard 5: Instructional Planning and Strategies** 5.0 Beginning special education professionals select, adapt, and use a repertoire of evidence-based instructional strategies to advance learning of individuals with exceptionalities.	**Standard 1: Assessment** 1.0 Special education specialists use valid and reliable assessment practices to minimize bias.	**1** Data-Based Decision Making and Accountability
Chapter 12 Response to Intervention (RTI) and a Multi-Tiered System of Supports (MTSS)	**Standard 4: Assessment** 4.0 Beginning special education professionals use multiple methods of assessment and data-sources in making educational decisions. **Standard 5: Instructional Planning and Strategies** 5.0 Beginning special education professionals select, adapt, and use a repertoire of evidence-based instructional strategies to advance learning of individuals with exceptionalities.	**Standard 1: Assessment** 1.0 Special education specialists use valid and reliable assessment practices to minimize bias.	**1** Data-Based Decision Making and Accountability **5** School-Wide Practices to Promote Learning
Chapter 13 How to Evaluate a Test	**Standard 4: Assessment** 4.0 Beginning special education professionals use multiple methods of assessment and data-sources in making educational decisions.	**Standard 1: Assessment** 1.0 Special education specialists use valid and reliable assessment practices to minimize bias.	**1** Data-Based Decision Making and Accountability **9** Research and Program Evaluation
Chapter 14 Assessment of Academic Achievement with Multiple-Skill Devices	**Standard 4: Assessment** 4.0 Beginning special education professionals use multiple methods of assessment and data-sources in making educational decisions.	**Standard 1: Assessment** 1.0 Special education specialists use valid and reliable assessment practices to minimize bias.	**1** Data-Based Decision Making and Accountability **3** Interventions and Instructional Support to Develop Academic Skills
Chapter 15 Using Diagnostic Reading Measures	**Standard 4: Assessment** 4.0 Beginning special education professionals use multiple methods of assessment and data-sources in making educational decisions.	**Standard 1: Assessment** 1.0 Special education specialists use valid and reliable assessment practices to minimize bias.	**1** Data-Based Decision Making and Accountability **3** Interventions and Instructional Support to Develop Academic Skills
Chapter 16 Using Diagnostic Mathematics Measures	**Standard 4: Assessment** 4.0 Beginning special education professionals use multiple methods of assessment and data-sources in making educational decisions.	**Standard 1: Assessment** 1.0 Special education specialists use valid and reliable assessment practices to minimize bias.	**1** Data-Based Decision Making and Accountability **3** Interventions and Instructional Support to Develop Academic Skills
Chapter 17 Using Measures of Written Language	**Standard 4: Assessment** 4.0 Beginning special education professionals use multiple methods of assessment and data-sources in making educational decisions.	**Standard 1: Assessment** 1.0 Special education specialists use valid and reliable assessment practices to minimize bias.	**1** Data-Based Decision Making and Accountability **3** Interventions and Instructional Support to Develop Academic Skills
Chapter 18 Using Measures of Intelligence	**Standard 4: Assessment** 4.0 Beginning special education professionals use multiple methods of assessment and data-sources in making educational decisions.	**Standard 1: Assessment** 1.0 Special education specialists use valid and reliable assessment practices to minimize bias.	**1** Data-Based Decision Making and Accountability
Chapter 19 Using Measures of Social and Emotional Behavior	**Standard 4: Assessment** 4.0 Beginning special education professionals use multiple methods of assessment and data-sources in making educational decisions.	**Standard 1: Assessment** 1.0 Special education specialists use valid and reliable assessment practices to minimize bias.	**1** Data-Based Decision Making and Accountability **4** Interventions and Mental Health Services to Develop Social and Life Skills